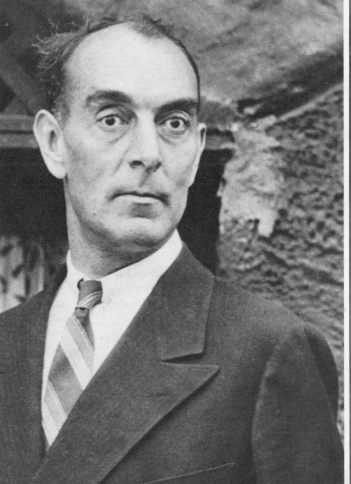

Dictionary of Literary Biography • Volume Twenty-five

American Newspaper Journalists, 1901-1925

Dictionary of Literary Biography

Dictionary of Literary Biography • Volume Twenty-five

American Newspaper Journalists, 1901-1925

Edited by
Perry J. Ashley
University of South Carolina

A Bruccoli Clark Book
Gale Research Company • Book Tower • Detroit, Michigan 48226

Manufactured by Edwards Brothers, Inc.
Ann Arbor, Michigan
Printed in the United States of America

Copyright © 1984
GALE RESEARCH COMPANY

Library of Congress Cataloging in Publication Data
Main entry under title:

American newspaper journalists, 1901-1925.

  (Dictionary of literary biography; v. 25)
  "A Bruccoli Clark book."
  Includes index.
  1. Journalists—United States—Biography. I. Ashley,
Perry J. II. Series.
PN4871.A5   1984   070'.92'2 [B]   83-25395
ISBN 0-8103-1704-4

for
Jon and Ric
Jan and Allison
David, Joanna, and Christopher

Contents

Contents

Plan of the Series

. . . Almost the most prodigious asset of a country, and perhaps its most precious possession, is its native literary product—when that product is fine and noble and enduring.

Mark Twain*

The advisory board, the editors, and the publisher of the *Dictionary of Literary Biography* are joined in endorsing Mark Twain's declaration. The literature of a nation provides an inexhaustible resource of permanent worth. It is our expectation that this endeavor will make literature and its creators better understood and more accessible to students and the literate public, while satisfying the standards of teachers and scholars.

To meet these requirements, *literary biography* has been construed in terms of the author's achievement. The most important thing about a writer is his writing. Accordingly, the entries in *DLB* are career biographies, tracing the development of the author's canon and the evolution of his reputation.

The publication plan for *DLB* resulted from two years of preparation. The project was proposed to Bruccoli Clark by Frederick G. Ruffner, president of the Gale Research Company, in November 1975. After specimen entries were prepared and typeset, an advisory board was formed to refine the entry format and develop the series rationale. In meetings held during 1976, the publisher, series editors, and advisory board approved the scheme for a comprehensive biographical dictionary of persons who contributed to North American literature. Editorial work on the first volume began in January 1977, and it was published in 1978.

In order to make *DLB* more than a reference tool and to compile volumes that individually have claim to status as literary history, it was decided to organize volumes by topic or period or genre. Each of these freestanding volumes provides a biographical-bibliographical guide and overview for a particular area of literature. We are convinced that this organization—as opposed to a single alphabet method—constitutes a valuable innovation in the presentation of reference material. The volume plan necessarily requires many decisions for the

placement and treatment of authors who might properly be included in two or three volumes. In some instances a major figure will be included in separate volumes, but with different entries emphasizing the aspect of his career appropriate to each volume. Ernest Hemingway, for example, is represented in *American Writers in Paris, 1920-1939* by an entry focusing on his expatriate apprenticeship; he is also in *American Novelists, 1910-1945* with an entry surveying his entire career. Each volume includes a cumulative index of subject authors. The final *DLB* volume will be a comprehensive index to the entire series.

With volume ten in 1982 it was decided to enlarge the scope of *DLB* beyond the literature of the United States. By the end of 1983 twelve volumes treating British literature had been published, and volumes for Commonwealth and Modern European literature were in progress. The series has been further augmented by the *DLB Yearbooks* (since 1981) which update published entries and add new entries to keep the *DLB* current with contemporary activity. There have also been occasional *DLB Documentary Series* volumes which provide biographical and critical background source materials for figures whose work is judged to have particular interest for students. One of these companion volumes is entirely devoted to Tennessee Williams.

The purpose of *DLB* is not only to provide reliable information in a convenient format but also to place the figures in the larger perspective of literary history and to offer appraisals of their accomplishments by qualified scholars.

We define literature as the *intellectual commerce of a nation*: not merely as belles lettres, but as that ample and complex process by which ideas are generated, shaped, and transmitted. *DLB* entries are not limited to "creative writers" but extend to other figures who in this time and in this way influenced the mind of a people. Thus there will be volumes for historians, journalists, publishers, and screenwriters. By this means readers of *DLB* may be aided to perceive literature not as cult scripture in the keeping of cultural high priests, but as at the center of a nation's life.

DLB includes the major writers appropriate to each volume and those standing in the ranks immediately behind them. Scholarly and critical counsel has been sought in deciding which minor figures to include and how full their entries should be.

---

*From an unpublished section of Mark Twain's autobiography, copyright © by the Mark Twain Company.

Wherever possible, useful references will be made to figures who do not warrant separate entries.

Each *DLB* volume has a volume editor responsible for planning the volume, selecting the figures for inclusion, and assigning the entries. Volume editors are also responsible for preparing, where appropriate, appendices surveying the major periodicals and literary and intellectual movements for their volumes, as well as lists of further readings. Work on the series as a whole is coordinated at the Bruccoli Clark editorial center in Columbia, South Carolina, where the editorial staff is responsible for the accuracy of the published volumes.

One feature that distinguishes *DLB* is the illustration policy—its concern with the iconography of literature. Just as an author is influenced by his surroundings, so is the reader's understanding of the author enhanced by a knowledge of his environment. Therefore *DLB* volumes include not only drawings, paintings, and photographs of authors, often depicting them at various stages in their careers, but also illustrations of their families and places where they lived. Title pages are regularly reproduced in facsimile along with dust jackets for modern authors. The dust jackets are a special feature of *DLB* because they often document better than anything else the way in which an author's work was launched in its own time. Specimens of the writers' manuscripts are included when feasible.

A supplement to *DLB*—tentatively titled *A Guide, Chronology, and Glossary for American Literature*—will outline the history of literature in North America and trace the influences that shaped it. This volume will provide a framework for the study of American literature by means of chronological tables, literary affiliation charts, glossarial entries, and concise surveys of the major movements. It has been planned to stand on its own as a vade mecum, providing a ready-reference guide to the study of American literature as well as a companion to the *DLB* volumes for American literature.

Samuel Johnson rightly decreed that "The chief glory of every people arises from its authors." The purpose of the *Dictionary of Literary Biography* is to compile literary history in the surest way available to us—by accurate and comprehensive treatment of the lives and work of those who contributed to it.

The *DLB* Advisory Board

Foreword

The years between 1901 and 1925 have been romanticized as the era of the wisecracking, hard-drinking reporter who outdid the police in solving crimes while seeking out scandals which would become the next day's titillating headlines. This stereotype, immortalized by Ben Hecht and Charles MacArthur in their 1928 play *The Front Page* and in countless films and television programs, has a basis in fact. The flamboyant personalities in the raucous world of *The Front Page*'s vaudeville-style journalism were patterned after real-life reporters and editors the playwrights had known during their own newspaper days in Chicago. Some journalists actually did succeed in solving crimes and tracking down malefactors where the police had failed.

The scandals were there, too, providing copy for two outbursts of sensationalism between 1901 and 1925. The "yellow journalism" of the turn of the century, fueled by the circulation war between William Randolph Hearst and Joseph Pulitzer in New York City, had run its course by the end of the first decade. Another wave of sensationalism, sometimes referred to as "jazz journalism," was initiated after World War I; it was brought to its absurd climax by the end of the 1920s in New York by Hearst's *Mirror* and Bernarr Macfadden's *Graphic*.

At the same time, however, a number of newspapers were establishing reputations for solid, factual reporting of the news. In New York, Adolph Ochs and his brilliant managing editor Carr Van Anda were making the *Times* "the newspaper of record" that published "all the news that's fit to print." The *Christian Science Monitor,* founded by Mary Baker Eddy in 1908 to "injure no man, but bless all mankind," was becoming a truly national newspaper which increased its daily circulation to almost 150,000 without emphasizing crime, sex, or violence. Strong regional newspapers devoted to community service included Fremont Older's *San Francisco Bulletin,* Melville Stone's *Chicago Daily News,* Clark Howell's *Atlanta Constitution,* and Lucius Nieman's *Milwaukee Journal.*

Editorial campaigns and crusades gained in intensity in the first quarter of the century, in both the responsible and the sensational press. Newspapers in many cities attacked party political machines while fighting fraud and corruption in local, state, and national government. They argued for reform in the penal system; advocated the initiative, referendum, and recall; proposed the popular election of U.S. senators; campaigned for the regulation of railroad and utility rates; and supported the labor movement. When World War I engulfed Europe, most of these newspapers reflected the isolationist sentiments of their readers; but after the U.S. entered the conflict, they gave vigorous support to the war effort.

The increasing power and influence of the press in the early part of the century provoked a reaction in the form of the first major examinations and criticisms of American journalism, as exemplified by Will Irwin's series on "The American Newspaper" in *Collier's* in 1911 and Upton Sinclair's muckraking novel *The Brass Check* (1919). Newspaper publishers, many of whom had become men of great wealth, found themselves under attack from two directions: they were distrusted by the wealthy for supporting reforms in their newspapers that were contrary to the interests of their own class; and they were suspected by progressive reformers of hypocritically seeking to curry favor with the working class only to sell more papers and thereby acquire even more wealth for themselves. E. W. Scripps summarized the attitude of some of these publishers when he said, shortly before his death: "The loneliness of my life is great. I am hated by the rich for being a renegade, and I am hated by the poor for being rich. I am not wise enough or learned enough to be an acceptable member of the highbrow club. I have learned too many things to make me a comfortable companion of the man in the field, or the street and in the shop." To try to overcome their feeling of isolation, some publishers began to share their riches with their communities and their profession. Hearst gave $1,000,000 to the University of California for a women's gymnasium to honor his mother, bought and gave to the state of Illinois the Lincoln homestead, and donated the Greek Theater to the city of Berkeley, California; *Chronicle* publisher M. H. de Young left his outstanding art collection to the city of San Francisco, where it is now housed in a museum bearing his name; Nieman's widow gave shares of stock in the *Milwaukee Journal* to Harvard University to establish a continuing educational program for working journalists; and Scripps provided funds for the Foundation for Research in Population Problems at Miami (Ohio) University and the Scripps Institute of Oceanography of the University of California.

The number of daily newspapers being published in the United States grew until a peak of about 2,600 was reached around 1915, and then began to decline. However, the circulation of those newspapers that remained showed a rapid growth: while the population of the United States increased 62 percent between 1900 and 1930, the aggregate circulation of all daily newspapers increased 231 percent. More Americans were reading newspapers than ever, but there were fewer newspapers for them to read.

The reduction in the number of newspapers being published was partly due to mergers and consolidations, which accelerated during the period. Journalism historian Frank Luther Mott suggests that the lack of reader interest in newspapers representing differing political viewpoints, as well as mounting production costs, led to the combining of morning and evening papers under common ownership in many major cities. This means that Frank A. Munsey, who has been criticized for causing a dramatic reduction in the number of dailies published in New York City between 1916 and 1924, was really only slightly ahead of his time. It would become a fact of economic life that only those newspapers which best served the needs of their readers would survive.

Many newspapers escaped mergers only to become parts of chains—or "groups," as the chain owners prefer to call the arrangement. Such multiple ownership increased strikingly during the period; in 1900, ten chains published thirty-two newspapers, representing less than fifteen percent of total daily circulation. By 1930, fifty-five groups controlled 311 dailies with about one-third of the total U.S. circulation. Scripps, one of the early leaders in group ownership, owned nine daily newspapers in 1900; by the time of his death in 1926, he had controlled thirty-two papers. Hearst owned one paper in San Francisco and one in New York in 1900; by 1931 he had acquired or founded forty-two newspapers, of which twenty-four still existed in that year.

Diversity among newspapers, even independent ones, was further reduced by the wide use of syndicates and wire services. Journalism historians Edwin and Michael Emery point out that syndicates have made available to newspapers "of all localities the work of talented artists and writers whose services could not otherwise be obtained by the average reader." They also note, however, that while wire services have contributed to the excellence of modern newspapers, "nevertheless they have become one of the 'common denominators.' Their usual style of writing—summary leads, inverted pyramid story structure, jampacked facts—affected all newspaper writing, to the detriment of original, individualistic reporting." Oswald Garrison Villard observed the same trend when he reported that as one traveled across the country buying papers in various cities, he would see "the same comics, Sunday magazines and special features in almost all of them. The newspaper profession has turned out to be a business and as a result there is bound to be standardization," and ultimately a decline in the number of newspapers being published.

Newspapers had traditionally provided not only information and opinion but also entertainment to their readers, and the quality of entertainment reached a high point in the period under consideration in this volume. In the first quarter of the twentieth century some of the great storytellers of American journalism were turning the incidents of everyday life into works of literary art which still endure as part of the national folklore. George Ade, Don Marquis, Ring Lardner, and Irvin S. Cobb made household words of such characters as Artie, Doc Horne, Pink Marsh, archy the cockroach, and mehitabel the cat. In addition to thousands of newspaper columns, these four writers alone produced over 150 books and plays.

During the same period, two other media were coming to the fore which would eventually prove to be even more effective at entertaining the average person, forcing newspapers to concentrate on their primary function of delivering the news. First there were the inexpensive, popular magazines which began in the cities in the 1890s and moved into the countryside with the inauguration of the rural free delivery system by the Post Office in 1897; the *Saturday Evening Post* began at this time to call itself the "in-home entertainment magazine for the whole family." Then there was the beginning of commercial radio broadcasting in 1920; by the end of the decade, radio antennas were "sprouting from the rooftops" as independent stations scrambled to affiliate with the new networks. The full impact of these new media would not be felt until after 1925.

In all, the first fourth of the twentieth century was a transitional period from the highly personalized journalism of the nineteenth century to the corporate journalism of today—a time when the existence of one newspaper publishing firm in each city was becoming the rule rather than the exception, and in which the surviving newspapers were increasingly being run as business enterprises by professional managers rather than as vehicles for the expression of the beliefs of individual editors.

–Perry J. Ashley

Acknowledgments

This book was produced by BC Research. Karen L. Rood is senior editor for the *Dictionary of Literary Biography* series. Philip B. Dematteis was the in-house editor.

The production manager is Lynne C. Zeigler. Art supervisor is Claudia Ericson. The production staff included Mary Betts, Patricia Coate, Lynn Felder, Kathleen M. Flanagan, Joyce Fowler, Laura Ingram, Walter W. Ross, Patricia C. Sharpe, Joycelyn R. Smith, Karen Campbell Totman, and Meredith Walker. Jean W. Ross is permissions editor. Joseph Caldwell, photography editor, did the photographic copy work for the volume.

Valuable assistance was also given by the staff at the Thomas Cooper Library of the University of South Carolina: Lynn Barron, Sue Collins, Michael Freeman, Gary Geer, Alexander M. Gilchrist, Jens Holley, David Lincove, Marcia Martin, Roger Mortimer, Harriet B. Oglesbee, Jean Rhyne, Karen Rissling, Paula Swope, and Ellen Tillett.

American Newspaper Journalists, 1901-1925

George Ade

(9 February 1866-16 May 1944)

Robert Carey
University of Arkansas

See also the Ade entry in *DLB 11, American Humorists, 1800-1950.*

MAJOR POSITIONS HELD: Reporter, columnist, *Chicago Morning News*, renamed the *News-Record* and later the *Record* (1890-1900).

SELECTED BOOKS: *The Chicago Record's "Stories of the Streets and of the Town,"* anonymous (Chicago: Chicago Daily News, 1894);
Second Series of the Chicago Record's "Stories of the Streets and of the Town," anonymous (Chicago: Chicago Daily News, 1894);
Third Series of the Chicago Record's "Stories of the Streets and of the Town," anonymous (Chicago: Chicago Daily News, 1895);
Fourth Series of the Chicago Record's "Stories of the Streets and of the Town," anonymous (Chicago: Chicago Daily News, 1895);
What a Man Sees Who Goes Away from Home (Chicago: Chicago Daily News, 1896);
Circus Day (Chicago & New York: Werner, 1896);
Stories from History, as John Hazelden (Chicago & New York: Werner, 1896);
Artie, A Story of the Streets and Town (Chicago: Stone, 1896);
Pink Marsh, A Story of the Streets and Town (Chicago & New York: Stone, 1897; London: Stone, 1897);
Fifth Series of the Chicago Record's "Stories of the Streets and of the Town," anonymous (Chicago: Chicago Daily News, 1897);
Sixth Series of the Chicago Record's "Stories of the Streets and of the Town," anonymous (Chicago: Chicago Daily News, 1898);
Seventh Series of the Chicago Record's "Stories of the

Culver Pictures

Streets and of the Town," anonymous (Chicago: Chicago Daily News, 1899);
Doc' Horne: A Story of the Streets and Town (Chicago & New York: Stone, 1899);
Fables in Slang (Chicago & New York: Stone, 1900; London: Pearson, 1900);

*Eighth Series. The Chicago Record's Stories of the Streets
　　　and of the Town,* anonymous (Chicago: Chicago
　　　Daily News, 1900);
More Fables (Chicago & New York: Stone, 1900;
　　　London: Pearson, 1902);
Grouch at the Game, or Why He Changed His Colors
　　　(Chicago?: H. Miller and W. Mabbett, 1901);
Forty Modern Fables (New York: Russell, 1901);
The Girl Proposition: A Bunch of He and She Fables
　　　(New York: Russell, 1902);
People You Know (New York: Russell, 1903);
The Sultan of Sulu: An Original Satire in Two Acts (New
　　　York: Russell, 1903);
In Babel: Stories of Chicago (New York: McClure,
　　　Phillips, 1903);
Breaking Into Society (New York & London: Harper,
　　　1904);
True Bills (New York & London: Harper, 1904);
In Pastures New (New York: McClure, Phillips,
　　　1906);
The Slim Princess (Indianapolis: Bobbs-Merrill,
　　　1907);
Verses and Jingles (Indianapolis: Bobbs-Merrill,
　　　1911);
Knocking the Neighbors (Garden City: Doubleday,
　　　Page, 1912);
Ade's Fables (Garden City: Doubleday, Page, 1914);
Hand-Made Fables (Garden City: Doubleday, Page,
　　　1920);
Single Blessedness and Other Observations (Garden
　　　City: Doubleday, Page, 1922);
The Mayor and the Manicure: Play in One Act (New
　　　York & London: French, 1923);
Nettie: A Play in One Act (New York & London:
　　　French, 1923);
Speaking to Father: Play in One Act (New York &
　　　London: French, 1923);
The College Widow: A Pictorial Comedy in Four Acts
　　　(New York & London: French, 1924);
Father and the Boys: A Comedy Drama (New York &
　　　London: French, 1924);
The County Chairman: A Comedy-Drama (New York &
　　　London: French, 1924);
Just Out of College: A Light Comedy in Three Acts (New
　　　York & London: French, 1924);
*Bang! Bang!: A Collection of Stories Intended to Recall
　　　Memories of the Nickel Library Days When Boys
　　　Were Supermen and Murder a Fine Art* (New
　　　York: Sears, 1928);
The Old-Time Saloon: Not Wet–Not Dry Just History
　　　(New York: Long & Smith, 1931);
One Afternoon with Mark Twain (Chicago: Mark
　　　Twain Society of Chicago, 1939);

Stories of the Streets and of the Town (Chicago: Caxton
　　　Club, 1941);
The Permanent Ade, edited by Fred C. Kelly (In-
　　　dianapolis: Bobbs-Merrill, 1947);
Chicago Stories, edited by Franklin J. Meine
　　　(Chicago: Regency, 1963).

Historians of popular culture have cause to
take George Ade into account in two areas: his
newspaper column work, which he periodically
gathered into bound anthologies that were as well
received around the country as they had been initially in Chicago, and his relatively brief though
prolific period as a playwright and librettist. He
enjoyed enormous popularity in both fields.

Ade is at once a delight and a disappointment.
His imaginative use of language, humor, and
characterization and his amusing approach to
everyday life can still bring a smile and a chuckle.
However, much of his work is dated, tied as it is to
the vernacular of the time. His ear was unerring and
he missed nothing. To say that Ade lacked substance, as some have, is to say that much of the life of
the average man is insubstantial. Ade heard music
and saw fun in commonplace comings and goings
and was able to capture them in an original prose
style that entertained millions of readers and
theatergoers.

His work was praised by some of the foremost
literary and journalistic personages of his time, including Mark Twain, William Dean Howells, and
H. L. Mencken. Howells, in particular, urged Ade
to stop turning out his journalistic vignettes and
write realistic novels couched in Ade's own style and
use of language. Although Ade promised Howells
he would do so, he never got around to it, and he
was still turning out newspaper syndicate work well
into his sixties. Ade's one novel—*The Slim Princess*
(1907)—was a burlesque and not what Howells had
in mind.

Ade was born 9 February 1866 in Kentland,
Indiana, a small farming community near the Illinois border. He was the next to youngest of three
boys and three girls born to John Ade, an immigrant from England, and his wife, Adaline, a native
of Ohio. The Ades lived a typical small-town existence centered around church and community activities. John Ade made only a small salary as cashier
at the local bank, and Ade recalled later that his
mother often washed out her children's underwear
each night and hung it to dry by the stove because
each child had but one set.

Ade did well in school, and an essay he wrote

in his early teens so impressed his teacher that she sent it to the editor of the *Kentland Gazette*, who published it. The essay stood out not so much for any original thought (those who prepared for life and were diligent and honest would do well; those who did not would not), but for the skill with which the author handled the language. The boy liked to read and spent much time doing that, far preferring the works of Mark Twain and Charles Dickens to the heavy farm work his parents required of him each summer. "I did not volunteer; I was drafted," Ade recalled later. "My parents thought that if they kept me away from the gaieties and temptations of a village of 800 people I might grow up to be a good citizen."

Ade's boyhood was spent pleasantly. His parents were kind and loving, the citizens of Kentland were friendly, and the community was comfortable. Growing up there was always a fond memory for Ade—despite the farming. John Ade did have some concern for his son's future when he graduated from high school, though, since the boy had shown no interest in or aptitude for any job opening that was likely to occur in Kentland. This problem was solved when the Newton County superintendent of schools asked John Ade if his son might be interested in a scholarship to Purdue, then a small agricultural college only ten years old. Despite the scoffings of business friends who regarded college as a waste of time, John Ade decided that this was the proper course. Ever since his essay had appeared in the paper, George Ade had captured the attention of his teachers, and they thought he had academic promise. John Ade, a religious man who sometimes served his church as a lay minister, had tried with no success to interest his oldest son, Will, in attending a seminary. George, then, would be the college man, even though it would be a financial strain: the scholarship would only cover part of the costs.

In the fall of 1883, seventeen-year-old George Ade made the fifty-mile trip to Lafayette and became one of twenty-nine members of the freshman class (there were only 200 students enrolled in Purdue at the time). Ade, who was to become one of the school's best-known alumni, chose a course leading to a bachelor of science degree. He took to college life eagerly, joined a literary society and later a social fraternity, Sigma Chi, and was popular among his fellow students. He also became a frequent visitor to the Grand Opera House in Lafayette. The entertainment at the opera house was far better than for the usual small town, since acts traveling between Chicago and Cincinnati would often stop over in Lafayette. Here he fell under the spell of Gilbert and Sullivan, an influence that continued into his own creative work in the theater.

Ade was not a brilliant student; indeed, the scientific curriculum he had chosen gave him problems—particularly math, where he recorded a 60 in higher algebra one term. But in English literature and composition he did much better. He edited the *Purdue*, a monthly literary magazine, for a semester.

During his junior year he met a fellow student who was to become his lifelong friend and collaborator, John T. McCutcheon. McCutcheon, who went on to pursue a successful career as an illustrator and cartoonist, later recorded his first memories of Ade: "He was thin and tall and wore a sedate blue suit with tight spring-bottomed trousers that flared out at the ankle. And he had three outstanding characteristics which made him an inviting subject for caricature: an unusual expanse of head behind the ears, a sweep of strongly marked eyebrows and a striking lack of abdominal fullness, described by realists as slab belly." In Ade's senior year he met a freshman named Lillian Howard, whom he saw steadily that year; she was probably the only serious love interest of his life.

The class of 1887 at Purdue was composed of eight graduates. Each senior delivered a paper as part of the commencement ceremony; the title of Ade's was "The Future of Letters in the West." He felt sure that one day he would be a part of it, and he was not wrong.

However, armed with his degree and no immediate means for achieving that end, he had to settle for something else. He knew for certain that he did not want to farm, but that was about all there was to do around Kentland. Ade returned to Lafayette and began reading law in a local firm, living on money sent by his father. Law reminded Ade of nothing so much as math, and Blackstone lacked the lyric language of Gilbert and Sullivan. The would-be lawyer ended his career after only seven weeks.

Something more to Ade's liking soon came along: a group of Lafayette Republicans were starting a political newspaper, and they hired Ade as its only reporter for $8 a week. The *Morning Call* was Ade's first newspaper job, and from the beginning he knew he had found a home. Attending political gatherings and writing about them were enjoyable. Ade might have stayed with the *Morning Call* indefinitely, but it folded. He was fortunate

Ade with Lillian Howard, the only serious love interest of his life. She later married a minister.

enough to land a similar job on the *Lafayette Call*, an evening paper, for $2 less per week. He did get paid every week, though, something that had not happened during the *Morning Call*'s final days.

However, Ade soon succumbed to a lure from the managers of a local patent medicine company who offered to double his salary to write ads for their products. He seemed adept at this too. He won a $3 raise by coining a phrase for Cascarets, a laxative: "They work while you sleep." The laxative and the phrase circulated throughout the country. Meanwhile, Ade was still seeing Lillian Howard, but was fast losing out to a Baptist minister. Lillian at last decided on the minister about the same time the patent medicine company was forced to reduce its payroll. The man who made Cascarets famous had now lost his job and his girl. Faced with these circumstances, Ade decided to take the advice of his old friend McCutcheon, who had joined the art department of the *Chicago Morning News* and for

months had been urging Ade to come to Chicago. Ade had no love of the big city, and all his life he was to write of it with the mild satire of a country boy who remained unconvinced. But he was twenty-four, out of work, and very nearly broke; he had no place else to go. His journalism career was about to begin in earnest.

Ade arrived in Chicago in June 1890. He had "a suitcase which looked like leather, which it was not, and a very small trunk which looked like pressed paper, which it was." McCutcheon scheduled an interview for Ade with Charles Dennis, the city editor of the *Morning News*. McCutcheon had been telling Dennis what a good reporter Ade would make, and Dennis apparently was convinced, offering him a job at $12 a week following the interview.

Ade's first assignment was turning out a daily weather story. Anxious to please, he attacked the subject with enthusiasm. His first efforts so pleased Dennis that he began running them on the front page. That Ade could take a routine assignment like the weather and infuse it with such freshness and sparkle that it interested everyone was his great strength and skill. It made him famous and it made him rich.

"After I went on the Morning News . . . I had small confidence in my ability," he wrote later. "I was afraid of the cable cars and my own shadow. I had only one asset which helped to shove me forward from the start . . . I was interested in all kinds of people and what they were doing and hoping to do." That kind of interest led him to question bank presidents, stable owners, bellhops—anyone who came within range and seemed a likely interview subject—about the weather. His ear for accents and dialogue combined with his writing skill made his stories about the weather among the most widely read items in the paper.

Ade was a hit from the start. For him it was a quick journey from cub to star reporter. Soon he was getting the choice assignments from the full range of news—stockyard strikes, trials, politics, city hall, major sports stories, and visiting personalities. He did it all with a dash and quickness that made him a journalistic natural. Even later, when he was turning out his syndicated "Fables," magazine articles, and plays, he seldom looked back, seldom rewrote. And if he usually opted for the glib over the profound, it must also be said that in doing so he was often funny and usually entertaining.

Ade's enthusiasms were for "people, journalism financial success, good talk and good times," biographer Lee Coyle wrote. "He was not particularly interested in national affairs, social problems, intellectual achievement, ideas, the arts, culture, religion or technological advancements. He was a youth with a ukelele; and life was to be one grand, sweet, happy song. He never changed, and he got what he wanted from life. The riches came; the talk was good and the good times were many."

By 1893, the *Morning News* had become the *Record* after a short existence as the *News-Record*, and Charles Dennis had been promoted to managing editor. When the Columbian Exposition, better known as the Chicago World's Fair, opened in May of that year, Dennis had set aside two columns on the editorial page to be filled with copy under the headline "All Roads Lead to the World's Fair." For the next six months Ade's one assignment was to fill that space, writing about whatever he wanted as long as it pertained to the fair. It would be hard to imagine a man better suited to a job. So successful was he and so widely acclaimed and read were the columns that when the fair was over Ade kept the columns under the new title, "Stories of the Streets and of the Town." He and John McCutcheon wandered about the city each day; Ade wrote between 1,200 and 2,000 words on a subject of his choice and McCutcheon provided an illustration. Much of what Ade turned out was gossipy in nature, snatches of overheard conversations, dialogues initiated with policemen, bartenders, delivery boys, whoever happened to be around and had something to say that Ade could use. Most of all it was fun and carried off in high good humor, and the readers loved it. George Ade was becoming a minor celebrity. Even though the columns were unsigned, many Chicagoans, particularly those in the arts and in journalism, knew it was Ade who wrote them. Light, breezy, humorous, deftly and seemingly effortlessly constructed, "Stories of the Streets and of the Town" ran for seven years in the *Chicago Record*.

The newspaper took advantage of Ade's popularity and published eight collections of the columns between 1894 and 1900 under the title of the column. In the collections each story was given a title, although they had originally appeared without titles. Some of those in the first series included: "Her Visit to Chicago," "A Victim of the Slot Machine Habit," "A Run to a Fire," "The Lonesome Passenger and the Porter," "About Arrests and Those Arrested," "The Conductor Has His Woes."

In 1894 Ade and McCutcheon began having $10 a week withheld from their salaries to save toward a trip to Europe. A year later, both decided to quit the paper and go on an extended tour (as far

as $520 apiece could take them) of Europe; they would take their chances on getting rehired when they returned. Dennis was not about to lose his two stars and made them a counterproposal: the two could tour the Continent much the same way they had been touring Chicago, sending home two illustrated travel articles a week; their salaries would continue. Ade and McCutcheon agreed, and soon their work from Europe was being seen in the *Record* under the heading "What a Man Sees Who Goes Away from Home."

The *Record* published a collection of Ade's stories and McCutcheon's illustrations as *What a Man Sees Who Goes Away from Home* in 1896. The stories were given titles for the collection, including "Ship Companions," "Sights in Brussels," "Boys in Europe," "Earthquakes in Florence," "Sights in Rome," "Italian Lotteries," "America as Viewed Abroad," and "Made Prisoners on a Paris 'Bus." Ade approached Europe with the same attitude and style that he had used so successfully in writing about Chicago, and his new articles proved just as popular with the readers as his earlier ones had been.

Ade returned from Europe having acquired a lifelong passion for travel and an itch to try something new. He again took over "Stories of the Streets and of the Town" but began to experiment with it. His stories became more and more fictionalized and characters began recurring. Ade also began experimenting with the use of slang. The first fictional character, based on an office boy Ade knew, was Artie Blanchard; Artie, with his jive-talking anecdotes about himself, was another immediate Ade hit. Ade began trying different literary forms in his column: dialogue, verse, the short story, the fable. The characters he created weaved in and out of his columns, to the delight of a growing and loyal fan club. Fred Kelly, who wrote a friendly and personable biography of Ade, was one of his fans, having become addicted to Ade as a "youngster in knee pants." Kelly had gone to the Chicago World's Fair with his mother in 1893; they had had to leave sooner than they intended because they ran out of money. Kelly remembered the experience in the preface to his biography, *George Ade* (1947):

> To console me in my disappointment, my mother said she had noticed in a morning paper, the *Record*, a daily department, "All Roads Lead to the World's Fair," delightful little stories of happenings at the fair. She would subscribe for that paper and we at least

could read about some of the things we had missed seeing.

After the fair was over, and "All Roads Lead to the World's Fair" was succeeded by "Stories of the Streets and of the Town," we continued to take the *Record*. I was entertained by the stories for years before I knew who wrote them. Then when "Fables in Slang" began to appear in the same department on the paper's editorial page I was one of the countless number to whom George Ade was a hero.

The "countless number" grew throughout the 1890s as Ade's nimble imagination expanded. Artie was succeeded by Pink Marsh, his black counterpart. Pink is the stereotype of the black as seen by whites, a characterization appearing repeatedly in popular art right up to the civil rights movement of the 1960s: a crap-shooting, high-stepping, amiably simpleminded fellow who loves his watermelon and fried chicken. Amos and Andy were his direct descendants. In Ade's columns the "Morning Customer" traded dialogue with Marsh, a bootblack in a basement barbershop. Though most of it seems offensive today, the characterization of Pink Marsh drew strong praise from Mark Twain in a letter to William Dean Howells: "Pink—oh, the shiftless, worthless, lovable black darling. Howells, he deserves to live forever." But Pink soon gave way to Doc' Horne, a roomer in a cheap hotel, a self-taught expert on almost any subject. Doc' Horne, like Pink, was a lovable bumbler, a windy buffoon who was almost always entertaining. Horne has more depth than either Pink or Artie; it is clear that Ade was giving more attention to his characterizations.

One of the reasons he was doing so was the success and acclaim given to publications of collections about each character. In 1896, the Chicago publishing house of Herbert S. Stone and Company asked Ade to link some of his best Artie pieces together for a book. This was not to be just another paperback effort by the *Record*, but a real book that would be distributed nationally by a respected publishing company. (It was Stone that introduced Bernard Shaw and H. G. Wells to American readers.) *Artie* was published initially in September 1896 and quickly went into second and third printings. Acclaim was widespread and reviews were exceptionally laudatory. This was the first Howells had seen of Ade and he was immediately smitten. Howells, perhaps America's leading literary critic at that time, was moved to write, "On the level which it

consciously seeks I do not believe there is a better study of American town life in the West." "It is brimful of fun and picturesque slang," said the *New York Recorder*. "Mr. Ade shows all the qualities of a successful novelist," said the rival *Chicago Tribune*. "Artie is a character, and George Ade has limned him deftly as well as amusingly," the *Detroit Free Press* said. "Under his rollicking abandon and recklessness we are made to feel the real sense and sensitiveness, and the worldly wisdom of a youth whose only language is that of a street-gamin." "George Ade is a writer, the direct antithesis of Stephen Crane," the *Albany Evening Journal* editorialized. "In 'Artie' he has given the world a story of the streets at once wholesome, free and stimulating." H. S. Stone published books on the other two Ade characters, *Pink Marsh* in 1897 and *Doc' Horne* in 1899. They, too, were very well received.

Artie, Pink Marsh, and Doc' Horne were only a few of the characters in the sketches, stories, and dialogues with which Ade filled his columns. The variety was endless. Ade was also doing some straight reporting, covering the Republican and Democratic national conventions in 1896 for the *Record*.

An experiment Ade first tried in his column on 17 September 1897 proved to be an extremely popular outlet for his talents, even by Ade standards. That was the day the *Record* printed the initial Ade "Fable." Ade used the antique form and stilted manner of presentation of Aesop, but he added his own inventive language and slang in the telling of the tale; also the whimsical use of capital letters added emphasis to particular words. Ade felt compelled to label that first effort "This is a Fable" so that his readers would be prepared.

In the meantime Ade's publisher had been urging him to write a novel. Ade outlined a proposal for "The College Widow" but then found he was too busy with newspaper work to do a novel; he later developed the story into one of his most successful plays. Ade suggested instead a compilation of his fables as his next book. Ade found he loved to write the fables, usually turning them out in one sitting and scarcely changing a word. He gave additional care and polish to them when they were published in book form. The very first one he wrote, "This is a Fable," became "The Fable of Sister Mae, Who Did as Well as Could Be Expected" when Stone came out with the anthology, *Fables in Slang*, in 1900. Other titles in the first of Ade's five fable books were "The Fable of the Slim Girl Who Tried to Keep a Date

That Was Never Made" and "The Fable of the Preacher Who Flew His Kite, but Not Because He Wished to Do So."

Ade had been flirting with fame with the publications of *Artie, Pink Marsh*, and *Doc' Horne*, but he certainly captured it with *Fables in Slang*. The public and the critics were at once generous. Ade had developed a wide following that was as diverse as it was large. Highbrows and lowbrows applauded, as did schoolboys and college professors, baseball players and literary critics. "I would have rather written *Fables in Slang* than be president," effused William Allen White. "His portrayal of life is almost absolute in its perfection," wrote William Dean Howells. "You experience something of the bliss of looking at your own photograph." It was at this point that Howells urged Ade to get out of journalism and write a novel of meaningful realism.

Ade was soon to get out of daily journalism but he never did get around to that realistic novel. He wrote about the problem himself: "I have promised William Dean Howells . . . that I will further consecrate my efforts to unadorned realism. But, hang it all, the circus vernacular brings in more royalties. . . . The dollar sign is luminous in the sky. Another good man gone wrong."

Ade had been negotiating with a New York publisher, R. H. Russell, to syndicate his stories to newspapers around the country. Ade had grown tired of the daily grind, and when he and Russell reached a deal, Ade left the *Record* in July 1900; his full-time journalistic career was over, although in later years he wrote scores of articles for newspapers and magazines on a free-lance basis.

After leaving the paper, Ade began writing plays; and for eight years, from 1902 to 1910, there was not a more successful playwright in America. He turned out Broadway hits almost as fast as he did newspaper columns. They ranged from *The Sultan of Sulu* (1902), a musical showing Ade's debt to Gilbert and Sullivan, to *The County Chairman* (1903), a comedy about small-town politics. Then, as quickly as he had captured the successful dramatic touch, he lost it. The reviews became less favorable and his dramatic efforts had shorter and shorter runs. Ade was so upset by the critical harshness to and short run of *U.S. Minister Bedloe* in 1911 that he virtually quit the theater. He wrote a few one-act plays and some theater sketches later, but he never returned to Broadway.

If his second career as playwright had left him disgruntled, it had also left him enormously wealthy. He had invested much of his money in

Ade with cartoonist John T. McCutcheon, his lifelong friend, in 1910

Indiana farmland and had built a spacious country estate, Hazelden, on 2,400 acres in his native Newton County. Clearly Ade would never again have to put pen to paper or do anything else to earn a living, but he continued to pour out a stream of essays, humor pieces, and reminiscences for a variety of markets. *Single Blessedness and Other Observations* (1922), a collection of these, contained material that had appeared earlier in the *American Magazine, Cosmopolitan*, the *Saturday Evening Post, Century*, and *Life*, among others.

Ade's seemingly limitless energies were involved in many other projects in his later years. He helped in a drive to build a football stadium at Purdue and did all manner of promotional work for the university and for his fraternity, Sigma Chi. He wrote a pamphlet for the Olds Motor Works; he wrote publicity for the American Merchant Marine Library Association, the Society for Preservation of American Ideals, and several other organizations. He was a much-sought-after speaker. He was awarded honorary doctorates from Purdue and Indiana University. Ade suffered a stroke and, after a

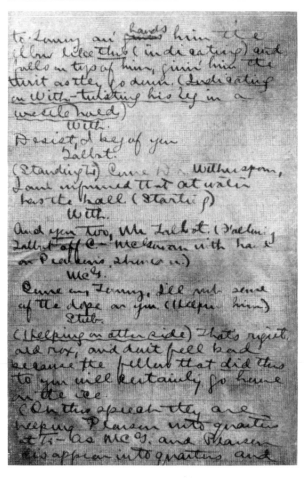

Page from the manuscript for Ade's 1924 play,
The College Widow *(Fred C. Kelly)*

and place as spoken by a representative of a particular stratum of society, which Ade could capture masterfully. What Ade did not and perhaps could not do was give the depth to Artie and Pink that Twain gave to Huck and Tom; when the moment was gone, so were the characters.

Ade put much stock in the standard Victorian virtues of his day. His stories were "wholesome" and "fun," filled with "good fellows" and "good morality." Ade made it a point not to create anything one could not read or show to his mother or sister. As a journalist he was primarily an entertainer, and his chief entertainment was humor that was not too taxing, never harsh, and always amiable.

His most original contribution and probably the work that endures best are the fables in slang. This excerpt is from *More Fables* (1900):

> When Uncle Brewster had put on his Annual Collar and combed his Beard and was about to start to the Depot, his Wife, Aunt Meeley, looked at him through her Specs and shook her Head doubtfully.
>
> Then she spoke as follows: "You go slow there in the City. You know your Failin's. You're just full of the Old Harry, and when you're Het Up you're just like as not to Raise Ned."
>
> "I guess I can take keer of myse'f about as well as the Next One," retorted Uncle Brewster. "I've been to the Mill an' got my Grist, if any one should ask. I ain't no Greeny."

short illness, he died on 16 May 1944. He was seventy-eight years old.

When news of Ade's death was reported, many people were surprised to learn that he had survived until 1944, so tied was his reputation to the decades immediately before and after the turn of the century. By the time of his death it is probably not an exaggeration to say that he was best known to crossword puzzle fans as a three-letter word for American humorist. His full-time newspaper career was comparatively brief, twelve years at the most, and his tenure as a playwright was even shorter. It is surprising that his impact was as great as it was and that he achieved such widespread popularity in such a short period.

Much of Ade's work can be criticized as superficial: Artie and Pink do not have the timelessness of Huck and Tom, although Mark Twain himself thought at the time that they did. What Twain heard was the music of the language of a given time

Who could resist following Uncle Brewster to the station? Not many.

Artie, who works in an office and holds court with whomever will listen, cannot understand how some women can go out with the men they do. The modern-day reader will have trouble understanding Artie's street argot. From *Artie* (1896): "What kills me off is how all these dubs make their star winnin's. W'y out there last night I see the measliest lot o' jays—regular Charley boys—floatin around with queens. I wish somebody'd tell me how they cop 'em out." Nobody ever does, and it is not hard to see why Artie did not endure.

In an introduction to a reprint of *Pink Marsh* in 1963, James T. Farrell says the character of Pink must be seen in perspective, as a black man serving white men in a turn-of-the-century setting, "before the racial strain in Chicago became menacing." Farrell says the use of phonetic spelling was necessary to capture Pink's dialect because of the sharp variance of speech patterns in a younger and more stratified America. The practice began with Twain and continued with Ade and Finley Peter Dunne and Ring Lardner. Still, the condescending treatment Pink receives in the barbershop from white customers who constantly bait his woeful ignorance will leave the modern reader uneasy rather than amused. In this handling Pink meets the fate of too many of Ade's characters: he becomes a caricature. For example, in this dialogue between Pink and a customer, Pink speculates as to what he might do if he found a million dollars; the customer says they would probably find Pink "at a fold table, with a watermelon on one side of him and fried chicken on the other."

> "That ain' no bad guess mistah! You can't tell neeteh—might be po'teh-house steak 'ith onions. You know I have all 'ese cullud men to wait on me—one to brush my close, one to shine my shoes, 'noteh to wait on 'e table, an' I'd have one cullud boy 'ith nothin' to do 'cept think o' what I want to eat. 'Heah boy, what you goin' o' gi' me f' suppeh?' 'Well,' he say, 'I got a little po'teh-house—an quail an' pohk-chops—le's see, sweet potatoes, ice cream, chaklum-rushe—' "
>
> "Look out there!"
>
> "O', got to have some 'at stuff—cla'et, an' fancy cakes an' champagne."
>
> "What are you talking about? You wuzn't built to stand anything better'n gin."

And so it goes. Obviously Ade drew this banter with the participants acting in good humor. But just as obviously this kind of humor is not humorous anymore.

Carl Van Doren said that Ade was for his time rather than for the ages. Lee Coyle describes Ade as a man "with a magnificent gift that he packaged for the marketplace" and says that "it is idle to speculate on what might have become of his rare talent had it been burnished at Princeton rather than at Purdue—or had he aspired to the *Atlantic Monthly*

rather than the Chicago *Record*. Ade was unequal to the discipline and the intellectual direction needed to make him other than he was. But what he was was quite enough. He was a skilled journalist, gifted with a talent that he turned to cash; and, if he grew rich upon the merriment of America, it was deserved, for America has always insisted upon enriching talent that sprinkles laughter across the land."

Bibliography:

Dorothy Ritter Russo, *A Bibliography of George Ade* (Indianapolis: Indiana Historical Society, 1947).

Biography:

Fred C. Kelly, *George Ade: Warmhearted Satirist* (Indianapolis & New York: Bobbs-Merrill, 1947).

References:

R. F. Bauerle, "A Look at the Language of George Ade," *American Speech*, 33 (February 1958): 77-79;

John Abbott Clark, "Ade's Fables in Slang: An Appreciation," *South Atlantic Quarterly*, 46 (October 1947): 537-544;

Lee Coyle, *George Ade* (New York: Twayne, 1964);

James DeMuth, *Small Town Chicago: The Comic Perspectives of Finley Peter Dunne, George Ade, and Ring Lardner* (Port Washington, N.Y.: Kennikat Press, 1980);

Bergen Evans, "George Ade, Rustic Humorist," *American Mercury*, 70 (March 1950): 321-329;

William Dean Howells, "Certain of the Chicago School of Fiction," *North American Review*, 176 (May 1903): 734-746;

Carl Van Doren, "Old Wisdom in a New Tongue," *Century*, 105 (January 1923): 471-480.

Papers:

George Ade's unpublished letters and other papers are in the Purdue University library.

Winifred Black
(Annie Laurie)

(14 October 1863-26 May 1936)

Faye B. Zuckerman
California State University, Northridge

MAJOR POSITIONS HELD: Reporter and feature writer, *San Francisco Examiner* (1889-1936), *New York Journal* (1895-1897), *Denver Post* (1898-1917).

BOOKS: *The Little Boy Who Lived on the Hill* (San Francisco: Privately printed, 1895);
"My Neighbor has Gone on a Long Journey, I Did Not Say Good-by" (San Francisco: Taylor & Taylor, 1917);
Roses and Rain (San Francisco: Black, 1920);
John Irby's Passing Creates a Void. He Lives on in Friend Memory. Stands Close to Door "Up Yonder" (San Francisco: Privately printed, 1925);
The Life and Personality of Phoebe Apperson Hearst (San Francisco: Nash, 1928);
Dope; The Story of the Living Dead (New York: Star Company, 1928).

PERIODICAL PUBLICATIONS: "Gold of the Burning Desert," *Cosmopolitan*, 39 (September 1905): 519-526;
"Case of Mrs. John Smith of London," *Cosmopolitan*, 49 (August 1910): 381-390;
"Child and Charity Trust," *Good Housekeeping*, 54 (June 1912): 740-749;
"Players and Lookers-on," *Playground*, 15 (February 1922): 694-695;
"Rambles through My Memories," *Good Housekeeping*, 102 (January 1936): 18-21; (February 1936): 36-37; (March 1936): 44-45; (April 1936): 84-85; (May 1936): 36-37.

Winifred Black in later life. Despite blindness and illness, she continued to write for William Randolph Hearst's publications almost to the day of her death in 1936 (Peter Stackpole).

One of the original women reporters to be called a "sob sister," Winifred Black wrote some 16,000 articles under the pen name "Annie Laurie" in her forty-seven-year career on the *San Francisco Examiner*. She interviewed President Benjamin Harrison and African explorer Henry Stanley; rode with William Jennings Bryan on his 1896 campaign train; became one of the first female reporters to interview a prizefighter; and befriended prostitutes, juvenile delinquents, criminals, policemen, and judges. As a "sob sister," she was a spokesperson for the downtrodden, children, and women. Her writing was prolific, empathetic, compassionate, and persuasive. Black successfully fought for civic reform, initiated crusades, and contributed to the development of a sensationalized form of news writing that became a genre for newspapers during the early twentieth century.

An extremely energetic woman, Black juggled a career in journalism with the rearing of three children at a time when women were considered only extensions of the men they married. Contemporaries said she had magnetism and a driving force which allowed her to become accepted in the then male-dominated profession of journalism. She became an editor, a syndicated columnist, and a reporter and paved the way for other women to enter the field of journalism.

Born 14 October 1863 in a secluded log cabin deep in the northeastern woods of Wisconsin, Winifred Sweet's life was influenced by her politically ambitious father, Gen. Benjamin Jeffrey Sweet, and her sister Ada, who was eleven years her elder. Her father brought noted figures of the day such as James Garfield, Ulysses S. Grant, Brigham Young, and Robert Ingersoll to visit the Sweet household. She frequently eavesdropped on her father's late-night debates with such politicians, which sparked her interest in local, national, and world affairs. In 1867, the Sweet family moved to a suburb of Chicago, where General Sweet worked as the United States pension agent for Chicago. When he died in 1874, Ada Sweet took over the position, providing some needed financial support for the family. Their mother, Lovisa Denslow Sweet, died in 1878, apparently after lapsing into a deep depression over the death of her husband.

Throughout her youth, Sweet was quite taken by one of her father's political friends, whom she described as shy and aloof; her father once predicted that this friend, James A. Garfield, would become president some day. Her father's forecast became a reality in the election of 1880. This election marked Winifred Sweet's first participation in a newsworthy event. She was quite surprised in 1880, at age seventeen, when Ada and friend Robert Ingersoll whisked her away from a New England finishing school to accompany them to the Republican convention in Chicago. The delegates were in a deadlock between General Grant and the magnetic James G. Blaine. Ingersoll solved the delegates' problem by running up to the podium and calling for the nomination of Garfield. Dark horse candidate Garfield won the nomination and chose Chester A. Arthur as his running mate to satisfy the conservative "stalwart" faction. Garfield beat the Democratic hopeful, Winfield S. Hancock, and became the twentieth president of the United States. He died a year later as the result of an assassin's bullet.

In 1882, Sweet, described as a stunning, blue-eyed redhead with a seventeen-inch waist, completed school. She picked acting as her first career and traveled with a small theatrical company, playing bit parts in small theaters throughout Canada,

New York State, and the South. She found her experiences in the theater depressing: being confined to following a script, receiving only small parts, and waiting around to appear on stage only to recite a few short sentences were boring to her. Instead of leaving the theatrical company, however, Sweet found solace in weeping, denouncing, and playing the heroine in a number of letters she wrote to her sister in Chicago. In her letters Sweet vividly described the hardships of touring with the theatrical company.

Touched by these letters, Ada would read them aloud at social gatherings. The editor of the *Chicago Tribune* was at one of these gatherings; he published one of Sweet's letters in his newspaper. This first publication sparked her interest in journalism. But having had few experiences with journalists and newspapers, she rejected the idea of journalism as a profession and continued to pursue her acting career.

In 1886, Sweet, twenty-three, found herself mixing in New York's literary circle when she was invited to stay with Mary Mapes Dodge, editor of the children's magazine *St. Nicholas*. There she was mesmerized by Dodge's literary friends and found herself eavesdropping on her host's conversations about political and social issues of the day. This was when Sweet started to consider journalism as a career. As in the old days when she had sneaked downstairs to the dining room and hidden behind the door to overhear her father's political discussions, she quietly sat at a separate table listening to the chatter of Dodge's friends, such as William Dean Howells, Mary Williams, Frank Stockton, Mary Wilkens Freeman, Richard Watson, and Samuel Clemens (Mark Twain).

After her stay with Dodge, Sweet continued to tour, even though theater life had become even more boring than before. She began to write more and more letters to her sister; the letters lost their trial-and-tribulation atmosphere and took on a more humorous and informative tone. She wrote lengthy accounts of lonely railroad stations, bizarre hotels, actors' dressing-room antics, and weird audiences. After a few more letters appeared in the *Tribune* during the late 1880s, Sweet decided to become a newspaper reporter.

In 1889 Sweet, then twenty-six, arrived in San Francisco to visit her brother-in-law, who was mourning the loss of his wife, Sweet's sister Minnie. She took one glance at the climbing streets of the most picturesque city in the western United States and made up her mind she was going to live there. As soon as she got a chance, she marched into the shabby offices of William Randolph Hearst's *San Francisco Examiner* on Montgomery Street and introduced herself as a woman of broad newspaper experience. This was probably one of her best acting jobs, as the managing editor, Sam Chamberlain, fell for her performance and hired her.

With her only knowledge of journalism being a few dramatic letters printed by chance in the *Chicago Tribune*, Sweet accepted her first assignment: to cover the 1889 California Flower Show. Devoid of any kind of news judgment, she planted herself atop a stepladder at the show and feverishly wrote down what she saw. When the show ended, Sweet whipped through the dimly lit streets of San Francisco and handed Chamberlain her first news story. Chamberlain needed only a quick glance at the article to see its weakness: it was stilted, filled with adjectives and long elaborations about the exhibits. Explaining that she was writing for an audience of middle-class people and not for the upper class, Chamberlain tore her story to shreds while he told her that good writing had no place in a newspaper.

But Sweet was determined to become a journalist. She swallowed her pride and rewrote the story, choosing words and descriptions carefully. After adding the pen name "Annie Laurie," from a song her mother used to sing to her when she was a child, she turned in her copy and left the office, sure that she no longer had a job. After a sleepless night, she was delighted to discover her story on page one; the editor had rewritten the first three paragraphs, but the rest was unchanged. It had never occurred to her, she later wrote in her memoirs, to tell the reader "where it [the flower show] was, who was giving it, who offered the prizes and who won them."

When she went back to the *Examiner* office, she learned that Chamberlain had hired her on a permanent basis for $15 a week. Her next few assignments were covering flower shows and writing about San Francisco high society. Again she knew she was doing only the bit parts, this time on a newspaper instead of on a stage. She studied the paper's style, trying to develop the simplistic, tight writing William Randolph Hearst wanted to see in his publication. Sweet soon learned that dramatic results were best obtained with short sentences and small words in a lucid sequence.

In January 1890, after only a few months on the *Examiner*, Sweet showed she was game to do anything in the pursuit of news. This was exactly the philosophy the newspaper was trying to instill in the young woman reporter. The plan was for Black to follow the lead of famed stunt reporter Elizabeth Cochrane ("Nellie Bly") of Joseph Pulitzer's *New York World*. Cochrane was then in the midst of performing her most famous promotional stunt: trotting the globe in an attempt to beat the fictitious record set in Jules Verne's *Around the World in Eighty Days* (1873) for Pulitzer's sensational, crusading newspaper.

Sweet's first stunt was to get herself admitted to San Francisco Receiving Hospital, where it had been rumored that the medical staff was negligent in its patient care. After a few obvious falls and stumbles and a final dramatic faint on a crowded street corner, she managed to get herself taken to the suspect hospital, where she took mental notes on how she was treated by the staff and doctors. An accusatory exposé titled "A City's Disgrace" appeared on the front page of the *Examiner*'s Sunday feature section on 19 January 1890. In the article, Sweet kept readers entertained with a description of the male staff members' lewd sexual advances and horrified by her account of the brutal treatment she received from doctors and nurses. She was indignant about being force-fed incorrect medication and getting taken to the hospital in a prison van rather than an ambulance. This time she wrote in clear, concise sentences and avoided "fine writing" and using too many adjectives; her article apparently contained the mix of civic reform and sensationalism that Hearst wanted in the newspaper. As a result of the exposé, city officials called for improved health care services and organized an adequate ambulance service for San Francisco. Her investigative news story not only brought changes in hospital procedure and personnel but became her initiation into the world of "yellow journalism."

The San Francisco Receiving Hospital story was the beginning of a long series of crusading and sensational articles in which Sweet called for various civic reforms. Later in 1890, she wrote an emotional story about juvenile delinquents, "Lads Who Know No Mothers." She vividly portrayed the hardships of female workers in "Women Clerks Who Make Over One Hundred Dollars a Month" in 1892. She spent three days working in a canning factory for poverty wages, which she described in a compelling front-page article, also in 1892. In addition to portraying the woman's angle while crusading for civic reform, Sweet wrote a series of articles about politics and politicians. She spent a day in Sacramento observing California Governor Markham at work. On 1 March 1890, in a front-page story headlined "Our Governor at His Work, Annie Laurie's Day with the Man Who Guides the Ship of State," Sweet de-

*Winifred Sweet as a young reporter for William Randolph
Hearst's* San Francisco Examiner

wangled her way into an interview with the king of
Hawaii, Kalakua I. "Annie Laurie Called on His
Majesty Kalakua I" appeared on 9 April 1890 on the
front page of the Sunday features section. This
article illustrates Sweet's personalized, emotional
writing style. The article's lead said: "The Sandwich
Islands are often called, in the flowery language of
the guide-book, the 'Paradise of the Pacific.' According to my experience, they could be as appro-
priately named the 'Paradise of Politicians.' " She
often interjected her opinions into her articles:

> The court is carried on with all the pomp and
> ceremony of an empire. There are all sorts of
> dignitaries with grand titles which fill the soul
> of the awe-struck republican with amazement
> and wonder. The rules of precedence are
> rigidly enforced, and the formalities of the
> Court of St. James are imitated with great zest
> by the courters. . . .
>   The Americans are the ruling power, of
> course, without any doubt and their republi-
> can ideas will creep out in the sort of amused
> tolerance with which they regard the at-
> tempts at monarchical state. The natives like
> display and royal magnificence, and are firm
> believers in the "divinity that doth hedge a
> King." It was not many years ago that the
> person of a sovereign was so sacred to them
> that no one was allowed to approach him
> standing, and as for any unlucky wight who
> was unfortunate enough to inadvertently
> walk through the shadow of his king, he was
> summarily punished by a hideous death.
> Much of this old reverence still remains with
> the natives. . . .

scribed Markham as a fair-minded, compassionate
official. But she had no qualms about bitterly
criticizing San Francisco's mayor in "He Who
Ruleth a City" in 1892.

Her forte was uncovering injustice and corruption through daring stunts which she could turn
into first-person descriptions of her experiences,
filled with editorial commentary and emotionalism.
She worked best when story assignments were
vague: it was on the scant instructions of her editor
that Sweet boarded a boat for Hawaii in pursuit of a
story on life in a leper colony. The *Examiner*'s front
pages followed her exploits in Molokai as she
examined the colony. In one article, "Among the
Lepers," she used highly charged prose to explain
the disease and describe the daily life of the colony's
inhabitants. Sweet also interviewed family members
who came to Molokai to remain near their loved
ones. Just before she was to leave for home, she

Managing to manipulate her way into interviews to get what she called a "scoop" won the
actress-turned-journalist much of her fame and
popularity. She was not back one week from her
Hawaii stunt before she performed another of her
exploits. Chamberlain told her that President Harrison's private train was due to arrive in San Francisco that day and that the press had been banned.
Determined to get an exclusive story, the twenty-
nine-year-old Sweet went to the station and hopped
aboard the train when an entrance was temporarily
left unguarded. As the train whistled out of the
station, Sweet was making her way to the president's
stateroom. By chance she met Governor Markham,
who offered to introduce her to Harrison. By the
time the train reached Nevada, Sweet had become
one of the few women journalists to interview a

president in the nineteenth century. (In the 1820s, Ann Royall reportedly sat on John Quincy Adams's clothes on the bank of the Potomac River until the president agreed to grant her an interview.)

While the name Annie Laurie had become a regular feature among the pages of the *Examiner* by 1892, the newspaper had doubled its circulation and passed its top competitor, the *San Francisco Chronicle*. William Randolph Hearst, who had taken over the *Examiner* in 1886, had turned the shabby, six-page Democratic political party organ into a successful big-city daily newspaper by 1892. He offered his staff generous salaries, for which he expected daring reporting methods and highly charged stories. The *Examiner* newsroom buzzed with talented journalists: humorist Bill Nye wrote a regular column, as did the cynical Ambrose Bierce; reporter "Petey" Biglow, who rode into the mountains to interview bandits, performed stunts similar to Sweet's. The primary cartoonist for the *Examiner* then was Homer Davenport.

The blue-eyed redhead from Wisconsin had found a niche for herself in journalism. She needed the feel of deadline pressure and the flexibility of choosing an angle for a story to make her life less confining. She, like other *Examiner* staff members, began to think nothing of sixteen-hour workdays; she felt sad at the thought of returning after work to her hotel room. Each morning she would jump out of bed and head for the newspaper office, which at that time had no typewriters or ticker tape machines spewing out news: all the energy was supplied by staff members who rushed around the office to get the news out; and in the early 1890s, news stories at the *Examiner* were still handwritten. Sweet aggressively pursued and wrote two or three major stories a week. She took on added responsibility by becoming the originator and editor of both the *Examiner* Christmas edition and the newspaper's Sunday children's page. In addition, she found time in 1892 to marry a fellow reporter, Orlow Black.

In 1895 Winifred Black received a telegram from Hearst instructing her to come to New York to help build the circulation of his newly acquired *New York Journal*. She left her husband and her son at her boss's call, and she, Davenport, and sportswriter Charlie C. Dryden all traveled to New York to join the *Journal*. To the East Black brought her vigor for finding and reporting the news. On the *Journal* she wrote as Winifred Black, continuing to write as Annie Laurie for the *Examiner*. Black became part of a close-knit network of professionals who were dedicated to Hearst and formed his inner council of advisers. Hearst, thirty-two in 1895, personally gave

Black, also thirty-two, assignments. In New York she wrote such stories as "Why Girls Kill Themselves" and "Strange Things Women Do for Love." During a cloak makers strike, Black roamed a soup kitchen Hearst had opened and financed, looking for human interest stories. Black's sympathetic style of writing, which overplayed issues to get emotional reactions from readers, had become perfected by 1895.

For Black, however, New York had lost the exhilarating appeal of 1886, when she had stayed with Mary Mapes Dodge. Now she said that the city was unbearable, the winters too cold and summers too fearful; she called New York "depressing." She looked for excuses to return to San Francisco, the city she had fallen in love with at first sight. In 1895, during one of her frequent trips to the West Coast, she again wrote for the *Examiner*; such articles as "House Hunting in New York," "Annie Laurie in New York," and "Odd Eastern Things" appeared in the Sunday feature section of the newspaper.

Because of her dislike for New York, Black chose assignments which took her to other cities or countries. After 1896 her beat virtually became the world. *Examiner* and *Journal* readers waited with bated breath to find out what injustice or corruption Black would weed out in some corner of the world. She turned up on board William Jennings Bryan's 1896 campaign train as the only female correspondent and received several exclusive interviews with Mrs. Bryan. A few months later, readers, via one of Black's news stories, learned the horrors of a bullfight Black attended in Mexico. She wrote about Mormon polygamy in "Polygamy Yet Vigorous in Utah." In Kentucky she tracked down and interviewed a state senator who was hiding from a band of assassins.

In 1897, Black returned to San Francisco, apparently because her husband had died. She was soon assigned to write from the woman's angle on San Francisco's murder trials. She described teary-eyed spectators, the forlorn family members of the accused, and trembling witnesses. She was perfecting her "sob sister" style. One of the first trials she covered was a gruesome murder by William Henry Theodore Durrant, the superintendent of a Baptist church, in 1898. Black and *San Francisco Chronicle* reporter Mabel Craft were the first women to sit at the press table in the courtroom. Black scooped all the other reporters when she followed and got an exclusive interview with a young girl nicknamed the "Sweet Pea Girl," whose custom it was to send a bouquet of flowers to the accused and wear a necklace of sweet peas around her neck. Black also interviewed Durrant in his cell; the interview appeared in a front-page story headlined "Annie Laurie Visits Durrant in Broadway Jail."

Soon after, for unknown reasons, Black moved to Denver with her son. There she began to write for the *Denver Post*. Although she was a reporter for the *Post*, several of Black's stories appeared in the *San Francisco Examiner* after 1898; she apparently always wrote for the Hearst chain regardless of where she was living and working. One of her greatest stunt stories was syndicated by the Hearst International News Service in 1900, while Black was living in Denver. This was her coverage of the Galveston, Texas, flood. Of all of Hearst's reporters, Black was the closest at the time to Galveston. Hearst wanted her to get to the city before competing newspapers could report on a tidal wave that had left a death toll of nearly 7,000. On Hearst's command, she took the next train to Texas and was one of the first reporters and the only woman journalist to witness the aftermath of the disaster. When Black returned to her hotel room after filing her first story about the flood, she was met with several telegrams informing her that four Hearst newspapers had organized relief programs to help the people of Galveston. Black's instructions were to find a hospital. In the end, she commandeered an eighty-bed hospital and raised nearly $350,000, $60,000 of it from Hearst's personal account. Additionally, she wrote a series of articles which asked readers to send relief. These disaster stories were typical of the kinds of crusades Hearst wanted in his newspaper.

On 17 September 1900, one such story, entitled "Many Lives Are Saved: Surgeons and Nurses Doing Heroic Work," revealed not only how Black covered news events but how her writing style had developed into what would later be called "sob sister journalism." This story's lead ran: "Houston (Tex). September 16—We took care of 150 people at Houston Hospital last night. Out of these 150 people 100 are seriously ill and 50 were hungry, dazed and worn out with the days of misery and distress. We are only just beginning to find out what this awful calamity has been to people in this vicinity. The first shock is wearing off, the long lists of dead and missing are getting to be an old story now and the sick and suffering are crawling into our places of refuge. Some of them have been sleeping on open prairies ever since the storm—most of them in fact; men with broken arms and broken legs, sick women and ailing children. They crawl out of the wreck of their homes and lie down on the bare ground to die."

In 1901, Black married Charles Bonfils, brother of *Denver Post* co-owner Frederick Bonfils; they had two children: an invalid son and a daughter, Winifred. She continued to use the name Black professionally.

In 1906, Black performed another crusade-stunt when a major earthquake struck San Francisco, toppling buildings and leaving thousands homeless. On the day of the earthquake, Black received a telegram in Denver from Hearst. The telegram said, "Go." She went. Black's instructions, once she arrived in San Francisco, were to quickly organize a crusade for the Hearst International News Service; Hearst wanted her to monitor how his newspapers brought in relief to San Francisco. Again, Black was instrumental in setting up a relief fund as well as a medical facility.

By 1907, after nearly nine years of rarely missing a major murder trial, Black—along with Dorothy Dix, Ada Patterson, and Nixola Greeley-Smith—had become a regular fixture in American courtrooms. They all wrote highly emotional news stories about how the people most affected by a trial behaved during the proceedings. The women reporters sat at a centrally located table, which was the customary position for the press, covering the trial as a running story. All other reporters and feature writers had a row of seats assigned to them in a corner. It was at the 1907 Harry Thaw trial in New York that a cynical colleague, Irvin Cobb, labeled Black and her associates "sob sisters," because of what he called their saccharine and emotion-charged prose. Black despised the label. She wrote, "I am not a 'Sob Sister' or a special writer. I'm just a plain, practical all-around newspaper woman. That is my profession and that is my pride. I'd rather smell the printers' ink and hear the presses go round than go to any grand opera in the world."

In twenty years of working for Hearst, Black had more than once proved her allegiance to him. She was one of the few who consistently defended Hearst as a decent employer and wrote for his publications. She contributed several articles to the Hearst-owned *Cosmopolitan*, and her memoirs appeared in *Good Housekeeping*.

In 1910, she ventured to England to write about the British suffragettes, a militant group who fought the police and protested the treatment of women by pouring acid in letter boxes. Her 1901 marriage to Charles Bonfils had turned into a charade, she said, and she clearly preferred traveling around the world in pursuit of the news to staying home in Denver with her husband. She complained that Bonfils had little interest in newspapers or newspaper work.

By 1915, at age fifty-one, Black had turned the name Annie Laurie into a San Francisco institution. She felt few qualms about openly attacking anyone who stood in the way of her crusades. She worked closely with Hearst's mother, Phoebe Apperson Hearst, to raise funds to save the famed Palace of Fine Arts building in San Francisco. "Every time there was a hint of Demolition, Black gave such loud shrieks of anguish in a public way that the matter was dropped cold," Ishbel Ross wrote.

Black left her husband in 1917 and moved back to San Francisco with her children, although the couple were never divorced. "Your paper was your sweetheart and your wife and your child and your smart outfit—it was your life and your heart's blood and the very soul of you," Black explained.

Shortly thereafter, Black was off on another adventure, this time traveling around Europe as an unofficial correspondent during World War I. Few of her stories appeared in the *Examiner*, because her articles rarely made it past the censors. When Black returned to San Francisco, she harshly berated the censors in the *Examiner* for halting the news. This type of acid writing often characterized Black's style of writing during the last fifteen years of her career.

One of the last articles Black wrote in her famed sob-sister style was an obituary of Phoebe Apperson Hearst in 1919. When his mother died, William Randolph Hearst insisted that Black write the obituary; he said that if Black could not be found, only a straight news account could appear in the newspaper. Forty minutes before deadline, the *Examiner* staff tracked Black down aboard a ferry in San Francisco Bay, heading toward Berkeley. She rushed back to the office and churned out a three-column feature article eulogizing Phoebe Hearst. Later, in twelve days, she wrote a 200-page pamphlet about Mrs. Hearst's life, which Hearst had printed on parchment paper with handset type and bound in vellum.

Black's acid attacks and conservative political leanings became more apparent near the end of her forty-seven-year career. She bitterly attacked the League of Nations narcotics conferences of 1931. From her reporter's position at the Geneva-based conferences, Black accused world leaders of making decisions which hurt Americans rather than helped them. As the head of this major crusade against drug abuse and trafficking, she used sensational writing techniques to taint the news.

By the 1930s, Black's glowing red hair had turned white and her seventeen-inch waist had

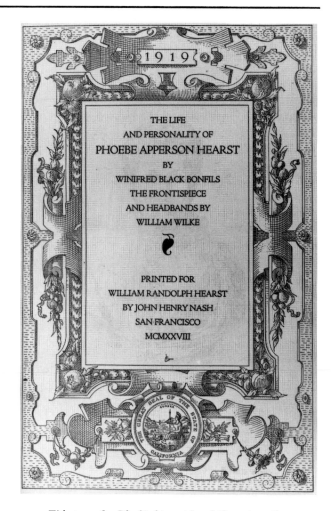

Title page for Black's biography of Hearst's mother, written at the publisher's request

grown plump with age. By 1936, Black, blinded as a result of diabetes and sickly from old age, was confined to her bed. Then seventy-two, she continued to keep up a healthy working pace, writing weekly about five articles for the Hearst syndicate and about three articles for the *Examiner*. Seven months before she died she was taken on her first airplane ride. On 26 May 1936, Black died, survived by her daughter, Winifred, and her estranged husband; her oldest son had drowned in 1926 off Carmel, California. The Little Jim Endowment Fund, a San Francisco charity she had set up in 1896 and named for an incurably ill child she had written about, lived on as well.

Winifred Black had a knack for vividly personalizing incidents so as to get an emotional response from readers. Typical of writers in the yellow journalist genre, she never let anything stand in the way of the pursuit of news: she once marched down a church aisle, interrupted the minister in the middle of his sermon, and received the information she desired. "If feminine wiles don't work, smash through the door," she once said.

One of the original and most famous of the sob sisters, Black contributed to the development of a newspaper genre in which editorializing, using the first person, and describing events with emotion were the accepted form. Black's flair for the dramatic was satisfied not by the theater, but by reporting assignments she sensationalized into front page news stories. A fighter for civic reform and the rights of the downtrodden, Black believed in yellow journalism, using its techniques long after the style had become obsolete; in doing so, she became one of its lasting symbols.

References:
"Annie Laurie," *Time* (October 1935): 50-51;

Edwin Emery and Michael Emery, *The Press and America* (Englewood Cliffs, N.J.: Prentice-Hall, 1978);

Edwin Ford and Edwin Emery, *Highlights in the History of the American Press* (Minneapolis: University of Minnesota Press, 1954);

Robert McHenry, *Liberty's Women* (Springfield, Mass.: Merriam, 1980): 34;

New York Times, May 1936, section 2, p. 26;

Ishbel Ross, *Ladies of the Press* (New York: Harper, 1936);

Patricia Schofler, "A Glorious Adventure . . . ," *American History Illustrated* (February 1981).

Papers:
While there is no formal collection of Winifred Black's papers, several of her letters can be found in the papers of various California public officials and journalists at the Bancroft Library at the University of California, Berkeley.

Oliver K. Bovard
(27 May 1872-3 November 1945)

Ronald T. Farrar
University of Kentucky

MAJOR POSITION HELD: Managing editor, *St. Louis Post-Dispatch* (1908-1938).

"O.K.B.," as the legendary Oliver Kirby Bovard became known throughout the newspaper world, is widely regarded—along with Carr Van Anda of the *New York Times*—as one of the ablest managing editors of his era. Bovard deployed the staff of the *St. Louis Post-Dispatch* with the brilliance of a great general, and under his leadership the newspaper built a distinguished reputation for aggressive reporting and journalistic integrity. In his newspaper's handling of day-to-day news, Bovard insisted upon a presentation that was accurate and unbiased; as a crusading editor in the Pulitzer tradition, he exposed waste and corruption at all levels—from local graft in St. Louis to the national scandal known as Teapot Dome. Although he was largely unknown to the general public—Bovard had a lifelong passion for self-effacement—he became a heroic figure of epic proportions to report-

ers and other editors as tales of his genius spread to newsrooms throughout the country. He was a newspaperman's newspaperman, an editor revered within a craft where reverence is not easily conferred.

Born in St. Louis on 27 May 1872 to Charles Wyrick and Hester Bunn Bovard, Bovard learned early about the press from his father, a printer and editor for several newspapers, including the *Post-Dispatch*. Bovard's formal education, however, ended with the seventh grade; although he passed the entrance examinations for high school, he was unable to attend and took a job instead. He worked in clerical positions for several years before being hired as a reporter by the *St. Louis Star* in 1896. His duties included general assignment reporting and at least one specialty—the bicycle beat. The cycling rage was sweeping the country, and Bovard, an ardent cyclist, wrote about the bicycle sprints and endurance races that were then in fashion. At one time Bovard himself cycled from St. Louis to

Oliver K. Bovard

Mexico City in a widely heralded, but unsuccessful, attempt to establish a handicap distance record. His reports were popular with bicycle enthusiasts—and with gamblers who bet heavily on the races. But Bovard soon was ready to take on more ambitious news stories. In 1898 he wrote an article exposing a transportation company's bribery of city officials in order to acquire a profitable street railway franchise. Sensing that the *Star*'s publisher would reject the article for political reasons, Bovard took the piece to the *Post-Dispatch* and offered it for publication in exchange for a job as a reporter. The story led to a massive criminal investigation and demands for municipal reform. None of the boodlers went to prison for some time, but Bovard's immediate ambition—to be a newsman for the *Post-Dispatch*— was realized.

Then only twenty years old, the *Post-Dispatch*,

the result of a merger of two weak papers brought about by the immigrant Joseph Pulitzer, had already moved into the lead among St. Louis's afternoon dailies. Under Pulitzer's driving leadership, the *Post-Dispatch* had enlivened the region with what would later be described as "the New Journalism," a powerful combination of aggressive investigative reporting, crusading editorials, and vigorous promotion. Pulitzer demanded that his newspaper do more than merely publish the news; it should, in his view, become a positive force operating in the public interest.

This milieu was an ideal one for young Bovard, and he flourished in it. Within two years he had been promoted to city editor, in immediate charge of the local reporting staff. Realizing that the *Post-Dispatch* must go beyond crusades and occasional scoops, Bovard became determined to upgrade the quality of the newspaper's daily news report. Through planning, hard work, and a strong competitive spirit, he swiftly shaped his reporters into the strongest staff in the city. Charles Chapin, himself a distinguished city editor in New York, visited the *Post-Dispatch* and wrote Pulitzer that "Bovard is the first city editor in St. Louis," adding that he "is quick to scent a news story and a good man to develop it. He works with unflagging zeal all of the time and I think the reporters respect and sustain him." Bovard's biographer, James W. Markham, says the young city editor "might have been a Roman patrician. His handsome finely cut features and his brilliant glacial blue eyes gave the impression of a man born to rule. He kept his emotions well under control. Most of the time he appeared calm, spoke in low tones, and was generally undemonstrative; but he could become surprisingly intense in discussing subjects close to his interests. Although he was a man of strong likes and dislikes, he apparently never permitted prejudices to govern his actions. His mind was receptive to new ideas. His judgment was quick, courageous, and decisive, reflecting self-confidence. His journalistic skill inspired trust and commanded respect."

Bovard remained a bachelor until he was thirty and, indeed, had openly deplored the idea of matrimony in his case, calling that institution a threat to his personal liberty. His attitude reversed itself, however, when he was introduced by a mutual friend to eighteen-year-old Suzanne Thompson, a visitor to St. Louis from San Antonio, Texas. They were married on 16 June 1902.

In the winter of 1908, a staff shake-up on the *Post-Dispatch* left the top job in the newsroom, that of managing editor, open. Bovard was the logical

Bovard (center) and some of his reporters in 1898 (St. Louis Post-Dispatch*)*

choice to receive the promotion, but his superiors felt that the young man needed additional seasoning. As a result the final decision was delayed: Bovard was awarded the job but not the title; he was designated "acting" managing editor. A year later, still carrying the title "acting" managing editor, Bovard was summoned to New York and assigned a position on Pulitzer's illustrious *New York World*. Actually he was in effect undergoing a prolonged audition for the managing editorship of the *World*. After some months, Pulitzer chose another man to head the *World*'s news operation, but he had been greatly impressed with Bovard and directed him to remain in New York as assistant managing editor. Bovard refused, calmly asserting to Pulitzer that he had no desire to be subordinate to a managing editor who was less of a journalist than himself. Pulitzer angrily accused Bovard of challenging his judgment, but Bovard held his ground—contending that he would rather go back to St. Louis than "play second fiddle" in New York. When he ultimately determined that Bovard's mind was made up, Pulitzer acquiesced, returning him to St. Louis "with increased salary and emoluments"—

and the managing editorship, with full and final authority for the news operations of the *Post-Dispatch*. This was the job he wanted, and he held it for nearly thirty years.

Once back in St. Louis, Bovard moved rapidly to consolidate and build his empire. Before long he brought under his tight control virtually all of the news-editorial side of the paper except for the editorial page itself—and he coveted even that. Next, Bovard undertook to expand the paper's national and international coverage. Correspondents were dispatched overseas, and plans were put in motion for a Washington bureau. Bovard could be ruthless in his quest for power, and his machinations earned him many enemies. One of them, Roy Howard, then a *Post-Dispatch* wire editor and later to head the worldwide operations of United Press, publicly regarded Bovard as "a classic example of the stuffy, high-hat, supercilious, cold-blooded, know-it-all type of executive." The reporters, the rank and file of the staff, regarded their managing editor with varying combinations of adoration, hatred, and fear. All agreed that he got results.

Bovard's unique managerial style became the

subject of tales told in newsrooms across the land. One anecdote involved a young reporter who, upon being told by Bovard that his services were no longer required, protested, "But Mr. Bovard, I've got to live!" To which Bovard replied, "Not necessarily." In another instance, a reporter's wife got into some difficulty with the police. The news story, as it moved across Bovard's desk, identified the woman as the wife of a *Post-Dispatch* reporter. Coldly, Bovard penciled in "former" before *"Post-Dispatch* reporter," and the unlucky young man learned when he read the paper that afternoon that he had been fired. To another reporter, a former theatrical press agent who was given to exaggerating the glamour of show business in the articles he wrote, Bovard handed a dismissal notice and remarked, "I have stood between you and a stage career long enough."

His dressing downs were frequent, and sometimes brutal. Once a reporter submitted a "think piece" (a speculative essay) which was poorly researched. Even worse, the author had signed his own by-line to the article—a breach of professional etiquette, since by-lines are customarily awarded by editors to reporters in recognition of better-than-average work. Bovard called the writer before him and said, "I have read your composition, and I am going to put both you and the *Post-Dispatch* under obligation to me by depositing it here," motioning toward the wastebasket. "You have attached your name to it, I see. Well, writing yourself down as a fool before me doesn't matter much, but you shouldn't advertise yourself in that character. Remember, the paper has a circulation of 150,000."

Another young reporter, Charles G. Ross, contributed to the legend by becoming a Bovard object lesson. Ross had been dispatched to an extreme corner of St. Louis for a story about a painter who had fallen from a smokestack. The accident occurred well beyond the outermost point of the streetcar line, and so Ross was required to trudge a considerable distance during the worst part of a hot, dusty day. After much exertion, he finally located the factory, gathered the information he thought he would need, and started back toward the newspaper office, arriving there late in the afternoon. Bovard looked over Ross's account of the accident, then stunned the young reporter with one question: "How *tall* was the smoke-stack?" Ross could not reply in specific terms, but said he had seen the smokestack, and that it was "quite tall." "Tall is a relative term," Bovard said crisply. "I want you to go back and find out the exact height." It was late that night when Ross returned to the city room once

again, this time with the precise information in feet and inches. It was a lesson etched deeply into his experience, and Ross—who later won a Pulitzer Prize and became press secretary to President Harry S Truman—never forgot it.

Those who saw only the harsh side of O. K. Bovard, however, were usually those who did not really know him—a point made by Paul Y. Anderson, who, under Bovard's tutelage, became one of the most effective investigative reporters in journalism history. "Despite legends which dramatize Bovard's sardonic humor and cruel wit," Anderson wrote, "the fact remains that he was the best friend of every competent man who ever worked for him."

By any standard, Bovard developed and gave direction to some of the greatest newspaper staffs ever assembled. Besides Anderson (who won the Pulitzer Prize for exposing the Teapot Dome scandal) and Ross, the *Post-Dispatch* could also boast of John T. Rogers, another Pulitzer Prize winner whose articles brought about the impeachment of a federal judge in Illinois; authors Silas Bent and Frederick H. Brennan; nationally prominent columnists Lowell Mellett, Marquis Childs, and Raymond P. Brandt; and a number of others who became famous as Hollywood screenwriters, magazine journalists, and foreign correspondents. Many of Bovard's finest newspapermen, notably Sam Shelton, Carlos Hurd, Frank A. Behymer, Rogers, and Anderson, remained with the *Post-Dispatch* for all or most of their careers.

Having no use for a private office, Bovard invariably sat at a desk in the newsroom personally checking copy, changing headlines, and talking with his troops. Although he was readily accessible to everyone on the staff, Bovard was always in command, something his subordinates rarely forgot. Challenged once by a reporter on the dictionary spelling of a word, Bovard replied, "Webster may be right, but he's not editing the *Post-Dispatch*!"

Bovard's own sure news judgment caused him to refuse to print one of the biggest news stories of the century—a story later proven to be wrong. This was the "false armistice" report mistakenly announcing the end of World War I. When the bulletin moved over the United Press telegraph on 7 November 1918, another St. Louis afternoon paper issued an extra with banner headlines trumpeting the armistice signing. Bovard discounted the report, and the *Post-Dispatch* carried no reference to it, except to note the wild celebrations in downtown St. Louis caused by the announcement. A few hours later the entire country learned what Bovard had suspected—that the armistice report was an error.

Fully vindicated, Bovard explained his editorial reasoning: "The extra (issued by another paper) said the signing took place at 11 a.m. French time. Analysis of the official news from France showed that the German armistice commissioners had not entered the French lines up to that hour, and that General Pershing's army was heavily engaged in front of Sedan as late as 1:45 p.m. It was further obvious that the signing could not take place for several hours after the meeting of the two parties. Finally, the message bore no inherent mark of truth, no authority was given. While this was not a factor in reaching the decision, it was interesting to note."

Bovard's hard work and executive ability won him professional accolades and a substantial income—his salary and bonuses in the pre-Depression era frequently topped $75,000 a year—but the restless managing editor was ambitious for even more power with the *Post-Dispatch*; he wanted control of the paper's editorial page.

Following the stock market crash of 1929, Bovard's ideas took a sharp leftward turn, and soon he began developing his own solutions for the country's economic problems. His thesis was set forth in a privately circulated essay which he entitled "Forward with Socialism and Democracy." In his biography of Bovard, Markham describes the managing editor's position as favoring public ownership of utilities and major national resources and a massive redistribution of the country's wealth. The New Deal, Bovard thought, was a sham; he contemptuously dismissed President Roosevelt as "a mere actor" and "the Kerensky of the American revolution."

As Bovard's views grew even more radical, those of his publisher, Joseph Pulitzer, Jr. (the senior Pulitzer had died in 1911 and had been succeeded by the youngest of his three sons) moved in the other direction; the managing editor found himself at odds with the paper's deepening conservatism. To the astonishment of many of the staff, the *Post-Dispatch* editorial page became ever more cautious, to the point of endorsing the Republican Alf Landon in the presidential election of 1936. The younger Pulitzer, who had idolized his managing editor—in his will he had named Bovard the guardian of his own children—now felt that Bovard's political activism, and his ambition, must be curbed. The two men clashed, with Pulitzer criticizing Bovard at one point for being "too radical for editorial control and too contemptuous of business for business office control." Eventually the publisher directed criticism at the news department of the

paper, a realm heretofore regarded as Bovard's alone. As Pulitzer, finally out of his illustrious father's shadow, continued to assert himself ever more, Bovard's frustrations increased.

The last straw for Bovard was a memorandum from Pulitzer in the spring of 1938, a lengthy critique of Bovard's judgment in handling and displaying the news. Comparing the front pages of the *Post-Dispatch* with those of the *New York Times* for a fifteen-day period, the publisher found the *Post-Dispatch* "disappointing and monotonous." That same afternoon, 13 May 1938, Bovard turned in his resignation:

> Dear J.P.:
>   Your comparative analysis of *Times* and *P-D* front pages prompts, but is not the cause of, my resignation, which please accept at your convenience.
>   I reached the decision to step out more than a year ago and there is no longer reason for deferring the action.
>   You will scarcely be surprised, I think, because you have always been familiar with my views on public questions and newspaper policy, and my inability to sympathize with much of the paper's general course.
>   Those differences eventually became a strain on my sense of propriety. As you know I feel the paper lacks a philosophy of its own and merely marks time in this stirring period. In this situation my work does not give me the satisfaction I formerly derived from it. . . .

Pulitzer attempted to dissuade Bovard, but the managing editor held firm, the two men finally agreeing that the resignation should take effect in one year. However, not long after that the paper's business office, presumably without Pulitzer's knowledge, proposed to cut some salaries in Bovard's news department; Bovard angrily demanded that his resignation be accepted at once. Pulitzer interceded in Bovard's behalf, overruling the proposed salary cuts, but Bovard insisted upon leaving anyway. Using the thick blue copy pencil that had become his trademark, Bovard scribbled a memorandum and posted it on the newsroom bulletin board. The shocked staffers, most of whom were unaware of the clash between Bovard and Pulitzer, read this message:

> With regret I have to tell you that I have resigned because of irreconcilable differences of opinion with Mr. Pulitzer as to the general conduct of the paper, and am leaving

office August 23. I recognize and respect the rights and responsibilities of ownership and make no complaints.

I salute you, a splendid body of men and an exceptional newspaper staff. I shall always be proud of my association with you, and my best wishes remain with you collectively and individually. . . .

Following his resignation, Bovard chose to live out his days at Windridge Farm, his ninety-two-acre estate near St. Louis. He jealously guarded his privacy, resisting invitations to lecture at journalism schools, to write articles dealing with press performance, and to serve as a newspaper consultant. He and his wife made few public appearances and from all indications enjoyed the quiet life. Bovard busied himself with the supervision of his farm acreage and orchards and left the estate only rarely, usually for hunting trips. It was on one of these, an expedition to Canada in the autumn of 1944, that he developed a bronchial illness which was followed by a persistent fever. The following year, on a hunting trip to Saskatchewan, he became ill again; he returned home and two weeks later entered a hospital suffering from pneumonia. A week later he was dead.

The eulogies that poured in from journalists throughout the world stressed Bovard's personal integrity, his intellectual honesty, his good taste, and his tireless quest for editorial excellence. Most moving of all were tributes from his former staff members. One of them, written by Paul Y. Anderson for the *Nation*, summed up Bovard's remarkable career: "For twenty years he was the most influential individual in St. Louis, but to the city's general public his name was unknown. It never appeared in 'Who's Who.' The exploits of many men who performed them under Bovard's guidance are recorded in that volume, but not his. Other editors made the after-dinner speeches and served on the reception committees; 'O.K.B.' was content to run the paper. He shunned society and never joined a club. Yet in the narrow circle where he chose to move outside the office he was prized as a rare and delightful companion. He deliberately cloistered his private life to avoid associations which might embarrass him in his single-minded determination to get and print all the news. In that implacable resolve, God knows, he never wavered."

References:

Paul Y. Anderson, "The Greatest Managing Editor," *Nation* (13 August 1938): 142;

Ronald T. Farrar, *Reluctant Servant: The Story of Charles G. Ross* (Columbia: University of Missouri Press, 1968);

James W. Markham, *Bovard of the Post-Dispatch* (Baton Rouge: Louisiana State University Press, 1954);

"O. K. Bovard Retires," *Newsweek* (8 August 1938): 33;

"Sealed Envelope," *Time* (8 August 1938): 56.

Arthur Brisbane

Lucas G. Staudacher
Marquette University

BIRTH: Buffalo, New York, 12 December 1864, to Albert and Sarah White Brisbane.

MARRIAGE: 30 July 1912 to Phoebe Cary. Children: Seward, Sarah, Emily, Hugo, Alice, Elinor.

MAJOR POSITIONS HELD: Editor, *New York Evening Journal* (1897-1921), *Chicago American* (1900-1936); owner, *Washington* (D.C.) *Times* (1917-1919), *Wisconsin News* (Milwaukee) (1918-1919); syndicated columnist (1917-1936); editor, *New York Mirror* (1934-1936).

DEATH: New York City, 25 December 1936.

SELECTED BOOKS: *Editorials from the Hearst Newspapers* (New York: Albertson, 1906);

Brisbane on Prohibition; a Forcible Address by the Famous Editor, the Doctrine of Moderate Indulgence (New York: U.S.B.A., 1908);

Mary Baker G. Eddy (Boston: Ball, 1908; London: Chatto & Windus, 1908);

Three Brothers: An Editorial (New York: Privately printed, 1916);

The Book of Today (New York: International

Arthur Brisbane (Culver Pictures)

Magazine Company, 1923);

Today and the Future Day: An Analysis of Two New Books, with Other Articles (New York: Albertson, 1925);

What Mrs. Eddy Said to Arthur Brisbane; the Celebrated Interview of the Eminent Journalist with the Discoverer and Founder of Christian Science (New York: Paige, 1930);

How to Be a Better Reporter (Eugene: University of Oregon, Fine Arts Press, 1933).

PERIODICAL PUBLICATIONS: "The Incubator Baby and Niagara Falls," *Cosmopolitan* (September 1901): 509-516;

"William Randolph Hearst," *Cosmopolitan* (May 1902): 48-51;

"Joseph Pulitzer," *Cosmopolitan* (May 1902): 51-54;

"William Randolph Hearst," *Independent* (4 October 1906): 785-787;

"Interview With Mrs. Eddy," *Cosmopolitan* (August 1907): 451-458;

"Fight Against Alcohol," *Cosmopolitan* (April 1908): 492-496; (May 1908): 549-554;

"Littlest Woman in the World," *Cosmopolitan* (August 1908): 74-79;

"Armours," *Cosmopolitan* (February 1909): 279-292;

"The Universe Is Only a Front Yard," *Golden Book Magazine* (July 1931): 86-87;

"Building Boulder Dam," *Golden Book Magazine* (February 1932): 191-192;

"As I See Them: The Women of 1934," *Pictorial Review* (January 1935): 18-19.

Arthur Brisbane was the most widely known editor, columnist, and writer in the United States in the decades from the Spanish-American War to his death in 1936. When he was hired away from Joseph Pulitzer's *New York World* by William Randolph Hearst to become editor of the *New York Journal*, the stage was set for a historic circulation battle. Sensationalism, called "yellow journalism," was deftly employed by Brisbane to earn the *Journal* an amazing surge in circulation and to earn Brisbane himself an annual salary of $70,000. His salary eventually rose to $260,000, and he was known as the most highly paid journalist of his time. He began a column of news comment in 1917 which was first extended to the Hearst newspaper chain and then syndicated in about 200 dailies and 1,200 weeklies with a circulation totaling about 20,000,000. He continued the column until his death. Probably no other editorial writer was read as regularly by so many people or was as influential in affecting American public opinion. He also briefly owned dailies in Washington, Detroit, Milwaukee, and other cities.

Brisbane was born in Buffalo, New York, in 1864, the son of Albert Brisbane, a well-to-do parlor radical who was impressed with the socialistic views of Charles Fourier. Arthur's mother died when he was two; his father married Redalia Bates when Arthur was eleven. His stepmother took him abroad at thirteen to study in France and Germany for five years, mainly with tutors.

Upon his return from Europe in 1882, he was hired by Charles A. Dana, editor of the *Sun*, and worked so hard for a couple of years that his parents, afraid that he would ruin his health, returned him to Europe for a rest. Instead, letters he wrote Dana were so interesting that he became the *Sun*'s London correspondent and did everything from interviewing statesmen to reporting prizefights.

He remained in Europe a few years, then came back to the United States at twenty-three to become editor of the *Evening Sun*, which was just starting. Brisbane later said the editors were determined to make it a literary paper. Those who worked for it included Richard Harding Davis, who began his Van Bibber series for the *Sun*, basing it on a tale by Manchecourt which Brisbane translated from *La Vie Parisienne*.

Brisbane later recalled that in these last decades of the nineteenth century, new and sensational methods were being introduced into journalism, that apparently the days of Greeley and Dana were over, and that Joseph Pulitzer himself had a hand in upsetting old ideas. But Brisbane said he believed that the *Evening Sun*, despite the fact that it depended on literary quality and news, had the largest circulation of any paper in New York at that time. He recalled some of the changes in the seven years he spent on the *Sun*: marvelous improvements in printing presses, which made the four-page paper a thing of the past; telephones; and incandescent lamps. Comic supplements and feature articles were added to the Sunday editions.

When Pulitzer hired Brisbane away from the *Sun* in 1890 to develop the *Sunday World*, the new editor had orders to engage anyone he wanted. At the end of ten weeks, circulation was increasing at the rate of 11,000 each Sunday and ultimately soared to more than 600,000. Brisbane thus sprang quickly to fame as New York's most able and aggressive managing editor. He developed the *Sunday World* into a strikingly original paper. Feature articles in the Sunday supplement were in 1893 illustrated by the first colored pictures ever attempted on a fast newspaper press. Some comic cuts by R. F. Outcault, picturing child life in "Hogan's Alley," were tried in colors—the first attempt in any newspaper to produce colored "comics." In experimenting with color, it was decided to print in bright yellow the dress of the leading figure, "The Kid of Hogan's Alley." The success of using solid colors in these Sunday comics was instantaneous. Outcault, the creator of the "Yellow Kid," was soon hired away by Hearst for his *Sunday Journal*, but the *World* secured George B. Luks, afterwards a painter of merit, to continue the "Yellow Kid" in its Sunday edition. Advertisements for the rival "Yellow Kids" in the two papers adorned the billboards of New York. This war of comics, coupled with the sensationalism that marked both papers, led an editor of one of the other New York newspapers to coin the term "yellow journalism."

One day Brisbane tried printing his simple editorial paragraphs on the *World*'s front page. From abroad Pulitzer cabled: "Stop column, don't want independent editorial opinions in my newspapers." Brisbane stopped; but in 1897 he applied for a job with Hearst, whose *Evening Journal* needed

help. Brisbane's plan was daily evening yellow journalism. Hearst offered Brisbane a salary of $8,000 a year and a commission of $1,000 for every 10,000 in circulation the *Journal* gained. That contract netted Brisbane $70,000 in the first year.

Brisbane began writing editorials for the *Journal*, planned coverage, and personally wrote many of the smashing headlines for the Spanish-American War coverage. The *Journal*'s circulation rose beyond the million mark, a first for any American newspaper. Brisbane's hostility toward President McKinley became more vicious after the war, and he printed editorials on political assassination. But when McKinley was shot, the *Journal* shifted policy quickly to words only of praise for the murdered president.

In 1900 Hearst sent Brisbane to Chicago, where he started the *American* on 4 July. Brisbane soon returned to New York, leaving Charles Edward Russell and Andy Lawrence in charge of the *American*.

An article he wrote for Hearst's *Cosmopolitan* magazine in 1901 involved a comparison of an incubator baby and Niagara Falls, in connection with the Buffalo Exposition: "Men stand in the spray on the high banks, as the rainbows form and the green water sweeps over with millions of horsepower. Eighteen million cubic feet of water every minute, dashing down to carve out the solid rock. . . . But what is that power beside the force that may originate in the tiny brain of an incubator baby? . . . That brain may start a work that will persist, and affect men's destiny, when the falls, working their own ruin, shall have dwindled down to an even, placid stream without so much as a ruffling of the water to tell where once the great power rushed by. . . . The river represents material force, the mere force of gravity. The child's brain represents spiritual force, the power of organization and of speculation."

In 1907, Brisbane interviewed seventy-six-year-old Mary Baker Eddy, the founder of Christian Science, at the request of *Cosmopolitan*. He reported her in good health and clear of mind at a time when she faced a lawsuit aimed at taking away from her control of her money and her actions. His clearly detailed, sympathetic report began: "Millions of people in this country will be interested in the personality of the very remarkable woman who founded Christian Science, and gathered together the great Christian Science following." Brisbane made it plain that "the first duty of a writer who sees a personality interesting to the world is to tell what he has seen, rather than what he thinks. For what one man has seen another would see, whereas one does not think what another thinks." (Mrs. Eddy won the competency suit.)

When *Cosmopolitan* asked Brisbane on another occasion to pick his own topic for an article, he chose "to discuss a small colored lady called Princess Weenie Wee, undoubtedly the smallest mature human being now living." Her real name was Harriet Elizabeth Thompson and she was from Bryn Mawr, Pennsylvania; at eighteen years of age she was no bigger than the ordinary four-month-old baby. Brisbane pointed out that with such a subject for a text he could discuss any dismal topic and retain attention. Rather than do that, he said that at one time she would have been the king's plaything, but in the twentieth century she belonged to the people.

Brisbane also contributed an article on the Armours to a series on "Owners of America" appearing in *Cosmopolitan*. The world's greatest meat packer and butcher also dealt massively in grain and refrigerator cars, Brisbane wrote. He called Armour "one of today's specialized kings. . . . The ruled . . . denounce kings and put republics where kingdoms were before. But kings rule within the republics."

His first article on Hearst—in *Cosmopolitan* in 1902—reported on the Chief's activities and ambitions in the newspaper world. Brisbane predicted that Hearst would add to the three newspapers he then owned in New York, Chicago, and San Francisco by founding papers in other large cities. Hearst's aim, according to Brisbane, was "to exercise public influence through the simultaneous efforts of opinion in newspapers all over the United States." Brisbane also praised Hearst for succeeding in spite of wealth:

> Who are the men in the United States who have succeeded, who have triumphed over the keenest competition, despite the possession of wealth? You can scarcely mention one. There is absolutely no such individual save W. R. Hearst among the successful editors of America. . . .
>
> The number of those [rich men] who have tried and failed is very great. Huntington owned the "Star" and it failed. Jay Gould owned the "World" and it failed. Duke, the head of the Tobacco Trust, owned the "Recorder" in partnership with another very rich man and it failed. . . .
>
> Scores of rich men have foolishly spent money in the belief that money could make newspapers or build up an editor. They all failed. . . .

> This writer believes that the actual intention of W. R. Hearst, through his newspapers, is to fight persistently the cause of genuine democracy, not merely the Democracy of a political party, but the real democracy upon which the government is founded.

This article was one of two which Brisbane wrote for *Cosmopolitan* in a series on "Captains of Industry"; the other was on Joseph Pulitzer. Brisbane said that Pulitzer's "great success was the establishment of the *St. Louis Post-Dispatch*. . . . The paper was made successful as was the *New York World* later by attacking injustice, by refusing to recognize the claims of the rich to especial privilege, by working honestly for the great mass of people who lived in the condition from which Pulitzer had emerged, thanks to favor and heredity."

Brisbane produced another article on Hearst in 1906 for the *Independent* magazine. Hearst, then a member of Congress, had been nominated for governor of New York by the Democratic party. The magazine editor noted that Brisbane's father, Albert, "in 1842 purchased the right from Horace Greeley to occupy one column daily on the front page of *The Tribune* to preach Fourierism. Now, within one generation, Mr. Arthur Brisbane, the son, is paid the highest salary of any editor in America to teach the same doctrines for which his father could not get a hearing except at advertising rates. Mr. Arthur Brisbane reaches a wider audience every day than any other writer in the world." Brisbane wrote that the nomination of Hearst "means a severe blow at trust and corporation government. . . . The situation is emphasized by the nomination of Mr. Hughes on the Republican ticket. Mr. Hughes is a corporation lawyer. He is very highly spoken of, but he is a corporation lawyer. . . . His income has been paid to him in large fees, thousands at a time, by a few corporation managers. Mr. Hearst may be called a journalistic lawyer of the people. His income has been paid to him by millions of citizens contributing one cent each." In spite of Brisbane's efforts, Hearst lost the election.

Brisbane—who in 1912 married his cousin's daughter, Phoebe Cary—was included in a feature in *Everybody's* magazine in 1916 entitled "Seven Super-pens." The others were William Allen White, editor of the *Emporia* (Kansas) *Gazette*; Clark Howell, editor of the *Atlanta Constitution*; Frank Cobb, chief editorial writer of the *New York World*; Robert F. Paine, chief editorial writer of the National Editorial Association; Fremont Older, editor of the *San Francisco Bulletin*; and Frank P. Glass, editor of the *Birmingham News*. The reference to Brisbane said: "It is not improbable that something like four million sturdy middle class Americans, including hundreds of writers, believe that Arthur Brisbane is the champion editorial writer of the world. For Brisbane has clarity, brevity, and euphony domesticated so they'll eat out of his hand. He can take the most complex material and translate it into a kindergarten epic. If he wanted to 'put over' a dissertation on hygiene and dietetics, he would entitle it 'Pity Poor Moses—He Had No Ice-Box.'"

The year after this feature appeared, Brisbane started his "Today" column for the Hearst newspapers. It was soon syndicated in 200 additional papers. Rewritten under the title "This Week," it appeared in 1,200 weekly papers. In 1937 his readership was estimated at 30,000,000.

In the process of preparing his simple, easily understood paragraphs, Brisbane scanned dozens of newspapers. He said that when he had decided on a column's content, he wrote it in fifteen minutes. He felt that "anyone who writes as rapidly as I . . . can never be a great writer." He was efficient in his working methods: most of "Today's" words were spoken into dictaphones which Brisbane installed in his limousine and carried on planes and trains. Sometimes his column was dictated as Brisbane's car stood on the deck of the ferry taking him from Manhattan to his 3,000-acre New Jersey estate. His writing speed left him plenty of time to devote to financial and real estate interests. He had a home also in Hempstead, Long Island, and a palatial town house on Fifth Avenue, along with investment properties in many states.

His superb gift was a common touch as an editorial writer. His millions of published words were more remarkable for smooth flow and clarity than for depth or originality of thought. He was an omnivorous reader with a sharp memory. He possessed a great stock of odds and ends of information, like an almanac, which was impressive to his readers. He admired science and material progress, and he often pondered on the vastness of the material universe as contrasted with the minuteness of man.

The acquisition by Brisbane of the *Washington Times* in 1917 raised some questions. One article asked, "Who Owns the *Washington Times*?" In an editorial in the *Times* of 23 February 1918, entitled "The Law Compels Editors to Tell Who Owns the Newspaper," Brisbane wrote that the law, "good as far as it goes, doesn't go far enough," and while "it is well enough to know who owns the newspaper, it is even more important to know who and what owns the man that owns the newspaper." In an affidavit, Brisbane stated that he and his wife were the sole owners and that there were no bondholders, mortgagees, or other security-holders. Brisbane said that he bought the paper from its previous owner, Frank A. Munsey, paying half in cash and allowing Munsey to keep all the stock in security for payment of the other $250,000. To finance the paper and put it on a paying basis, Brisbane arranged for a credit of up to $500,000 with Christian W. Feigenspan of Newark, a brewer. It was necessary to use only $375,000 of the amount borrowed. The loan was made without security, although Brisbane said he offered real estate as collateral. At first no interest was asked by Feigenspan, although Brisbane said he insisted on paying interest on the five-year loan. A Washington correspondent of the *New York Evening Sun* said that the *Times* under Brisbane had frequently published editorials and news articles supporting the sale of beer and light wines but opposing the sale of whiskey. In one article Brisbane wrote: "My attitude on the temperance question is well known. For more than twenty years opposing the sale of whisky, I have advocated temperance, which I believe can best be promoted by forbidding the sale of all alcoholic spirits, permitting only the manufacture and distribution of light wine and beer in which the alcohol content is reduced to an innocuous percentage." (On this point, at least, Brisbane showed himself to be consistent with a discussion a decade earlier in *Cosmopolitan* magazine. He had pointed out in a series of articles on the fight against alcohol that "total abstinence enthusiasts report that the maximum of efficiency is attained with the minimum of beer or wine. . . . A man does his best work with a mind free of any artificial stimulant, but between efforts that mind requires the relaxation and rest, freedom from nervousness and facility of digestion that mild stimulants alone can give.")

Brisbane confessed, however, that his chief concern as editor was the "false accusation that I and my paper are, or have been at any time, in any way, pro-German" in World War I. He flatly denied the accusation: "I have never written one line in favor of Germany, and I have written hundreds of columns in denunciation of Germany and her methods and purposes in this war. I do not think there is any paper in the United States, or any editor in the United States who has been as bitterly, as violently, and as persistently pro-Ally and anti-German as I have been." Feigenspan, trustee of the pool of brewers that advanced the money to Brisbane, in turn defended their loyalty: "More than 95 per cent of all the brewers in the United States are American-born"; and in many cases their parents were American-born, he added.

Brisbane wrote of the purpose of the *Times* in his anniversary number: "This newspaper was purchased to tell the news as accurately as possible, to reflect in editorial columns the thoughts and feelings of good citizens, to entertain and inform in the evening the working people, rich and poor, to support the President and the Government of the United States, from the first to the last word through every hour of the war. The owner of this paper may truly say in a very small way, to his readers, what Michelangelo said to the Pope for whom he built St. Peter's: 'I have made nothing from the building unless it be by adding to my reputation and my soul's salvation.'"

In 1918 Brisbane acquired the *Evening Wisconsin* and the *Daily News* in Milwaukee and combined them into the *Wisconsin News*. Brisbane was widely regarded as a front man for Hearst, who a few months later bought the *Milwaukee Free Press* but retained only the Sunday edition under the name *Telegram*. When Brisbane moved into Milwaukee, he said that it had become his permanent home. Some considered the announcement quite a boost for the city because Brisbane was considered a newspaper genius. But Brisbane left only three weeks later, after introducing a full page of comics and printing his editorials in fourteen-point type.

John Gregory, who had been editor of the *Evening Wisconsin* and had been retained by Brisbane, soon realized that his new boss did not appreciate his editorials. "The editorials you write make people think," Brisbane complained. "Editorials should make people think they think." Gregory thought about that remark and then quit. Other changes in the new newspaper included headlines presenting the latest Broadway and Hollywood gossip; more crime news; Hearst columnists, led by Brisbane; and serialized novels, two to four running at one time. The *Milwaukee Journal* met these changes by reviving a feature section with some sensational content, adding more comic strips, and starting a women's section and a magazine for its Sunday edition, but mainly by strengthening its local and state news coverage. In 1919 Hearst took over the *Wisconsin News* and the *Washington Times*.

For a time, Brisbane exercised important influence in Hearst's financial affairs. It was Brisbane who got Hearst into Manhattan real estate in a big way; the two co-owned the Ziegfeld Theatre and several hotels. Brisbane never had an official position in the business end of the empire, but he certainly had Hearst's ear. By 1929 Hearst had been persuaded to have more liquid funds available in case the world did not get better and better forever. Brisbane then wrote the Chief a note in which he offered the opinion that there was no reason to fear the future, that a new economic era had dawned upon the world, and that far from conserving cash, it was Hearst's capitalistic duty to expand. The Chief fortunately listened to others and had cash when the Depression came. In 1927 Hearst had created Hearst Magazines, Inc., and sold debentures to the public to raise $10,000,000. In 1930 the Hearst empire began raising some $42,000,000 on the Class A stock of Hearst Consolidated. An analysis by *Fortune* magazine experts in 1935 concluded that Brisbane no longer was close to the business ear of Hearst.

In *Golden Book* magazine in 1931, a reprint of one of Brisbane's daily editorials was described: "But as a sincere and stimulating statement of a universe-minded point of view, it has not been bettered since it was written twenty-five years ago. Arthur Brisbane, one of the greatest single forces shaping public opinion in the world today, exerts an incalculable influence on the possibly twenty-five million readers of Hearst newspapers." The article indulged in some dreamy idealism:

> So it will be some day with us who are now engaged in the detailed organization of the little home which we call the earth. We are fixing up our moral plumbing—fighting poverty, injustice and above all, ignorance. We are fighting the meanness that comes of competition and the greater meanness that is based upon the dread of poverty in the future. Some of us are piling up millions that we can never use, while others suffer for lack of that which could be abundantly supplied. All these little earthly questions that seem so big will be settled in time.
>
> But a few years in the sight of Time—a few hundred centuries, perhaps, as we count them—and our earthly habitation will have been made fit to live in. We shall have eliminated the unfit—not by killing them off, but by educating them. We shall have solved the question of poverty by solving the question of production, and especially of distribution. We shall have developed a citizenship capable of earnest work, of sobriety and of moral decency, without the spur of want, imprisonment or the scaffold. . . .
>
> Then we shall appreciate the cosmic wisdom which has divided our day into darkness and light—the light for the enjoyment of the

material beauties of our earthly home; the night for the study and enjoyment of the vast, mysterious universe spread out around us.

Brisbane's clear, simple style continued to prove attractive to magazines. The editor of *Golden Book Magazine* in 1932 offered this preface: "There is no pen in the world whose day-by-day records give us such vivid pictures of contemporary life and work as that of Mr. Brisbane. He travels, observes, chronicles, interprets, philosophizes." The magazine offered a reprint of notes on Boulder Dam which had appeared in Brisbane's "Today" newspaper column. He reported that "you must start your motor at Hodge, California, two hundred miles away, early, to spend the day here. You drive down from California, through a pass between snow-covered mountains, cross the Nevada line, pass through the city of Las Vegas . . . and on, twenty-three miles to this new-born city in Nevada mountains that had no road, not even the narrowest, until it was decided to harness the power rushing through the deep boulder canyon. You realize that the three thousand men here are in primitive country when you hear that mountain sheep, of which a flock may be seen on the mountain tops, come down occasionally for a close view of automobiles, never seen by them before."

After he became editor of the Hearst tabloid daily *New York Mirror* in 1934, Brisbane turned out eight columns of special editorials a week in addition to his "Today" and "This Week" columns. For the Hearst Sunday editions he furnished the text for an illustrated page which dramatized some portentous, if obvious, thought or outlined the contents of a classic biography or history. But Brisbane's labors for the *Mirror* failed, and he was asked to leave the staff after two years.

Brisbane wrote about any topic, small or large, easy or difficult, in a popular vein attractive to readers who were beginning to set their sights on obtaining high school diplomas. When he picked "The Women of 1934" for *Pictorial Review*, his choices came from a wide variety of occupations: Mme Curie, Eleanor Roosevelt, Mme Dionne, Mae West, Aimee Semple McPherson, Evangeline C. Booth. But Brisbane offered a dedication to the mothers of 1934: "No woman has painted one of the world's great pictures or written one of the great poems. 'Nice' pictures and poems, yes, but not 'great' ones. But women have created the men who painted the pictures and wrote the poems. And women, therefore, have created all that the great men have done."

In 1935, Brisbane visited Alf Landon at the

Brisbane (right) with William Randolph Hearst on the publisher's seventy-second birthday in 1935

governor's mansion in Kansas when Landon seemed a likely prospect for Republican nomination for the presidency. Brisbane was, along with Hearst, Paul Block, and Eleanor Medill Patterson, a powerful supporter of Landon. When the group arrived at the railroad station, Brisbane proceeded to interview the local reporters on Landon: "How does Landon stand?. . . Has he a good radio voice?" The following year, Brisbane called the completion of the 200-inch telescopic reflector the most important event of 1936 because it would enable man to see at least one million light-years into space, "and that is a long distance." But the fact was that a smaller 100-inch telescope already had penetrated 500 million light-years into space, and the new one was expected to pierce space for 1,500 million light-years.

Brisbane, of course, attracted the attention of critics. J. M. Gillis, columnist for the *Catholic World*, for example, called Brisbane's excursions into theological topics comic relief. He said Brisbane had an "irresistible penchant for theology, and his little lessons in the divine science are always amusing." Gillis titled his comments "Rev. Arthur Brisbane, D.D." In one column, Gillis said that Brisbane presented the "ever alluring theory of reincarnation with a novel twist. . . . If a black man behaves well in this existence, and is by way of reward reincarnated white, what about the black man who behaves badly? . . . These . . . questions call for clarification, Dr. Brisbane." On another important matter, judgment beyond the grave on those who commit suicide, Gillis quoted Brisbane: "Everybody appearing in the next world will feel foolish if obliged to say, 'I killed myself,' when asked: 'How did you come here?' " Gillis commented:

> Now the reader will understand the vast reputation for originality that has been acquired by our leading popular theologian. How many preachers have treated that theme of the private judgment of the soul immediately after death. And how many have strained their imagination in trying to visualize the scene! Yet how few, if any, have had the insight to anticipate the Judge's salutation to the suicide, "Now don't you feel foolish!" It is all so graphic that the reader hears the question almost as if it were addressed to himself.
>
> And there you have the secret of the success of the only professor of theology in America who is paid a hundred thousand dollars a year.

For the ordinary reader, Brisbane produced his most effective and simplest writing when he treated difficult subjects: "To many fear of death is worse than death. . . . Death is soon over, fear is dreadful and prolonged agony. . . . Crillon, greatest fighter of them all, laid out in death, was found to have wounds on every inch of his body in front, not a scar on his back. Of him it could be said he never feared the face of any man."

Mildly eccentric in his later years, Brisbane himself showed no fear of death, but took sensible health precautions. On his Allaire, New Jersey, estate he built not only a palatial residence and racing stable but also a brick tower which he called "a machine for living." Each of its five floors had one large room. On the roof was a sleeping arrangement, for Brisbane argued that if outdoor sleeping was helpful to consumptives, it must also be good for people in normal health. When the morning sun

waked him, he merely adjusted a light-proof mask of black silk and slept peacefully on. In 1936 a stubborn ailment was followed by a series of heart attacks. By November he was bedridden, although he continued his work.

Death came to Brisbane on Christmas Day, 1936. He had murmured into a dictaphone the day before a timely "Today" column: "Another Christmas has come. . . . Nineteen hundred and thirty-six years ago. . . . peace on earth, good will toward all men. . . ." But Brisbane was too tired to finish. His son Seward furnished the last paragraph, the only writing not actually by Arthur Brisbane to have appeared in his daily editorial column in its entire nineteen years. Brisbane's last words were from Voltaire's *Candide*: "This is the best of all possible worlds." Thus ended perhaps not the most distinguished but certainly in many ways the most remarkable career achieved to that time by a writer for the press. His fortune was estimated at $25,000,000 to $30,000,000.

The *Review of Reviews* wrote: "Many members of this new public have encountered the name as well as the daily wisdom of Arthur Brisbane . . . the country's foremost newspaper editor . . . the most widely known American journalist and his influence reaches all classes." The *Literary Digest* said: "Editor, historian, philosopher, columnist—'defender of the yellow press'—Brisbane was known, liked, hated, praised, scorned by millions. Along with Dana, Greeley, Pulitzer, Bennett, he is expected to join journalistic immortals. If for no other reason, because he was the highest-salaried writer the business ever knew—at $260,000 a year." Hearst wrote the day after Christmas: "I know that Arthur Brisbane was the greatest journalist of his day. I know that he was one of the most powerful factors behind the social and political progress of the Nation. I know that he was one of the most patriotic supporters and conservators of true American ideals and institutions. I know that he was kind and understanding, and deeply sympathetic with the struggles and sorrows of humanity."

On the other hand, the *New Republic* said:

> During the last twenty years we have often found it necessary to take issue—sometimes harsh issue—with Arthur Brisbane. . . .
>
> We should be less than fair if we did not point out that Brisbane was gifted with a special kind of journalistic brilliance. A master of the stripped reportorial style, keen and alert, he spoke the simple language of millions of American people—especially those millions

who read as they run. We should also be less than fair if we overlooked the fact that it was his dream to bring culture to the masses: and if his conception of culture was not ours—or yours—it does not negate his sincerity or his hope.

The duty of fairness, however, demands an examination of both sides of the coin. With all his gifts—his sense of the accurate word, his indefatigable energy—he never ventured beyond the horizons seen from the slopes of San Simeon. A good reporter, loyal to the man who gave him his chance, he made Mr. Hearst's battles his own. He was a militarist and an impassioned defender of the present order. His nuggets of wisdom, generally set in bold-faced type, were not always sound. His enthusiasms were often trivial and his great discoveries (that a prize-fighter was no match for a gorilla, for example) were equally so. A master in his field, he was also a master of the commonplace. He did not quite deserve his lifetime reputation and it will probably not long outlive his death.

The *New Republic* probably came closest to evaluating Brisbane's journalistic life in a realistic manner. Brisbane certainly used some sound principles in preparing his articles and editorial campaigns: simple words, sentences, and paragraphs; large readable type; color; and pictures. But he mixed facts with fake stories to achieve his aim—a strong form of yellow journalism.

Biography:
Oliver Carlson, *Brisbane: A Candid Biography* (New York: Stackpole, 1937).

References:
James Wyman Barrett, *Joseph Pulitzer and His World* (New York: Vanguard Press, 1941);

Willard G. Bleyer, *Main Currents in the History of American Journalism* (New York: Houghton Mifflin, 1927);

Oliver Carlson and Ernest Sutherland Bates, *Hearst: Lord of San Simeon* (Westport, Conn.: Greenwood Press, 1970);

Hartley Davis, "The Journalism of New York," *Munsey's* (November 1900): 217-233;

"Seven Super-pens," *Everybody's* (March 1916): 357;

John Swinton, "The New York Daily Papers and Their Editors," *Independent* (18 January 1900): 168-171; (25 January 1900): 237-240;

Robert W. Wells, *The Milwaukee Journal: Its First 100 Years* (Milwaukee: Journal Company, 1981);

"Who Owns the Washington Times?" *Literary Digest* (5 October 1918): 16-17;

John K. Winkler, *William Randolph Hearst: A New Appraisal* (New York: Hastings House, 1955).

Abraham Cahan
(6 July 1860-31 August 1951)

James Glen Stovall
University of Alabama

See also the Cahan entry in *DLB 9, American Novelists, 1910-1945*.

MAJOR POSITIONS HELD: Editor, *Arbeiter Zeitung* (New York) (1891-1894); reporter, *New York Commercial Advertiser* (1897-1901); editor, *Jewish Daily Forward* (New York) (1897, 1902, 1903-1951).

SELECTED BOOKS: *Social Remedies* (New York: New York Labor News Co., 1889);

Yekl: A Tale of the New York Ghetto (New York: Appleton, 1896);

The Imported Bridegroom and Other Stories of the New York Ghetto (New York & Boston: Houghton Mifflin, 1898);

The White Terror and the Red: A Novel of Revolutionary Russia (New York: Barnes, 1905; London: Hodder & Stoughton, 1905);

Raphael Naarizoch (A Story) (New York: Forward Press, 1907);

The Rise of David Levinsky (New York & London: Harper, 1917);

Bleter fun Mein Leben, 5 volumes (New York: Forward Association, 1926-1931); volumes 1 and 2 republished as *The Education of Abraham Cahan*, translated by Leon Stein, Abraham P.

Abraham Cahan in 1940 (Culver Pictures)

Conan, and Lynn Davison (Philadelphia:
Jewish Publication Society of America, 1969);
Palestina (New York: Forward Publishing Associa-
tion, 1934).

OTHER: *Hear the Other Side: A Symposium of Democratic Socialist Opinion*, edited by Cahan (New
York, 1934).

Abraham Cahan was a spellbinding speaker, a
fine writer, a brilliant editor, and a deep and creative thinker. Cahan dominated the thinking of the
immigrant Jewish community on the Lower East
Side of New York City in the first two decades of this
century; the newspaper he edited for nearly fifty
years, the *Jewish Daily Forward*, commanded a widespread loyalty among the immigrant Jewish society.
Yet, according to Irving Howe, Cahan had "a rather
grim and acrid temperament, as if all Jewish frustrations had come to rest on his soul. He could be
narrow, philistine and spiteful; his personal culture
was limited; but when it came to apprehending relations between the immigrant Jews and the world

surrounding them, his mind was wonderfully
keen." Cahan's accomplishments were impressive:
he brought the *Forward* from obscurity to domi-
nance; he was constantly in demand as a speaker,
especially for labor and socialist groups; he was an
effective political and labor organizer. He was an
amateur naturalist and an author with numerous
short stories and novels—including one minor
masterpiece—to his credit.

Cahan was born on 6 July 1860 in Podberezy, a
small Lithuanian village near Vilna, to Schachne
and Sarah Goldarbeiter Cahan. The area had a
large Jewish population (Napoleon, on his march to
Moscow, had called Vilna the "Jerusalem of
Lithuania") which had suffered periodically from
the anti-Semitism of czarist Russia. Though his
grandfather had been a rabbi, Cahan's father, a
teacher of Hebrew, wanted to provide a secular
education for his only son but was too poor to do so.
His only choice was to enroll Abraham in the Jewish
Teachers' Institute of Vilna when he was seventeen.

Russia was closer to revolution than at any
other point in her history, and Cahan was soon
caught up with visionaries who imagined that the
right spark could set off a peasant revolt. He joined
an underground *kruzhok* (circle) in 1880 and received his first exposure to socialism. Cahan eagerly
delved into the literature of the movement and became a devoted follower. When word of the assassination of Czar Alexander II came in 1881, Cahan,
who had graduated that year and was teaching in
Velizh, waited with his fellow revolutionaries for the
inevitable peasant uprising. It never came; instead,
the assassins were rounded up, tried, and executed.

Next came a general crackdown on all subver-
sives. Cahan's room was visited by the police, and
while they found nothing incriminating, Cahan
knew he was being watched. Others in his revolutionary circle had been arrested, and he realized
that his days of freedom in Russia were numbered.
His first plan was to emigrate to Switzerland. Then
he was tempted to settle in Palestine, but Cahan was
at a point in his life when he wished to set aside his
Jewishness. Finally, he decided to join the stream of
immigrants to America.

Cahan docked in Philadelphia in June 1882
and went to New York City by train. Although
Cahan considered himself an exiled Russian radical
rather than a Jewish immigrant, he found a home
on the Lower East Side of Manhattan along with
Jewish immigrants of every national stripe. Cahan
found jobs as a common laborer, including one in a
cigar factory. He also found friends, many of whom
were deeply interested in the budding labor union

Cahan, age twenty-three, the year after he immigrated to the United States (Jewish Daily Forward)

English by sitting in on classes at an elementary school. He also began contributing articles about the Lower East Side to English-language newspapers such as the *New York World* and the *New York Sun*.

Cahan was hired by a night school to teach English to immigrants. This job gave him an income and an opportunity to engage in his two favorite activities: writing and union organizing. He helped form the first Jewish labor union, one for garment workers, and soon there was talk among his fellow organizers of beginning a newspaper. Cahan was naturally suited for such work, and in 1886 he began editing *Neie Zeit (New Era)*. Other labor papers soon made their appearances, few of them lasting very long. *Neie Zeit* existed for only a few months, but Cahan had no trouble finding outlets for his writing. He was a frequent contributor to the *Workman's Advocate*, the organ of the Socialist Labor party, of which he was a member. On 11 December 1886 he married Anna Bronstein from Kiev, an educated woman with literary and artistic interests. They had no children.

Anna Bronstein at the time of her marriage to Cahan in 1886 (Jewish Daily Forward)

movement in America. These radicals, like those in Russia, had their romantic streaks, and the attraction for Cahan was irresistible. He joined the Propaganda Verein, a group formed to promote socialist ideas, and gave speeches in both Russian and Yiddish. Cahan's abilities as a stump speaker were soon apparent, and after only a few public appearances, he was widely known for his oratory and his socialist leanings.

Cahan had come to America knowing little English. Initially he found that this lack of knowledge of the language meant little, since he spent most of his time among other immigrants. As his feelings about his adopted country grew, however, so did his desire to learn the native tongue. Working with only a grammar book and a stack of newspapers every night, he learned English so swiftly that he was soon making money teaching other immigrants to read and write; he later perfected his

In 1890 a number of labor groups got together to start the *Arbeiter Zeitung*, a Yiddish-language labor newspaper. Because of his fluency in Yiddish and his knowledge of Yiddish folkways, Cahan became an avid contributor. The paper was an immediate success, largely due to Cahan's ability to communicate in this fluid and half-formed language. Cahan still thought of himself more as a labor organizer and socialist than as a journalist: in 1891 he was temporarily president of the Cloak Makers Union and a delegate to the second congress of the Second Socialist International in Brussels. Later that year he was named the editor of the *Arbeiter Zeitung*. Within two years he was also editing *Die Zukunft*, the Yiddish organ of the Socialist Workers party of America.

Friction, rivalries, and personality conflicts were abundant in the labor movement of that time, and Cahan's abrasive personality did nothing to shield him from involvement in these conflicts. By 1894 he was growing somewhat disenchanted with the labor movement and with his colleagues. He had also developed a new love as a writer—fiction; he had published his first works of fiction in the *Arbeiter Zeitung*. He felt he could use fiction as a better means of expressing himself and of teaching his readers (his writing almost always took a didactic tone). Consequently, he left his editing jobs and devoted more of his time to writing. In 1895 he published his first English-language story, "A Providential Match," in *Short Stories* magazine. This work attracted the attention of William Dean Howells, a writer and critic who prided himself on finding new talent and who had met Cahan in 1891 while doing research for a book. Howells encouraged Cahan and helped get a publisher for Cahan's first novel, *Yekl: A Tale of the New York Ghetto* (1896).

Cahan's commitment to the labor movement was too deep for his absence to be permanent. Many of his friends, still dissatisfied with the publications associated with the movement, felt that yet another newspaper should be tried, and they felt that Cahan was the only one who could edit it properly. They were right, although it was several years before Cahan was allowed enough control to do the job. Cahan decided to put his budding literary career aside and try to make a success of this new paper, and on 22 April 1897 the first issue of the *Jewish Daily Forward (Vorwärts)* appeared, with Cahan as its editor. The old feuds quickly revived, however: the *Forward* suffered from a surplus of talent and ego, and by August Cahan had resigned.

At almost the same time, Cahan lost his job as an English teacher, mainly because of his socialist activities. He wanted to devote himself to his fiction, but he realized that he could not make a living doing so. For a while free-lancing was his only means of support, but he was soon offered a salaried position on the *New York Commercial Advertiser*.

Cahan had doubts about how well he would do on an English-language, Republican-oriented newspaper; the idea that a journalist could work for a publication that he opposed ideologically was foreign to him. His editors convinced him otherwise, however, and Cahan's work came under the direction of the city editor, the soon-to-be-famous Lincoln Steffens. At the time Steffens was experimenting with his own concept of journalism: he was trying to hire "writers" rather than "journalists," people who could use language well but had little training as reporters; his intention was to produce a newspaper with high-quality writing. Hiring Cahan was Steffen's boldest move in this bold experiment. Cahan was the office "exotic," a Russian immigrant, a Jew, a Socialist, and a man possessed of an intimate knowledge of the Lower East Side of New York City. Steffens and his colleagues had never known anyone like Cahan, and Cahan played his role well: he would hold discussions on socialism and anarchism in the city room during the afternoons after the paper had gone to press; he took his colleagues to his Lower East Side haunts and introduced them to characters even more exotic than he was. For Cahan, too, the time he spent with the *Commercial Advertiser* was a learning experience. His was the police beat, and he saw many sides of New York life. He was introduced to the American mainstream concept of the journalist as a fact gatherer rather than a polemicist. All in all, he gained a knowledge and insight about America outside the Lower East Side that few of his immigrant colleagues could match.

This heady time for the *Commercial Advertiser* staff came to an end in 1901, when Steffens quit to join *McClure's* magazine. The series of exposés on abuse and corruption Steffens conducted for this publication rocketed him to fame and established his place in American journalism. The *Commercial Advertiser* was not the same with Steffens gone, and Cahan soon lost interest in working for the paper. He quit, again with the intention of devoting himself to his fiction. He had been collecting material which he hoped one day to use in a novel, and he took this chance to begin that work. Cahan had maintained an active interest in writing fiction, and his first collection of short stories, *The Imported Bridegroom and Other Stories of the New York Ghetto*, had been published in 1898. But he had also maintained his contacts with his labor colleagues during his stint with Yankee journalism—even to the point of writing a series for the *Forward* while still with the *Commercial Advertiser*—and he found it hard to resist a call to return to the ranks.

By 1902 the *Forward* was doing badly. It was a drab six-page paper, three pages of which were generally taken up by advertisements. Cahan was persuaded to return to the paper as editor, despite his misgivings and his desire to work on his novel, and also despite the opposition of his wife. He was determined to make the paper meaningful to the working men and women whom it was intended to help. Cahan began including features and anecdotes about everyday life, and his own leading articles began telling stories instead of spouting ideology. In changing the face of the paper, however, Cahan encountered strong opposition from the intellectuals, who felt the original purpose of the socialist organ was being subverted. Cahan and the *Forward* were accused of low taste and vulgarity, but circulation soared. This irritated the intellectuals even more; they did not like what Cahan was doing, and they certainly did not want him to be successful at it. After only six months, Cahan was again forced to resign.

Anna Cahan was happy about this resignation, and she tried to ensure its permanence by persuading Cahan to move to a Jewish agricultural community in Woodbine, New Jersey, while she rented a furnished room in the city. During this time in the country, Cahan became keenly interested in bird watching, and after a few months he moved to New Milford, Connecticut, to pursue the hobby. He became locally famous for his persistence in this activity, but during those months pressures built on him to return to the *Forward*. These pressures included his own financial condition.

In 1903 he did return to the paper, again with assurances of absolute control. He remained there for more than forty years and built the paper into the leading voice not only of the Lower East Side community but of Jews around the world. Cahan continued to lead the paper in the direction of appealing to the common laborer and housewife; his reporters focused on the everyday lives of the readers. Cahan resumed his never-ending feud with the intellectuals, who thought the paper had become a Jewish version of yellow journalism.

Cahan's most effective device for reaching his readers was the "Bintel Brief" (Bundle of Letters) section. Cahan encouraged his readers to pour out their hearts in this section, and they did so in abundance. The first Bintel Brief on 20 January 1906

included a mother's lament: "My boy, who's now the breadwinner in the family, is as deaf as the wall; he can't even hear his unhappy parents when they cry." The letter went on to tell how the son had saved up his lunch money and bought a watch and chain, "so he can tell when slack-time is coming"; but after the writer had asked a neighbor woman to "look after things" while she left the house for five minutes, "now the watch is at your pawnbroker's. Not at mine." The letter concluded with a promise to forgive the neighbor if she would "only mail the pawn-ticket to me!" Cahan was not above assigning his reporters to write the letters when printable copy ran short, but after the section became popular, there was little need for this practice. The writing in the Bintel Brief columns ranged from pedestrian to poetic, but there was no doubt about its readership. The section covered a wide variety of topics, and the public response was astonishing. Hundreds of letters came to the *Forward* office each week. Some who were unable to write came to the office and asked reporters to take down their thoughts. Others, not connected with the paper, hired themselves out to write for those who could not. The Bintel Brief became part of immigrant Jewish terminology and folklore.

Despite this appeal to the masses, the *Forward* stuck by its socialist position—as defined by Cahan himself. This position was often more pragmatic than many more rigorous socialists would have liked, but they could not argue with the paper's success. The paper was a friend of the Jewish trade unions and often contributed money, coverage, and tactical advice to them. The paper had been established as a nonprofit organization, but its spiraling readership allowed it to prosper.

Cahan did not neglect his fiction. In 1913 he wrote a four-part series for *McClure's* entitled "The Autobiography of an American Jew." These articles formed the basis for his novel *The Rise of David Levinsky* (1917). This novel is generally thought to be Cahan's best work and is often quoted to give insight into Cahan's own life.

World War I presented Cahan and the *Forward* with their first major political crisis. Pro-German feeling was strong among Jewish immigrants, many of whom had fled Russia and had no use for the czar. Cahan echoed these feelings and endangered the third-class mailing privilege of the paper. To maintain this privilege, Cahan backed off from publishing sentiments against the war and conscription. While many thought this position lacking in courage, Cahan argued that he had saved the paper from harassment and possibly from extinction. By 1918 circulation approached 200,000, and the paper was the chief voice of Jews rather than of socialism.

Cahan gave the paper's full support to the Russian Revolution—support which caused it considerable embarrassment in later years. When Lenin and the Bolsheviks seized power and sought to consolidate their rule by terror, Cahan continued to defend the revolution and the Communists. In January 1922 Cahan wrote an editorial entitled "No Freedom of Speech in Russia: Is That Wrong?," in which he defended the actions of the Bolshevik dictatorship in suppressing its opposition, arguing that the Communists were moving toward "reason and tolerance" and should be allowed to continue. This stance was not palatable to many of Cahan's colleagues, and a major rift developed which the *Forward* reflected in its pages. Soon, however, the actions of the Communists became too much for Cahan, and he retreated from his position of full support. After a 1923 trip to Europe during which he interviewed a number of Russian refugees, Cahan finally had to acknowledge that there was less freedom in Russia under the Bolsheviks than under the czars. He reaffirmed this position after a 1927 trip to the Soviet Union itself.

The *Forward*'s position on communism reversed itself completely, and it became a shrill critic of the Stalin regime. It published information about Siberian concentration camps and editorialized on the bond between socialism and democracy. This stance moved the paper toward the mainstream liberal-labor movement, so that after Franklin Roosevelt took office in 1933, the *Forward* found much in the New Deal that it could support.

Another issue on which the *Forward* reversed itself during these decades was Zionism and the creation of a Jewish state. In the early years, the *Forward* opposed a Jewish move into Palestine, but as such a move became more feasible, particularly with the support of the major world powers, the paper gradually came to support the idea. Cahan visited settlements in Palestine in 1925 and was impressed with the people he met, particularly David Ben-Gurion. "I must marvel at the heroic fire that burns in them," he wrote of the settlers when he returned to America.

The *Forward* began a long, slow decline in power and prestige after World War II. The destruction of the Jewish community in Europe by the Nazis dried up the *Forward*'s source of immigrant writers; the Jewish community on the Lower East Side was losing its cultural force. Most importantly, however, Abraham Cahan had become a very old

The Jewish Daily Forward *Building, New York City, as it looks today (Sol Zaretsky)*

man. In 1946 Cahan suffered a stroke, and control of the paper passed to Hillel Rogoff, the managing editor. Cahan retained the title of editor until his death on 31 August 1951, shortly after the death of his wife.

Few editors of his time could claim the kind of influence that Cahan exerted on his readers, who included people in every part of the world. Few also could claim his experience, intellect, and insight. His paper was described by Oswald Garrison Villard, editor of the *Nation*, as "the most vital, the most interesting, the most democratic of New York's daily journals." Those same adjectives—vital, interesting, and democratic—could also describe its editor, Abraham Cahan.

Bibliographies:
Ephim Jeshurin, *Abraham Cahan Bibliography* (New York: 1941);

Sanford E. Marovitz and Lewis Fried, "Abraham Cahan (1860-1951): An Annotated Bibliography," *American Literary Realism, 1870-1910*, 3 (Summer 1970): 197-243.

References:

Jules Chametzky, *From the Ghetto: The Fiction of Abraham Cahan* (Amherst: University of Massachusetts Press, 1977);

Hutchins Hapgood, *The Spirit of the Ghetto* (Cambridge, Mass.: Belknap Press, 1967);

Irving Howe, *World of Our Fathers* (New York: Harcourt Brace Jovanovich, 1976);

William Dean Howells, "New York Low Life in Fiction," *New York World*, 26 July 1896, p. 18;

Moses Rischin, *The Promised City: New York Jews, 1870-1914* (Cambridge: Harvard University Press, 1962);

Ronald Sanders, *The Downtown Jews: Portraits of an Immigrant Generation* (New York: Harper & Row, 1969).

Samuel S. Chamberlain
(25 September 1851-25 January 1916)

James S. Featherston
Louisiana State University

MAJOR POSITIONS HELD: Founder and editor, Paris *Le Matin* (1884-1886); managing editor, *San Francisco Examiner* (1889-1895), *New York Journal* (1895-1905); editor in chief, *New York American* (1905-1907); editor, *San Francisco Examiner* (1909); publisher, *Boston American* (1910-1916).

Sam Chamberlain was a brilliant but erratic newspaperman who spent most of his career as an executive with the William Randolph Hearst publishing empire. For two years, he was the secretary of another towering but enigmatic figure of American journalism, James Gordon Bennett, Jr. Chamberlain played a key role in revitalizing two newspapers, the *San Francisco Examiner* and the *New York Morning Journal*, while an employee of Hearst. He helped Bennett start the Paris *Herald*, and with the backing of tycoon John Mackay he founded *Le Matin* in Paris. Chamberlain, however, was best remembered by some of his contemporaries for his sartorial splendor and his drinking escapades.

Samuel Selwyn Chamberlain was born 25 September 1851 in Walworth, New York, the son of Ivory C. and Mary Ingalls Chamberlain. He came by his journalistic talents naturally: his father was an editorial writer for the *New York World* before its purchase by Joseph Pulitzer. Sam Chamberlain has been described by one writer as a "true child of the newspaper business, ill educated but well informed, who cut his teeth on copy pencils and went to work as a reporter when he out-grew knee pants." In fact, however, Chamberlain graduated from New York University in 1871. Two years later, he married Mary T. Munson; their son, William Henry Chamberlain, was also destined to become a noted newspaperman.

Chamberlain worked on the *Newark Advertiser* and elsewhere before coming to Park Row, the fabled thoroughfare on which the New York dailies then clustered. Chamberlain worked in various reporting and editing capacities for the *Herald* (1875-1879), the *World* (1879-1880), and the *Evening Telegram* (1881-1883) and was widely known for his journalistic talent, dandified dress, and conviviality. In his lively biography, *The Scandalous Mr. Bennett*, Richard O'Connor writes: "In those years he gained two distinctions among his fellows, aside from his professional brilliance. He drew fewer sober breaths than any of them, and he was the best dressed man on Park Row until Richard Harding Davis came along. . . . Booze and dandyism, however, did not interfere with his cool handling of the news."

In 1883, Chamberlain left for Paris, where he joined the expatriate James Gordon Bennett, Jr., who was operating his *New York Herald* by remote control. In 1884 Chamberlain founded *Le Matin*, a French-language newspaper, with the financial backing of John Mackay, a multimillionaire who had struck it rich in Comstock Lode mining. Chamberlain had met Mackay through Bennett, with whom Mackay had been involved in a scheme to

S. S. Chamberlain

break the transatlantic cable monopoly held by Jay Gould and Western Union. Mackay and a partner, James Fair, who became a United States senator from California, had conspired with agents of Louis Napoleon to corner the world's wheat market; *Le Matin* was an offshoot of this grandiose scheme, which almost ruined Mackay and Fair. (*Le Matin* later was to become one of the most successful Parisian newspapers under the ownership of Maurice Bunau-Varilla and his brother, Philippe.)

Bennett hired Chamberlain as his secretary in 1886, although Chamberlain functioned more as an executive assistant; in 1887, Chamberlain helped Bennett start the European edition of the *Herald*. The two men usually got along famously with each other. Bennett, an even more erratic individual whose own drinking sprees were legendary, had few friends other than sycophants who catered to him in hope of reward; others were repulsed by his tantrums, recklessness, and unpredictability. Chamberlain, whose appetite for the high life was enormous, was able not only to keep up with his employer but to view Bennett's most outrageous acts with aplomb. Both men were about the same age, and, according to O'Connor, they seem to have shared "a quality of despair and rootlessness which

they chose to conceal under a carnival spirit."

While in Paris, Chamberlain sometimes protected Bennett from wild excesses. Bennett, after sustained drinking, once decided to attack the Catholic church editorially. He then dictated or ordered Chamberlain to write a venomous editorial containing such phrases as "to hell with the Pope," "tear down the monasteries," "drive out the monks," and "no more interference from Rome." Then Bennett ordered Chamberlain to accompany him to his own cable company to file the editorial. Later, he sobered up enough to remember the indiscretion. He nervously asked Chamberlain if the editorial had reached New York. Straight-faced, Chamberlain replied, "Yes, but I thought it might not be strong enough, so I got it back so you could read it over again." Bennett breathed a sigh of relief and said, "Thank God." That afternoon Bennett stopped at a jewelry store and purchased an expensive cats-eye ring for Chamberlain.

About a year later, another episode cooled the relations between the two men. Bennett, a yachtsman who was called the "Commodore," was cruising his craft in the eastern Mediterranean when it approached an American warship on maneuvers. Bennett's yacht was on a collision course that would have sent it crashing into the naval vessel amidship. The yacht's sailing master pointed this out to Bennett, who was standing beside him on the bridge. Chamberlain, white-faced with fear, was also standing nearby, and he protested that deliberately colliding with an American warship would have serious repercussions in addition to smashing up the yacht. "Keep right ahead," roared Bennett. "That ship has no right to cross my bow. Keep her on course." Chamberlain could take no more; suddenly he leaped for the helm, swung the wheel, and avoided the collision. Infuriated, Bennett then marooned Chamberlain on a tiny, uninhabited island with only a few days' supply of food and water and a white shirt to wave at passing ships. Other guests on the yacht protested, however, and Bennett relented and lowered a boat to return Chamberlain to the yacht. Neither man would apologize, but Bennett later forgave Chamberlain.

Chamberlain first met William Randolph Hearst at the bar of the Hoffman House in New York City during the summer of 1888. Hearst was impressed with Chamberlain's fashionable dress, his sophistication, and his worldliness. Chamberlain also had the sort of experience Hearst was seeking, and he hired Chamberlain to become managing editor of his *San Francisco Examiner*. In his critically acclaimed biography *Citizen Hearst*, W. A. Swanberg writes that Chamberlain "proved an ideal Hearst lieutenant, a practical psychologist whose New York and Paris experience had taught him what it took to startle, amaze, and stupefy the public."

In San Francisco, Chamberlain helped Hearst assemble a brilliant staff that included, among others, Arthur McEwen. McEwen, who lent his brilliance to the editorial page, once said that what Hearst wanted was the "gee whiz" emotion. Chamberlain headed a staff of able young men who would go to great extremes in search of that emotion. Chamberlain assigned one reporter, Frank Peltret, to have himself committed to an insane asylum, which he did by jumping off a ferry boat and talking wildly when fished out. Peltret spent a month in the asylum and then wrote a bloodcurdling story about his experiences. Chamberlain also hired Winifred Sweet (later Black), a good-looking, red-haired chorus girl who came to San Francisco with a touring theatrical group, and he taught her Hearst journalism. Miss Sweet became famous as the nation's first "sob sister" under the pen name of Annie Laurie. One of her first stunts was to expose conditions at San Francisco's City Receiving Hospital. To do so, she dressed in shabby clothes and collapsed on a downtown street. A policeman with liquor on his breath tried to smell whiskey on hers as she waited a long time for a jolting express wagon to take her to the hospital. Upon her arrival, she was insulted and pawed by interns, given an emetic of hot water and mustard, and released. Her front-page story resulted in a shake-up at the hospital and the suspension of the physician in charge.

The *Examiner* began to attract national attention. It was the first to print the news of the hoisting of the American flag in Honolulu. It sent a special trainload of public schoolchildren to the World's Fair in Chicago. It published the largest paper ever printed until that time in the United States—120 pages. When the federal census of 1890 came out, the *Examiner* filled an entire page with figures for every state and city on the West Coast. Hearst and Chamberlain lived by the creed that "the story's the thing," and they carried personal journalism to its extremes. A big story could always lure Chamberlain from his desk.

One of Chamberlain's successful reporting feats came during a political upheaval in the Sandwich Islands (Hawaii). Chamberlain assigned himself to cover the story and arrived in the islands with a number of other correspondents. The lordly, impressive Chamberlain mingled with the people of Queen Liliuokalani's court, gave wine suppers, and so ingratiated himself with the queen that she spent

pleasant hours with the magnetic Chamberlain and told every detail of what would be described as her "true life story." Chamberlain wrote the story in the presence of the queen and remained with her until the San Francisco-bound steamer was ready to leave. He then rushed to the vessel waving the manuscript of his exclusive story at his disconsolate rivals.

Chamberlain, a personal favorite of Hearst's, was a lively companion, and his small office was a gathering place for the staff of the *Examiner*. Although Hearst had a much larger and finer office, he seemed to feel more at home in Chamberlain's little eight-by-ten cubbyhole. There was much merriment there as the staff joked and made its plans. Hearst and Chamberlain each tried to outdo the other with daring schemes.

Chamberlain was a genius at directing the type of saturation and sensational news coverage favored by Hearst. He also, unfortunately, was not above fabricating stories. Many of these fabrications came from the fertile imagination of a talented reporter named Eddie Morphy. Morphy freely admitted writing such "hot air" stories, and he also recalled writing the story about the funeral of Sen. George Hearst, the father of William Randolph. The reporters assigned to cover the funeral drank too much and failed to return to the office. Chamberlain, frantic for a front-page story, asked Morphy if he could write a stirring and dignified account of the funeral. "Sure thing," Morphy told Chamberlain. "I'll do a masterpiece for you. But tell me something about the length of the procession, and what the old man looked like. Was he tall and thin or short and fat?"

Within a few years, Hearst was ready to invade New York and challenge Joseph Pulitzer's *World* and Bennett's *Herald* for newspaper supremacy in the nation's largest city. He purchased a failing newspaper, the *Morning Journal*, for only $180,000 in 1895. Hearst then sent for Chamberlain, McEwen, Ambrose Bierce, Winifred Black, and his other San Francisco stars to duplicate the success of the *Examiner* in New York. In addition to importing his own talented staff from San Francisco, Hearst raided other New York newspapers for talent, particularly Pulitzer's Sunday *World*. Within a few years, the *Journal* and the *World* were in an all-out war for circulation.

Chamberlain took charge of the news operation with his usual aplomb, and he was confident in his knowledge of what would "sell papers" in New York. A young reporter, according to one story, once rushed into the city room to announce there had been a murder on a streetcar. Chamberlain calmly asked, "What streetcar line?" Told it was the Bleecker Street crosstown line, Chamberlain sadly shook his head and said indifferently, "What happens on a crosstown line never attracts any attention. Now, if only it had happened on a Broadway car. . . ."

Chamberlain headed what became known as the "Wrecking Crew." Allen Churchill, in his highly readable history, *Park Row*, describes how this group covered the news:

> When a good story broke, the entire Hearst staff ran to cover it. Park Row began calling the mass exodus from the Hearst office the departure of the Wrecking Crew, but it resembled more an officer leading a battalion into battle. Sam Chamberlain, after hurried consultation with Cosey Noble [the city editor], would shout excited commands. Members of the staff would leap into coats and follow the running Noble out to the streets. . . . At first the exodus of the Wrecking Crew was a helter-skelter operation, but in time the Hearst reporters formed into a wrecking crew which, it was said, left the citizens gasping.
>
> Ahead sped bicycles, shouting to make way for the carriages whose plunging horses set up sparks from pounding hoofs. When the Hearst affluence became known, the city's wildest cabmen made Park Row their headquarters. To supplement their own talents, some bought fire and cavalry horses to pull carriages. After this wildly careening cavalcade always followed a trail of small boys, delivery wagon drivers, and a legion of stray, yelping dogs. When the story was big enough, Hearst himself went along, leaping wild-eyed and long-legged into a carriage. . . .

Chamberlain played a key role in the sensational coverage the *Journal* gave the Spanish-American War. During the early stages, Chamberlain was described as the "generalissimo of the Hearst forces shuttling between New York and Key West, urging his men to mount a genuine offensive." It was Chamberlain who assigned reporter Karl Decker to rescue Evangelina Cisneros, the so-called "Cuban Joan of Arc," from a prison cell. Chamberlain instructed Decker about how to accomplish the international jailbreak and added significantly, "I can assure you of Mr. Hearst's ample appreciation if you succeed." Decker, his pockets full of Hearst money, succeeded. Chamberlain also played a key role in securing the damaging letter in

which Depuy de Lôme, the Spanish minister in Washington, had described President McKinley as a low politician who "catered to the rabble." This letter created a sensation when published and added to the growing war hysteria. The *Journal* used its entire front page to publicize the letter and headlined it "THE WORST INSULT TO THE UNITED STATES IN ITS HISTORY." Chamberlain was much addicted to big screaming headlines four or five inches high. Hearst himself intervened when Chamberlain and others in the *Journal* city room devised a font of wooden letters a full seven inches tall. "We've gone far enough in that direction," Hearst said.

Chamberlain also was addicted to excitement, and the atmosphere in the city room was sometimes chaotic. Chamberlain obviously liked it this way, and he sometimes was offended when the city room did not have an atmosphere of madness. "Get excited, everybody," he would shout, "everybody get excited." In the early days, when the *Journal* city room had only one hand-crank telephone, it was difficult to respond to Chamberlain's order. Later, when more phones were installed, a reporter would call the switchboard and tell the operator to ring all the city room phones. At the same time, the staff would rush about, hammer at typewriters, shout for copyboys, and otherwise create as much confusion as possible. This seemed to satisfy Chamberlain.

Much has been written about Chamberlain's intemperance, and it was fortunate that he chose employers who were tolerant of insobriety. Hearst considered it sort of an occupational hazard that some of his key employees were heavy drinkers—particularly Chamberlain and McEwen, both of whom would sometimes disappear on drinking sprees. Once during the *Examiner* days, Chamberlain showed up drunk, and E. B. Henderson, then the manager, wired the absent Hearst, "Chamberlain drunk again. May I dismiss him?," to which Hearst replied, "If he is sober one day in thirty this is all I require." Hearst biographer W. A. Swanberg notes: "Sam Chamberlain, after months of reasonable sobriety, would disappear, board a transatlantic steamer, and make for a certain waterfront saloon in Antwerp. Hearst's London representative would go to Antwerp and coax him to return. Arthur McEwen, when he strayed, was apt to head for South America." On one occasion Chamberlain disappeared from the *Journal* office and headed for Holland, where he was joined by McEwen several days later. Hearst's London man was able to track them down in an Amsterdam bar and persuade them to go home. John K. Winkler recreated the scene of their return in these words: "When they arrived, there was a new man in charge of the editorial page and a new managing editor sat in Chamberlain's chair. 'Pardon me,' said Chamberlain, 'just a moment.' He hung up his smart English hat, disposed of his smart English overcoat, sat down at his suddenly vacated desk without disarranging a petal of the flower in the lapel of his smart morning coat, opened his mail and telegrams and stepped into the city room, inquiring as was his wont: 'Well, what is this array of talent and beauty doing to make the world brighter and better this morning?' The new editorial writer stepped down and out, the nice new managing editor was no more, and life resumed in the *Journal* office with its hectic but customary course."

Chamberlain continued with Hearst in various executive positions until his death, except for a brief interlude during which he helped the merchant Thomas B. Wanamaker build up a newspaper in Philadelphia. For about a year (1907-1908), Chamberlain was editor of *Cosmopolitan* magazine, which Hearst had purchased in 1905. Historian Frank Luther Mott noted that Hearst made *Cosmopolitan* more sensational and that his "idea of a magazine was a Sunday supplement raised to a higher degree, but just as readable and attractive." Chamberlain, of course, was an expert at this type of journalism.

At the time of his death, Chamberlain was publisher of the Hearst-owned *Boston American*. Chamberlain died 25 January 1916 of heart disease at the age of sixty-four. He was survived by his wife and his son, who at the time of his father's death was a member of the *New York Evening World* staff. Chamberlain's obituary in the *New York Times* noted that he was a newspaper executive who was known nationwide. Chamberlain, however, was much more than that; he was a journalistic legend whose career spanned five decades and two continents.

References:

Ernest Sutherland Bates and Oliver Carlson, *Hearst: Lord of San Simeon* (New York: Viking, 1936);

Oliver Carlson, *Brisbane: A Candid Biography* (New York: Stackpole, 1937);

Allen Churchill, *Park Row* (New York: Rinehart, 1958);

Roy Everett Littlefield, *William Randolph Hearst: His Role in American Progressivism* (Lanham, Md.: University Press of America, 1980);

Ferdinand Lundberg, *Imperial Hearst: A Social Biography* (New York: Equinox Cooperative Press, 1936);

Frank Luther Mott, *A History of American Magazines, 1835-1905* (Cambridge, Mass.: Harvard University Press, 1957);

Richard O'Connor, *The Scandalous Mr. Bennett* (Garden City: Doubleday, 1962);

Mrs. Fremont Older, *William Randolph Hearst: American* (New York: Appleton-Century, 1936);

Don C. Seitz, *The James Gordon Bennetts: Father and Son* (Indianapolis: Bobbs-Merrill, 1928);

W. A. Swanberg, *Citizen Hearst* (New York: Scribners, 1961);

John Tebbel, *The Life and Good Times of William Randolph Hearst* (New York: Dutton, 1952);

John K. Winkler, *W. R. Hearst: An American Phenomenon* (New York: Simon & Schuster, 1928).

Frank I. Cobb

(6 August 1869-21 December 1923)

William David Sloan

University of Alabama

MAJOR POSITIONS HELD: Chief editorial writer, *Detroit Free Press* (1900-1904); editorial writer, chief editorial writer, editor, *New York World* (1904-1923).

BOOKS: *Woodrow Wilson—An Interpretation* (New York: New York *World*, 1921);
Cobb of the World: A Leader in Liberalism, edited by John L. Heaton (New York: Dutton, 1924).

PERIODICAL PUBLICATIONS: "Are Newspapers Declining in Influence?," *New York World*, 30 December 1909;
"Mr. Pulitzer's Journalism," *New York World*, 31 October 1911;
"Thirty Years—A Retrospect," *New York World*, 10 May 1913;
"The Press and Public Opinion," *New Republic* (31 December 1919): 144-147;
"Economic Aspects of Disarmament," *Atlantic Monthly* (August 1921): 145-149;
"Is Our Democracy Stagnant?," *Harper's* (June 1923): 1-6.

In an era when corporate ownership of newspapers was making editorial writers little more than mere hirelings, Frank I. Cobb enjoyed the freedom to speak his mind—and he spoke it well, for few editorial writers of the twentieth century have matched Cobb for forcefulness and clearness of style. He was fortunate to work for the *New York World*, where publisher Joseph Pulitzer's attitude toward journalism left little doubt that Cobb could write with authority. The combination of style and freedom made Cobb's editorials among the most respected of his time and Cobb among perhaps the ten best editorial writers in American history. The *World's* editorial page was considered by many contemporaries the most influential in the nation and is credited by some journalism historians with inspiring a renaissance of the newspaper editorial function.

Francis Irving Cobb was born in Shannon County, Kansas, on 6 August 1869, a raw place and time at which buffalo, Indians, and outlaws still roamed the plains. His youth, spent with the working people of the country and small towns of the developing Midwest, and his education in the public schools helped shape the style and outlook he later brought to his role as editor of America's outstanding newspaper in its greatest newspaper city. Driven from the family farm by an infestation of grasshoppers, Minor H. Cobb moved with his wife, Mathilda, and his son to the forests of Michigan, where Frank Cobb worked in the lumber camps and sawmills. He received his education in the public schools and at Michigan State Normal School. In 1890, at the age of twenty-one, he was appointed superintendent of the high school at Martin, Michigan. Instead of continuing his career as an educator or going to law school, he decided to go into journalism. After one year as superintendent, he joined the *Grand Rapids Herald* as a reporter, later becoming its political correspondent and city editor. At the age of twenty-four he transferred to the *Grand Rapids Eagle* as city editor and the following year to the *Detroit Evening News*, where he served first as political correspondent and later as editorial writer. In 1897 he married Delia S. Bailey. At the age of thirty he joined the *Detroit Free Press* as its leading editorial writer and remained there for four years.

In 1904 Joseph Pulitzer, the absentee owner and editor of the *New York World*, began a search for a new editor who could revive the paper's editorial strength and stature. William H. Merrill, the chief of the editorial page, was growing old, and his writing lacked the punch it once had. The *World's* editorial staff was filled capably by such men as John Heaton, Horatio Seymour, and Ralph Pulitzer (the owner's son), but the elder Pulitzer could look to none of them to succeed him as editor. He wanted a young man who knew history and politics; who had a keen perception and a concise, direct, forceful style; who could write with clarity, brevity, and punch; and who could provide dynamic and persuasive leadership for the liberal causes Pulitzer espoused: in short, he wanted another, younger Joseph Pulitzer. To find the right man, Pulitzer dispatched one of his personal secretaries, Samuel M. Williams, on a nationwide hunt. Journeying from city to city, Williams read the editorials in the local papers. In Detroit, he sensed he was nearing completion of his mission.

Most editorials he had read were ponderous and uninspired, but those in the *Detroit Free Press* were impressive in the tradition of Pulitzer. Williams purchased back copies of the *Free Press*, read and reread the editorials, found out that the writer was Cobb, and invited him to dinner, where he probed Cobb's mind without revealing his purpose. "At the table," Williams recounted, "Cobb proved himself a brilliant conversationalist, an omnivorous reader, a shrewd observer, a forceful talker, and a keen analyzer of men and affairs. He had vitality of brain and body, yet was so simple in manner, so modest, so lovable, that I knew immediately I had found the Ideal Editor." Williams then wired Pulitzer of his find, but the demanding *World* owner wanted to know much more and told Williams to quiz Cobb further. "What," Pulitzer wanted to know, "has Cobb read in American history, Rhodes, McMaster, Trevelyan, Parkman? What works on the Constitution and constitutional law? Has he

read Buckle's History of Civilization? . . . Search his brain for everything there is in it." Williams took Cobb to lunch and satisfied himself on Cobb's knowledge of history and politics, his political opinions, even his table manners. Finally, after several months of attempting to persuade Cobb, who was none too eager to leave the *Free Press* for the institutionalized, anonymous journalism of New York City, Williams convinced him to visit Pulitzer. After the interview, the owner announced to Williams, "Cobb will do. He knows American history better than anyone I have ever found. . . . in time, we can make a real editor of him." In the spring of 1904 Cobb, at the age of thirty-four, reported to the *World* as one of its several editorial writers, not knowing that he had been picked to replace the legendary Pulitzer as its chief.

The new editorial writer brought to his job a wide-ranging knowledge, an inquisitive mind, a thorough grasp of American political life, and a keen insight. Although his formal education was not uncommon, he had an eager desire to learn through ceaseless study, travel, and discussion with other astute people. He possessed a marked ability to pick up information from various sources and to apply it confidently. Although he had never studied either German or French formally, he mastered both languages. Neither had he studied classical music or modern science, but those subjects also fell within his understanding. His knowledge of American political history was extraordinarily detailed and broad. However, he did not get lost in the subtleties and complexities of his vast knowledge. His editorial writing was notable because of his ability to analyze and simplify bewildering topics and situations and make them understandable to readers.

With his knowledge and insight Cobb combined a clean, forceful, and interesting writing style. He was one of the first editorial writers whose style was marked by modern conciseness and economy. Hating florid phrases and bombast, he stated his ideas clearly and simply. Neither was he afraid to say what he believed. Targets, whether corrupt officials or dangerous ideas, were attacked boldly, unrelentingly, and vigorously. His style was versatile: it was said that he "could swing the bludgeon or wield the rapier at will." He might attack deserving targets with brilliant sarcasm or biting irony, but he also could write with a lightness of touch when the subject merited such treatment. For his mastery of editorial style, he ranked at the top of his profession with his contemporaries Henry Watterson of the *Louisville* (Kentucky) *Courier-Journal*, William Allen

White of the *Emporia* (Kansas) *Gazette*, and Arthur Brisbane of the Hearst newspapers. Watterson called Cobb "the strongest writer of the New York press since Horace Greeley." While his editorials were anonymous, contemporaries declared that "Cobb's work was signed by his style."

Despite such ability, Cobb at the beginning of his employment with the *World* was subjected constantly to intensive criticism by Pulitzer. The petulant owner was often merely hypercritical, but his ultimate motive was to turn the promising young man into America's most outstanding editor. In regard to his training under the master of the *World*, Cobb once explained: "Mr. Pulitzer conducts a school of journalism in regard to me. He often says he expects that I shall be able to carry on the principles of the *World* for the next twenty years." That explanation came after Cobb had been with the paper five years and after he already had become the heir apparent to Pulitzer. In earlier years, he had not acquiesced so readily to Pulitzer's methods. The old man's tactic was to criticize harshly anything which did not please him, and the editorials of Cobb were not excepted. After he read two editorials mailed him by Merrill, the editorial chief, Pulitzer wrote back: "I hope Cobb will improve with age, but I must tell you that the first two editorials you sent as excellent specimens of irony . . . were to my mind or taste, very poor. Flippancy, dear old fellow, triviality, frivolity, are not irony—please underscore these words and put them in Cobb's brain."

Such continual criticism the first year finally determined Cobb to quit the *World*. The owners of the *Free Press* had been urging him to give up New York journalism and return to Detroit, where an interest in the paper awaited him. Cobb, wishing to accept the offer, requested that Pulitzer release him from his contract. Pulitzer was indignant and ordered Cobb to meet with him. By the time of their interview, however, Pulitzer had calmed down; he applied all his charm to the young writer, explaining that he was genuinely sorry for having hurt Cobb's feelings. He remained adamant in his intolerance for imperfections in writing, but he assured Cobb that he was only encouraging him to reach his potential. It was not the last difference of opinion the two had, but Cobb consistently distinguished himself and gradually began his inexorable rise in the *World* hierarchy. Despite his criticisms, Pulitzer considered Cobb the best writer in the country. It was also Cobb who, among the younger members of the editorial staff who occasionally got to try their hand at running things, most pleased Pulitzer with

his work. Indeed, Pulitzer had found in Cobb just the man he wanted, one who shared his editorial views, who could make decisions and act, and who could express the paper's opinions forcefully and cogently.

Within a year of his arrival, Cobb replaced Merrill as chief editorial writer. Horatio Seymour became editorial supervisor, a position he held until 1920, although his authority was limited to final approval of what went on the editorial page and steadily dwindled under the ascendancy of Cobb. Indeed, after Cobb became chief writer, he was virtually in charge of the *World*'s editorial operation, and therefore of the *World* itself, but the title of editor did not pass to him as long as Pulitzer lived. The sick, egoistic, absentee owner did not allow anyone to presume to have authority to run Pulitzer's paper.

Much of the stature of the *World* was a result of the role Pulitzer had set for it and the authority he vested in Cobb. The relationship between the owner and the editorial writer was one of mutual respect, and the prerogative Pulitzer gave Cobb resulted largely from the fact that the two shared similar attitudes about journalism. Cobb was willing to work under Pulitzer's direction because of his esteem for the great newspaper owner's philosophy of journalism. When once asked by a grand jury (investigating a possible libel by the *World* of Theodore Roosevelt) whether he "regard[ed] Mr. Pulitzer as the Big Man of the *World*," Cobb responded, "I regard Mr. Pulitzer as the Big Man of all American newspapers." Even though American newspapers were fast becoming corporate enterprises often dictated to by profit motives, Pulitzer gave Cobb a free hand in determining editorial policy and writing editorial opinions unhampered by financial concerns. Pulitzer ran the *World* until his death, but his editorial director still enjoyed a liberty which was unheard of for employees of corporate papers. As a result, Cobb wrote with a stronger sense of authority than did most other editorial writers on big newspapers. Although his editorials were unsigned, they did not reflect the depersonalized, institutionalized voice of a corporation. Instead, they were the statements of an individual in a newspaper which was the manifestation of the individual. In a period during which most editorial writers have been merely hired hands, Cobb "became a power and a personality in the United States," said Ralph Pulitzer, "writing editorials he did not sign in a paper he did not own."

With Joseph Pulitzer's death in 1911, the leadership of the *World* was bestowed on Cobb, and along with it the office of editor. During the twelve years he occupied the post, the *World* became the nation's most prominent editorial journal, and the one whose opinions were most eagerly followed.

Cobb believed Pulitzer's prime motivation in the operation of the *World* had been to make it a public servant, a paper that would fight for liberal causes in the interest of the masses, rather than a corporation with the basic purpose of making a profit. In an editorial at the time of Pulitzer's death, Cobb wrote that Pulitzer "was the first of the great editors to regard a newspaper not as private property but as public property . . . independent of everything except public interest—independent even of its own proprietor when occasion required. . . . His aim was to make a newspaper that . . . would hold itself beyond every form of influence except that of the public welfare. . . . Although he was the owner of *The World* . . . he was in no sense a newspaper publisher. Practically all his knowledge of counting-room affairs was second-hand. He once told [me] . . . that in all the years of his journalistic career he never spent an hour at any one time in the business office. Nothing connected with *The World* appealed to him less than its income and profits. . . . Its prosperity was a means, never an end. . . . To him journalism was never a business; it was the most powerful and responsible profession in which any man could engage." Two years later, on the thirtieth anniversary of Pulitzer's purchase of the *World*, Cobb wrote in similar fashion that the day Pulitzer took over the paper "marked the beginning of a new journalism in the United States—a journalism that was to be independent of individuals, of private interests, of personal ambition, of political factions and of parties—a journalism devoted unreservedly to public purposes and public principles regardless of all other considerations." Although Cobb only infrequently stated his own views on journalism, it is quite clear that they mirrored Pulitzer's.

In 1913 Cobb married his second wife, Margaret Hubbard Ayer, a writer for the *World*; they had two children, Jane and Hubbard.

Cobb's leadership was recognized in a number of causes. Above all, he was an advocate of political liberalism and of human freedom. Especially notable were his efforts in behalf of insurance reform, integrity in government, Woodrow Wilson, American and democratic interests in World War I, the League of Nations, constitutional government, and freedom of expression. The *World*'s campaign against corruption by the Equitable Insurance Company from 1905 to 1907 had encouraged government investigation and reform legislation in New York which served as a model for laws in other states. Its investigation of the construction of the Panama Canal had uncovered much corruption and focused public attention on the financial dealings of government officials involved; that campaign had resulted in Theodore Roosevelt's institution of a libel prosecution against Pulitzer. The *World*'s defiance of Roosevelt's high-handed attacks still stands as one of the most worthy defenses of the concept of freedom of the press. Cobb, one of Wilson's trusted advisers, was credited by some contemporaries with having persuaded the Democrats to give Wilson his first presidential nomination in 1912. Being close to Wilson and at the same time independent in thought, Cobb was the leading editorial writer voicing the prevailing American attitude of restraint toward entering Word War I. An editorial for 1 August 1914, titled "An Indictment of Civilization," read in its entirety:

> In Vienna, there is a doddering old man, the offspring of a tainted house, who sits on the throne of the dual empire.
>
> In St. Petersburg, there is a weak, well-meaning neurotic who by the accident of birth happens to be the Czar of All the Russias.
>
> In Berlin there is a brilliant, talented, ambitious manipulator of politics who is German Emperor by grace of the genius of Bismarck, Moltke, and Roon.
>
> Of these three men, only the one in Berlin has more than mediocre abilities; yet the three are permitted to play with the lives of millions of men, with property worth thousands of millions of dollars, with the commerce and industry and prosperity and laws and institutions not merely of empires and kingdoms but of continents. It is left to them to determine whether the world is to witness the most deadly and devastating war of all history.
>
> The thing would be laughable, ridiculous, if it were not so ghastly.
>
> War of itself may be wise or unwise, just or unjust; but that the issue of a world-wide war should rest in the hands of three men—any three men—and that the hundreds of millions who will bear the burden and be affected in every relation of life by the outcome of such a war should passively leave the decision to those three men is an indictment of civilization itself.
>
> Human progress is slow indeed when a whole continent is still ready to fight for anything except the right to life, liberty and self-government.

After American entry into the war, Cobb was one of the most forceful advocates of wholehearted efforts toward victory and was a member of the American mission sent to Europe to prepare for the signing of the armistice. After the war, he was American journalism's strongest and most consistent supporter of the League of Nations and opponent of tyranny. He was recognized also for his insight into the problems of the United States' constitutional form of government in the twentieth century and for his strong advocacy of human freedoms, especially liberty of expression.

Fellow journalists admired Cobb not only for his editorial ability but for his personal characteristics. He was kind, unassuming, lacking in conceit, a man of honesty and personal charm, gentle and generous. Cobb enjoyed the company of other, less important staff members of the *World*, and he was a favorite among the staffers in the newsroom. While he was a dynamic, engaging, and knowledgeable conversationalist, he did not condescend toward anyone of lesser knowledge or station. He was known as a man who had received no special favors but had earned every benefit he had gotten out of life. Cobb was a director and first vice-president of the American Society of Newspaper Editors, chairman of the publicity committee of the Woodrow Wilson Foundation, and a chevalier of the French Legion of Honor and the Belgian Order of Leopold.

With Cobb's death on 21 December 1923, a large vacuum was left at the *World*. He had been a ceaseless fighter in the causes of liberalism and of responsible journalism. His ambition was not for personal success but to continue the tradition of quality in the *World*. Woodrow Wilson eulogized him as an enlightened leader of American thought. "I have known no man," the former president wrote, "whose sturdiness of character and clear vision of duty impressed me more than those of Frank I. Cobb. He completely won my confidence and affection and I recognized in him a peculiar genius for giving direct and effective expression to the enlightened opinions which he held. I consider his death an irreparable loss to journalism and to the liberal political policies which are necessary to liberate mankind from the errors of the past and the partisan selfishness of the present. His death leaves a vacancy in the ranks of liberal thinkers which someone should press forward to fill if the impulse of progress is not to be stayed." Walter Lippmann, Cobb's replacement, had served first as an assistant to Cobb; but neither his intellect nor his temperament was suited to carrying on the paper as a leading popular journal. The *World* itself expired in a merger with the *New York Telegram* in 1931.

References:

"Appreciation," *New Republic* (2 January 1924): 137;

James L. Barrett, *Joseph Pulitzer and His World* (New York: Vanguard Press, 1941);

"Cobb, a Leader in Liberalism: An Editor Who Made the Nation His Debtor," *Current Opinion* (August 1924): 163-164;

Lindsay Denison, "Cobb, The Man," in *Cobb of the World: A Leader in Liberalism,* edited by John L. Heaton (New York: Dutton, 1924): xi-xxv;

"An Editor of the 'World' and the World," *Literary Digest* (12 January 1924): 40-42;

"Frank I. Cobb," *Nation* (2 January 1924): 3;

"Great Editor," *Outlook* (2 January 1924): 8-9;

Heaton, *The Story of a Page* (New York & London: Harper, 1913);

J. Schermerhorn, "Editorial Writer," *American Magazine* (January 1913): 29-30;

Don C. Seitz, *Joseph Pulitzer: His Life & Letters* (New York: Simon & Schuster, 1924);

"Sketch," *Everybody's* (March 1916): 356.

Irvin S. Cobb

Sam G. Riley
Virginia Polytechnic Institute and State University

See also the Cobb entry in *DLB 11, American Humorists, 1800-1950.*

BIRTH: Paducah, Kentucky, 23 June 1876, to Joshua Clark and Manie Saunders Cobb.

MARRIAGE: 12 June 1900 to Laura Spencer Baker; child: Elisabeth.

MAJOR POSITIONS HELD: Managing editor, *Paducah Evening News*, 1895; reporter and columnist, *Louisville Evening Post*, 1898-1901; managing editor, *Paducah News-Democrat*, 1901-1904; reporter and humor writer, *New York Sun*, 1904-1905; reporter and humor columnist, *New York World*, 1905-1911; staff contributor, *Saturday Evening Post* (1911-1922), *Cosmopolitan* (1922-1932).

AWARDS AND HONORS: Honorary degrees from Dartmouth and the University of Georgia; adopted by Blackfoot and Iroquois tribes; Chevalier of the Legion of Honor (France), 1918.

DEATH: New York, 10 March 1944.

Culver Pictures

BOOKS: *Cobb's Anatomy: A Guide to Humor* (New York: Doran, 1912; London: Hodder & Stoughton, 1915);

Back Home; Being the Narrative of Judge Priest and His People (New York: Doran, 1912; London: Heinemann, 1912);

Cobb's Bill-of-Fare (New York: Doran, 1913; London: Hodder & Stoughton, 1915);

The Escape of Mr. Trimm: His Plight and Other Plights (New York: Doran, 1913; London: Hodder & Stoughton, 1914);

Europe Revised (New York: Doran, 1914);

Roughing It De Luxe (New York: Doran, 1914);

"Speaking of Operations—" (Garden City: Doubleday, 1915; London: Hodder & Stoughton, 1916);

Paths of Glory: Impressions of War Written At and Near the Front (New York: Doran, 1915); expanded and republished as *The Red Glutton: Impressions of War Written at and near the Front* (London & New York: Hodder & Stoughton, 1915);

Fibble, D. D. (New York: Doran, 1916);

Local Color (New York: Doran, 1916);

Old Judge Priest (New York: Doran, 1916; London: Hodder & Stoughton, 1916);

Those Times and These (New York: Doran, 1917; London: Brentano, 1927);

"Speaking of Prussians—" (New York: Doran, 1917);

Lost Tribes of the Irish in the South (New York: American Irish Historical Society, 1917);

The Thunders of Silence (New York: Doran, 1918);

The Glory of the Coming: What Mine Eyes Have Seen of Americans in Action in this Year of Grace and Allied Endeavor (New York: Doran, 1918; London: Hodder & Stoughton, 1919);

Life of the Party (New York: Doran, 1919);

Eating in Two or Three Languages (New York: Doran, 1919; London: Hodder & Stoughton, 1919);

"Oh Well, You Know How Women Are!" (New York: Doran, 1919);

The Abandoned Farmers (New York: Doran, 1920);

From Place to Place (New York: Doran, 1920);

A Plea for Old Cap Collier (New York: Doran, 1921);

One Third Off (New York: Doran, 1921);

J. Poindexter, Colored (New York: Doran, 1922);

Sundry Accounts (New York: Doran, 1922);

Stickfuls; Compositions of a Newspaper Minion (New York: Doran, 1923);

A Laugh a Day Keeps the Doctor Away (New York: Doran, 1923; London: Hodder & Stoughton, 1924);

Snake Doctor, and Other Stories (New York: Doran, 1923);

Irvin Cobb at His Best (Garden City: The Sun Dial Press, 1923);

Goin' on Fourteen: Being Cross-sections out of a Year in the Life of an Average Boy (New York: Doran, 1924);

Indiana: Cobb's America Guyed Books (New York: Doran, 1924);

Kansas: Cobb's America Guyed Books (New York: Doran, 1924);

Kentucky: Cobb's America Guyed Books (New York: Doran, 1924);

Maine: Cobb's America Guyed Books (New York: Doran, 1924);

New York: Cobb's America Guyed Books (New York: Doran, 1924);

North Carolina: Cobb's America Guyed Books (New York: Doran, 1924);

Alias Ben Alibi (New York: Doran, 1925);

"Here Comes the Bride—" and So Forth (New York: Doran, 1925);

Many Laughs for Many Days (New York: Doran, 1925; London: Hodder & Stoughton, 1925);

On an Island That Cost $24.00 (New York: Doran, 1926);

Prose and Cons (New York: Doran, 1926);

Some United States: A Series of Stops in Various Parts of this Nation with One Excursion across the Line (New York: Doran, 1926);

Chivalry Peak (New York: Cosmopolitan, 1927; London: Hodder & Stoughton, 1928);

Ladies and Gentlemen (New York: Cosmopolitan, 1927; London: Hodder & Stoughton, 1927);

All Aboard: Saga of the Romantic River (New York: Cosmopolitan, 1928);

Red Likker (New York: Cosmopolitan, 1929; London: Jarrolds, 1930);

This Man's World (New York: Cosmopolitan, 1929; London: Brentano, 1929);

To Be Taken before Sailing (New York: Cosmopolitan, 1930);

Both Sides of the Street (New York: Cosmopolitan, 1930);

Incredible Truth (New York: Cosmopolitan, 1931);

Down Yonder with Judge Priest and Irvin S. Cobb (New York: Long & Smith, 1932);

Murder Day by Day (Indianapolis: Bobbs-Merrill, 1933);

One Way to Stop a Panic (New York: McBride, 1933);

Faith, Hope and Charity (Indianapolis & New York: Bobbs-Merrill, 1934);

Judge Priest Turns Detective (Indianapolis & New York: Bobbs-Merrill, 1937);

Azam, the Story of an Arabian Colt and His Friends (New York: Rand, 1937);

Favorite Humorous Stories of Irvin Cobb (New York: Triangle Books, 1940);

Glory, Glory Hallelujah (Indianapolis: Bobbs-Merrill, 1941);

Exit Laughing (Indianapolis & New York: Bobbs-Merrill, 1941);

Roll Call (Indianapolis & New York: Bobbs-Merrill, 1942);

Cobb's Cavalcade (New York: World, 1945).

PERIODICAL PUBLICATIONS: "Trail of the Lonesome Laugh," *Everybody's*, 24 (April 1911): 467-475;

"Kipling Interviewed at Last," *Literary Digest*, 47 (27 December 1913): 1277;

"I Am Strangely Moved by the Movies," *Woman's Home Companion*, 44 (July 1917):15;

"Advantages of Being Homely," *American Magazine*, 86 (July 1918): 43-45;

"I Admit I Am a Good Reporter," *American Magazine*, 88 (August 1919): 60-61;

"Story That Ends Twice," *Saturday Evening Post*, 193 (4 September 1920): 8-10;

"Darkness," *Saturday Evening Post*, 194 (20 August 1921): 3-5;

"His Mother's Apron Strings," *Good Housekeeping*, 76 (March 1923): 10-13;

"Eminent Dr. Deeves," *Current Opinion*, 74 (June 1923): 692-701;

"My Free Recipe for Getting Rich," *Rotarian*, 43 (September 1933): 11-13;

"Trial and Error," *Reader's Digest*, 41 (December 1942): 32.

Though Irvin S. Cobb was an accomplished reporter of straight news, he is mainly remembered in present-day journalistic circles for his contributions as a humor columnist. Much of his surviving humor copy was done between 1904 and 1911, the period during which he worked as a reporter and humor columnist for two major New York City newpapers. Cobb had entered newspaper journalism in his hometown at age sixteen and worked for Kentucky papers until 1904, when he left his native state for the "big city." After getting out of newspapering in 1911, he concentrated on writing humor articles and short stories for the magazine market—notably the *Saturday Evening Post* and *Cosmopolitan*—and in addition had more than sixty books published.

Irvin Shrewsbury Cobb was born in 1876 in the rollicking frontier town of Paducah, Kentucky, into a family whose descendants were among the first settlers of that state—"a story stiff with proud adjectives," as he put it. Cobb's grandfather was a Paducah frontiersman when hostile Indians were still in the area; his father, Joshua Cobb, was an alcoholic, upon whose death Cobb had to begin earning a living at age sixteen. The skinny, narrow-shouldered, gangling Cobb, whose boyhood friends called him "Shrivly," was described as "about as homely a kid, except for his eyes and brow, as ever hit Kentucky since Abe Lincoln left home." He was six feet tall, with Irish coloring—pale skin, blue eyes, and black hair. Prior to his father's demise, Cobb had driven an ice wagon for two summers, delivered circulars, and collected bills to bolster his family's modest income. His original ambition was to go to a military college, then law school, or, failing that, to become a cartoonist; but when his father drank himself to death, Cobb took the best-paying job he could find—cub reporter for the *Paducah Evening News* at $1.75 a week.

On his first day, Cobb was given a pencil and paper and was told to go out into the street and find some news. "Always before this street had seemed to me fairly to throb with life and movement. Now, all of a sudden, it had become as cold and empty as an open grave. It looked as if nothing had ever happened there; as if nothing ever was going to happen there." Soon, however, he discovered that he preferred writing to cartooning, and by age nineteen he was the *News*'s managing editor—possibly the youngest in the nation and, as he later remarked, "in the light of fuller knowledge I'm sure I must have been the worst managing editor of any age in the United States. I was reckless, smart-alecky, careless, gaudy in my enthusiasms, a dynamic

builder of lurid headlines. I rarely let dull fact hamper my style."

After involving the paper in a number of libel suits, young Cobb was relieved as managing editor and reduced to the rank of reporter. Even so, he reported in his autobiography, *Exit Laughing* (1941), at this time in his career he could "work at high-pressure fifteen hours on a stretch, play dime-limit draw poker all night, drink my share of the drinks, and come to work the next morning, blear-eyed perhaps and a trifle drowsy, but without a twitching nerve in my body." At age twenty he was making $12 a week, a good salary for a small-town reporter in those days, and he always spoke of himself "as a journalist, never as a mere newspaperman." He also served as Paducah correspondent for several other papers (including the *Chicago Tribune*) and in a good week could double his income in this way.

Cobb was the *News*'s sole reporter, though the paper had several other editorial employees, all older men: a river editor who did a steamboat column; an exchange editor "who seemed to live entirely on chewing tobacco and clippings"; an editorial writer; and "others of nebulous positions," three of whom were Confederate veterans, the fourth a Union vet, and all of whom wrote "what pleased them when it pleased them."

His first editor, known around Paducah as "Boss Jim," had pointed him in a new direction, telling him he had a flair for writing "funny stuff" and printing Cobb's first jingles and other humor copy. After his demotion from managing editor, he again had time to write humor pieces, and a few other Kentucky papers began to use them, though without a by-line.

From 1898 to 1901 Cobb worked for the *Louisville Evening Post*, doubling as political reporter and humor columnist. Some of the copy for his "Kentucky Sour Mash" column was done in verse. "My poetry," he wrote much later, "was so wooden that it fairly creaked at the joints, but I could turn it out by the yard. For 20 years now I have done no versifying, and I find it almost impossible to frame lines that will scan or rhyme, whereas this used to be the easiest thing I did."

Undoubtedly his most exciting assignment during his years with the *Post* was covering the murder of Gov. William Goebel of Kentucky, a political forebear of Louisiana's Huey Long and "a Mussolini of politics if one ever lived. He had audacity, ruthlessness, a genius of leadership, an instinct for absolute despotism, a gift for organization, a perfect disregard for other men's rights or their lives where his own wishes were concerned. . . . He loved power as drunkards loved their bottle and he would have waded through blood up to his armpits to have his way. . . . I think it was always snowing in his wintry soul." Cobb had sat in the press stand on the stage of Louisville's Music Hall where the Democratic convention was held and a half-dozen times had flattened himself when guns were drawn. He was in Legislative Hall when he heard the shot that struck the newly sworn-in Goebel, and he rushed from the building to help carry the governor away, after which he got the details from Goebel's bodyguards and wired the story to the *Post*. (Cobb later admitted that he went along with the wishes of Goebel's aides and reported that the dying man's last words were, "Be brave and fearless and loyal to the great common people." In his autobiography, Cobb reveals that the governor expired after having eaten an oyster, his favorite food, and that his actual last words were "Doc, that was a damned bad oyster.") Cobb was a witness for the defense at the trial of a black man named Ireland who was acquitted of the murder, and he later covered the arrests of Kentucky Secretary of State Caleb Powers; Henry Youtsey; and James Howard, the man who actually fired the fatal shot. This long, involved case kept Cobb busy for "upwards of a crowded year" and gave him the confidence to handle big stories. He felt that it especially prepared him for the biggest news assignment of his career, which came seven years later—the Harry Thaw-Stanford White-Evelyn Nesbitt murder case.

During a recess in the trial, Cobb traveled to Savannah and married Laura Spencer Baker, whom he described as "five feet-one of steadfastness, wholesomeness and spunk." The couple honeymooned in Washington, D.C., in June, "when the asphalt melted to chewing gum in the streets and the draft horses wore straw hats and fell down in their tracks and the salamander in the zoo perished by a heat stroke." During another break in the Goebel proceedings, Cobb went to Cincinnati. The trial recommenced unexpectedly, and after a painfully slow train ride back, in his desperation he filed a duplicate of the trial's transcript—over 4,000 words. To his surprise, it made good reading. "Songbirds began chirping in the cage of my ribs," he reported, as his managing editor at the *Post* wired congratulations and asked how Cobb ever managed to think of such a clever idea.

For about two years the couple lived in Louisville, and Cobb worked his way up to $18 weekly plus free-lancing; then they moved to Paducah, where Cobb again became managing editor of the

local paper, renamed the *Paducah News-Democrat*. From ages twenty-five to twenty-eight, the space of time during which he held this post, he wrote no humor copy at all. His editorial duties required an eighteen-hour workday; he got out six weekday editions, a weekly, and a Sunday paper.

Cobb's first big break came at this time and was like a plot straight out of an improbable short story. "Before the buoyant imaginations of moving-picture producers, as reflected on the silver screen, taught us that all great reporters were drunken geniuses, with a dashing way about them though, and that all women writers were beautiful abnormalities, and that a city room somewhat closely resembled feeding time at the zoo, a favorite fiction story was the one about the despised cub, whom even the copy boy snubbed and the Neroesque city editor sneered at and the rest of the staff ignored; but he went forth and all by himself, through a superhuman stroke of brilliancy, outslicked the supercilious star of the opposition sheet right down to his union suit. This was known as a 'scoop'." The only real-life occurrence of this wishful-sounding plot that he ever encountered, Cobb said, happened to himself. An accused wife-murderer named Christopher Merry had escaped from the Chicago police and with an accomplice named Smith had headed south. Frostbitten feet slowed Merry's progress, and he was captured and placed in the county jail at Princeton, Kentucky, about 100 miles from Paducah. As country correspondent for the *Chicago Tribune*, Cobb was telegraphed instructions to rush to Princeton and get an interview with the prisoners. When he arrived, he found that two far more experienced Chicago reporters had arrived before him but were pacing and swearing in such a way that he could tell "their preconceived notions of Southern hospitality had suffered a severe jolt." The rifle-toting jailer had been ordered to allow no strangers to see his prisoners, and he had told the city reporters that "the Twelve Apostles could not get into that jail except over his dead body." At this point Cobb remembered that his father and Princeton's mayor had served in the same regiment in the Civil War. He had but to ask, and the mayor led him past the fuming Chicago reporters and into the jail for an exclusive interview. "That there Chicago officer told me not to admit any strangers," the jailer allowed, "and I ain't aimin' to do so; but son, you ain't no stranger—you're homefolks." After wiring a synopsis to the *Tribune*, Cobb was advised: "LET IT ALL COME. SPREAD YOURSELF AND KEEP SENDING UNTIL WE SAY STOP." Cobb, who had never before done a story of such length for a city paper, produced thousands of words of "flamboyant and be-adjectived" copy and tied up the telegraph wires so that the Chicago men were completely scooped.

The next week he received word of a $50 bonus in a personal note from *Tribune* editor Joseph Medill, who complimented the job he had done. Later, Cobb said that the $50, plus an added $50 for expenses, was the largest sum he had ever owned in his life; but he admitted that the Medill note had not been properly treasured, as the only editors who really mattered to him at the time were Henry Watterson of Louisville, Henry W. Grady of Atlanta, and Edward Carmack of Memphis. It was this profitable experience that prompted him to look for newspaper work with a big-city paper. "I wanted to get there," he said, "before mad extravagance plunged them into bankruptcy." His first thought was to go to Chicago and work for the *Tribune*. The Associated Press's Harry Beach, whom he had met while covering the Goebel murder, took him in hand and recommended him to the *Tribune*'s city editor, Eddie Beck. Beck wanted to hire Cobb but was overruled by managing editor James Keeley. "Chicago's loss was New York's gain," Cobb later wrote, "not that Chicago didn't somehow contrive to continue getting out daily newspapers." Five months later, in August 1904, he sent his wife and daughter to Savannah to stay with her parents, borrowed $200 from his father-in-law, and left for New York City.

Cobb rented a room at a boardinghouse and spent two fruitless weeks trying to get a job with a city paper. In exasperation he composed a letter and had thirteen copies made. The letter read: "This is positively your last chance. I have grown weary of studying the wall-paper design in your anteroom. A modest appreciation of my own worth forbids me doing business with your head office boy any longer. Unless you grab me right away I will go elsewhere and leave your paper flat on its back right here in the middle of a hard summer, and your whole life hereafter will be one vast surging regret. The line forms on the left; applications considered in the order in which they are received; triflers and professional flirts save stamps. Write, wire or call the above address." The next morning he called at the *New York Sun* and was promptly hired at $15 a week. Afterward he found that his nervy letter had netted him five other job offers, including one from Arthur Brisbane for the *Evening Journal*.

Cobb remained with the *Sun* for only a year and a half, making his first friends among New York-based journalists in Sam Blythe, who was later a Washington columnist and champion of the California redwoods, and Charley Hand of the London *Daily Mail*. Though he contributed humor copy to the *Sun*, it was a straight-news assignment that led to his accepting a better-paying job at Joseph Pulitzer's *New York World*. Cobb was sent by the *Sun* to cover Theodore Roosevelt's Portsmouth (New Hampshire) Peace Conference, and another journalistic chum, Bob Davis, described the situation as follows: "Cobb cast his experienced eye over the situation, discovered that the story was already well covered by a large coterie of competent, serious-minded young men, and went into action to write a few columns daily on subjects having no bearing whatsoever on the conference. . . . There wasn't a single fact in the entire series ['Making Peace at Portsmouth'] and yet the *Sun* syndicated them throughout the United States." Shortly thereafter, Cobb accepted an offer from the *World*, serving there as a reporter, rewrite man, staff correspondent on out-of-town assignments, and humor writer. Here he remained for the next six years. It was at this point that he began to put on weight. As his daughter, Elisabeth, put it, "One day he was a long, lean Gary Cooper-legged boy, the next a fat man." In his *World* humor column, "New York Through Funny Glasses," Cobb described himself thus: "I should say that in appearance he is rather bulky, standing six feet high, not especially beautiful, a light roan in color, with a black mane. His figure is undecided, but might be called bunchy in spots. He has always, like his father who was a Confederate soldier, voted the Democratic ticket. He has had one wife and one child and still has them. In religion he is an innocent bystander." Cobb's weight gain disconcerted him little. He took advantage of his corpulence and cast himself as the comic fat man in much of his humor work. "Past a certain age," he observed, "the average man either stays thin and becomes a trellis for his varicose veins to climb on, or he takes on a contour which, being viewed sideways, suggests that he swallowed a parasol and after it got down in him it blew open."

Between reporting jobs and humor columns, he wrote an average of three signed humor pieces a week for the *World*'s magazine page, and during his last four years with the paper, he wrote a page of humor for the magazine section of the Sunday edition under the heads "The Hotel Clerk Says" and "Live Talks With Dead Ones." These humor pieces were syndicated, and for the entire four years he never missed filling his Sunday page. His colleagues on the *World* could always tell when he was about to begin a humor piece, Cobb said. He would sit down at his typewriter, insert a sheet of paper, and look as though he were about to cry. "I still regard humorous writing as about the most serious work a writing-man can do," he said. "I've never yet got a laugh out of anything I wrote in the line of humor. I trust that others have, occasionally, but I haven't."

While Cobb was obviously happy to have gained national prominence through his humor work, he did not wish to be known as merely a humorist. He was proud of his ability to handle straight news, but at the same time he indulged in self-criticism, saying of his writing: "My weakest point is a tendency to over-write, to over-elaborate, a story which interests me personally. (Perhaps I am over-writing now.) My strongest point is a sense of news values. . . . My heaviest liability in the line of outstanding reportorial shortcomings is an almost complete absence of the deductive quality, wherefore effects appeal to me rather than causes. As an analyst I would never shine unless it were with the same shininess which we associate with a brass dime." Being interviewed for a chapter in Thomas Masson's *Our American Humorists*, Cobb said: "One curious thing I have discovered: A man may write serious fiction for ten years or do straight reportorial work for ten years, but let him turn out one piece of foolery that tickles the public in its short-ribs and, from that hour, he is branded as a humorist." However much or little he liked the label "humorist," his ability to make the reading public laugh was responsible for his *New York World* salary of $150 a week, which reportedly made him the highest paid newspaper writer of his day.

A curious aspect of the Cobb humor technique is revealed in the somber halftone of himself that appeared over his column. The incongruity of the woebegone face and the hilarious copy is reminiscent of the technique used by the late Emmett Kelly, the famous circus clown. A vivid description of Cobb's picture is provided by Bob Davis: "The first glimpse I had of him was in a half-tone picture in the New York *Evening World*. . . . It was the face of a man scarred with uncertainty. . . . Grief was written on the brow; more than written—it was emblazoned. The eyes were heavy with inexpressible sadness. The corners of the mouth drooped, heightening the whole effect of incomprehensible sadness. . . . If Cobb were an older man I would go on the witness stand and swear that the photograph was made when he was witnessing the Custer Massacre or the passing of Geronimo through the winter quarters of his enemies."

The biggest straight-news story of Cobb's newspaper career was the 1906 murder of promi-

nent architect Stanford White by millionaire Harry K. Thaw over the affections of Thaw's wife, international beauty Evelyn Nesbitt. This was a case to make any reporter's heart beat faster. It was close to being the ideal crime story, as described by Cobb: "It had in it wealth, degeneracy, rich old wasters; delectable young chorus girls and adolescent artists' models; the behind-the-scenes of Theaterdom and the Underworld, and the Great White Way, as we called it then; the abnormal pastimes and weird orgies of overly aesthetic artists and jaded debauchees. In the cast of the motley show were Bowery toughs, Harlem gangsters, Tenderloin panders, Broadway leading men, Fifth Avenue clubmen, Wall Street manipulators, uptown voluptuaries and downtown thugs. . . ." Irvin Cobb was a reporter at Thaw's 1907 trial, sometimes writing as much as 12,000 words a day. When doing his humor pieces, he composed at the typewriter, but in covering a major news story he preferred to write in longhand. Covering the Thaw trial, Cobb had his own copyboy, who relayed the handwritten sheets to a stenographer at the *World*. Cobb was, he said in *Exit Laughing*, proud of his "agility at hand galloping."

He was appalled by the conflicting testimony of paid "expert witnesses" at the trial and personified them in a single character—"Dr. J. Mumble Viceversa." He later wrote of the "scurvy, sweated smear of pseudoscientific poppycock which was spread, like batter on a hot griddle, all over the fraud-tinged transcript." Of Thaw's principal defense lawyer, Delphin Michael Delmas, an attorney past his prime, Cobb wrote: "To the sympathetically inclined, a practically extinct crater which still fancies itself an active volcano is a pitiful sight to see," and he reported in detail how the district attorney "ate him alive, bite by wriggling bite." Cobb also covered Thaw's second trial—which resulted in a term for Thaw not at Sing Sing, but at the State Asylum for the Criminally Insane at Matteawan—and after that, the efforts of Thaw's family to extricate him from even this modest punishment. "In no time at all he was much dissatisfied with the accommodations and craving to depart therefrom," wrote Cobb. "He was ever a restless spirit."

One of Cobb's pet peeves was the indecisive editor "who isn't sure of himself and so can't be sure of anyone else. . . . He worries to a lather and drives competent contributors half crazy by futile, meaching little suggestions. Doesn't Mr. Soft Lead agree with him that it would strengthen the introduction were the second paragraph shifted to where the third paragraph now is? He has been fretting over it all night and his poor head is fit to split. Would Miss Fountain Penn consent to the substitution on Page 24 of the word 'pale' for her choice 'pallid'? With the context, 'pale' is stronger, somehow, more emphatic. At least so it seems to him." As much as he disdained weak, ineffective editors, he valued strong, decisive ones. His favorite city editors, he said, were Tommy Dieuaide of the *New York Sun*, fellow Kentuckian Keats Speed of the *New York Evening Journal*, and Charley Chapin of the *World*. In Chapin he saw "something of Caligula, something of Don Juan, a touch of Barnum, a dash of Narcissus, a spicing of Machiavelli." Cobb was amazed by Chapin's singleness of purpose and further described him: "Features, specials, comics, supplements and all such circulation-getting side issues he despised. By his estimates these merely cluttered up the space which should be devoted to what was immediate, what was exciting or distressing or funny in the day's grist. His idol, and the only one he worshiped except his own conceitful image, was the ink-nosed, nine-eyed, clay-footed god called News." (Editor Chapin eventually murdered his wife and was sent to Sing Sing, where he edited the prison paper, the *Star of Hope*.)

Toward the end of his years with the *World*, Cobb began experimenting with other outlets for his talent. He wrote the script for a musical comedy, *Funabashi* (1908), in five days and remarked later that only the absence of a guillotine in New York accounted for his escape from punishment for the offense. Next he took a six-week vacation from the *World* to try his hand at short-story writing, urged to do so by Mrs. Cobb; by Sam Blythe, political columnist for the *Saturday Evening Post*; and by the *Post*'s editor, George Horace Lorimer. The result, "The Escape of Mr. Trimm," was published by Lorimer in 1909, but Cobb retained his *World* position for another two years and wrote short stories on the side. Lorimer bought them all, and finally, in 1911, Cobb left newspapering for the more lucrative fields of magazine and book writing. Soon after joining Lorimer's employ, the Cobbs were sent to Europe; the articles Cobb did on this trip were collected in *Europe Revised* (1914), a big seller and one of his finest humor books. As his daughter expressed it, "He had caught the wave, and was to roll along on top of it for a long time."

Through his long career writing for the

Frontispiece and title page for Cobb's 1914 book about a Western trip

magazine and book trade, Cobb said, he retained a nostalgic love for newspaper work. Often as he read the paper, he would find himself rewriting headlines, mentally altering makeup, and reordering whole stories. When the *Titanic* sank on 15 April 1912, Cobb helped cover the story as an unpaid volunteer. He interviewed surviving crew members and passengers as they came ashore from the *Carpathia* and "for two days and nights had a gorgeous time."

During the eleven years he wrote for the *Post*, Cobb was twice more sent to Europe, but on these trips he covered World War I. He reported the Chateau-Thierry campaign, the fall of Louvain, the occupation of Brussels, and the Battle of Mons. He was sick in bed in the Savoy Hotel in London when German Zeppelins raided that city in 1918; did battle coverage from an observation balloon over the river Aisne; developed an umbilical hernia carrying men from hospital trains in Maubeuge, France; helped amputate three gangrenous fingers that "looked like rotted bananas" from the hand of a German private; and was nearly shot as a spy by a Prussian sergeant near Louvain. After each experience covering the war, he returned to the United States and went on the lecture circuit, on one occasion under contract with the promoters Edgar and Archie Selwyn. In the spring of 1915 Cobb was given a dinner at New York's Waldorf-Astoria, "presumably in celebration of the fact that I had gone on lecture tour during the winter and had escaped alive. (I always got out of town before popular indignation could crystallize.)"

Cobb left the *Saturday Evening Post* in 1922 to join the staff of William Randolph Hearst's *Cosmopolitan* magazine. When Cobb had left the *Sun* for Joseph Pulitzer's *World*, Pulitzer had been blind and a bundle of nerves; few members of the *World* staff had ever seen their publisher. In the six years Cobb worked for Pulitzer, he never met the boss and spoke with him only once by telephone. For the over nine years he wrote for *Cosmopolitan*, by contrast, he had frequent contact with the flamboyant Hearst and was even entertained by him at San Simeon, Hearst's palatial California retreat. In *Exit Laughing*, Cobb says that he always felt he had failed to penetrate Hearst's shell and had never met the *real* Hearst, but that the great man had "a redeeming sense of humor . . . a genuine drollery. He can laugh at himself. The joke which is aimed at him . . . is the one over which he laughs the heartiest and remembers the longest and repeats the oftenest . . . although on occasion, he does seem to fancy himself as chosen to be God Almighty's ghost writer." Of

Hearst's famous spending habits, Cobb said: "At the top of his success Mr. Hearst spent money, not as some tremendously affluent brother capitalist might, nor yet as the unhampered monarch of a barbaric despotism might, but like a wildly extravagant government." While Cobb was a Hearst "star" and was royally paid, he conceded that the average Hearst employee was poorly compensated and concluded that "considering what they give in ability and energy and devotion, . . . newspapermen are as overworked and as poorly paid as any like class in the whole economic frame."

During the course of his writing career, Cobb met seven U.S. presidents. He played poker with Warren Harding and both liked and sympathized with this most hapless of presidents. Cobb interviewed Grover Cleveland and met William Howard Taft on a train. Of Theodore Roosevelt he once wrote, "Always on leaving him, I found myself wondering whether he relaxed, even for just a little bitsy bit, in his sleep," and observed that Roosevelt "had a compassionate sympathy for all mankind, excepting that contemptible segment of it which couldn't see eye to eye with him." It was revealing of the nature of Roosevelt's appeal, Cobb said, that the nation called him "Teddy," whereas it was impossible to imagine anyone calling Woodrow Wilson "Woody," even when he was a boy. Of President Wilson Cobb wrote that "the only man who ever could convince me that Woodrow Wilson wasn't the safest shepherd our government had had since Lincoln, would be Woodrow Wilson. And so he did." Originally on cordial terms with this president, Cobb began disagreeing with Wilson's policies and after a year "couldn't have got into the White House with burglar's tools." Cobb met Calvin Coolidge at a banquet, where they shared the head table; and of Herbert Hoover, Cobb observed that here was a man with a big heart. "He may not wear it on his sleeve, but it's not very far up the cuff." The U.S. Congress was to Cobb "the chief assembling plant of coagulant dullness," and of the average politician he said, "Open his front door and you're in his back yard." The humorlessness of politicians appalled Cobb. "What's more," he said, "they have taught the public to believe that any man capable of jesting, either at himself or at the follies of this lamentable but ludicrous world, is unfitted for high authority."

"Life," Cobb observed, "can be pretty monotonous to the literary truck horse that grazes always in the same pasture and feeds always at the same trough." To ward off boredom, he worked in radio; did some advertising copywriting, including five jobs for the Ford Motor Company; wrote vaudeville sketches for Ed Wynn and other performers; and wrote several plays, none of which was successful. Of his last play, he said that by the end of the third act, "you almost could hear the horses pawing impatiently in the alley, waiting to carry the corpse away to that cemetery of expired theatrical hopes." His first film-writing experience was in 1926 for Metro-Goldwyn-Mayer, and in his later years he spent considerable time in Hollywood. He collaborated on *Boys Will Be Boys*, which first played in New York and then was made into a silent film starring Cobb's friend Will Rogers. Cobb's most successful piece of writing was the book *"Speaking of Operations—"*(1915) which sold over 300,000 copies in its first five years; unquestionably the most popular literary character he created was Judge Priest, who was modeled after Judge William S. Bishop of Paducah. Over a thirty-year period Cobb produced roughly seventy Judge Priest stories as well as a novelette and a mystery novel featuring the judge.

The stock market crash of 1929 marked the beginning of a decline in Cobb's health and productivity. After suffering heavy financial losses on the market, he convinced himself that his well of short story material had run dry. He resigned from *Cosmopolitan* in 1932, dabbled in radio for a short while, then moved to California to act in movies for Hal Roach. He wrote a number of screenplays, including that for the movie version of *Judge Priest* (1934), in which Will Rogers played the title role. In 1935 he costarred as the riverboat captain in Rogers's last film, *Steamboat Round the Bend*. A daily syndicated column he had begun since moving West was abruptly cancelled by the syndicate, and his illnesses became more frequent and more severe. Shortly after moving back to New York City, Cobb slipped into a coma and died.

Cobb professed to find the company of newspapermen more interesting than that of any other occupational group. In 1940 he wrote of four distinct journalistic phases he had detected during his years in the business. The first he termed the age of the flaring editorial voice, personified by men like Charles Dana, Murat Halstead, Henry Watterson, Samuel Bowles, and Henry W. Grady. Phase two, he said, was the age of the reporter. Many of his favorites are all but forgotten today: Sam Blythe, "Ham" Peltz, Johnnie O'Brian, Tommy Ybarra, Will Irwin, and Frank O'Malley. He felt that the forgotten hero of journalism was the rewrite man, the greatest of whom, he said, was Max Fischel, Jacob Riis's mentor. Phase three was the age of the publisher: Hearst, Frank A. Munsey, William Rockhill Nelson

Cobb presenting a special miniature Academy Award to Shirley Temple in 1935 (Academy of Motion Picture Arts and Sciences)

of Kansas City, Adolph Ochs, Roy Howard, Clifford Copley, Frank Gannett, and Bernarr MacFadden. His final phase was the age of the columnist—a development Cobb did not like and criticized as "warmed-over semi-editorial pap with an illustrious name tacked on to give it weight; the volunteer moralizer, the self-elected philosopher, the featured scientific contributor, the fashion arbiter, . . . the social wiseacre, the whist wizard, the untiring traveloguer, . . . the cocksure interpreters of foreign events, . . . the financial prognosticator who with almost godlike precision predicts the next market crash within two weeks after it occurs. . . ."

To maintain his prolific outpouring of written copy, Cobb professed to have three rules:

(I) I have never waited for inspiration.

(II) I go to my desk at a certain hour.

(III) I stay there a given number of hours. If for long enough I look a sheet of paper in its reproachful but otherwise empty face, I know that sooner or later I'll cover it with words, not necessarily the choicest or the handsomest words in the lexicon but, nevertheless, words.

Writing, Cobb claimed, is the most laborious and wearing of the creative arts: "When not giving concerts, a musician finds joy in playing for his own delectation. An actor not professionally engaged delights to take part in benefits. In his off hours a portrait painter does water-color sketches, largely to amuse himself. . . . But show me a writer who, when not writing for pay, deliberately writes for fun or for self-expression, and I'll show you one of the rarest cases of freakish misapplication in the entire dime museum of the human race."

Among humorists, Cobb admired Mark Twain, Bill Nye, George Ade, Don Marquis, Ring Lardner, Ellis Parker Butler, Ed Howe, Walt Mason, Will Rogers, and Charles Russell. Though Russell is better known (along with Frederic Remington) as one of the two greatest artists of the American West, Cobb called him "probably the greatest repositer and expositor of the frequently ribald but always racy folklore of forgotten mining camps and plowed-under cattle trails that ever lived." In *The American Humorist: Conscience of the Twentieth Century* (1964), Norris Yates says Cobb and Rogers were similar in that each preferred the rural to the urban, each regarded himself as a spokesman for the everyday American, each was quite literate but affected a pose of semiliteracy, and each used a variety of media—newspapers, magazines, books, radio, the lecture circuit, film—to reach a wide public. Their differences, Yates said, were that Cobb was a storyteller, whereas Rogers was not; that Cobb relied more on the use of quaint characters and tall tales, often written in dialect; and that Rogers was better at penning quotable epigrams. While this is generally accurate, it should be added that while Cobb's production of epigrams was modest in quantity, the quality was there: "Britons never will be slaves, except to their adenoids," for instance. Yates's summation of Cobb's contribution is that Cobb deserves credit for having been one of the first nationally prominent humorists to portray the Lit-

tle Man as a victim of the twentieth century.

William Allen White, writing in the *Saturday Review of Literature* in 1941, called Cobb's Southern view of the South "a nice blend of hiccuping nostalgia and conscious, deliberate, downright deception," but admired Cobb's style nevertheless, considering him a partial holdover from the late 1800s era of the crackerbox oracle. Certainly Cobb's humor had the common touch; for the most part it was gentle and avoided giving offense or hurting people's feelings. He always took care to let the reader know that he considered himself at least as fallible as the reader was. His daughter, Elisabeth, attributed his success to his letting the public know he considered himself one of them: "He was themselves, grown famous."

Biographies:

Fred Gus Neuman, *Irvin S. Cobb: His Life and Achievements* (Paducah, Ky.: Young, 1934);

Elisabeth Cobb Chapman, *My Wayward Parent: A Book About Irvin S. Cobb* (Indianapolis & New York: Bobbs-Merrill, 1945).

References:

R. H. Davis, "Introducing Mr. Cobb," *Golden Book* (January 1934): 15-16;

Davis, "Irvin S. Cobb, a Paducah, Kentucky, Gentleman," *American Magazine* (May 1917): 14;

Davis, *Irvin S. Cobb, Storyteller* (New York: Doran, 1924);

"Exit Laughing, With Excerpts from the Classic Letter He Left His Friends," *Newsweek* (20 March 1944): 98;

Thomas L. Masson, *Our American Humorists* (New York: Moffat, Yard, 1922), pp. 91-103;

F. G. Neuman, "Irvin S. Cobb: His Hobbies," *Hobbies* (August 1944): 102;

William Allen White, "The Humor of the Self-Kidder," *Saturday Review of Literature*, 23 (22 March 1941): 5;

Norris Yates, *The American Humorist: Conscience of the Twentieth Century* (Ames: Iowa State University Press, 1964), pp. 127-133.

Elizabeth Cochrane
(Nellie Bly)

(5 May 1867-22 January 1922)

Lea Ann Brown
Southern Illinois University

MAJOR POSITIONS HELD: Reporter, *Pittsburgh Dispatch* (1885-1887), *New York World* (1887-1895), *New York Journal* (1919-1922).

BOOKS: *Ten Days in a Mad-house; or, Nellie Bly's Experience on Blackwell's Island* (New York: Munro, 1887);
Six Months in Mexico (New York: Lovell, 1888);
Nellie Bly's Book: Around the World in Seventy-two Days (New York: Pictorial Weeklies, 1890).

Nellie Bly is a part of American folklore—a larger-than-life figure who beat Jules Verne's fictional character Phileas Fogg around the world. But traveling the circumference of the globe in seventy-two days is not the only reason she is noteworthy: she was a woman reporter in the male-dominated 1880s; her first-person writing style was uncommon in the newspapers of the period; her investigative methods were also atypical, but her experiences in factories, with the insane, and on the stage enabled her to write stories that caught the interest of the average person. Her articles not only increased circulation for her newspapers but also enlightened an ignorant public and helped initiate reforms.

Entering the world as Elizabeth Cochran, she was the third child of Michael Cochran's marriage to Mary Jane Kennedy. She was born and raised in Cochran's Mill, Pennsylvania, a town her father had founded. She learned to take care of herself in a male-dominated world by competing with six older brothers (three of them half-brothers). Her father, a judge, was an important influence even though he died during her childhood. Except for one year of boarding school, Cochran was self-educated, drawing her knowledge from his personal library and his own writings. The young girl also had a strong feminine role model in her mother: Mrs. Cochran's instruction in proper social conduct is the most likely explanation for later descriptions of her daughter that always noted her femininity, her manners, and the correctness of her dress. She may

Elizabeth Cochrane (Nellie Bly) (Culver Pictures)

have been a reporter, but she was also a lady.

Cochran took her first step toward a writing career when she persuaded her mother to move from Apollo, Pennsylvania, their home since shortly before her father's death, to Pittsburgh in the mid-1880s. But writing was a man's job, and Cochran encountered continual rejection as she attempted to find work. These obstacles forced them to find cheaper lodging; in a matter of months, mother and daughter went from renting in the city's fashionable districts to sharing lodging with women from the shops and factories. Although she could have become as workworn as the women with whom she was living, luck intervened to keep Cochran out of the schoolroom and out of the clutches of wealthy old ladies who needed companions. As she was considering these positions, the *Pittsburgh Dispatch* ran an editorial, "What Girls Are Good For," denouncing the practice of hiring women in shops and offices.

The piece brought Cochran's anger forward in a caustic reply directed to the managing editor, George A. Madden. This reply has been lost, but it must have been well written because Madden ran a classified ad asking the author to write to him. Madden assumed the writer was a man. Knowing this, Cochran signed her first response "E. Cochrane," adding a final *e* to her surname which she retained thereafter. Madden requested a second article: "Girls and Their Spheres in Life." Knowing the attitude of most of his readers, Madden had not printed Cochrane's angry retort to the editorial, but he ran this second article as presenting the other side of the issue. He directed a second letter to the writer about the possibility of "E. Cochrane" working for the *Dispatch*. He got an answer he never expected: Cochrane showed up at his desk to accept his offer. Surprise at discovering that Cochrane was a woman did not keep Madden from giving her another assignment. Her second article for the *Dispatch* was on a topic she chose herself: divorce. Her skillful handling of what in 1885 was a sensitive issue secured her official employment by the newspaper—the first woman on the *Dispatch*.

There are two versions of how Elizabeth Cochrane adopted her famous pen name. The first gives Cochrane credit for quick thinking as she was persuading Madden to accept her piece on divorce: the editor wanted her to use a pen name; Erasmus Wilson, his assistant, was humming the popular Stephen Foster song "Nellie Bly," and Cochrane seized upon it. The second gives all the credit to Madden: he had made inquiries, learned of Cochrane's old family name, and decided it would be improper to link the family with commentary on divorce; this time an unidentified office boy was the whistler who gave Madden the idea. The choice proved to be symbolic: the girl in the song uses a broom to "sweep de kitchen clean"; Nellie Bly the reporter used her writing to clean up abuse and corruption.

Cochrane's first crusade was a series of articles describing the slums of Pittsburgh, with special emphasis on the conditions of working-class women—the very women among whom she and her mother were living. Her writing brought the stories of these faceless factory laborers into the homes of the middle and upper classes, fanning a spark that led to a public outcry to end the starvation, filth, and despair she reported. Even as she was channeling interest into finding solutions for the problems of the poor, the public's fascination with the identity of Nellie Bly was gaining momentum; the question of her gender was a popular topic for speculation. The preservation of her anonymity by the *Dispatch* had a twofold purpose: the curiosity of the reading public to find out who Nellie Bly really was boosted circulation, and she would be more successful as an investigator if she was not easily recognized.

Not all readers were cheering Nellie on, however. Factory owners and civic leaders exerted pressure on Madden to stop Bly, and he finally gave in. During the early part of 1886, Bly went to the opera, the theater, and any society affair that came along. Cochrane resented being restricted to such innocuous events and demanded to be allowed to do more feature stories. She finally got two assignments she wanted: she interviewed the warden of Western Penitentiary, a modern facility for its time, and she returned to the factories. Again the city leaders forced Madden to reassign her to "safer" stories.

Even as the business community attempted to have her silenced, her peers acknowledged her work: she was the first woman invited to join the fledgling Pittsburgh Press Club. But even with that honor, she was becoming discouraged by the restrictions being placed on her. She convinced Madden to send her to Mexico: reports in the Mexican press did not always correspond with the stories done by American writers living there, and Cochrane took this inconsistency as an invitation to do some digging of her own; besides, the trip would get her out of Pittsburgh. She traveled to Mexico with her mother accompanying her as chaperone. Mrs. Cochran endured the trip until they reached Mexico City. Frightened by the strange surroundings and ill from the food, Mrs. Cochran allowed her daughter to send her home—defying conventions of the period that frowned on unescorted women. Cochrane was left to begin an investigative series that lasted for six months, drawing the sharp contrast between the rich enjoying their Parisian luxuries and the masses who slept, hungry, in the streets. She learned both Spanish and the common people's Mexican dialect. She met and traveled with Hoosier poet Joaquin Miller, who was doing investigations of his own. Miller dubbed her "Little Nell, the second Columbus."

Cochrane was allowed to travel freely throughout Mexico. She explored small villages and documented the extent of marijuana use among the males. She also reported the executions of Americans. Although she was aware of the Mexican government's power to censure her for negative commentaries, she wrote an exposé denouncing President Porfirio Díaz and his immediate predecessor, Manuel Gonzáles, for improperly receiving money from the national lottery. She also raised the possibility of an impending revolution and admonished the powerful elite for its denial of freedom of expression. When this article made it back to Mexico, she was criticized in the press, and she received a threatening note. Recognizing that her freedom to work was finished, she formulated a plan that would get both her and her notes out of the country. Secret police were her constant companions as she put on a grand show of buying souvenirs, lingerie, and a traveling costume from the latest Parisian fashions. Back in her hotel room she hid her notes under the gaudy mementos in her suitcase. On the day of her departure, she dressed herself in the alluring outfit and marched out into the street to summon a hansom cab to take her to the station. Her acting ability came to her rescue that day as it would time and time again: the secret police surrounded her before she could board the cab; appealing directly to their leader, she prattled out a story about buying "ladies' things" for friends back home. He personally escorted her to the train, delivering her luggage to the conductor with instructions that it not be searched. It was not until the train arrived in El Paso that she was sure her ruse had worked. Her material wound up on the pages of the *Dispatch* and not in the hands of the Mexican government.

Cochrane's return to Pittsburgh was short-lived. She was convinced that she was ready for a new challenge—New York. With less than $100, her personal clipping file, and her belief in herself, Cochrane left Pittsburgh in the summer of 1887 to confront the New York press. She wanted to be a reporter on Park Row, home of the *New York Times*, the *Herald*, the *Tribune*, the *Sun*, and Joseph Pulitzer's *World*. The *World* and Pulitzer had been together less than five years when Cochrane darkened the newspaper's office lobby that summer. Since his first edition on 10 May 1883, Pulitzer had built a newspaper strong in both reputation and subscriber support. His objective for the *World* he had printed in that first issue: it was to be a "journal dedicated to the cause of the people rather than that of the purse potentates . . . that will expose all fraud and sham, fight all public evils and abuses—that

will serve and battle for the people with earnest simplicity." Cochrane's stories fit into this philosophy perfectly, although Pulitzer would not know that until she told him; but despite repeated attempts to meet Pulitzer or managing editor John A. Cockerill, for the first few months she talked to no one but a copy boy.

She was pushed into achieving victory or admitting defeat and returning home when she was mugged and robbed of all her savings in Central Park. Her last attempt was a three-hour siege—she waited until the men in the city room were all arguing about what to do with her and then walked past them into Pulitzer's office. Her first meeting with the publisher and managing editor of the *World* was uncomfortable for all three, but something appealed to the two men as it had appealed to Madden when she barged into his office. There was always determination in her voice and purpose in her words. When she suggested an investigative piece about the treatment of patients in the asylum on Blackwell's Island, she aroused their reluctant interest. After more persuading, she obtained their support for the story and a $25 advance on her salary. The one stipulation of their unwritten agreement was that once she started the assignment she must conclude the job; the *World* would not be party to any stunt that could backfire in humiliation.

Cochrane became "Nellie Brown" as the first step in her penetration of Blackwell's Island. She haphazardly chose a shabby lodging house, "The Temporary Home for Females," from which to launch her assignment. She had left home with seventy-three cents; the room cost thirty cents. She fabricated a story for the matron of the rooming house about being from Cuba, using the Spanish she had learned in Mexico to give credibility to her story. The hours she had spent practicing facial expressions in the mirror she put to use from the moment she entered the house: she wore a dreamy expression during her interview with the matron; for her first meal with her new peers, she projected a frightened look into her eyes. Never one to procrastinate about getting a job started, Cochrane staged her first episode of illogical behavior during supper that first night. She began by shaking, contorting her face, and running from the table to a corner of the sitting room; she responded to questions in broken Spanish. The matron attempted to control the situation by excusing her behavior as travel fatigue. When the woman attempted to lead her back to her room, Cochrane reacted violently, demanding that they let her go home. Then she began ranting about a pistol. As the hours of the night passed, the other lodgers took turns watching the performance Cochrane was giving. The next day her acting convinced a judge, newsmen, and a panel of doctors that Nellie Brown was insane and gained her access to the Bellevue insane pavilion, the first stop for patients bound for Blackwell's Island. Once inside the pavilion, she found several of the victims she had come to write about: there was Anne Neville, sick in body but not in mind; and Mrs. Shanz, old and displaced but hardly insane. Cochrane mentally documented that the structure was a dangerous firetrap, that the routine contributed to physical and mental discomfort. She was locked up in the pavilion on a Tuesday; it was Sunday before she was reexamined. Again she feigned the symptoms of insanity, and again she was successful. On Sunday, 25 September 1887, she was committed to Blackwell's Island Madhouse with the diagnosis of "dementia with delusions of persecution."

She was transferred by ambulance, manned by a drunken attendant, to the Blackwell's Island barge docked at the East River, and finally delivered into the confines of the madhouse itself. She witnessed the inadequate provisions of food and clothing for the patients; she found herself subjected to ice-cold baths; she encountered filth everywhere as people were forced to use the same bath water, linens, and hair combs. From the moment she had set foot in the madhouse, she had discarded her charade; but despite her "normal" behavior, she was never reexamined. She continually protested the rough treatment given to other inmates, but she never pushed the nurses to the point that they would have her sent to the "Retreat" or to the "Lodge," the sections reserved for violent patients. She relied on second-hand accounts of the abuse that the patients in these wards received from the attendants. She was convinced that beatings and ice-cold baths were not warranted under any circumstances. Although she was learning more about the horrors of institutional life every day, Cochrane began to worry about the preservation of her own sanity. Ten days after her commitment to Blackwell's Island, the *World* obtained her release. Following her return to freedom, she wrote a narrative that initiated a formal inquiry and a grand jury investigation. Blackwell's Island, "the human rat-trap, easy to get into, impossible to get out of," was given $3,000,000 to implement changes, and Cochrane was given a regular reporting job on the *World*.

Employment bureaus' fees and tactics for matching domestic servants and employers were the focus of her next crusade. Cochrane argued for regulation to protect both the employer and the

employee from the unscrupulous agencies; her articles were the basis of one of the first public outcries for fair labor practices. Mistreatment of female prisoners, poor working conditions in New York factories, and the false promises of expensive "educational" programs directed at simple factory girls were other targets for her untiring pen.

Cochrane's life seems to have been totally taken up by her work as a reporter. No biographical accounts mention even one close female friend. Her chances for romance, too, seem to have occurred very infrequently: Erasmus Wilson, Madden's assistant in Pittsburgh, and James Metcalf, the editor of *Life* in New York, are the only two men given any space in the major biographies. During her years in New York, she did enjoy a brief period of parties and attention from colleagues in the press, but her fun was abruptly ended when she was assigned to a big political story—an assignment the men on the staff wanted.

Cochrane was assigned to investigate the activities of "the Fox," Edward R. Phelps, the "king of the lobbyists." Phelps was suspected of being involved in every dishonest project throughout the state, but no one had been able to prove the allegations. Cochrane, masquerading as the wife of a patent medicine manufacturer, called on Phelps and asked him to kill a legislative bill that would eliminate the sale of quack remedies in the state; she indicated she was willing to pay $2,000 for his help. Acting the part of the innocent, ignorant female, she arranged to meet Phelps in his New York office to give him a check for helping her—a check he instructed her to make payable to a relative of his. Cochrane persuaded Phelps to give her a receipt, and only then "discovered" that she had left her checkbook in her hotel room. Phelps agreed to meet her at the hotel; but Cochrane went straight to the newsroom, where she began writing her exposé even while the corrupt lobbyist was waiting for her in the lobby of the Hotel St. James. Her article on Phelps's involvement in graft resulted in a public outcry for honesty in government. The same piece ended the camaraderie between Cochrane and the male reporters: she had overstepped her bounds by getting involved in lobby politics. Hurt by their rejection, she poured her heart into more stories about slums, tenements, and public health.

She exposed herself to malaria, yellow fever, tuberculosis, and cholera to get stories; her articles invited the wrath and retribution of factory owners, shop proprietors, and shady public officials. But occasionally, the lighter side of life would find its way into her writing: she took readers with her as she made unsuccessful attempts to perform in a ballet and a stage show; she helped to rid New York of a clever beggar who would scatter bread crusts and, when a likely handout walked by, would pretend to eat the crusts; she ended the career of a Central Park "masher" by describing the way he approached girls.

Her position and reputation gained her entrance to the homes of President Harrison's cabinet members to interview their wives. She also talked with widows of former presidents and with Belva Lockwood, the presidential candidate on the Woman Suffrage ticket. Cochrane had never associated herself with the suffragettes, even though every battle she had fought and won had been applauded by the members of the movement. Just as people were always surprised at Cochrane's femininity, she was surprised by Mrs. Lockwood's: "Mrs. Lockwood does not look like the cuts newspapers have published of her. . . . She is a womanly woman; what greater praise can one give her?" When Mrs. Lockwood learned of Cochrane's addiction to work without the benefits of leisure, she advised her to look for friends and to learn to need people. This advice might have had a more immediate effect, but work once again was given the center ring in Cochrane's life. Her request to go around the world faster than Jules Verne's Phileas Fogg in *Around the World in Eighty Days* (1873) was approved by Pulitzer.

For the stunt to be a success, it had to be kept an absolute secret until it was underway. When the word finally came that she was scheduled to leave for England on the *Augusta Victoria*, she had only two days to prepare for the trip, but not much preparation was required. If she attempted to travel with trunks, she would be continually delayed. Her entire traveling wardrobe consisted of two dresses, a coat, and three ghillie caps; everything else, from needles and thread to pencils, paper, and a nightgown, were folded into one carry-on bag. At exactly six seconds past 9:40 on the morning of 14 November 1889, Cochrane left American soil. She promised to be back in seventy-five days. After she was at sea, the *World* broke the story. Nellie Bly once again caught the imagination of the American people, and circulation climbed as people clamored to know of her progress. The crossing was extremely rough, but after docking at Southampton and taking a tugboat to London, she had some exciting news from the *World* correspondent who met her: Jules Verne had heard about her trip and wanted to meet her. She immediately rearranged her plans to include a side trip to Amiens, France.

Cochrane preparing to leave on her trip around the world in November 1889 (Bettmann Archive)

Her route from London took her across the English Channel to Calais, France, and then 179½ miles on her excursion between Amiens and Calais. Verne was delighted with Cochrane even if he had doubts about her achieving the task she had set for herself. Back in Calais, she caught the mail train to Brindisi, Italy, where she purchased passage to cross the Mediterranean Sea. During this part of her journey, the nation's fascination with her grew: there was a national contest to guess how long it would actually take her, and all types of speculation about "who is Nellie Bly?" found its way into print. The *World* gave readers stories on these related topics when they did not know where Cochrane was; cables at that time were not efficient enough to keep the editors informed of her precise location.

From Brindisi, she made her way to Port Said, Egypt, on the Pacific and Oriental steamer *Victoria*, arriving on the afternoon of 27 November. The Suez Canal, she wrote, "is an enormous ditch enclosed on either side with high sandbanks." The trip through the man-made waterway took twenty-four hours. The *Victoria* dropped anchor in the Bay of

Suez where, Cochrane was told, the Israelites crossed the Red Sea. The next morning the *Victoria* made her way onto the Red Sea, paused at Aden, and continued to Colombo, Ceylon, where Cochrane was to take the steamer *Oriental* to China; she was forced to wait, however, for the arrival of the steamer *Nepal* before they could leave. After all the connections were resolved, the *Oriental* departed, introducing Cochrane first to Penang or Prince of Wales Island and two days later to Singapore, where she bought a monkey. They sailed out of Singapore into a monsoon but arrived in Hong Kong safely. Cochrane's impressions of the East were not favorable: she reported that she found poverty and despair everywhere. While touring the East she learned that another female reporter had left the day after she sailed from New Jersey, going the other way, and was ahead. Devastated but determined, Cochrane decided to finish her trip, win or lose. After spending Christmas in China, the *Oriental* took her to Yokohama, Japan. She wrote that the Japanese had taken the best of European culture and combined it with their own with brilliant success. She sailed for home on 7 January.

Storms continued to plague the voyage. The sailors blamed the bad weather on Cochrane's pet monkey, calling it a jinx, but she refused to throw the animal overboard. The ship finally docked in San Francisco—sixty-eight days after Cochrane had left New Jersey. Another obstacle was averted when she was given a special medical clearance while health officials tried to determine how long the ship should be quarantined because of rumors of smallpox. Her trip across the continent took four days, and at exactly 3:51 P.M. on 25 January 1890 she was back in Hoboken, New Jersey: she had traveled around the world in seventy-two days, six hours, ten minutes, and eleven seconds. And she had done it first: the other reporter, Elizabeth Brisland of *Cosmopolitan* magazine, required seventy-six days to make her trip.

Cochrane's trip made her a star, and life became a routine of parties, concerts, and evenings with the wealthy. Cochrane was now wealthy in her own right, earning over $20,000 per year; she no longer went to the slums to get stories, but she did continue to write about rights for working people and similar themes in a Sunday column that she pioneered. Her interview subjects included the socialists Eugene Debs and Emma Goldman.

But still she was looking for more: she was in need of the human companionship Mrs. Lockwood had advised her to look for. Cochrane found that need fulfilled by seventy-two-year-old millionaire bachelor Robert Seaman, president and owner of the Ironclad Manufacturing Company, a prosperous hardware firm. They were married 5 April 1895, and Cochrane took on the roles of wife and hostess until Seaman's death in 1904. She then tried to manage his business, but eventually lost her entire fortune. She spent World War I in Austria, where she had gone to escape her financial problems. In 1919, she returned home penniless.

A friend from the *World*, Arthur Brisbane, had moved to the *Evening Journal* and gave her a job. But it was not the same: women were becoming more and more accepted in the field; the public was no longer responsive to her type of crusading stories. She had spent most of her life alone, and she died alone, of pneumonia, on 22 January 1922 in St. Mark's Hospital. She was buried in the Church of the Ascension cemetery in New York. There were no headlines to salute her passing and only modest obituaries, but the *Journal* paid her a compliment she would have been proud of: "She was considered the best reporter in America."

Cochrane's entire reporting career lasted only a little over ten years, but she earned more fame for herself than many other journalists who work at their typewriters for four and five times as long. If she had not been connected with Joseph Pulitzer, who supported her ideas, she probably would not have been as successful; but her ability to convince the man who could most effectively help her in her career that she was capable of carrying out her plans was another facet of her talent. A champion of the downtrodden and abused, Cochrane was so preoccupied with her work that she had little time left to develop relationships with her own peers. She may in fact have chosen work as an escape from having to deal with people on a personal level: Cochrane could handle people as long as they were sources for stories from whom she could remain detached. So she lived her life alone except for her nine-year marriage to Seaman. She made strides for women in journalism but refused to align herself with the suffragettes. She returned to the newspaper world because she was broke, only to find herself outdated. Her success as a reporter gave her neither personal happiness nor security, but it did leave history with a colorful character.

Biographies:
Nina Brown Baker, *Nellie Bly* (New York: Holt, 1956);
Mignon Rittenhouse, *The Amazing Nellie Bly* (New York: Dutton, 1956);

Iris Noble, *Nellie Bly, First Woman Reporter* (New York: Messner, 1957).

References:
Mignon Rittenhouse, "They Called her the Amaz

ing Nellie Bly," *Good Housekeeping* (February 1955): 48-51;

Ishbel Ross, *Ladies of the Press* (New York: Harper, 1936).

George Creel
(1 December 1876-2 October 1953)

Warren T. Francke
University of Nebraska at Omaha

MAJOR POSITIONS HELD: Editor/publisher, the *Independent*, Kansas City weekly (1899-1909); editorial writer, *Denver Post* (1909-1911), *Rocky Mountain News* (1911-1912).

SELECTED BOOKS: *Quatrains of Christ* (Kansas City, Mo.: Independent Press, 1907);
Measuring up Equal Suffrage, by Creel and Benjamin Lindsay (New York: National American Woman Suffrage Association, 1912);
Children in Bondage, by Creel, Lindsay, and Edwin Markham (New York: Hearst's International Library, 1914);
What Have Women Done with the Vote? (New York: National Woman Suffrage Publishing Co., 1915);
Chivalry Versus Justice: Why the Women of the Nation Demand the Right to Vote (New York: National Woman Suffrage Publishing Co., 1915);
Wilson and the Issues (New York: Century, 1916);
Ireland's Fight for Freedom (New York & London: Harper, 1919);
Complete Report of the Chairman of the Committee on Public Information (Washington, D.C.: Government Printing Office, 1920);
The War, the World and Wilson (New York: Harper, 1920);
How We Advertised America (New York: Harper, 1920);
Uncle Henry, anonymous (New York: Reynolds, 1922);
The People Next Door: An Interpretive History of Mexico and the Mexicans (New York: Day, 1926);
Sons of the Eagle; Soaring Figures from America's Past (Indianapolis & New York: Bobbs-Merrill, 1927);

George Creel (Harris & Ewing)

Tom Paine-Liberty Bell (New York: Sears, 1932);
War Criminals and Punishment (New York: McBride, 1944);
Rebel at Large: Recollections of Fifty Crowded Years

(New York: Putnam's, 1947);

Russia's Race for Asia (Indianapolis: Bobbs-Merrill, 1949).

OTHER: *Men Who Are Making Kansas City*, compiled by Creel and John Slavens (Kansas City, Mo.: Hudson-Kimberly, 1902);

White House Physician, by Vice-Adm. Ross T. McIntire in collaboration with Creel (New York: Putnam's, 1946).

PERIODICAL PUBLICATIONS: "Shame of Ohio," *Cosmopolitan,* 51 (October 1911): 599-610;

"Carnival of Corruption in Mississippi," *Cosmopolitan,* 51 (November 1911): 725-735;

"Denver's Uprising Against Misrule," *Collier's,* 48 (6 January 1912): 13;

"Denver Triumphant," *Everybody's,* 27 (September 1912): 314-315;

"Why Industrial War?," *Collier's,* 52 (18 October 1913): 5-6ff.;

"High Cost of Hate," *Everybody's,* 30 (June 1914): 755-770;

"Poisoners of Public Opinion," *Harper's Weekly*, 59 (7 November 1914): 436-438; (14 November 1914): 465-466;

"Poisoners of Public Health," *Harper's Weekly,* 60 (2 January 1915): 4-6;

"Press and Patent Medicines," *Harper's Weekly,* 60 (13 February 1915): 155;

"Can Wilson Win?," *Century Magazine,* 92 (June 1916): 266-272;

"Four Million Citizen Defenders," *Everybody's,* 36 (May 1917): 545-554;

"Fight for Public Opinion," *Scientific American*, 118 (6 April 1918): 298;

"American Newspapers," *Everybody's,* 40 (April 1919): 40-44;

"Makers of Opinion," *Collier's,* 65 (15 May 1920): 20;

"The 'Lash' of Public Opinion," *Collier's,* 74 (22 November 1924): 8-9.

When President Woodrow Wilson named George Creel to head the World War I censorship and propaganda effort, Creel's career as a newspaper editorialist became the center of controversy. The *New York Times* of 16 April 1917 noted the entanglement of Creel's journalistic and political activities and concluded that neither revealed "any evidence of the ability, the experience, or the judi-

cial temperament required to gain the understanding and cooperation of the press." In a *Collier's* magazine article, journalist Mark Sullivan judged the new chairman of the Committee on Public Information, the man who would govern the newspapers and reporters of the United States, in more definite terms: "For such a job Creel is the most unsuitable of men." Comparing him to the flamboyant evangelist Billy Sunday, Sullivan labeled Creel "temperamental, excitable and emotional to the last degree . . . the most aggressive and daring of newspaper men . . . the most violent of muckrakers. Creel is a crusader, a bearer of the fiery cross. His ten years as a newspaper man in Kansas City and five in Denver were devoted to the championship of one form after another of idealism." Sullivan charged that Creel classified men into two classes, "skunks and the greatest man that ever lived," and knew no shadings, only black and white. To this, Creel responded, "An exaggeration, of course, but not entirely untrue." He defended his suitability for the wartime assignment, nevertheless, and soon other writers were praising him under such headlines as "Our Uncensorious Censor." Eventually even Sullivan would laud Creel's activity as prodigious, his style as exuberant, and his results as sweeping: with Wilson's ideas and Creel's dissemination, "the two would conquer the world."

While the national spotlight shone most brightly on Creel during those two years of World War I, the glare of controversy had followed him through most of his newspaper experience, particularly in Denver. He started quietly enough, however, in Kansas City, the nearest metropolis to his Missouri origins. His mother's grandfather Fackler had left Virginia for Missouri and settled in Saline County in 1842. His father's family also came from Virginia, and Missouri became the home of Henry Clay Creel "as a measure of reformation," according to son George. After election to the Virginia House of Delegates, Henry Creel fell in with a wild crowd; "roistering left little time for lawmaking," and grandfather Creel sent him off to farm in Missouri. Henry left to serve as a Confederate captain, then returned to a Lafayette County farm, where he married Virginia Fackler in 1868 and fathered three sons. George, the middle son, flatly summarized his father's farming career as "a flop from the first." He grew up viewing his father as a burden upon his mother, who supported the family by sewing, gardening, and taking in boarders, and explained his early passion for women's suffrage by declaring, "It was because I knew my mother had more character, brains, and competence than any man that ever lived."

More important to his future career, she reared Creel in the towns of Independence and Odessa and offered influences that ranged from a "Southern Colonel" image of manhood to a love for literature, evidenced both by her vividly written diaries and by her inspiring her sons to read Dickens and *The Iliad*. Creel resisted formal education (one biographical sketch puts him in Odessa College, but he claimed only eighth grade) but credited his mother for his "fair" knowledge of history and the classics. While in his teens, he ran off to follow the county fairs around Missouri for a year; later he roamed the Southwest, where he came across a ten-volume set of popular novels by Ouida. Reading her romantic works for three days and two nights on a train from Texas, he arrived back in Kansas City with a writing style.

The *Kansas City World*, part of the Scripps chain, was struggling to compete with William Rockhill Nelson's *Kansas City Star* when its city editor hired Creel for $4 a week. Neither Creel nor the *World* was destined for a long run. Part of a three-man news staff, he served as a "leg man" for the more experienced reporters and covered the federal building, railroad offices, and undertakers; later he wrote feature articles suggested by two librarians, started a book-review column, and covered social happenings. His first reporting job ended on a note to become common in Creel's turbulent career when Creel behaved too much the Southern Colonel to suit his hard-boiled city editor from the East. A wealthy man's daughter had eloped with the coachman; the teary-eyed, broken-voiced magnate gave Creel the full story but pleaded with him not to run it in the *World*. Asked for the story, Creel said, "The gentleman was feeling very badly and didn't wish to be quoted." The city editor's teeth "ground out a bulldog growl. 'You fool! Go the back door, see the cook, and get the story out of her.' 'Go the back door yourself,' exclaimed Creel in sudden anger; 'I'm not a back-door worker.' "

Fired, he hopped a cattle train to New York and found himself rejected by every newspaper and magazine before meeting a free-lance joke writer in a saloon. Creel learned that William Randolph Hearst and Joseph Pulitzer were buying jokes and poems for their comic supplements, paying a dollar for squibs and a quarter a line for verse. As a 1913 *Collier's* profile put it: "Shutting himself in his cheap room in a mechanics' hotel, he ground out jokes by the dozens, by the hundreds, jokes in bales and

jokes in bundles." But he sold none for a month and survived by shoveling snow.

After spending his last dime, he finally sold four items to Hearst's *Evening Journal*; soon he scored regularly with *Puck*, *Judge*, and other periodicals. In early 1898, he accepted a staff position on Hearst's *American* comic supplement, which allowed him to sell independently to the *Journal* for a combined income of $40 a week. It also allowed him not only to appear in the company of "The Katzenjammer Kids," "Foxy Grandpa," and "Buster Brown," but to catch glimpses of Hearst, Arthur Brisbane, and Morrill Goddard. As head of Hearst's Sunday supplement, Goddard invited Creel to move up from jokes to "page thrillers," but the young Missourian, who saw the editor as a "gaunt, nerve-wracked man with a pair of mad eyes," declined the offer after seeing what that kind of work had done to Goddard.

As for the *Journal*, Creel called its city room "Bedlam." When the Spanish-American War broke out, he later recalled, the Hearst-Pulitzer rivalry reached "a stage of utter madness"; other recollections involved editors carted off to asylums. Creel confessed that he saw himself "as the cheapest sort of a hack" at age twenty-two, "nothing more than a penny-a-liner!" Creel came to see his cronies in the Park Row saloons as tosspots rather than artists and poets. However, when his efforts to enlist in both the Cuban and Philippine campaigns failed on technicalities, one of those aspiring poets, Arthur Grissom, lured him back to Kansas City with visions of a new journal. Grissom had married the daughter of a Kansas City millionaire and had moved to the Missouri city, where he corresponded with Creel about his plan for a quality "journal of opinion" until Creel joined him in the enterprise.

The first issue of the *Independent*, 11 March 1899, gave Kansas Citians a blend of editorials, the arts, sports, social news, and politics, written by Grissom and Creel with some help from New York City friends as prominent as Edwin Markham and Winifred Black. Grissom soon left for New York to start *Smart Set*, and Creel, at twenty-three, became the sole owner and editor of a financially shaky weekly. He flirted with socialism but professed to be revolted by everything in Marx but the theory of surplus value. Henry George's *Progress and Poverty* (1879) converted him to the single-tax idea, and he aligned himself with the Democratic party; when he worked for Woodrow Wilson's campaign in 1916, he claimed to have "boomed" his candidate for the presidency as early as 1905 in the *Independent*. On the local front, editor-publisher Creel had to choose between two Democratic factions, Thomas Pendergast's Goats and the Rabbits of Frank Walsh and Joe Shannon. He fought the Pendergast gang then and continued to be troubled by their relationship with Harry Truman when his fellow Missourian gained the presidency forty years later. The Creel style, replete with epigrams and alliteration, is represented in this 25 August 1905 commentary: "Policemen were crowded thick at every polling place, and urged on by the Police Commissioners and favorite saloon keepers, bullied those whom they could and battered those whom they could not. Many were drunk, and all were fully armed; that the day passed without bloodshed was a wonder. It was the last stand of the Police Machine, and like a pack of wolves brought to bay, they fought fiercely and ignobly. Police Commissioner Gregory and Saloon Keeper Pendergast, riding behind a pair of blooded bays, drove from place to place, whipping recalcitrants into line, mouthing threats and maledictions at every turn."

Creel crusaded with enthusiasm on social issues, declaring his opposition to the view that a woman's place was in the home: "A hermetically sealed home at that," he later observed, "through which no wind of change was ever allowed to blow. Out of love and admiration for my mother, I resented it, and . . . I clamored that women had just as much right as men to be regarded as people." In retrospect, he took greatest pride in campaigns against quacks—particularly one Dr. Carson, who cured by laying on of hands until crowds grew too large, then prescribed the placing of slips the size of cigarette papers between the shoulder blades. Carson fought Creel with testimonial advertisements in the other Kansas City papers, but when he pressured the *Independent*'s printer to refuse publication, Creel sued for libel. After several weeks in court, he dropped the suit but gained satisfaction from Carson's conviction for practicing medicine without a license. Less satisfying was a crusade against prostitution and venereal disease: "Absolutely unable to put such words as gonorrhea and syphilis into cold print, I skated all around the subject, getting more and more vague and involved, and accomplishing nothing except to have a number of subscribers rebuke me for my 'preoccupation with prurience.'"

In 1908, a clergyman convinced him to convert his publication to the *Newsbook*, projected as the first in a chain of weekly newspapers representing the National Fellowship of the University Militant, a group of prominent progressives and reformers promoting artistic and scientific achievement. After

four months of accumulating debts, he revived the *Independent* and pursued advertising "with all the ferocity of a starved timber wolf." The whole ten years in Kansas City involved a series of advertising ups and downs—here snaring a new account, there losing it after an editorial controversy. When he decided to depart for Denver in 1901 with $50 in his pocket, however, Creel claimed the *Independent* was financially sound; he convinced a magazine writer, at least, to suggest that "if he had been content to await a buyer, he might have sold his paper for five or six thousand dollars; but he was not content." Marketable or not, he gave it to two women job printers and left for a position as editorial writer with the *Denver Post*.

The volatile personality and the vivid journalism that later prompted such strong reactions to his World War I appointment by President Wilson would become more visible in Denver. Creel soon engaged in controversies not only with political foes but with his employers, the flamboyant Fred Bonfils and Harry Tammen. Just as he had characterized the New York journalism of 1898, he called the *Post* of 1909 "Bedlam," "the Coney Island of journalism." Because Bonfils and Tammen also owned a circus and reveled in promotion, the newspaper building bulged with bands, bearded ladies, and elephants, and human flies crawled over its facade; when performers were not giving shows on the balcony, Bonfils would grab a canvas bag and throw pennies to the crowds in the streets. Creel was allowed to write daily signed articles and fill an entire page on Sunday; but after six months of the publishers' stalling on crusades, and still lacking the editorial control he had expected, he offered to resign. Instead, Bonfils convinced Creel to accompany him to Africa to meet Theodore Roosevelt. The trip stuttered at the start when Creel lost his expense money, picked up steam in Khartoum when he bought an Arab costume and leased a camel, but ended with more haggling about the lost money and other penny-pinching by Bonfils.

The *Post* had brought Creel to Denver at a time when Judge Ben Lindsey was battling "the Beast," as Lindsey called the corporate-backed political machine. The *Times*, controlled by Mayor Robert Speer, and the *Republican* defended the corporations against the Progressive *Rocky Mountain News*; the *Post*, according to a history of the *News*, "was the journalistic mercenary of the wars, shifting back and forth as fortunes changed and influential callers came visiting. . . ."

Before such shifts struck home to Creel, Bon and Tam, as they were known, endorsed his editorial campaigns for a commission form of government, municipal ownership of utilities, and other causes dear to their editorial writer's heart. The controversial Creel style burst forth when eleven state senators blocked his pet project, a bond issue to enable the city to purchase the water company. He later confessed, "I branded the eleven as traitors, pinned the Scarlet Letter on each breast, and carried their names on a Roll of Dishonor. I even went so far as to shout that lynching would be a good thing." When one senator sued for libel, the reference to hanging became a point of cross-examination, and Creel's response became an anecdote that was irresistible to the magazine writers who profiled him in the next few years. Had not Creel used the word *rope* in a purely figurative sense? In one widely read version, "He replied excitably in a high voice that rang out to the auditors above every other sound in the courtroom: 'No— the hemp! the hemp! the hemp!' They tried to stop him, but he kept beating the arms of the witness chair and shouting dramatically: 'The hemp! the hemp! the hemp!'" He clearly wanted the offending eleven hanged by a rope. Other displays of emotion, other episodes of shouting and fist-pounding pockmark his public career, but this single outburst probably contributed most memorably to the reputation that preceded his CPI appointment by Wilson.

At whatever future damage, Creel won in court and went on to write a fervent editorial supporting the full slate of a Citizen's party, whose organization he had first urged. "On Tuesday every man and woman will have opportunity to strike a blow for a free state, a free city," he began. He described the ballot as "a gleaming sword," the fight for justice as "the Great Adventure," and it was all "For the People! Say that word over. People! PEOPLE! Why, it grows electric! It thrills!" Any danger that the *Post*'s type fonts would run short of exclamation points subsided when he read the next day's paper and learned that Bonfils and Tammen had substituted machine politicians for the Citizen's candidates for three key offices. Creel resigned in a flurry of public speeches and was puzzled that a majority of his colleagues condemned his actions as disloyal.

Creel moved to New York, where from spring through September of 1911 he wrote for Hearst's *Cosmopolitan*. In that fading day of the muckraking era, Creel could characterize the magazine as the only one "that still believed in the value and righteousness of exposing rotten conditions wherever rottenness could be found." Living in Greenwich Village, he sallied forth to discover Mississippi's new senator, James K. Vardaman, and to meet "my first REAL [political machine] boss," George Cox of Cincinnati. But a western assignment took Creel back to Denver, where he accepted the offer of former senator Thomas Patterson to write editorials for the *Rocky Mountain News*.

Armed with the publisher's pledge of full backing, Creel undertook a "finish fight against the corporations that had a strangle hold" on Colorado. He protested the "brazen defiance, shameless venality, and depraved servility" of their political hirelings. When Mayor Speer removed a thorn from his side by physically deposing assessor Henry Arnold from office, Creel called for a mass rally "to consider the many outrages perpetrated by Robert W. Speer and his venal council, particularly the crowning villainy that has resulted in the midnight raid of thugs upon the courthouse, and the violent and ruffianly ejection of Assessor Henry J. Arnold. . . ." The midnight raid in mid-December prompted not only his trumpeting editorial but a 6 January 1912 article in *Collier's* carrying Creel's byline. He quoted his own editorial but identified it only as a "call to the people . . . made through the columns of the *Rocky Mountain News*." His magazine version of the response counted 30,000 who "braved the bitter wind that swept the lawns." Evidently the weather worsened; he went on: "This amazing, well-nigh incredible outpouring may not be dismissed as 'sensationalism,' 'mere emotionalism,' or the 'idle curiosity of a mob.' Those patient, storm-swept thousands stood as the priests of the religion of democracy, the beat of their feet the organ music of a strengthened faith, and the shine of their faces the altar lights of new hope." In short, his man Arnold became mayor; but Creel, suspicious when the *Post* also backed Arnold's candidacy, became police commissioner to keep an eye on Arnold. Also in 1912, Creel married a well-known actress, Blanche Bates.

Police Commissioner Creel became a prime target of the press, particularly when he ordered billy clubs taken from the policemen. The *Republican* ran a series of "Lochinvar Creel" poems which began:

> George Lochinvar Creel came out of the West
> His ideas were naked, his reforms undressed,
> And save his good nerve, he weapons
> had none,
> But he boomed into office like a 13-inch gun.
> . . . .
> He stayed not for horse sense, and stopped
> not for reason

He flew into the air at most any

old season. . . .

He flew, for example, into prostitution and venereal disease by proposing a 266-acre farm for "Denver's human wreckage." In 1913, the *Post* revived the African adventure by pretending in print that Creel had stolen the expense money, but the generous owners "forgot all about it." Creel countered in the 3 February *News*, "What is one thousand dollars to the *Post*? A bagatelle! A trifle! Does it not offer million-dollar rewards for the first humming bird that flies over Pike's Peak? For the first trip to Mars? . . . Who does not know that money is the heart's blood of these men? Why, until every cent of the lost money was repaid them, they never knew rest, nor did I know peace."

Creel's term as police commissioner came to an early end when he began pushing Mayor Arnold to live up to campaign promises; Arnold countered by returning clubs to policemen and putting the police under the command of the fire commissioner. Creel then proposed a resolution, directed

at Fire Commissioner McGrew, forbidding officials from drinking in public bars. McGrew protested, and Creel, rising to his full height of five feet seven inches, exploded, "You have rarely drawn a sober breath since you came on this board. There have been mornings when you have lurched in here with your eyes blackened as the result of low saloon rows, looking like a bum. You have turned the department's automobiles into midnight joy wagons, and the fire chief into an attendant during your circle of bars and disorderly resorts." Creel concluded by defying those present "to recall a single intelligent or even intelligible sentence you have ever uttered."

Mayor Arnold suspended his police commissioner, and a hearing upheld the action on the ground of "creation of dissension." Creel took pride, however, in resulting commendations, particularly from Kansas City, where William Rockhill Nelson pointed out editorially that "in Kansas City Mr. Creel was doing the same sort of fighting against shams and frauds and crookedness that he is doing in Denver." The city where his *Independent* had struggled also produced a telegram, signed by

CHILDHOOD IS SACRIFICED DAILY THAT PROFIT MAY FLOW
FROM EVERY TURN OF A MILL-WHEEL

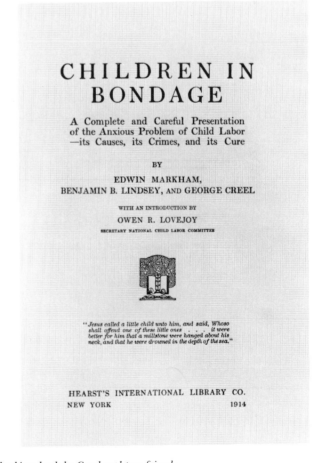

Frontispiece and title page for a muckraking book by Creel and two friends

judges, civic leaders, and editors. It reported that McGrew was trying to get "something on you. . . . we have a story of your fight for a decade against corruption and dishonesty, almost entirely at your own expense. . . ."

Thus ended not only Creel's days as police commissioner but his full-time newspaper career. It did not end his important role in newspaper journalism, however. Creel had the luxury of blending free-lancing with volunteer work for social and political causes. He moved to New York, where he devoted three months in 1915 to women's suffrage and wrote a series on boxer Jess Willard for Arthur Brisbane. After muckraking for *Harper's Weekly*, *Everybody's*, and other periodicals, he became active in President Wilson's 1916 reelection campaign.

The Wilson campaign found him working for Bob Wooley, publicity head for the Democratic National Committee; Creel wrote newspaper features, leading off with an interview with Thomas Edison. Soon he was concentrating on a defense of Secretary of the Navy Josephus Daniels, under heavy attack by the opposition for, according to Creel, his "democratization" of the navy. Eventually his contribution to Wilson's reelection included a book, *Wilson and the Issues* (1916), and formation of a support committee of authors, including Irvin Cobb, Ida Tarbell, and Lincoln Steffens, among many others.

An assistant secretary's post in the administration was offered but rejected; Creel considered the salary too low to bring his wife and two children, George Bates and Frances Virginia, to Washington. Word spread in March 1917, however, that with war a certainty, military leaders were pushing for strict censorship rules. Creel sent a brief on the subject to the president in which he urged a voluntary agreement with the press; argued for expression, not suppression; and proposed an agency to fight for what Wilson had called "the verdict of mankind." Wilson approved the proposal and appointed Creel chairman of the Committee on Public Information, which included Secretary of State Robert Lansing, Secretary of War Newton D. Baker, and Secretary of the Navy Daniels.

The cabinet members were to play only a small part in the elaborate efforts of the CPI, although Lansing added to the conflict surrounding Creel. The committee's work is fully recorded in many sources, including Creel's own *How We Advertised America* (1920) and J. R. Mock's and Cedric Larson's *Words That Won the War* (1939). Creel organized authors, artists, and the Four-Minute Men, a bureau of 75,000 public speakers; he recruited ad-

vertising men and photographers and published a 100,000 circulation daily newspaper, the *Official Bulletin*; a government wire service rushed news to the world. In short, the Creel Committee, as it came to be known, used every means of written, pictorial, and oral communication to promote the national cause and yet resisted war hysteria and avoided censorship of American journalists.

Whatever the accomplishments, however, criticism was unavoidable, and it would inevitably focus on the chairman's journalistic career and his personality. The reaction combined outrage against anticipated censorship with denunciations of Creel as the administrator of this ominous new agency. According to William L. Chenery, a colleague from the Denver days (and later, as editor of *Collier's*, Creel's employer), any appointee faced instinctive opposition, although "another man might have lacked George Creel's reckless wit and his disconcerting capacity for infuriating those with whose opinions he differed." In Mock's and Larson's summary, Creel "was one of the most disliked and traduced members of the national government while the war was in progress," and the caricature of Creel remained in force.

The chairman allowed his performance to quiet the press, but he battled on the committee with Secretary Lansing and managed to offend the Congress. Creel characterized Lansing as envious of his direct access to the president and accused the secretary of "losing no opportunity to hound me with the petty complaints of a humorless man." In turn, the *War Memoirs of Robert Lansing* (1935) sniff at Creel's "socialist tendencies" and accuse him of personal hostility and attempting to "discredit me as Secretary of State." Congressmen were not so gentle: in a chapter of his autobiography headed "The Plague of Partisanship," Creel lists "licensed liar," "depraved hack," "pro-German," and "Bolshevik" among the charges directed at him. He was asked about Congress in a public forum and quipped, "Oh, it has been years since I went slumming." The *New York World* demanded his firing; Creel offered his resignation, but Wilson settled for "a padlock on my lips." When a budgetary change required that the chairman appeal to Congress for funds, the House committee inquired in Kansas City and Denver about his "temperamental qualifications." His old editorial words sounded shrill as read by the congressmen, Creel admitted, "and I expressed regret for certain extravagances of expression, explaining that they were due to the 'emotionalism of the moment.'" He received his funds, but the feuding continued. Creel frequently faulted the

Covers for four of the most famous publications of Creel's Committee on Public Information

press for failing to report properly his side of such controversies as the so-called "fake" submarine attack on U.S. transports. Still, his service ended with the highest praise from President Wilson and the eventual acclaim of critics such as Mark Sullivan, who worked as one of the committee's legion of volunteers. Creel's public career continued for another quarter of a century but was never again so fully the focus of press attention. He wrote more books, starting with *The War, the World and Wilson* (1920), and in 1920 accepted a staff position with *Collier's*, writing leaders, historical romances, and wide-ranging articles.

Never returning full-time to newspaper jour-

nalism, Creel, who moved to San Francisco in 1926, switched frequently from magazine work to politics and back again over the next twenty years. In the 1930s he worked on political campaigns, including Franklin Roosevelt's; served FDR as a regional administrator for the National Recovery Act; ran for governor of California in 1934 (losing to Upton Sinclair in the Democratic primary); was rehired by Chenery as *Collier's* Washington correspondent; and in 1938 accepted another FDR offer to head the Golden Gate International Exposition in San Francisco. He had planned to head east again in 1941, but his wife fell ill before Pearl Harbor and died on Christmas Day. Two years later, in 1943, he married

Creel in New York on 1 November 1941, telling reporters the United States should enter World War II without delay (Culver Pictures)

Alice May Rosseter. When he did reach Washington, he volunteered to replay his World War I role but was rejected, and found his only comfort in sharing a park bench with another discarded advisor from 1917, Bernard Baruch. Writing at age seventy, he decried the decline of standards, denounced "slack-jawed heirs to great wealth" who "pour money into left-wing sheets," and scorned the banalities of broadcasting. He later called for harsh postwar reprisals against Japan and Germany and became a strident anti-Communist cold warrior.

He was still the Creel of strong sentiments, so richly portrayed as two distinct persons by Mark Sullivan in the *Over Here* volume of *Our Times* (1936): the private Creel "was fecund with the spirit of comedy, rich in sensitiveness and kindness, likable to the last degree. But the instant Creel arose on a public platform or took up his pen, he became a raging reformer, compound of the more berserker

qualities of Danton, Marat, or Charlotte Corday. . . . he passed into a different personality, became tense, bitter, bellicose, angrily emotional. . . . Wherever he was, in whatever public role, trouble, commotion, angry controversy arose about him as surely as smoke goes upward." And all his writings, Sullivan concluded, whether in Kansas City, Denver, New York, or Washington, served the purpose of "denouncing diverse aspects of the world that seemed to Creel imperfect." Still, the stormy, public Creel could claim not only success in the war for world opinion but could proclaim before Congress in 1918, "Every single thing for which I have fought is today law, in either federal statutes, state statutes, or municipal ordinances. There is not an advocacy of mine that has not been approved by American majorities. My crime is that I fought for these reforms before they were fashionable." To repeat Creel's reply to his critics, "An exaggeration, of course, but not entirely untrue." He continued to write and speak out for his beliefs—now conservative rather than liberal—until his death in San Francisco at the age of seventy-six.

References:

Walton E. Bean, "George Creel and His Critics: A Study of the Attacks on the Committee on Public Information, 1917-1919," Ph.D. dissertation, University of California, Berkeley, 1941;

William L. Chenery, *So It Seemed* (New York: Harcourt, Brace, 1952);

Robert Lansing, *War Memoirs of Robert Lansing* (Indianapolis & New York: Bobbs-Merrill, 1935);

Peter C. MacFarlane, "Fortunes of Citizen Creel," *Collier's*, 51 (19 July 1913);

James R. Mock, *Censorship 1917* (Princeton, N.J.: Princeton University Press, 1941; reprint, New York: DaCapo Press, 1972);

Mock and Cedric Larson, *Words That Won the War* (Princeton, N.J.: Princeton University Press, 1939);

Robert L. Perkin, *The First Hundred Years* (New York: Doubleday, 1959);

C. C. Regier, *The Era of the Muckrakers* (Chapel Hill: University of North Carolina Press, 1932);

Mark Sullivan, *Our Times, 1900-1925*, vol. 5, *Over Here, 1914-1918* (New York: Scribners, 1936);

Donald Wilhelm, "Our Uncensorious Censor," *Independent*, 93 (5 January 1918): 20-21.

Papers:

George Creel's papers are in the Library of Congress.

M. H. de Young

(30 September 1849-15 February 1925)

Stephen D. Bray

MAJOR POSITION HELD: Publisher, *San Francisco Chronicle* (1880-1925).

M. H. de Young was associated with the *San Francisco Chronicle* from the time he was fifteen until his death in 1925. In those sixty years he built it into one of the major newspapers in California. Along with the *Los Angeles Times*, the *Chronicle* under de Young was known as one of the leading conservative voices in the state. After guiding the paper from its birth through its growth into a stable institution, he devoted much of his time to the interests of the Republican party and to public affairs. His direction of the paper coincided with the development of San Francisco from a frontier town into a distinctive, cosmopolitan community, and he played a significant role in that transformation; as a civic leader and art collector, he promoted the economic and cultural development of the city. The *Chronicle*, which is now the highest-circulation paper in northern California, and the M. H. de Young Memorial Art Museum remain as monuments to his contributions to San Francisco.

Michael Harry de Young, Jr., was born in St. Louis, Missouri, on 30 September 1849. His father, Michael H. de Young, Sr., was a prominent banker who chose to move his family to California. The elder de Young suffered a stroke and died during the journey, but his widow, Amelia, and three sons arrived in San Francisco, which was still a young, tough village, in June 1854. Michael attended the local schools and got his first taste of journalism when he helped his older brother, Charles, put out a paper, the "School Circle." He was still in high school when he helped Charles, only nineteen himself, start the *Chronicle*.

With a twenty-dollar gold piece borrowed from their landlord, the brothers found space in a job printing shop to put out a four-page tabloid called the *Dramatic Chronicle*. The first issue appeared on 17 January 1865 and consisted of advertising and literary material. The paper was intended as a program sheet for local theaters, which were a very popular diversion. It was paid for initially by the theater owners and delivered free around the city to the theaters, cafés, and hotels. Michael distributed the paper and served as its business manager. In its debut, the youthful editors proclaimed,

"We shall do our utmost to enlighten mankind in '*esse*,' and San Francisco in '*posse*,' of actions, intentions, sayings, doings, movements, successes, failures, oddities, peculiarities, and speculations, of 'us poor mortals here below.'"

The paper quickly received a colorful reputation for its robust and uninhibited writing. In one month it was circulating 2,000 copies. It attracted the attention of a young *Carson City Appeal* correspondent living in San Francisco; his name was Samuel Clemens, but he wrote under the name of Mark Twain. Twain used the *Chronicle* offices as his headquarters and penned occasional squibs for the paper. Another early contributor was Bret Harte, who was then a secretary at the San Francisco mint. The paper soon became a magnet for other bohemians in the city.

At night the young editors would study issues of the *New York Herald*, the country's leading sensationalist paper. By copying the *Herald*'s tech-niques, the *Chronicle* rapidly became a financial success. It contained, M. H. de Young recalled later, "just enough reading matter for men to read during lunch, and it was of a character to attract special attention. There were criticisms of public men, crisp references to important events, shots at conspicuous people, and other such information." The *Chronicle*'s first major scoop was its initial report and subsequent extras on the assassination of President Abraham Lincoln. Its accounts mobilized an angry, patriotic mob which stormed the offices of seven copperhead newspapers in the city.

Within two years the successful paper was using its own equipment and had moved into more spacious offices. With circulation exceeding 10,000, it had outgrown its original market. On 1 September 1868 it became the *Daily Morning Chronicle*, sold for five cents on the street, and was ready to compete with the older city dailies, the *Alta California*, the *Bulletin*, and the *Call*. With its new format, an editorial declared, it was planning to publish "what will prove a novelty in San Francisco journalism, a bold, bright, fearless and truly independent newspaper." The new *Chronicle* built its circulation on a formula of crusades against various monopolies—railroad, land, water, gas, and telegraph—and heavy doses of sensationalism. One titillating piece, which appeared in 1869 under the heading "The Course of True Love," was a detailed account of irregular married life in exclusive social circles. The *Chronicle* was also known for its spirited attacks on public persons; by 1871 Charles de Young had already been sued twelve times for criminal libel, a record even by San Francisco standards.

The period still belonged to the frontier days of journalism where disputes were not confined solely to the editorial columns, and Charles's differences with political enemies sometimes involved physical as well as verbal assaults. His association with Denis Kearney, a labor agitator who was building a powerful political base in the city, climaxed in one of the most violent episodes in San Francisco journalism and led to M. H. de Young's career as sole proprietor of the *Chronicle*. The greatest political battle fought by the de Young brothers was in 1879 on behalf of a new, more liberal state constitution which drew the resistance of the state's corporate interests and most of the press; among newspapers, the *Chronicle* was alone in its enthusiastic support. This reform-oriented document was also strongly endorsed by Kearney and his Workingmen's party. After the constitution was approved by the voters, the private ambitions of

Kearney and Charles de Young collided. Their conflict focused on Kearney's choice for mayor of San Francisco, the Reverend Isaac S. Kallach: de Young not only fired a barrage of verbal shots against Kallach's character in the *Chronicle* but also fired real gunshots at his person. Kallach recovered, however, and proceeded to win the election. A short time later Kallach's son took revenge: on 23 April 1880, he entered the *Chronicle*'s inner offices and shot and killed Charles de Young.

After his brother's death, M. H. de Young took complete control of the paper and steered it on a more temperate and politically conservative course. By 1884 it enjoyed the highest circulation figures in the city. It supported civic improvements and economic growth in San Francisco, fought for exclusion of the Chinese, and identified with the principles of the Republican party. His father had been a Whig, and de Young had promised his father that he, too, would always be a Whig; but when the Whigs succumbed and were succeeded by the Republican party, he reneged on his promise and transferred allegiance to the Republicans. In 1888

Memorial to de Young's brother Charles, who was killed by the son of a man he had wounded in a political dispute (Bancroft Library, University of California)

he attended the Republican national convention as a delegate for the first time. He was chairman of the California delegation and assumed a dominating role on behalf of the candidacy of James G. Blaine, who had been the party's candidate in 1884. Unfortunately for de Young, Blaine did not want the nomination a second time, and it went instead to Benjamin Harrison. De Young was also a delegate in 1892 and 1908. In 1892 he made his only attempt at political office when he unsuccessfully sought the Senate seat being vacated by George Hearst, whose son, William Randolph Hearst, was rejuvenating the *San Francisco Examiner*, the leading competitor of the *Chronicle*.

With the *Chronicle* firmly established, de Young was interested in improving the newspaper's physical plant. To replace the five-story building constructed in 1879, he erected in 1888 the first steel structure in the city; ten stories high, it was San Francisco's first skyscraper. The building was destroyed in the earthquake and fire which gutted the city in 1906; de Young took pride in the fact that with borrowed equipment the paper never missed an issue. In the wake of the catastrophe, de Young served on the special executive committee of the Red Cross. The building was rebuilt on the same site, but in 1923, de Young constructed a newer facility on its present location; it, too, was one of the most modern buildings of its time.

He also devoted much of his time to acting as a kind of civic ambassador from San Francisco. In 1889 he went to the Paris Exposition as a representative of the United States. In 1892 he was appointed by President Harrison as a national commissioner to the upcoming World's Columbian Exposition in Chicago. While acting in that capacity and holding discussions with visitors from abroad, he conceived of the idea of an exposition to be held in San Francisco. He returned home to organize what became known as the Midwinter Fair, which opened in 1894 on a newly developed site in Golden Gate Park. In order to ensure that potential guests might not be deterred by the title, he included the motto "The Land of Sunshine, Fruit and Flowers" on all official correspondence. The fair was an enormous economic and cultural success for the city: constructed during a national depression, it provided jobs for many unemployed men, and the setting and exhibits became a wondrous advertisement for the city. Soon afterwards, using the Fine Arts building constructed for the fair as its temporary home, de Young founded the Golden Gate Park Memorial Museum. An avid and respected art collector who traveled abroad extensively in search

Front page of the San Francisco Chronicle *for 26 January 1915, the thirty-fifth year of de Young's ownership of the paper*

of art treasures, he contributed many of his private acquisitions to the permanent collection. In honor of his efforts, a new home was built on the old site and renamed the M. H. de Young Memorial Museum. In 1898 he was named commissioner-general from California to the Trans-Mississippi Exposition in Omaha, Nebraska, and in 1900 he returned to France as a national commissioner to the Paris Exposition. In 1915 he acted as vice-president and director of concessions of the Panama-Pacific International Exposition in San Francisco.

De Young was not known as an editor who expressed his own views in his paper. As a journalist he was overshadowed in San Francisco by William Randolph Hearst and Fremont Older, but he was primarily concerned with managing the business side of the paper. He came to be appreciated by his peers while acting for twenty-four years as a director of the Associated Press.

De Young had married Kate I. Dean in 1880. In 1913 his only son, Charles, who was being groomed as his successor, died from typhus. De Young's own death came on 15 February 1925; he was seventy-five. Ownership of the paper passed to his four daughters and their families, where it still resides. His passing was mourned by city leaders and by members of the newspaper profession across the nation. He was eulogized as perhaps the last of an era of personal journalists who created and were identified with their papers.

References:

John Bruce, *Gaudy Century* (New York: Random House, 1948);

Robert W. Davenport, "Fremont Older in San Francisco Journalism," Ph.D. dissertation, UCLA, 1969;

"Life of M. H. de Young," *San Francisco Chronicle*, 16 February 1925, pp. 2-9;

Irving McKee, "The Shooting of Charles de Young," *Pacific Historical Review*, 16 (August 1947): 271-284;

John P. Young, *Journalism in California* (San Francisco: Chronicle Publishing Co., 1915).

Papers:

M. H. de Young's papers are in the Bancroft Library, University of California, Berkeley.

Rheta Childe Dorr
(2 November 1866-8 August 1948)

Susan G. Motes
University of Alabama

MAJOR POSITIONS HELD: Reporter, *New York Evening Post* (1902-1906); reporter and war correspondent, *New York Evening Mail* (1915-1918).

BOOKS: *What Eight Million Women Want* (Boston: Small, Maynard, 1910);

Inside the Russian Revolution (New York: Macmillan, 1917);

A Soldier's Mother in France (Indianapolis: Bobbs-Merrill, 1918);

A Woman of Fifty (New York: Funk & Wagnalls, 1924);

Susan B. Anthony: The Woman Who Changed the Mind of a Nation (New York: Stokes, 1928);

Drink: Coercion or Control (New York: Stokes, 1929).

PERIODICAL PUBLICATIONS: "Regeneration of the O'Tools," *Everybody's*, 12 (April 1905): 561-564;

"Women Strikers of Troy," *Charities and the Commons*, 15 (18 November 1905): 233-236;

"Crowning a King in Norway," *Harper's Weekly*, 50 (28 July 1906): 1054-1057;

"Bulling the Woman-Worker," *Harper's Weekly*, 51 (30 March 1907): 458-459;

"Christmas from behind the Counter," *Independent*, 63 (5 December 1907): 1340-1347;

"Woman's Invasion," *Everybody's* (November 1908): 579-581; (December 1908): 798-810; (January 1909): 73-85; (February 1909): 236-248; (March 1909): 372-385; (April 1909): 521-532;

"What's the Matter with the Public Schools?," *Delineator* (January 1909): 99-100;

"Institutional Church," *Delineator* (April 1910): 315-316;

"Prodigal Daughter," *Hampton's*, 24 (April-May 1910): 526-538, 679-688;

"Making Over the Backward Child," *Hampton's*, 24 (June 1910): 809-822;

"Fighting Chance for the City Child," *Hampton's*, 24 (July 1910): 103-116; (August 1910): 249-258;

"Rebuilding the Child World," *Hampton's*, 24 (October 1910): 489-498;

"Child's Day in Court," *Hampton's*, 24 (November 1910): 633-643;

"Another Chance for the Bad Boy," *Hampton's*, 25 (December 1910): 797-807;

"Problem of Divorce," *Forum*, 45 (January 1911): 68-79;

"Reclaiming the Wayward Girl," *Hampton's*, 26 (January 1911): 67-78;

"Women Did It in Colorado," *Hampton's*, 26 (April 1911): 426-438;

"Breaking into the Human Race," *Hampton's*, 26 (April 1911): 317-329;

"Deathproof Versus Fireproof," *Hampton's*, 26 (June 1911): 687-698;

"Keeping the Children in School," *Hampton's*, 27 (July 1911): 55-66;

"Westmoreland Strike," *Hampton's*, 27 (July 1911): 125-126;

"Twentieth Child," *Hampton's*, 27 (January 1912): 793-806;

"When Is a Factory Not a Factory?," *Hampton's*, 27 (February 1912): 34-39;

"Child That Is Different," *Century*, 83 (April 1912): 924-930;

"Child Who Toils at Home," *Hampton's*, 28 (April 1912): 183-188;

"Ellen Key," *Bookman*, 37 (July 1913): 510-512;

"Mrs. Pankhurst—the Woman," *Good Housekeeping*, 57 (December 1913): 759-763;

"Mothers, Sisters and Sons," *Harper's Weekly*, 60 (May 1915): 448-449;

"120 High-School Girls Who Failed," *Ladies Home Journal*, 32 (May 1915): 32;

"Putting It up to the Fathers," *Good Housekeeping*, 60 (May 1915): 497-502;

"Eternal Question," *Collier's*, 66 (30 October 1920): 5-6;

"Children's Crusade for Peace," *Ladies Home Journal*, 41 (March 1924): 12;

"Last of the Ural Cossacks," *Current History Magazine of the New York Times*, 16 (August 1924): 775-781;

"Secret Gardens of Konopiste," *Current History*

Magazine of the New York Times, 20 (August 1924): 770-775;

"Should There be Labor Laws for Women?," *Good Housekeeping*, 81 (September 1925): 25;

"Ellen Key," *Saturday Review of Literature*, 2 (8 May 1926): 773;

"How to Get Rich," *Collier's*, 78 (17 July 1926): 38-39;

"A Convert from Socialism," *North American Review*, 224 (November 1927): 498-504;

"Free and Equal Citizens," *Good Housekeeping*, 87 (July 1928): 38-39;

"Other Prohibition Country," *Harper's*, 159 (September 1929): 495-504;

"England Going Sober," *World's Work*, 59 (January 1930): 61-64;

"Let's Compromise on Prohibition," *World's Work*, 59 (September 1930): 49-52.

Rheta Childe Dorr achieved distinction as a female war correspondent during World War I. She was among the first women to be hired as a newspaper reporter, holding jobs ranging from woman's page editor to foreign correspondent. An ardent feminist, she spent a great deal of energy advocating the ratification of the nineteenth amendment. The topics of her newspaper stories, magazine articles, and books reflected her devotion to causes—particularly those of working women and children.

On 2 November 1866 Rheta Louise Child was born in Omaha, Nebraska, to Edward Payson Child, a druggist, and Lucie Mitchell Child. Later in life she embellished her name to Childe, possibly to reflect her mother's French heritage. As a child Rheta was disturbed by poverty she saw in her community. On several occasions she came home with some of her clothes missing and no explanation why; the truth was not discovered until her mother returned one day to find Rheta distributing the contents of the linen closet to several poor children who had followed her home.

At the age of twelve Rheta read in the newspapers that Elizabeth Cady Stanton and Susan B. Anthony would be in Lincoln, where the family had moved, for a lecture on women's rights. Although she was not completely certain what it was about, she resolved to attend the meeting and convinced her older sister to do likewise. When her father uncovered the plot, he was adamant in his refusal of permission for them to attend. The strong-willed child considered this a direct challenge and went anyway. She was later to write of the meeting in her autobiography: "I have experienced perhaps more than my share of thrills, but rarely have I thrilled as

I did at that first exposition, by those two great women, of equal suffrage." Their inspiration led her to donate a silver dollar to the cause and to join the National Woman Suffrage Association; unfortunately, the next day's issue of the *Nebraska State Journal* carried a report of the meeting with a list of those who had joined the organization. Rheta was punished for her disobedience, but rather than repentance, the result was the development of a deep conviction that there was a class war between men and women based on what she called "unjustifiable sex distinctions." She felt that women were not inferior to men and should not be denied rights and opportunities because of their sex.

Rheta began working at the age of fifteen, despite the fact that women did not generally work; in fact, the only moderately acceptable jobs for a woman were teacher, dressmaker, milliner, or domestic. Since her father had suffered financial reverses and was unable to provide her with new school clothes, she decided the best opportunity for her to earn money would be at the upcoming state fair. She used all of her persuasive skills to talk a reluctant family friend into hiring her for six days as a window washer. She worked hard during the day and argued with her family about the necessity of her work at night. At the end of the week she triumphantly held $15 in her red, swollen hands.

The following fall her father sent her to Nebraska State University. During her second year, in 1885, a professor lent her a copy of Henrik Ibsen's *A Doll's House*. The play and the character of Nora impressed her so much that the next day she began to seek a permanent job in order to assert her economic independence. She wrote in her autobiography that at that time most people thought "that all jobs in the world belonged by right to men, and that only men were by nature entitled to wages. If a woman earned money, outside domestic service, it was because some misfortune had deprived her of masculine protection. That any sane or normal woman would elect a life of wage earning was unthinkable. Woman's place was in the home. . . ." Another reluctant family friend employed her at the post office. It took three days of arguing before her parents acquiesced. She worked for two years at the general delivery windows.

Feeling restless and unfulfilled, she moved to New York in 1890 to study at the Art Student's League. After a short time she decided that writing was to be her medium of self-expression:

> I remembered that I had always written, that
> it had always been natural for me to scribble.

. . . I began to write. Anything that came into my head, verse, fiction, little newspaper stories, and because I was so young it did not astonish me that my stuff sold. . . . Of course my earnings were small but I required little. . . . Like other personable young women I had attendant swains who gave me luncheons and dinners several times a week, brought me flowers and books and took me to the theater. . . . If I had had fewer swains I should have felt poor, and perhaps I should have done better work. . . . I wrote a great deal of verse. In fact, every time I fell in love, which was rather often, I burst into the emotional sort of thing which is perennially salable. . . . I scarcely know where I should have arrived if something had not fortunately happened. I married. Not one of the devoted youths who bestowed dinners and flowers and inspired erotic verse, but a comparative stranger, a man twenty years my senior, one whom I had known, altho not very well, in my home town. He was a New Yorker born and on one of his eastern visits we met again. The attraction was instant and mutual, and within a short time we were married. . . . His straight, lithe body and clear brown eyes were no small part of his attractiveness to me, but it was really his mind that I longed most to possess. . . . He had read deeply and could talk of his books almost better than anybody I had ever met.

Childe and John Pixley Dorr were married in 1892 and lived briefly in Nebraska before moving to Seattle, where John and his brother were in business. It was in Seattle that their son, Julian Childe Dorr, was born in 1896. The first two years of the marriage were quite happy; however, her desire to explore ideologies concerning the role of women caused a philosophical conflict which later proved to be insurmountable. Her husband suggested that writing might be a good way for her to express herself, and that it might help return their marriage to its former state. Unable to find subjects for stories through her routine activities, she began mingling with the life of Seattle: "I haunted the streets, the docks, the outfitting stores, interviewing miners, successful and unsuccessful, getting wonderful yarns. . . . I began to write newspaper stories, sending them to New York where they were promptly accepted and printed." Her husband found this work "incomprehensible and repellent," and in 1898, by mutual agreement, she left him and returned to New York with $500, their two-year-old child, and an English nurse, to find her place in the world as a journalist.

Rheta Dorr had sent articles from Seattle which the *New York Sun* had purchased, so she went to that paper first for a job; however, they were not interested in hiring a woman. The next three years were difficult as she unsuccessfully looked for a job with every newspaper in New York City, meanwhile earning money by selling stories at $5 per column. She later wrote: "I was at this time, and for a long time after, in danger of becoming what I dreaded to be, a man-hater. As far as I could see I lived in a world entirely hostile to women; a world in which every right and every privilege were claimed by men. Men exacted everything, gave nothing, throwing contempt into the bargain. Every man's hand was held out to help young fellows beginning life. Almost any recent college graduate could get a trial week in a newspaper city-room. The brightest woman waited in the office-boy's coop. No man's hand was held out to help a woman struggling to support a child. . . . There were other aspects of the case too. I discovered, after coming back to New York, that I occupied a doubtful position with men. As a young girl I had a train of respectfully devoted admirers. As a woman yet young and pretty, but a woman separated from her husband, I had a train of men openly game-hunters. Not all but most of the men with whom I was acquainted, sooner or later became in speech and behavior over-familiar. They told me stories they would never dare tell to a girl. When they took me to dinner they frequently tried to make me drink too much. If they took me to the theater it was oftener to a music-hall or a Broadway farce than to Daly's. The worst of it was—how shall I express it—the worst was that I was young and warm-blooded and sometimes I did not know how to hide the effect of the second cocktail or the too-amusing story. I could protest, I could say sharp and sarcastic things, but I had not yet acquired the armor with which a woman of the world protects her dignity."

She was forced to sell almost everything, except her silverware, to support herself and her young child, but despite the lack of success she remained determined to stay in New York. Her first regular work came from selling a weekly fashion column to the American Press Association for syndication. Occasionally she was assigned a photographer, and together they were sometimes able to fill a Sunday page.

A break came when Dorr was offered the large sum of $25 to secure photographs of the formal announcement of Theodore Roosevelt's nomination to run for vice-president with William McKinley. The pay was high for this job because Colonel Roosevelt refused to be photographed, but Dorr persuaded him to have the pictures taken on the condition that she be in charge of the photographers and keep them in line. The colonel's request was honored, and the event was successfully photographed. After this the *Tribune* and the *New York Evening Post* bought copy from her regularly. In 1902 Hammond Lamont, managing editor of the *Post*, invited her to join the staff to cover women's activities. Despite its prestige, the *Post* had found that women did not read the paper and that the advertisers were aware of this fact. She was hired at $25 a week. Later, when she found that she needed more money to support herself and her child, she was told that she would not get a raise because the *Post* could hire all the females it wanted for $25 or less. To earn additional money she wrote editorials, reviewed books, and wrote special articles for the Sunday supplement, bringing in as much as $10 a week more. She later wrote of her experience at the *Post*: "I was taught to write good, clear English, I was forced into habits of straight thinking and accurate statement. . . . But the best thing that the 'Evening Post' did for me was done accidentally." She was sent to cover a story about goldbeaters striking because women were invading their trade and they wanted to replace the girls with boy apprentices. She was told: "Girls, you see, couldn't never reely learn the trade, and they wouldn't if they could. Girls just work temporary till they get married." Not long afterward a similar strike occurred in the Tiffany glassworks. Here, too, women were being excluded from the work force because they were seen as only temporary workers. She resolved to get a closer look at the problem of working women and moved to New York's East Side for the next two years; she wanted to live among the toilers in the heart of a ghetto. She became allied with the Women's Trade Union League, endorsing minimum-wage laws, the eight-hour workday, and woman suffrage. "I have always believed that citizenship is better for women than special protective legislation, which seems to me dangerously to label us permanent inferiors and dependents." From 1904 to 1906 she served as chairman of the committee on the industrial conditions of women and children of the General Federation of Women's Clubs, and she was instrumental in securing the first official investigation of the conditions of working women in 1905.

Dorr left the *Evening Post* in 1906 after being told that she had no future with the paper since a woman could never be a city editor and her thinking was too nontraditional for her to become an editorial writer. Lamont recommended that she write magazine articles or books.

That summer she left for Europe with enough commissions to pay her expenses for three months: the *Evening Post*, the *Boston Transcript*, and *Harper's Weekly* had agreed to publish her stories of the crowning of King Haakon of Norway and the news of that country's independence from Sweden. Dorr traveled from Norway to St. Petersburg, Russia, where she lived with revolutionary terrorists. From St. Petersburg she went to Copenhagen to cover a meeting of the International Woman Suffrage Alliance; her financial resources were dwindling by this time, and she hoped to get a newspaper story from the meeting. It was there that she first learned of Emmeline Pankhurst, who had led a number of aggressive suffragists from Manchester to London and had tried to force a woman suffrage bill on the British government. In October she traveled to England to find out firsthand what the British women were doing.

On her voyage home in November she vowed that she "would battle not only for myself but for freedom and opportunity for everything living that wore chains, especially sex chains." Returning to the United States almost penniless and without a job, she decided that she had had enough of women's fashions, women's clubs, and social events, and that magazines might be more challenging than newspapers. However, she did write some newspaper pieces about the suffragettes, making then sensational enough to guarantee publication. She convinced the editor at *Everybody's* magazine to hire her to write a series of articles called "The Woman's Invasion." She wanted to tell the story of women in industry: "What I proposed to do was to drop my identity completely, become a factory worker and to tell from the inside the story of women who worked."

She was able to persuade John O'Hara Cosgrave, editor in chief of *Everybody's*, to pay her $35 a week to collect her personal experiences. She later remembered: "Altho many women have since made personal investigations of the trades, I believe that I was the first woman to throw herself into the ranks of manual workers with a view of surveying their conditions in relation to the whole social fabric." Her plan was "to take up, one after another, the historic trades of women, cooking, sewing, washing and ironing, spinning and weaving, canning, preserving, and other household arts, following from the home where they began to the factory which had absorbed them. My articles would describe the transformation of the trades themselves, and would also describe the effect of the change on the work-

ers, their homes, and their point of view on life. My great object, of course, was to demonstrate that women were permanent factors in industry, permanent producers of the world's wealth, and that they must hereafter be considered as independent human beings and citizens, rather than adjuncts to men and to society."

She spent more than a year working as a seamstress, laundress, department store clerk, and assembly-line worker and sending her notes weekly to the editors of *Everybody's*; but they wanted completed articles, which she was too mentally overwhelmed and too physically exhausted to write. William Hard was selected as her collaborator to produce twelve articles; but their first meetings revealed that he saw his role as author and hers as data collector, and she did not pursue their joint efforts. She was then shocked to see the magazine announcing that " 'The Woman's Invasion' by William Hard" would begin in the next issue, October 1908. She hired an attorney and forced the magazine to cease publication of the series until she was added as coauthor. However, once the article appeared she found that "the title was mine, the idea was mine, most of the material was mine, but the intent and meaning of the whole thing was distorted beyond recognition. . . . The only thing I had left to hope was that this series, altho it bore my name, would soon be forgotten and that other articles I should write would give me a better reputation." She was able to prevent the publication of a book by Hard based on these articles.

In June 1910, Benjamin B. Hampton of *Hampton's* magazine gave her use of the office but not a place on the staff. "On 'Hampton's' I was given unlimited opportunity to express my own ideas in my own fashion, and I had a certain authority in directing the magazine's policy," she recalled. Dorr contributed from six to ten articles a year to the magazine. These articles were the basis for her first book, *What Eight Million Women Want* (1910), which she later described as "a survey and analysis of the collective opinion of women as it had, up to that time, been expressed in what they tried to do in women's clubs, in suffrage associations, trade unions, Consumers' Leagues, and in the allied organizations known as the International Council of Women." In November 1912 she went to Sweden to interview Ellen Key and then to Germany to interview other feminist leaders. Upon her return *Good Housekeeping* editor William F. Bigelow asked her to go back to Europe to get Emmeline Pankhurst to write a series of articles for the magazine. Dorr stayed in Paris most of the winter helping Pankhurst

WHAT EIGHT MILLION WOMEN WANT

BY

RHETA CHILDE DORR

BOSTON
SMALL, MAYNARD & COMPANY
PUBLISHERS

Title page for Dorr's 1910 book about the women's club movement in the United States

write her autobiography, which was published in 1914 as *My Own Story*.

In 1915 Dorr went to work for Dr. Edward E. Rumely at the *New York Evening Mail*. She wrote a special page in support of the reelection of New York mayor John Purroy Mitchel, who advocated better schools. She also authored a daily editorial, "As a Woman Sees It," which was widely syndicated. These signed editorials concerned topics of her choosing and gave her a fulfilling outlet for her ideas.

Her concern for women's rights diminished as she developed a strong interest in World War I. Her interest in politics also grew. In 1916 she rode on the Republican campaign train supporting Charles Evans Hughes, who favored the ratification of the nineteenth amendment. In addition to making speeches each day she also filed a 1,000-word story

for the *Evening Mail* and continued to write her editorial column.

When the Russian Revolution began in 1917, Dorr decided that she wanted to cover it. Since she had been to Russia twice already and had kept up with revolutionary activities for the past ten years, it was logical that the paper would send her; that they did so was an indication of the changing climate for working women. It is possible that her enthusiasm for going to Russia stemmed from her admiration of Arthur Young, the British journalist who had reported on the French Revolution; she indicated in her autobiography that to cover a revolution and be like Young had been the greatest adventure she could hope for. During her five months in Russia, she hired a university student, partially educated in England, to be her interpreter. This allowed her much more freedom than most reporters had to mingle with the people in factories, on the streets, and in the parks. When she returned she found that Americans were uninformed about Russia and were eager to read her work. She spent the next five weeks writing from memory, since her notes had been confiscated in Russia. Her stories were published in the *Evening Mail* and, subsequently, in her book *Inside the Russian Revolution* (1917).

A short time thereafter she was able to convince her editors to send her to France. In addition to the fact that she liked being a war correspondent, she wanted to see her son, who was serving in the army there. Her first stop was England, where she visited factories and saw women doing men's jobs very effectively. The pay and working conditions for the women were good; Dorr was optimistic that this treatment would continue after the war, but it did not. During the time she had been in Russia and on her subsequent return to the United States, she had not had time to find out what was going on in France and was much less informed about the situation there than her editors thought. Before leaving England she arranged an interview with Sir John Buchan of the press bureau of the English Foreign Office, and through his briefing she was able to enter France knowledgeable of the situation. When she arrived, the French authorities refused to recognize her credentials and told her that her newspaper should have sent a man. She finally concluded that the solution to her problem was to join the YMCA; through this organization she was able to get bookings for informal lectures on the Russian Revolution wherever she needed to go in the country. During this trip she saw her son twice before he was wounded.

In May her paper called her back to begin

writing about her experiences. In addition to these articles, she wrote *A Soldier's Mother in France* (1918) for mothers of soldiers. Not long after she returned, Dr. Rumely was arrested for buying the *Evening Post* with German money, and Dorr resigned from the paper. She free-lanced articles partly to be with her son, who was recovering from his injuries in a New York military hospital, and also because no other position was offered her. After her son had sufficiently recovered, Dorr went to Washington, D.C. Returning to her hotel late one night, she was run over by a motorcycle; her serious injuries affected both her mental and physical health. Deciding that work was the best cure, she campaigned for Harding and Coolidge. "But afterwards I realized that I had to do a little more for my shattered nerves. I had to go away from every reminder of that ghastly accident. I decided to go to some far corner of Europe, and I chose Czecho-Slovakia, simply, I suppose, because I knew that its capital, Prague, was a quaint, medieval town where in past years Goethe had retired for meditation, Mozart had written some of his best music, George Sand and other writers had lived." Shortly after her arrival in Prague an internal injury from the accident was discovered. After surgery she had more months of difficult recovery ahead of her. She was advised that she must relax before she could return to her former state of health. In November 1921 Dorr was able to get in touch with Anna Viroubova, a woman she had met on her first trip to Russia. She convinced Viroubova to write her recollections of Nicholas II and the Empress Alexandra. They began to work on the book in April 1922 and produced *Memories of the Russian Court*, which was published in 1923. Dorr spent three years in Europe, during which she wrote a series of articles on the Dawes Committee for the *New York Herald Tribune*,

traveled to Bulgaria during the Communist outbreaks, covered Mussolini's march into Rome, and wrote articles on Bulgaria and Rumania for the *Herald Tribune* and other papers.

In 1924 her autobiography, *A Woman of Fifty*, was published. Her impetus to write the book came from a desire to record not the story of Rheta Childe Dorr but the plight of a woman living during that time. As a result, details in the book are not always accurate: for example, she says she married John Pixley Dorr, a man of forty who was twenty years her senior; in 1892 she would have been twenty-five or twenty-six years old, not twenty. The autobiography expresses ideas that are quite advanced for the time in which it was written. In 1936 Dorr's son died while serving as American vice-consul in Mexico; his death came as a severe blow. Several years later she became an invalid, living in a sanatorium in Bucks County, Pennsylvania, before moving to the home of her physician, Dr. Aileen Von Lohr, in New Britain, Pennsylvania. It was here that Rheta Childe Dorr died at the age of eighty-one.

References:

Louis Filler, *Crusaders for American Liberalism* (New York: Harcourt, Brace, 1939);

"Leading Articles: A Convert From Socialism," *Review of Reviews* (December 1927): 650;

Frank Luther Mott, *History of American Magazines*, volume 5 (Cambridge, Mass.: Harvard University Press, 1968), p. 149;

Robert E. Riegel, *American Feminists* (Lawrence: University of Kansas Press, 1963), pp. 173-177;

Ishbel Ross, *Ladies of the Press* (New York: Harper, 1936), pp. 109-116.

Floyd Gibbons
(16 July 1887-24 September 1939)

Richard M. Brown

MAJOR POSITIONS HELD: Reporter, war correspondent, foreign correspondent, director of foreign news service for Europe and North Africa, editor of the European edition, *Chicago Tribune* (1912-1926).

BOOKS: *How the Laconia Sank; The Militia Mobilization on the Mexican Border: Two Masterpieces of Reporting* (Chicago: Daughaday, 1917);
"And They Thought We Wouldn't Fight" (New York: Doran, 1918);
The Red Knight of Germany: The Story of Baron von Richthofen, Germany's Great War Bird (Garden City: Doubleday, Page, 1927; London: Heinemann, 1927);
The Red Napoleon (New York: Cape & Smith, 1929).

A restless, unorthodox roving reporter, Floyd Gibbons brought high excitement, courage, and ingenuity into his foreign and war correspondence to earn his reputation as the premier war correspondent of his generation. He also pioneered, along with Graham McNamee, the reporting of news events by radio in the 1920s and, among other firsts, broadcast on-the-scene reports using the portable "knapsack" transmitter.

Christened Raphael Floyd Phillips Gibbons in Washington, D.C., Gibbons was the eldest of five children of Edward Thomas and Emma Theresa Phillips Gibbons. A Roman Catholic, Gibbons was enrolled in Washington's Gonzaga College at the age of eleven but attended public schools in Des Moines, Iowa, and Minneapolis, Minnesota, when his father, a produce dealer and business promoter, took the family to those cities. He returned to Washington to continue his education in the preparatory department of Georgetown University, but the pranks which were characteristic of his boyhood led to his dismissal in his fourth year.

Heading west, Gibbons got a job shoveling coal in Lucca, North Dakota, where he also helped the editor of the local weekly and was inspired with the ambition of becoming a reporter. Returning to Minneapolis in 1907, he went to work for the *Daily News*; but Gibbons soon lost that position and went

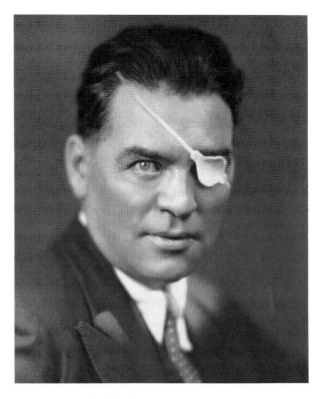

Floyd Gibbons (Culver Pictures)

to work for the *Milwaukee Free Press* as a police reporter a few months later. While the loss of his first newspaper job has been attributed to his colorful reporting on the federal courts, his brother said that their father got Gibbons discharged from what he considered an unsuitable job. In 1910, Gibbons returned to Minneapolis to take a job on the *Tribune*. He gained a reputation for handling unusual assignments, and his first big scoop came in the "Battle of Cameron Dam" outside Winter, Wisconsin, in 1910. This incident, in which John Dietz, a farmer, was disputing a lumber company's effort to gain control of a dam on his property with the collusion of the local sheriff, enabled Gibbons to score a number of beats on the twenty-five other reporters on the story. At one point his chief rival, "Red" Schwartz of the *Minneapolis Journal*, tried to breach the reporters' agreement to share the single telephone and single telegraph wire out of Winter by hiring a lumberman to hold the telephone wire until Schwartz could file his story. Gibbons planted a hatchet at the foot of a telephone pole outside the general store where the phone was located and, as Schwartz rushed to file his story, climbed the pole and chopped the wire before heading for the telegraph office to file his own account. He was jailed on a felony charge for cutting the wire but was freed when his paper paid $500 for the four hours the phone was out of service.

By 1912, Gibbons felt ready for big-time newspapering and went to Chicago. Arriving the first week in May, he found the newspapers all but shut down by strikes. Only the socialist *World* was publishing, and Gibbons worked there for several months until the paper folded when the strike ended. He finally landed a job on the *Chicago Tribune*, where he built a reputation for solid, factual reporting and ingenious, thorough news gathering in spite of his bohemian and devil-may-care attitude. He was beginning to acquire the knack of giving drama and distinction to his stories,

Gibbons covering the "Battle of Cameron Dam" in Wisconsin for the Minneapolis Tribune *in 1910*

but not at the expense of fact.

In 1914, Gibbons married Isabelle Pherrman of Minneapolis and also began his adventurous career as a roving correspondent. The *Tribune* sent him to cover the mobilization on the Mexican border sparked by Pancho Villa's raids. Gibbons not only provided a thorough documentation of the weaknesses in the calling up of the National Guard, but he provided exciting eyewitness reports of combat in Ciudad Juárez, across the border from El Paso. He culminated his success by joining Villa, in spite of Villa's threat to hang the first American reporter to fall into his hands. Villa was so taken by Gibbons that he provided a special car for him on his personal train. Gibbons was promoted to the *Tribune*'s Washington bureau following this success, but he returned to Mexico with Gen. John J. Pershing's punitive expedition after Villa's raid on Columbus, New Mexico, in 1916.

Gibbons's next great exploit came with his assignment as war correspondent to Europe in 1917. Ignoring instructions to obtain passage on the S. S. *Frederick VIII*, which was carrying Ambassador Count von Bernstorff and had been assured safe crossing, he deliberately chose the S. S. *Laconia*, a Cunard passenger liner facing an extreme risk of U-boat attack. He foresaw the extent of the newspaper scoop he could achieve with an eyewitness account of such a disaster. His gamble paid off eight days out when the *Laconia* was sunk 200 miles off the Irish coast. His story on the event was read before both houses of Congress and is included today in anthologies of great reporting. In France, he frequently beat other reporters in his coverage. Dissatisfied with the carefully conducted group tours imposed on the press, he disappeared for six weeks while secretly training with the Sixth Field Artillery. While the other seventeen correspondents were being held five miles from the front, where the Americans were about to take over their first sector, Damon Runyon of the *New York American* spotted the familiar hulking form on a passing caisson. Gibbons scooped them and even ended up as custodian of the shell casing of the first American shot fired in the war.

Gibbons was covering the Marine attack at Belleau Wood when he was hit in the arm, shoulder, and head; his left eye was destroyed. At the time he was hit, he was trying to reach a badly wounded major trapped in an open field by machine gun fire. While convalescing, he returned to the United States as a war lecturer at the request of Marshal Foch and General Pershing. With his tailored uniform, one arm in a sling, his cane, the white

Gibbons's mother pinning the Croix de Guerre with Palms on him in Chicago, 28 September 1918. Gibbons's father is between them (Chicago Tribune).

eyepatch that was to become his trademark, and the Croix de Guerre with Palms on his chest, Gibbons was a heroic figure and was widely acclaimed during his speaking tour.

He was able to return to Paris on New Year's Day, 1919, taking over as the director of the *Tribune*'s foreign news service for Europe, the Near East, and North Africa and as editor in chief of the European edition. His was not to be a management career alone, however: he retained the desire for on-the-scene reporting, the personal courage, and the graphic style which told the story in human terms.

As a reporter he was priceless to his paper, and the *Tribune* used him for its most demanding stories. He was in Ireland before the year was out, covering the Sinn Fein rebellion. The next year he bluffed his way to the front in the Polish-Russian war after a plane crash thwarted his effort to circumvent the border controls. After the war, the great famine of 1921 was sweeping Russia and carrying away millions of its people, yet no American correspondent could get to the famine area along the Volga. In Riga, Gibbons met the redoubtable Ambassador Litvinoff and ended up accompanying him to Mos-

cow, where he received permission to enter the famine region and tell the world of the horrors there; Walter Duranty of the *New York Times* called this "one of the biggest newspaper triumphs in postwar history." Gibbons capped this exploit with an exclusive interview with Joseph Stalin.

In 1923, Gibbons was assigned a newspaper stunt which proved to be one of his roughest adventures. With *The Sheik* and Rudolph Valentino capturing the American public's imagination, the editor of the *Tribune* assigned Gibbons to organize a camel caravan across the Sahara. Gibbons not only undertook the crossing from Colomb-Béchar, Algeria, to Timbuktu at a season during which native caravans avoided the desert, but he made the crossing in only half the usual time. Fifteen years earlier, when he was fired from the *Minneapolis Daily News*, editor Bill Sheppard had suggested he go to Timbuktu; one of Gibbons's first acts upon arrival was to notify Sheppard that he was carrying out his assignment. The French honored Gibbons with the Cross of the Legion of Honor upon completion of this expedition.

In 1924, Gibbons's marriage to Isabelle Pherrman ended in divorce. The continual separations as Gibbons pursued his career had resulted in estrangement of the couple, and his wanderings gave no possibility of normal home life. There were no children.

Following an around-the-world trip, Gibbons returned to Africa in 1925 for the war the French and Spanish were fighting against the Riff in Morocco. Again it was a time of harrowing front-line adventure and scooping the other correspondents. More honors came to him now, including promotion to Chevalier of the Legion of Honor and the award of the Medal of Morocco. The latter entitled him to a harem of eighteen—only two fewer than the sultan—whenever he was in Morocco.

Upon the death of his mother in Paris late in 1925, Gibbons returned to Chicago, and this return marked the beginning of new directions in his career. On Christmas night, he made his first broadcast over the *Tribune*'s new radio station, WGN. Speaking without a prepared script, he talked of Christmases he had experienced during his wanderings. His sincerity and his colorful storytelling ability made him an overnight sensation, but he did not immediately move into broadcasting. Instead he accepted a roving assignment in Europe that included covering Marshal Pilsudski's coup d'état in Poland in May 1926. In July, he ended his fifteen years of service with the *Tribune*

Gibbons tells Ahaamouk, king of the Tauregs, about his trip across the Sahara from Colomb-Béchar to Tamnarasset, the Taureg capital, in 1923 (Chicago Tribune).

and wrote a biography of Baron Manfred von Richthofen, the German war ace, which was serialized in Capt. Joseph Medill Patterson's *Liberty* magazine for twenty-three weeks. This led to his only attempt at writing fiction, *The Red Napoleon* (1929), which was also serialized in *Liberty* as well as becoming a newspaper serial.

Gibbons's radio career began when he contacted M. H. Aylesworth, president of the National Broadcasting Company, for technical information for *The Red Napoleon*. Aylesworth, who saw in Gibbons the potential for becoming a star, invited him to do an audition when the book was completed. Late in the spring of 1929, Gibbons accepted the invitation. He was not told that the NBC board of directors was gathered to listen to the tryout. Impressed with his speed, clarity, and dramatic presentation, they voted to put him under contract, and his program, "The Headline Hunter," was born. Sponsored by General Electric, it took less than three months to become one of the nation's most popular programs. A staccato delivery that averaged up to 217 words per minute without loss of

clarity fascinated audiences, and his intimate knowledge of the people and places in the news made him one of the most respected commentators of his time. His ability to hold his listeners spellbound with almost any subject and his graphic storytelling ability gave him an ever-growing audience. Along with Graham McNamee, Gibbons pioneered the reporting of news events by radio and was the first to use a portable shortwave transmitter for on-the-scene reporting. With a crude twenty-four-pound transmitter strapped to his chest and two men holding his antenna aloft on upright bamboo fishing poles, Gibbons covered the arrival of the airship *Graf Zeppelin* at Lakehurst, New Jersey, on 5 August 1929.

While successful as a radio commentator, Gibbons considered himself primarily a reporter and, in particular, a war correspondent. To protect his freedom to cover any conflict, every radio contract he signed contained a provision that the contract was null and void if war broke out; thus he was free to cover the Sino-Japanese War in 1931 and 1932 for the International News Service. However, he

Gibbons using the first portable radio transmitter to broadcast the arrival of the Graf Zeppelin *at Lakehurst, New Jersey, 5 August 1929. Behind him, two men are holding up the antenna for the equipment.*

interspersed his cabled reports with broadcasts for NBC; and an interview in Mukden with Gen. Shigeru Honjo, commander of the Japanese forces, was the first broadcast ever made from the headquarters of an army in the field and the first broadcast to span the Pacific from continental Asia. It was rebroadcast worldwide. Under fire from both ground and air on numerous occasions, Gibbons was able to provide extensive coverage of both sides.

Returning to the United States in 1932, he became increasingly busy. Besides his newspaper and radio work, he had been making movie short subjects for several years and was heavily in demand as a speaker and celebrity. Among his other activities that spring and summer, he produced a series of articles, broadcasts, and speeches warning of weaknesses in the United States' Asian policy, particularly concerning Hawaii; covered both the Republican and Democratic conventions; pioneered the first radio broadcast from a moving train; and covered the Bonus March on Washington, where he reported the brutal manner in which the troops dispersed the marchers and burned their shelters. Following a scathing article on the administration's defense of its actions, he was barred from his assigned broadcast coverage of the

American Legion convention, although NBC, the White House, and the Federal Communications Commission all denied responsibility for that censorship. At a banquet on the first night of the convention, Patrick J. Hurley, then secretary of war, stated on his "sacred word of honor" that Gibbons's accounts were not fact and that no soldier had done the burning. Gibbons replied that he was only one of the newspaper reporters and photographers who had witnessed the burning of the shacks and who had pictures verifying the facts. He concluded, "A camera doesn't have a word of honor, either." Gibbons was invited to give the convention assembly an eyewitness account, for which he received a standing ovation. Later that day, the government retracted its version of the event.

The strenuous pace which Gibbons had maintained for over twenty-five years was beginning to tell on him, and in early February 1934 he was stricken with a heart attack while on a short vacation at Hot Springs, Virginia. The doctors informed him that he would have to cut his activities drastically. Not only was his heart in poor condition, but his rapid-fire speaking had begun to damage his lungs as well. He attempted to slow down, but the efforts were sporadic and temporary. The follow-

*Gibbons interviewing the chief of the District of Columbia police
before the veterans' Bonus March in July 1932
(International News Photo)*

ing year he was again serving as a war correspondent in Ethiopia for INS and NBC, covering the Italian side of the war. The hardships proved too much for him, and he collapsed from high-altitude breathing problems during his second shortwave broadcast. After a short convalescence, he resumed his hectic schedule, covering rioting in Cairo, doing articles on Jerusalem, interviewing Mussolini, and reporting the funeral of George V of Great Britain. Six months after his return to the United States he was back in Europe to cover the Spanish Civil War. This, his ninth war, was particularly dangerous for him since he was covering both sides and vulnerable to being shot as a spy by either. Of all the wars he had covered, he found this the most brutal and inhumane, and he was horrified at the callous disregard for both human life and property.

Upon returning to New York, he resumed his round of radio shows, adventure films, and personal appearances, but at a slower pace. At the end of 1937 he retired to two farms he had purchased near Stroudsburg, Pennsylvania. While he enjoyed the life of a gentleman farmer, he carried on limited media activities. He continued work on his true-adventure films, and on 16 January 1939, he made a special broadcast for the "Lux Radio Theater."

The arduous life of adventure, war correspondence, writing, public appearances, broadcasting, and motion pictures had taken its toll, and he was ill, although not even his closest relatives knew the severity of his illness. As World War II approached, he recognized that he would feel obligated to cover it, and he even signed a contract with INS to go to Europe. When war broke out in September, however, he was too ill to go on the air for three fifteen-minute broadcasts on war developments each week. On Sunday, 24 September 1939, he died in his bedroom at his farm, where war maps covered the walls. After a life of danger and wandering, the fatal heart attack came in the old family bed in which he had been born fifty-two years before. His funeral mass was at Georgetown University with burial at Mount Olivet Cemetery in Washington, D.C.

A man of physical and moral courage who went for the story against any odds, Gibbons was noted for the clarity and empathy in his writings. His keen sense of humor and other personal qualities endeared him to both his readers and his listeners. He was not awed by greatness nor impressed by his own achievements. He always saw the dignity of the common man and sought to convey that dignity in his war reporting, his accounts of the Russian famine, and his stories of the Depression and the Bonus March; this was, perhaps, his greatest strength.

Biographies:

Douglas Gilbert, *Floyd Gibbons, Knight of the Air* (New York: McBride, 1930);

Edward Gibbons, *Floyd Gibbons, Your Headline Hunter* (New York: Exposition Press, 1953).

Morrill Goddard

(7 October 1865-1 July 1937)

James Boylan
University of Massachusetts, Amherst

MAJOR POSITIONS HELD: Sunday editor, *New York World* (1889-1896), *New York Journal*, renamed the *American* (1896-1922); editor, *American Magazine*, renamed *American Weekly* (1896-1937).

BOOK: *What Interests People—and Why* (New York: American Weekly, 1932).

Morrill Goddard's reputation as an editor rests largely on his innovations in the relatively brief period when he helped the leading New York newspaper impresarios of the 1890s, Joseph Pulitzer and William Randolph Hearst, create yellow journalism. Goddard's peculiar contribution to the sensational genre embraced bizarre pseudo-science, mildly risqué human interest features, and flamboyant, colorful graphics—the characteristics that came to be associated with the term *Sunday supplement*. Goddard spent his later career as a secure member of Hearst's high command, continuing to apply for forty years the formulas he had developed before the turn of the century.

Goddard almost obsessively avoided public attention. Late in life, he wrote to his college alumni magazine: "I have been most of my life printing facts and photos of famous and infamous persons, but it is my opinion that I do not belong in either category and thus do not qualify for extended notice or a portrait." It is unclear why he chose obscurity, but a Hearst biographer, John K. Winkler, to whom Goddard gave what may have been his only interview, concluded that the " 'greatest Sunday editor' looks upon his achievements with mingled feelings."

Goddard was born in Auburn, Maine, on 7 October 1865, to a Portland family. He was the third son and third child of seven born to Charles William and Rowena Caroline Morrill Goddard. His father was a lawyer and public official who had served as United States consul in Constantinople during the Civil War and eventually became a state judge. The Goddard side of the family traced its roots back to seventeenth-century Massachusetts; his mother was the daughter of a Maine governor of the 1850s.

After attending Portland public schools, Morrill Goddard was sent off to his father's alma mater, Bowdoin College. In the spring of his sophomore year, he was expelled for participating in the hazing of freshmen. He immediately transferred to Dartmouth. He was remembered there as a quiet, retiring undergraduate, who came out of his shell only to work on student publications. He was nineteen—the youngest member of the class of 1885—when he finished his studies. Without waiting to collect his diploma—and, it appears, to foil his father's plan to set him to studying law—Goddard left Hanover for New York City.

He immediately set out to win a position on the *World*, purchased and rehabilitated in the previous two years by Joseph Pulitzer and on its way to becoming one of the most prosperous newspapers ever published in America. A flagship of the new mass urban journalism, the *World* used energetic reporting and self-promotion to thrust itself ahead of the field. Goddard applied for a staff position, but was given only the cub's customary opportunity of developing stories on his own, to be paid only for what was printed. He shrewdly cultivated, with gifts of cigars and whiskey, the friendship of the peg-legged Civil War veteran who managed the city morgue. The resulting flow of stories so impressed managing editor Ballard Smith that within weeks Goddard was put on the staff.

His feats of aggression and intrusion as a reporter, strangely contrasting with his quiet personality, became legend. During the funeral procession of U. S. Grant in July 1885, he talked his way into a carriage near the front, where he could observe the Grant family's vehicle. He was able to interview an inaccessible papal delegate in Washington by memorizing questions in Latin. As a fellow native of Maine, he was able to get in to interview presidential candidate James G. Blaine at home; he then interviewed Blaine's kitchen servants for good measure. He was in the pack of reporters that pursued President Cleveland on his Maryland honeymoon in 1886. So impressed was Smith that Goddard, barely twenty-one, was made the city editor of the *World*.

Despite Goddard's affinity for handling hard news, Pulitzer decided to make him Sunday editor.

The Sunday edition had been a key ingredient in the prosperity of the *World*, and Pulitzer wanted to build it further. Goddard was reluctant at first, but he consented when he was empowered to hire his own artists and writers—a new departure in Sunday journalism and a recognition of the status of the Sunday paper. Goddard plunged into the job vigorously and extravagantly, so much so that he stirred opposition in other departments. In 1892 he received a summons from Pulitzer, who had been running the *World* from Paris since his sight had failed in 1890. Goddard underwent a cooling-off period in Paris of some weeks, but was eventually returned to New York with his position reaffirmed.

Granted new powers, he moved to expand the Sunday *World*. On Easter Sunday 1893, the tenth anniversary of Pulitzer's acquisition of the newspaper, Goddard printed an edition of 100 pages. When the *World* bought a new color press to illustrate women's fashions, Goddard persuaded the management to let him use it for comics, in which slightly off-register color would matter less than in fine illustration. Goddard hired Richard F. Outcault to do the drawings, and on 18 November 1894, the newspaper published what was evidently the first American newspaper color comic, the forerunner of the famous "Yellow Kid," which was also developed under Goddard's supervision.

Goddard was also developing his own style of sensationalism. He is credited in some texts with being the originator of the banner headline. His illustrations tended to be large, and his specialty was the cutaway drawing, showing, for example, human innards or the interior of a ship. On 13 October 1895, he created a stir with a story headed " 'The Girl in the Pie' at Three Thousand Five Hundred Dollar Dinner in Artist Breese's New York Studio." Beneath the headline was a page-wide drawing of a young woman, clad in gauze, emerging from a large basin on a table surrounded by ogling, respectable-looking men. Beneath the drawing was a long story that described the party and identified the guests (to their consternation).

This story caught the eye of William Randolph Hearst, who had just secretly bought a decrepit New York newspaper, the *Morning Journal*, and was shopping for talent. Not long after the publication of "The Girl in the Pie," Goddard got a message from Hearst; and in January 1896, by which time Hearst had come out into the open as owner of the *Journal*, he made a serious bid to hire away Goddard. Goddard resisted on two grounds—that Hearst might not last in New York and that he did not want to leave the staff he had built at the *World*.

The spendthrift Hearst met both objections. The first he answered by guaranteeing Goddard $35,000 a year. The second response was the most notorious theft of talent in the history of the American newspaper business—the hiring away of the entire *World* Sunday staff, except one secretary. Pulitzer bought back the staff with a higher bid, but within twenty-four hours, Hearst responded with a winning offer. Goddard and his staff left a thriving Sunday *World*, with a circulation of 450,000, for a Sunday *Journal* selling fewer than 100,000.

Goddard set about at once to make up the deficit. No longer restrained by Pulitzer's caution, Goddard had a free hand with the Sunday *Journal*. He was spurred further by competition with a former colleague, Arthur Brisbane, who then headed the Sunday *World* but who also ultimately joined Hearst. Goddard offered new twists of pseudoscience and pseudosex. His banners became famous:

MARS PEOPLED BY ONE VAST THINK-
ING VEGETABLE
MLLE. ANNA HELD RECEIVES ALAN
DALE, ATTIRED IN A 'NIGHTIE'
DOES MODERN PHOTOGRAPHY INCITE
WOMEN TO BRUTALITY?
A SOUTH SEA ADAMLESS EDEN WHERE
HUSBANDS ARE WELCOME

Such offerings, plentifully illustrated and supported by a minimum of documentation, helped drive up the Sunday *Journal*'s circulation to more than 435,000 before the end of 1896, although it was not able to hold that level. The paper became a hefty package, usually of eighty pages, including three color supplements—one for women, one for humor, and one, which was Goddard's specialty, called the *American Magazine*.

The *American Magazine*, which in 1916 was renamed the *American Weekly*, occupied Goddard for the rest of his life. Although he carried the title of Sunday editor of the *American* (as the *Journal* was renamed in 1901) until 1922, his duties centered increasingly on the magazine, especially after Hearst decided in 1911 to distribute it through all of his Sunday newspapers. This meant a circulation of 2,000,000, which became, by the time of Goddard's death, more than 5,000,000. The supplement also became a major money-maker for the Hearst organization when Arthur Kobler, another Hearst deputy, persuaded Hearst to let him sell advertising in it. It is said, however, that advertisers were unable to exert any influence over Goddard's choice of material.

Goddard's editing techniques did not change greatly with the passage of years. He distilled his philosophy in a series of presentations to *American Weekly* sales conferences from 1928 to 1931; these works were published in 1932 as: *What Interests People—and Why: Modern Miracles; Underneath the Veneer of Civilized Man; The Sixteen Elements of Universal Interest.* The philosophy was not complicated but expressed the credo of what Michael Schudson, in *Discovering the News* (1978), calls "story" journalism. Goddard wrote:

> If the imaginary doings of fictitious characters who never existed in real life, and who never really did any of the things the novelist portrays, are of interest—how much more gripping would be the interest if these novelists were able to make their stories narratives of the actual romances, intrigues, crimes or extraordinary exploits of genuine living human beings. . . .
>
> *The American Weekly* was the first to realize this, and was the originator of what has been called "true life stories."
> . . . .
> *The American Weekly* has been called sensational. The great events of history have been sensational. The great events which sell newspapers have, for the most part, been sensational. The great events of the Old Testament which stand out in our minds are sensational, and miracles performed by the Saviour were, every one of them, sensational.

Not until after Goddard's death were these principles seriously modified: after 1937, the *American Weekly* was reduced to tabloid size, much toned down, and slicked up. The Hearst organization terminated it in 1963.

Having cast his lot with Hearst at the age of thirty, Goddard made no major move thereafter. He turned down Pulitzer's effort to rehire him in 1901. Secure in his place in the Hearst organization, he turned his working life inward and avoided celebrity. He took no apparent part in professional journalism activities, nor did he collect any of the awards and degrees that customarily fall to aging editors. So intent was he on remaining out of sight that he is said to have destroyed the only two photographs taken of him.

His private life seems to have been that of a typical prosperous executive of his era. He was a member of a handful of scholarly or charitable organizations. He and his wife—Jessamine Rugg,

whom he had married in Hot Springs, Arkansas, in 1889—raised five children. As he aged, he began to ease off his load of responsibilities. His aide, Abraham Merritt, who succeeded him as editor, gradually became an alter ego who could put out issues of the *American Weekly* so much like Goddard's that Goddard said he could not tell the difference. Late in the 1920s, Goddard was negotiating to raise his salary from $3,000 to $5,000 a week, but he decided he would rather take three months a year off to pursue his chief recreation, yachting, and his salary stayed at $3,000. But he never retired, and it was during one of his summer leaves that he died of a heart attack at his vacation house at Naskeag Point, Maine.

Appraisals of Goddard's work have not been numerous. One appeared in *Tide*, a magazine of the advertising business: "To Goddard and his astonishing skill, the American Sunday newspaper is unendingly in debt, the magazine field along with it. He knew, possibly, with greater surety than any editor of his time, what interested people and why. On that knowledge he built a vast circulation and an enormously profitable property for Hearst. . . ." Frank Luther Mott, in *American Journalism* (1962), notes that Goddard has been called "the father of the American Sunday paper" and credits him with setting "the model for this type of journalism."

References:

Willard Grosvenor Bleyer, *Main Currents in the History of American Journalism* (Boston: Houghton Mifflin, 1927), pp. 357-371;

"Class of 1885" notes, *Dartmouth Alumni Magazine* (October 1937): 33-34;

William A. Hachten, "Sunday Magazines: End of an Era," *Columbia Journalism Review* (Summer 1963): 24-28;

Will Irwin, "The American Newspaper," *Collier's* (January-July 1911); reprinted by Iowa State University Press, 1969;

"Memoirs of a Great Editor" (reprinted from *Tide*), *Dartmouth Alumni Magazine* (October 1937): 13-14;

Frank Luther Mott, *American Journalism: A History: 1690-1960*, 3d ed. (New York: Macmillan, 1962);

Glen W. Peters, *"The American Weekly,"* *Journalism Quarterly*, 48 (Autumn 1971): 466;

W. A. Swanberg, *Pulitzer* (New York: Scribners, 1967), pp. 206, 216, 226, 279, 280;

John K. Winkler, *W. R. Hearst: An American Phenomenon* (New York: Simon & Schuster, 1928), pp. 103-109.

Charles H. Grasty
(3 March 1863-19 January 1924)

Daniel W. Pfaff
Pennsylvania State University

MAJOR POSITIONS HELD: Managing editor, *Kansas City Star* (1884-1889); publisher, *Baltimore Evening News* (1892-1908), *St. Paul Dispatch* and *St. Paul Pioneer Press* (1908-1909); president and general manager, *Baltimore Sunpapers* (1910-1914); war correspondent, *Kansas City Star* and Associated Press (1915-1916); treasurer, *New York Times* (1916-1917); special editorial correspondent, *New York Times* (1917-1924).

BOOK: *Flashes from the Front* (New York: Century, 1918).

Charles H. Grasty began and ended his forty-four years in newspapering doing what he considered the most important work in journalism—reporting. Had he done only that, he would be remembered at least for his correspondence from Europe for the Associated Press and the *New York Times* during World War I. He is a larger figure, though, chiefly because of his important influence upon journalism in Baltimore between 1892, when he became publisher and part owner of the *Evening News*, and 1914, when he stepped down as president and general manager of the *Baltimore Sunpapers*.

Charles Henry Grasty was born 3 March 1863 at Fincastle, Virginia, the son of a Presbyterian minister, the Reverend John Sharshall Grasty, and the former Ella Giles Pettus. The family moved to the small town of Mexico, Missouri, 100 miles northwest of St. Louis, when he was a small child. He was a precocious youngster, who taught Latin while he was in high school, then entered the University of Missouri to study law. The law lost out to journalism in 1880, however, after he took a summer reporting job paying $6 a week on the *Mexico Intelligencer* and chose not to return to the university. In 1882 his work caught the eye of William Rockhill Nelson, who offered him $7 a week to join the *Kansas City Star*. He did, and rose to managing editor in eighteen months. At twenty-one, he probably was the youngest managing editor in the country.

Nelson's fierce independence as a crusading newspaperman became the model for Grasty's career as an editor and publisher. He remained at

the *Star* until 1889. On 29 May of that year, he married Leota Tootle Perrin of St. Joseph, Missouri. In 1890 he became general manager of the *Manufacturers' Record*, a weekly business journal in Baltimore.

At the same time he became involved in business affairs by helping to find investors to develop Roland Park, a Baltimore suburb. By late 1891 he was eager to get back into daily journalism and was in a position to find backers to help him buy and revive the anemic *Baltimore Evening News*. He did so following principles he had learned in Kansas City, making the formerly Democratic paper militantly independent. It immediately came out against the powerful Gorman-Rasin Democratic machine that had long dominated Maryland politics. He also pledged to his backers that the *News* would fight the corruption in Baltimore government that often had been tolerated or ignored by the prosperous morning *Sun*, owned by the Abells. Grasty joined forces with the old Reform League of Baltimore, to which many influential Baltimoreans belonged, and held many of its conferences in his office. According to H. L. Mencken, "He was no aloof publisher like the Abells, with a distaste for personal political contacts and articulating only through his editorials." Instead "he was a warm, charming, friendly fellow, a grand companion, who loved to talk, liked his drink, and understood not only the newspaper game, but the game of politics, too. He comprehended the fact that fighting the machine was the soundest possible business policy for his newspaper, that the harder he fought the bosses and the worse the bosses hated him, the stronger his property became and the surer his prosperity." The result was that the *Sun* "was practically forced into fighting. Had it refrained, with the sort of impetus Grasty had then achieved, he might easily have emerged from the battle, even if he lost, the dominant newspaper figure in the field, with the strongest paper." Thus it was Grasty who got the credit for having "made a fighting force of the thousands of independent Democrats who were disgusted with the Gorman-Rasin regime." The machine began to fall apart in 1895 as voters in great numbers turned to Republican candidates.

The big losers were Arthur Pue Gorman, who lost the state senate seat from which he had dominated Maryland politics for years, and I. Freeman Rasin, Gorman's ally in control of Baltimore, who was defeated for city council. Republican Alcaeus Hooper was elected mayor of Baltimore, and Lloyd Lowndes became Maryand's first Republican governor since the Civil War.

Another of the *News*'s triumphs followed its charge in 1893 that several of the city's prominent Democratic politicians were involved in gambling schemes. In the resulting criminal libel suit the *News* was found not guilty, and gambling in Baltimore became much more covert, though it did not disappear. Years later, Grasty would credit this episode with establishing the power of the *News* in Baltimore. "The important thing journalistically, he always argued, is to assume the sound position and make a good fight. If that be done, you always win, no matter how badly you lose. No newspaper man ever believed more completely in this paradox than Grasty. It was one of the basic axioms in his newspaper creed," according to Mencken.

A challenge of another kind faced Grasty in the aftermath of the great Baltimore fire of 7 February 1904 in which a large part of the city, including the *News* plant, was destroyed. The *Washington Post* agreed to print the paper until Grasty could make other arrangements. He remembered that two years before, *New York Times* publisher Adolph S. Ochs had bought and combined the *Philadelphia Public Ledger* and *Philadelphia Times*, leaving the *Times* plant idle. Grasty went to New York and called Ochs: "Everything was destroyed down there," he said. "How about your *Philadelphia Times* plant?" With no hesitation, Ochs replied: "It's at your service." When Grasty inquired about the price, Ochs said, "Just take it. It's yours. Take it to Baltimore. If we can't agree on a price later, we'll leave it up to some third party. Don't let the details worry you." Within ten days the Philadelphia plant had been moved by train to a temporary building in Baltimore. It was to be powered by the boiler in an old Pennsylvania Railroad locomotive, an arrangement in which the pressmen had less than full confidence. Therefore, on the first day, the *News* was set in duplicate both in Baltimore and in Washington. The precaution proved unnecessary, and Grasty telegraphed the staff in Washington: "Tell Washington good-by and come home."

Grasty and the *News* did not always prevail. Perhaps his greatest reversal came in 1907, when the paper launched a crusade to replace incumbent governor Austin L. Crothers with the Republican challenger, George R. Gaither. More than any other battle he had been in, Grasty wanted to win this one, but Crothers was elected. Associates said this disappointment led to Grasty's sale of the *News* on 27 February 1908 to chain-maker Frank A. Munsey for $1,500,000—a sum that testified to the success of his management, and a move that took Baltimoreans by surprise. Part of the agreement with Munsey was that Grasty would become the general manager of all the Munsey newspapers. However, the two men discovered within a matter of weeks that they could not get along, and Grasty resigned.

Now a wealthy man, but not one accustomed to idleness, Grasty got back into newspapering in St. Paul, Minnesota, where in late 1908 he bought a half-interest in the evening *Dispatch*. Early the next year he bought the *St. Paul Pioneer Press*, which had both morning and evening editions, and combined its evening edition with the *Dispatch*. This gave his papers circulation leadership in both the morning and the evening, and Grasty made bold changes in the editorial operations of the newspapers as well. He insisted that both be fully independent of influence by stockholders and advertisers and that they be open to all points of view. "His individuality," said *Advertising Magazine* in September 1909, "is the dominating influence in the greatest change in newspaper policy ever known by the Northwest." The excitement, however, was short-lived. St. Paul was not as impressed as the writer of that magazine piece, and, sensing that his goals were not being realized, Grasty sold the papers back to the previous owners and took a vacation in Europe with his family.

There was another reason for leaving Minnesota. Grasty knew that there were some serious differences among the two brothers and their cousin—all descendants of founder Arunah S. Abell—who were partners in running the *Baltimore Sun*. He sensed an opportunity to gain control of the *Sun* and thereby get back into the midst of Baltimore and Maryland politics, in which he still had an intense interest. Even though he did not have enough money of his own to take over the *Sun*, he had no trouble finding nonpartisan backers in Baltimore. He had an offer of support from former Maryland governor Edwin Campbell, but he rejected it in order to avoid any direct association with political interests.

Grasty raised the necessary funds and established himself in full and absolute command of the newspaper. Under a somewhat complex stock-distribution and voting-rights agreement he became president with "full managerial and editorial control of the company." He could not be removed by a vote of the other stockholders, nor could his duties be redefined by them. The explanation of this extraordinary grant of power seems to lie mainly in the reputation and connections Grasty had built during his sixteen years in charge of the *Evening News* and his thorough understanding of the Baltimore scene. In short, the Abells were aware that if they did not let him take charge on his terms, they might well have him again as a competitor. They feared that he might buy back the *News* from Munsey, acquire one of two other Baltimore dailies, or even start a new paper. Once in charge at the *Sun*, Grasty saw to it that the other major stockholders—except Arunah S. Abell II and Charles S. Abell, whom he regarded as professional newspapermen—were kept in the dark about his plans for change until they were accomplished facts. He especially wanted to prevent any attempt by the nonprofessional stockholders to let business or advertiser interests influence editorial policies.

In a manner reminiscent of his St. Paul strategy, he quickly moved to dominate both morning and evening circulation in the city by buying the *Baltimore World* at auction in April 1910, for the astonishing price of $63,000. The *World* was a down-at-the-heels operation "worth, at most," wrote H. L. Mencken, "$10,000, including editorial equipment, bills receivable, United Press franchise, office cat and good-will." But Grasty wanted to establish an *Evening Sun* and feared there was truth to the rumor that William Randolph Hearst might buy the *World* and make it a dangerous evening competitor. Thus he felt he had no choice but to keep ahead of a bidder later discovered to have been planted by the *World*'s owners to run up the price.

In fact, the *Evening Sun* already faced a determined rival in Grasty's old newspaper, the *Evening News*. But because running that paper had been such a positive experience for him, he found the idea of getting back into the evening field irresistible. According to Mencken, his attraction to evening papers lay in "their rapid turnover of news and ideas. When a notion for an editorial occurred to him, he liked to write it down at once, and print it within a few hours, and see people reading it before the end of the day. And when there was exciting news afoot he liked to see it pass from the reporters' desks to the composing room, the pressroom and the street with all possible speed. Moreover, he was convinced, and with sound reason, that evening papers were destined to go ahead faster in the United States than morning papers, both in circulation and advertising."

Mencken was in an excellent position to know Grasty's thoughts on that subject because he was, as Mencken biographer William Manchester puts it, "chief workhorse" on the *Evening Sun*. His title was associate editor, but because the editor, John Haslup Adams, was in poor health, the bulk of the work of both jobs fell on his shoulders. Mencken, already a *Sun* employee when Grasty took over, had expected the new publisher to fire rather than promote him: four years earlier he had quit as Grasty's news editor on the *Evening News* after working for him for just six weeks. Grasty quickly let Mencken know he bore no lingering resentments; he wanted Mencken to stay because his experience on afternoon papers would be valuable in launching the *Evening Sun*.

He also thought—mistakenly, as it turned out—that the *Evening Sun* could instantly gain a solid circulation base by being forced upon subscribers to the morning and Sunday *Suns*. He began this effort on 18 April 1910, the day the *Evening Sun* first appeared, by setting a combination rate of ten cents a week for all three papers, just a penny more than for the morning and Sunday combination, and requiring all carrier subscribers to buy the package. But the subscribers balked. Thousands who wanted an evening paper made it clear that they preferred the *News*, and the package requirement was dropped within a month. For the remainder of Grasty's proprietorship, the *Evening Sun* struggled to sell half the number of papers sold by the morning *Sun*, whose circulation ranged between 80,000 and 91,600. But it often fell short of the mark and never made money while Grasty was in charge, though it did overtake the *News* in both circulation and advertising linage after he left.

Because he was inclined to behave like the personal journalists of the previous century, Grasty frequently was the subject of controversy. One of the most heated disputes erupted in 1911, when the *Evening Sun* and the *Evening News* took different sides on the then-developing Taft-Wilson-Roosevelt presidential campaign. Grasty's *Sun* was for Wilson; Munsey's *News* was for Roosevelt. Their political differences quickly deteriorated into a personal feud between Grasty and Munsey. Munsey charged that Grasty had returned to Baltimore in hopes of getting control of the *News* again at a bargain price and had violated a tacit agreement made at the time he sold the *News* to Munsey not to compete against it. Grasty denied this and argued that he had set up no new newspaper, since the *Evening Sun* was a reincarnation of the *World*. The tone in which the dispute was conducted is illustrated in this excerpt from an *Evening Sun* editorial: "On the whole, Mr. Grasty's return to Baltimore has been helpful to Mr. Munsey's interests by preventing him from transplanting to Baltimore the men and methods that have caused the failure of his newspaper enterprises elsewhere, and certainly the men in the *News* office have no reason to feel otherwise than gratified at the improved conditions since Mr. Grasty has come back into the Baltimore field."

Similarly, when the rival *American* suggested that Grasty expected an ambassadorship in return for the *Sunpapers'* support of Woodrow Wilson's nomination and election, he used the opportunity to respond with more bravado. Under the headline "The Sun Will Send No Bill to Governor Wilson for Services Rendered," he reproduced a letter he had written six weeks earlier to *New Orleans Item* editor James M. Thomson: "I do not think there is any office that you, or I, or any other earnest and intelligent editor can afford to accept. This is particularly and preeminently true in a case where an editor has been useful to a cause and his acceptance of an office would put him and his paper in the position of making a sordid swap of his support in return for office. But aside from that consideration, office means nothing to me. There is one thing in Maryland better worth doing than any other thing. That thing is the piloting of Maryland's great newspaper—*The Sun*." The statement clearly identified Grasty's sense of his role. His title was president and general manager of the A. S. Abell Company, but, as Mencken expressed it, "he was always the editor first and the publisher only afterward, and he was intensely jealous of every encroachment, however slight and indirect, upon the editorial freedom of his papers." It was for this reason that he maintained a wall of separation between editorial management and politicians, advertisers, stockholders, and even most of his associates in the operation of the company. As a result he made some lasting enemies, particularly among politicians. This was amply demonstrated when the *Sun* waged a bitter campaign against the election of machine-sponsored candidate James H. Preston for mayor. Preston and the machine arrayed against Grasty and the *Sun* all the enemies Grasty had made in his twenty-five years of militant journalism. After Preston was elected, he took every opportunity to strike back at the newspaper and its publisher. While he made many enemies, it also was true, as the *Sun* observed after his death, that "he also made many friends. In any gathering where he was he was the center. There was a sparkle and charm, an unexpectedness and appeal about him that few had.

More beautiful things could flash through his mind in a short time than most men have in a lifetime. One of his friends said about him years ago: 'Grasty can be the biggest man and the smallest boy of anyone I have ever known.' "

Grasty's determination to operate the papers so single-handedly from the editorial point of view caused several problems that proved to be beyond his ability to resolve. When it came to matters of advertising and circulation, he would have been wise to seek advice from persons in the company knowledgeable on those subjects. But he did not, fearing that this would compromise the papers' editorial independence. Instead he had established the *Evening Sun* and enlarged the Sunday *Sun* with virtually no business consultation. The result was a severe drain on profits. The morning paper continued to make money, but the *Evening Sun* especially, and to some extent the enlarged Sunday *Sun*, erased those gains and incurred growing indebtedness, despite slow gains in circulation. In mid-1914, with the company's deficit nearly $1,000,000, Grasty's fellow directors proposed that he retire from supervision of the company's business affairs. He did so, though under the agreement making him president he could have refused. He retained his title and complete control of the editorial department, but he quickly lost interest in continuing under the new arrangement. On 12 September 1914 he resigned as president and general manager, and on 30 November he resigned also as a director of the corporation. The *Sunpapers'* fortunes began to improve within a year, largely through the efforts of board chairman Harry C. Black, whom Mencken described as a more astute businessman as well as a man with an "essentially editorial point of view" who held to "most of the articles of the Grastian code."

Grasty had been vacationing in Europe when World War I erupted in the summer of 1914; he returned there in 1915 as a war correspondent for the *Kansas City Star* as well as for the Associated Press, of which he had been a director from 1900 to 1910. He came back to New York to serve for a short time in 1916 as treasurer of the *New York Times*, but he had little real interest in that and returned to Europe as a special editorial correspondent for the *Times*. Many of his dispatches were also printed in the *Sun* and other newspapers.

Grasty's was not battlefield reporting but behind-the-scenes detail and commentary on the military and diplomatic aspects of the war. He had access to and the confidence of a long list of important leaders, including American general John J.

Pershing, British prime minister David Lloyd George, French marshals Joseph Jacques Joffre and Ferdinand Foch, and many others. The interview with Foch, considered a "beat," was telegraphed around the world the day after it was printed in the *Times*. In it Grasty had asked the marshal the key question, "What is the chance of the Germans' being able to break through?" Then he described the reply: "General Foch, before answering, took a few whiffs from his 2-cent cigar and looked at me with a smile of quiet confidence in his bright brown eyes. 'They won't break through,' he said, and the words were as percussive as pistol shots." In the same interview, Foch urged America's entry into the war: "Don't lose half a minute," he said.

Leaders other reporters considered "interview proof" would speak readily to Grasty, partly out of respect for his ability, partly because they were sure he could be trusted not to reveal certain details given him in confidence. Because of this, while Grasty was in Europe Americans undoubtedly learned more about the war and its aftermath than could have been possible otherwise. The *Sun* observed on his death that "he was probably the best-informed journalist in Europe and none had higher standing or reputation." A book containing some of his best World War I reporting and commentary was published in 1918 as *Flashes from the Front*. He remained in Europe after the war as a roving correspondent for the *Times*, writing "when and what he pleased." He spent the rest of his life in that job, returning to the United States for only a few weeks each year. He died in London at the age of sixty; he was survived by his wife and stepdaughter.

On the day following his death, an editorial in the *Sun* described Grasty as the "apt pupil" of Joseph Pulitzer and William Rockhill Nelson, both of whom "had faults, and some of them were very serious ones. . . . But from one fault, at least, both of them were free; neither knew how to bend the knee, neither ever truckled to any man or group of men, high or low." Grasty, the editorial said, carried the same trait to Baltimore:

> He introduced into the journalism of this town, then extraordinarily flabby and old-fashioned, all the devices of enterprise that

Nelson had invented. He detached the *Evening News* from every tie of party; he augmented its circulation by putting fresh and lively news into it; he got a sturdy vigor into its editorial utterances; he employed its growing power in a courageous and relentless war upon every sort of political corruption. The politicians then in harness squirmed beneath his strokes, and some of them tried to meet him with reprisals, legal and otherwise. But he stood out against them in a truly magnificent fashion, and before he sold the *News* many of the worst were disposed of and almost forgotten and the survivors had learned a caution that has never abated since. Probably no citizen of Baltimore ever performed greater public services. Our municipal government today, whatever its defects, is at least a hundred times as honest, intelligent and efficient as it was in 1892. For that change we may thank Charles H. Grasty more than we may thank any other man. . . .

In the end he took service with the New York *Times*—service that relieved the old hardy skipper from duties on the bridge and made him a comfortable passenger in the cabin. He did good work in that new role, but it was not as dramatic, not as arduous, and above all not as important as the work of his youth. His monument belongs in Baltimore, not in New York or in London, where he served the *Times* so long. He left an indelible mark upon journalism here, and he left a no less indelible mark upon municipal history. He changed our newspapers and he changed our politics, and both changes were for the better.

References:

Baltimore Sun, 20 January 1924, pp. 4, 6, 16;

Meyer Berger, *The Story of the New York Times 1851-1951* (New York: Simon & Schuster, 1951), pp. 142-143;

Gerald W. Johnson, Frank R. Kent, H. L. Mencken, and Hamilton Owens, *The Sunpapers of Baltimore* (New York: Knopf, 1937), pp. 285-339;

William Manchester, *The Sage of Baltimore* (London: Melrose, 1952), pp. 56-61;

New York Times, 20 January 1924, p. 9.

William Randolph Hearst

Stephen Vaughn
University of Wisconsin, Madison

BIRTH: San Francisco, California, 29 April 1863, to George and Phoebe Elizabeth Apperson Hearst.

EDUCATION: Harvard University, 1882-1885.

MARRIAGE: 28 April 1903 to Millicent Willson; children: George Randolph, William Randolph, Jr., John Randolph, Elbert Willson, Randolph Apperson.

NEWSPAPERS OWNED: *San Francisco Examiner* (1887-1951); *New York Journal*, renamed *American and Journal*, then *American* in 1901 (1895-1937); *New York Evening Journal*, renamed *American and Journal*, then *Journal* in 1901, renamed *Journal-American* in 1937 (1896-1951); *Chicago American*, merged to form *Herald-American* in 1939 (1900-1951); *Chicago Examiner*, merged to form *Herald-Examiner* in 1918 (1902-1939); *Boston American* (1904-1951); *Los Angeles Examiner* (1904-1951); *San Francisco Call*, merged to form *Call-Bulletin* in 1929 (1913-1951); *Boston Daily Advertiser* (1917-1951); *Washington Times* (1919-1937); *Wisconsin News* (Milwaukee) (1919-1937); *Boston Record* (1920-1951); *Detroit Times* (1921-1951); *Los Angeles Herald*, merged to form *Herald-Express* in 1931 (1922-1951); *Seattle Post-Intelligencer* (1922-1951); *Washington Herald* (1922-1937); *Rochester Journal* (1922-1937); *Oakland Post-Enquirer* (1922-1950); *Syracuse Telegram*, merged to form *Journal Telegram* in 1925 (1922-1939); *Baltimore News*, merged to form *News-Post* in 1934 (1923-1951); *Baltimore American* (1923-1951); *Fort Worth Record* (1923-1925); *Albany Times-Union* (1924-1951); *San Antonio Light* (1924-1951); *Milwaukee Sentinel* (1924-1951); *New York Daily Mirror* (1924-1951); *Pittsburgh Sun-Telegraph* (1927-1951); *Pittsburgh Post-Gazette* (1927-1937); *Omaha News-Bee* (1928-1937).

MAGAZINES OWNED: *California Orchard and Farm*, renamed *Orchard and Farm* in 1897 (1888-1922); *International Studio,* merged into *Connoisseur* in 1931 (1897-1931); *Motor* (1903-1951); *Cosmopolitan* (1905-1951); *Motor Boating* (1908-1951); *Pall Mall* (England), renamed *Nash's and Pall Mall* in 1914, *Nash's* in 1927, *New Nash's and Pall Mall* in

William Randolph Hearst

1935, merged into *Good Housekeeping* in 1937 (1910-1937); *Good Housekeeping* (1911-1951); *The World Today*, renamed *Hearst's Magazine* in 1912, *Hearst's* in 1914, and *Hearst's International* in 1921, merged into *Cosmopolitan* in 1925 (1911-1925); *Harper's Bazaar* (1912-1951); *Puck* (1917-1918); *Good Housekeeping* (England) (1922-1951); *Smart Set* (1924-1928); *Town and Country* (1925-1951); *McClure's* (1926-1928); *American Druggist* (1927-1951); *Connoisseur* (England) (1927-1951); *Home and Field* (1929-1933); *Harper's Bazaar* (England) (1929-1951); *American Architect* (1929-1938); *House Beautiful* (1933-1951); *Pictorial Review* (1934-1939).

OTHER NEWS ENTERPRISES OWNED: Hearst News Service, International News Service, Universal Service, King Features, Newspaper Feature Service, Premier Syndicate, International Film Service, International News Reel Corporation.

AWARDS AND HONORS: LL.D., Oglethorpe University, 1927.

DEATH: Beverly Hills, California, 14 August 1951.

BOOKS: *Editorials from the Hearst Newspapers* (New York: Hearst's International Library, 1914);
Let Us Promote the World's Peace (New York: McConnell, 1915);
The Obligations and Opportunities of the United States in Mexico and in the Philippines (New York: Allied Printing Trades Council, 1916);
Truths about the Trusts (Rahway, N.J.: Privately printed, 1916);
On the Foreign War Debts (N.p., 1931);
Selections from the Writings and Speeches of William Randolph Hearst, edited by E. F. Tompkins (San Francisco: Privately printed, 1948);
William Randolph Hearst: A Portrait in His Own Words, edited by Edmond D. Coblentz (New York: Simon & Schuster, 1952).

William Randolph Hearst presided over one of the great financial and communications empires in American history. Truly one of the giants of the publishing industry, he did not confine his interests and influence to journalism alone. He was fascinated with politics and aspired to political office, dreaming of nothing less than occupying the White House. Hearst was a curious personality—a combination of Dr. Jekyll and Mr. Hyde, as one biographer put it—and his legacy for American journalism and history is, at best, mixed.

The Hearst fortune may not have been as large as those of the Rockefellers, the Mellons, or the Fords, but it was large enough, with assets totaling at one time between $200,000,000 and $400,000,000. The name Hearst, of course, is identified with newspapers, and Hearst during one period owned more than a score of them. But the empire involved much more: there were magazines; radio stations; mines; ranches; New York City hotels and real estate; motion picture companies; one of the world's great private collections of art and antiques; and castles, the most stunning of which was San Simeon, overlooking the Pacific. In 1935, before the Great Depression threatened to destroy this empire, *Fortune* magazine estimated that Hearst employed 31,000 people with an annual payroll of $57,000,000. Almost 100 executives were paid $25,000 or more a year and a

few made more than $100,000. Even after the Depression sheared away a sizable part of the organization, Hearst in the last years of his life still ruled over King Features, which had 52,000,000 readers, the largest feature service in the United States. In addition, he controlled the Sunday supplement *American Weekly*, which, with its circulation of nearly 10,000,000, was the most widely read magazine in the country; the Independent News Service (INS); radio stations in Baltimore, Pittsburgh, and Milwaukee, with television applications pending in those cities; eight magazines including *Cosmopolitan*, *Harper's Bazaar*, and *Good Housekeeping*, which brought in revenues of $50,000,000 annually; and sixteen large urban daily newspapers with a combined circulation of over 5,000,000.

Hearst was born 29 April 1863 and named after his paternal and maternal grandfathers. He grew up in a privileged and overly protected environment. His father, George, was an amiable man who became a multimillionaire by speculating in land and by investing in such lucrative mining enterprises as the Ontario, the Anaconda, and the Homestake. He also had political ambitions and served in the California legislature, made an unsuccessful bid for the California governorship, and eventually gained national prominence as a United States senator. George Hearst did not marry until he was forty, when he took a bride, Phoebe Elizabeth Apperson, who was twenty-two years his junior. The strong-willed Phoebe became a formidable figure in her own right and achieved national attention for gifts to educational institutions and poor students. Phoebe was a nominal Presbyterian, her husband a nominal Episcopalian; apparently the Hearst family was not deeply religious, and William Randolph was never baptized. The relationship between the father and mother was not an entirely happy one, in part because George took up with another woman. The marriage remained an uneasy truce, and Phoebe's affections were consequently focused on her only child.

Hearst's personality remains an enigma. Some contend that his emotional stability was permanently crippled by the excessive pampering from his mother and by the fact that his relationships with adults during his early years were largely with women. There was a soft, almost feminine side to Hearst, and he had a great capacity for sentiment and sympathy. He was painfully shy and found speaking in public to be a great struggle. He could be sincere and compassionate yet he possessed a large, compulsive ego and an apparently deep need to manipulate others. He dreamed great dreams

William Randolph Hearst's parents, George and Phoebe Hearst (Brown Brothers)

and had a monumental urge toward sensation and showmanship. He was an aggressive man who possessed a great talent for getting what he wanted.

Hearst's penchant for showmanship and his interest in journalism revealed themselves early. He entered Harvard in the fall of 1882 and was later described by one of his classmates as a young fellow of "amiable indolence" whose inactivity was occasionally "broken by spasms of energy." Although he frequently showed more enthusiasm for practical jokes than for serious work, in his second year he did become business manager of the *Harvard Lampoon*, a job formerly held by his friend Eugene Lent. The *Lampoon* had been a financial drain, and it was the business manager's plight to make up the losses out of his own pocket. Because Hearst received a large allowance from his father he seemed a logical replacement for Lent. Upon assuming the position he immediately launched an aggressive circulation campaign and sought out advertising, and the publication soon began to show a profit.

Harvard suspended Hearst at the end of his junior year, in part because of a series of practical jokes played on professors and others. On one occa-sion he sent chamber pots to his instructors with their names inscribed in the bottom. Another time he purchased a jackass and corralled it in a professor's home with a sign reading "Now there are two of you."

While suspension from Harvard might have been traumatic for most young men, it is probably safe to assume that it hardly fazed Hearst, who turned his attention to his real interest: running a newspaper. His father had purchased the *San Francisco Examiner* in October 1880, not so much because he was interested in journalism—he was scarcely literate—but rather to use the paper as an organ to further his political fortunes. William's first interest in newspapers may have come from his visits to the offices of the *Examiner*. His work for the *Lampoon* further stimulated his curiosity about the San Francisco paper, which came to him regularly while he was at Harvard. In Hearst's opinion the *Examiner* was in poor shape financially and was edited badly because of his father's journalistic amateurishness. Hearst followed the Boston and New York dailies carefully and was especially enthusiastic about the *Boston Globe* and Joseph

Pulitzer's *New York World*. He made numerous visits to the *Globe* after receiving a letter of introduction to *Globe* publisher Col. Charles H. Taylor, and during what should have been his senior year at Harvard, he went to work as a reporter for the *World*. Pulitzer's publication fascinated him because it combined sensationalism and idealism and was aimed at the masses. In just three years Pulitzer had raised its circulation from 15,000 to a quarter of a million.

Hearst wrote a long letter explaining how the *Examiner* might be improved and convinced his father to subscribe to the *New York Herald*'s telegraph service, thus broadening the San Francisco paper's coverage. George Hearst was not enthusiastic about the idea of his son forging a career in journalism; but the paper had lost a quarter-million dollars, and in early 1887 he was in Washington preparing to enter his first full Senate term. He therefore yielded to his son's wishes and turned the *Examiner* over to the young man, who was not yet twenty-four.

Hearst probably envisioned himself as the Pulitzer of the West Coast. He vowed to increase

Hearst performing in an amateur theatrical for the Hasty Pudding Club at Harvard

circulation while at the same time launching the paper on a campaign to purify California. Like Pulitzer, he tried to hire the best talent available and soon Arthur McEwen, William H. Hart, Edward "Pop" Hamilton, and Ambrose Bierce were on the Hearst payroll. In addition to the money invested in large salaries, he also bought expensive new presses from New York. If the paper did not immediately become a money-maker, at least its circulation and advertising picked up dramatically. Under Hearst the *Examiner* launched several crusades, including an effort to defeat a new city charter which would have strengthened boss control in San Francisco. Hearst also battled for lower water rates. Of perhaps greater long-term significance, he began a sustained drive against the powerful Southern Pacific Railroad and the moguls behind it, including Collis P. Huntington and Leland Stanford. Delighting in such endeavors, Hearst apparently saw journalism, as his correspondent James Creelman later remarked, as "an enchanted playground in which giants and dragons were to be slain simply for the fun of the thing."

Hearst embarked on an almost endless series of efforts to enliven the *Examiner*. Certainly he covered the news in a grand manner: for example, he dispatched a chartered train to report on a disastrous fire at the Hotel Del Monte in Monterey. Often, where news did not exist it was created: in early 1888 he took half of his staff to Washington to put out a special edition of the *Examiner* urging that the Democratic national convention be held in San Francisco that summer. His was "a childlike dream world," writes one of his biographers, "imagining wonderful stories and then going out and creating them." Other observers were less kind. The *North American Review* referred to Hearst's work as "a blazing disgrace to the craft." Will Irwin remarked that in the Hearst press "the music of the spheres became a screech." Oswald Garrison Villard likened the coverage found in Hearst papers to "gathering garbage from the gutters of life." Hearst writer Arthur James Pegler said that "a Hearst newspaper is like a screaming woman running down the street with her throat cut."

Still, despite the increase in circulation, the *Examiner* lost nearly $300,000 during the first couple of years under its new owner. This amount was more than had been lost in the previous seven years when the paper had been under the elder Hearst's control. George Hearst became reluctant to support his son further, and upon his death in 1891 he left not a penny to William, giving everything instead to Phoebe. But Phoebe soon sold her

The offices of the San Francisco Examiner, *which were destroyed in the 1906 earthquake (Bancroft Library, University of California)*

seven-sixteenths interest in the Anaconda Copper Mining Company to the Rothschilds of London for $7,500,000 and turned the money over to her son, so Hearst was hardly destitute.

When Hearst began to think of expanding beyond the West Coast, he almost instinctively turned toward New York, the stronghold of Joseph Pulitzer. Several papers in that city were available for sale, including the *Times*, the *Advertiser*, and the *Recorder*, but Hearst settled for the less expensive *Morning Journal*, a scandal sheet founded by Pulitzer's brother, Albert, in 1882. Albert had sold this paper in 1894 for $1,000,000 to John R. McLean, publisher of the *Cincinnati Enquirer*, a publication which also specialized in the sensational. Although McLean tried to breathe life back into the *Morning Journal*, it lost so much money that he offered Hearst a half interest for $360,000. Hearst finally obtained the entire paper for half that amount, together with the German-language *Das Morgen Journal*, which was thrown in for good measure. With *Morning* dropped from the title, the

Journal first appeared under its new owner's direction on 7 November 1895.

Within a year the *Journal* had become one of the city's major papers, second only to the *World*. Hearst brought with him from San Francisco some of his best people, including the *Examiner*'s managing editor, Samuel Chamberlain; McEwen and Winifred Black also came. Hearst hired such outstanding literary figures as Stephen Crane, Bob Davis, and Julian Hawthorne to be feature writers. Gus Dirks and others in the art department created such immortal comic strips as the "Katzenjammer Kids," "Foxy Grandpa," "Alphonse and Gaston," and "Happy Hooligan." George Pancoast, who came from San Francisco, developed a color press from which emerged the Sunday comic section. By the end of 1895 the *Journal*'s circulation neared 100,000, and in early November of the following year—the day after the presidential election—the paper printed a record 1,500,000 copies. In September 1896, Hearst put out his first late-afternoon paper, the *Evening Journal*, and the next year purchased the *New York Morning Advertiser* to obtain its Associated Press franchise.

This open warfare infuriated Pulitzer, who heard himself denounced by Hearst as an editor who dealt in "bogus news" and pandered "to the worst tastes of the prurient and horror-loving." Taking note of Pulitzer's own tactics some years earlier, Hearst raided the *World*'s staff, taking away some of its best people, including Arthur Brisbane, Richard Outcault, Morrill Goddard, and Solomon Solis Carvalho.

The competition between Hearst and Pulitzer took on international significance in the events leading up to and surrounding the Spanish-American War. Hearst is still regarded by many to have been the single most important factor behind the United States' entry into this brief but important military engagement. In the late nineteenth century, Americans became increasingly interested in developments beyond their national boundaries; the mass media often stimulated this interest. By the time William McKinley entered the White House in 1897, presidents had begun to realize, if only intuitively, that they had to pay close attention to public opinion and that policy decisions often required the persuasion or control of opinion. McKinley was one of the first chief executives who tried to deal with the press and opinion in a calculated way. How successful he was in this regard remains a matter of debate among historians: most writers have assumed that the jingoism of the Hearst and Pulitzer presses overwhelmed McKinley and pushed the

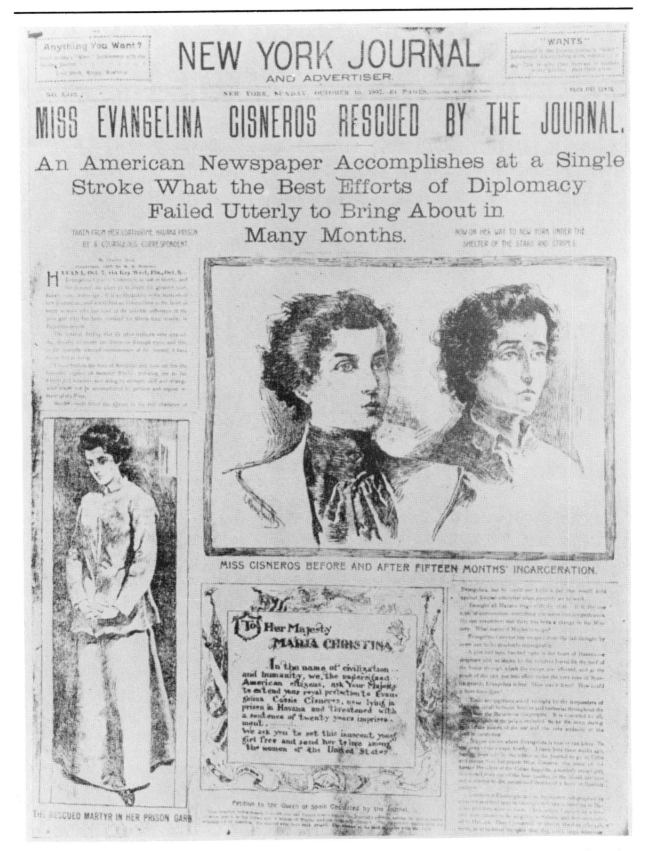

Front page of Hearst's New York Journal, *10 October 1897: an example of the sensationalistic reporting that inflamed American sentiments before the Spanish-American War*

United States into the Spanish-American War; but more recently, Robert Hilderbrand has suggested in *Power and the People* (1981) that McKinley had greater control over events than hitherto suspected. Whatever the strength of McKinley's leadership, Hearst's actions during the Cuban revolution and the subsequent war revealed how powerful and dangerous an irresponsible press can become.

It is simplistic to argue that Hearst, Pulitzer, and yellow journalism caused the Spanish-American War; the causes are more varied and complex. Spain's empire in the New World had been crumbling for decades and the Cubans were restive, especially after the American tariff of 1894 placed higher duties on Cuban sugar. The tariff contributed to the extreme economic hardship on the island, and the following year a rebellion broke out against the Spanish authorities.

The Cuban revolution came as a boon for Hearst in his circulation battle with Pulitzer. There were marvelous opportunities for an editor who was not afraid to play fast and loose with the truth. It has been said of Hearst that he "snooped, scooped, and stooped to conquer" his New York rival. The *Journal* presented the war in stark terms of good versus evil. In reality, however, neither side in this struggle had a monopoly on ruthlessness. The insurgents, for example, carried out a scorched-earth policy in the hope that either the Spanish would withdraw or the Americans, who had nearly $50,000,000 invested in Cuba, would come in.

When the pace of events slowed and it appeared that there might be no large-scale fighting, Hearst did not hesitate to take action. When artist Frederic Remington, who had been sent to Cuba to draw pictures of the fighting, reported that everything seemed quiet and war unlikely, Hearst reputedly cabled back: "You furnish the pictures and I'll furnish the war." After three Cuban women were searched by Spanish authorities—albeit by female authorities—on a ship flying the American flag, the *Journal* ran a story under the headline "Does Our Flag Protect Women?" Accompanying the story was an illustration showing three male Spanish officials undressing a woman.

Hearst papers displayed a special interest in the plight of Evangelina Cisneros, a young Cuban woman who was apparently implicated in the revolt but who had been imprisoned, the *Journal* claimed, merely because she tried to protect her honor from a Spanish officer. Hearst embarked on a crusade to "Enlist the women of America" in the Cuban girl's behalf; a petition was circulated that obtained 20,000 signatures, including those of Mrs. Mark Hanna; Mrs. John Sherman, the wife of the secretary of state; and Mrs. Nancy McKinley. So moved was Jefferson Davis's widow that she signed an appeal to the queen regent of Spain asking that she save Miss Cisneros "from a fate worse than death." When interest in the case was at its peak a Hearst reporter, acting under orders, aided Senorita Cisneros's escape and smuggled her into the United States. The *Journal* ran headlines saying "An American Newspaper Accomplishes at a Single Stroke What the Best Efforts of Diplomacy Failed Utterly To Bring About in Many Months." Miss Cisneros was given an enormous reception, first at Madison Square Garden and then in Washington, where she met the president. One state governor suggested that Hearst might wish to send 500 reporters to Cuba to emancipate the entire island.

The *Journal* proved adept at using atrocity stories, a staple of nearly all war propaganda. The paper publicized the activities of Spanish general Valeriano Weyler—or "Butcher" or "Wolf" Weyler, as he was better known in the United States. This "human hyena," this "mad dog," massacred prisoners, dragging the sick and wounded from their beds to be executed, pausing only long enough to feed their bodies to the dogs and sharks. "It is not only Weyler the soldier" that was the problem, the *Journal* contended, "but Weyler the brute, the devastator of haciendas, the destroyer of families, and the outrager of women. . . . Pitiless, cold, an exterminator of men. . . . There is nothing to prevent his carnal, animal brain from running riot with itself in inventing tortures and infamies of bloody debauchery."

Both Hearst and Pulitzer worked to turn the turmoil in Cuba into a crisis of international proportions. Both editors emphasized incidents in which American property was destroyed in that country but ignored the fact that Cuban rebels were responsible for much of the destruction. The American public seemingly had an insatiable appetite for such fare, and during 1898 Hearst and Pulitzer sold 800,000 newspapers daily, their influence extending far beyond New York as many smaller editors around the country patterned their copy on that of the *Journal* and the *World*. Not every publisher was impressed, though. E. L. Godkin of the *New York Evening Post* wrote that "Nothing so disgraceful as the behavior of these two newspapers . . . has ever been known in the history of journalism."

Despite the energetic efforts of Hearst and Pulitzer to keep Cuba front and center stage, public interest shifted in 1896 to William Jennings Bryan's rousing presidential campaign against McKinley and to the Turkish massacres in Armenia. The Republican McKinley entered the White House in early 1897. Later that year a more liberal Spanish ministry came to power and recalled Weyler, moderated its policies in Cuba, emptied its prisons of American citizens, and took steps toward granting Cuban autonomy. When Spanish sympathizers (known as "loyalists") rioted and appeared to endanger American lives in January 1898, McKinley dispatched the battleship *Maine* to Cuba.

Meanwhile, the *Journal* managed to gain possession of an indiscreet private letter written by the Spanish minister in Washington, Dupuy de Lôme. In the letter de Lôme revealed bad faith in his dealings with the United States on an impending commercial matter and referred to the American president as "weak and a bidder for admiration of the crowd." Although de Lôme resigned, the incident inflamed American opinion.

The clamor over de Lôme had hardly died when an even more sensational story broke on 15 February 1898—perhaps the biggest news event since President James Garfield's assassination in 1881: a tremendous explosion sank the *Maine* and killed 250 men in Havana harbor. To this day no one is certain why the *Maine* blew up: the Spanish government, already beset with problems, hardly wanted to give the United States an excuse for entering the war on the side of the rebels. Such reasoning, however, made little impression on Hearst, whose headlines proclaimed that "THE WARSHIP MAINE WAS SPLIT IN TWO BY AN ENEMY'S SECRET INFERNAL MACHINE"; "THE WHOLE COUNTRY THRILLS WITH WAR FEVER." A few days later the *Journal* declared that "Intervention is a plain and imperative duty."

Hearst spent nearly a half-million dollars and even covered the war in person. Altogether, approximately 500 representatives of the press were in Cuba—more than the entire number that covered the Civil War over four years. Hearst, along with about twenty photographers, writers, and artists from his *Journal* staff, were in the vanguard. Hearst chartered a tramp steamer on which he operated a small printing plant. A special edition of the *Journal* originated from this ship. Hearst and his staff were involved in several engagements; on one occasion the publisher led a foray onto a beach where twenty-six Spanish sailors were captured. On another occasion, James Creelman, a veteran correspondent for the *Journal*, led a successful assault on the fort at El Caney. Wounded in the attempt,

Creelman was taken to the rear where he looked up to see Hearst, replete with revolver, straw hat, and pen and notebook, waiting to take down Creelman's story.

This war forced Pulitzer to draw on his financial reserves as never before, and he ultimately withdrew from his battle with Hearst. Thus left to his own devices, Hearst began to create a vast newspaper chain. The *Evening Journal* became simply the *Journal* after 1901, while the morning paper's name was changed to the *American*. To these papers and the *Examiner* in San Francisco, Hearst in 1900 added morning and evening papers in Chicago, the *Examiner* and *American*. In Boston, four years later, he founded the evening *American*. These six papers formed the nucleus of the Hearst chain.

Hearst sensed, as did many other journalists in the late nineteenth and early twentieth centuries, that the press was "the greatest force in civilization" and that under a republican government it formed as well as expressed public opinion. Newspapers, in Hearst's view, controlled the nation because they represented the people. They could "suggest and control legislation, . . . declare war, [and] punish criminals, especially the powerful," while rewarding with "approving publicity the good deeds of citizens everywhere." What some writers have found disturbing about Hearst is that in addition to understanding the press's power, he was also a consummate showman. Newspapers were for Hearst not merely instruments of information designed to inform the public. "Putting out a newspaper without promotion," he once said, "is like winking at a girl in the dark—well-intentioned but ineffective." His papers, as biographer W. A. Swanberg has written, "were not newspapers at all. They were printed entertainment and excitement—the equivalent in newsprint of bombs exploding, bands blaring, firecrackers popping, victims screaming, flags waving, cannons roaring, houris dancing, and smoke rising from the singed flesh of executed criminals." Hearst believed that "the public is more fond of entertainment than it is of information," and this was his credo throughout his life.

Hearst's attitude toward the press is also alarming because he was apparently never content merely to publish newspapers. He had strong political ambitions, and in fact his ultimate goal was to become president. His political career provides an interesting odyssey. He began as a champion of progressive causes in the late nineteenth and early twentieth centuries and played an important part in liberalizing the Democratic party. Although he was never underprivileged, he considered himself and his papers to be the champion of the underdog. The *Journal* and the *Examiner* had a crusading, muck-raking quality in the years around the turn of the century. Editorials attacked "criminal" corporations and sided with organized labor, writers produced exposés on packing houses, and the papers supported a range of reforms, including woman suffrage, municipal ownership of utilities, federal income taxes, direct election of United States senators, and the eight-hour day. These were popular causes in many quarters during the Progressive Era, to be sure, but there is reason to believe that Hearst was sincere about such reforms even though he became increasingly conservative in later years.

Critics have contended that Hearst was never overly concerned with principle, since his position on issues shifted so frequently. The perception of him as an unprincipled egoist who would stop at nothing to further his own ends was an image he never fully overcame, despite his abilities in propaganda, advertising, and showmanship. There were other liabilities, too, for a man who aspired to high political office. He was painfully shy and had a deep-seated fear of public speaking, a problem compounded by a high-pitched voice which did not project well in a time before public address systems. Ambrose Bierce called it "a voice like the fragrance of violets made audible." Through sheer determination and good coaching, however, Hearst largely overcame this handicap and became a competent orator.

He sought several political offices. He ran twice for Congress, twice for New York City mayor, and once for the New York governorship. His real objective, though, was to become president of the United States; and with his powerful publishing empire behind him, he came closest to that goal in 1904, when he placed second in the balloting for the nomination at the Democratic convention.

Hearst had first sought the vice-presidency, hoping to run with William Jennings Bryan in 1900. He had supported Bryan in 1896 when many other Democratic papers had bolted the party, partly from fear of free silver. But the problem remained of how a relative newcomer to politics, one who had had little practical experience, could rise in the party. In May 1900, Hearst struck a bargain. The Democrats realized that if they were to win in November they would need a publication in Chicago. Hearst agreed to publish a Chicago paper in return for being elected president of the National Association of Democratic Clubs. With Bryan's blessing, on 2 July Hearst began publishing the

Chicago American. When the Democrats convened for their convention in Kansas City two days later, the *American* was distributed among the delegates. To Hearst's dismay, however, the Great Commoner selected Adlai Stevenson of Illinois as his running mate. Bryan ran on a platform that year opposing imperialism, demanding free silver, and calling for control of the trusts. Hearst opposed two-thirds of this program, favoring only the regulation of trusts, but he remained silent.

When Bryan's bid for the White House was defeated for the second time in 1900, Hearst's attention turned to 1904. He had powerful tools at his disposal with his expanding chain of newspapers, which began to publicize the Hearst name as never before. "W. R. Hearst" appeared on the front-page flags and on the mastheads of the newspapers, and an increasing number of news stories focused on Hearst as well. As Moses Koenigsberg later observed, Hearst sought to expand his newspaper empire and yearned "for the ownership of a newspaper in every advantageous center in America." By fulfilling this ambition, he hoped to command the passage of any program he favored, in addition to installing himself in the White House. The presidency of the National Association of Democratic Clubs was a powerful post, too, with 3,000,000 members, most of whom were influential in persuading voters, in 12,000 clubs nationwide.

The assassination of President McKinley in September 1901 was a serious setback for Hearst. The Hearst papers had been scathing in their criticism of the president, and this abuse had reached a point in February where Ambrose Bierce, following the assassination of Governor Goebel of Kentucky, had written: "The bullet that pierced Goebel's breast/ Can not be found in all the West;/Good reason, it is speeding here/ To stretch McKinley on his bier." A few weeks later the *Journal* had printed an editorial which said in part that "if bad institutions and bad men can be got rid of only by killing, then the killing must be done." The public therefore reacted violently when word circulated that McKinley's assassin, the young, self-proclaimed anarchist Leon F. Czolgosz, carried a copy of the *Journal* in his pocket. For a time the paper was boycotted by many libraries, businesses, clubs, and patriotic organizations, as well as by some newsstands. Hearst was hanged in effigy on more than one occasion.

Hearst was able to overcome this episode, and within less than a year he was a candidate for the United States Congress. He knew that it would be good to hold some lesser position before driving for

Hearst, with arm raised, making a speech during his unsuccessful campaign for mayor of New York City in 1904 (Brown Brothers)

the presidency in 1904. Hearst probably really wanted the nomination for New York governor, but with the aid of Charles Francis Murphy and Tammany Hall, he secured the nomination for Congress and easily won election, outpolling his Republican opponent by three to one. The victory was marred, though, when a celebration at Madison Square Garden ended in tragedy after fireworks exploded prematurely, killing eighteen and injuring scores more. Lawsuits from this unfortunate incident followed Hearst for decades.

In Congress, Hearst favored controlling the trusts and ending secret rebates by railroads. He wanted government ownership of railroads, telegraphs, and mines. He was for the eight-hour work day and the graduated income tax, as well as the direct election of United States senators. He strongly supported improvement of public schools, which perhaps reflected his mother's influence. In foreign affairs, he favored a navy second to none and wanted either a Nicaraguan or Panamanian canal. Yet Hearst during this time was obsessed with the presidency and he was frequently absent from Congress, making few if any speeches in the House. What influence he did exercise usually occurred behind the scenes as the leader of about a half-

dozen representatives known as the "Hearst Brigade." Through them he introduced such progressive measures as an amendment to the Sherman Antitrust Act, which would have strengthened its power to investigate the railroad-coal trust, and an amendment to increase the Interstate Commerce Commission's power to fix railway rates. Hearst by this time had powerful enemies in Washington, and almost anything he proposed, however worthy, met strong opposition.

Hearst faced considerable opposition from both Republicans and conservative Democrats by 1904, not only in Washington but in his home state as well. The boss of Tammany Hall, Murphy, favored Alton B. Parker for the presidency and the state Democratic leader, David B. Hill, supported Grover Cleveland. The *New York Post*, Hearst's old enemy, opposed him, saying: "It is not simply that we revolt at Hearst's huge vulgarity; at his front of bronze; at his shrieking unfitness mentally, for the office which he sets out to buy. All this goes without saying. There never has been a case of a man of such slender intellectual equipment, absolutely without experience in office, impudently flaunting his wealth before the eyes of the people and saying, 'Make me President.' This is folly."

Parker and Hearst, nevertheless, emerged as the two front-runners for the nomination. Delphin M. Delmas, a San Francisco attorney and longtime supporter of the family, placed Hearst's name in nomination; Clarence Darrow seconded it. Bryan, however, obviously disapproved of the Hearst candidacy. Hearst received 263 convention votes, considerably short of the number needed for nomination. This convention was the closest Hearst came to occupying the White House, although he remained a force in American politics throughout most of his life. The ambition of becoming president died hard, however, and he remained obsessed with the dream for many years.

Hearst continued to believe that he could win the nomination in 1908, but he realized that he was politically weak in the East and he therefore laid plans to win the governorship of New York. But first he was reelected to Congress in 1904, running ahead of Parker and the Democratic ticket in his district. The following year he ran for mayor of New York City under the banner of the Municipal Ownership League and lost by less than 4,000 votes to the Democrat, George B. McClellan, Jr., placing well ahead of the Republican candidate, William H. Ivins. The loss did not substantially damage Hearst's political fortunes; in fact, he may even have emerged stronger. He had, after all, run without a party and against Tammany Hall and had only narrowly been defeated. Moreover, by this time he had developed a slashing campaign style, overcoming his earlier problems as a speaker. He therefore loomed as a power to be considered in the upcoming governor's race.

The Republican candidate for governor in 1906 was Charles Evans Hughes, fresh from his much-publicized participation in the New York insurance fraud investigations. The campaign for governor was hard-fought and bitter. Theodore Roosevelt sent his secretary of state, Elihu Root, to New York to campaign against Hearst. Root's presence may have been decisive, as he assailed Hearst's character and, perhaps more damaging, revived the charge that Hearst bore responsibility for McKinley's death. Hearst lost the election by 58,000 votes, the only Democrat on the ticket to be defeated. Just as quickly as Hearst's political star had risen, it had now fallen. For all practical purposes his political career was at an end. He did run for mayor again in 1909 but lost decisively and was defeated the following year in a race for lieutenant governor. He finally renounced his political ambitions, which may have cost him nearly $2,000,000. In 1912, the year

of the three-way race between Woodrow Wilson, Theodore Roosevelt, and William Howard Taft, Hearst supported his old friend Champ Clark for the Democratic nomination.

The outbreak of war in Europe in 1914 launched the world into a new era and Hearst into more controversy. During the war Hearst was accused of being sympathetic to the German cause, the most damaging of accusations at that time for a man who still deep down aspired to political office. It is probably more accurate to say that Hearst was "anti-British" rather than "pro-German"; but whatever the truth, he reaped enormous criticism and unpopularity.

Hearst and his papers had not always been accused of being pro-German. During the Spanish-American War he had talked of fighting when a German admiral had insulted Admiral Dewey at Manila Bay. Although Hearst's ancestry was British, he was suspicious of the English and believed they had outsmarted the Americans at every turn. As early as 1896 the Hearst press had criticized Britain in the Venezuela-British Guiana boundary dispute. The first Hay-Paunceforte treaty, which prohibited fortification of the Panama Canal, outraged Hearst. He distrusted American bankers who made loans to the Allies, believing that such loans made neutrality impossible. He apparently was concerned about "foreign entanglements" and deeply worried about the "yellow peril," fearing that as soon as the United States was preoccupied in Europe the Japanese would attempt to take advantage of the situation. Hearst was thinking about Mexico, too, because he and his mother had nearly $4,000,000 in oil, ranch, timber, and mining holdings there. Since the exile of Porfirio Díaz in 1911, the country had been in chaos; and in 1916, when Gen. John J. Pershing pursued Pancho Villa into Mexico, Hearst applauded enthusiastically, writing: "Our flag should wave over Mexico as the symbol of the rehabilitation of that unhappy country and its redemption to 'humanity'. . . . " He pictured Mexico as a potential ally of the Japanese against the United States.

The obsession with Japan and Mexico culminated in a motion picture. Hearst's International Film Service started work in 1915 on a fifteen-part film, *Patria*, a "serial romance of society and preparedness" starring Irene Castle and featuring Warner Oland; the story concerned a Japanese-Mexican plot to overthrow the United States. The first episode was released to the public in January 1917 by Pathé, which recently had become the outlet for Hearst pictures. The film was explicit in its attack on a country supposedly friendly to the United States. It accused the Japanese of perpetrating the explosion of U.S. munitions stores on Black Tom Island, New Jersey, in July 1916 and of inciting labor violence. In a later episode the film showed the Japanese invading the United States from Mexican soil. The picture played to full houses across the country. It deeply offended Japanese Ambassador Hanrihara; many people, including Canadian censor Ernest Chambers and American writer Samuel Hopkins Adams, speculated that the film was part of a German plot to stir up anti-Japanese sentiment in America. President Wilson, upset after seeing it, insisted that everything derogatory to the Japanese be deleted, and the film was held up by state and federal authorities while changes were made. Eventually, the film was allowed to run after all of the characters were given Mexican names, even though they continued to wear Japanese uniforms.

Hearst's warm support of the Irish, including Sir Roger Casement, the Irish patriot who was executed for conspiring with the Germans, antagonized the British. In October 1916, British Prime Minister Lloyd George denied the International News Service, started by Hearst in 1909, access to the country's mail and cable facilities. Less than three weeks later the French government instituted similar measures. In early November the Hearst papers were banned in Canada; henceforth anyone found reading them was subject to a $5,000 fine or five years in prison.

Hearst, who believed the Germans likely to win the war, attempted to counter the massive Allied propaganda campaign in the United States. As support for the Allies grew into hysteria, Hearst's popularity declined. The *New York Tribune* began a weekly series called "COIL IN THE FLAG— HEARS-S-S-T" condemning Hearst's alleged "pro-Germanism." By 1918, the anti-Hearst uproar had cut into profits as well as into the Hearst image. Antagonism was so great, for example, that Oregon citizens burned Hearst papers while singing "Keep the Home Fires Burning," and so loudly was the Hearst name booed in some movie houses that Hearst-Pathé News was shortened simply to Pathé News. After the armistice, the Hearst papers launched a campaign attempting to show what Hearst had done to help America win the war. New York City Mayor John F. Hylan infuriated many people when he appointed Hearst chairman of a committee charged with welcoming home return-

Hearst and his wife, Millicent Willson Hearst, at the time of their marriage in 1903 (Culver Pictures)

ing soldiers, and a Senate judiciary committee investigating German and Bolshevik propaganda during the war began looking into Hearst's wartime activities.

Hearst had married a former Broadway dancer, Millicent Willson, in 1903, and their first son, George, had been born the following year. William Randolph, Jr., was born in 1908; John Randolph was born in 1910; and twin boys, Elbert Willson (who later changed his name to David Whitmire Hearst) and Randolph Apperson, were born in late 1915. Hearst's mother, Phoebe, died on 13 April 1919, one of the many thousands of victims of the influenza epidemic which swept western Europe and the United States. She was a remarkable woman, who had given some $21,000,000 to philanthropic and educational causes. Her son inherited her $11,000,000 estate.

However unpopular the Great War made Hearst, his empire continued to expand. By 1919 he owned twelve newspapers across the country, including the *Boston Daily Advertiser*, the *Washington*

Times, the *Chicago Herald*, the *Wisconsin News* (Milwaukee), and the *San Francisco Call*. Four years later he could claim twenty-two dailies with a total circulation of over 3,000,000 and fifteen Sunday papers with a circulation of better than 3,500,000. In addition, by 1923 he owned nine magazines—two in England and seven in the United States, including *Cosmopolitan, Good Housekeeping, Hearst's International*, and *Harper's Bazaar*—with a total circulation of more than 2,700,000. It has been estimated that one out of every four American families read a Hearst publication. Certainly it was an expensive operation, costing over $90,000,000 a year. The Hearst organization was probably the biggest single user of paper in the world: it took thirty-two tons of paper to turn out a single page of all the daily newspapers. More than 38,000 people were on the Hearst payroll.

Hearst retained the loyalty of his subordinates through a combination of compassion and cruelty. He paid his executives enormous salaries, far greater than they could receive anywhere else. Men like Brisbane and Goddard became wealthy in their own right working for Hearst. Brisbane earned more than a quarter-million dollars a year near the end of his career and left an estate estimated at $25,000,000. There are numerous stories of Hearst workers who had suffered bad luck or fallen on hard times who were generously aided by their employer. Yet Hearst had a brutal side: with salaries in excess of $100,000 waiting for those who made it to the top, the competition was fierce, and Hearst relished and encouraged the tension it created. An employee who reached the top knew that he would remain there only so long as he was able to please Hearst. One could tell where a worker fit into the Hearst hierarchy by how he addressed the boss. At the lower echelons one called him simply "Mr. Hearst"; at a higher level he was addressed as "Chief"; and at the very top a very small circle of friends and workers such as Brisbane, Chamberlain, and a few others referred to him as "W. R." His wife and mother may have called him "Will" or "Bill"; no one else did.

By the 1920s Hearst's empire, which had been increased by his mother's bequest, included mines; a burgeoning collection of antiques and art objects purchased both in America and abroad; millions of dollars invested in New York real estate; and ranches, the most impressive of which was San Simeon, an estate between Los Angeles and San Francisco which, at 270,000 acres, was nearly as big as Rhode Island. Hearst, it is said, spent nearly $40,000,000 on this estate, and no other private

Hearst's castle at his estate, San Simeon, California (Robert E. Waltz–Blackstar)

residence in the United States could rival it. Filled with art treasures, it had four large buildings (one for the owner and three for guests), a private zoo, two swimming pools, and a private railroad. Hearst also owned castles on Long Island and in Wales, a townhouse in New York City, and a Bavarian village in the mountains of northern California.

Early in the post-World War I period Hearst increased attention to his motion picture holdings, properties which previously had interested him only sporadically. Much of his interest was undoubtedly stimulated by a young chorus girl, Marion Davies (whose real name was Marion Cecilia Douras), whom he had first met in 1917. Hearst respected the idea of fidelity and was against sin in the abstract, but he was also a romantic who had a healthy lust for life. The relationship with Miss Davies, which began during the war, lasted for more than three decades. It was by no means Hearst's first controversial liaison: his affair with Tessie Powers had raised eyebrows many years before he had married. Hearst labored mightily to make Miss Davies into the country's biggest screen star, sparing no expense in training her and promoting her in his publications. Hearst wanted to marry Miss Davies,

Hearst's longtime companion, actress Marion Davies, reaching for the brass ring at the publisher's seventy-fifth birthday party in 1938. The party was held under a circus tent at Hearst's Santa Monica beach house. (Courtesy of Ken Murray, The Golden Days of San Simeon)

but his wife refused to grant a divorce. Eventually an understanding was reached: the Hearsts officially remained married, raised their children, and appeared together at political and social functions. But the marriage was a pretense, although the couple remained on friendly terms.

Politically Hearst was still powerful well into the postwar period. As late as 1920 he considered making another run for the presidency or at least the governorship of New York. But he managed only one vote at the Democratic convention in San Francisco that year as another editor, James M. Cox from Ohio, was nominated. Hearst eventually supported the Republican Warren Harding for president even though he disliked Harding's platform; he also backed Al Smith for New York governor. Both Harding and Smith were victorious. Hearst was still a powerful political boss, even if he was not universally loved. With three newspapers in California he had great influence in that state; he was strong in Chicago, where his friend William Hale Thompson was mayor; and through Mayor Hylan he was able to move New York City Hall. Moreover, he had the respect of such important political leaders as James Reed and Hiram Johnson.

In Al Smith, Hearst found a formidable opponent, one who would ultimately shatter whatever remaining dreams for high office he might have

had. The Smith-Hearst quarrel dated back to before the Great War. When Hearst had sought the governorship in 1918, it was Smith who had won the nomination; Hearst had swallowed hard and supported Smith, no doubt helping him to a narrow victory. But the Hearst papers had soon begun to criticize Smith's record, and the attack had reached a fevered level in 1919 when a milk producer's strike cut the flow of milk into New York City. The *American* and the *Journal* had published material inferring that Smith's part in the affair had caused the deaths of slum children. Outraged by what he considered irresponsible and grossly unfair charges, Smith had challenged Hearst to a public debate. Hearst had refused, and his attack on Smith had backfired as Smith's response won widespread public approval. In a clash between New York State's two most powerful Democrats, Smith had emerged the winner.

In 1922, Hearst, still hoping to be governor, let it be known that he would concede that office to Smith if Smith would agree to support Hearst for the senatorial nomination. A Smith-Hearst ticket appeared potentially strong in terms of money and publicity. But Smith refused to have anything to do with Hearst, and in a showdown he was backed by the party regulars. Hearst supported Smith in the fall, but his hatred for Smith ran deep and hurt Smith's later political career.

Hearst was a bundle of contradictions given to bewildering political shifts. Critics always suspected that he would willingly sacrifice principle for political power and would resort to whatever methods were needed to obtain his goals. When he had been younger he had espoused progressive ideas and championed liberal causes. But in the postwar years he became increasingly conservative, and liberals eventually became disillusioned with him. Both the public and the politicians who had once supported him turned away.

Hearst's growing conservatism, which was reflected in his newspapers, became evident in several ways during the 1920s and 1930s. An early advocate of the graduated income tax, he opposed it at every turn once it became a reality. He admired Calvin Coolidge, agreed with his opposition to the Boston police strike, and was grateful for the president's reluctance to spend federal funds. Hearst was an even more ardent admirer of Coolidge's secretary of the treasury, Andrew Mellon. A fellow art collector who, like Hearst, had large property holdings in Mexico, Mellon managed to cut the taxes on large incomes, gifts, and inheritances. His policies probably saved Hearst hundreds of thousands, if not millions, of dollars. Indeed, when Coolidge let it be known that he would not run for reelection in 1928, Hearst supported Mellon for president.

Hearst also opposed the unionization of newspaper workers. Although Section 7A of the National Industrial Recovery Act of 1933 guaranteed workers the right to bargain collectively without employer interference, the American Newspaper Guild's effort to organize workers encountered stiff resistance from Hearst, who in the early 1930s was the nation's most powerful publisher, controlling thirteen percent of the daily press circulation. Hearst publicly maintained that as professionals, newsmen could not be paid on a union scale, since the differences in ability required that a publisher deal with each on an individual basis. Besides, Hearst contended, unionization would take the romance out of newspaper work. Hearst's motives in taking this posture are difficult to discern, but he probably was serious about professionalism and romance; money does not seem to have been uppermost. Many of his papers were incurring deficits at this time, which were paid by his mining and ranching operations. Hearst no doubt also saw the press as a means to maintain power over public opinion, and unionization seemed to threaten that power.

Proving that an employee had been dismissed because of his union work was often difficult. Intimidation or the threat of dismissal was sufficient to bring most workers into line, and there were relatively few dismissals from the upper echelons of the Hearst organization. The Newspaper Guild did challenge some firings in the Hearst camp, however, such as those of Louis Burgess, an editorial writer on the *San Francisco Examiner*, and Dean Jennings, a rewrite man on the *San Francisco Call-Bulletin*. Although the National Labor Relations Board found in Jennings's behalf, its decision was overturned by President Franklin D. Roosevelt's executive order in early 1935.

Many writers speculate that the reason Roosevelt supported Hearst in the Jennings case was to repay a political debt incurred during the 1932 Democratic convention. Hearst had still had political clout in 1932 and had used it to influence the outcome of the convention in FDR's behalf. Hearst had hoped that Hoover would step aside for Coolidge in 1932; but when it became apparent that Hoover would be renominated, Hearst went back to the Democrats and threw his support to Speaker John Nance Garner of Texas, with whom he had served in Congress. At the convention Garner ran a distant third in the balloting behind Roosevelt and

behind Hearst's bitter enemy, Al Smith, but Garner controlled forty-two delegates from Texas and forty-four from California. Ultimately Hearst persuaded Garner to throw his support to Roosevelt; and thus did he influence the selection of the Democratic nominee, the election of the president, and the course of the nation.

Actually, FDR's motives in the Jennings case were more complex than merely repaying a political debt: publishers were threatening to resign en masse from the NRA in 1935 if he did not help Hearst. Roosevelt was shrewd enough to realize that their support might be critical for his beleaguered program.

A direct strike was called against the Hearst organization in 1936 in Milwaukee, where the guild sought recognition as the bargaining agent for the editorial workers at the *Wisconsin News*. They hoped to obtain a contract for minimum salaries and a forty-hour week for the writers. An anti-Hearst boycott in the city took several forms and met with limited success. Even though this walkout gathered nationwide publicity and support, the strikers were unable to gain all their demands and accepted a compromise in August. Guild members voted to affiliate themselves with the AFL, and further negotiations were conducted by the local and state AFL units rather than directly between the Hearst management and the guild. The *Wisconsin News* eventually announced pay raises and a forty-hour week unilaterally, although the Hearst organization was not required to enter into a contract. Another strike against the Hearst operation took place in Seattle after the dismissal of photographer Frank Lynch and drama critic Everhardt Armstrong. Occurring in late July 1936, it further broadened support for the guild and hardened Hearst's antiunion image. Hearst's actions probably contributed to the guild's emergence as one of the most militant of the white-collar unions.

Hearst eventually became one of the strongest critics of New Deal domestic and foreign policy and supported Alf Landon in 1936 and Wendell Willkie in 1940. Many contend that he became a supporter of fascism in the 1930s. He did in the beginning apparently see hope in Adolf Hitler, stating in 1934 that "if Hitler succeeds in pointing the way of peace and order . . . he will have accomplished a measure of good not only for his own people but for all of humanity." During a trip to Germany that year he interviewed Hitler and was photographed with Dr. Alfred Rosenberg and other Nazis. At home in California, he occasionally dined at San Simeon with such right-wing figures as Father Coughlin. By the 1930s Hearst had become strongly anticommunist and his papers launched a vigorous anti-Red campaign. He strongly opposed Upton Sinclair's efforts to become governor of California, assailing him as a communist. Swanberg believes that had Hearst been presented with a choice between fascism and communism he would have chosen the former, but that he preferred above all else what he perceived as traditional American democracy. During the 1930s Hearst was a capitalist whose empire was tottering, who had lost faith in Roosevelt, and who saw his country mired in depression; the future seemed uncertain and collapse appeared possible. But Hearst was also repelled by fascism's brutality and totalitarianism; his admiration for Hitler was never unqualified, as his editorial attacks against fascism in Italy and Germany indicate.

Hearst's criticisms of Roosevelt's foreign policy are noteworthy and have been subject to misconceptions. He is often regarded as one of the country's leading isolationists, but his views on foreign policy during the 1930s and early 1940s were more complicated. He was anticommunist and militantly nationalistic. He held deep-seated suspicions about the British and French, and especially about the Russians and the Japanese. Hearst frequently made reference to George Washington and Thomas Jefferson and used much of the language employed by the isolationists of the 1930s, but many of his ideas could hardly be characterized as isolationist. He believed that the United States should play a strong role in Latin America; he advocated strengthening American air power and the merchant marine in order to maintain military preparedness; and in the late 1930s he consistently supported FDR's defense expenditures, even though they were opposed by other isolationists and pacifists.

Hearst's position on foreign policy as enunciated in his editorials between 1936 and 1941 resembled not so much the isolationists, according to historian Rodney Carlisle, as the bipartisan "internationalist" foreign policy of the post-World War II period. Hearst was convinced that the real threat to America lay not in Europe but across the Pacific, primarily from the Soviet Union and to a lesser extent from Japan. He favored a strong deterrent

(Left to right) Joseph Cotten, Orson Welles, and Everett Sloane in a scene from Welles's 1941 film Citizen Kane, *loosely based on Hearst's life. Hearst's lawyers and his Hollywood columnist, Louella Parsons, tried unsuccessfully to have the film suppressed.*

force which would include universal military training, a revitalized navy and air force, and the creation of new weapons and technology. He thought that the United States should avoid limiting its ability to take unilateral action in foreign affairs; thus, he opposed doing anything which would support the Versailles Treaty or the League of Nations or, for that matter, which would threaten Germany. He accepted Hitler's view of the Versailles Treaty as unfair and he believed that nazism offered a barrier to communism. He was critical of Nazi excesses, but thought that the United States should offer advice and otherwise stay out of German affairs. He was unenthusiastic about aiding Great Britain or France, believing that neither was democratic, the former being characterized by aristocracy and monarchy and the latter by socialist and communist tendencies. Finally, he urged that a careful watch be kept on both the Soviet Union and Japan.

Although remaining critical of many of Roosevelt's policies and supporting Willkie in the 1940 campaign, Hearst nevertheless endorsed FDR's request for more defense spending in the spring of 1940, and the following year he approved of Roosevelt's call for the creation of a mutual de-

fense system for the Western Hemisphere. After the attack on Pearl Harbor, Hearst's opposition to war disappeared and he patriotically supported American victory. In his advocacy of military preparedness to turn back aggression, in his belief that the Soviet Union was America's major potential enemy, in his strong anticommunism, in his opposition to French and British overseas empires, and in his willingness to work with the Germans to oppose the Soviets, Hearst's position was remarkably like the views of American foreign policymakers in the 1950s and 1960s.

Hearst's empire was brought near collapse during the Depression. Always a compulsive buyer, he had purchased an enormous volume of art objects and antiques at inflated prices; he had also invested heavily in New York real estate, whose value plunged in the 1930s. By 1937 the Hearst organization's debt approached $126,000,000 and there were fears that bankruptcy could not be avoided. Hearst relinquished financial control of his publishing enterprises to longtime friend Clarence Shearn (with Hearst retaining technical editorial control), who began closing down papers that were losing heavily. Those which fell under the ax

Hearst in 1941

included the *New York American* and *Sunday American* and the *Rochester Journal*. The *Washington Herald* was leased to Cissy Patterson. In addition, Hearst was forced to sell much of his art treasure as well as to drop his movie enterprise in Hollywood. The latter was especially painful because Hearst's hope of making his companion, Miss Davies, a star of the first magnitude was never quite fulfilled. Ironically, Hearst had to borrow $1,000,000 from Miss Davies, whose financial situation was for a time better than his. Perhaps the low point was reached when Hearst, unable to pay the mortgage on San Simeon, discovered that it was his longtime enemy Harry Chandler who held the note. In 1933, Hearst had borrowed $600,000 from a Los Angeles bank and put San Simeon up for security, unaware that Chandler, the publisher of the *Los Angeles Times*, was a stockholder in the bank and the one who had put up the cash personally. Fortunately for Hearst, no one apparently wanted San Simeon and Chandler extended the loan. In another irony of this period, it was the Second World War, which Hearst had so ardently hoped America would avoid, that saved his publishing empire. Circulation and advertising rose, and the organization was revived.

During the postwar years Hearst's health declined. He developed a serious heart condition and was forced to move from the remote San Simeon to a smaller home in Beverly Hills. There, an invalid, he spent his last years and died on 14 August 1951. In illness and in death Hearst received accolades he had never obtained earlier. Among the honorary pallbearers at his funeral were Herbert Hoover, Gen. Douglas MacArthur, Bernard Baruch, Gov. Earl Warren, John Nance Garner, and Arthur Hays Sulzberger.

Hearst's will, 125 typewritten pages, distributed a personal estate of almost $60,000,000. In the will, the Hearst sons became trustees of three trusts. One trust gave Mrs. Hearst $1,500,000 cash and $6,000,000 in Hearst Corporation preferred stock. A second trust gave the Hearst sons 100 shares of Hearst Corporation voting stock and sufficient preferred stock to guarantee a $150,000 return annually. A third trust gave money for various educational and charitable purposes.

Without question, Hearst was one of the most powerful Americans of his generation, and his legacy is still difficult to assess. Surely his unrestrained sensationalism must weigh heavily against his positive accomplishments. With a publishing empire virtually unrivaled, he aspired to the White House and on at least one occasion came reasonably close to obtaining his goal. The American public, how-ever, aware of his many flaws, wisely rejected him. He was a man of tremendous vigor, industry, intelligence, and wealth, and he might have been one of the truly great men of this century had those qualities been matched by a greater sense of integrity and a firmer commitment to principle.

Biographies:

Oliver Carlson and Ernest Sutherland Bates, *Hearst: Lord of San Simeon* (Westport, Conn.: Greenwood Press, 1936);

Ferdinand Lundberg, *Imperial Hearst: A Social Biography* (New York: Equinox Cooperative Press, 1936);

Mrs. Fremont Older, *William Randolph Hearst, American* (New York: Appleton-Century, 1936);

John Tebbel, *The Life and Good Times of William Randolph Hearst* (New York: Dutton, 1952);

John K. Winkler, *William Randolph Hearst: A New Appraisal* (New York: Hastings House, 1955);

W. A. Swanberg, *Citizen Hearst: A Biography of William Randolph Hearst* (New York: Scribners, 1961);

Lindsay Chaney and Michael Cieply, *The Hearsts: Family and Empire–The Later Years* (New York: Simon & Schuster, 1981).

References:

Rodney P. Carlisle, "The Foreign Policy Views of an Isolationist Press Lord: W. R. Hearst and the International Crisis, 1936-1941," *Journal of Contemporary History*, 9 (July 1974): 217-227;

Carlisle, *Hearst and the New Deal: The Progressive as Reactionary* (New York: Garland, 1979);

Carlisle, "William Randolph Hearst's Reaction to the American Newspaper Guild: A Challenge to New Deal Labor Legislation," *Labor History*, 10 (Winter 1969): 74-99;

Wilber Cross, "The Perils of Evangelina," *American Heritage*, 19 (February 1968): 104-107;

Robert C. Hilderbrand, *Power and the People: Executive Management of Public Opinion in Foreign Affairs, 1897-1921* (Chapel Hill: University of North Carolina Press, 1981);

Roy Everett Littlefield III, *William Randolph Hearst: His Role in American Progressivism* (Washington, D.C.: University Press of America, 1980);

Frank Luther Mott, *A History of American Magazines: Volume IV: 1885-1905* (Cambridge: Harvard University Press, 1957), pp. 491-505;

Theodore Peterson, *Magazines in the Twentieth Century* (Urbana: University of Illinois Press, 1964);

David Sarasohn, "Power Without Glory: Hearst in the Progressive Era," *Journalism Quarterly*, 53 (Autumn 1976): 474-482;

Kenneth Stewart and John Tebbel, *Makers of Modern Journalism* (New York: Prentice-Hall, 1952), pp. 103-120.

Papers:

The William Randolph Hearst papers, and other collections pertaining to the family, are housed in the Bancroft Library of the University of California, Berkeley.

Ben Hecht

(28 February 1894-18 April 1964)

A. J. Kaul
Western Kentucky University

See also the Hecht entries in *DLB 7, Twentieth-Century American Dramatists*, and *DLB 9, American Novelists, 1910-1945.*

MAJOR POSITIONS HELD: Reporter, *Chicago Journal* (1910-1914); reporter, foreign correspondent, columnist, *Chicago Daily News* (1914-1923); columnist, *PM* (1940-1941).

SELECTED BOOKS: *The Wonder Hat*, by Hecht and Kenneth S. Goodman (New York: Shay, 1920);

The Hero of Santa Maria, by Hecht and Goodman (New York: Shay, 1920);

Erik Dorn (New York & London: Putnam's, 1921);

1001 Afternoons in Chicago (Chicago: Covici McGee, 1922);

Gargoyles (New York: Boni & Liveright, 1922);

Fantazius Mallare: A Mysterious Oath (Chicago: Covici McGee, 1922);

The Florentine Dagger: A Novel for Amateur Detectives (New York: Boni & Liveright, 1923; London: Heinemann, 1924);

Cutie, A Warm Mamma, by Hecht and Maxwell Bodenheim (Chicago: Hechtshaw, 1924);

Humpty Dumpty (New York: Boni & Liveright, 1924);

Broken Necks and Other Stories (Girard, Kans.: Haldeman-Julius, 1924);

Tales of Chicago Streets (Girard, Kans.: Haldeman-Julius, 1924);

The Kingdom of Evil: A Continuation of the Journal of Fantazius Mallare (Chicago: Covici, 1924);

The Wonder Hat and Other One-Act Plays, by Hecht and Goodman (New York & London: Appleton, 1925);

Broken Necks (Chicago: Covici, 1926);

Count Bruga (New York: Boni & Liveright, 1926);

Infatuation, and Other Stories of Love's Misfits (Girard, Kans.: Haldeman-Julius, 1927);

Jazz, and Other Stories of Young Love (Girard, Kans.: Haldeman-Julius, 1927);

The Unlovely Sin and Other Stories of Desire's Pawns (Girard, Kans: Haldeman-Julius, 1927);

Christmas Eve (New York: Covici Friede, 1928);

The Front Page, by Hecht and Charles MacArthur (New York: Covici Friede, 1928; London: Richards & Toulmin, 1929);

The Champion from Far Away (New York: Covici Friede, 1931);

A Jew in Love (New York: Covici Friede, 1931);

The Great Magoo, by Hecht and Gene Fowler (New York: Covici Friede, 1933);

Actor's Blood (New York: Covici Friede, 1936);

To Quito and Back (New York: Covici Friede, 1937);

A Book of Miracles (New York: Viking, 1939; London: Nicholson & Watson, 1940);

Ladies and Gentlemen, by Hecht and MacArthur (New York, Los Angeles & London: French, 1941);

Fun to Be Free, Patriotic Pageant, by Hecht and MacArthur (New York: Dramatists Play Service, 1941);

1001 Afternoons in New York (New York: Viking, 1941);

Miracle in the Rain (New York: Knopf, 1943);

A Guide for the Bedevilled (New York: Scribners, 1944);

I Hate Actors! (New York: Crown, 1944);

The Collected Stories of Ben Hecht (New York: Crown, 1945);

A Flag Is Born (New York: American League for a

Ben Hecht (Culver Pictures)

Free Palestine, 1946);

A Child of the Century (New York: Simon & Schuster, 1954);

Charlie: The Improbable Life and Times of Charles MacArthur (New York: Harper, 1957);

The Sensualists (New York: Messner, 1959);

Perfidy (New York: Messner, 1961);

Gaily, Gaily (Garden City: Doubleday, 1963);

Letters from Bohemia (Garden City: Doubleday, 1964).

SELECTED PLAYS: *The Wonder Hat*, by Hecht and Kenneth S. Goodman, 1916, Arts and Crafts Theatre, Detroit;

The Hero of Santa Maria, by Hecht and Goodman, 12 February 1917, Comedy Theatre, New York;

The Egotist, 25 December 1922, Thirty-ninth Street Theatre, New York;

The Front Page, by Hecht and Charles MacArthur,

14 August 1928, Times Square Theatre, New York;

The Great Magoo, by Hecht and Gene Fowler, 2 December 1932, Selwyn Theatre, New York;

Twentieth Century, by Hecht and MacArthur, 29 December 1932, Broadhurst Theatre, New York;

Jumbo, by Hecht and MacArthur, 16 November 1935, Hippodrome, New York;

To Quito and Back, 6 October 1937, Guild Theatre, New York;

Ladies and Gentlemen, by Hecht and MacArthur, 17 October 1939, Martin Beck Theatre;

Christmas Eve, 27 December 1939, Henry Miller Theatre, New York;

Fun to Be Free, Patriotic Pageant, by Hecht and MacArthur, 1941, Madison Square Garden, New York;

Lily of the Valley, 26 February 1942, Windsor Theatre, New York;

We Will Never Die, 9 March 1943, Madison Square Garden, New York;

Swan Song, by Hecht and MacArthur, 15 May 1946, Booth Theatre, New York;

A Flag Is Born, 5 September 1946, Alvin Theatre, New York;

Hazel Flagg, 11 February 1953, Mark Hellinger Theatre, New York;

Winkelberg, 14 January 1958, Renata Theatre, New York.

SELECTED SCREENPLAYS: *Underworld*, Paramount, 1927;

Scarface, United Artists, 1932;

Design for Living, Paramount, 1933;

Twentieth Century, Columbia, 1934;

Crime Without Passion, by Hecht and Charles MacArthur, Paramount, 1934;

Viva Villa!, M-G-M, 1934;

Once in a Blue Moon, by Hecht and MacArthur, Paramount, 1935;

The Scoundrel, by Hecht and MacArthur, Paramount, 1935;

Barbary Coast, by Hecht and MacArthur, United Artists, 1935;

Gunga Din, by Hecht and MacArthur, RKO, 1939;

Wuthering Heights, by Hecht and MacArthur, United Artists, 1939;

Angels Over Broadway, Columbia, 1940;

Spellbound, United Artists, 1945;

Notorious, RKO, 1946;

Miracle in the Rain, Warner Bros., 1956;

A Farewell to Arms, 20th Century-Fox, 1957.

Ben Hecht gave to the popular culture of American journalism a vaudeville-style, behind-the-front-page picture of the newspaper reporter, tinted with an absurd "cinematic" realism that made him the master human-interest storywriter during the Chicago Literary Renaissance. His newspaper reports of the human comedy staged in the streets, whorehouses, and police courts of Chicago spliced journalism with the literature of popular art.

Born 28 February 1894 in New York City, Ben Hecht was descended from "a long line of humiliated Jews." When he was a young boy, his parents, Joseph and Sarah Swernofsky Hecht, peasant immigrants from southern Russia, moved to Racine, Wisconsin, where Joseph Hecht, a tailor, became a designer of women's clothes and set up a small factory.

Hecht's formal education ended on graduation from Racine High School in 1910. His extracurricular activities included membership on the football, track, and cheerleading teams, performances as a circus acrobat, and collaboration on the school play. Voracious reading compensated for his lack of higher education. For his thirteenth birthday, Joseph Hecht gave his son four large boxes of books containing the works of Shakespeare, Dickens, and Twain. In high school, he read Harte, Hawthorne, Gogol, Balzac, Maupassant, Poe, Thackeray, and "a man of marvels," Dumas. The common thread running through his reading list is criticism of manners, morals, and customs laced with the flash and dazzle of words and the well-turned phrase. "The magic of words still remains for me," Hecht wrote in his autobiography, *A Child of the Century* (1954). "I prefer them to ideas. They are more precious currency. No ideas have ever filled me with wonder. Phrases have."

Three days at the University of Wisconsin in July 1910 convinced Hecht that a college education for him was a waste of time. He had already read the books prescribed in the arts and sciences curriculum, and he said so. His fraternity brothers, piqued by such an outspoken affront to university honor, demanded an apology at a fraternity dinner. Hecht agreed, but walked out of the fraternity house before the appointed hour of apology with his "university budget" of $50 and took a train to Chicago.

On his first day in Chicago, a relative introduced the sixteen-year-old Hecht to Martin Hutchens, managing editor of the *Chicago Journal*. For a tryout, Hutchens asked Hecht to write a poem based on a ribald plot that the managing editor devised impromptu. The six verses of doggerel that

Hecht scribbled in an hour earned him a $12.50-a-week job as a "picture chaser" assigned to track down photographs of criminals and their victims for use in the newspaper. Hecht's resourcefulness and skill in this work, which at times led him to the fringes of the law and respectability, boosted his weekly pay to $15, which virtually vanished on Saturdays when he was paid. Book-buying binges—"I bought books as a drunkard orders drinks"—left him nearly penniless between paydays. "I read constantly," he recalled. "I read on my way to cover stories, while waiting for cardinals to die, murderers to hang, embezzlers to confess, fires to ebb, celebrities to speak."

By his own admission, Hecht was "a Robinson Crusoe in a newspaper office" when he ventured into reporting. His first accounts were fictional (proclaiming, for instance, "an outbreak of piracy on the Chicago River") and initiated him into the world of reporters—"outside an adult civilization, intent on breaking windows." Conversations with newsroom aficionados were spoken in "the language of Dickens, Twain, Carlyle and Rabelais come out of book covers and gladdening bars, city rooms and whorehouses." The bawdy-house humor Hecht deployed throughout his prolific writing career was learned from prostitutes: "Their talk became my well-worn dictionary to be used forever—much as reporters' talk still is in my ears with its special language." Hecht confessed: "The whiplash phrase, the flashing and explosive sentence, the sonorous syntax and bull's eye epithet—if I have any literary forebears, these barroom confabulators are mine."

In 1914, Hecht joined the *Chicago Daily News*, hired by managing editor Henry Justin Smith for $45 a week, $10 a week more than *Journal* owner John C. Eastman was willing to pay. (Eastman's shop rule posted on the *Journal* newsroom's bulletin board announced: "Any reporter who is worth more than $35 a week does not belong on my newspaper.") To Hecht, Smith was a man of intelligence and literary sensibilities who "saw the paper as a daily novel written by a score of Balzacs. Its news stories were reports of life to him."

Life's seamier side, found in police courts and jails, barrooms, and brothels, attracted Hecht's journalistic and literary interests. "Up to a point," he wrote in *Gaily, Gaily* (1963), "I have found man's vices more interesting than his virtues, his flaws more diverting than his perfections. There are limits beyond which wrong-doing hurts and frightens even its onlookers. But within these limits, the didoes of the wicked are the world's chief entertainment. What else does the press report of on a good day for news—and of what else is most literature made?"

Hecht covered, by his own reckoning, seventeen hangings during his fifteen-year Chicago newspaper career. On 14 August 1914, he was covering the hanging of a murderer in Wheaton, Illinois, near Chicago, when he received a telegram from Smith: "Keep story of hanging brief. Omit all gruesome details. The world has just gone to war." World War I ended the nation's political isolationism and its giddy youthful innocence— what Hecht called "the last narcissus years of America."

He married Marie Armstrong in November 1915, and they had a daughter, Edwina. His salary boosted to $75 a week in December 1918, Hecht was sent to a defeated Germany as a foreign correspondent in Berlin for the *Daily News* syndicate's seventy American newspaper subscribers. In early 1920 he returned to the streets of Chicago, declining Smith's offer to tour Europe and to write feature stories on his travels. "I was a youth of twenty-four when I entered Germany," he said later. "When I emerged

Marie Armstrong Hecht, Hecht's first wife

from it my young cynicism had lost much of its grin."

The Chicago of 1912 to 1922, according to Hecht, "found itself, mysteriously, a bride of the arts." Hecht participated in the Chicago Literary Renaissance that included Maxwell Bodenheim ("more ignored than any literary talent of his time"), Edgar Lee Masters ("a short, square-faced, ill-tempered man"), Sherwood Anderson ("He was Modernism—the unwanted orphan on the doorstep of complacency"), and Carl Sandburg ("his smokey eyes, oracle voice, herring catcher's cap still unknown beyond our Local Room"). Sandburg was a reporter, then an editorial writer, for the *Daily News*, and Hecht later recalled that he first heard Sandburg recite "Chicago" in the county building's pressroom in the summer of 1914. Margaret Anderson, editor of the *Little Review*, which published Hecht's earliest writings, and Harriet Monroe's *Poetry* magazine gave expression to the colloquial Midwestern voice of the Chicago Literary Renaissance. "The 'Chicago School' produced a number of books of varying merit," Hecht explained. "No common concept brought us together nor were we animated by any notions of being 'modern' or 'different.' "

"A literary renaissance is of small use to a city editor," observed Hecht, whose first novel, *Erik Dorn* (1921), was overshadowed by his *Daily News* columns, "One Thousand and One Afternoons," which started in June 1921—three months before *Erik Dorn* was published. His daily columns, Henry Justin Smith wrote in a preface to a selection of them published as *1001 Afternoons in Chicago* (1922), "were presented to the public as journalism extraordinary; journalism that invaded the realm of literature, where in large part journalism really dwells. They went out backed by confidence in the genius of Ben Hecht." Every day for a year the *Chicago Daily News* published a Ben Hecht sketch, "and still the manuscripts dropped down regularly on the editor's desk," Smith went on: "Comedies, dialogues, homilies, one-act tragedies, storiettes, sepia panels, word-etchings, satires, tone-poems, fugues, bourrees,—something different every day. Rarely anything hopelessly out of key."

Moodily subjective and psychologically sophisticated, the self-revelatory descriptions in the Kafkaesque columns displayed the linguistic bravado of imagist poetry, while, as Smith confessed, "making his editor stare and fumble in the Dictionary of Taboos." Prostitutes, flappers, and fops, the marginal men and women of urban life, were cast in the minidramas of street scenes nestled among skyscrapers. The "newspaper reporter" in his columns was an existential metaphor for modern man, who saw, Hecht claimed, that "the city was nothing more nor less than a vast, broken mirror giving him back garbled images of himself." Forty-two years later, Hecht commented: "There is always self in any poetical description of a street, a sky, or a fellow human being."

The newspaper reporter of "One Thousand and One Afternoons" sought answers to questions:

What were the men in the grass waiting for? In the street? On the porches and stone steps? They were images of himself—all "waiting images" of himself. Therefore the answer lay in the question: "What had he been waiting for?"

The newspaper reporter bit into his pencil. "Nothing, nothing," he muttered. "Yes, that's it. They aren't waiting for anything. That's the secret. Life is a few years of suspended animation. But there's no story in that. Better forget it."

So he looked glumly out of his bedroom window, and, being a sentimentalist, the huge inverted music notes the telephone poles made against the dark played a long, sad tune in his mind.

The nation's leading newspapers applauded the journalistic performance of *1001 Afternoons in Chicago*. "Hints of gray pathos, traces of black tragedy" beneath "the colorful surface narratives," a *New York Times* critic declared, suggested "the quality of the snapshot rather than the finished painting; . . . his sketches can hardly be said to rise to the dignity of literature," though few would deny their "high order of journalistic attainment." His staunchest defender, Burton Rascoe, whom Hecht called "the brilliant high-strung Tory of letters" in charge of the *Chicago Tribune*'s book section, wrote in the *New York Tribune*: "There is no newspaper writer in America who can touch him in imaginative and literary treatment of police court happenings, hospital cases, street curb incidents—all the multitudinous events of city life. He is a poet; he is a wit; he is clever; he has feeling, and he has a sense of drama." Stanley Walker, city editor of the *New York Herald Tribune* after the 1924 merger, reported that America's journalists considered *1001 Afternoons in Chicago* "something of a Bible" and "the perfect example of how 'human interest' stories should be handled."

Critical response to *Erik Dorn* was profuse and mixed. The "verbal patterns, the pungently evoca-

tive word-combinations, the strange richness of metaphor" made the novel "a distinct new model in the mechanics of expression," said Rascoe: "Hecht is our first great epithetician." Another critic said *Erik Dorn*'s "verbal glitter" and "the hero's penchant for talking in newspaper headlines, in snatches of epigram and metaphor that sound like the imagist stirrings of a vers-librettist" added "a character and personality to American fiction." A less enthusiastic critic felt that the book was a "descent from literature to journalism—first-class journalism, to be sure, vivid and brilliant and interesting, brimful of ideas and opinions . . . untouched with emotion or philosophy" that became "weary platitudes at the second reading." "Too much chattering comment," held another, critical of the "pert cynicism" and "tiresome stridency which is characteristic of Ben Hecht not less than Erik Dorn."

Significantly, several critics observed in *Erik Dorn* a display of literary cinema. *Dial* drama critic Gilbert Seldes commented on Hecht's "movie technique" of "alternately retarding and speeding up his film." Others called the novel "a series of word pictures of amazing strength and realism," yet marred by "an intolerable scurry of noise and jar and strain, a roaring machinery of existence in which the soul of man is ground and ground until it becomes no more than a bundle of twitching nerves." Said a *Literary Review* critic: "Dorn is the author's dramatic mask."

Erik Dorn is a cynical but brilliant journalist who thrives on the veneer of the world's images: "The crowds moving through the streets gave Erik Dorn a picture. Above the heads of the people the great spatula-topped buildings spread a zigzag of windows, a scribble of rooftops against the sky. . . . The city alive with signs, smoke, posters, windows; falling, rising, flinging its chimneys and its streets against the sun, wound itself up into crowds and burst with an endless bang under the far-away sky. . . . Dorn was most pleased to look upon the world, to observe it as one observes a pattern—involved but precise. Life as a whole lay in the streets . . . legs moving against the walls of buildings, diagonals of bodies, syncopating face lines. . . . The nature of Erik Dorn was a shallows. Life did not live in him. He saw it as something eternally outside. To himself he seemed at times a perfect translation of his country and his day."

In many respects, *Erik Dorn* reflected the world of T. S. Eliot's "The Hollow Men" (1925), whose "quiet and meaningless" voices are "rat's feet over broken glass." Hecht wrote of Erik Dorn: "Into this emptiness of spirit, life had poured its excitements as into a thing bottomless as a mirror. He gave it back an image of words. He was proud of his words. They were his experiences and sophistications. . . . They enabled him to amuse himself with complexities of thought as one improvising difficult finger exercises on the piano."

Like Eliot's hollow men trapped in a twentieth-century "wasteland," Hecht's fictive persona viewed life as "a tawdry pantomime" and "a pouring of blood, a grappling with shadows, a digging of graves. . . . Laws, ambitions, conventions— froth in an empty glass. Tragedies, comedies—all a swarm of nothings. Dreams in the hearts of men—thin fever outlines to which they clung in hope. Nothing . . . nothing. . . ."

Erik Dorn the journalist, perhaps like Hecht, viewed newspapers with the existentially absurd lens with which he viewed life: "The perfunctory hysterics of the stories of crime, graft, scandal, with their garbled sentences and wooden phrases; the delicious sagacities of the editorial pages like the mumbling of some adenoidal moron in a gulf of high winds; headlines saying pompous 'amen' to asininity and a hopeful 'My God!' to confusion— these caressed him and brought the thought to him, 'if there is anything worthy the absurdity of life it's a newspaper—gibbering, whining, strutting, sprawled in attitudes of worship before the nine-and-ninety lies of the moment—a caricature of absurdity itself."

The cynicism and iconoclasm Hecht and his Chicago coterie of journalists, literati, and artists embraced in those days were reflected in the pages of H. L. Mencken's *Smart Set* magazine. "The H. L. Mencken tuning fork awoke the iconoclast in me," Hecht recalled. Verbal broadsides against America's conventional Puritan morality typified Hecht's intellectual and literary stance:

> Removing masks in general became an intellectual passion with me. I disbelieved with a violence that made me seem an embittered philosopher long before I had become even a man of intelligence.
>
> I sought to remove the mask from the world, to look behind it, to disprove loudly the virtues it proclaimed. . . . My earliest writings were full of excited contempt for all moralists. I dedicated myself to attacking prudes, piety-mongers and all apostles of virtue.

Mencken was a hero to Hecht, who sold a short story, "The Unlovely Sin," to *Smart Set* ("I considered the magazine . . . a sort of monthly Gospel")

for $45; he had expected to receive $1,000 for his masterpiece and to relieve part of his $3,000 in debts. When the federal government charged Hecht with having written a "lewd, obscene and lascivious" novel in *Fantazius Mallare* (1922), illustrated by former Hearst artist/reporter Wallace Smith ("His drawings spoke elegantly of an inner writhing"), Mencken offered to travel from Baltimore to Chicago to testify as an expert witness for the defense led by attorney Clarence Darrow. Darrow's defense was unsuccessful, and Hecht and Smith were fined $1,000 each for using the mails to send obscene material.

The period of his first novels and widely acclaimed newspaper columns represented, Hecht recalled, "the three most favorite years of my life." His books, including *Gargoyles* (1922)—"an immature effort to shout 'Boo!' at the flappers," a critic said—brought Hecht recognition as a journalist and street-level literatus. His literary apprenticeship in a newsroom of aspiring Balzacs had set the subject and tone for his later writings, which appeared in the *Chicago Literary Times* and, later, the flickering images of film.

Started in 1923, the *Chicago Literary Times* was Hecht's own creation. It was financed by bookseller-publisher Pascal Covici, according to Hecht, "under the delusion he was investing in a house organ." Hecht wrote most of the literary and advertising copy and helped distribute the paper. The *Literary Times* displayed the braggadocio style of America's jazz journalism of the 1920s. The $30-a-month assistant editor, Maxwell Bodenheim, described the tabloid's format as "streamers and scareheads, with poetry, prose and the other arts treated in a breezy, jovial, unassuming or unpretentiously serious way . . . we violated all of the sacred rules of the United High Brow Critics Union." For Hecht, "The policy of my paper was to attack everything." Newspapers were not spared a jab in the *Literary Times*: "Trying to determine what is going on in the world by reading the newspaper is like trying to tell the time by watching the second hand of a clock."

The *Chicago Literary Times* did more to enhance Hecht's literary reputation than his bank account; the newspaper folded in June 1924. While he edited the tabloid, three more of his books were published—*The Florentine Dagger* (1923), *Humpty Dumpty* (1924), and *The Kingdom of Evil* (1924)—and a year after he left Chicago, Covici published *Broken Necks* (1926), "Containing More '1001 Afternoons.'"

Hecht's exodus from Chicago in 1925 rep-

Hecht's second wife, Rose Caylor Hecht

The MacArthur-Hecht collaboration yielded *The Front Page*, a play staged by George S. Kaufman on 14 August 1928 at the Times Square Theatre in New York City; the 1931 movie adaptation became the first classic of the newspaper film genre. The raucous world of *The Front Page*'s vaudeville-style journalism was patterned after the real-life exploits of the reporters and editors the playwrights had known in the Chicago days. The main character of the play and film, reporter Hildy Johnson, was "a rough amalgam of the two playwrights at their wildest," according to a *New York Times* writer, and the managing editor character was modeled after Walter Howey of the *Chicago Tribune* and *Chicago Herald-Examiner*. The play's rapid-fire dialogue was the source for Hildy Johnson's now-famous movie line, "Hello sweetheart, get me rewrite," and his crack that a newspaperman is "a cross between a bootlegger and a whore."

In an epilogue to the published play (1928), Hecht and MacArthur admitted: "It developed in writing this play that our contempt for the institution of the Press was a bogus attitude; that we looked back on the Local Room where we spent half our lives as a veritable fairyland.... The iniquities,

resented a decisive break in terms both of his personal life and of his writing career. His unhappy marriage to Marie Armstrong Hecht ended in divorce, and in March 1925 he married Rose Caylor, the mother of his second daughter, Jenny. Shortly after arriving almost penniless in New York City, Hecht received a telegram from a writer friend in Hollywood: "Will you accept three hundred per week to work for Paramount Pictures. All expenses paid. The three hundred is peanuts. Millions are to be grabbed out here and your only competition is idiots. Don't let this get around." Hecht accepted and joined the first wave of writers to move west in the Hollywood "gold rush" of the 1920s. During his significant and prolific forty-year career as a screenwriter, Hecht translated his Chicago newspaper experiences into memorable films. His first movie script, *Underworld* (1927), was based on a condemned criminal's escape from the Cook County jail while the sheriff was testing the gallows before the hanging ("straining a number of points in this story"), and won an Academy Award; another script, *The Scoundrel* (1935), coauthored and codirected by Hecht and former Chicago newspaperman Charles MacArthur, also won an Oscar.

Hecht and his frequent collaborator on plays and screenplays, Charles MacArthur (Bettmann Archive)

double dealings, chicaneries and immoralities which as ex-Chicagoans we knew so well returned to us in a mist called the Good Old Days. . . . As a result *The Front Page*, despite its oaths and realism is a Valentine thrown to the past. . . . In writing it we found we were not so much dramatists or intellectuals as two reporters in exile."

Hecht ended his exile from newspapers in 1940 when he joined *PM* in New York as a columnist, contributing sketches as he had in Chicago. In addition to columns about his old friends Maxwell Bodenheim and Sherwood Anderson, Hecht wrote about the Nazi extermination of Jews. "No statesmen or journalists spoke out," Hecht recalled later. "Art was also silent. . . . The silence, then, shamed me." As a *PM* columnist, "only part of me was a newspaperman now. I was as much Jew as reporter, and I wrote often of Jews. My column reported the incredible silence of New York's Jews in this time of massacre."

His *PM* columns were published as *1001 Afternoons in New York* (1941). Critics called Hecht "the master of the iridescent phrase, the startling image, the grotesque turn of thought" and "without doubt, one of our most facile word painters"; his columns were "more roving and fanciful and literary than standard newspaper stuff." Another critic confessed: "While the rest of us merely push into print the short-lived anecdotes and news-events of each day, Ben Hecht stamps his output with timelessness and with that strange rhythm of words which he alone beats out. We write for the day. He writes for the years."

In 1941, Hecht was back in Hollywood grinding out movie scripts to grubstake his literary career. Hecht was afflicted with what he called "a duality often to be found among writers. I was eager to write like a beggar but live like a king. I managed to do both for a long time, sliding constantly from penury to riches in a fashion often startling." Frequently working on two or more scripts at a time, Hecht wrote more than thirty movies in less than two weeks each, never spending more than eight weeks on any of his more than seventy filmscripts. He earned between $50,000 and $125,000 a script; his movie-writing salaries brought him $5,000-plus a week, once as much as $3,500 a day. During the peak of his scriptwriting days, he earned more than $300,000 a year. "I never hid it, invested it or even spent it," Hecht admitted. "I allowed it to blow away—while I sat for six months doing what I liked—writing a book, mooning in the garden and studying the Hudson . . . I sometimes had to earn two hundred thousand dollars during the first half

of the year in order to be able to sit out the second half as a prose writer."

His credits for stories or original screenplays include the classic gangster film *Scarface* (1932); *Twentieth Century* (1934); *Gunga Din* (1939); *Wuthering Heights* (1939); the Alfred Hitchcock movies *Spellbound* (1945) and *Notorious* (1946); *Miracle in the Rain* (1956); and *A Farewell to Arms* (1957). He also collaborated (without credit) on *Gone with the Wind* (1939), *Foreign Correspondent* (1940), and *Roman Holiday* (1953). Hecht held cinema in contempt: "The movies are one of the bad habits that corrupted our century. . . . an eruption of trash that has lamed the American mind and retarded Americans from becoming a cultured people."

British film exhibitors boycotted his films in retaliation for Hecht's outspoken support of Jewish resistance movements in Palestine in the late 1940s. Hecht's film credits were stripped from movies screened in England for five years.

The Hollywood film factory's extravagant salaries allowed Hecht to continue his literary production, which included *A Jew in Love* (1931); *Actor's Blood* (1936); *A Book of Miracles* (1939); *Miracle in the Rain* (1943); *A Guide for the Bedevilled* (1944); *I Hate Actors!* (1944); *The Collected Stories of Ben Hecht* (1945); *A Child of the Century*, his autobiography (1954); *Charlie* (1957), recollections of Charles MacArthur; *Perfidy* (1961), a polemic against the leadership of Israel; *Gaily, Gaily* (1963); and *Letters from Bohemia* (1964), reminiscences of his newspaper days and the characters he knew—"all of them wild men in print, in music or on canvas."

"My main goal was to remain 18, never to grow up or grow old," Hecht told an interviewer on his sixty-fifth birthday. "I missed that goal." Hecht collapsed while reading in his fourteenth-floor apartment at 39 West Sixty-seventh Street, New York City, on 18 April 1964, the victim of an apparent heart attack at age seventy; he had been working on a script for *Casino Royale* (1967). The story of his death appeared on the front page of the *New York Times*. "Human tribulation," the *Times* said, "frequently touched the heart that Mr. Hecht wore on his sleeve." The *Chicago Daily News* called Hecht "a pivotal figure" in the great Chicago Literary Renaissance.

Beneath the shirt-sleeve surface, Ben Hecht was a moralist tutored in the comic wisdom of lost innocence and Valentine remembrances of bygone days—a child of the century and, as author John Gunther put it, "a dreamer, a romantic teller of tales" who penned his epitaph in "Some Introductory Thoughts" to his *Collected Stories*:

> My short stories are my chief social effort to escape the gloomy pits of information in my mind.
>
> One does this by entering the happy storehouse of the imagination. Here is a world not yet gone to pot, here are people and events still as dreamy and charming as filled the days of one's innocence. Sitting down to write them, I enjoy myself.
>
> Yet in my stories, after they are written, I find always that I have actually invented nothing, that the people I have written about are actually people I have known, and that the anecdotes in which I wrap them up are truly adventures which have befallen me or those around me.
>
> It becomes obvious to me, then, that the only fictional thing in my stories is my point of view. My point of view in most of my stories is that of a child who finds the world full of exuberant and engrossing matters, who dramatizes what he sees so he may enjoy it more, and who asks as a reward for his labors only the illusion that existence is a fine thing.... The folly and poison of life manage to unhorse my sturdiest efforts at cheer. I am full of contempts that my wit and Arabian-Nights plots do not entirely conceal.
>
> And try as I may to cheer myself up with sparkling tales and a jolly point of view, a moan lurks in the corners of my tales.
>
> I apologize for this unseemly sound. It belongs in me and not my tales. For I have had always a picture of myself as a story teller. I have seen myself like those sunny and cackling fellows who once upon a time stood on the street corners of Bagdad and unfolded tales to the harassed citizens who paused to listen—and fling grateful kopecks at their feet.

Biography:

Doug Fetherling, *The Five Lives of Ben Hecht* (Toronto: Lester & Orpen, 1977).

References:

Harry Hansen, *Midwest Portraits: A Book of Memories and Friendships* (New York: Harcourt, Brace, 1923), pp. 305-357;

Chaim Lieberman, *This Man and His "Perfidy"* (New York: Bloch, 1964);

Thomas H. Zynda, "The Hollywood Version: Movie Portrayals of the Press," *Journalism History* (Spring 1979): 16-25, 32.

Papers:

The largest collection of Hecht's papers is at the Newberry Library in Chicago.

E. W. Howe
(3 May 1853-3 October 1937)

William I. McReynolds
University of Colorado—Boulder

See also the Howe entry in *DLB 12, American Realists and Naturalists*.

MAJOR POSITIONS HELD: Publisher-editor, *Atchison* (Kansas) *Globe* (1877-1910); *E. W. Howe's Monthly* (1911-1933).

BOOKS: *The Story of a Country Town* (Atchison, Kans.: Howe, 1883; London: Cape, 1933);

The Mystery of the Locks (Boston: Osgood, 1885);

A Moonlight Boy (Boston: Ticknor, 1886; London: Trübner, 1886);

A Man Story (Boston: Ticknor, 1889);

An Ante-Mortem Statement (Atchison, Kans.: Globe Publishing, 1891);

The Confession of John Whitlock, Late Preacher of the Gospel (Atchison, Kans.: Globe Publishing, 1891);

Daily Notes of a Trip Around the World (Topeka, Kans.: Crane, 1907);

The Trip to the West Indies (Topeka, Kans.: Crane, 1910);

Country Town Sayings (Topeka, Kans.: Crane, 1911);

Travel Letters from New Zealand, Australia and Africa

Culver Pictures

(Topeka, Kans.: Crane, 1913);

Success Easier than Failure (Topeka, Kans.: Crane, 1917);

The Blessings of Business (Topeka, Kans.: Crane, 1918);

Ventures in Common Sense (Topeka, Kans.: Crane, 1919); republished as *Adventures in Common Sense* (London: Melrose, 1922);

The Anthology of Another Town (New York: Knopf, 1920);

Notes for My Biographer (Girard, Kans.: Haldeman-Julius, 1926);

Sinner Sermons (Girard, Kans.: Haldeman-Julius, 1926);

Preaching from the Audience (Girard, Kans.: Haldeman-Julius, 1926);

Dying like a Gentleman and Other Stories (Girard, Kans.: Haldeman-Julius, 1926);

When a Woman Enjoys Herself and Other Tales of a Small Town (Girard, Kans.: Haldeman-Julius, 1928);

The Covered Wagon and the West (with Other Stories) (Girard, Kans.: Haldeman-Julius, 1928);

Her Fifth Marriage, and Other Stories (Girard, Kans.:

Haldeman-Julius, 1928);

Plain People (New York: Dodd, Mead, 1929);

The Indignations of E. W. Howe (Girard, Kans.: Haldeman-Julius, 1933).

PERIODICAL PUBLICATIONS: "Loafing Round in Florida," *Country Gentleman* (February 1920): 30, 100;

"The Apologies of an Old Fogy," *Saturday Evening Post*, 193 (11 December 1920): 27;

"Confessions of a Common Man," *American Magazine*, 95 (June 1923): 34, 92-100;

"What Life Has Taught Me," *Collier's* (January 1925): 25;

"My Home Town, Atchison," *Rotarian*, 43 (September 1933): 21-23, 55.

E. W. Howe was well known as a small-town Kansas journalist, but on a smaller scale of fame than his younger friend, William Allen White. Centering his career almost exclusively in Atchison, Kansas, Howe was probably more representative of deep Midwestern currents than White was. The *Atchison Globe* served as Howe's platform for thirty-three years, from its founding in December 1877 until he sold it to his son Gene on 31 December 1910. Even after 1910, Howe continued as a columnist.

At the time of his death, his former employees recalled that Howe most wanted to be remembered as a country journalist. He chose the path of common sense, and he became known as the Sage of Potato Hill—the name of his rural home near Atchison—and also as an eccentric. A reporter for the *Nation* magazine called him "something of a crank" principally because "he has refused to surrender his rustic illusion not only that the world is a very simple place to those who can see it simply but that those who do not so see it are deliberately perverse."

Edgar Watson Howe was born near Treaty, Indiana, on 3 May 1853, the first of five children of Henry and his second wife, Elizabeth Irwin Howe; the family also included two children from Henry Howe's first marriage. Henry Howe was a farmer, schoolteacher, and Methodist circuit rider who moved his family by covered wagon to Fairview in Harrison County, Missouri, before the Civil War. The elder Howe built a church on his Missouri land and continued to preach and ride circuit, sometimes taking Ed with him on these crusades against sin. Henry Howe was an outspoken abolitionist at a time when such a stand in Missouri invited personal danger; he was tried and acquitted for inciting rebellion among the slaves. In his autobiography, *Plain People* (1929), Howe remembered his father as a hard, stern parent who showed his son no affection and berated him for not producing enough for the family. "One of my recollections is of his saying that I had been an expense to him until I was seven years old." Whippings from his father were common until Howe was thirteen, by which time he was working on his own as a printer.

Incapacitated after a year's service in the Civil War as a captain in a company of army volunteers, the elder Howe moved his family to Bethany, Missouri, where he purchased a weekly newspaper, the *Union of States*, to carry on his crusade. It was there that young Ed began his first work in a print shop; he was only eleven or twelve years old at the time. The elder Howe deserted his family in 1865 by running away with a woman in his congregation; this traumatic incident was instrumental in setting the attitudes that the agnostic and misogamist Howe maintained throughout his life. Calder M. Pickett, Howe's biographer, says that Howe believed selfishness, not Christian belief, would save mankind: "It pays to behave yourself, because good conduct is more profitable than bad conduct."

His father's desertion brought an end to Howe's life at home. By then an accredited journeyman, he took to the road as a tramp printer. At the age of fifteen, Howe went to work on the *North Missourian* in Gallatin, Missouri, for $5 a week and board. From Gallatin, he went to Maysville and then to St. Joseph, where he worked on the *Herald* as a "sub," or extra man. It was in St. Joseph that Howe began to develop a contempt for the alcoholic and the intemperate, a theme that became a constant in his writings: he got drunk once, was caught, and was humiliated by the experience. He wrote: "I have been a tiresome preacher of temperance ever since. I have never been able to see any sense in intoxicants; if I want to play the fool, I can find a dozen things more promising than whisky." Howe delighted in quoting the Kentucky editor Henry Watterson, who had said he "would walk seven miles barefooted over a turnpike to the funeral of a fool who would try to make a corkscrew out of a mule's tail" but that he never could shed "a tear for the idiot who had no better sense than to kill himself drinking whisky."

Following his mother's death in Bethany in 1868 or 1869, Howe returned home. His father also reappeared and moved the family to Council Bluffs, Iowa, where he had established a place for them to live. Howe got a typesetting job on the local paper, the *Nonpareil*.

Howe stayed in Council Bluffs only a short time before he quit the *Nonpareil* in anger at the new foreman. He went to Chicago, but soon found that the big city was not for a country boy. The *Omaha Republican* was his next destination; but life proved dull in Omaha, so Howe and an adventurous friend decided to go west. They stayed briefly in Cheyenne, Wyoming, before moving on to Salt Lake City, where Howe worked for the *Deseret News*, the Mormon church paper run by Brigham Young.

Soon Howe was on the road again, returning east to visit in Omaha and Council Bluffs. Learning that a printer's job was available on the *Nemaha Valley Journal* in nearby Falls City, Nebraska, Howe obtained the position, for which he was soon earning the good salary of $20 a week. Howe was happiest in Falls City, and he once had unusual responsibilities thrust upon him when the paper's owner married and left him in charge of the paper for two weeks.

Following a disagreement with the owner, Howe was on his way west again. He worked briefly as a sub on the *Rocky Mountain News* in Denver and then went to work twenty miles away in Golden, where he and a friend, Joe Franklin, saved enough money to buy the *Golden Eagle*. For two years, from 1873 to 1875, Howe was publisher-editor of the paper, whose name he changed to the *Golden Globe*.

In the midst of his Golden days he returned to Falls City to marry Clara Frank, a woman he had met there. After a honeymoon in Atchison, Kansas, Howe returned with his bride to Golden, where their first child was born in the summer of 1874. Howe finally sold the newspaper and returned to the *Nemaha Valley Journal* in Falls City, where his second child was born in the winter of 1876.

After so many wanderings and now with family responsibilities, Howe was ready to settle down; he moved to Atchison in 1877. Howe often said he did not know why he chose Atchison, but Pickett questions this: after all, Howe had honeymooned there, and it was relatively close to other towns with which he had had close relationships: Falls City, Omaha, Council Bluffs, and St. Joseph. Also, Atchison was at that time something of a boom town: it was a railroad center, and a foundry and a seed company established a few years before Howe's arrival had helped to establish it as a regional agricultural center.

Howe's start in Atchison was not auspicious. He had two competitors, the *Champion* and the *Patriot*. He had to borrow money to buy a Gordon job press, but he was able to bring a font of brevier type with him from Falls City. With this and with the assistance of his half brother, Jim, Howe started the *Atchison Globe* on 8 December 1877. It was a newspaper of one sheet, 10½ inches by 15 inches, with two pages. The Gordon press was able to accommodate only two pages, but the Howes soon managed to print four pages by running each sheet through the press twice. Bigger and faster presses followed later: a drum-cylinder model, turned by hand power at first, and then by a water motor; next, a two-revolution model run by a steam engine; and finally, a Goss perfecting press.

Howe acquired a national reputation for the universally quotable "paragraphs" that he wrote for the *Globe* and for his first novel, *The Story of a Country Town* (1883). A pioneering example of realistic fiction, *The Story of a Country Town* marked an early and sharp departure from the nineteenth-century image of the "idyllic" rural life. Howe's portrait of an American small town was a damning indictment of an arid way of life that corrodes the spirit and cripples the mind. *The Story of a Country Town* is basically a series of shattered dreams. Life in the fictitious Missouri communities of Fairview and Twin Mounds is depicted through the tragic story of the central figure, Jo Erring. An unwanted child, Jo is taken into the home of his sister, whose son, Ned Westlock, becomes Jo's best friend. It is through Ned's eyes that the narrative unfolds. Other characters include Jo's beloved Mateel Shepherd, the local preacher's daughter, who Jo suspects has never forsaken her love for the lazy, good-for-nothing Clinton Bragg, an interloper from the wicked East. Jo's suspicion leads to destruction. Howe's view of village and farm was colored by harsh pessimism and filled with a pervasive sense of human waste. After Howe came other American writers who were equally willing to expose realistically the miserable state of life in rural America: Harold Frederic, Hamlin Garland, Edgar Lee Masters, Sherwood Anderson, and Sinclair Lewis.

Following completion of the novel, Howe sent the manuscript unsolicited to various publishers. After eight rejections, the *Globe* publisher decided to print it himself, late at night after putting his newspaper to bed. In 1927, Howe recalled that ordeal: "As Kelley set the type (it was a new font of minion purchased for the purpose) the printing was done four pages at a time, on a medium Gordon job press. Two thousand copies were run off. And when the sheets were ready, a local bindery bound them in cases purchased in St. Louis." Howe sent copies of the novel to William Dean Howells, the literary czar of the time, and to Mark Twain, Howe's

writing idol. Twain, who made it a practice not to comment on works by new authors, made an exception in Howe's case by writing him a letter of congratulations for the "simple, sincere, direct, and at the same time so clear and so strong" style. In a "Private Section" of the same letter, Twain said Howe "may have caught the only fish there was in your pond." Although Howe was to write more novels, none was a popular or critical success; Twain had been correct.

By the mid-1880s, the years of struggling for financial success were coming to an end for Howe. *The Story of a Country Town* had made him a celebrity, and he had become a man of some local, as well as national, prominence. He was now able to get out of the provinces and see the big world. Howe began to publish reports of his travels, which were a staple in his writings until the end of his career. His travel impressions were gathered into books, typical of which were *Daily Notes of a Trip Around the World* (1907) and *Travel Letters from New Zealand, Australia and Africa* (1913). In his travel commentaries, Howe demonstrated a capacity to universalize situations and to make his readers understand foreign customs by relating them to their own lives.

Howe's most lasting fame was gained, however, by his widely quoted epigrammatic "paragraphs," most of which first appeared in his popular column, "Globe Sights," and some of which had been written as early as the Golden, Colorado, days. These mainstays throughout the early years of the Atchison paper were often interspersed with straight news; sometimes they became the concluding sentences of news stories. Typical "paragraphs" were such as the following: "There are two ways of raising boys; but judging from the men turned out, both ways are wrong." "If you go slow others will overtake you; if you go fast, you will exhaust your strength and die young." Howe's journalism was intensely local. Most of his paragraphs dealt with immediately identifiable persons, things, or situations. Howe knew that a newspaper must be founded upon human nature and, also, that entertainment was an important part of the total package.

Howe and his reporters were likely to be seen tramping the streets and roads and coming to know almost everyone in Atchison and in the nearby countryside. (Although much of his basic attitude seemed sour, Howe liked people and was a great conversationalist.) But Howe certainly must have touched a national and international nerve through his "universal" paragraphs, because they were soon published everywhere. H. L. Mencken was one who

Howe (left) and fellow Kansas editor William Allen White around 1900 (Laura M. French)

championed the small-town editor. The two were seen as writers dedicated to cutting away sham and hypocrisy in American society. In the introduction to the 1919 collection of Howe's paragraphs, *Ventures in Common Sense*, Mencken wrote that what set Howe apart from the vast herd of national sages was his "relentless honesty, sacrificing every appearance, however charming, to what he conceives to be the truth."

Howe had an astonishing repertory of prejudices, and he was famous for his blunt exposition of them, often expressed with laconic humor. He enjoyed his role as debunker and iconoclast, and he counted himself the eternal enemy of phonies. He once wrote that Daniel Webster's last words had not been the popularized "I still live"; instead, the great politician had really said "Give me some brandy." A conservative Republican himself, Howe believed that politicians were frauds. He complained that newspapers that would not allow any advertising on the editorial page would turn over columns to "the praise of some two-cent candidate." He also held most reformers in contempt: he once sneered that a Populist "is a man who declares that industry is

'discreditable,' that thrift is a crime, and respectability suspicious." To Howe the worst muckraker was Ida Tarbell, because she attacked reputable and successful businessmen such as Howe's hero, John D. Rockefeller: "In the interest of reform, is it possible that a gentle, refined woman has been lying about an inoffensive old man?" Yet Howe had good things to say about another muckraker, Lincoln Steffens, who was exposing the evils of government and placing the responsibility where it belonged — upon the people.

In a sense, as biographer Pickett says, Howe was a reformer and "meddler" himself in that he wanted to change conditions stemming from marriage and relations between the sexes, from religion, and from the idea of success. Howe believed that a man could choose success over failure and plan his life accordingly. Perhaps Howe read success in his own rags-to-riches career, in which he gained fortune and fame through his talents. His own secular religion was rooted in what he identified as *The Blessings of Business*, the title of his 1918 tract: business was the cement of society. Howe was an admirer of the acquisitive instinct, and it seemed quite admirable to him that people should be able to make money through energy and hard work: "The first principle is life; the second, maintenance of life. The thing of greatest human interest and importance, therefore, is the production and distribution of food, the manufacture of necessities; or what we call 'Business.'" Howe's was essentially a Social-Darwinian view; he simply viewed life as a struggle for existence: "It is a fight from the cradle to the grave, and the man who makes a great success, is a genius, and entitled to admiration." Simply put, the fittest to survive are businessmen. To Howe, labor agitators, prohibitionists, women's righters, agrarians, and preachers of the Social Gospel were all wasteful, malicious, and in some cases downright evil.

Howe had a reputation as a misogynist, although he did have a happy and longtime relationship with at least one woman: his niece, Adelaide, who took care of him for many years and was his traveling companion. Over the years, a host of editorials in the *Globe* denounced the woman suffrage movement; Howe never abandoned the belief that woman's place was in the home. In an editorial, he considered what the equal rights movement had meant to Susan B. Anthony, one of its leading proponents: "She never had a love affair serious enough to make moonlight look any different to her than high noon . . . and she never knew what it was to love and care for one's own baby"; in other words, Anthony had missed out on the real joys of life. The suffrage movement annoyed him because Howe felt women already were living in the best of all possible worlds. On the other hand, Howe believed disillusionment was in store for anyone undertaking matrimony and that love itself is suspect: "The love stories give examples of a maiden who looked into a spring at midnight and the face of a Prince appeared over her shoulder, and she married him. But how is Daughter to find her Prince in real life, when there isn't a spring on the place, and one can't see the reflection of a Prince's face in the hydrant?"

Howe's own marriage ended in bitterness and divorce in 1901. Relationships with others in his immediate family were less than satisfactory. His first two children had died in 1877; three more had been born later: James in 1879, Mateel (named after the heroine of *The Story of a Country Town*) in 1883, and Eugene in 1886. Howe's relationship with Jim was strained, although Jim's success as an Associated Press writer was the occasion for fatherly pride. Howe loved Mateel when she was young, but the two became estranged as she got older and more independent-minded. In 1927, the newly married

Mateel Howe Farnham received the $10,000 *Pictorial Review* prize for her first novel, *Rebellion*, which described the conflicts between a father and daughter. Gene, who worked on the *Globe*, had a better relationship with his father, but he sadly labeled Howe the "most wretchedly unhappy man I ever knew" in the article he wrote for a *Saturday Evening Post* series about famous journalists. Gene had a successful career as a celebrated regional editor in Amarillo, Texas, where he purchased the *Amarillo News* and changed it to the *News-Globe* in 1924, shortly before the oil boom hit the Panhandle area.

Howe was suspicious of affection and fearful of sentiment. Religion, in particular the organized kind, was especially suspect to Howe, who aired his feelings throughout his career. "I do not believe that Christ was the son of God; I do not believe the history of Christ found in the Bible," he once said. "It is positively known that men wrote every line of the New Testament without any assistance from Christ or from God." According to Pickett, Howe was the best-known newspaper critic of religion in America. This was a particularly daring stance since he lived among Midwesterners, who were more religious than many others in the country. Christmas was a fraud to Howe; he finally sold his *Globe* in 1910 when the traditional "Christmas Gloom" was on him, son Gene recalled.

After a few months, the writing bug hit Howe and he began a new publication, *E. W. Howe's Monthly*; the first issue appeared in March 1911. The *Monthly* was a small, pocket-size magazine, at first consisting of sixty-four pages and priced at ten cents a copy or $1 a year. Howe wrote everything in the *Monthly*, which was mainly a collection of his views and prejudices. It was a highly personalized publication, and Howe refused to argue with readers; he simply instructed his "country-girl secretaries" to burn all letters that were disagreeable and to return money to all dissatisfied subscribers.

It was the astonishing quantity of Howe's prejudices and his humor that had kept the *Globe* going, and the same held true for the *Monthly*, which adopted a newspaper format in February 1914. By the 1920s Howe was acquiring a truly national audience and the *Monthly* was being widely quoted, just as the *Globe* had been. Howe was becoming an almost legendary figure: writing for *Scribner's*, Gerald Carson identified the Atchison writer as "The Village Atheist" whose maxims and apologues, "as Franklin's were a hundred and fifty years ago, have been repeated and bandied about until they have in many instances quite lost their paternity."

Howe started spending his winters in Florida; the remainder of the year he lived at Potato Hill and made trips to other parts of the country, all the while writing about his travels as he had in the earlier days. He also went on speaking tours, although he was always uneasy about his abilities as a public speaker. Although he had made attacks on higher education for most of his writing days, Howe received honorary degrees in 1927 from Washburn College in Topeka and from Rollins College in Winter Park, Florida.

In 1929 Dodd, Mead and Company published Howe's autobiography, *Plain People*, which Pickett calls "a moving, prejudiced, funny and infuriatingly un-thorough book." Reviews at the time of the book's publication were generally favorable.

Howe's eyesight began to fail during the 1930s, and with no prior announcement, he suspended operation of *E. W. Howe's Monthly* with the November 1933 issue. On 17 July 1937, Howe suffered a slight stroke of paralysis. On 1 October, wire services carried the news that his former wife had died at the age of ninety. Two days later, on 3 October, Howe died in his sleep at his Atchison home. He was eighty-four.

E. W. Howe's "Globe Sights" are still quoted throughout the world, and one appears as an overline every day on the front page of the *Atchison Globe*. His portrait hangs in the Newspaper Hall of Fame at the University of Kansas's William Allen White School of Journalism. *The Story of a Country Town* is read in literature classes as the earliest example of realism in the American novel. Howe and his views and prejudices would mostly be anachronisms today, but from 1877 until 1933—almost sixty years—he was the epitome of the country-town journalist to much of America.

Biography:

Calder M. Pickett, *Ed Howe: Country Town Philosopher* (Lawrence: University Press of Kansas, 1968).

References:

Ernest Boyd, "The Sage of Potato Hill," *Nation*, 139 (August 1934): 247-248;

Gerald Carson, "The Village Atheist," *Scribner's*, 84 (December 1928): 733-739;

Rolla A. Clymer, "A Golden Era of Kansas Journalism," *Kansas Historical Quarterly*, 24 (Spring 1958): 97-111;

Kenneth S. Cooper, "E. W. Howe—A Self-Educated Educator," *Educational Forum*, 26 (January 1962): 233-237;

"Ed Howe: Sage of Potato Hill Ends Long Publishing Career," *Newsweek*, 3 (January 1934): 34;

Editorial obituary, *Nation*, 145 (October 1937): 390-391;

Grover C. Hall, "E. W. Howe and H. L. Mencken," *Haldeman-Julius Monthly* (July 1925): 163-167;

Gene A. Howe, "My Father Was the Most Wretchedly Unhappy Man I Ever Knew," *Saturday Evening Post*, 21 (25 October 1941): 25, 44-46, 49;

William Dean Howells, "Two Notable Novels," *Century*, 28 (August 1884): 632-633;

Wilbur L. Schramm, "Ed Howe versus Time," *Saturday Review of Literature* (February 1938): 10-11;

Carl Van Doren, "Prudence Militant: E. W. Howe, Village Sage," *Century*, 106 (May 1923): 151-156;

John William Ward, "Afterword" to *The Story of a Country Town* (New York: Signet, 1964);

D. P. Wilson, ed., "Edgar Watson Howe," in *Eminent Men of the State of Kansas* (Topeka: Hall Lithographing Co., 1901), p. 125.

Papers:

Letters of E. W. Howe are held by the University of Kansas, Indiana University, and the University of Southern California.

Clark Howell, Sr.

(21 September 1863-14 November 1936)

Wallace B. Eberhard
University of Georgia

MAJOR POSITIONS HELD: Managing editor, editor, publisher, *Atlanta Constitution* (1889-1936).

BOOKS: *Eloquent Sons of the South: A Handbook of Southern Oratory* (Boston: Chapple, 1909);
History of Georgia, 4 volumes (Atlanta: S. J. Clarke, 1926);
Genealogy of the Southern Line of the Family of Howell (Atlanta, 1930).

PERIODICAL PUBLICATIONS: "Our Family Skeleton," *North American Review*, 159 (July 1894): 88-89;
"World's Event for 1895: Cotton States and International Exposition," *Review of Reviews*, 11 (February 1895): 158-166;
"Henry W. Grady," *The Chatauquan*, 21 (September 1895): 703-706;
"Aftermath of Reconstruction," *Century*, 85 (April 1913): 849-853.

"He is now 33 years old, and it may safely be said that what he has done in his profession is a mere experiment compared with what he will do. His mind is broad, conservative and sympathetic. He has an intuitive knowledge of the relation that even the smallest political event bears to the future. He has a complete understanding of public affairs. He is not a partisan in any sense but he stands for pure democracy in every sense. The work that his predecessors began he will carry on and make perfect, and the *Constitution*, under his editorial control, will continue to grow in power and influence, not merely as a newspaper, but as the organ and representative of the people and the people's interests." The words are those of a Southern newsman — Joel Chandler Harris — written in 1897 to describe a colleague who had just been appointed his editor in chief: Clark Howell, Sr. For the thirty-nine years that followed, Howell was the *Constitution*'s editor and guiding force, active literally until his dying day in 1936. But, for whatever reason, Howell has been largely ignored by historians. He is relegated to a line or two in the general media histories; the latest history of the state of Georgia does not mention him at all; Southern histories either neglect him entirely or say little of his life and work in relation to the life of the South or the growth of the *Constitution*. He was a journalistic bridge between the editorships of two better-known Southern journalists: Henry W. Grady, who was hired by Howell's father, Evan Park Howell; and Ralph McGill, who joined the *Constitution* as a sportswriter in 1929 and soon was pressed into service as a political writer by Clark Howell. And he was a political bridge between Grady's version of the New South and McGill's.

By the fortunes of war, Clark Howell was born in South Carolina. His father was commanding a

Confederate artillery battery in Tennessee and Julia Erwin Howell had returned to her home in Erwinton, South Carolina, when Clark arrived on 21 September 1863. His grandfather had moved to Georgia from North Carolina as a boy, and Evan Howell had grown up in Atlanta and had been educated at the Georgia Military Institute and the University of Georgia Law School. The Howells could trace their American lineage back to 1637, when John Howell arrived in Virginia from England.

One tale of Clark Howell's involvement in the Civil War claims that he and his mother were at the Howell family home on the Chattahoochee River north of Atlanta when Sherman began to close in; mother and child fled before the Yankees. The cook baked some biscuits which Mrs. Howell folded in her apron, and, with a cow tied behind the wagon to furnish milk for the baby, the trio escaped. Clark Howell's sister Rosalie maintained late in life that it was this incident, told to a family friend named Margaret Mitchell, that wound up as the classic scene in *Gone with the Wind* (1936) in which Melanie ties a cow to the wagon as the O'Haras abandon their plantation.

There is little doubt about Howell's essential Southernness, which meant so much more in his time than it may today. His roots and family ties undoubtedly controlled his life and behavior to a large extent, but it does not appear that his regionalism restricted his personal growth or shackled him with a provinciality that kept him from larger service and recognition.

Evan Howell returned to a desolate land at war's end. Atlanta lay in ruins, but Sherman's bonfires meant a shortage of lumber which Capt. Howell turned to advantage. For two years he cut, sawed, and sold timber from his father's lands before moving into Atlanta to become a reporter and then city editor on the *Atlanta Intelligencer*. He then returned to the practice of law and was elected solicitor general and then state senator. He turned to journalism again on 17 October 1876, when he purchased a half-interest in the *Atlanta Constitution*, which had been established in 1868 by Carey Styles. A chance meeting with Henry Woodfin Grady—on his way to catch a train for a new editorial position in Augusta—led to Grady's being hired on the spot by Howell. Grady, in turn, urged the employment of Joel Chandler Harris as an "editorial paragrapher." These three remarkably complementary journalists began to build the *Constitution* into a newspaper of regional and national reputation.

Clark Howell, one of seven children, com-

pleted his degree at the University of Georgia in 1883 and plunged into the world of journalism. His apprenticeship took him to the *New York Times*, where he worked as a reporter under Henry Lowenthal, who was later a *Times* managing editor. From there he moved to the *Philadelphia Press* news desk, where he worked under Charles Emory Smith, later U.S. postmaster general. One of his reportorial assignments at the *Press* earned him national recognition. The aging Samuel Tilden had yet to make known his availability as a nominee on the Democratic ticket; Howell paid him a visit in Gramercy Park and learned from the man himself that he was in failing health and would not seek office. The resulting story got wide play in leading papers across the country. Within a few weeks Howell was back in Atlanta; in a year he was night city editor of the *Constitution* under Grady. By this time, Grady was coming into his own as spokesman for the New South, and Howell's tutelage frequently must have been unsupervised. Still, he did work closely with Grady and the others assembled by his father and Grady in the editorial department of the *Constitution*.

Politics, it would seem, meant as much to Howell as journalism and the South. His grandfather had been an Atlanta judge and his father a state legislator. Shortly after his return to Atlanta, he was nominated for the legislature in August 1884, a month before he became twenty-one. He was elected and went on to serve five terms in the House of Representatives. In 1887 he married Harriet Glascock Barrett of Augusta, a member of a prominent Georgia family; they had one child, Clark, Jr.

By 1889 Howell was assistant managing editor of the *Constitution*, even more heavily engaged in being the alter ego of Grady. When Grady died that year, Howell was a young but seasoned newsman, and he stepped into Grady's shoes. He served his last term in the Georgia House (1890-1891) as speaker; the following year, he became a Democratic national committeeman from Georgia and retained the position until 1924. By 1895 all significant editorial questions at the *Constitution* were being decided by Howell; when Evan Howell retired two years later, Clark Howell was made editor in chief.

Howell was finally free to set editorial policy on his own, out from under any shadow that may have been cast by his father. He soon showed his independence and judgment in several editorial campaigns. In 1897, he took on the state's notorious convict lease system, which permitted firms to bid for the unrestricted use of state prisoners in private enterprises. Although the legislature did not abolish the system, it did act to moderate some of the abuses and assume more control. At the same time, Howell stood firm in support of Atlanta's policy of accepting all refugees fleeing the yellow fever epidemic then raging in a number of Southern cities. No cases had ever been documented as originating in Atlanta, and his voice of mercy and compassion helped prevent panic and a siege mentality in the community. Also in the same year, the *Constitution* stood almost alone against a move to outlaw football at the University of Georgia after a student died while playing the game there. The governor vetoed the bill—the only veto used on any of the 235 bills passed during the session. Howell also helped to fight off repeated attempts to weaken the university and reduce its funding that cropped up that year. His devotion to the university led to his appointment to its board of trustees in 1896. These campaigns—some of them waged concurrently—established early in his editorship that he would be his own man and that he could work aggressively and responsibly toward well-defined editorial objectives. The newspaper supported good roads and other causes and spoke as moderately as was possible on racial matters.

Howell's wife died in 1898, but he continued his varied activities. In addition to journalism and politics, he was becoming a nationally known speaker, somewhat in the mold of Grady. When the 1898 Chicago Peace Jubilee climaxed with a dinner feting President William McKinley, it was the Hon. Clark Howell who spoke on the topic "Our Reunited Country," to which the president responded. Other speaking engagements included an appearance in Buffalo, New York, in 1899, where he spoke on the "Man with His Hat in His Hand."

In 1900 Howell was elected to the Georgia Senate, of which he was chosen president. The following year was an important one for Howell: he gained control of a majority of the *Constitution*'s stock, which his father had sold when he retired; and he married Annie Comer of Savannah, the daughter of a railroad president. They had three sons: Hugh Comer, Albert, and Julian Erwin. His speaking engagements continued, including an appearance in New York City as the keynote speaker at a Grant Day dinner in 1901 and an address in Des Moines in 1903 at the seventeenth annual meeting of the Grant Club on "Grant's Life as a Peace Lesson."

Given his roles as the editor in chief of a well-known and respected Southern newspaper and as a young and articulate politician, it is easy to see why *Harper's Weekly* commented after the Grant Day speech in New York that he had "prospered in all directions, and been elected speaker of the Georgia legislature, which will send him in time no doubt, to the U.S. Senate."

Howell's eye was not on the Senate but on the governor's chair, and it was in this race that he ran into a political buzz saw. Georgia had long been dominated politically by the Bourbons, who controlled the Democratic party, and Howell was one of them. Continued rule by the Bourbon element seemed assured when Howell announced in the spring of 1905 that he would be a candidate for governor in the 1906 primary. What he could not predict was the growing discontent with the Bourbons on the part of other Democrats, the fixation on the issue of disenfranchising black voters, and the campaigning ability of Hoke Smith, one-time owner of the *Atlanta Journal* and secretary of the interior for three years under President Cleveland. The race was as ruthless and vigorous as any in the history of Georgia. Smith, supported by the Populist Tom Watson, spoke out for a state constitutional provision that would effectively end the black man's right to vote. Perhaps the high—or low—point of the campaign was a debate between the two leading candidates in the Columbus Opera House in January 1906. Howell opposed the amendment, but not because he favored universal voting rights for blacks; rather he thought the white primary and other mechanisms were sufficient as a control and that the amendment would be found unconstitutional if tested in the federal courts. Smith countered Howell's one-hour opening oration with an endorsement of the disenfranchisement amendment and an attack on the Bourbon domination of Democratic politics. Fears of growing black voting power were kindled by Smith in the debate and in dozens of stump speeches. Thanks to the voting issue, party discontent, and a wide field of candidates which split the vote, Smith won easily. He received 104,796 popular votes and 312 county unit votes, to the 79,477 and 52 received by the other four candidates. Howell received only 23,006 popular votes and 12 county unit votes.

Howell never ran for office again, but he never divorced himself from politics or active public service outside the field of journalism. He maintained his position as an active member of the Democratic party, both in Georgia and at the national level. He corresponded regularly with every president after he became editor. His friendship with Franklin D. Roosevelt began sometime in the second decade of the twentieth century, and they wrote to each other on a "Dear Franklin," "Dear Clark" basis for many years. When Roosevelt began to visit Warm Springs, Georgia, to engage in therapy for his polio-afflicted legs, Howell visited the health spa frequently for chats with FDR. Presidents of both parties called on him to serve on national commissions. Warren Harding appointed him to a National Coal Commission in 1921. Calvin Coolidge asked him to serve on a National Transportation Commission.

Howell's second wife died in 1922. Two years later he married Margaret Cannon Carr of Durham, North Carolina.

Howell was always involved in editorial decisions and in writing editorials. His close reading of a routine city council story led to the newspaper's first Pulitzer Prize in 1931. A particular sentence in the story sparked a question in his mind. He followed the clue and his instincts and wrote what was said to have been one of the finest editorials of his career. A reportorial investigation and a series of articles followed, leading to indictments of a number of prominent officeholders on charges of accepting kickbacks for virtually all goods and services purchased by the city. Several wound up on chain gangs, and others faded from the public eye. Because of his lengthy friendship and support for FDR, Howell was offered a choice of several minor ambassadorships in rather out-of-the-way places such as Turkey, but he declined. Perhaps his most significant public service came in a totally unexpected and unlikely field: when the Federal Aviation Commission was organized in 1934 to study the fledgling aviation industry, FDR named Howell to chair it. As far as can be determined, Howell had never flown or shown more than minimal interest in the airplane and its role in American transportation. This was precisely why Howell was picked, said Roosevelt: he needed a man of ability, but one without commitments or preconceived stands on the issues. In the end the commission, after extensive hearings and investigation, put forth a list of recommendations which have, over the years, been accepted in one form or another.

Howell's newsroom involvement was legendary, though hardly unbiased. Ralph McGill wrote of his being called into Howell's office in early 1936, when Richard B. Russell's campaign for the Senate appeared to be foundering. McGill described the event this way:

> [Howell] asked me if I had not written politics in Tennessee. (I was then sports editor.) I said

I had. He then told me that Dick Russell had opened his campaign for the Senate a few days before and it had not got off the ground. He asked me to join Gov. Russell the next day at his home near Winder and cover that day's speech at Royston. His opponent was former Gov. Talmadge. "In Tennessee politics," I said, "you write hard." "Just give me a factual story," he said. (Papa Howell carried a small bamboo cane. It was his habit to whack friends across their rear as he met them. He patted me on the shoulder as he spoke and whacked me gently across the rear as I left. "Just the facts," he said.)
>
> I recall that Major Howell [Clark's son, also active on the newspaper by this time] winked at me.
>
> The next afternoon I wrote about Gov. Russell lighting the watch fires of democracy on the thousand hills of North Georgia and of how the lights from their purifying flames burned away the darkness of demagogic distortions and destroyed the curtains of falsehood.
>
> It was days before I got back. I went in to see Papa Howell. He whacked me joyfully across my ample bottom and said, "Just what I wanted, Ralphie. Just what I wanted. Dick is going to win." [He did.]

Among other distinctions, Howell served as a member of the official U.S. delegation to the Philippines when Manuel Quezon was made president in 1935; he was made a chevalier of the French Legion of Honor on 1 January 1936. He was a member of the Democratic National Committee for twenty-six years and a director of the New York-based Associated Press from its founding in 1900 until his death.

A newsman to the end, Howell was writing and editing as he fought the cancer that claimed him, and he dictated a Roosevelt victory editorial titled "The Path Ahead" to his chief editorial writer, Francis Clarke, from his bed. Ralph McGill, then primarily a sportswriter, was in the press box in New Orleans, where Georgia and Tulane were battling on the gridiron, when he heard the news of Howell's death. He stopped his note-taking in midsentence, rolled fresh copy paper into his typewriter, and wrote an eloquent, two-column tribute to "Papa" Howell, his friend and editor.

Howell was a dedicated, enthusiastic journalist, able to attract a superior editorial staff and stimulate it to carry out the day-to-day work. Because of his frequent absences he needed subordinates who could operate in tune with his editorial concept of the *Constitution*; Frank Stanton, Quimby

Melton, Sr., Joel Chandler Harris and his son Julian, columnist "Bill Arp," McGill, and many others did just that. Although the *Constitution* did not run away from its rivals, it stayed competitive in a newspaper-dominated communications environment: it climbed from an 1889 daily circulation of 11,000 to 99,000 in 1937, when the *Georgian* was selling 84,500 and the *Journal* 95,000 daily.

Howell was also a sought-after orator in the tradition of his predecessor, Grady, and his best-known successor, McGill. His skill on the platform gave him an opportunity to act as one of the spokesmen for the New South, picking up where Grady left off. He was a bridge between his region and the nation, both in journalism and politics. His oratory was in a conciliatory, heal-the-wounds-of-the-conflict vein; much of his writing for journals has the recurring theme of the regeneration of the South, perhaps to the point of boosterism. His service on the board of directors of the Associated Press—both the older, Illinois corporation and its post-1900, New York State-based successor—kept him in contact with journalism leaders from all parts of the nation. Through them he stayed in touch with journalistic innovation; they, in turn, respected him, his newspaper, and his region. Presidential appointments to commissions may be risky barometers of respect and ability, but the frequency with which he was called upon for service by presidents of both parties is evidence of his national standing.

Howell was deeply involved in explaining and rationalizing the South to the nation and was said to be instrumental in persuading Booker T. Washington to speak at the 1895 Atlanta Exposition. Washington's message there set white minds at ease, as he disclaimed for his race any aspirations of social equality. Howell called the speech a "platform upon which blacks and whites can stand with full justice to each other." Thus, though he was a decent man and a moderate on racial matters, he joined others in perpetuating the separate-but-equal myth and postponed the beginning of full equality of opportunity for blacks in the South.

References:

Wallace B. Eberhard, "Clark Howell and the *Atlanta Constitution*: A Preliminary Assessment," *Resources in Education*, 15 (October 1980);

Dewey W. Granthem, Jr., "Georgia Politics and the Disenfranchisement of the Negro," *Georgia Historical Quarterly*, 32 (1948): 4-21;

Joel Chandler Harris, "The New Editor-in-chief of the *Constitution*," *Review of Reviews*, 15 (May 1897): 558-560;

Dennis J. Pfennig, "The Captain Retires: Clark Howell Takes the Helm," *Atlanta Historical Journal*, 25 (Summer 1980): 5-20;

Pfennig, "Evan and Clark Howell and the *Atlanta Constitution*: The Partnership (1888-1897)," Ph.D. dissertation, University of Georgia, 1975.

Papers:

Clark Howell's papers are held by the Atlanta Historical Society, Emory University, and the University of Georgia.

Will Irwin

(14 September 1873-24 February 1948)

Robert V. Hudson
Michigan State University

MAJOR POSITIONS HELD: Subeditor and editor, *San Francisco Wave* (1899-1900); reporter, development editor, Sunday editor, *San Francisco Chronicle* (1900-1904); reporter, *New York Sun* (1904-1906); war correspondent, *New York Tribune* (1915).

BOOKS: *Stanford Stories*, by Irwin and C. K. Field (New York: Doubleday, Page, 1900);
The Reign of Queen Isyl, by Irwin and Gelett Burgess (New York: McClure, Phillips, 1903);
The Picaroons, by Irwin and Burgess (New York: McClure, Phillips, 1904; London: Chatto & Windus, 1904);
The Hamadryads, music by W. J. McCoy (San Francisco: Bohemian Club, 1904);
The City That Was (New York: Huebsch, 1906);
Pictures of Old Chinatown, text by Irwin, pictures by Arnold Genthe (New York: Moffat, Yard, 1908);
Warrior the Untamed (New York: Doubleday, Page, 1909);
The Confessions of a Con Man (New York: Huebsch, 1909);
The House of Mystery (New York: Century, 1910);
The Readjustment (New York: Huebsch, 1910);
Old Chinatown, by Irwin and Genthe (New York: Kennerley, 1912; London: Sidgwick & Jackson, 1913);
Where the Heart Is (New York & London: Appleton, 1912);
The Red Button (Indianapolis: Bobbs-Merrill, 1912);
Why Edison Is a Progressive (New York: Privately printed, 1912);
Beating Back, by Irwin & Al Jennings (New York & London: Appleton, 1914);
Men, Women and War (London: Constable, 1915; New York: Appleton, 1915);
The Latin at War (New York: Appleton, 1917);
A Reporter at Armageddon (New York & London: Appleton, 1918);
"The Next War" (New York: Dutton, 1921);
Columbine Time (Boston: Stratford, 1921);
Christ or Mars? (New York & London: Appleton, 1923);

Will Irwin (Culver Pictures)

Youth Rides West (New York: Knopf, 1925);
How Red Is America? (New York: Sears, 1927);
Highlights of Manhattan (New York: Century, 1927; revised and enlarged edition, New York & London: Appleton-Century, 1937);
The House That Shadows Built (Garden City: Doubleday, Doran, 1928);
Herbert Hoover: A Reminiscent Biography (New York: Century, 1928);
Cecilie and the Oil King (London & New York: Brentano's, 1928);
Propaganda and the News (New York & London: Whittlesey House/McGraw-Hill, 1936);
Scituate, 1636-1936 (Scituate, Mass.: Scituate Tercentenary Committee, 1936);
Spy and Counterspy, by Irwin and E. V. Voska (New

136

York: Doubleday, Doran, 1940; London: Harrap, 1941);

The Making of a Reporter (New York: Putnam's, 1942);

What You Should Know about Spies and Saboteurs, by Irwin and Thomas M. Johnson (New York: Norton, 1943);

Thirty-Eighth Anniversary of the Dutch Treat Club (New York: Privately printed, 1943);

A History of the Union League Club of New York City, by Irwin, E. C. May, and Joseph Hotchkiss (New York: Dodd, Mead, 1952);

Lute Song by Kao-Tong-Kia, adapted by Irwin and Sidney Howard (Chicago: Dramatic Publishing Co., 1954);

The American Newspaper, edited by C. F. Weigle and D. G. Clark (Ames: Iowa State University Press, 1969).

OTHER: *The Complete Works of Frank Norris*, volume 4, introduction by Irwin (Garden City: Doubleday, Doran, 1928);

"My Religion," in *They Believe*, as told by Otis Skinner and others (New York & London: Century, 1928);

Letters to Kermit from Theodore Roosevelt, 1902-1908, edited by Irwin (New York & London: Scribners, 1946).

PERIODICAL PUBLICATIONS: "The New York Sun," *American Magazine*, 67 (January 1909): 301-310;

"The American Newspaper," *Collier's*, 46 (21 January 1911) - 47 (29 July 1911);

"What's Wrong with the Associated Press?," *Harper's Weekly*, 58 (28 March 1914): 10-12;

"The United Press," *Harper's Weekly*, 58 (25 April 1914): 6-8;

"Detained by the Germans," *Collier's*, 54 (3 October 1914): 5-6, 23-24, 26-27;

"The Press in Europe," *Collier's*, 54 (7 November 1914): 13, 24;

"If You See It in the Paper, It's—?," *Collier's*, 72 (18 August 1923): 11-12, 26-27;

"Newspapers and Canned Thought," *Collier's*, 73 (21 June 1924): 13-14, 29;

"The Job of Reporting," *Scribner's*, 90 (November 1931): 492-497.

Will Irwin, one of the great reporters of the twentieth century, began his long and varied writing career as a newspaperman. He was later also a magazine writer and editor, novelist, playwright, poet, and propagandist. Upon his death, *Time* aptly called him a "Jack-of-all-letters." The *New York Times*, for which he had occasionally written, described him in this way: "Wide ranging, versatile, personally genial, a story-teller who delighted his cronies, he searched and wrote in just about every field available to an extraordinary curiosity." He was a close friend and the official biographer of Herbert Hoover and the author or coauthor of more than thirty factual and fictional books. But it is as a reporter that he is best remembered.

William Henry Irwin was born 14 September 1873 in Oneida, New York, and spent his early childhood in the Finger Lakes region. His mother, Edith Greene, the daughter of a Canandaigua, New York, painter and poet, infused in Irwin and his younger brother Wallace, who would become a famous humorist, the idea that art was the really important thing in life. Irwin's father, David, was a bookkeeper and lumber salesman from Erie, Pennsylvania, who unsuccessfully sought his fortune in the silver fields of Colorado in the late 1870s and early 1880s. From him Irwin acquired a sense of humor and a roving bent.

In Leadville, high in the Rocky Mountains, "Willy" Irwin liked school, imitated Shakespeare's sonnets, became interested in theater, and found his first newspaper job. He was a printer's devil, then newspaper carrier for C. C. Davis, who was campaigning in his *Herald-Democrat* to clean up the Wild West mining camp.

In the late 1880s the Irwin family, now five after the birth of Herman, moved to Denver, where Bill (as he was called by his family and close friends) and Wallace Irwin excelled in composition and oratory. A teacher at West High School, Sara Graham, recognized Bill's talent and encouraged him. After his mother died in 1892, a few months after his graduation, Miss Graham lent him money to attend Stanford University in Palo Alto, California.

He went to Palo Alto in September 1894. At Stanford he met Hoover, beginning a lifelong friendship that would generate a great deal of copy for him, and entered campus politics. He won prizes for poetry and stories in student publications and worked his way up to editor of the student newspaper. He was also active in debate and theater. His courses emphasized the classics. Late in his senior year he was considering a career in either theater or newspaper work, when he was asked to withdraw from the university or be expelled for writing rowdy lyrics to a drinking song that was sung by an inebriated baseball team to one of the most Victorian faculty members. He withdrew in the spring of 1898 and volunteered for the Spanish-American War,

Irwin with Samuel Hopkins Adams, who persuaded him to leave San Francisco and go to work for the New York Sun

but was rejected for varicose veins. While he waited for reinstatement at the university, he secretly married a classmate, Harriet (Hallie) Hyde. He was eventually allowed to graduate, and on 24 May 1899, he received a bachelor of arts degree.

The next month, at the urging of a friend, he began his newspaper career on the *San Francisco Wave*, an illustrated ten-cent tabloid with literary leanings. The regular editorial staff consisted of Irwin and J. O'Hara Cosgrave, the supervising editor and business manager. Irwin did most of the writing, including theater reviews, celebrity interviews, and compilations from foreign and domestic exchanges, often under pen names; he developed the ability to present facts authoritatively and interestingly, two attributes of his best journalism. Irwin also sent the weekly to press and, when Cosgrave was ill, took over the business and editorial sides, earning the title of editor. When Cosgrave sold the *Wave* in 1900, Irwin went to work for the *San Francisco Chronicle*.

As a reporter, he covered a wide variety of events, including murder investigations, trials, the public welcome of Vice-President Theodore Roose-

velt, the visit of President McKinley, and the sinking of a liner at the Golden Gate. After several months, he was appointed development editor to put out a Saturday page extolling the assets of northern California counties. Although he disliked desk work, he was lured by its regular, higher pay. In 1902 he accepted the Sunday editorship.

As he had done while on the *Wave*, he also free-lanced articles and stories for weeklies and magazines and collaborated on novels. After the Irwins' secret marriage was discovered, they were married in a formal ceremony to satisfy Hallie's dowager aunt. In October 1903 Hallie gave birth to a son, William Hyde Irwin.

At the Bohemian Club, a group of professional men and artists, Irwin met Samuel Hopkins Adams, a former *New York Sun* reporter who was working for publisher S. S. McClure. Adams eventually helped Irwin get a job on the *Sun*, which, Irwin later recalled, was at that time "the newspaperman's newspaper, the ambition of half the reporters in the United States."

The morning *Sun* had gained its reputation under the late Charles A. Dana and was still shining under management by some of his associates. Dana had put a premium on the reporter as writer: the reporter had to master the art of the plain tale "decked mainly with those details which the trained eye of the good reporter comes to perceive." The newspaper's style called for its reporters to write lucidly and concisely, with an effect of ease; to avoid stock phrases; to avoid the flamboyant; and never to overlook color and human interest. The techniques of writing for the *Sun* were similar to those of writing fiction, and from both the morning and evening *Suns* emerged novelists, essayists, and playwrights.

In June 1904 Irwin arrived in New York without his family and immediately began work. Covering train wrecks, murders, banquets, fake spiritualist mediums, fires, police court cases, burglaries, parades, demonstrations, highbinder wars, visiting celebrities, ship collisions, and the Russo-Japanese peace conference, he gradually earned status as the newspaper's highest-paid reporter. But this success did not satisfy his literary ambition, and his job became frustrating. Sometimes the copydesk butchered his writing, and sometimes assignments were dull or irritating. Just at quitting time one evening he was assigned to interview a Kansas City man about an unimportant bank deal, but by 1:30 A.M. the man had not arrived at his hotel, and Irwin went home swearing. Disgusted with the "newspaper game," he envied people who could make a living writing in more literary forms.

In 1906 S. S. McClure, whose book house and magazine had published some of Irwin's fiction, offered him an opportunity to become a writing editor of the magazine. It looked like a financially secure way to move from newspaper reporting to magazine writing, although it involved desk work. He gave notice of his resignation at the *Sun*, and while he learned his new job he worked for both the newspaper and McClure.

During this transitional period Irwin wrote his best-known newspaper story, one that reflected both his and the *Sun*'s styles at their best. In the local room, with little sleep, he had been writing running front-page accounts of the earthquake and fire that ravaged San Francisco for two days in April 1906, when he passed into a strange state. As he later explained, he could "work through every waking hour, without the slightest symptom of flagging mental energy." His faculties seemed to function "with preternatural acuteness," especially his memory. He could remember familiar blocks of San Francisco in detail, often even to the number of stories in buildings and to the legends on their signs. His sudden flood of consciousness may have been

released by a telegram from San Francisco that his relatives and friends were "all safe, well."

At noon on the third day the city editor asked him to prepare a description of San Francisco. Writing in pencil, as usual, Irwin drew on his highly sensitized memory for a word picture of the San Francisco he had known and loved. He began: "The old San Francisco is dead. The gayest, lightest hearted, most pleasure loving city of the western continent, and in many ways the most interesting and romantic, is a horde of huddled refugees living among ruins. It may rebuild; it probably will; but those who have known that peculiar city by the Golden Gate and have caught its flavor of the Arabian Nights feel that it can never be the same. It is as though a pretty, frivolous woman had passed through a great tragedy. She survives, but she is sobered and different. If it rises out of the ashes it must be a modern city, much like other cities and without its old atmosphere." Irwin vividly described the old city, its hills and waters and woods and winds and rains, creating moods and pictures with scenes like this: "Yet the most characteristic thing after all was the coloring. For the sea fog had a trick of painting every exposed object a sea gray which had a tinge of dull green in it. This, under the leaden sky of a San Francisco morning, had a depressing effect on first sight and afterward became a delight to the eye. For the color was soft, gentle and infinitely attractive in mass." He remembered in detail the steep flight of stairs up Vallejo Street leading to the winding path to the summit of Russian Hill, where he had lived among artists in small villas whose windows overlooked the "city of romance and a gateway to adventure." He recalled that "loud bit of hell," the Barbary Coast, then concluded with a paragraph about an old "sixty foot cross of timber. Once a high wind blew it down, and the women of the Fair family then had it restored so firmly that it would resist anything. As it is on a hill it must have stood. It has risen for fifty years above the gay, careless, luxuriant and lovable city, in full view from every eminence and from every valley. It must stand tonight above the desolation of ruins." Under the headline "THE CITY THAT WAS," the story was played on page five of the 21 April 1906 morning *Sun*. Although, as was the newspaper's practice, no by-line appeared, word of Irwin's authorship spread; suddenly he was famous in the "newspaper game." The story was polished for hard covers and was often reprinted.

By the eighth and last night of Irwin's journalistic marathon, he had written more than seventy-five columns about the disaster, helping the

Front cover of Collier's *magazine for 21 January 1911, containing the first of Irwin's series of articles on the history of American journalism. The completed series actually ran to fifteen installments, rather than the fourteen originally planned.*

Sun's little Laffan News Bureau successfully compete against the mighty Associated Press. Managing editor Chester S. Lord tried to convince him to stay, but Irwin hardened his heart and went to work for *McClure's* magazine.

He was unable to get along with McClure, and after less than a year with the magazine, starting as managing editor and being promoted to editor, he left with unpleasant memories. He could have returned to the *Sun*, but he thought that would forever prevent him from branching into other kinds of writing.

So he turned to free-lancing full-time, mostly for *Collier's*, in which he earned a reputation as a muckraker, exposing phony spiritualists and illicit liquor traffic, and as a press critic. For his fifteen-part series on "The American Newspaper" for *Collier's* in 1911, he drew not only on extensive research but also on his experiences with C. C. Davis, the *Chronicle*, and the *Sun*. He placed his hope for truthful newspapers on the reporters and editors in the newsrooms rather than on their publishers. Pieces on the liberal United Press and the conservative Associated Press for *Harper's Weekly* extended his reputation as a journalist. But in 1914 he gave up journalism to write fiction full-time.

He could not, however, tolerate for very long working alone at a desk. When the Germans invaded Belgium, he made arrangements with *Collier's* and the *American Magazine* to cover the war. After many adventures, including surviving house arrest by the invading German army in Louvain, he returned to the United States to do publicity work for the Commission for Relief in Belgium, headed by Herbert Hoover. In January 1915 he arranged with some magazines and the *New York Tribune* to resume his war correspondence.

In London he discovered that censorship prevented information about British soldiers from getting back home. Newspapers printed only brief communiqués, such as "We repulsed a heavy assault on the Ypres sector." There was no atmosphere, no description, no hero stories that would boost civilian morale; the public was getting restive. Irwin learned that confused fighting he had glimpsed three months before had been part of a general engagement fought with great valor by outnumbered and outgunned British soldiers who had blocked the Germans' path to channel ports. Three months had passed since the battle of Ypres, and the British public still had not been informed of the details, although this looked like a heroic, strategic victory. For three weeks superior German forces had stormed the British line, unsuccessfully trying to

break a hole between the French and Belgian armies. For numbers engaged and for casualties, this looked like the greatest battle the British army had ever fought. Here was a big story—if Irwin could break the censorship.

With help from confidential government sources, Irwin pursued his story, defying the British War Office. "You'll get your fingers burned," Hoover warned him. Lord Northcliffe (Alfred Harmsworth), publisher of the *Daily Mail* and *Times* of London, offered to cooperate but also warned him, "We may face a jolly row, you and I." Since the story could not be cabled without being killed or ruined by the censor, Lord Northcliffe and Irwin sent it by courier aboard a fast ship to the *Tribune*. The story was played high on page one on 18 March 1915. By arrangement with the *Tribune*, the *Times* of London published "The Splendid Story of Ypres" in the morning, the *Daily Mail* in the afternoon. Except for the lack of fine detail, the story was a *New York Sun*-style report of a big event, organized chronologically, without sensationalism and with emphasis on clarity.

With the perspective of three months after the retreat that Field Marshal French and his Tommies had turned into victory, Irwin could effectively blend analysis and narrative. His description of the last desperate assault by the Germans was such a blend: "Ypres is the old historic capital of French Flanders; and the British observers noted a curious fact about the operations against Ypres. However heavy the German bombardment, the famous old Cloth Hall, the most beautiful building of its kind in Flanders, went unscathed by shells. It was saved, we know now, for a special purpose. Kaiser Wilhelm himself was moving forward with a special force to a special assault which should finally and definitely break the allied line at Ypres. To do this was to clear Flanders of the Allies; then, as by custom he might, he intended to annex Belgium in the Cloth Hall of Ypres. He came with his own Prussian Guard; it was that Guard which, on the 15th, led another terrible massed attack. It was no less vigorous than the attack of the 31st, but the English, reinforced now by the French, met it better. Again the dense masses poured in; again the very officers fired until their rifles grew too hot to hold. When, that night, the strength of the German attack was spent, the better part of the Prussian Guard lay dead in a wood—lay at some places in ranks eight deep. . . . A fortnight more, and the line from La Bassée to the sea had been locked as thoroughly as the line from Switzerland to La Bassée. It had cost England 50,000 men out of a 120,000 engaged—a proportion of loss greater than any previous war ever knew. It had cost the French and Belgians 70,000. It probably cost the Germans 375,000. That is a half-million in all. The American Civil War has been called the most terrible in modern history. In that one long battle Europe lost as many men as the North lost in the whole Civil War." The story made a great impact.

He did not consider the story extraordinary, but readers did. The *British Weekly* declared that "no message from any correspondent during the war has surpassed in merit and interest" Irwin's report, which would "live as one of the greatest in history." Few Britons disagreed with the *Daily Mail* that the story was "a noble epic." Northcliffe's newspaper called the attention of its readers to Irwin's power of visualization, one of the strongest attributes of his journalism and fiction: "In the power to visualize the great moments of the war and bring them up before the reader, as in a picture, Mr. Irwin excels among the correspondents of to-day." Elsewhere the story was called "an amazing performance."

The British were craving real news and glorification of their army, and Irwin became a sensation in London. He was guest of honor in the homes and clubs of political leaders and aristocrats, and people followed him on the street like a heavyweight champion. Readers cried over his story. Northcliffe yielded to popular demand and reprinted "The Splendid Story of Ypres" in a pamphlet, with a first edition of half a million. The story subsequently reappeared as the climax of Irwin's first collection of war correspondence, *Men, Women and War*, published in London in 1915. He relished the popularity.

But the British War Office, whose censorship he had thwarted, and the French, who felt he had given them insufficient credit, barred his way to the front. Finally, he got a pass to Boulogne, the Royal Army Medical Corps hospital center in France, and to any point where the RAMC worked.

On the night of 22 April 1915, he learned of a poison-gas attack that day by the Germans in the Ypres sector, violating the Hague Convention of 1907. He headed toward the front on an empty hospital train, which stopped shortly before dawn at a first-aid dressing post where British soldiers lay in rows, choking. Ambulances added more wounded and dead to the rows on the platform, while in the distance could be heard the drum of artillery. As Irwin helped carry stretchers, he noticed a peculiar smell, and he began coughing; the air burned in his lungs. It seemed like an eternity before the loaded train backed out for Boulogne.

The poison-gas attack was Irwin's "second battle of Ypres," as he called it in his dispatch of 24 April to the *Tribune*. At first the gas from the "asphyxiating shells" did not seem especially lethal but "one that rather overpowers its victims and puts them hors de combat for a few days without killing many. Its effect at Bixschoote may have been due to panic caused by the novelty of the device." But the effect of "the noxious trench gas" was deadlier than he had at first thought. "Some of the rescued have already died from the after effects," he reported two days later. "How many of the men left unconscious in the trenches when the French broke died from the fumes it is impossible to say, since those trenches were at once occupied by the Germans." Irwin did not report that he, too, was a victim of the gas.

The effects of the gas and an attack of tonsillitis forced him back to London and to bed. After his recovery he was still barred from the front, so he returned to the United States. In the winter of 1915-1916 he besieged the British and French embassies in Washington for permission to return to the war zone; he was successful with the French. Having been divorced in 1908 by Hallie, who had stayed in California, he married writer Inez Haynes Gillmore in 1916 and then returned with her to France as a correspondent exclusively for the *Saturday Evening Post*. After a shake-up in the British government, he got an appointment with the secretary of state for war, David Lloyd George, who erased his name from the War Office blacklist.

Now Irwin was free to travel wherever reporters could go. It was a mixed blessing: near Gorizia a shell exploded near him, knocking him down and injuring his right eardrum. Gradually his hearing in that ear vanished.

In 1918 he joined the Committee on Public Information, headed by George Creel, as chairman of its new foreign division in Washington. After six months he was back in Europe for the *Saturday Evening Post*. He reported events there before and after the signing of the peace treaty.

In 1920 he returned home to crusade for international cooperation and against war in lectures, magazine articles, and books, notably his bestselling "*The Next War*" (1921). He left the *Saturday Evening Post* to champion the League of Nations in *Collier's*. He continued to write other journalism and fiction, including his best novel, *Youth Rides West* (1925), which he researched in Leadville.

Through the Depression and World War II he wrote for the North American Newspaper Alliance and other syndicates, for *Liberty* and other magazines, and for book publishers. His polemical

Propaganda and the News (1936) included a history of journalism, and his autobiographical *The Making of a Reporter* (1942) emphasized his career as a reporter. For the American stage, he adapted (with Sidney Howard) an ancient Chinese play, which eventually became the Broadway musical *Lute Song by Kao-Tong-Kia*. He still took pride in his skills as a newspaperman, however.

On 7 January 1944 at 9:15 P.M. he was getting ready for bed when United Press called him. "Mrs. Hoover dropped dead at 7:30 tonight," the newsman said. "Will you turn us out a column appreciation right away and telephone it in?" Irwin wrote for an hour and spent an additional half hour phoning in his 800-word story, revising as he talked. "Seemed quite like old newspaper days," he wrote to his son, "and with all my grief—I'd known Lou Henry for 49 years—I felt bucked up to think that I could still do a rush, emergency newspaper story."

Early in 1948 Irwin suffered a series of strokes. On 24 February he died of a cerebral occlusion in St. Vincent's Hospital, near his Greenwich Village town house.

His death ended a life—as he described it—"led more for experience than for achievement," although he had received many honors for both. They included the Legion of Honor, King Albert Medal, Olympic Games medal, and a Doctor of Humane Letters from Knox College. Also he had served his professional organizations in several capacities, including as president of both the American Centre of P.E.N. and the Author's Guild of the Author's League of America. Above all, he prized his profession for its variety. As an editor he had quickly tired of the "sober routine work" at a desk, and as a fiction writer he had found it impossible to sustain the solitary task of daily writing. He had enjoyed newspaper reporting because each day brought something new, something unexpected, some adventure. He had the restless curiosity of a natural reporter.

Most of Irwin's works—and almost all of his best works—were factual. Even much of his fiction was founded on fact, sometimes on his experiences as a newspaper reporter. He could recreate, as in *The City That Was,* better than he could create. Ironically, some of what he wrote for only a day, such as his *Sun* classic, has outlived his more intentionally literary endeavors.

Biography:
Robert V. Hudson, *The Writing Game: A Biography of Will Irwin* (Ames: Iowa State University Press, 1982).

References:
William Rose Benét, "The Phoenix Nest," *Saturday Review of Literature*, 31 (12 June 1948): 36;
Robert V. Hudson, "Organizing U.S. Propaganda in World War I," *Grassroots Editor* (July-August 1973): 20-22, 32;
Hudson, "Will Irwin's Pioneering Criticism of the Press," *Journalism Quarterly* (Summer 1970): 263-271;
"That Grave, Gay Irwin," *Independent*, 100 (15 November 1919): 96;
"War as National Suicide," *Literary Digest* (7 August 1915): 252-253.

Papers:
Will Irwin's papers are at Beinecke Rare Book and Manuscript Library, Yale University.

James Keeley

(14 October 1867-7 June 1934)

Norman H. Sims
University of Massachusetts, Amherst

MAJOR POSITIONS HELD: Managing editor, general manager, *Chicago Tribune* (1898-1914); owner, *Chicago Herald* (1914-1918).

BOOK: *Newspaper Work: An Address by James Keeley* (Chicago, 1912).

James Keeley ushered the *Chicago Tribune* into the twentieth century. As managing editor and general manager from 1898 to 1914, he shaped the *Tribune* to meet his idea of the modern newspaper: an independent institution that gave "personal service" to its readers. He tried to make the *Tribune* a "friend" of its readers at a time when the city was becoming an impersonal place. A model of the incorruptible, tough, cigar-chewing editor, Keeley won the loyalty of his reporters and readers. When the *Tribune* referred to itself in advertisements as "The World's Greatest Newspaper," it cited Keeley's principles as the reason why.

Keeley was born 14 October 1867 in London. He told friends that his first memories were of a foundling home and that he grew up scrambling for a living as a newsboy in the Whitechapel district. Passing a booking agent's shop one day, he said, he spotted a leftover ticket to Leavenworth, Kansas; he saved his money until he could buy it, and then he came to the United States. This story of his youth Keeley maintained until his death, but according to his biographer, James Weber Linn, it was a fiction. Linn discovered that Keeley's parents were James and Elizabeth Rawlings Keeley. His mother was a stubborn, puritanical, and industrious woman who had been disinherited by her family when she married. The marriage was a stormy one, and Keeley's father departed in 1875. Elizabeth Keeley taught school to support herself and her two sons.

Keeley was regarded as an excellent pupil at school, but at fourteen he was sent to work for an uncle who ran a book and stationery business in London. The job involved folding and delivering newspapers in the morning, buying publications during the day in Fleet Street and the Strand, and delivering papers again in the evening. Keeley jostled with the other newsboys during twelve-hour

James Keeley in 1913

workdays on London's streets, where determination was a necessity. "It's an education, in its way," he later said.

His mother corresponded with a family named Perryman who had immigrated to Leavenworth; they suggested that Keeley come to live with them, and his mother bought him a ticket to America. He immigrated in 1883, stopping for half a day in Chicago to change trains along the way. He got a job at a jewelry store in Leavenworth, and four years later became engaged to Annie Perryman. The engagement apparently caused the split with his family, which resulted in Keeley's tale of an orphan's childhood in London. In one version of the story, told by Keeley's brother, Elizabeth Keeley wrote a damaging letter about Keeley to Annie Perryman, who then broke the engagement. Keeley left

144

Leavenworth filled with hatred for his mother and never spoke of her again. In Annie's version, another woman stole Keeley away, but her story does not account for Keeley's sudden dislike for his mother. Whatever happened, Keeley left Leavenworth around 1887, and his English childhood underwent a complete transformation that he carried to his deathbed.

While living in Wyandotte, Kansas, Keeley began supplying "items" to the *Kansas City Journal*, and he soon won a regular job as a reporter. Watching what happened to his copy at the editor's desk, Keeley learned to eliminate the surplus words. "I starved in Wyandotte," he said, "but I learned there how to write a newspaper story." Between 1887 and 1889 he also worked on the *Memphis Commercial* and the *Louisville Commercial*. From the beginning of his career, Keeley was known as someone who would stubbornly dig out a story. His first big story involved chasing down and capturing a murder suspect in the Arkansas swamps. Keeley held

Keeley at age fifteen, shortly before he left England for America

the man at gunpoint until a fellow reporter arrived with the sheriff.

Keeley went to Chicago in 1889 and immediately won a job at the *Tribune*, where he was to remain for twenty-five years. Most of the great Chicago reporters of the 1890s shared an apprenticeship on the night police beat. Breaking into the newspapers along with Keeley during that decade were George Ade, James O'Donnell Bennett, E. S. "Teddy" Beck, Finley Peter Dunne, John Kelley, H. E. "Hek" Keough, Wallace Rice, Charley Seymour, Henry Justin Smith, Bert Leston Taylor ("B. L. T."), and Brand Whitlock. On the police beat, Keeley established a reputation as a reliable newsman. After two years, he was promoted to general assignment reporter.

In the spring of 1892, word was received in the *Tribune* office that a "rustler's war" had broken out in Wyoming. Keeley was given his first chance to make a splash on the front pages: he was handed $300 and told to catch the next train for the West. When he arrived in Wyoming, he heard stories of 100 gentlemen besieged at a ranch by an army of "rustlers," with the Sixth Cavalry on its way to the rescue. Keeley displayed his talents for industrious reporting and for squeezing all the drama from a story. At one point he drove forty miles in a buggy through snow-covered country to catch up with the cavalry, along the way cutting the telegraph line so a rival reporter could not beat him with the story. In the end, the "rustler's war" turned out to be more of a local ranchers' dispute that involved the killing of two persons who lived 2,000 miles from Chicago. Yet Keeley's reports made the front page eleven times in two weeks.

Keeley married Gertrude Small on 5 June 1895. She had grown up in Maine and attended Boston University before beginning a career as a reporter on the *Boston Post*, and she had worked on the *Tribune* from 1893 until their marriage. During that period Keeley had risen to a position of power, first as assistant city editor and then, at age twenty-seven, as city editor. Keeley had plans for the *Tribune*: "I'll make it the world's greatest newspaper," he told his wife.

Keeley's work brought him into the shadowy zone between reporting and editing. As an editor, Keeley literally kept an eye on the streets. He walked to work to keep the images of Chicago's bustling streets fresh in his mind. When a big story broke, such as the tornado that struck St. Louis in 1896, Keeley reacted as a reporter, leading the *Tribune* expedition that was sent to cover the story. One of his greatest moments as an editor occurred in May 1898, during the Spanish-American War. Coverage of the war created an atmosphere where speed, excitement, and drama were crucial to newspaper success. Keeley knew how to play the game. When Adm. George Dewey destroyed the Spanish fleet in Manila Bay, Keeley got his chance. The *New York World* and *Chicago Tribune* had an arrangement to share the reports of Edward Harden, who had accompanied Dewey to the Philippines. Two other reporters were also present when Dewey said to Capt. Charles Gridley, "You may fire when you are ready, Gridley," and launched the attack. Dewey cabled Washington that a battle had been drawn, but nothing more. Then he cut the telegraph cable. Washington and the rest of the world had no further news of the massacre. Returning four days later to Hong Kong, Dewey filed his report to the secretary of the navy while the correspondents anxiously lined up behind him. Dewey's message went first. But Harden, who knew how the telegraph worked, filed his report as an "urgent" at $5 a word. Dewey's message traveled slowly; each relay station repeated the message to assure accuracy. Meanwhile, Harden's forty-five-word dispatch sped on its way, arriving in America three hours before Dewey's. The message was too late to make the *World*, but Keeley had posted a man to wait every night in the *World* office for Harden's report. Keeley was notified at 3:20 A.M. and stopped the *Tribune* presses. In stacked headlines the *Tribune* proclaimed, "DIRECT NEWS FROM DEWEY! NO AMERICAN SHIP LOST! NOT ONE AMERICAN KILLED! ONLY SIX AMERICANS INJURED! ELEVEN SPANISH SHIPS SUNK! 300 SPANIARDS ARE KILLED! 400 SPANIARDS INJURED!" The other morning papers reported no news from Dewey. Keeley capped his triumph by telephoning President McKinley to inform him of the American victory. While it was hardly a milestone in newspaper history—everyone would have the same story by the next news cycle—it was the kind of stunt that made journalism so dramatic in the 1890s, and it proved that Keeley had the flair needed by great reporters and editors in that age. In 1898, at age thirty-one, Keeley was promoted to managing editor.

The interests of ordinary people could dictate policy to Keeley. Once he ran four columns of an Elihu Root speech on the front page when other papers gave it far less attention. Keeley had passed through the composing room and noticed the printers gathered around reading the speech. "If half a dozen hardboiled printers stopped work to read it, I knew the public would eat it up," he explained. When breaking news was flowing into the *Tribune*, Keeley took his lead from the demands for information heard on the telephone and in the street. One example was the 1903 Iroquois Theater fire, when most of the requests coming into the office were for names of the dead. Other newspapers put narrative stories of the disaster on the front page, but Keeley's *Tribune* devoted the entire front page to a list of 571 names and addresses of people who were dead or missing. Even Burton Rascoe, who was not fond of Keeley, admitted that this was "a stroke of genius" that satisfied the question uppermost in the minds of most Chicagoans. Another writer said of Keeley's rather strange-looking front page, "No other paper did it, but each editor recognized the minute he saw the *Tribune*, that Keeley had beaten him."

As an editor, Keeley scored some of his greatest reporting scoops. On a December night in 1905, Keeley left the *Tribune* around midnight after putting the finishing touches on the morning's paper. Passing the First National Bank building, he noticed a meeting in progress which included some of the wealthiest financiers in the city. Keeley quickly joined the meeting and acted as if he belonged. The bankers and financiers were conferring about John R. Walsh. Walsh had made a fortune in publishing and banking, but now his financial ship was sinking, and only this gathering of bankers—and James Keeley of the *Tribune*—knew it. Once the bankers realized that Keeley had the story, they would not let him leave until the *Tribune* was on its way to the city. Keeley took off his coat and settled in for a long evening. Soon he wandered off to the toilet, where he found an empty bucket. Casually he carried the bucket to an outside door of the building, told the guard, "These guys want more coffee," and escaped. Dashing back to the office, Keeley recalled the delivery wagons and ordered the front page done over. Only the *Tribune* carried the Walsh scoop the next morning. Eventually, Walsh's newspaper, the *Chronicle*, failed along with his banks, thousands lost their money, and Walsh went to jail. Keeley considered the story his finest triumph as a reporter.

Keeley's reputation was built on Chicago stories, pursued regardless of who might be offended or damaged. Among his contemporaries he was called "ruthless" and recognized as a man with many enemies. Keeley did not lack compassion, but he was tenacious. When he got his teeth into a story, he set his jaw and held on.

The *Tribune* was among the last of the Chicago newspapers to drop an official party designation.

Although labeled Republican or Independent-Republican, under Keeley's leadership it was one of the most independent papers in the city. Keeley strictly separated the editorial side from the advertising side. The story is told that in 1905, a wealthy gentleman visited Keeley's office to ask that a damaging story about his son not be printed. The man told Keeley, "I have been a friend of the *Tribune* for forty years." Keeley snapped back, "The *Tribune* has no friends and wants none."

His fierce independence and tough manner may have cost him a price in friendships at the time, although his later life shows that not even the businessmen he attacked in print held a grudge against him. Keeley is said to have once told his wife that he had no best friends. "If you should die," she asked, "whom shall I ask to be your pallbearers?" "Gertrude, there are ten thousand men in Chicago right now that would give their right eyes to be my pallbearers," Keeley responded.

Keeley's reporters lived in fear of his sharp rebukes; high praise from the young managing editor might consist of a brief note which said, "Good work," and nothing more. He was heavyset—not fat, but solid like an English bulldog. When the pressure was on, Keeley chewed unlighted cigars down to stubs and then threw them away. When things quieted down again, he might light the ever-present cigar, but he was never known as a drinker. While most reporters who worked under Keeley were loyal, Burton Rascoe, who was on the *Tribune* staff but not directly under Keeley, was critical. Rascoe described Keeley as "a particularly vicious bulldog" who was "both pompous and tyrannical." Other editors and reporters constructed their days around Keeley's demanding schedule, but Rascoe said, "If I had been directly responsible to him I should have been so frightened and intimidated by him that I should never have worked more than a day or so under his direction."

The famous *Tribune* cartoonist, John T. McCutcheon, remembered a more sympathetic figure. "Keeley loved music; he had a very sentimental side which came out occasionally in spite of his efforts to smother it. Behind his abrupt way of giving his staccato orders, he had a venturesome soul; he would have liked to be off doing the things his correspondents were doing. He was always sympathetic with my desire to go adventuring and with any departure I made from the routine cartoon. In after years I had many occasions to be grateful for the permissions of absence he granted, and the way he played up my stuff."

Two things suggest that Keeley's reputation as a ruthless man did not do him justice. One is the story of the capture of Paul Stensland in 1907. Stensland was a Norwegian immigrant who became the president of the largest state bank in Chicago, a millionaire who had served on prestigious public boards. One day Stensland disappeared, and it was discovered that hundreds of thousands of dollars were missing from the bank. Keeley assumed the role of detective and personally went in search of the man. Following tips, Keeley chased rumors about Stensland across Europe and into North Africa. With the determination that had given him the "ruthless" reputation to begin with, Keeley finally found Stensland in Tangier. He had captured an old, tired, and scared man. "After that I lived with a naked tortured soul for quite a while," Keeley said. "I don't want any more. From then on I mean to let policemen capture any law violators. I'm through." Stensland was returned to Chicago, convicted, and sentenced to jail. After the trial, Keeley's compassion emerged. When it was clear that the bank's affairs were straightened out and the depositors would be paid in full, Keeley successfully campaigned for Stensland's immediate parole and secured him a job with Chicago businessman Samuel Insull.

More significant as an indication that Keeley was not a hard and ruthless man was his dedication to "personal service," which reveals a genuine concern for the problems of ordinary people. Keeley's definition of *news* meant that the *Tribune* should have no friends and want none, indeed, could not afford to have any. But his definition of the role of the *newspaper* in modern life was quite different. "Personal service" was the highest aim of the modern newspaper, according to Keeley. "It must enter into the everyday life of its readers, and, like the parish priest, be guide, counselor, and friend," he said. In the early twentieth century, Keeley saw the changes sweeping over the city. Chicago was filling up with immigrants, migrants from the farm, and new types of individuals who did not have the ties of family and tradition that bound them to stable communities. The newspaper, then, had a role to play in the community that *was* like that of the parish priest; the newspaper could be a reliable friend, a trusted informant, even a confessor.

The standard definition of news—reports of government, public affairs, crime—was not enough to satisfy Keeley's theory of "personal service." Although William Randolph Hearst saw the need for "departments" in the newspaper before Keeley did, nevertheless Keeley was among the leaders in pioneering the omnibus newspaper of the

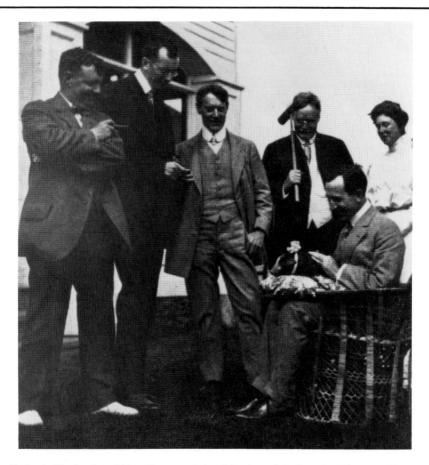

*Keeley (with cigar) and his wife entertaining friends at their farm in Wheaton, Illinois.
The man with the pig in his lap is cartoonist John T. McCutcheon.*

twentieth century. He opened a health department in the *Tribune* written by Dr. W. A. Evans. The *Tribune* was among the first major newspapers to refuse patent medicine ads—which Keeley said cost the paper $200,000 annually—as a "matter of conscience, a dislike for dirty dollars." There was a column of advice to the lovelorn, written by Laura Jean Libbey, which drew 3,500 letters a week. A column by actress Lillian Russell gave beauty advice and attracted as many as 200 letters a day. The poet and columnist Bert Leston Taylor ("B. L. T.") wrote "A Line o' Type or Two," Finley Peter Dunne's "Mr. Dooley" appeared in the *Sunday Tribune*, H. E. Keough and Ring Lardner wrote sports, and McCutcheon's cartoons appeared in the paper. Marion Harland's "Helping Hand" department functioned as a clearinghouse for the exchange of items no longer needed by their owners; even a dozen orphaned children found homes through Mrs. Harland's column. The *Tribune* advised its readers on how to earn money at home, how to fight the increased cost of living, and on dietetics, travel,

and cooking. The whole idea of "personal service" was epitomized in "The Friend of the People" department. Keeley explained: "This is where the citizen with the grievance files his complaint—the lion's mouth of today. Here come the simple annals of a broken sidewalk, street lamps that fail to light the way, insanitary alleys, unlighted halls in tenement houses, uncollected garbage, inattention on the part of public officials or servants of a public service corporation, the petty burdens of the poor and the uninfluential. The number of small wrongs that afflict the citizens of a community is equaled only by the lack of success that attends the ordinary man in his efforts to secure redress. But it would astonish you to observe the celerity with which 'The Friend of the People' secures results." Following the tradition pioneered by Keeley, newspapers and television stations still gain public support today by seeking to correct the commercial and governmental injustices suffered by ordinary citizens. Hundreds of people were killed or injured annually in Fourth of July celebrations, and Keeley began a campaign for a Sane Fourth. His paper ran a clearinghouse at Christmas that permitted the wealthy to anonymously donate gifts to needy children in the city.

The *Chicago Tribune*'s motto has always been exaggerated and the subject of jokes, but Keeley could take real pride in the full-page *Tribune* advertisements labeled "Why 'The World's Greatest Newspaper'?" Printed under that headline were Keeley's public remarks on the role of the modern newspaper as an organ of personal service.

When none of the family owners of the *Tribune* were prepared to assume leadership in 1910, the more experienced Keeley was promoted to general manager. From that position he exercised "absolute" control, as he once told a Senate committee. Soon after coming into "absolute control" of the *Tribune*, Keeley took the paper to the brink of financial disaster by fearlessly, stubbornly sticking to his guns. The issue was political corruption; Keeley knew he was right and refused to back down. The story involved William Lorimer, who had been chosen by the Illinois Joint Assembly in 1909 as U.S. Senator. The assembly had been deadlocked through ninety-four ballots, but on the ninety-fifth there was a sudden switch from the leading candidate to Lorimer. Despite suspicions, no evidence of bribery on the ninety-fifth ballot could be found. Lorimer entered the Senate. But soon a story appeared in the *Tribune* under the headline "Democratic Legislator Confesses He Was Bribed to Cast Vote for Lorimer for United States Senator." Keeley had purchased a story testifying to the exchange of money. The source was a legislator, a not entirely savory character himself. Keeley thoroughly investigated the story and was convinced of its authenticity. But the hard evidence was lacking. The Senate failed to eject Lorimer. The source of the bribe money was in question, but Keeley thought he knew. Two one-line editorials written by Keeley appeared in the *Tribune*: "Who furnished the 'dust'—to use a colloquialism—to bribe the legislators?" and "Who provided the grease to lubricate the wheels of the senatorial chariot?" "Dust" referred to the lumber interests who were supposed to profit from Lorimer's position, and "grease" suggested the meatpacking industry was involved. Trials of alleged participants failed to bring convictions. Libel suits were filed and Keeley responded that if anything libelous had been printed the injured parties could have the *Tribune* building, then worth $1,500,000. Keeley owned not one penny of *Tribune* stock. As his biographer said, "If Keeley's foot slipped he would be splashed, but

they [the McCormicks and Pattersons, owners of the *Tribune*] would be drowned in the flood of libel suits." As the floodwaters rose, it was a rival paper, Herman H. Kohlsaat's *Record-Herald*, that came to Keeley's rescue. A friend in the wealthy Chicago Club told Kohlsaat that his firm had supplied $10,000 of the $100,000 used to bribe the legislators. In testimony following this revelation, the truth emerged: the lumber and meatpacking interests had organized the bribes. The Senate unseated Lorimer, and the threat of libel suits faded away. Keeley had risen from night police reporter on the *Tribune* to city editor, managing editor, and general manager whose authority "in all departments" was "absolute" even to the point where he could risk the fortune of a newspaper he did not own. He was cool under pressure and pursued the lumbermen and packers mercilessly, although they were men for whom he held no personal dislike, and in fact, they owned companies for which Keeley would later work.

During his editorship, Keeley put into practice his theory of the newspaper. As early as 1895, he said, "News is a commodity, and for sale like any other commodity." The commercial metaphor implied that only honest news, independently reported and edited, would be rewarded by the buying public. Like a produce stand, the newspaper would prosper as long as it had the freshest and highest quality commodity in town.

Keeley thought suppression of the news was among journalism's cardinal sins. "By improper suppression a newspaper sells its soul and betrays its readers. To my mind it is the high treason of journalism," Keeley told a Notre Dame class in 1912. He added, "The man who thinks he can betray his readers, the man who thinks he can let dollars supersede duty, the man who thinks he can let private interest dictate his policy—and doing these things secretly imagines that he can pose as a leader of public opinion, an exponent of right and honesty—is fooling himself, not the public. The public is canny and its eye teeth are getting sharper every minute. The day of invisible government in the newspaper world, as in the political world, is vanishing."

Part of the paper's duty was to report events fairly. "There should be no partisanship in politics, no prejudice in religion, no hostility to organized labor, no antagonism to wealth per se, no color of opinion, in fact, opinion would be barred from the report of every happening, every meeting, every public discussion, everything that goes to make up the daily grist of news," Keeley said. In the role of impartial friend, Keeley found a justification for the ideology of objectivity that transformed the newspaper world early in this century. His was not an abstract faith in science, but a knowledge of how a friend must act to gain the confidence of others.

In May 1914, Keeley's long relationship with the *Tribune* ended. According to biographer Linn, Joseph Medill Patterson and Robert R. McCormick were ready to assume control and would have pushed Keeley out anyway. Burton Rascoe claims the parting was more of a coup engineered by Patterson and McCormick, in which they seized power from Keeley at a stockholder's meeting. In any event, Keeley had already been involved in negotiations for the purchase of Herman Kohlsaat's *Chicago Record-Herald*. With the help of wealthy backers such as Ogden Armour, Victor Lawson, and Samuel Insull, Keeley took over the *Record-Herald* on 11 May 1914. The reputation of the *Tribune* changed after Keeley departed, as it tried to exercise more influence upon national policy, but it continued to develop along the lines of "personal service" that he had first carved out.

In other ways, however, the *Tribune* acted like a jilted lover. When the "Official History" of the *Tribune* was published by the firm in 1922, Keeley rated scant mention. At his death, he was given only a minor obituary in the paper. The man who at one time aspired to make it the "world's greatest newspaper," and was given some credit toward that goal in *Tribune* ads, nearly became a nonentity. For some time, Keeley disappeared from the *Tribune* almost as completely as had his own mother after Keeley left Leavenworth.

The move to the *Record-Herald* represents a dramatic shift in Keeley's attitude. While he had been a social acquaintance of many businessmen before, he was not associated with them financially. His bulldog manner now softened. "Along the line somewhere," writes Linn, Keeley turned into a "house pet." The paper, renamed simply the *Herald*, became something the financial backers would approve. It was less ferocious than the *Tribune*.

Keeley held his ground in competition with the *Tribune* and other Chicago newspapers until World War I, but the paper lacked adequate funding from the start. The *Tribune* had always geared up for war coverage. But Keeley was an expert on Chicago, not on European affairs. When the archduke Ferdinand was assassinated, an event the *Tribune* realized would ignite all of Europe, Keeley editorialized in the *Herald* that "the fortunes and calamities of the House of Hapsburg are far away from us and of little interest." Fighting hard to recover lost ground in war coverage, Keeley gathered facts firsthand during a European trip in 1916, but the *Tribune* always stayed a few steps ahead. Robert J. Casey, who then worked on Hearst's *Examiner*, said Keeley was no longer feared after he left the *Tribune*. "Nobody in the city room [of the *Examiner*] ever thought of wasting his animosity" on the *Herald*, Casey wrote. "We were gunning for the *Tribune*." On 30 April 1918, Keeley sold the *Herald* to Hearst, who combined it with his paper to become the *Herald and Examiner*. Keeley accepted an offer to work in the Department of Public Information of the British government and left for England, although he expected to return to another Chicago newspaper. He never did. The *Herald* was his last newspaper position.

After the war, Keeley worked for the remainder of his career as a publicist, often for the businessmen he had attacked as editor of the *Tribune*. Keeley's friends and backers, people like Samuel Insull and Julius Rosenwald, were immigrants, too. But Keeley differed from them. He was a man in need of money. He became a commercial press agent for a group of Chicago meatpackers ("Who provided the grease to lubricate the wheels of the senatorial chariot?"), for the Warren Harding presidential campaign, and for the Pullman Company, where he later became a vice-president.

The last decade of Keeley's life was spent in relative prosperity, among close friends who frequently visited his home and in traveling with his wife. After Gertrude's death in 1926, Keeley continued his social rounds, contributed to the creation of a new wing in a Chicago hospital, and was honored on 20 March 1933 — the fiftieth anniversary of his arrival in Chicago as a young boy on his way to Kansas — by one hundred people who considered him a close friend. A statement made about him in the *Chicago Evening Post* some twenty years earlier, "Nobody ever spoke of him as a good fellow," became an amusing line from the past.

Keeley died on 7 June 1934 at his home in Lake Forest, Illinois, from complications associated with heart disease and a cerebral hemorrhage.

Biography:
James Weber Linn, *James Keeley, Newspaperman* (Indianapolis: Bobbs-Merrill, 1937).

References:
Robert J. Casey, *Such Interesting People* (Indianapolis: Bobbs-Merrill, 1943);
Charles H. Dennis, *Victor Lawson; His Time and His*

Work (Chicago: University of Chicago Press, 1935);

Peter Clark Macfarland, "Explaining Keeley," *Collier's Weekly* (28 June 1913): 5;

John T. McCutcheon, *Drawn From Memory* (Indianapolis: Bobbs-Merrill, 1950);

Burton Rascoe, *Before I Forget* (New York: Literary Guild of America, 1937).

Moses Koenigsberg

(16 April 1879-21 September 1945)

Alice A. Parsons

MAJOR POSITIONS HELD: Publisher, *San Antonio* (Texas) *Evening Star* (1892-1895); editor, *Chicago American* (1903-1907), *Boston American* (1908-1909); president, Newspaper Feature Service (1913-1928), King Features Syndicate (1915-1928), International News Service (1919-1928).

BOOKS: *Southern Martyrs* (Montgomery, Ala.: Brown, 1898);
The Elk and the Elephant (N.p., 1899);
King News: An Autobiography (Philadelphia & New York: Stokes, 1941).

Moses Koenigsberg was, in his own words, "educated in public schools and in newspaper offices." He reported for, edited, or owned approximately twenty newspapers, and demonstrated talent and integrity as a journalist and as a businessman; but he is little remembered today. He spent the most productive part of his career as an employee of William Randolph Hearst, and his accomplishments have often been attributed to the Hearst organization rather than to him personally. Koenigsberg conceived of, established, and ran the first modern newspaper features and comics syndicates; the features and news dispatches distributed by organizations under his control appeared regularly in newspapers having a mass circulation of 16,000,000 readers on weekdays and 25,000,000 on Sundays.

Koenigsberg says in his autobiography, *King News* (1941), that his father, Harris Wolf Koenigsberg, a Russian Jew, was permitted to marry Julia Foreman, the daughter of a Polish Jewish patriot, only after he promised her father that he would escape with her from czarist rule. Following their wedding, they were smuggled across the border hidden in a chest under a load of hay. They reached the United States after the Civil

War. The Koenigsberg family, including Moses, three older brothers, and a sister, settled in San Antonio, Texas, where Harris Koenigsberg opened a tailoring business.

Moses was an ambitious boy who printed and published a monthly newspaper, the *Amateur*, when he was nine. He was precocious in school and was whipped when he was twelve for suspected plagiarism. Since he was innocent of this charge, he left school, and shortly afterward he and a Mexican boy traveled with a band of revolutionaries in Mexico. By his own account, his physical exercise program enabled him to pass as an adult, and since he felt all professions paled beside newspaper work, he became a reporter for the *San Antonio Times* in 1891 as the result of winning a $100 essay prize. Koenigsberg soon lost this job when he was sued for criminal libel for exposing corruption among prosecuting attorneys, who were pocketing fines from prostitutes. After the suit was dropped, he went to Houston to continue his newspaper career.

Koenigsberg worked briefly for the *Houston Age*, a newspaper he described as "a pitiable relic of a tempestuous past," and was traded to the *Texas World*, where he was made editor, for a small sum of cash and the settlement of an overdue account between the newspaper owners.

Koenigsberg soon moved eastward and became a reporter for the *New Orleans Item*. "Ever since I decided to be a journalist," he confided to an *Item* coworker, "I have kept my eye on one goal. I want to do such work as will earn a prize beyond valuation in dollars. We don't have such an emblem or reward in the United States. But there is an international trophy for distinguished service to society. It is membership in the French Legion of Honor. Of course, it's only a dream, but that's my target." Koenigsberg would later realize this dream, and it would result in the loss of his position with Hearst.

Returning to San Antonio, in 1892 Koenigsberg launched the *Evening Star* with three partners. The first distribution consisted of 5,000 free copies of an "amateurish" but "refreshing" paper, according to Koenigsberg. It contained sophomoric items such as this editorial paragraph:

> There was a classic forecast of the stellar course of San Antonio's new daily newspaper. A proper sympathy will find it in this stanza by Lord Byron:
>
> > ...'Tis sweet to hear
> > at midnight on the blue and moonlit deep,
> > The song and oar of Adria's gondolier,
> > By distance mellow'd o'er the waters sweep;
> > 'Tis sweet to see the *Evening Star* appear...

After three months, the *Evening Star* claimed the largest circulation of any afternoon paper in south Texas. The growth of the subscription list was attributed to the copious volume of neighborhood news. The *Evening Star* faded out after weathering

monetary problems, a disagreement with the *Star*'s financial sponsor concerning "sacred cows" to safeguard, and, later, competition with the *Evening News*. Koenigsberg, now sixteen, job-hopped from newspaper to newspaper in Kansas City, St. Louis, Chicago, Pittsburgh, and New York. Koenigsberg was not shy or modest about presenting his abilities to editors, and the newspaper business was characterized by heavy turnover at the time.

During the Spanish-American War, Koenigsberg served briefly with an Alabama volunteer unit and with the First Division of the Seventh Army Corps in Miami; he wrote a book, *Southern Martyrs* (1898), about military censorship during the war.

Koenigsberg became city editor of Hearst's *Chicago American* in 1903. The Hearst newspapers used all the known methods of promoting circulation, including exciting headlines. Koenigsberg's autobiography likens the function of a startling headline to the Salvation Army's device for attracting street crowds: "The Gaity of the Salvationist band's music—tunes often more befitting a sailor's revel than a prayer meeting—was an ethical companion to the boldness of the daily's head lettering. The evangelist musicians were sent forth to halt vagrant souls. The newspaper headline was set out to halt vagrant minds."

Koenigsberg launched a campaign to prevent theater tragedies after the matinee performance of *Bluebeard, Junior* at the Iroquois Theatre on 30 December 1903 was interrupted by a fire that left 200 charred bodies piled high against the emergency exits; the victims had been unable to escape because the doors opened inward. Koenigsberg wrote: "That was one exposé to which passion drove me with a fury no mere professional feeling could equate." Diagrams, sketches, cartoons, and photographs stressed each lesson of the catastrophe. The fireproof asbestos curtain required in auditoriums throughout the world may be traced to a campaign launched in the *Chicago American* on the day following the catastrophe, according to Koenigsberg. It started with his demand for the arrests of the mayor of Chicago, the building commissioner, one of the fire inspectors, and the owners and managers of the theater. The indictments failed, but the *American* had focused attention on methods to prevent a recurrence of the Iroquois Theatre horror.

Between 1903 and 1907, the *Chicago Evening American* published a ceaseless torrent of sensational stories. Chicago was the center of operations of ex-convicts, and homicide was rampant. Vast numbers of unassimilated immigrants milled around in their new environment. Koenigsberg hunted for hidden crime tips among the municipal bureau's daily lists of weddings, interments, and building permits. The name Johann Hoch jumped at Koenigsberg from the roll of burial permits: it seemed that Hoch had had numerous wives, few of whom survived more than a few weeks' honeymoon. Hoch had evidently studied burial permits as well, and had sought out widows whom he offered to assist in the collection of insurance funds. He preferred women in their late forties who seemed to display menopausal symptoms. Posing as a physician who was not licensed to practice in the United States, and using a sprinkling of therapeutic terminology, Hoch approached his victims with medical advice. Each new wife had welcomed Hoch's plan of rejuvenation, which required the recruitment of a female relative of the bride to administer rectal injections of arsenic. Koenigsberg advised the police of his suspicions, and Hoch was caught in New York with the collaboration of *Das Morgen Journal*, a German daily owned by Hearst. The scoop was published on 20 January 1905. Koenigsberg's habit of closely reading every line that came into his office resulted in journalistic history.

Hearst began to visit Chicago frequently while Koenigsberg was the managing editor of the *American*. The activities of his boss's political advisers disturbed Koenigsberg, whose professional code prescribed "singleness of devotion to newspaper duty" and required "complete independence from divergent accountability or commitment." He maintains that during the quarter of a century of his membership in the Hearst organization, he never wrote or directed the writing of one article intended to advance Hearst's personal ambitions in politics.

In Koenigsberg's stilted and torturously written autobiography, he says: "the art of intrigue prospered considerably under the patronage of W. R. Hearst. Some of the conspiracies and machinations practiced under his indulgent eye measured up to the most exacting Machiavellian standards. There was convincing evidence that Hearst enjoyed hugely the plotting and counterplotting of lieutenants vying for his favor." In 1907 Hearst informed Koenigsberg that he wished him to consolidate and manage the classified advertising departments of the *Chicago Evening American*, the *Chicago Morning Examiner*, and the *Chicago Sunday American*. Koenigsberg declined the offer, as he had no taste for business and wished to remain an editor. Shortly afterward he was sent to New York.

Raids by Hearst's *New York Journal* on Joseph Pulitzer's *New York World* stars had been followed by

"retaliatory depredations" that led to the erection of legal barricades around certain personnel in each newspaper office. "Master and man" agreements—as ironclad as leading attorneys in New York could draft them—were used with every employee the opposition might try to tempt. When almost ten years of court tests had stabilized the structure of these agreements, a standard form was adopted. "It makes bondmen of us," commented T. E. Powers, a cartoonist who had several times slipped back and forth between the Hearst and Pulitzer camps. Koenigsberg's first "personal service contract" was signed in New York under the direction of Hearst's general manager, S. S. Carvalho, and Koenigsberg was sent on to Boston to manage the *Boston American*. His $125 weekly salary did not change.

In Boston, Koenigsberg found that the *American* was deeply in debt and had other formidable problems. Working like a slave and exercising tight cost controls—even saving string—he managed to reduce the paper's deficit. Hearst wired him joyously: "Fine! Now please add a 'Metropolitan' and an 'Outing' section in colors." Koenigsberg reluctantly obeyed. Soon the paper was again in desperate financial straits; Koenigsberg was unable even to use his own office because of the many bill collectors hounding him. Finally, Koenigsberg managed to raise a loan through a former Chicago friend. He begged to be transferred from Boston, and always recalled his stay there as a nightmare.

Fortunately for Koenigsberg, Hearst at this time was aiming to acquire more newspapers to help publicize his policies and blaze a trail to the presidency. He rescued Koenigsberg from Boston and sent him on a tour of the nation's larger cities to appraise newspapers that could be bought. "It revolved around an obsession," Koenigsberg later wrote, "a yearning for the ownership of a newspaper in every advantageous center in America. By gratifying that ambition, he could command the performance of any program he favored, including his installation in the White House." For some time Hearst was unable to add to his chain, possibly because he was short of money, but Koenigsberg continued to travel, selling the Hearst syndicated comics and columns. When he arrived in a city to talk to a newspaper owner, the man was usually terrified that Hearst planned to start a paper there and force him out of business. Often he would buy the features in the belief that this was the best way to keep Hearst out, so Koenigsberg found his tours highly profitable.

The four years beginning in August 1909 surpassed all of Koenigsberg's expectations. He wrote that his accomplishments would have been impossible anywhere except under the leadership of Hearst. Koenigsberg became the confidant of publishers from Shanghai to London. "Publication problems of the most intimate and complicated character were submitted to me for analysis." For weeks at a time newspapers were operated under his direction from the private offices of the owners without the knowledge of their subordinates.

When Koenigsberg was thirty-five he decided to found his own feature syndicate, but under an interpretation of the law by the New York State Court of Appeals, he was still bound to the Star Company, the Hearst holding corporation. Hearst allowed him to establish the new syndicate and to operate semi-independently within the Hearst empire. In August 1913 the Newspaper Feature Service came into being, beginning a fifteen-year span of Koenigsberg's life that left an enduring mark on newspapers. Syndicates had existed for thirty years, but Koenigsberg expanded their range and volume and increased circulation. In 1915 he started an additional Hearst service, King Features Syndicate (the name was taken from Koenig, German for king), which was successful from its inception due in large part to popular comic strips such as "Bringing up Father." This syndicate endured long after Hearst enterprises had faded away.

Hearst gave Koenigsberg another responsibility in 1919 when he placed him in charge of the International News Service. According to W. A. Swanberg, author of *Citizen Hearst* (1961), the INS, with its mythical writers, its "pro-Germanism," and its pilfering of news, had sunk to such depths of discredit and unreliability that even the Hearst editors, who had to use it, were fearful to do so. Koenigsberg brought the INS back to life and profitability, and soon he was managing eight different Hearst services, including Newspaper Feature Service, International Feature Service, Universal Service, Premier Syndicate, and Star Adcraft Service.

Koenigsberg married Virginian Vivian Carter, the daughter of a banker, on 10 December 1923 in New Haven, Connecticut. They had a daughter, Virginia Rose, who later worked in the library of the *New York Times*. Not much has been written concerning Koenigsberg's personal life; what is contained in his autobiography is obviously selective. Emile Gauvreau, managing editor of the *Hartford Courant* and later of the *New York Graphic* and the *Mirror*, wrote in his book *My Last Million Readers* (1941): "He [Koenigsberg] was a large, fat man busily engaged in a glass cage from which he sur-

veyed a line of writers bent over their tasks in separate compartments. Down his damp forehead fell a Napoleonic lock, which he twisted about with a nervous forefinger. He was addicted to telephonic hysteria, answering two calls at one time, necessitating desperate pantomime with the help of underlings waving papers and signaling. . . .his eyes seemed to glow in his fat face, which had the mark of good fellowship, of illness, of care and wine. . . ."

Koenigsberg was certainly an energetic and ambitious journalist who did not shrink from what he felt was his moral responsibility as a newsman. In 1925 he accused the Associated Press of using INS material; in retaliation, the AP directors threatened to withdraw AP service from Hearst newspapers. Koenigsberg believed that the AP was trying to monopolize news distribution. When he represented the INS at a League of Nations conference of press officials in 1927, he opposed the Associated Press's resolution supporting private property rights in news. He was central in the adoption of a counterresolution stating that "no one may acquire the right of suppressing news of public interest." For this feat it was announced in France that he would be made a Chevalier of the Legion of Honor, the award he had dreamed of receiving since boyhood. In his autobiography, Koenigsberg wrote: "The sole sovereignty that has stood unmoved by the assaults of world revolution is that dominion of the mind in which man's soul subsists on current intelligence. At the conference of press experts convened by the League of Nations at Geneva in 1927, I remarked that news was a process of civilization. Lord Burnham, the presiding officer, retorted that he had considered civilization a process of news. Between the observations emerges a truth of supreme importance to mankind. If, from the blood-drenched wreckage through which humanity has staggered, only one sovereignty shall survive, let it be King News."

Koenigsberg's award angered Hearst, who wrote a full-page editorial suggesting the resignation of any of his employees who accepted foreign decorations. Koenigsberg, who had worked for Hearst for twenty-five years, knew that the editorial was aimed at him; he also knew that Hearst resented France for not paying her war debts. On 19 February 1928, at a dinner at the Astor Hotel attended by 1,500 people, Koenigsberg simultaneously accepted the decoration and resigned from the Hearst organization. (In 1933 Koenigsberg returned the award to France to protest her failure to pay the war debts.)

With the Hearst world behind him, Koenigsberg again job-hopped; first, he tried to build a newspaper chain with a department store tycoon; then he failed in an attempt to buy the *Denver Post* when the stock market crashed in 1929. He became executive director of the Song Writers' Protective Association and briefly helped produce a Sunday magazine at the *Philadelphia Inquirer*. He died at the age of sixty-six of a heart attack in his home in New York City. He was survived by his widow and daughter; a brother, Simon Koenigsberg of Dallas; and a sister, Mrs. Sol Dalkewitz of San Antonio.

Koenigsberg often stated his conviction that journalism is the greatest potential instrument for the advancement of mankind. He believed that a publisher could render no better service than by extending circulation and providing matter to lighten the hearts of people: "We [Americans] are an emotional people, and on more than one occasion our sense of humor alone has saved us." The newspaper features released under his control included serial and short fiction, signed editorials, magazine pages in color, illustrated Sunday news stories, a wide range of daily departments, and the largest group of comics ever published.

References:

Emile Gauvreau, *My Last Million Readers* (New York: Dutton, 1941);

Alfred McClung Lee, *The Daily Newspaper in America: The Evolution of a Social Instrument* (New York: Macmillan, 1937);

W. A. Swanberg, *Citizen Hearst: A Biography of William Randolph Hearst* (New York: Scribners, 1961).

Ring Lardner

(6 March 1885-25 September 1933)

Alfred Lawrence Lorenz
Loyola University

See also the Lardner entry in *DLB 11, American Humorists, 1800-1950*.

MAJOR POSITIONS HELD: Sportswriter, *Chicago Examiner* (1908), *Chicago Tribune* (1908-1910); managing editor, *Sporting News* (1910-1911); sports editor, *Boston American* (1911); columnist, *Chicago Tribune* (1913-1919), Bell Syndicate (1919-1927).

BOOKS: *March 6th: The Home Coming of Charles A. Comiskey, John J. McGraw, and James J. Callahan* (Chicago: Blakely, 1914);

Bib Ballads (Chicago: Volland, 1915);

You Know Me Al (New York: Doran, 1916);

Gullible's Travels, Etc. (Indianapolis: Bobbs-Merrill, 1917; London: Chatto & Windus, 1926);

My Four Weeks in France (Indianapolis: Bobbs-Merrill, 1918);

Treat 'Em Rough (Indianapolis: Bobbs-Merrill, 1918);

The Real Dope (Indianapolis: Bobbs-Merrill, 1919);

Own Your Own Home (Indianapolis: Bobbs-Merrill, 1919);

Regular Fellows I Have Met (Chicago: Wilmot, 1919);

The Young Immigrunts (Indianapolis: Bobbs-Merrill, 1920);

Symptoms of Being 35 (Indianapolis: Bobbs-Merrill, 1921);

The Big Town (Indianapolis: Bobbs-Merrill, 1921);

Say It with Oil (New York: Doran, 1923);

How To Write Short Stories [With Samples] (New York: Scribners, 1924; London: Chatto & Windus, 1926);

What of It? (New York: Scribners, 1925);

The Love Nest and Other Stories (New York: Scribners, 1926; London: Allan, 1928—augmented with works from *What of It?*);

The Story of a Wonder Man (New York: Scribners, 1927);

Round Up: The Stories of Ring W. Lardner (New York: Scribners, 1929; London: Williams & Norgate, 1935);

June Moon, by Lardner and George S. Kaufman (New York: Scribners, 1930);

Lose with a Smile (New York: Scribners, 1933);

Ring Lardner (Culver Pictures)

First and Last, edited by Gilbert Seldes (New York: Scribners, 1934);

Shut Up, He Explained, edited by Babette Rosmond and Henry Morgan (New York: Scribners, 1962);

Some Champions: Sketches and Fiction by Ring Lardner, edited by Matthew J. Bruccoli and Richard Layman (New York: Scribners, 1976);

Ring Lardner's You Know Me Al: The Comic Strip Adventures of Jack Keefe (New York: Harcourt Brace Jovanovich/Bruccoli Clark, 1979).

PLAYS: *Elmer, the Great,* by Lardner and George M. Cohan, New York, Lyceum Theatre, 24 September 1928;

June Moon, by Lardner and George S. Kaufman, New York, Broadhurst Theater, 9 October 1929.

Rats drove Ring Lardner into journalism.

As he told the story, he was working as a meter reader for a gas company in his hometown of Niles, Michigan, but too often he found "a rat reading the meter ahead of me." At one point, the editor of the *South Bend Times* came to the gas company office to try to hire Lardner's brother, Rex, a reporter for the *Niles Daily Sun*. Lardner volunteered that he often helped Rex with his work; that was an untruth, but as he later said, "I was thinking of those rats."

The year was 1905, and Ringgold Wilmer Lardner was twenty. In taking a job with the *Times* he embarked on a journalistic career which, though relatively short, would win him a place as one of America's outstanding journalist-humorists. Over the next twenty-eight years Lardner would find in the social pretensions of the lower middle class grist for column after column of newspaper reportage and some 125 short stories for magazines—collected in fifteen books.

Lardner was born on 6 March 1885 to Henry and Lena Lardner. The Lardners were one of the wealthiest families in Niles: Henry Lardner had inherited a farm from his father and, from a cousin, cash which he put into mortgage notes; the family lived handsomely off the interest while Ring was growing up. Ring was the youngest of their nine children, and his mother kept him and the two children closest to him in age, Rex and Anna, protected at home during his first dozen years. The mother, a woman of catholic literary interests who wrote essays and poetry, educated her children at home; they read widely at her urging in the family's rather extensive library. A woman of musical talent, she encouraged them to play the piano and the organ and to sing. They performed little plays, some written by their mother and some, later, which Ring wrote. Ring and Rex, at least, also came to know baseball—came to have a passion for it, in fact—and very early they could recite the batting orders of each of the twelve teams in the National League. Lardner said later that he wondered whether he would ever see enough baseball games to satisfy his love for the sport.

Ring, Rex, and Anna Lardner did not go to formal school until Ring was twelve, when the three were enrolled at Niles High School; Ring was graduated when he was sixteen. His main distinction was being selected to write the class poem, a work which in no way presaged his later journalistic accomplishments.

On graduation, Lardner showed no interest in going on to college. Instead, he spent the next four

Lardner (right) with his brother Rex and sister Anna during their high school days

years working desultorily at a variety of low-level jobs in Chicago and Niles, winding up finally with the Niles Gas Company. He was much more interested in his involvement with the American Minstrels, an amateur theatrical group in which he was a performer and for several of whose productions he also wrote music and lyrics.

Lardner signed on with the *South Bend Times* as "sporting editor," but the small-town newspaper of his day, as of today, could not afford the luxury of a specialist, so he was not only sports editor but sports staff, "dramatic critic, society and court house reporter, and banquet hound. My hours were from 8 A.M. on." During the baseball season he would make the rounds of the police station and the courts, then head to the ball park where he was official scorer for the South Bend team at $1 a game.

He vacationed from the sports desk in the autumn of 1907 by going to Chicago for the World Series between the Cubs and the Detroit Tigers, and there he met Hugh Fullerton, a baseball writer for Hearst's *Chicago Examiner* and later a columnist for the *Tribune*. They sat together during the Series and

Fullerton was impressed by Lardner's knowledge of the game. He helped the young man win a job on the sports desk of the *Chicago Inter Ocean*. Before the next baseball season began, however, Lardner had signed on with the *Examiner* as a baseball writer, and at the start of the season he went on the road with the Chicago White Sox. At last he could see all the baseball games he wanted. His stories appeared under the name "James Clarkson," a convenience by-line later used for the newspaper's crime exposé stories.

Lardner got along well with the ball players. He played poker with them in Pullman cars, sang with them in saloons, whiled away the hours with them in hotel lobbies just talking—and listening. One of the players he came to know particularly well that season was a young infielder; Lardner referred to him in telling about the episode as "Jack Gibbs." Lardner noticed that in restaurants or dining cars Gibbs would spend long minutes studying the menu, then invariably order steak and potatoes or ham and eggs, and sometimes both. Realizing that Gibbs was illiterate, Lardner took to reading his own

menu aloud, pretending that was his normal practice. He also began reading the sports pages aloud
for Gibbs's benefit.

As they got to know one another better, Gibbs
brought Lardner letters from his wife Myrtle and
urged Lardner to read them aloud, ostensibly so
that Lardner could enjoy them, too. Gibbs even had
Lardner write letters to Myrtle for him. She would
get a kick out of having typed letters, he told Lardner, then proceeded to dictate: "Well I guess you
better tell her where we are first. No. Start out this
way: 'Dear Myrt.' And then tell her she knows damn
well I don't get no pay till the last of April, and
nothing then because I already drawed it ahead.
Tell her to borrow off Edith von Driska, and she can
pay her back the first of May. Tell her I never felt
better in my life and looks like I will have a great
year, if they's nothing to worry me like worrying
about money. Tell her the weather's been great, just
like summer, only them two days it rained in Birmingham. It rained a couple of days in Montgomery and a week in New Orleans. My old souper feels
great. Detroit is the club to beat—them and Cleveland and St. Louis, and maybe the New York club.
Oh, you know what to tell her. You know what they
like to hear." Years later Lardner would say that his
success as a writer could be summed up in three
words: "I just listen." What he listened to would
become a new journalistic and literary idiom.

At the close of the 1908 season, Lardner
moved from the *Examiner* to the *Tribune*, even then
the largest newspaper in Chicago. For the next two
years he covered both the White Sox and the Cubs
during the baseball season and a variety of other
sports during the off-season, and he matured as a
journalist. Sports reporters had long before moved
away from simply setting the box scores of ball
games in type to giving running accounts, play by
play, inning by inning. The better writers later went
a step farther and began to focus on the personalities of the players or bits of high drama within
the game. Lardner was one of those writers: he was
a careful observer who recounted the human aspects of the games he covered. He also began to
insert humor into his stories.

After Lardner became engaged to Ellis Abbott, a young girl from Goshen, Indiana, in 1910, he
looked for a job that would involve less travel and
more salary. He found one in St. Louis, as managing
editor of Charles Spink's *Sporting News*. He did not
like Spink, however, and believed that Spink on
several occasions had forced him to compromise his
integrity as a journalist. Just what those compromises were, he never said publicly. He told his

fiancée in a letter only that "Mr. Spink was dishonest" and had done "everything . . . without my
knowledge that was against all newspaper
rules. . . ." Within two months he quit and moved
east to become a baseball writer for the *Boston
American*. He and Ellis were married in the spring of
1911; shortly thereafter he was named sports editor
of the *American*.

Again, it was a short-lived editorship. Lardner
had hired his brother, Rex, and another Chicago
sports reporter during the baseball season, and
when he went off to cover the World Series in the
fall, higher management fired the two. Lardner
quit in protest, and after borrowing money from the
front offices of the Red Sox and the Braves, he took
his bride back to Chicago. He was a copyreader with
the *Chicago American* for a short time, then rejoined
the *Examiner* as a sports reporter.

Lardner began to take more license with his
stories. He put more humor into them; from time to
time he told them in crude verse, something of a
convention of the day and practiced regularly by
Lardner's friend and colleague, Grantland Rice.
Utilizing his musical talent, Lardner also parodied
popular songs of the day (during the 1919 "Black
Sox" World Series his refrain was "I'm forever
blowing ball games/Pretty ball games in the
air. . . ."). He also occasionally wrote dialogue in the
vernacular of baseball players, a practice he had
begun during his short stay on the *Sporting News*.
Readers more and more took note of him.

One of Lardner's friends in the world of
Chicago sports journalism was a *Tribune* reporter,
Hugh E. Keogh, an excellent writer who, about the
time Lardner was getting into journalism, had been
tapped by the *Tribune*'s innovative managing editor,
James Keeley, to write a daily sports column. Keeley
had seen the popularity of columns in other sections
of the newspaper, and he thought the same sort of
thing might prove popular among readers of the
sports pages. Keeley was right, both about Keogh
and the column—"In the Wake of the News."
Keogh made it the best of its kind in the country and
attracted a devoted following. (The column is still a
fixture of the *Tribune* sports section and is still
popular.)

When Keogh died in 1913, Lardner was at
spring training with the White Sox. The *Tribune*
contacted him and offered him the column. He
accepted, and he soon made the column his own.
Under Lardner it was a crazy quilt of both content
and style. He adopted the tried-and-true one-
paragraph comment when it suited him, or even
just a one-line wisecrack. He might insert a piece of

Lardner about the time he started writing the "In the Wake of the News" column for the Chicago Tribune *in 1913 (courtesy of Ring Lardner, Jr.)*

purported breakfast table conversation at the Lardner house; another was a column supposedly written by one of the children.

Early in his first year Lardner used a series of columns to entertain readers with a novel, "The Pennant Pursuit," purportedly written by a copyboy. It was a parody of a popular type of novel of the day, especially the Frank Merriwell stories, which glorified athletes as heroes; it was deftly drawn and designed to point up the nonsense, even the hypocrisy, in those stories. Shortly after the novel was concluded, Lardner took aim at the then-current practice of newspapers printing the-way-it-was stories ghostwritten by staff members under the by-lines of famous athletes. The first was an account, printed a week before the game, of the first game of the 1913 World Series between the New York Giants and the Philadelphia Athletics as it actually would have come from one of the Giants players. The ghostwritten stories had the athletes speaking in the language of the drawing room; Lardner had his player speaking the vernacular of the dugout: "We ought to of trimmed 'em. When Egan, the big shot, said I was out at second he musta been full o' hops, the big boob. I like t' known where he was at las' night, the big bum. Some o' them umps oughta be on the chain gang, the big boobs." And so it went, the first among many columns in the idiom of the American baseball player as Lardner heard it in Pullman car poker games among players and coaches, in dugouts, and in locker rooms. By the end of the first year of his proprietorship of "In the Wake of the News," Lardner had gone a long way toward perfecting both the spoken and written idioms of the players and had installed them as regular devices. They were the most endearing and most enduring devices he would use as a columnist; they would also serve as vehicles for his entry into fiction.

The *Tribune*'s Sunday editor encouraged Lardner to try a longer piece in the same vein, a short story for the feature section. Lardner wove a story out of all he had heard in spending "about ninety nights per annum in lower berths," and, especially in being privy to the correspondence between "Jack" and "Myrtle Gibbs." The story, "A Busher's Letters Home," was a series of letters from a rookie pitcher with the White Sox to his friends back home. When he was finished with it, however, the editor decided it was not quite right for *Tribune* readers. Lardner put it in the mail to the *Saturday Evening Post*, and *Post* editor George Horace Lorimer sent back an acceptance letter and a check for $250.

doggerel. He kept readers up on the doings of the Lardner family and used a variety of forms to do so. That meant verse on some occasions, as on the birth of his second son, James:

> If you were Barbara, I know
> You'd cost your dad a lot more dough.
> And when you married, it would be
> Like last night's second round—on me.

On other occasions he ran what he headed "Riverside Locals," one-line reports on the comings and goings of his family much like the reports of country correspondents for small-town newspapers: "J. B. and B. Lardner will be guests of honor at an adenoid and tonsil party on Chicago Avenue this A.M." One favorite device was a recounting of the

Ring and Ellis Lardner with their children (left to right): Jim, David,
Bill (Ring, Jr.), and John (courtesy of Ring Lardner, Jr.)

From then on Lardner continued to write not only his daily column but also short fiction. Five other series of Busher letters appeared in the *Saturday Evening Post* and were collected into the book *You Know Me Al* (1916). Lardner also published his fiction in *Redbook* and other magazines and, when he had enough of the short pieces, he collected them into books. It was grueling work at the typewriter, but his responsibilities had grown considerably over the years. He and Ellis had four sons: John, born in 1912; James, in 1914; Ringgold Wilmer, Jr. (Bill), in 1915; and David, in 1918.

When America entered World War I, Lardner went to Europe for a short time as a war correspondent. He sent back columns of sidelight comment headed "In the Wake of the War" for the *Tribune* and wrote a series of articles on the war for *Collier's*. That work did not match his sports reporting; he was much more at home on the playing field than in the trenches.

Lardner's contract with the *Tribune* expired in June 1919, and he did not renew it. Instead, capitalizing on his national fame, he signed with the Bell Syndicate of John N. Wheeler to write a weekly column and moved his family to New York. He ranged far and wide across the country covering major sports events for the Bell Syndicate during the next eight years. At the same time, he continued writing fiction for magazines. He tried writing for the Broadway stage in the late 1920s. His first full-length effort, with George M. Cohan, was *Elmer, the Great*, which was performed at the Lyceum Theatre in New York in 1928 to less than laudatory reviews from his newspaper chums. More successful was the next year's *June Moon*, on which he teamed with George S. Kaufman. In 1932 he published a series of autobiographical articles for the *Saturday Evening Post*, and later that year and into 1933 a series of columns on radio for the *New Yorker*.

In 1926 his health began to fail him. He was discovered to have tuberculosis in that year, and he was further weakened by years of heavy drinking. He died on 25 September 1933, following a heart attack. The obituaries and later critical comment centered on his fiction and reckoned him a serious literary figure. But Lardner always considered himself to be a journalist, and it was his success at that work which initially brought him fame and which put him alongside such other journalist-humorists as George Ade, Finley Peter Dunne, and Samuel L. Clemens.

Letters:

Ring around Max: The Correspondence of Ring Lardner and Max Perkins, edited by Clifford M. Caruthers (De Kalb: Northern Illinois Press, 1973);
Letters from Ring, edited by Caruthers (Flint, Mich.: Walden Press, 1979).

Bibliography:

Matthew J. Bruccoli and Richard Layman, *Ring Lardner: A Descriptive Bibliography* (Pittsburgh: University of Pittsburgh Press, 1976).

Biographies:

Donald Elder, *Ring Lardner, A Biography* (Garden City: Doubleday, 1956);
Ring Lardner, Jr., *The Lardners: My Family Remembered* (New York: Harper & Row, 1976);
Jonathan Yardley, *Ring: A Biography of Ring Lardner*

(New York: Random House, 1977).

References:

Sherwood Anderson, "Four American Impressions: Gertrude Stein, Paul Rosenfeld, Ring Lardner, Sinclair Lewis," *New Republic* (11 October 1922): 171-173;
Anderson, "Meeting Ring Lardner," *New Yorker* (25 November 1933): 36-38;
F. Scott Fitzgerald, "Ring," *New Republic* (11 October 1933): 254-255;
Thomas L. Masson, "Ring Lardner," in his *Our American Humorists* (New York: Moffat, Yard, 1922);
Allan Nevins, "The American Moron," *Saturday Review of Literature* (8 June 1929): 1089-1090;
Walton R. Patrick, *Ring Lardner* (New York: Twayne, 1963);
Howard W. Webb, Jr., "The Development of a Style: The Lardner Idiom," *American Quarterly*, 12 (Winter 1960): 482-492.

Papers:

Lardner's papers are in the Newberry Library, Chicago.

Victor F. Lawson

(9 September 1850-19 August 1925)

David Paul Nord
Indiana University

MAJOR POSITIONS HELD: Publisher, *Chicago Daily News* (1876-1888); editor and publisher, *Chicago Daily News* (1888-1925); board of directors, Western Associated Press and Associated Press (1889-1925).

When Victor F. Lawson died in 1925 after nearly fifty years as proprietor of the *Chicago Daily News,* some of the obituary writers proclaimed him "the last of the old-time editors." He was not; he was in fact the first, or one of the first, of the new breed of editor/publishers that came to dominate American newspaper journalism in the twentieth century. Unlike the great nineteenth-century editors of his own time, Lawson was a business manager, not a writing editor; an organization man, not a flamboyant individualist; an organizer, not a thinker; a

joiner, not a prophet. At his death Lawson was hailed as a giant by his peers, but he was little known by the public. He was the prototypical progressive businessman who happened to find his way, quite by accident, into journalism. Because of the nature of the times and of the enterprise, such a man was well suited to build the first medium of mass communication in Chicago—one of the first in the world.

Lawson lived all his life in Chicago. He was born in his parents' modest house on Superior Street on 9 September 1850, when Chicago was a youthful frontier city of 28,000 people. He died in his Lake Shore Drive mansion, a mile away, on 19 August 1925, in a great metropolis of 3,000,000. Lawson's close ties to Chicago during its adolescence and rise to adulthood greatly influenced his

From a painting by George R. Boynton

own life and the life of the newspaper he created for Chicago's citizens. The *Daily News* was not only the first mass-circulation newspaper in Chicago, it was the first self-consciously urban newspaper in that city—the first newspaper of the modern metropolis.

Lawson's parents, Iver and Melinda Nordvig Lawson, were Norwegian immigrants who had come to America as youngsters in the 1830s. Iver Lawson grew rich in Chicago by following a well-trodden path to prosperity in those early, booming times: buying and selling real estate. Success in business led to politics, and Iver Lawson became the first Norwegian-American in Chicago to achieve political prominence, first as a member of the city council and then as a state senator in the 1860s. He was also a devout Christian, and in 1848 he helped to establish Chicago's first Norwegian Lutheran Church. Already by 1850 the Lawsons were devoted to their new country. When their first son was born in that year they named him Victor Fremont, in honor of Gen. John C. Frémont, hero of the Mexi-

can War and victor in California. The Lawsons left their son a legacy of individual enterprise, family affection, religious faith, Chicago loyalty, and American patriotism.

Victor Fremont Lawson (called Fremont by his family and close friends) was the favored of the Lawson's three children and a success at school, both in his studies and among his peers. He attended public grammar school and high school in Chicago, and he liked to remember in later years his satisfaction at earning his own spending money working in the circulation department of the *Evening Journal* during school vacations. In 1869, Lawson was enrolled in Phillips Academy at Andover, Massachusetts, to prepare for entrance into Harvard. At Andover he made his mark in the manner that would become his lifelong style—quiet, elusive, reserved, almost diffident; yet well liked and admired by those few who came to know him well. Lawson never made it to Harvard, however: illness and the Chicago fire kept him from enrolling as planned in 1871. The illness affected his eyes; the fire wiped out his father's fortune. Like many other Chicago businessmen, Iver Lawson quickly recouped at least part of his fortune, but then he died suddenly in 1874. Management of his estate fell to his firstborn son.

One of his father's businesses was a partnership in the *Skandinaven*, a Norwegian-language daily edited by young Lawson's great-uncle, Knud Langland. Lawson took an office in the *Skandinaven* building and began to manage the accounts of the family enterprises. One of the lesser tenants in the same building happened to be a struggling little penny newspaper called the *Chicago Daily News*. The *Daily News* was the creation of Melville E. Stone, with the financial backing of Percy Meggy and William H. Dougherty. Stone was an energetic and ambitious young man only two years older than Lawson but already by 1875 an experienced and much-admired Chicago journalist. When the first regular issue of the *Daily News* appeared on 23 December 1875, it was a new kind of newspaper for Chicago: cheap, politically independent, and drastically condensed. This was Stone's design. Stone ridiculed the "blanket sheets" of Chicago that sold for four or five cents and bored their readers with arcane political harangues and endless miscellany and trivia. In contrast, his was a tiny, four-page paper about the size of a modern tabloid. At first, most of the stories were only a few sentences long. It was designed to be a paper for modern, busy, urban men and women of all classes.

Within six months of its founding, the *Daily*

162

News was both a success and a failure, as new publications often are. It had a circulation just under 10,000, a large figure for an evening paper of that time, and about fifty percent of the paper's space was given over to advertising, a remarkably high figure. But advertisers were skittish, rates were low, and debts mounted; Stone's backers pulled out after a few months. In July 1876, with the paper at the maw of bankruptcy, the desperate Stone enlisted the aid of his former schoolmate (Stone had been two years ahead of Lawson at Chicago High School) and current landlord, Victor Lawson. Somewhat recklessly, in the opinion of his financial advisors, Lawson not only agreed to help Stone out but bought the entire property for $6,000, of which $4,000 immediately went for payment of outstanding debts. Stone stayed on as editor and also retained a one-third interest in the paper's profits—if profits ever appeared—but Lawson was now the boss. On 1 August 1876, the masthead read for the first time: "Victor F. Lawson, Publisher."

Stone and Lawson worked well together. They became not just business partners but friends, and

Lawson at about the time he bought the Chicago Daily News *from Melville Stone's backers*

they remained so for fifty years. They were similar enough to understand each other, yet different enough to complement each other. Like Lawson, Stone came from a middle-class, Middle Western family that believed in hard work, individual initiative, and the values of Protestant Christianity. They both preferred a newspaper that would be chaste as well as cheap, tasteful as well as truthful. But Stone was by far the more lively and audacious of the two. While Lawson, in his ever-present dark frock coat, counted pennies and agate lines of advertising in the austere business office, Stone presided as ringmaster over one of the merriest, drunkest, but most talented editorial staffs in town. Stone's favorite and most famous staffer was Eugene Field, whose brilliant feature "Sharps and Flats" (the first modern newspaper "column") lit up the pages of the *Daily News* from 1883 until his death in 1895.

Under Lawson's sharp-penciled business management and Stone's lively and pugnacious editorial direction, the *Daily News* prospered. A failing paper, the *Post and Mail*, was taken over in 1878 for its Associated Press membership. A morning edition, the *Morning News*, was added on 21 March 1881. In the summer of 1885, less than ten years after its birth, the afternoon *Daily News* achieved a steady circulation of 100,000, one of the largest in the world at that time, matched only by Joseph Pulitzer's *New York World*. To mark the occasion, Lawson borrowed a battery of artillery from the state armory and fired a salute along the lakefront.

The *Daily News* became the first mass-circulation newspaper in Chicago because it served the whole city—that is, it spoke to a broad cross section of the heterogeneous urban population. Stone's and Lawson's formula was not to publish a large "smorgasbord" paper, with something for everyone, in the style of the *Chicago Times, Chicago Tribune*, and other popular papers; their aim was to print a small newspaper that was heavily edited, so that a majority of the content would appeal to a majority of readers. Rather than serve the individual tastes of individual readers, Stone and Lawson sought out the common tastes of a community of readers in Chicago. Thus, from the beginning the *Daily News* included popular fiction, household tips, consumer protection advice, and other information relevant to the lives of most people in the modern city. And always, as Lawson liked to say, it was "a 'short and to the point' paper . . . for busy people."

Its editorial philosophy also reflected the *Daily News*'s roots in the new urban environment of

Chicago. Though both Lawson and Stone embraced many of the individualistic values of nineteenth-century American businessmen, they made their newspaper a spokesman for a new kind of urban community based upon voluntary association, activist government, and mass communication. The editorials of the *Daily News* were much more attuned to the idea of interdependence than to the notion of individualism in the great metropolises of the late nineteenth century. The paper promoted the creation of all sorts of philanthropic organizations, including shelters for prostitutes and homeless waifs, public baths, mutual aid building societies, and unemployment relief agencies. The *Daily News* itself established a sanitarium for sick babies along the cool lakefront in Lincoln Park. While the other local papers in this age of laissez-faire decried high taxes and paternalistic government, the *Daily News* urged increased government action for sewers, schools, parks, streets, hospitals, baths and pools, utilities, air pollution control, and other public works and services, including the great Chicago drainage canal. Twenty-five years before the so-called Progressive Era, the *Daily News* was promoting the idea that the imperatives of modern urban existence required a new kind of organized, formal, even governmental approach to the creation and maintenance of community life in America.

While Stone worked to produce a paper that people would read, Lawson worked to place it into their hands. By all accounts, he was a genius at building circulation—within the city for the afternoon *Daily News* and throughout the Midwest for the *Morning News* and the short-lived *Weekly News*. Lawson used all the standard gimmicks of the trade and invented some new ones. He advertised in other publications and on posters, handbills, postcards, calendars, rulers, letter openers, blotters, fans, clocks, and postage stamp cases. In the newspaper, he ran contests, games, mystery serials—anything to spark interest and conversation. But more important than the gimmicks was the organization. Lawson planned strategies and tactics like a general in a military campaign. Through painstaking devotion to detail, he and his agents came to know every corner in Chicago and every village in the Midwest—and to get the right supply of papers there at the right time. Typical of Lawson's attention to detail were his instructions to a *Morning News* circulation agent in 1885: "If in your opinion it is unadvisable to work the Nebraska towns, you may leave them at present and go to the Minnesota River towns, taking Clinton, Iowa, on your way; before

you do this, however, you had better get matters on a satisfactory basis in Omaha and at Lincoln. We have sent advertising matter to the latter place as follows, which you had better put up: 200 Black and Yellow Cards, 20 Lithographs on Rollers, 100 Posters, 100 Comparative Exhibits, 800 Circulars, 5 lbs. tacks, 100 Boards."

Lawson's approach to building advertising, the consort of circulation, was perhaps even more effective and more modern than his circulation-building efforts. By insisting upon two fundamental principles, Lawson helped to change forever the nature of newspaper advertising. The principles, then nearly unknown in America, were: accurate, detailed, and frequent sworn statements of circulation; and uniform, fixed rates for ad insertions. Lawson's purpose was to rationalize the suspicious and chaotic relations between newspapers and advertisers in a way that he believed would benefit both. At the *Daily News*, no advertiser was granted special treatment, such as cut rates, rebates, special placement, or extra puffery in the news columns; extra charges for cuts or multicolumn ads were clearly spelled out and adhered to; "reading matter ads" (ads that looked like news stories) were marked "adv." These rules were designed to protect the paper's interest. In exchange, Lawson guaranteed the advertiser a fair buy: equal treatment with other advertisers and assurance that he was reaching precisely the circulation he paid for.

Lawson found it a slow, sometimes aggravating task in the 1870s to convince advertisers and agents that he was serious about his fixed rates and immutable rules. He was constantly telling ad agencies that "we wish it distinctly understood that the Chicago *Daily News* does not *receive* propositions from advertisers—it *makes* propositions *to* advertisers." To nationally prominent ad agencies, such as George P. Rowell of New York, he was courteous but firm: "Now the simple fact is this—we do not allow advertisers to make any conditions at all. We are not selling advertising space in that way." To a firm of lesser prestige that sought a special deal he wrote: "The insolence of your proposition can only be compared with its stupidity. Did it ever occur to you that possibly we made our own rates and didn't assign that part of our business to an 'enterprising' firm of advertising agents in Cincinnati, Ohio?"

Some advertisers were miffed and took their business elsewhere. Many more grew to appreciate Lawson's forthright business style. By the 1880s, the *Daily News* was one of the most desirable and profitable advertising media in America, and other publishers began to copy the Lawson formula.

On 15 May 1888, with the *Daily News* firmly established as the largest circulation newspaper west of New York and the *Morning News* on the rise as well, Melville Stone unexpectedly announced his retirement from the newspaper business at age thirty-nine. Lawson was shocked, but Stone was adamant. Stone felt exhausted and imprisoned after thirteen years of fourteen- and fifteen-hour days. Reluctantly, Lawson agreed to buy out his partner's one-third interest in the paper for $350,000. Lawson also agreed to pay Stone another $100,000 over ten years for Stone's promise not to reenter the Chicago newspaper field during that time. Now Lawson, the acknowledged master of the business office, was editor as well as publisher—and Stone's staff of easygoing, hard-drinking reporters nervously anticipated life with the reclusive, frock-coated puritan as their new chief. Eugene Field immediately offered his resignation, but Lawson talked him out of it and did the same with other staffers. It soon became clear that Lawson would continue the Stone tradition by working through managing editors of the Stone style. Lawson was too good a manager to change a successful combination.

For Victor Lawson and his *Daily News* the decade of the 1890s was perhaps the golden age. The *Daily News* completely dominated the afternoon field, reaching a circulation of 200,000 by 1894. The *Morning News*—called the *News Record* from 9 May 1892 to 12 March 1893, then the *Record*—after 1893 had one of the best staffs of writers and reporters ever assembled, including Field, George Ade, Finley Peter Dunne, Slason Thompson, and cartoonist John T. McCutcheon. Ads flooded the business office, and Lawson grew rich; but he did not slow down. In the 1890s, he increasingly devoted his personal time and wealth and his newspapers' prestige to the social and political reform movements that were growing in Chicago.

Lawson believed in philanthropy as well as business. As he became wealthier he gave more and more to charity. Lawson's understanding of philanthropy was broad, encompassing political as well as social welfare organizations. Though he avoided partisan politics entirely, he was a strongly political citizen and editor. He participated personally and financially in almost every nonpartisan "good government" movement that arose in Chicago during his fifty-year association with the *Daily News*. He was an especially ardent and faithful supporter of the Municipal Voters' League, which was founded in 1896 to fight public utility corruption and to elect "good men" to the Chicago city

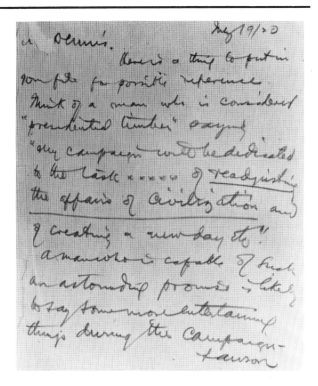

A memorandum from Lawson to Charles H. Dennis, managing editor of the Chicago Record *(Charles H. Dennis,* Victor Lawson: His Life and His Work*)*

council. Whenever advice or money was needed, Chicago reformers called on Victor Lawson. On the national level, he was a leader of the postal savings bank movement, which achieved success in 1910.

Though Lawson was not an editorial-writing editor, he was an incessant memo writer, and he steered his newspapers to serve his ends. In the 1890s, the *Daily News* became a champion of urban reform. Moving early away from laissez-faire, Lawson and the *Daily News* became outspoken advocates of expanded public authority. The paper continued its campaign, begun by Stone, for better city services. Under Lawson the *Daily News* also became increasingly obsessed with public utility control as the key to the salvation of the city, holding that government abdicated its social duty when it turned over to private corporations the provision of utilities and other public services. Lawson used his newspapers to promote vigorously the efforts of the Municipal Voters' League to "purify" the Chicago city council, because the expansion of services and the municipal ownership of utilities would require an honest and "businesslike" city government.

Lawson and his newspapers were especially hostile to "special privileges" that permitted the growth of private monopolies in the provision of essential services. The two great malefactors in Chicago, according to the *Daily News*, were the Illinois Central Railroad and the street railway system controlled by Charles T. Yerkes. Because of its "hoggish" control of Chicago's lakefront in defiance of city efforts to reclaim it, the paper regularly referred to the I.C., even in news stories and headlines, as the "All Hog Line." Yerkes, in Lawson's view, was simply the personification of social irresponsibility. The *Daily News* had a favorite epithet for any arrogant use of corporate power: "Yerkesism." The paper maintained throughout the 1890s that "organized capital is well enough so long as it does not trench upon the rights of the people."

Lawson's enemies, especially Yerkes, viewed the *Daily News*'s talk of corporate responsibility and antimonopoly as sanctimonious claptrap. In a sense, the charge was just, for Lawson was himself a grasping monopolist. He was the chief organizer of the Associated Press, which controlled the news, and of the Daily Newspaper Association of Chicago, which controlled advertising, labor, and other business policies in the newspaper world of Chicago. In the fashion of the times and in the manner of the progressive businessman that he was, Victor Lawson could denounce monopoly and special privilege while at the same time doing everything possible to organize, stabilize, and rationalize his own business and industry. Like Theodore Roosevelt, Lawson possessed the gift of being able to distinguish between good and bad monopolies. His were good.

Particularly good, in Lawson's view, was the Associated Press. Lawson was the midwife of the modern AP. He was not, of course, the father; the AP traced its origin back at least to 1849 and the establishment of the Associated Press of New York. What Lawson did was to participate in the combination of the New York AP and the Western AP in the 1880s and, more important, to lead in the building of a virtual news monopoly for the reorganized AP between 1892 and 1897. The aim of the principal members of the AP during the 1890s was to put the rival United Press (no relation to the later UP) out of business by providing an essential news service (under the direction, incidentally, of Melville Stone) and then by prohibiting members from subscribing to any other news service. The leaders also arranged that most of the power of the organization would be retained in the hands of a few large publishers. The AP won its battle with the United Press, largely through the organizational efforts of Victor Lawson and several other Midwestern publishers. Lawson was president of the AP from 1894 to 1900 and a director from 1893 until his death in 1925. (In

honor of his work during this era, Lawson was proclaimed, by resolution of the AP board of directors shortly after his death, "The Founder of the Associated Press.") Because the AP was a mutual, cooperative association, Lawson liked to view this fight as a quest for democracy of the press. Opponents of the AP, such as the *Chicago Inter Ocean* after 1898, viewed it as monopolization of the press—which, of course, is precisely what it was.

Lawson was also the leader of a successful effort to achieve cooperation among rival publishers for the reduction of competition in Chicago through the Daily Newspaper Association. Again his enemies called it monopoly; he called it "commercial sanity." The purpose of the association was to rationalize and coordinate the newspapers' business in the areas of promotional activities, advertising, and labor relations. As Lawson put it, "there is no advantage to any one in maintaining expensive methods that will produce no additional business when adopted by all." To this end, many of the gimmicks and schemes that Lawson himself had used to promote circulation in the 1870s and 1880s were banned in the 1890s by mutual consent of the daily newspaper publishers. Rules regulating advertising were also adopted. Color ads, for example, were prohibited, on the theory that soon most ads would be in color, which would raise costs without benefiting anyone. Most important, the newspapers agreed to present a united front against organized labor. In a remarkable display of unity, for instance, all the Chicago dailies shut down for four days in the middle of the Spanish-American War in 1898 to resist the demands of the stereotypers' union. The association held tight, and the union was broken.

Lawson was not really a hypocrite on the subject of monopoly. He was, from the 1870s until his death, a businessman and a progressive. His purpose was to regulate economic activity to achieve efficiency and rationality. He sought government regulation of private power where it touched the public interest; he sought self-regulation of private power where, in his opinion, it did not touch the public interest.

In the first quarter of the twentieth century, the *Daily News* continued to thrive, while its publisher gradually drifted more into the background. (While the afternoon *Daily News* thrived, the morning paper, called the *Record-Herald* after its merger with the *Times-Herald* in 1901, languished. Lawson severed his connection with it by stages between 1901 and 1918.) The spirit of cooperation in the Chicago newspaper field ended with the arrival of William Randolph Hearst in 1900, and the early

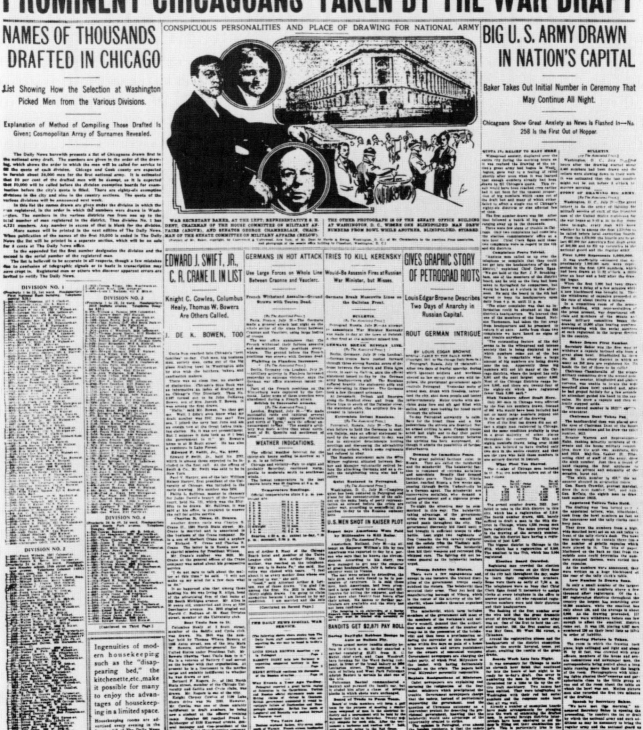

Front page of Lawson's Chicago Daily News *for 20 July 1917*

years of the new century were times of intense competition. Sometimes the competition took the form of violent street battles for circulation; sometimes it was conducted on a loftier plane, through the development of new features and better news reporting to capture the readers of the growing city. One of the *Daily News*'s new features earned it the permanent admiration of the newspaper community world-wide: the *Daily News* Foreign Service.

The Foreign Service was the brainchild of Lawson, who felt in 1898 that the United States was embarking on a new era of expansion and world involvement; the American people would need a direct source of international news, not filtered through London or controlled by foreign powers. He ordered that such a service be created. It started in 1898 as a service of the *Record*; Lawson transferred it to the *Daily News* in 1901. It survived until 1976, the longest-lived and one of the most distinguished foreign services of any newspaper in the United States. During the Lawson era, the service was staffed by such legendary reporters as Paul Scott Mowrer, Edgar Ansel Mowrer, Edward Price Bell, Raymond Swing, and John Gunther. The service was extremely costly to the *Daily News*, even in its early years. Though it was syndicated to many other papers, the net cost to the *Daily News* was still more than a quarter of a million dollars per year by 1919. Lawson paid it gladly, because he viewed his foreign service as a great public service, and thus as a solemn obligation.

In fact, Lawson always viewed the *Daily News* in general more as a public service than as a private business. Of course, all publishers say such things, and Lawson was a publisher's publisher. But for Lawson the notion had actual meaning; it was part of his code of conscience. This attitude grew partly out of Lawson's understanding of public life in a modern city—of public property, public interest, and public utility. It also grew from his religious convictions. He believed in the social gospel. Throughout his life, he gave many thousands of dollars to charity. In his will, Lawson left three-fourths of his multimillion-dollar estate to various philanthropic and community causes, the largest bequest going to the Chicago Congregational Missionary and Church Extension Society. He believed that a newspaper, like an individual citizen, should serve the community on which it depends for its existence.

Throughout his life, Lawson was as devoted to his family and friends as to his church and community. He married Jessie Strong Bradley on 5 February 1880 and was completely devoted to her

until her death in 1914. The couple had no children. Mrs. Lawson was a strict Sabbatarian, and it was partly in deference to her beliefs that Lawson never allowed the *Daily News* or the *Record* to publish Sunday editions. During much of their thirty-five years together, Mrs. Lawson was chronically ill. From the 1880s on, the couple made frequent and lengthy trips to Europe in search of rest and health for her. As much as possible, Lawson remained at her side. Lawson was nearly as loyal to his old friends: his most intimate friends throughout his life were those he had known from childhood. But though he was devoted to family and friends, he could be stern and businesslike in personal relationships. In 1885, for example, while acting as financial guardian for his brother Iver (fifteen years his junior), Lawson continually badgered the young man to give up his frivolous ways and to settle down to hard work and hard study. He upbraided the staff at Iver's boarding school for coddling the boy. "His business with you is to study," Lawson lectured the headmaster, "not to travel or to go to theaters." In short, Lawson was a loving husband, an honest business associate, and a loyal friend, in the serious, somber manner of the self-conscious, self-righteous Christian gentleman.

By 1920, Lawson was a somewhat shadowy figure at the *Daily News*, like a character out of history. Bob Casey, then a young reporter on the paper, remembered that Lawson would quietly come and go in his early-model Rolls Royce and square-topped brown derby, looking a lot like the old pictures of President Garfield. He never spoke to Casey. While the old retainers and the gray-haired matrons of the business office addressed Lawson in hushed tones of reverence, the younger staffers pretty much ignored him and went about their business. But, though they hardly seemed aware of it, these young men were working for what was still, as Casey called it, "Mr. Lawson's Newspaper." The great writers, the legendary editors, the loyalty to the news and to the city, the creative chaos of the newsroom—all embodied the Lawson legacy. Though Lawson never spoke to him directly, Casey felt the old man's ways. "The Chicago *Daily News*," Casey said, "was then not only the only paper I had ever worked on but the only paper I had ever heard about that threw ads into the hellbox to make way for news."

Lawson was not unhappy that the *Daily News* had grown beyond his control, for he looked upon his newspaper as an institution superior to himself. Unlike many other newspaper entrepreneurs of his era, such as Joseph Medill or Adolph Ochs, who continually tinkered with their wills and intimidated their heirs, Lawson did not attempt to perpetuate his rule beyond the grave. When his will was read shortly after his death in August 1925, Chicago and the entire country were shocked to learn that no provision had been made for the future of the *Daily News*; the paper was not even mentioned. Along with the rest of his property, the *Daily News* was simply to be administered briefly and sold by the Illinois Merchants Trust Company. Lawson believed that "the dead hand can't rule"; the paper would have to take care of itself. The *Daily News* was sold in 1925 to a close Lawson associate, Walter Ansel Strong; it was sold again in 1931 after Strong died to Frank Knox, and again in 1944 to John S. Knight, and yet again in 1959 to Marshall Field IV. The paper itself died (of "evening metro newspaper disease") on 4 March 1978.

Throughout its frequent ownership changes, the *Chicago Daily News* maintained the standards and the character established over fifty years by Victor Fremont Lawson. Lawson was right: the paper was superior to him; it had a life of its own. Unlike many great newspapers that began in the nineteenth century, the *Daily News* was never merely the extension of its publisher. Lawson was never a writer, seldom an editor. He was an organizer and a manager. In modern, twentieth-century fashion, while employees wrote and edited, he organized and managed his newspaper to greatness.

Biography:
Charles H. Dennis, *Victor Lawson: His Life and His Work* (Chicago: University of Chicago Press, 1935).

References:

Willis J. Abbot, "Chicago Newspapers and Their Makers," *Review of Reviews*, 11 (June 1895): 646-665;

Donald J. Abramoske, "The Chicago *Daily News*: A Business History, 1875-1901," Ph.D. dissertation, University of Chicago, 1963;

Abramoske, "The Founding of the Chicago *Daily News*," *Journal of the Illinois State Historical Society*, 59 (Winter 1966): 341-353;

Abramoske, "Victor Lawson and the *Chicago Weekly News*: A Defeat," *Journalism Quarterly*, 43 (Spring 1966): 43-48;

Robert J. Casey, *Such Interesting People* (Indianapolis: Bobbs-Merrill, 1943);

Chicago Daily News, 4 March 1978 [last edition];

"The Lawson Bequests to Charity," *Literary Digest*, 86 (26 September 1925): 32-33.

Paul Scott Mowrer, *The House of Europe* (Boston: Houghton Mifflin, 1945);

"Mr. Lawson's Will," *Christian Century*, 42 (17 September 1925): 1140-1141;

David Paul Nord, *Newspapers and New Politics: Midwestern Municipal Reform, 1890-1900* (Ann Arbor, Mich.: UMI Research Press, 1981);

Jason Rogers, *Newspaper Building: Application of Efficiency to Editing, to Mechanical Production, to Circulation and Advertising* (New York: Harper, 1918);

Royal J. Schmidt, "The *Chicago Daily News* and Illinois Politics, 1876-1920," Ph.D. dissertation, University of Chicago, 1957;

Henry Justin Smith, *A Gallery of Chicago Editors* (Chicago: The *Daily News*, 1930);

James D. Startt, *Journalism's Unofficial Ambassador: A Biography of Edward Price Bell, 1869-1943* (Athens: Ohio University Press, 1979);

Melville E. Stone, *Fifty Years a Journalist* (Garden City: Doubleday, Page, 1921);

Graham Taylor, "Chicago Reclaims Its *Daily News*," *Survey*, 55 (1 February 1926): 572-573;

Taylor, *Pioneering on Social Frontiers* (Chicago: University of Chicago Press, 1930);

Robert L. Tree, "Victor Fremont Lawson and His Newspapers, 1890-1900: A Study of the Chicago *Daily News* and the Chicago *Record*," Ph.D. dissertation, Northwestern University, 1959;

"Victor F. Lawson, 1850-1925," *Journal of the Illinois State Historical Society*, 18 (October 1925): 773-775;

Benedict K. Zobrist, "Edward Price Bell and the Development of the Foreign News Service of the Chicago *Daily News*," Ph.D. dissertation, Northwestern University, 1953;

Zobrist, "How Victor Lawson's Newspapers Covered the Cuban War of 1898," *Journalism Quarterly*, 38 (Summer 1961): 323-331.

Papers:
Victor F. Lawson's papers are at the Newberry Library, Chicago.

Alfred H. Lewis

(20 January 1857-23 December 1914)

Richard M. Brown

MAJOR POSITIONS HELD: Reporter, *Kansas City Star* (1890-1891); Washington correspondent, *Chicago Times* (1891-1894); Washington bureau chief, *New York Journal* (1894-1898); editor, *Verdict* (New York) (1898-1900).

BOOKS: *Wolfville* (New York: Stokes, 1897);
Sandburrs (New York: Stokes, 1900);
Richard Croker (New York: Life, 1901);
Wolfville Days (New York: Stokes, 1902);
Wolfville Nights (New York: Stokes, 1902);
Peggy O'Neal (Philadelphia: Drexel Biddle, 1903);
The Boss and How He Came to Rule New York (New York: A. S. Barnes, 1903);
The Black Lion Inn (New York: R. H. Russell, 1903);
The President (New York: A. S. Barnes, 1904);
The Sunset Trail (New York: A. S. Barnes, 1905);
Confessions of a Detective (New York: A. S. Barnes, 1906);
The Throwback: A Romance of the Southwest (New York: Outing, 1906);
The Story of Paul Jones (New York: G. W. Dillingham, 1906);
When Men Grew Tall: The Story of Andrew Jackson (New York: Appleton, 1907);
An American Patrician; or, The Story of Aaron Burr (New York: Appleton, 1908);
Wolfville Folks (New York: Appleton, 1908);
The Apaches of New York (New York: G. W. Dillingham, 1912);
Faro Nell and Her Friends: Wolfville Stories (New York: G. W. Dillingham, 1913);
Nation-Famous New York Murders (New York: G. W. Dillingham, 1914).

PERIODICAL PUBLICATION: "Confessions of a Newspaperman," *Human Life* (November 1905-December 1906).

Alfred Henry Lewis (Culver Pictures)

Better known for his fiction, Alfred Henry Lewis was one of the most prolific political reporters of the "yellow journalism" era, an expert feature writer who was equally facile in covering national and local government. A Washington correspondent from 1891 to 1898, first for the *Chicago Times* and then as chief of William Randolph Hearst's Washington bureau, Lewis was a tireless and effective opponent of the political intrigue and corruption rampant during the period in which the "robber barons" were at the height of their power. A firm believer in the watchdog function of a free press, he saw its role as scrutinizing activities of politicians in the same manner as that of the policeman in keeping watch over "the plans and deeds of burglars, or what others are at criminal warfare with the law."

An individualist and an idealistic Democrat, Lewis produced highly partisan, often trenchant and bitter writings as he sought to inform the public of the scandal and corruption he found at all levels of government. Although he fought vigorously for reform, he finally became cynical about its success, viewing government as an accurate reflection of the moral climate of the electorate. "Be pure and your government will be pure; be brave and it will have courage.... Be dogs and you will have a dog government—a kennel, a collar, a bone to gnaw and a chain to clank," he wrote in the *Verdict*, a weekly Democratic paper he edited in New York City.

Lewis was born in 1857 to Isaac J. and Harriet Tracy Lewis in Cleveland, Ohio, and attended the public schools there. As a young man, he read law and was admitted to the Ohio bar in 1876, placing first among twenty-two in the examination. He became Cleveland's prosecuting attorney in 1880. The following year, when his father, a carpenter, decided to move west, Lewis gave up his practice to accompany his family to Kansas City, Missouri. For the next several years he roamed the Southwest as a cowboy, gathering the experiences and stories which he later wove into popular newspaper fiction as the "Old Cattleman" stories and which provided the material for his most enduring books.

During this period he worked on ranches in the Cimarron country of Kansas and drove cattle to Dodge City and other shipping points before drifting into the Texas panhandle and on into New Mexico, where he gained his first exposure to newspapering when he became the editor and entire newsroom staff of the *Mora County Pioneer*. Later, taking charge of the *Las Vegas* (New Mexico) *Optic* while the regular editor was indisposed, his freewheeling humor caused an uproar with the first issue. Among other tongue-in-cheek items was his response to a note that was handed in, saying: "Editor, Optic. I read your paper only when I am drunk. Yours truly, Alonzo Green." He wrote a paragraph saying that Green was indubitably, by his own showing, the miscreant who had been annoying the *Optic* with notes signed "A Constant Reader." Threatening to seek Green out and beat him, he cheerfully marked the item "First Page Must" and dispatched it to the printer. From New Mexico, his wanderings carried him to the frontier territory of southeastern Arizona at the time of the Tombstone silver boom and the expansion of the cattle industry as the Apache threat waned and new markets sprang up with the growing populace.

In 1885, Lewis returned to Kansas City to resume his interrupted law career and to marry Alice Ewing of Richfield, Ohio. Shortly after the marriage, at the urging of his brother, who was city editor of the *Kansas City Times*, he began writing his "Old Cattleman" stories. The first of these, an un-

paid effort, was widely reprinted and the second earned him $360. They also led to a reporting job on William Rockhill Nelson's *Kansas City Star* in 1890.

These stories, all introduced by the "Old Cattleman" conversing with his friends, were immensely popular. The "Old Cattleman" is a philosophizing septuagenarian bachelor living in retirement in the St. James Hotel with his servants and friends. He reminisces about the mythical town of Wolfville and its brave and humorous denizens. Wolfville closely parallels Tombstone in its early days, and the characters are often drawn from its inhabitants, only thinly disguised; in some cases, Lewis used actual persons without even changing their names. These stories, written initially as newspaper fiction, were eventually collected into a series of books which were his major literary contribution. Some authorities on Western literature consider his keen portrayal of the opening Western frontier to be more realistic and comprehensive even than that of Bret Harte.

After a year on the *Star*, Lewis went to Washington, D.C., as correspondent for the *Chicago Times*. There he eventually became a close friend of Theodore Roosevelt, then a civil service commissioner and a fan of Lewis's stories. It was Roosevelt who saw the further potential of the stories and encouraged Lewis to gather his "Old Cattleman" writings into his first book, *Wolfville* (1897). Roosevelt edited the manuscript and arranged for Frederic Remington to illustrate it. The book was an immediate success.

When the *Times* was sold to the *Chicago Herald* in 1894, Lewis was offered editorship of the combined paper. He declined, however, choosing to become chief of the Washington bureau of Hearst's *New York Journal*.

Particularly important to the *Journal*, which was handicapped by lack of an Associated Press franchise, were what it called "news novelettes," which were precursors of a dramatized, human-interest form of portraying events. Lewis was one of the most prolific producers of this form. Resembling the "New Journalism" of the 1970s, these accounts focused upon background and setting as well as the events themselves. They often dealt with pressures upon the legislators and the efforts of lobbyists to corrupt the legislative process. Lewis's muckraking frequently dealt with the actions of the railroad interests.

Hearst enjoyed the companionship of Lewis both on a personal and a professional basis and was attracted by the strength and freedom of his manner as well as his biting humor. Above medium height, solidly built with a square jaw and high brow, Lewis was an attractive individual with a forthright, alert expression. Pleasant and friendly, with a humorous outlook, he had an alert, well-trained mind that absorbed the nuances of situations. His dress was dapper, often tending toward the fashionable checked suits of that era and flowing white bow ties. Lewis's extemporaneous sayings were widely repeated and were often as hard-hitting as his writing. Once when Andrew M. Lawrence was in temporary charge of the *Journal* and was dashing around pompously stirring things up, Lewis halted him: "Calm yourself, Andy, calm yourself. You remind me of a little dog barking after an express and thinking he is making the train go."

As a Washington correspondent, Lewis set a grueling pace for himself. "I don't get down until about 4 in the evening," he wrote to Albert Bigelow Paine in 1895. "After that hour, and indeed until 5 the next morning, you will find me at my office in the Post building." In addition to his Congressional exposés, reform stories, and wire news, Lewis was also turning out articles for Hearst's *Cosmopolitan* and a steady stream of "Wolfville" fiction. His capacity for both volume and versatility made him a star among Hearst's writers, even after he severed his formal ties in 1898.

Moving to New York that year, he sought to devote more time to free-lance political and crime writing and to fiction. He did, however, edit a Democratic paper, the *Verdict*, until 12 November 1900. Most of this weekly, sponsored by O. H. P. Belmont, was written by Lewis.

A growing cynicism toward party politics seems to lie behind his decision to give up his last direct connection with newspaper journalism. He later wrote: "At that time I was a Democrat: I have since become politically nothing, my disgust with the Democrats being exceeded only by my disgust of Republicans. If I'd stayed away from Washington, I might have remained a Democrat. . . . "

Lewis's departure from a direct role in newspapers and from partisan politics did not mark a retreat from his crusade for clean government and a better society. Rather, it was a change in form. He continued the muckraking tradition in his magazine articles, largely for Hearst publications, dealing with the continuing battle of the police and the underworld and with the corruption that infested New York City government. He was fascinated with the Harry K. Thaw murder case and wrote several

extensive articles on it. His close study of Tammany Hall resulted in numerous articles and several books dealing with the evils of bossism in urban government.

A vitriolic and sensational writer closely attuned to working-class tastes of the time, Lewis reflected both the best and worst of the journalism of his era. A utopian crusader and a fearless advocate of clean government, he excelled in ferreting out and exposing the scandalous and predatory conduct of turn-of-the-century politicians and of the economic tycoons who corrupted them. Yet he was an unabashed racist who wrote of Negroes and Chinese as inconsequential menials and of Mexicans as low-down, untrustworthy, and dangerous "Greasers" in his stories. His work is peppered with such titles as "Sheeny Joe." Like many in his era and setting, he took for granted the superiority of his own kind and its manifest destiny. This was not without ambivalence, however, since people of these same races are sometimes placed in leading roles where they are portrayed sympathetically as noble individuals. His writings, at times, were intensely cynical and bitter. In politics and social ideals, his views reflected his early experience in the frontier towns. His ideal was the man who had a clear sense of right and wrong and a willingness to put his position on the line for his ideals, no matter what the risk. Western pioneers, with their refusal to tolerate any assault upon their freedom, integrity, or sense of propriety, were his ideals in both his personal conduct and his writing.

Lewis's decision to give up his law career for journalism reflects the working of those ideals in his personal life. Just as the lawyer in "The Clients of Aaron Green" (*Wolfville Nights*, 1902) was anachronistic to the simple, direct, and unswerving justice of Wolfville, the role of lawyer conflicted with Lewis's values of independence and intolerance toward corrupt and predatory practices in government.

He died in New York City after a short illness at the age of fifty-seven. His wife and several newspaper friends were present. The Lewises had no children.

While most of his major work is somewhat shallow and ephemeral, predicated largely on mass tastes of the time, his "Wolfville" fiction has been more enduring for its portraiture of the early West and its picturesque denizens. Throughout his life as an author and journalist, Lewis remained one of the most popular and productive writers of his time, both as a producer of popular fiction and as one of the most influential of the "muckraking" reporters.

References:
Abe C. Ravitz, *Alfred Henry Lewis* (Boise, Idaho:

Boise State University, 1978);
J. K. Winkler, *W. R. Hearst: An American Phenomenon* (New York: Simon & Schuster, 1928).

Charles MacArthur
(5 November 1895-21 April 1956)

John DeMers

See also the MacArthur entry in *DLB 7, Twentieth-Century American Dramatists*.

MAJOR POSITIONS HELD: Reporter, *Chicago Examiner* (1919-1921), *Chicago Tribune* (1921-1924).

BOOKS: *A Bug's-Eye View of the War* (Oak Park, Ill.: Pioneer Publishing, 1919);
The Front Page, by MacArthur and Ben Hecht (New York: Covici Friede, 1928; London: Richards & Toulmin, 1929);
War Bugs (Garden City: Doubleday, Doran, 1929);
Ladies and Gentlemen, adapted by MacArthur and Hecht (New York, Los Angeles & London: French, 1941);
Fun to Be Free, Patriotic Pageant, by MacArthur and Hecht (New York: Dramatists Play Service, 1941);
The Stage Works of Charles MacArthur, edited with introduction and notes by Arthur Dorlag and John Irvine (Tallahassee: Florida State University Foundation, 1974)—includes *Lulu Belle, Salvation, The Front Page, Twentieth Century, Ladies and Gentlemen, Johnny on a Spot, Swan Song*, and *Stag at Bay*.

PLAYS: *Lulu Belle*, by MacArthur and Edward Sheldon, New York, Belasco Theatre, 9 February 1926;
Salvation, by MacArthur and Sidney Howard, New York, Empire Theatre, 31 January 1928;
The Front Page, by MacArthur and Ben Hecht, New York, Times Square Theatre, 14 August 1928;
Twentieth Century, by MacArthur and Hecht, New York, Broadhurst Theatre, 29 December 1932;
Jumbo, by MacArthur and Hecht, New York, Hippodrome, 16 November 1935;

Culver Pictures
Charles MacArthur

Ladies and Gentlemen, by MacArthur and Hecht, adapted from Ladislaus Bus-Fekete's play, New York, Martin Beck Theatre, 17 October 1939;
Fun to Be Free, Patriotic Pageant, by MacArthur and Hecht, New York, Madison Square Garden, 1941;
Johnny on a Spot, New York, Plymouth Theatre, 8 January 1942;
Swan Song, by MacArthur and Hecht, adapted from Ramon Romero and Harriett Hinsdale's *Cre-*

scendo, New York, Booth Theatre, 15 May 1946;

Stag at Bay, by MacArthur and Nunnally Johnson, Tallahassee School of Theatre, Florida State University, 6 February 1974.

SELECTED SCREENPLAYS: *The Sin of Madelon Claudet*, M-G-M, 1931;
Rasputin and the Empress, M-G-M, 1933;
Crime Without Passion, by MacArthur and Ben Hecht, Paramount, 1934;
Barbary Coast, by MacArthur and Hecht, United Artists, 1935;
Once in a Blue Moon, by MacArthur and Hecht, Paramount, 1935;
The Scoundrel, by MacArthur and Hecht, Paramount, 1935;
Gunga Din, by MacArthur and Hecht, RKO, 1939;
Wuthering Heights, by MacArthur and Hecht, United Artists, 1939;
The Senator Was Indiscreet, United Artists, 1948.

PERIODICAL PUBLICATION: "Rope," *American Mercury*, 40 (February 1937): 182-195.

Though he spent much of his mature life in New York as a playwright and in Hollywood as a screenwriter, it is as a Chicago journalist that Charles MacArthur left an indelible mark on the American scene. More than any other twentieth-century newsman, MacArthur served as a model for the tough, wise-cracking reporter—a freewheeling archetype that remained for decades an American original. Noted for his elaborations on normal social usage, he was in some ways as colorful and unpredictable as the characters in his plays and movies. His second wife, the actress Helen Hayes, once said of him, "There is no rule of reason that he follows, so far as I can discover, and there is no telling, ever, what will happen next."

As a reporter for the *Chicago Tribune* and earlier for William Randolph Hearst's colorful *Examiner*, MacArthur demonstrated that he was neither awed by wealth nor impressed by social position. Once, waiting to interview arts patron Otto H. Kahn, he removed a few Greek volumes from the bookshelf and inscribed them: "To my friend Otto, without whose help this could not have been written. Socrates." Not even middle age—which crept up on him along with the success of his play *The Front Page* (1928) and such movie scripts as *Gunga Din* (1939) and *Wuthering Heights* (1939)—could shake MacArthur's conviction that most people took themselves too seriously. It was his job, as he

saw it, to deflate all pomposity.

As a reporter, playwright, and screenwriter, MacArthur's greatest creation was inarguably himself. His antics, especially those encouraged by *Examiner* managing editor Walter Howey, were legendary. They also revealed a curiosity, perseverance, irreverence, and tough-minded compassion that became the standard against which other newspapermen were measured. "You may picture MacArthur, if you will, in Lincoln green and a pointed cap," wrote critic Alexander Woollcott of the *New York World*. "He clearly belongs in the 13th century, astray, as like as not, from Robin Hood's band, and vaguely headed for the Holy Land."

MacArthur was born in Scranton, Pennsylvania, on 5 November 1895 to the Reverend William T. and Georgiana Welstead MacArthur. His father was an evangelist who heard the call while watching his threshing machine go up in flames, and ordained himself on the spot. His mother was one of nineteen children of an English remittance man who had served as an officer in the East India army—a fact that helps account for MacArthur's lifelong fascination with the military.

The preacher was rough on young Charles and his four brothers and two sisters. "He was constantly uncovering some new streak of wickedness in us," MacArthur remembered. "He would line us up at night, all still hungry as wolves, beseech God in a firm voice to forgive us, uncover our backs and whale the hell out of us."

By the age of thirteen, MacArthur had learned to take refuge in the bathroom of the family's home in Nyack, New York. There he indulged in the forbidden pleasures of Charles Dickens, Sir Walter Scott, and *The Rubaiyat of Omar Khayyám*. As soon as his mother's death freed him from family ties to Nyack, MacArthur went to Chicago in 1915 to seek a newspaper career. He managed to land a job on a small publication called *Oak Leaves* in suburban Oak Park before doing a short hitch on the *City Press*, whose editors ran him ragged and paid him just $10 a week.

In 1916, MacArthur interrupted his cub-reporter days to march off to Mexico with the Illinois militia under Col. Milton Foreman. The cavalry unit was dubbed by the expedition's commander, Gen. John Pershing, "Colonel Foreman's Dog and Pony Show." During the entire operation, MacArthur never expressed any interest in Pancho Villa, the villain they tried in vain to track down, or in the fact that Villa turned out to be a liberator. "War is war," he declared, "and politicians are politicians."

MacArthur in his Rainbow Division uniform

During the militia's return to Chicago—which was heralded with great patriotism despite the mission's failure—MacArthur was arrested weaving through the crowd in a military car, waving a top-heavy American flag and shouting, "Down with Tin-Pants Milton." In jail at Fort Sheridan, he caught Colonel Foreman's eye by decorating his blue denim prisoner suit with gold radiator paint, epaulets, and other ornaments and impersonating a general while picking up trash. The colonel ordered MacArthur removed from his clean-up duties— and from the army. "I don't know what the hell's going to become of you," Foreman told him. "But

I'm sure of one thing. You're never going to make a soldier."

When the United States entered World War I, MacArthur again found himself in uniform, serving in France with the famed Rainbow Division. The experience led to humorous accounts of the battles for Cantigny, Château-Thierry, and the Argonne. It also helped refine the cynicism that distinguished his life and work. "I don't think God is interested in us after puberty," MacArthur said at the time. "He is interested only in our births, for this requires His magic. Our dying requires only his indifference."

Back from his duties with Battery F in France, MacArthur plunged wholeheartedly into Chicago—which he later described in *The Front Page* as a "sort of journalistic Yellowstone Park offering haven to a last herd of fantastic bravos that once roamed the newspaper offices of the country." He enrolled at the *Examiner* under Howey, and their colorful love-hate relationship became the basis for that between reporter Hildy Johnson and editor Walter Burns in the play. According to Ben Hecht, Howey was able to hand the city's first $100-a-week reporter scoop after scoop because he kept a high Illinois official's resignation in his desk. The editor blackmailed the document out of the politician after catching him in some foul deed. From then on, Howey had an extremely cooperative news source.

"Of all the young journalists drinking and slugging their way to fame in that day, Charlie was one of the most popular and attractive," Hecht remembered. "Curly black hair, smoky eyes, a pointed nose, sledge-hammer fists, a capacity for alcohol that won a nod from the old-timers—these were Charlie MacArthur. Plus a firecracker mind and a vocabulary sired by the poets."

Innumerable tales of adventures and pranks sprang from MacArthur's tenure at the *Examiner*. But the case of the little girl locked in the safe in Moline, Illinois, reveals the nature of the 1920s Chicago journalism and the lengths Howey would go to lead the pack. When he learned a girl was trapped in a safe with only a few hours of air, Howey sent MacArthur on a special train to the state penitentiary in Joliet, where the reporter picked out two safecracking experts. Along with three prison guards, the warden, assistant warden, doctors, nurses, and railroad officials, MacArthur and his inmates hired another train to Moline. There the two safecrackers worked feverishly to open the door. With only minutes of air left inside, the safe door swung open—and revealed no little girl. She was home in bed after hiding in the attic, angry with her grandmother for getting drunk in front of her schoolmates. Enraged, MacArthur told Howey over the phone that his big story was no story and that all the *Examiner* had on its hands were two weary inmates mad about not getting a governor's pardon. "It's a terrific story," Howey shouted into the phone. "I'll give you a rewrite man. Give him every detail you've got. Everything all those wonderful people said. How everybody from the lowest to the highest rode to the rescue of that little girl." The story in the next morning's *Examiner* covered half the front page under the seven-column headline "It's a Wonderful World."

Switching over to the *Chicago Tribune*, MacArthur perfected his style under the direction of managing editor James Keeley—known as "J. God Keeley" to those who toiled on his newspaper. One of the reporter's successes was an interview with Spanish literary lion Vicente Blasco-Ibáñez, whose novel *Blood and Sand* was being reworked for Rudolph Valentino in Hollywood. Instead of a few short paragraphs on the visitor's impressions of Chicago, MacArthur offered a 1,000-word account of Blasco-Ibáñez's blistering critique of American culture. He accompanied this, however, with a description of the activities of Blasco-Ibáñez's toes, which had been sticking out from under a bedsheet as the aging wordsmith spoke. The story, which made page one, tickled Chicagoans.

When he was twenty-two, MacArthur married Carol Frink, the *Examiner*'s new "Little Girl Reporter." The quick collapse of their relationship, however, mixed with his growing literary ambitions, convinced him it was time to leave Chicago for New York in 1924. Carol stayed behind, to fluctuate for several more years between wanting to rid herself of her estranged husband or to hang on for the day he would strike it rich. As it turned out, MacArthur disliked the bigger city's noise and grime, but New York fell in love with him. For three years, he roomed with humorist Robert Benchley, writing for Hearst's *New York American* and penning occasional articles for Harold Ross's upstart publication the *New Yorker*. After a time, he left the *American*'s staff in hopes of following Benchley to fame as a "flourishing fat-cat freelancer." Mostly, however, he wrote plays.

With Edward Sheldon, a romantic stiffened into an invalid by arthritis, MacArthur turned out *Lulu Belle* (1926). With Sidney Howard he wrote *Salvation* (1928). Through these early plays he gained the approval and friendship of Woollcott, who expounded from the pages of Herbert Bayard Swope's *New York World*. MacArthur became a regular drinking companion of Benchley, F. Scott

Fitzgerald, and Dorothy Parker, who regaled the Round Table at the Algonquin Hotel with wordplay. At a Halloween party, Miss Parker was invited to join a group "ducking for apples." She replied: "Change one letter in that phrase and you have my life story."

In November 1924 MacArthur met Helen Hayes, who was playing the lead in *To the Ladies* by George S. Kaufman and Marc Connelly. Until she met MacArthur, Miss Hayes's life had been the stage, a hall bedroom shared with Mama Brown, and then a tiny flat shared with another girl—and Mama Brown. As the actress describes their meeting, she was at a party with Connelly, listening to his conversations with Benchley, Woollcott, Irving Berlin, and George Gershwin. "A beautiful young man came up to me with a bag of peanuts in his hand and said 'Want a peanut?' Somebody had spoken to me! I was amazed, but I answered correctly, 'Yes, thank you.' The young man poured several peanuts out of his bag into my hands. Then he smiled at me and said, 'I wish they were emeralds.' "

Any plans for marriage were delayed by difficulties with MacArthur's divorce from Carol Frink MacArthur, who fought against the proceedings for seven years. While he waited for his freedom, MacArthur settled in with Hecht to write a play—establishing a collaborative procedure that served them through twenty years of writing for Broadway and Hollywood. Hecht sat with a pencil, paper, and a lapboard. MacArthur paced, stretched out on the couch, looked out the window, and drew mustaches on magazine cover girls, spouting lines of dialogue in character. Each writer edited the other, and when they finished the play they flipped a coin to see who got top billing. MacArthur called heads, and the coin came up tails.

The Front Page drew less on the playwrights' vivid imaginations than on their sometimes comic, sometimes grotesque adventures as Chicago newspapermen. In the fast-talking vermin of the Criminal Courts pressroom, Hecht and MacArthur captured a seamy slice of American history. "Journalists!," complains reporter Hildy Johnson, who tries in vain to escape his overbearing managing editor. "Peeking through keyholes! Running after fire engines like a lot of coach dogs! Waking people up in the middle of the night to ask them what they think of Mussolini. Stealing pictures off old ladies of their daughters that got raped in Oak Park. A lot of lousy, daffy buttinskis, swelling around with holes in their pants, borrowing nickels from office boys! And for what? So a million hired girls and motormen's wives'll know what's going on."

After tryouts in Atlantic City, *The Front Page* opened at the Times Square Theatre in New York in 1928. The success of the play, however, interested MacArthur less than his impending marriage to Helen Hayes on 17 August. He wanted to keep the ceremony private, ordering Hecht to keep reporters and photographers away from the judge's chambers. To MacArthur's disgust, the judge actually delayed the wedding because some of the reporters he had invited had not yet arrived. One picture appeared on the front page of the *New York Daily News* with a headline needling MacArthur for his divorce difficulties: "Bridegroom or Bigamist?" (Carol MacArthur had finally agreed to a divorce, then claimed the divorce was fraudulent; later, she backed down.)

The marriage to Miss Hayes produced one child on 15 February 1930, a daughter they named Mary. Considerable publicity surrounded her birth because it forced the actress to withdraw from a show. Because of a term used in the legal tiff, Mary was known as the "Act of God Baby." The couple later adopted an infant named Jamie. The boy grew up to become actor James MacArthur and a source of great pride to his father, but Mary's death from polio at the age of nineteen was one of the major tragedies of his life. On her Nyack Hill tombstone,

MacArthur on vacation with Helen Hayes, their daughter, Mary, and adopted son, James (Freddie Maura)

MacArthur had the inscription chiseled: "Here beneath this stone doth lie / As much beauty as could die."

MacArthur and Miss Hayes went to Hollywood in the 1930s mainly for the money—he could pick up $25,000 to $50,000 per picture without the gamble of the theater or books. But it was hardly easy money, especially for that "firecracker mind and a vocabulary sired by the poets." MacArthur would rewrite scenes ten times, improving them in subtle ways, only to have the whole segment cut out by a studio boss. "I know less about writing than you do," one boss told him. "But so does the audience. My tastes are exactly those of the audience."

There was, however, something MacArthur had that Hollywood wanted—himself. "Make a hero out of MacArthur" was the order of the day, and the screen witnessed a parade of graceful heroes brimming with offbeat rejoinders. Clark Gable, Spencer Tracy, Cary Grant, George Sanders, Robert Taylor, and even Jimmy Durante played MacArthur in the movies. Among his most successful screenplays were *Crime Without Passion* (1934), *The Scoundrel* (1935), *Gunga Din*, and *Wuthering Heights*—all written in collaboration with Hecht.

MacArthur and Helen Hayes at the time of their marriage in 1928

While cultivating glittering intimacies with John Barrymore, Joan Crawford, Sam Goldwyn, and David O. Selznick, MacArthur and Hecht were also revolutionizing the financial side of movie-making. Peppering the moguls with suggestions, they pioneered cost cutting in the industry, shooting films in 80,000 feet that without them would have used 500,000. They cut the usual number of camera setups in half and reduced the number of retakes. To economize on movie scores, the two writers visited Richard Rodgers to listen to his Beethoven records; picking out passages they liked, they saved the cost of composing and orchestrating every time a bit of Beethoven was used.

Before the United States joined World War II, Hecht and MacArthur worked on propaganda pageants, such as "Fun to Be Free," put on by Billy Rose at Madison Square Garden. After Pearl Harbor, MacArthur wanted more. He wanted the real war his age and physical condition kept from him. In order to reach the front lines, MacArthur accepted a commission as a major and served around the world as a courier, escort, and military observer. In letters to his wife, he described the battlegrounds of Europe and Asia as though they were playgrounds, but he omitted mention of his trips to the hospital as an ulcer patient or the collapses that inevitably climaxed his drinking bouts.

After the end of hostilities, MacArthur decided to dabble as an editor between Hollywood writing projects. The publication was *Theatre Arts*, a magazine of the stage. In short order it had gone through its funds, and MacArthur decided a reorganization was necessary. He raised more money, and, as he wrote in a letter to his readers, "we sent for The Experts" and were "wheeled into the operating room while The Experts did a complete plastic job. We felt as good as new. No squeak, no stoop, even no squawk. While we were under the anesthetic, a soft rain of $1,000 set in." MacArthur resigned as editor of *Theatre Arts* in 1950.

In his final years, MacArthur was a victim of illness, bitterness, and drink. Yet he continued to write, despite fingers swollen to the size of bananas, despite ulcers and kidney poisons. He turned out movies and plays by himself and with such collaborators as Nunnally Johnson, Ludwig Bemelmans, Anita Loos, and, of course, Ben Hecht. On 21 April 1956 MacArthur died at New York Hospital of an internal hemorrhage suffered on his fourth day of hospitalization for nephritis and anemia; he was sixty. Earlier that week, Miss Hayes had canceled an appearance in the televised version of *The Cradle Song*, saying she was unable to continue in rehearsal because of her husband's illness. She was at MacArthur's side when he died.

Hundreds turned out for the memorial service at the Frank E. Campbell Funeral Church on New York's Madison Avenue, mostly people from MacArthur's glory days on Broadway or in Hollywood. Richard Rodgers and Oscar Hammerstein II were there, along with Irving Berlin, Lillian Gish, and Paul Muni. Walter Howey, the gruff editorial half of the duo immortalized in *The Front Page*, had died years before; many of MacArthur's other newspaper compatriots had also passed away. But one old Chicago reporter, Ben Hecht, played the role of collaborator one last time, telling the gathering of MacArthur's zest for a good story, his persistence in tracking it down—and his style in building these everyday activities into an American legend. The tales of MacArthur's newspaper days would brighten the mundane corners of the profession for generations; Hecht said: "They were stories that added love and a sense of wonder to our world. From his youthful days to his last ones, Charlie was a man of adventure. He loved life and threw his wit at people and events like a man scattering inexhaustible treasure."

Biography:

Ben Hecht, *Charlie: The Improbable Life and Times of Charles MacArthur* (New York: Harper, 1957).

References:

Helen Hayes, "The Most Unforgettable Character I've Ever Met," *Reader's Digest*, 51 (September 1947): 16-22;

Ben Hecht, *A Child of the Century* (New York: Simon & Schuster, 1954);

Hecht, *Gaily, Gaily* (Garden City: Doubleday, 1963);

New York Times, 24 April 1956, p. 31;

H. Allen Smith, *The Life and Legend of Gene Fowler* (New York: Morrow, 1977).

Papers:

Charles MacArthur's papers are held at the University of Wisconsin.

Bernarr Macfadden
(16 August 1868-12 October 1955)

William H. Taft
University of Missouri

MAJOR POSITIONS HELD: Founder, publisher, *New York Graphic* (1924-1932).

SELECTED BOOKS: *The Athlete's Conquest* (New York & St. Louis: Brown, 1892; revised edition, New York: Physical Culture Publishing Co., 1901);

Mcfadden's [sic] *System of Physical Training* (New York: Hulbert, 1895);

Physical Training (New York: Macfadden, 1900);

Fasting, Hydropathy, and Exercise, by Macfadden and Felix Oswald (New York: Physical Culture Publishing Co., 1900);

Virile Powers of Superb Manhood: How Developed, How Lost, How Regained (New York: Physical Culture Publishing Co., 1900);

New Cookery Book, by Macfadden, Mary Richardson, and George Propheter (London: 1901);

Power and Beauty of Superb Womanhood (New York: Physical Culture Publishing Co., 1901);

Strength from Eating (New York: Physical Culture Publishing Co., 1901);

Strong Eyes (New York: Physical Culture Publishing Co., 1901);

Natural Cure for Rupture (New York & London: Physical Culture Publishing Co., 1902);

Vaccination Superstition (New York: Macfadden, 1902);

What a Young Husband Ought to Know (New York: Macfadden, 1902);

What a Young Woman Ought to Know (New York: Macfadden, 1902);

Marriage a Lifelong Honeymoon: Life's Greatest Pleasures Secured by Observing the Highest Human Instincts (New York & London: Physical Culture Publishing Co., 1903);

Building of Vital Power (New York & London: Physical Culture Publishing Co., 1904);

Creative and Sexual Science (New York: Macfadden, 1904);

Diseases of Men (New York & London: Physical Culture Publishing Co., 1904);

Health, Beauty, and Sexuality, by Macfadden and Marion Malcolm (New York & London: Physical Culture Publishing Co., 1904);

Bernarr Macfadden (Bettmann Archive)

How Success Is Won (New York & London: Physical Culture Publishing Co., 1904);

How to Box (New York: Macfadden, 1904);

A Perfect Beauty, by Macfadden and Barbara Howard (New York: Macfadden, 1904);

Physical Culture for Babies, by Macfadden and Marguerite Macfadden (New York & London: Physical Culture Publishing Co., 1904);

Strenuous Lover (New York: Physical Culture Publishing Co., 1904);

Muscular Power and Beauty (New York: Physical Culture Publishing Co., 1906);

Macfadden Prosecution–A Curious Story of Wrong and Oppression under the Postal Laws (New York: Macfadden, 1908);

Vitality Supreme (New York: Macfadden, 1915);

Brain Energy-Building and Nerve-Vitalizing Course (New York: Physical Culture Publishing Co., 1916);

Manhood and Marriage (New York: Physical Culture Publishing Co., 1916);

Womanhood and Marriage (New York: Macfadden, 1918);

Strengthening the Eyes (New York: Physical Culture Publishing Co., 1918);

Making Old Bodies Young (New York: Physical Culture Publishing Co., 1919);

Eating for Health and Strength (New York: Physical Culture Corp., 1921);

Truth about Tobacco (New York: Physical Culture Corp., 1921);

The Miracle of Milk (New York: Macfadden, 1923);

Fasting for Health (New York: Macfadden, 1923);

How to Keep Fit (New York: Macfadden, 1923);

Keeping Fit (New York: Macfadden, 1923);

Preparing for Motherhood (New York: Macfadden, 1923);

Constipation, Its Cause, Effect and Treatment (New York: Macfadden, 1924);

How to Raise Strong Baby (New York: Macfadden, 1924);

Physical Culture Cook Book, by Macfadden and Milo Hastings (New York: Macfadden, 1924);

Physical Culture Food Directory (New York: Macfadden, 1924);

Walking Cure, Pep and Power from Walking–How to Cure Disease from Walking (New York: Macfadden, 1924);

Hair Culture (New York: Macfadden, 1924);

Diabetes, Its Cause, Nature and Treatment (New York: Macfadden, 1925);

Headaches, How Caused and How Cured (New York: Macfadden, 1925);

Strengthening the Nerves (New York: Macfadden, 1925);

Strengthening the Spine (New York: Macfadden, 1925);

Tooth Troubles: Their Prevention, Cause and Cure (New York: Macfadden, 1925);

Asthma and Hay Fever (New York: Macfadden, 1926);

The Book of Health (New York: Macfadden, 1926);

Colds, Coughs, and Catarrh (New York: Macfadden, 1926);

Foot Troubles (New York: Macfadden, 1926);

How to Raise the Baby (New York: Macfadden, 1926);

Plain Speech on a Public Insult: Bernarr Macfadden Replies to Atlantic Monthly (New York: Macfadden, 1926);

Predetermine Your Baby's Sex (New York: Macfadden, 1926);

Rheumatism, Its Cause, Nature and Treatment (New York: Macfadden, 1926);

Skin Troubles, Their Nature and Treatment (New York: Macfadden, 1927);

Digestive Troubles, How Caused and Cured (New York: Macfadden, 1928);

Good Health, How to Get It and Keep It (New York: Macfadden, 1928);

Talks to a Young Man about Sex (New York: Macfadden, 1928);

Exercising for Health (New York: Macfadden, 1929);

Health for the Family (New York: Macfadden, 1929);

Tuberculosis (New York: Macfadden, 1929);

Home Health Manual (New York: Macfadden, 1930);

Home Health Library (5 volumes, New York: Macfadden, 1933);

After 40–What?, by Macfadden and Charles A. Clinton (New York: Macfadden, 1935);

Man's Sex Life (New York: Macfadden, 1935);

Practical Birth Control and Sex Predetermination, by Macfadden and Clinton (New York: Macfadden, 1935);

Woman's Sex Life (New York: Macfadden, 1935);

How to Gain Weight (New York: Macfadden, 1936);

How to Reduce Weight (New York: Macfadden, 1936);

Be Married and Like It (New York: Macfadden, 1937);

Exercise and Like It (New York: Macfadden, 1937);

Handbook of Health (New York: Macfadden, 1938);

More Power to Your Nerves (New York: Macfadden, 1938);

New Handbook of Health with First Aid (New York: Macfadden, 1940);

Stomach and Digestive Disorders (New York: Macfadden, 1946);

Confessions of an Amateur Politician (New York: Macfadden, 1948).

OTHER: *Mary and Bob's True Story Book*, compiled by Macfadden (New York: Macfadden, 1930).

Bernarr Macfadden is better known for his lifelong interest in physical culture and the founding of *True Story* magazine, but he also gave New Yorkers the *Graphic,* called by his critics the "Pornographic." Macfadden was credited by Oswald Garrison Villard with starting the war of "gutter journalism" in New York. In addition to the *Graphic*, Macfadden owned newspapers in Michigan, Connecticut, and Pennsylvania. For a decade (1931-1941) he owned *Liberty* magazine. Yet today his influence lingers on through *True Story*, the grandfather of all such "true" and "confessional" periodicals that have cluttered the newsstands since 1919.

Macfadden's name at his birth was Bernard Adolphus McFadden. His family, which reached Missouri by way of Virginia and Kentucky, had a Scottish or Irish background. After he became more involved with the public, Macfadden thought his name should be changed. He considered "Bernard" too weak and too commonplace, so he shifted to "Bernarr," with the emphasis on the last syllable. This made it different. Obviously "Adolphus" had to go; it did. "McFadden" was commonplace, mediocre. "Mac" had a stronger connotation, being symbolic, to Macfadden, of one of the most powerful vehicles of its day, the Mack truck. Thus evolved "Bernarr Macfadden," as he has been known since the start of this century.

Macfadden was born in a Missouri Ozarks farmhouse in Mill Spring on 16 August 1868 to John R. and Elizabeth Miller McFadden. Macfadden was a puny, sickly, half-starved child, mainly because his alcoholic father spent what money he could get on liquor and horse races. The family survived on handouts from friends, neighbors, and Elizabeth McFadden's relatives. Macfadden's father died when the boy was about four years old; his mother died of tuberculosis six years later. Raised by relatives and others in Chicago and St. Louis, Macfadden received little formal education, a situation he later termed a blessing.

While holding numerous jobs in St. Louis, Macfadden became involved in body-building exercises. Dumbbell drills became a daily routine; long walks, too, were important to Macfadden, who added a ten-pound bar of lead to his backpack to build up his endurance.

Dazzled by Barnum's Circus when it appeared in St. Louis, Macfadden erected his own gymnasium in order to improve his physical condition so that he could duplicate the feats of the trapeze artists and other acrobats he had seen. He also set out to reform the world, at least physically. He took up wrestling and then went to various towns in Missouri offering to take on anyone; he won in several weight classes. Macfadden used wrestling to make some quick cash but, more important, to hold the crowd's attention for a speech at the end of the match on the virtue of good health and physical culture. Macfadden learned to be a public speaker during these exhibitions. Other activities followed, including a brief time when he was a hobo in Kansas. In that state, Macfadden had his first exposure to publishing when he became a printer's devil on

the *McCune Brick*, probably in 1886. Historians indicate that the people in McCune apparently did not concur with the newspaper's objective, "to hurl advice at the community," and soon ignored it out of existence. This brief incident must have had some effect on Macfadden's interests, since he sought a job as typesetter after his return to St. Louis around 1887. However, the union turned him down, which was probably best for both Macfadden and the union, since this young man would never have been happy with an inside job, especially one that involved as little physical activity as setting type did. Macfadden held a number of jobs in his youth, including driving a beer wagon, working as an assistant bookkeeper in relatives' businesses, coal mining, farming, teaching, coaching, and working in a hotel. He once ran a dry-cleaning establishment with a partner, an experience that made him determined never again to go into partnership with anyone else.

In 1893 Macfadden visited the World's Fair in Chicago and encountered Florenz Ziegfeld, who had Sandow, "the world's strongest man," on display in a midway show. Macfadden became excited about this show, especially the way Ziegfeld manipulated the lights to overplay Sandow's muscles. Ziegfeld became more famous for his ability to manipulate lights for his Follies girls in New York. Macfadden and Ziegfeld remained friends, and one of the publisher's daughters later appeared briefly in a Ziegfeld sketch on Broadway.

Macfadden reached New York in 1894 and opened a gymnasium. He also toured England, where his love of muscles was more acceptable than in the United States. From a four-page leaflet distributed in England to promote these exhibitions, Macfadden established *Physical Culture* magazine in 1899. Although this magazine never reached the circulation that *True Story* and the *Graphic* acquired, *Physical Culture* always remained Macfadden's greatest love. From its pages one can learn much of Macfadden's philosophy, his loves and desires, and his goals. One major goal was "to make each and everyone of my readers as broadminded" as he was trying to make himself.

During these early years in New York, Macfadden engaged in bitter conflict with Anthony Comstock, the chief agent of the New York Society for the Suppression of Vice. Macfadden's desire for freedom to print what he considered appropriate to assist his readers in reaching their goals conflicted with Comstock's views on decency. Comstock, labeled the "king of the prudes" by Macfadden, raided the publisher's offices in 1905 and confiscated posters advertising a physical culture exhibition scheduled for Madison Square Garden. The censor labeled such posters "filthy literature"— pornographic, lewd, and vulgar. Comstock even removed some pictures of ancient Roman and Greek gods, calling these "dirty."

In *Physical Culture* Macfadden waged a continuous editorial attack on the censor, who became the "quintessence of prudery" and who stood for "mystery, secrecy, ignorance, superstition, and for the most depraved conception of all that should be divine and holy." Some newspapers supported Macfadden in his struggles with Comstock. The *St. Louis Post-Dispatch*, for example, said, "Artists search for the truth; Comstock looks for the impure, the base, the lewd." George Bernard Shaw, some of whose writings appeared in Macfadden's magazines, wrote, "Comstockery is the world's standing joke at the expense of the United States."

Macfadden's next entry in the publishing

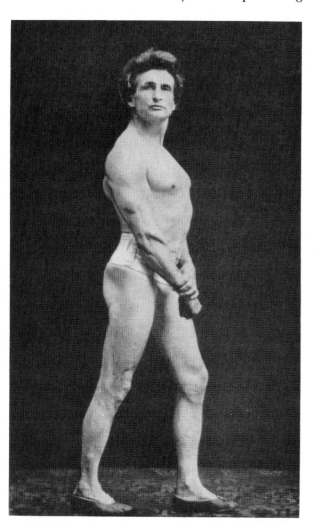

Macfadden displaying his physique at the age of fifty-six

business provided the funds that were to keep the *Graphic* and other projects operating. In 1919 he founded *True Story* "to assist in building the right sort of principles, add strength to your character and force and stability to your life purposes." Macfadden received so many letters from his faithful fans that he viewed *True Story* as a practical way to share with others his answers to their questions. He became the "Dear Abby" of the post-World War I era.

At *True Story* the editors were not allowed to edit, except to correct grammatical errors. Macfadden hired "average people," such as dime-store clerks and taxi drivers, to read and evaluate the articles submitted. It is said that when Macfadden found out that two of his staffers had taken a creative writing course at Columbia University, he fired them. The letters were to convey the human experiences of the writers and to be totally authentic in their content and feelings; Macfadden did not want them interfered with by trained editors or writers. Macfadden's formula was certainly successful: he earned $10,000 a day from *True Story* at its peak. Magazine historian Theodore Peterson considers *True Story* "the keystone of Macfadden's publishing business," turning the once-poor Missouri orphan into a millionaire. *True Story* was a product of the times. Frederick Lewis Allen wrote in *Only Yesterday* (1931) that "a bumper crop of sex magazines, confession magazines, and lurid motion pictures" had "their effect on a class of readers and movie-goers who had never heard and never would hear of Freud and the libido."

Macfadden always believed that only the prudes pointed a forbidding finger at sex. "You can't do anything about such an attitude. You can only lift sex to its proper dignity." Historians tend to feel that Macfadden never raised sex to its "proper dignity," in either *True Story* or the *Graphic*. In addition to providing Macfadden the funds he needed for his many projects, *True Story* helped to prepare Macfadden followers for the *New York Graphic*.

"The world's zaniest newspaper" appeared in New York on 15 September 1924, seeking to capture a portion of a market already served by fifteen dailies. Macfadden, however, was confident of his ability to penetrate this market with his *Graphic*. "As the publisher of ten magazines with a total yearly distribution of nearly fifty million, I am egotistical enough to believe that I can direct the making of a newspaper that will teem with life as it is being lived now and here today." One of his close associates, Fulton Oursler, believed his boss looked upon the *Graphic* as "the magic carpet that would carry him to

Macfadden at his cluttered desk in 1924 (Culver Pictures)

the White House." Obviously it failed to achieve this goal.

Macfadden leased the old plant of the *Evening Mail*, where the *Daily News* had also been printed for a time. His first editor, Emile Gauvreau, recalled that on his initial visit to the plant, "all machinery was covered with rust." Two years later the *Graphic* moved to a new eight-story building, where the flamboyant, headline-seeking Mayor Jimmy Walker, "the Pied Piper of Tabloidia," started the new presses.

Macfadden never really intended to publish what most readers would term a *news*paper; rather, he sought to promote physical culture on a daily basis and to provide a forum for his continuous attacks on the medical profession. Originally, the newspaper was to be called the *Truth*, with the slogan "Nothing But the Truth." Macfadden's staffers, feeling that title would not be appropriate for the sort of publication they would be putting out, convinced him that *Graphic* would be better; the paper

would, after all, be heavily illustrated. Macfadden told Gauvreau that he wanted "a paper wholly human, with a serious purpose behind it—which makes it different from all other tabloids I've ever heard of. We're going to play up physical culture in it from the start. That's why I'm starting it. And I want you to editorialize the news too. Don't stop with the bare skeleton of the facts. Point out the moral, the social lesson." As one biographer aptly noted, "The ideal was not entirely realized."

Macfadden's plan to "dramatize and sensationalize the news and some stories that are not news" fit into the era of the "terrible tabloids." Samuel Taylor Moore wrote in the *Independent*: "There is one thing to be said for the tabloids. Never, so far as is known, have these purveyors of journalistic filth engaged in blackmail. But nobody, high or low, is immune from their peering and prying, and when they succeed in spotting an act of moral turpitude they fall upon it with cries of joy. Such is the postwar trend in Manhattan journalism;

may common decency rise against it."

The *Graphic*'s initial staff of sixty editors and writers kept to a rustic, unsophisticated, rather than an urban, approach. It was the nation's eighth tabloid, following the *New York Daily News* and *Mirror* and others in Boston, Baltimore, Washington, Los Angeles, and San Francisco. (Cornelius Vanderbilt, Jr., owned the California papers that had brief careers, since he attempted to publish only the good news, avoiding the emphasis on crime.)

From the beginning the *Graphic* was different. As with the other tabloids, however, page one was designed to attract street sales; banner headlines were routine. But the *Graphic*'s use of first-person singular news accounts "as told to a *Graphic* reporter" set it apart. These stories carried such headlines as: "I Am Now the Mother of My Sister's Son," "Friends Dragged Me in the Gutter," "I Know the Man Who Killed My Girl," and "Must I Die Because I Am a Poor Boy?" Obviously, there were echoes of *True Story* in such accounts.

Criminal stories became the major component of the *Graphic*, which was "interested in the speedy solution of crime in order to bring criminals to justice." Movie actors seeking additional public exposure often posed for *Graphic* photographers who provided illustrations for crime stories.

Contests long have been associated with tabloids. The *Graphic* did not differ, except in some of the subjects. One prime promotional gimmick provided $10,000 in prizes for America's Apollos and Dianas, the ten men and ten women in perfect physical condition as determined by Macfadden's standards. Echoes of *Physical Culture* magazine are evident here.

Macfadden told *Editor & Publisher* that "sensationalism was nothing more than a clear, definite, attractive presentation of the news and is perfectly proper as long as one adheres to truth. . . . It is just a convenient word your critics use to throw at you."

Walter Winchell and Ed Sullivan were among many journalists who made their debuts on the *Graphic*. Winchell's Broadway gossip column became the newspaper's major drawing card, a situation Macfadden never fully comprehended. Winchell at first earned $100 a week plus a share of the advertising revenue he produced. It was estimated that his column lured from 75,000 to 100,000 extra readers to the *Graphic*. Macfadden and Winchell eventually engaged in a heated argument prompted by Winchell, who had a better offer from the *Daily News*. Macfadden fired the columnist, who was most happy at this outcome. Sullivan moved from the sport page to take over the Broadway

column. Macfadden was remembered by Sullivan as "the doughty old gentleman" who rarely came to the office. Frank Mallen's book, *Sauce for the Gander*, tells about many others who "served time" on the *Graphic* before going on to greater fame. Noted evangelist Aimee Semple McPherson covered several famous murder cases for the *Graphic*. Louis Weitzenkorn, the second editor of the *Graphic*, finally told Macfadden to "go to hell and take his slimy sheet along with him."

The *Graphic* carried many other features, including cute sayings by kids for which it paid a dollar each, a love diary, bedtime stories, and Macfadden's physical culture comments. Two pages were devoted to a fiction story. Broadway plays were reviewed by "common folks" rather than by experienced critics—who, no doubt, would have written over the heads of most *Graphic* readers.

Macfadden always viewed himself as a crusader. He called for the abolishment of graft in politics and business, the repeal of legislation preventing ownership of firearms, and the annulment of all prohibitory laws infringing constitutional rights. He called for the nonmedical investigation of healing methods, the registration of all citizens to detect crooks, and compulsory suffrage with fines for nonvoters.

In a talk before Parliament in 1927, Macfadden told the British that "the power of the press has been greatly over-estimated. A newspaper has to form certain policies and adhere to them to hold its readers. The present-day tendency toward combinations is to be deplored. Many big newspapers are becoming huge news-reporting machines, without feeling or personality." Such comments are still voiced by critics of the press.

If Macfadden's primary goal was to publish a feature-type newspaper for "home, father, mother, sister, brother" as he promised, he apparently failed to pass along any instructions to his staff. What his editors interpreted as "hard news" involved love, murder, holocaust, marital disputes, and similar subjects. After numerous layout experiments, the *Graphic*'s physical appearance became more like that of the *Daily News* and the *Mirror*. The newspaper never offered any significant innovations in its makeup, but it did differ in its use of photographs. The "composograph" became a *Graphic* trademark. This was a tasteless yet effective blending of photographs when more conventional pictures were not available. These represented the cooperative efforts of photographers, editors, and artists. Readers apparently enjoyed them, but while such scenes were identified in small type as being a

New York Graphic *columns by Ed Sullivan and Walter Winchell. Sullivan took over the Broadway column when Winchell left to join the* Daily News.

composograph, one can only speculate as to how many readers fully understood the composition process. Macfadden's assistant art editor, Harry Grogin, has been credited with inventing the composograph. Some were not so bad, such as a picture showing Mayor Walker riding in a gondola down the Grand Canal in Venice; in the 1920s it would have taken several weeks for such a photograph to reach New York from Italy.

The lurid Rhinelander case in late 1925 offered the staff its major challenge. A wealthy socialite, Rip Rhinelander, had charged his bride of only a few months with having some Negro blood. The judge, for some unexplained reason, ordered the girl to disrobe to her waist to prove a point for the defense. The *Graphic* took the case from that point. The entire courtroom scene was recreated in a composograph. A secretary was posed in similar fashion and her picture inserted in the scene. The public loved it. The presses were required to run for several extra hours to meet the demand for copies.

A similar reaction resulted from the *Graphic*'s coverage of the 1927 "Peaches" Heenan-"Daddy" Browning divorce case, involving a teenage wife and her eccentric and publicity-hungry millionaire husband. The New York Society for the Suppression of Vice again battled a Macfadden publication. John S. Sumner, now its secretary, termed the *Graphic*'s stories "simple, inane, and foolish, with a strain of dangerous filth running through them harmful to all society." This time the *Graphic* did not receive support from other newspapers. The *Sun*, for example, thought the *Graphic* had "violated the law in letter and spirit." The standard-size dailies branded the tabloids "a public nuisance." The *Graphic* was banned, along with the *Mirror*, in White Plains, New York, and Princeton, New Jersey.

When the vice charges reached the court, only to be thrown out, editor Gauvreau and the firm were the only ones sued. However, one can assume that the staff would have curtailed its coverage had Macfadden offered any protest. Later Macfadden said, "The fact that every newspaper in New York had to print the details of . . . the Browning case . . . proves beyond all possible argument that an alarmingly large number of people everywhere have distorted and perverted ideas." He admitted that his daughters read the *Graphic* daily but "they

A Graphic "composograph"—a composite photograph—purportedly showing Alice Rhinelander partially disrobing in court in 1925. The actual faces of other participants in the trial have been inserted into the picture, but Mrs. Rhinelander is portrayed by a Graphic *secretary (Harry Grogin).*

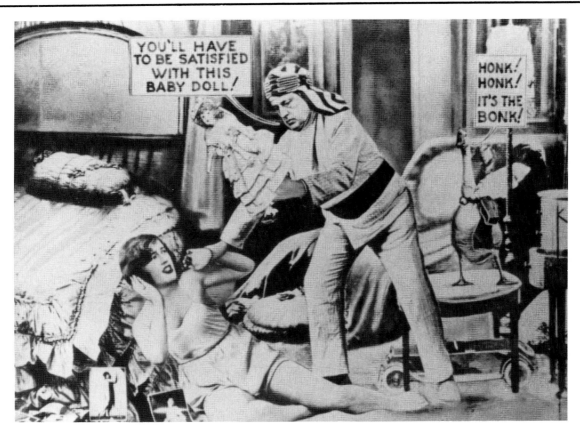

A composograph illustrating a Graphic *story about the "Peaches" Heenan-"Daddy" Browning divorce case in 1927 (Harry Grogin)*

pick out what they like." He also admitted the series of Heenan-Browning stories bored him, but "to the great mass of well-informed people it was amusing."

Rudolph Valentino, a friend of the Macfadden family, became the subject of several composographs. When the movie star died suddenly in New York, the *Graphic* posed a reporter in a casket and then replaced his face with Valentino's. The presses ran for many hours to satisfy a hungry public. Later, a composograph showed Valentino meeting Enrico Caruso in heaven.

Macfadden's use of the *Graphic* for personal recognition came through the newspaper's annual Graphic Sports Dinner, Lonely Hearts Ball, Music Festivals, and other events that attracted well-known personalities who gloried in the publicity such incidents provided. For example, the after-dinner entertainment for the 1928 Graphic Sports Dinner included Clayton, Jackson, and Durante; Texas Guinan; Ruth Etting; Bill Frawley; Helen Morgan; George Raft; Paul Whiteman; Vincent Lopez; and George M. Cohan. At the speaker's table were Mayor Walker and James A. Farley.

As Ed Sullivan pointed out, Macfadden did not maintain close contact with the *Graphic*. It was his habit to lose interest in a project once it was underway. After an absence of about two years he told *Graphic* readers on 11 January 1932 that he was back "to guide its general policies." He admitted that the newspaper had committed some mistakes, but he placed most of the blame on "persons who do not read the paper or have ulterior motives." His return failed to solve the situation, and the *Graphic* died on 7 July 1932.

Printer's Ink magazine noted that Macfadden had stressed "entertainment, inspiration and information." A *Saturday Evening Post* writer thought "the only value claimed for the *Graphic* was that it educated readers up to a point where they were able to understand the other tabloids." Oursler recalled some other plus-factors, such as Macfadden's proposals for a bridge across the Hudson and the use of double-decked subway cars to handle more riders.

Macfadden once rejected an offer of $2,000,000 from Hearst, believing that if Hearst were willing to pay that much, the *Graphic* must be worth more. As the newspaper neared its end, efforts to sell it to the employees failed. No one will ever know how much money Macfadden lost on the *Graphic*, although estimates have reached as high as $16,000,000. Macfadden wisely organized each of his projects on an individual basis so that when one corporation, such as the *Graphic*, failed it did not damage the others, such as *True Story*. Liabilities on the *Graphic* were listed at $3,132,521, mostly funds owed to Macfadden Publications, Inc. Assets were only $252,618. With a circulation of 180,000 at the end, the *Graphic* had 400 employees, many due back pay.

Oursler wrote that "with the *Graphic* Macfadden became a journalist, a newspaper publisher, with his interests touching the commercial and political life of the country; his contacts bringing him into high places and confronting him with serious problems. It was a long way from the wrestling championship of the world," a title Macfadden had earned in his early days in Missouri.

Macfadden owned other newspapers, but none brought him the recognition the *Graphic* did. In 1926, he held a half-interest in the tabloid Philadelphia *Daily News*, which he sold in 1932 for a slight profit. Macfadden once owned five Michigan newspapers. In 1929 he established the tabloid *Detroit Daily*, which he later sold to Robert McCormick and Joseph M. Patterson as part payment for their *Liberty* magazine. Renamed the *Mirror*, this Detroit newspaper folded in 1932. Also in Michigan, Macfadden owned the *Lansing Capital News*, *Greenville Daily News*, *Wyandotte Daily Record*, and *Mt. Pleasant Times*, with their circulations varying from 2,000 to 12,500. By 1932 he had disposed of all four. From 1929 to 1932, he owned the *New Haven* (Connecticut) *Times*. Some critics felt he acquired this publication to so impress the Yale community that the university would award him an honorary degree. One report said that "the employee who could have secured him a honorary degree would have received a cold million." The *Times* was sold for $10,000 to the *Journal-Courier*, which junked it. In 1925 Macfadden founded the *Automotive Daily News* in New York. Its circulation stayed around 10,000, but the newspaper went out of existence in the early 1930s. In addition to *True Story*, Macfadden at one time or another owned seventy-six other magazines.

Free from any pretense, Macfadden was never interested in accumulating money other than to use it for new projects. Nor was he interested in the style of living associated with a millionaire. He pioneered in the use of airplanes, often flying his own planes and sponsoring contests to promote more enthusiasm for the young aviation industry. He was involved unsuccessfully in the motion-picture business. He was a pioneer in conducting exercise programs on radio. At the New York World's Fair in 1939 the Macfadden Theatre was a promotional outlet open to all. His numerous books offering "medical cures" aroused the American Medical Association into waging a campaign to have these volumes banned from the mail.

Macfadden failed to gain any political office which he had expected to achieve through the use of his publishing empire. Worth at one time $30,000,000, he lost control of his publishing concern, and he lost a fortune operating hotels in Florida and California as well as health centers in New York State.

His married life was hardly more successful. The first of his four wives was Tillie Fontaine, whom he married some time shortly before the turn of the century; the marriage lasted only a short time. His second marriage, in 1901, was to Marguerite Kelly, a Canadian-born nurse who shared his interest in health and who wrote for *Physical Culture*; this marriage, too, was brief. His longest marriage, and the one which produced his nine children, was to Mary Williamson in 1913; she won a beauty contest he sponsored while on a tour of England. They were divorced in 1946. In 1948 he married a promoter, Johnnie McKinney Lee; they were separated in 1954.

In his eighties Macfadden was called a "frisky colt" with a disposition as "stubborn as a Missouri mule." In his only visit to a hospital, Macfadden died on 12 October 1955 at the age of eighty-seven. Stricken with jaundice, he had gone into his usual three-day fast, which he thought was a cure for most of his problems; this had weakened him, and he had collapsed in his hotel room. His death in the Jersey City Medical Center brought an end to a life which he had predicted would continue for at least 125 years. He died with only the income from a small annuity that had been set up by one of his auditors against his wishes. The *Chicago Daily News* reported that his death "removes a memorable figure from the American scene." It certainly did.

Macfadden sought to change America. His emphasis on physical culture was somewhat ahead of the times; in the 1980s, his message would be received more readily. His *New York Graphic* would today compete on the marketplace with the weekly *National Enquirer*, *Star*, and other tabloids. Publishers must give him some credit for his fight for freedom of expression; they need not give him credit for any innovations in the newspaper world.

He was more successful with his magazines, opening the world to the confession-type periodicals. Macfadden was a product of the excesses of the 1920s and the problems of the 1930s. His appeal was to the physical with less attention focused on the mental.

H. L. Mencken once wrote that Macfadden's "chief intellectual possession is a vast and cocksure ignorance." But Macfadden never sought to appeal to such individuals as Mencken through his publications. Macfadden reached a wider audience.

Biographies:

Fulton Oursler, *The True Story of Bernarr Macfadden* (New York: Lewis Copeland, 1929);

Grace Perkins Oursler, *Chats With the Macfadden Family* (New York: Lewis Copeland, 1929);

Clement Wood, *Bernarr Macfadden: A Study in Success* (New York: Lewis Copeland, 1929);

Mary Macfadden and Emile H. Gauvreau, *Dumbbells and Carrot Strips: The Story of Bernarr Macfadden* (New York: Holt, 1953).

References:

Frederick Lewis Allen, *Only Yesterday* (New York: Bantam, 1931);

Simon M. Bessie, *Jazz Journalism, The Story of the Tabloid Newspaper* (New York: Dutton, 1938);

Lester Cohen, *The New York Graphic* (Philadelphia: Chilton, 1964);

Michael L. Friedman, "Macfadden's *Graphic*," M.A. thesis, University of Missouri, 1967;

Oliver H. P. Garrett, "Another True Story," *The New Yorker* (19 September 1925): 9-10;

Emile H. Gauvreau, *My Last Million Readers* (New York: Dutton, 1941);

Alva Johnston, "The Great Macfadden," *Saturday Evening Post*, 213 (21 June 1941): 9-11, 97-100; (28 June 1941): 9, 21, 90-93;

Frank Mallen, *Sauce for the Gander* (West Plains, N.Y.: Baldwin, 1954);

Harland Manchester, "True Stories: The Confession Magazines," *Scribner's*, 104 (August 1938): 25-29;

Alexander Markovich, "The Publishing Empire of Bernarr Macfadden," M.A. thesis, University of Missouri, 1967;

Samuel Taylor Moore, "Those Terrible Tabloids," *Independent* (6 March 1926): 266;

Henry F. Pringle, "Another American Phenomenon, Bernarr Macfadden—Publisher and Physical Culturist," *The World's Work*, 56 (October 1928): 659-666;

William H. Taft, "Bernarr Macfadden," *Missouri Historical Review* (October 1968): 71-89;

Taft, "Bernarr Macfadden: One of a Kind," *Journalism Quarterly* (Winter 1968): 627-633;

Allene Talmey, "Millions From Dumb-bells," *Outlook and Independent*, 155 (3 June 1930): 164-168;

Robert Lewis Taylor, "Profiles," *New Yorker*, 26 (14 October 1950): 39-40, 42, 44-45; (21 October 1950): 39-51; (28 October 1950): 37-50;

Oswald G. Villard, "Sex, Art, Truth and Magazines," *Atlantic*, 137 (March 1926): 388-398.

Don Marquis

(29 July 1878-29 December 1937)

Sam G. Riley

Virginia Polytechnic Institute and State University

See also the Marquis entry in *DLB 11, American Humorists, 1800-1950.*

MAJOR POSITIONS HELD: Columnist, New York *Evening Sun* (1912-1922), New York *Tribune* and *Herald Tribune* (1922-1925).

BOOKS: *Danny's Own Story* (Garden City: Doubleday, Page, 1912);

Dreams & Dust (New York & London: Harper, 1915);

The Cruise of the Jasper B. (New York & London: Appleton, 1916);

Hermione and Her Little Group of Serious Thinkers (New York & London: Appleton, 1916);

Prefaces (New York & London: Appleton, 1919);

Carter, and Other People (New York & London: Appleton, 1921);

Don Marquis (Culver Pictures)

Noah an' Jonah an' Cap'n John Smith, A Book of Humorous Verse (New York & London: Appleton, 1921);

The Old Soak, and Hail and Farewell (Garden City & Toronto: Doubleday, Page, 1921);

Sonnets to a Red-Haired Lady (by a Gentleman with a Blue Beard) and Famous Love Affairs (Garden City: Doubleday, Page, 1922);

The Revolt of the Oyster (Garden City: Doubleday, Page, 1922);

Poems and Portraits (Garden City & Toronto: Doubleday, Page, 1922);

The Old Soak's History of the World (Garden City: Doubleday, Page, 1924; London: Heinemann, 1924);

The Dark Hours, Five Scenes from History (Garden City: Doubleday, Page, 1924; London: Heinemann, 1924);

Pandora Lifts the Lid, by Marquis and Christopher Morley (New York: Doran, 1924; London: Cape, 1924);

Words and Thoughts, A Play in One Act (New York & London: Appleton, 1924);

The Awakening, and Other Poems (London: Heine-

mann, 1924; Garden City: Doubleday, Page, 1925);

The Old Soak: A Comedy in Three Acts (New York & London: French, 1926);

The Almost Perfect State (Garden City: Doubleday, Page, 1927; London: Heinemann, 1927);

Out of the Sea, A Play in Four Acts (Garden City: Doubleday, Page, 1927; London: Heinemann, 1927);

Archy and Mehitabel (Garden City: Doubleday, Page, 1927; London: Benn, 1931);

Love Sonnets of a Cave Man and Other Verses (Garden City: Doubleday, Doran, 1928);

When the Turtles Sing, and Other Unusual Tales (Garden City: Doubleday, Doran, 1928);

A Variety of People (Garden City: Doubleday, Doran, 1929);

Off the Arm (Garden City: Doubleday, Doran, 1930);

Archys Life of Mehitabel (Garden City: Doubleday, Doran, 1933; London: Faber & Faber, 1934);

Chapters for the Orthodox (Garden City: Doubleday, Doran, 1934);

Master of the Revels: A Comedy in Four Acts (Garden City: Doubleday, Doran, 1934);

Archy Does His Part (Garden City: Doubleday, Doran, 1935; London: Faber & Faber, 1936);

Her Foot Is on the Brass Rail (New York: Marchbanks Press, 1935);

Sun Dial Time (Garden City: Doubleday, Doran, 1936);

Sons of the Puritans (Garden City: Doubleday, Doran, 1939);

the lives and times of archy and mehitabel (New York: Doubleday, Doran, 1940);

The Best of Don Marquis, edited by Christopher Morley (Garden City: Doubleday, 1946);

Everything's Jake (Tacoma, Washington: Non-Profit Press, 1978).

PLAYS: *The Old Soak*, New York, Plymouth Theatre, 22 August 1922;

Out of the Sea, New York, Eltinge Theatre, 5 December 1927;

Everything's Jake, New York, Assembly Theatre, 16 January 1930;

The Dark Hours, New York, New Amsterdam Theatre, 14 November 1932.

PERIODICAL PUBLICATIONS: "Being a Public Character," *American Magazine* (September 1917): 19-23, 68;

"Into the Literary Big Time," *Bookman* (June 1919): 405-408;

"Fits and Starts," *Harper's Magazine* (July 1919): 277-279;

"Hermione the Bolshevik," *Outlook* (23 July 1919): 482;

"Mother Goose, Propagandist," *Harper's Magazine* (August 1919): 439-440;

"Don Marquis, by Himself," *Everybody's Magazine* (January 1920): 29, 85;

"Your Cousin Mehitabel," *American Magazine* (October 1928): 44-45, 112, 114;

"Confessions of a Reformed Columnist," *Saturday Evening Post* (22 December 1928): 6-7, 53;

"Stage Struck," *Saturday Evening Post* (8 March 1930): 78, 81;

"The Other Woman," *Collier's* (13 December 1930): 14-15, 44;

"What Happens to Grouches," *Collier's* (8 April 1933): 28.

In any selection of important American humor columnists, Don Marquis deserves a place in the front row. Mainly remembered today for his characters archy the cockroach and mehitabel the cat, Marquis was also remarkable for his ability to intertwine the humorous and the melancholy, and for two other denizens of his imagination: Prohibition-era tippler Clem Hawley (the Old Soak) and Hermione, the air-headed New York dilettante, both of which are largely forgotten today but were household names in the 1920s and 1930s.

At age forty-seven Marquis left newspaper journalism to devote his time to a mixture of humorous and serious book writing—poetry, short stories, novels, and plays. Though most of his thirty-two books are out of print, and though his fame has faded badly, most of his work as a humorist was deftly done and is worth resurrecting. It was, in the words of E. B. White, "full of sad beauty, bawdy adventure, political wisdom, and wild surmise; full of pain and pity, full of exact and inspired writing."

He was born—during a solar eclipse— Donald Robert Perry Marquis (pronounced Markwis), the son of James Stewart Marquis, a country doctor in Walnut, Illinois, and Virginia Whitmore Marquis. His unpublished "Egobiography," as he called it, reveals that from his tender years he wanted to write a column, influenced in that ambition by the work of Eugene Field and George Ade. In the meantime he worked in a pharmacy (where he once caused an explosion), plucked chickens, attended Knox College for one term but left for financial reasons, and became a country school-teacher and railroad section hand.

Marquis's newspaper experience began when he signed on as a printer for an Illinois weekly, where he was later allowed to write an unpaid column. He moved to another weekly and was made its editor. (Sadly, the "Egobiography" includes no names or dates concerning his early employment.) As editor he wrote editorials, gathered news, sold ads, wrote ad copy, set type, sawed boiler plate, did layout, ran the press, folded and wrapped papers, and wrote his own column. A Democrat running a Republican paper, he became an embarrassment for a local GOP candidate, who solved the problem in 1900 by helping arrange a job for Marquis with the Census Bureau in Washington, D.C. During his one year with the bureau, Marquis took a second job as a reporter for the *Washington Times*. Next he moved to Philadelphia, hoping to land a column of his own. Though he managed to find a newspaper job (again, details are not available), he failed to get his column and in 1902 moved to Atlanta, Georgia, as associate editor of the recently founded *Atlanta News*. Here he wrote two columns of editorials daily, working under Col. John Temple Graves.

In early 1904 he defected to the *Atlanta Journal*, again as an editorial writer, occasionally doubling as a reporter or theater critic. He roomed at the Aragon Hotel with fellow journalist Grantland Rice and was befriended by Joel Chandler Harris. With Rice and Frank L. Stanton, Marquis spent frequent evenings in the bar of the Aragon writing barroom poetry and talking journalism. Though a prodigious worker, Marquis liked to affect a post of indolence—to remind himself, he said, that his goal was to succeed and someday be able to lead a lazy life.

In 1907 he left the *Journal* to become associate editor of Harris's newly formed *Uncle Remus's Magazine*, for which Marquis also wrote poetry and short stories. While employed there he married aspiring writer Reina Melcher on 8 June 1909. The magazine was a successful venture and at Harris's death in 1908 had a circulation of 200,000. Without Harris, whom Marquis had admired enormously, Marquis's prospects with the magazine began to pale, and on Thanksgiving Day 1909, he arrived in New York City in search of a newspaper that would allow him to do a signed column. After a short stint with a news service, he was employed by the *American* as a rewrite man and was also allowed to do signed features, which were run on the *American's* back page. The "Egobiography" indicates that he was fired from this position with no explanation. He then became a reporter and rewrite man for the *Brooklyn Daily Eagle* and free-lanced for other New York papers. His first book, a picaresque novel titled *Danny's Own Story*, was published in 1912 and helped establish his name, which led to a new job that year as editor of the *New York Sun*'s magazine page.

In his first year on the *Sun*, Marquis was allowed space for a regular column but was required to run it unsigned under the bland heading "Notes and Comment." When George M. Smith came to the *Sun* as managing editor in 1913, Smith suggested that Marquis call his column "The Sun Dial" and allowed him a by-line. Finally Marquis had the column he had so longed for, and with the increased recognition came lucrative offers from national magazines. "When the tide finally does turn in New York," Marquis observed, "it turns swiftly and with a rush."

It is said that his first desk at the *Sun* was a packing case marked "1 Gross Tom Cat," which actually referred to tomato catsup. Marquis liked this desk, the story goes, because no one would expect a man to keep a packing case tidy. Here he filled "The Sun Dial" with a variety of verse, sketches, fables, satire, and an occasional serious piece, rapping out his copy on an old Remington that, according to a colleague, made almost as much noise as a printing press. One day in 1916 he remarked to Frink Dana Burnet, a coworker and chum, that a big cockroach had crawled across his desk. "I believe he could damn near play my typewriter," Marquis said, and with this began the unlikely journalistic career of "the insect Voltaire," as writer Christopher Morley called archy the cockroach.

Almost every literate person past callow youth knows that the name *archy* begins with a lowercase *a* because the insect journalist, who typed his stories by night on Marquis's typewriter, had no means of depressing the uppercase key and in fact had to type each letter by diving headfirst onto the proper key. "expression is the need of my soul," wrote the sensitive archy in his introductory column, going on to reveal that he was once a vers libre poet (free verse was Marquis's pet peeve) whose soul had transmigrated into the body of a cockroach.

Alternately humble and proud, but always convinced that in his quest to write about the city from the underside he is superior to most humans, archy is upset by freddy the rat, his critic, and fascinated by the sex and violence that mark the life-style of mehitabel, a promiscuous alley cat of archy's acquaintance. "Toujours gai" is the motto of the

what have i done to deserve all these kittens

Illustration by George Herriman for Marquis's the lives and times of archy and mehitabel

enigmatic mehitabel, Marquis's vehicle for satirizing the free-spirited flappers of the 1920s. The essence of the good-bad character mehitabel is contained in Marquis's lines:

> my past is shady
> but wotthehell
> thank god i m a lady
> and class will tell

Hard on the many heels of the famous archy, Marquis created Hermione and Her Little Group of Serious Thinkers—fine satire on pretension in Greenwich Village, which Marquis called a "cultural bordello" and further described in verse as peopled by:

> Tame Anarchists, a dreary crew
> Squib Socialists too damp to sosh
> Fake Hobohemians steeped in suds,
> Glib Females in Artistic Duds
> With Captive Husbands cowed and gauche.

Writer Louis Hasley, quoted in the recent biography *Don Marquis* by Lynn Lee, suggests that Hermione should be "required reading for all superficial young intellectuals who believe that history began only when they became aware of it."

Hermione was taken in by anything Far Eastern, Marquis's comment on American gullibility when confronted with the exotic. The Hermione columns also provided his forum for repeated jabs at the free-verse style that was all the rage at that time. Hermione's favorite artist, the effete Fothergil Finch, was the vehicle for this satire.

Having achieved good results by inventing literary characters to speak for him, Marquis went on to create Clem Hawley, the Old Soak, a lovable hip-flask philosopher in the mold of Josh Billings, Artemus Ward, and the other cracker-barrel literary characters of the nineteenth century, a man who said he believed in old-time religion, calomel, and straight whiskey. The Old Soak was Marquis's means of speaking out against Prohibition ("the Eighteenth Commandment") and parodying *The Drunkard* and other temperance melodramas, but the character was not really an alcoholic. He stopped just short of the screen character portrayed by W. C. Fields, though he was once described by Marquis as "one whose devotion to alcoholic fellowship and endearing generosity of spirit superseded the practical concerns of work and family support."

Both of Marquis's children were born during his years with the *Sun*: Robert Steward (Bobby) in 1915 and Barbara in 1918. Reina published a novel, *The Torch Bearer*, in 1914, and Marquis's free-lance work was in great demand. These were perhaps his happiest years. Then, suddenly, Bobby died at age five, adding a bittersweet edge to Marquis's writing that only intensified with tragedies later in his life. The Old Soak began to draw fire from the clergy, who appreciated neither his satirical attacks on ballplayer-evangelist Billy Sunday nor his stance on Demon Rum in general.

On the positive side, producer Arthur Hopkins asked Marquis if he thought he could write a play. Later Marquis described the scene for his friend, cartoonist Clive Weed: "Of course what you say is: 'Yes, boss. When do you want it? Tomorrow? Or will the day after do?' " *The Old Soak* was successful on Broadway, opening in August 1922 and running for 423 performances.

Also in 1922 Marquis turned down *Sun* owner Frank A. Munsey's offer to become editor of that paper. Instead he moved to the *New York Tribune* (renamed the *Herald Tribune* later in 1922), where his column was retitled "The Lantern" and was syndicated to about twenty other papers.

In 1923 he sailed for Europe aboard the *Tus-*

Marquis's first wife, Reina Melcher Marquis, with their children, Bobby and Barbara (Katherine Glover)

cania with his wife, daughter, and their maid Agnes. The columns he sent back were among his best; many of them appeared the next year in Marquis's book *The Old Soak's History of the World*. In these columns, the Old Soak describes for the folks back home in the U.S.A. the glories of Paris, with all its "arkytextured up" churches "erected to the memory of Saint Somebody or other"; its "pallises and fromages and elegant tombs and frogs legs and good likkers and politeness"; the Loov, Van Sann, the Eyefull Tower, and the Notary Dom, "all arkytextured up with gargle oils with theyer necks stretched out over the roof. . . . Annybody ought to see they call them gargle oils because they are cleering theyer throats. They are carved that natural you can almost hear them hawk and spit." Archy also sent back impressions from abroad, and "The Lantern" carried a series Marquis called "French without a Struggle."

On 2 December 1923, shortly after returning

from Europe, Reina Marquis died unexpectedly at age forty, adding to the tragicomic tinge that marked Marquis's work. Despite his personal sorrows, he continued writing his humor column for two more years and continued publishing books. Financially, these were among his best years, his book sales, column, and play rights to *The Old Soak* swelling his coffers. In these days, he disdained the keeping of check stubs, preferring to phone the bank occasionally to ask his balance—a technique he dubbed the "Marquis System of Strainless Accountancy."

In 1925 the pressure of producing six humor columns a week and a desire to devote more time to his "long-pull jobs"—his books and plays—finally caused him to ask the *Herald Tribune*'s publisher, Ogden Reid, to release him from the three remaining years on his contract. Reid consented, and Marquis left the paper in August 1925, never to return to newspaper journalism. "I was nervously ill," he explained later. "It became an obsession with me that I must quit or die. I got to seeing that column as

Marquis portraying the title character in his play The Old Soak *in summer stock in Skowhegan, Maine, in 1926 (W. H. Langley)*

a grave, twenty-three inches long, into which I buried a part of myself every day—a part that I tore, raw and bleeding, from my brain."

Free of his daily newspaper obligations, Marquis kept up a steady stream of books and plays and had more time to spend with Barbara and with kindred spirits (the "Poolist Fathers") at the card and billiard tables of his favorite watering place, New York's Players Club. In February 1926 he married Marjorie Vonnegut, an actress and aspiring director. The couple rented out an apartment in their East Sixty-Second Street brownstone; among their various tenants were actress Ethel Barrymore and philosopher John Dewey.

Though the demands of daily journalism were behind him, Marquis frequently drew on his newspaper experience, as in these lines from *Love Sonnets of a Cave Man and Other Verses* (1928) satirizing interviewers:

> "Caesar," I said to him as I pulled out a pad of
> paper,
> "You've seen, no doubt, what Cassius says
> about your latest caper?"
> C. Julius smiled and coughed into his
> purple-hemmed bandanna,
> He gave your representative a very fine
> Havana;
> He clicked his sandals on the tiles, he trifled
> with his vesture—
> We interviewers never miss the smallest little
> gesture!
> In building up the characters, of statesmen
> or of wretches,
> It is these telling little strokes that vitalize our
> sketches. . . .

As he had in his newspaper days, he continued turning out an abundance of maxims: "Never change diapers in midstream"; "When a man tells you he got rich through hard work, ask him: 'Whose?' "; "Pity the Meek, for they shall inherit the earth."

In the late 1920s Marquis began a series of short-term writing jobs for various Hollywood movies studios, which he appears to have done strictly for the money. Of California, he once said, "This country consists of great sunshiny stretches of Blah. It is a country that has never been thought in," and of his experience with screenwriting, he observed, "You've got to know when to leave bad enough alone." On one of these writing assignments in 1929, he suffered his first heart attack and never again enjoyed good health. Barbara Marquis died of pneumonia two years later, in October 1931.

Marquis's second wife, Marjorie Vonnegut Marquis, in costume for her role in the Theatre Guild production of Eugene O'Neill's Ah, Wilderness! *in 1933 (New York Public Library Vandamm Collection of Theatrical Photographs)*

In November 1932 Marquis's play *The Dark Hours*, a serious drama about Jesus Christ, opened in New York City with Marjorie as director and Marquis himself as the principal financial backer. The production was not well received and was a disaster to the family's finances. In February 1933 Marquis attempted to establish a four-page newspaper of his own, *The Column*, which was to be written entirely by himself. Only one issue was printed, and the project was scrapped, probably for lack of funds to back it.

Marquis then suffered three strokes. The third, in 1936, completely ended his writing career. Marjorie died at the end of 1936, Marquis a year later. The wonder is that a man whose personal life had held so much sadness could rise above his troubles to produce so much excellent humor copy. Perhaps the explanation is simple and is revealed in

one of Marquis's own couplets: "We cannot help it, we are cursed/With an incorrigible mirth."

Summing up Marquis's contribution as a writer is not as simple, primarily because he divided his effort among so many types of writing. It would be difficult, as biographer Lee points out, to make a case for him as a major American literary figure—a "man of letters"—in the same way that honor is ascribed to Samuel Clemens; yet without doubt Don Marquis was one of the finest newspaper humor columnists America has produced.

New York Times drama critic Brooks Atkinson called Marquis "America's most ruminative humorist," and *Herald Tribune* columnist Franklin P. Adams said Marquis is "far closer to Mark Twain than anybody I know and am ever likely to know." The Mark Twain parallel was drawn even more strongly by Marquis's friend and admirer Christopher Morley, who stressed the two humor writers' similar small-town beginnings, brief formal educations, dislike of pretense and hypocrisy, interest in the religious but distrust of organized religion, dramatic instinct, and retention of the rural touch even after their success and urbanization. John Farrar, editor of the *Bookman*, went so far as to call Marquis "one of our truly great literary figures" and to praise his "sense of musical phrases, his mysticism and his great humanity." Bernard De Voto of *Harper's Magazine* praised Marquis's verse style "that delights you and frequently holds you breathless while you watch a jagged and vertiginous imagination shoot through the air like a skyrocket, giving off odd-shaped and slightly drunken stars of gold."

In his superb introduction to *the lives and times of archy and mehitabel* (1940), E. B. White recalled editing an anthology of American humor and the difficulty he had deciding in which category to include Marquis. "The book had about a dozen selections; something by Marquis seemed to fit almost every one of them. He was parodist, historian, poet, clown, fable writer, satirist, reporter, and teller of tales. . . . We could have shut our eyes and dropped him in anywhere. . . . Whatever fiddle he plucked, he always produced a song."

Biography:

Edward Anthony, *O Rare Don Marquis* (Garden City: Doubleday, 1962).

References:

Anonymous, "Don Marquis—American Minstrel," *Current Opinion* (November 1922): 662-664;
Anonymous, "The Literary Spotlight, xxxi: Don Marquis," *Bookman* (July 1924): 539-543;

Jesse Bier, *The Rise and Fall of American Humor* (New York: Holt, Rinehart & Winston, 1968);

Walter Blair and Hamlin Hill, *America's Humor: From Poor Richard to Doonesbury* (New York: Oxford University Press, 1978);

Chester Crowell, "The Fun of Don Marquis," *Atlantic Monthly*, 178 (November 1946): 129-131;

Benjamin De Casseres, "Portraits En Brochette: Don Marquis," *Bookman*, 73 (July 1931): 487-491;

Corey Ford, *The Time of Laughter* (Boston: Little, Brown, 1967);

Louis Hasley, "Don Marquis: Ambivalent Humorist," *Prairie Schooner* (Spring 1971): 59-73;

Hamlin Hill, "Archy and Uncle Remus: Don Marquis's Debt to Joel Chandler Harris," *Georgia Review* (Spring 1961): 78-87;

Rollin Kirby, "Don Marquis: Delayed Elizabethan," *American Mercury*, 64 (March 1947): 337-340;

Lynn Lee, *Don Marquis* (Boston: Twayne, 1981);

Thomas Masson, *Our American Humorists* (Freeport, N.Y.: Books for Libraries Press, 1966);

George Middleton, *These Things Are Mine* (New York: Macmillan, 1947);

Grantland Rice, *The Tumult and the Shouting* (New York: A. S. Barnes, 1954);

Carl Van Doren, "Day In and Day Out; Adams, Morley, Marquis, and Brown, Manhattan Wits," *Century 70*, 107 (December 1923): 308-315;

Norris Yates, "The Many Masks of Don Marquis," in his *The American Humorist: Conscience of the Twentieth Century* (Ames: Iowa State University Press, 1964), pp. 195-216.

Papers:

Don Marquis's papers are held at the Butler Library, Columbia University; the New York City Public Library; the Henry E. Huntington Library, San Marino, California; the Walter Hampden Memorial Library of the Players Club, New York City; the Houghton Library, Harvard University; and the Library of Congress.

C. K. McClatchy
(1 November 1858-27 April 1936)

Stephen D. Bray

MAJOR POSITIONS HELD: Editor (1884-1923), editor/publisher, *Sacramento Bee* (1923-1936); publisher, *Fresno Bee* (1922-1936), *Modesto Bee* (1927-1936).

BOOK: *Private Thinks by C. K. and Other Writings*, (New York: Scribners, 1936).

As editor of the *Sacramento Bee*, C. K. McClatchy expressed his independent and outspoken views for over fifty years. Relying solely on his paper for his platform, he was known as one of the leaders of the progressive movement in California politics. He was also recognized as a regional spokesman who helped shape the development of California's capital city and the Sacramento Valley. He founded the McClatchy chain of newspapers which circulated his commentary on regional and national affairs throughout California's great central valley. A lifelong progressive, McClatchy belonged to an era of spirited personal journalism and had much in common with the famous editors he admired: Fremont Older, Henry Watterson, and Josephus Daniels.

Charles Kenny McClatchy was born in Sacramento on 1 November 1858, the year after his father, James McClatchy, founded the *Bee*. James McClatchy arrived in New York from Ireland at the age of eighteen in 1842 and soon made the acquaintance of Horace Greeley. James McClatchy caught the gold fever in 1849 and traveled to California, where he served as correspondent for the *New York Tribune*. He worked for several papers before starting the *Bee* on 3 February 1857, three years after Sacramento became the capital of the young state. He immediately established a reputation as an independent, fearless editor, qualities which he passed along to his son. The elder McClatchy supported the Union cause and in his own frontier region fought against the interests of large miners and landowners.

C. K. McClatchy was the second of four children born to James and Charlotte McCormack McClatchy. He attended the local schools and in 1872 entered Santa Clara College. But he was a poor student in math and left school in 1875 to become a cub reporter on the *Bee*. He became a full partner on his twenty-first birthday in 1879, and assumed the position of editor after his father's death in 1883. In January 1884, McClatchy and his brother, Valentine, bought the one-third interest of their father's former partner and turned the *Bee* into a fully family-owned newspaper. Valentine acted as publisher until 1923, when, after a disagreement over policy, he sold his share to McClatchy. In 1885, McClatchy married Ella Kelly, a schoolteacher from Philadelphia, with whom he raised three children.

From the outset, McClatchy guided the policy of the *Bee*, which was always recognized for its unintimidated and uncompromising style of journalism. Two incidents, one from the beginning and one from the end of McClatchy's career, illustrate his editorial independence and personal integrity. In 1886, McClatchy refused to kill a story after visitors to his office complained that certain information would be embarrassing if revealed. He explained his decision in print: "Some queer notions obtain among the people as to the duty which a newspaper owes its readers, but the most prevalent one is that it should leave out important items of public interest at the request of those who may be injured by their publication. The object of this newspaper is to give the news. It is not the duty of a newspaper to wait until half its readers know a fact before it thinks of publishing it." In the 1930s, a spokesman for a candidate for governor protested the *Bee*'s endorsement of another candidate on the grounds that the latter could not win. McClatchy replied, "My friend, I want it distinctly understood that *The Bee* never editorially endorses candidates on the basis of their ability to win. Its endorsements are based on the integrity, ability, and general background of the candidates, and on the issues."

In 1904 McClatchy introduced a Northern California section of the *Bee*, which reached an area of five million acres and required the services of 125 special correspondents. He launched the first addition to the *Bee* chain, the *Fresno Bee*, in 1922. In 1925 he bought the *Sacramento Star* and merged it into the *Bee*, and in 1927 he purchased the *Modesto News-Herald* and renamed it the *Modesto Bee*.

In 1922 McClatchy became the first West Coast newspaper publisher to operate a radio station. In the next eight years he acquired stations in Stockton, Modesto, Fresno, and Bakersfield, and in Reno, Nevada.

McClatchy was a successful businessman; but he always felt that running a newspaper was a special form of business and that editing was a privilege. In order to ensure his independence, he refused to belong to any political party or social organization, and he declined all offers of political appointments. He told his associates that "the ring of the cash register must never have any influence on editorial policy." In his paper he described for his readers his conception of the purpose of journalism: "The editor occupies a position where it is his duty to battle for the right as God has given him to see the right. If he does not, he is false to every tradition of honest journalism; he is false to his profession; he is false to himself." McClatchy always demanded accuracy and fairness from his reporters, an achievement which was recognized by other publishers. In 1923, the *Carson City Daily-Appeal* commented that "C. K. McClatchy is probably the greatest journalist on the Pacific Coast. His newspaper is read and believed by more people than any other coast publication, although there are several newspapers with larger circulation."

McClatchy never accepted the idea of schools for journalism. Like other graduates of the "old school," he advised prospective reporters to begin at the bottom and work their way up; of course, not all cub reporters had fathers who owned the paper. As far as training was concerned, however, he believed that journalists needed only be familiar with three sources: the Bible, Shakespeare, and Dickens. In his home library, his personal bookplate read "These Are Enough."

McClatchy was best known for the strong convictions which he expressed in a personal column called "Notes" from 1883-1897 and "Private Thinks" from 1897 to 1936. He spoke out candidly on all the major economic, political, and social issues which faced the growing nation and state over a tumultuous half-century. He battled for his own views whether he was part of a movement or all alone, whether he was attacking the powers of trust or supporting legislation to check the activities of radicals. His ideal of the model citizen was the moderate person who avoided all extremes, and his ideal of the model paper was one which saw itself "as a tribunal that desires to do justice for all."

McClatchy was a tenacious critic or immovable defender regardless of the magnitude of the issue.

In 1933-1934 his crusade against organized crime in Nevada politics forced President Roosevelt to withdraw a judicial appointment, and earned the *Bee* the first Pulitzer Prize for meritorious public service ever awarded a California newspaper. McClatchy battled with equal vigor for civic improvements and environmental considerations in his hometown. His longtime progressive ally, Sen. Hiram Johnson, said that McClatchy "would fight as hard to preserve a shade tree as to drive a rogue from office." It was joked on the streets of Sacramento that when the flag on the *Bee* building was lowered to half-staff, it commemorated the passing of another oak tree.

Beginning with his support of the Sherman Antitrust Act in 1890, McClatchy was an early, vociferous, and consistent defender of progressive legislation. He aligned himself with the cause of late nineteenth- and early twentieth-century reformers who opposed the political dangers of accelerating economic concentration as well as the social effects of rapid industrialization. He was not reluctant to attack industrial and financial giants such as John D. Rockefeller and J. P. Morgan. He demanded more strict and better-enforced antitrust legislation and believed that the guilty tycoons should be placed in jail rather than merely having fines assessed against their companies.

McClatchy was an early crusader against the powerful railroad interests. From 1890 on, he fought the Southern Pacific, which controlled California state politics. In 1906, according to McClatchy, the issue was whether "California is to be governed in the interest of one arrogant and exclusive corporation or whether she shall be governed in the interests of the People." He strongly supported Hiram Johnson, the Progressive party candidate, in his bitterly contested but successful campaign for governor in 1910, despite powerful opposition from the Southern Pacific and its conservative ally, the *Los Angeles Times*. As a result, he was able to celebrate in 1911 "the splendid uplift given the politics and morals of the state by the change from railroad rule and official debauchery to freedom and independence and devotion to the public welfare."

McClatchy was an advocate of other Progressive Era legislation that aimed to ameliorate the social costs of industrial progress and thwart the rise of more radical alternatives such as socialism. He fought for public ownership of utilities; the conservation of natural resources; the initiative, referendum, and recall; primary elections; and the direct election of senators and presidents. He also cam-

paigned for women's suffrage, workmen's compensation, a minimum wage, and health and sanitation laws. In Sacramento he favored municipal ownership of water, garbage, and transportation services.

In national elections McClatchy proved his independence of party ties by always supporting the most progressive candidate running. In 1900 and 1908 he campaigned for the Democrat William Jennings Bryan; he backed Theodore Roosevelt when Roosevelt ran as a Republican in 1904 and on the Bull Moose ticket in 1912; and in 1916 he supported Woodrow Wilson.

In his views on the labor movement, McClatchy demonstrated the basic outlook of progressive leaders. He believed passionately in the rights of organized labor as a counterforce to organized capital, but he intensely disliked the closed shop, strikes, and the goals of the more militant labor leaders. Although he endorsed the principle of unionism, he argued that disagreements should always be settled through collective bargaining and, if necessary, compulsory arbitration. He felt that strikes, no matter how justified they might seem, injured the public. In 1934 he vehemently opposed the general strike in San Francisco led by Harry Bridges of the International Longshoreman's Association. McClatchy's ideal of a labor leader was American Federation of Labor president Samuel Gompers.

McClatchy was especially opposed to labor radicals such as the Industrial Workers of the World. He preferred that labor extremists, as he saw them, be stopped through legal channels, so in 1910 he defended the IWW's right to speak. But during the antired campaign which followed World War I, McClatchy supported the California Criminal Syndicalist Act, which was designed specifically to break up the IWW.

Another prominent example of McClatchy's contempt for radicalism was his longstanding opposition to labor agitator Tom Mooney. A bombing during the 1916 Preparedness Day parade in San Francisco led to a death sentence—later commuted to life imprisonment—for Mooney, who became a hero to the labor movement; many intellectuals believed in his innocence and campaigned for his release. But to McClatchy, Mooney was a "red agitator" and deserved to be executed. McClatchy scorned liberals, such as Lincoln Steffens, who came to Mooney's defense.

As it did with many others, the disillusioning outcome of World War I marked the beginning of McClatchy's isolationism. He opposed United States participation in the League of Nations on the grounds that the league could not be effective and was hypocritical. Although he wanted to see American defenses strengthened, he strongly opposed American military intervention in Central America at the bidding of American business interests. In 1924, when troops were sent to Honduras, he wrote: "Every step in this American invasion of Honduras has been a travesty on justice." In 1932 he opposed President Hoover's decision to send troops to Nicaragua to fight the rebel leader Sandino, whom he regarded as a patriot. It was the marines, he wrote, who were the "bandits."

McClatchy also took strong positions on the domestic social issues of the 1920s. He personally disliked the effects of alcohol and believed in regulation of the liquor industry, but he adamantly opposed Prohibition.

McClatchy frequently accused the colleges of acting as breeding grounds for subversive ideas. In 1923 he saw them as disseminating propaganda which struck "at the very roots of red-blooded Americanism and progressivism."

One of the most controversial issues in California was the 1924 Exclusion Act, which was intended to ban Asians from entering California. McClatchy supported the act primarily on economic grounds, but he also revealed some underlying racial prejudice. While insisting that no new Japanese settle in California, he recognized "the rights of those who have already come under invitation of this government, and particularly of those who have acquired American citizenship under our laws." Yet he also stated that "California merely asks that she be allowed to keep her wonderful lands for the white race and the children's children of the white race." According to McClatchy, the act would keep out "those who can never be assimilated in the dominant American racial strain." However, McClatchy attacked the ideas and practices of the Ku Klux Klan.

In 1924 McClatchy enunciated his own political philosophy when he defined progressivism. A progressive, McClatchy wrote, "avoids alike the pitfalls of bigoted opposition to any political or social change . . . and also the menace of that spirit which rebels against all existing things and sees only in violent revolution any hope of betterment." In the presidential election of that year he supported the Progressive party candidate, Robert La Follette, whom he saw as steering a course between the twin evils of corporate domination and unthinking radicalism.

When the Depression struck, McClatchy blamed President Hoover. In 1932 he strongly endorsed Franklin Roosevelt, who, he felt, "far more nearly represents the cause of humanity, the cause of right and righteousness, the cause of truth, and the cause of true Americanism than does the present executive."

McClatchy supported the long list of Roosevelt's programs to stimulate the economy and help the unemployed. He backed the NRA, the CCC, and the PWA. He especially liked the projects which not only created jobs but established government supervision over natural resources and public utilities. He enthusiastically defended the Tennessee Valley Authority, the Boulder Canyon Project, and, in his native region, the Central Valley Project, which, he told his readers, "conforms in every way to the president's program of creating jobs for the unemployed by constructing useful public works. . . . It will power the way to provide cheap electricity for a vast valley empire." He supported the New Deal's Wagner Act, which gave workers the right to organize unions, but he issued warnings against the influence of suspected Communists in certain unions. In this respect he found himself aligned with the red-baiting Hearst press.

By 1936, McClatchy was ready to back Roosevelt for another term. He wrote: "*The Bee* sees in the person and in the principles of Franklin Delano Roosevelt the national expression of the progressive ideas and ideals for which it has been battling during the past quarter of a century."

Shortly before his death from pneumonia on 27 April 1936, McClatchy wrote an editorial which summarized his outlook. The New Deal, he said, "has dramatized and made more vivid some truths that thinkers have long realized: that underpaid workers do not provide an adequate market for American goods; that child labor is not only inhumane, but replaces adult labor; that slums are not only unsanitary and crime breeders but are costly to the community; that to prevent the growth of unrest we must see that all who are able and willing to work are given opportunities to do so, and that those who are helpless should be cared for humanely."

At the time of McClatchy's death, the circulation of the *Sacramento Bee* was 50,000 compared to only 10,000 for the rival *Union*. McClatchy left an estate valued at $1,500,000, most of it stock in McClatchy papers. McClatchy's daughter, Eleanor, succeeded him as publisher. In his will, McClatchy instructed his successors to "ally themselves with no political party, to be fair to all, to decide questions by the light of principle, never under the slavery of petty or partisan politics." These were the standards that he preached and practiced while he was living. The papers that he left behind stood as a monument to his devotion to and expectations for journalism.

At the time of his death, many papers praised the veteran editor. Hearst's *San Francisco Examiner* acknowledged that "Mr. McClatchy conducted his newspaper as a public trust." The *New York Times* called McClatchy "the crusading type of journalist. No matter what the battle, he fought for it with wholehearted determination."

It was a fitting tribute to an editor who lived for journalism, who conducted his valley newspaper as a classroom in national politics, and who never swerved from his valiant and vigorous support of progressive values and ideals.

References:

New York Times, 28 April 1936;

Sacramento Bee, Centennial Album, Part 9, 3 February 1958;

Bernard A. Shepard, "C. K. McClatchy and the *Sacramento Bee*," Ph.D. dissertation, Syracuse University, 1960.

W. O. McGeehan
(22 November 1879-29 November 1933)

Ronald T. Farrar
University of Kentucky

MAJOR POSITION HELD: Sports editor, *New York Herald Tribune* (1924-1933).

BOOK: *Trouble in the Balkans* (New York: Dial Press, 1931).

PERIODICAL PUBLICATIONS: "Barber of Broadway," *Collier's*, 74 (1 November 1924); "Glorified Tomboy," *Ladies Home Journal*, 45 (July 1925); "Baseball: Business as Usual," *North American*, 224 (March 1927); "Ivory Industry," *Saturday Evening Post*, 200 (11 February 1928); "But They Do Come Back," *American Mercury*, 111 (April 1931).

One of the most admired and authoritative sports journalists of his time, William O'Connell McGeehan did much to enhance American sports pages with a dignity and a literary quality they had not enjoyed previously. His powerful columns, in San Francisco and later in New York newspapers, were praised for their honesty as well as for their tough professionalism. While many sportswriters of the period took refuge in clichés, jargon, and boosterism, McGeehan wrote in a style that was direct, clear, and respectful of the reader's intelligence. He crusaded tirelessly for clean sport in an era when charges of bribery and corruption, especially in boxing, were commonplace. Author and journalist Paul Gallico regarded McGeehan as "the greatest sports writer that ever lived."

McGeehan was born in San Francisco, the eldest of six children of Hugh and Theresa O'Connell McGeehan. He attended public schools, then enrolled at Stanford University. He left college, however, to enlist with the First California Volunteers in the Spanish-American War of 1898 and the Philippine Insurrection of 1899. Returning to San Francisco in 1900, he elected to forego his college plans and, instead, move directly into newspaper work. Hired by the *Call*, he quickly won the boxing "beat" and was assigned to cover prizefights throughout the region. The enormous popularity of boxing, plus McGeehan's crisp reporting of it, quickly won him a reputation as a "comer." At that time the metropolis of the West, San Francisco was known as a lively newspaper city, and some of the country's most colorful newspapermen won their spurs there in that period. McGeehan worked a total of fourteen years in San Francisco, moving from the *Call* to the *Chronicle*, then to William Randolph Hearst's splashy *Examiner*, and eventually to the *Evening Post*, where he was successively city editor and managing editor. The dog-eat-dog competition made San Francisco an excellent training ground for young journalists, many of whom eventually gravitated to newspaper jobs in New York.

On 27 January 1910 he married Sophie

Treadwell, a newspaper reporter and playwright. They had no children.

In 1914 McGeehan decided to make the move east, following a number of his former colleagues there, but he quickly learned that his considerable achievements on the West Coast would count for little in Manhattan. He had been a top executive in San Francisco, but in New York he found himself again a sportswriter, this time for Hearst's *Evening Journal*. Once more he wrote mostly about boxing, and he was assigned a regular column which he entitled "Right Cross." A year later he moved to the *New York Tribune*—still as a sportswriter, but with more freedom to choose his own assignments. His intellect, hard work, and comprehensive understanding of sports—and sports fans—impressed his superiors, and they named him sports editor shortly after he joined the paper. His newspaper work was interrupted by another military tour in 1917; he was not sent overseas during World War I but helped train infantrymen. Commissioned a captain, he later was appointed a major in the reserves.

In 1921, McGeehan became the *Tribune*'s managing editor. A year afterward, however, with his paper slipping in the fierce New York competition, McGeehan joined the larger and more prosperous *Herald*, where he was given the title of sports editor and responsibility for a daily column, "Down the Line." The *Herald* and *Tribune* merged two years later, forming what would become one of the country's most respected newspapers. McGeehan was retained as sports editor, and under his leadership the *Herald Tribune* sports section was regarded by many as the most readable and authoritative of its day.

McGeehan's writing was lean and timely, but it also reflected a dramatic flair and a sense of history. His rapid-fire account of "the fight of the century," the heavyweight boxing match between the champion, Jack Dempsey of Manassa, Colorado, and the Argentine challenger, Luis Angel Firpo, contained such vivid passages as these:

> The Manassa matador dropped the Wild Bull of the Pampas, but not until the matador was gored by the bull so that he will remember it for many a day. Fifty-seven seconds after the bell rang for the second round at the Polo Grounds last night, Luis Angel Firpo, the hope and pride of Latin America, rolled over near the ropes at the south end of the ring inert, unconscious—knocked out.
>
> But what happened before this was as hard to follow as the shifting colors of a kaleidoscope. It was the most savage heavyweight bout that was ever staged, while it lasted. . . .
>
> Seven times Dempsey dropped the Argentine giant last night, and seven times the giant pulled himself up to his feet. He came up fighting, and lashing savagely but blindly at the champion. It was a right to the jaw that dropped Firpo the first time. The other six times the giant was felled by volleys of blows, on the head, on the body, all over his huge hulk. As he dropped for the fourth time it seemed that he could not rise.
>
> Charles Schweiger, the old prize fighter who was at the bell, rose in his chair and counted. Firpo turned his seemingly sightless eyes in the direction of the bell as the counter shouted "Nine!" He dragged himself upward painfully and slowly, only to be knocked down again and again. But every time the Argentino came up he lashed at the champion. Some of these blows landed, for Dempsey seemed reckless and determined to carry the fight to the Argentino to the end. He rushed in, disregarding the clublike right of the giant. . . .
>
> This was no boxing match. It was a fight, and a most primitive one at that.
>
> Only in the jungle would you find a replica of the rapidly shifting drama that over 85,000 at the Polo Grounds saw last night. A pair of wolves battling in the pines of the North Woods, a pair of cougars in the wastes of the Southwest, might have staged a faster and more savage bout, but no two human beings. . . .

Despite the intensity of his writing, McGeehan was not a cheerleader for the sports world. Though he wrote of athletes—especially amateur athletes—with respect, he came down hard on promoters who dominated several professional sports during that era. In this he had the full backing of his newspaper; when he was hired, the *Herald* had boasted in an editorial announcement that "the fighting pen of McGeehan has been secured in the interest of clean sport." McGeehan refused to take wrestling seriously, dismissing it as "the cauliflower industry," and he once described boxing as "the manly art of modified murder";

> Prize fighting is not a sport. It is a business. As a business it is probably as honest as American politics or the average business, and probably a little more honest than the stock market.

Prize fights today are merely entertainments staged for the box office. The sporting element went out when the business became respectable and legal. In the old days, when the fighters had to hop across the country ahead of the Sheriff and stage a bout on the quiet, prize fighting was more of a sport than it is today.

For all his cynicism, however, McGeehan was known as a sentimental Irishman, fond of good company and lively conversation. "Those who knew him more intimately cherished his dry humor and his seemingly inexhaustible fund of anecdotes, not by any means limited to sport," a fellow newspaperman wrote about him. "His journalistic colleagues observed a flattering silence when Mr. McGeehan was in a story-telling mood, for he was an excellent raconteur who managed to stay aloof from the Broadway jargon and who, moreover, had read and digested a good deal."

A tireless traveler, McGeehan left New York whenever he could. He regularly visited Canada—fly-fishing in New Brunswick during the summers, moose hunting in the winters—and frequently journeyed to Mexico and Europe. These trips served as inspiration for some of his most memorable columns, satirical pieces filled with literary references not often found on sporting pages of the period. In addition to his grueling schedule of newspaper columns, he wrote numerous articles and short stories for the leading magazines of the day.

McGeehan's pungent observations, as reflected in his column and the numerous magazine pieces he wrote, went far beyond the sporting scene. He commented frequently on news and public affairs, and readers of his column never knew whether they would be treated to a sports profile or a whimsical essay. But they read McGeehan anyway; his column was consistently one of the most popular features in a newspaper staffed by many of the journalistic stars of the period. In 1925, his paper dispatched him to Dayton, Tennessee, to cover the famous Scopes trial in which the teaching of evolution in the public schools had come under fundamentalist challenge. Sidestepping the religious and educational issues involved in that courtroom drama, McGeehan chose instead to write tongue-in-cheek, offbeat revelations that were widely quoted—and welcomed by many for the light touch they brought to an otherwise ponderous news event. McGeehan did produce one book, *Trouble in the Balkans*, which was published in 1931. That work, a comic account of some of his travels, was favorably reviewed. "*Trouble in the Balkans*," one critic wrote, "is a continuous chuckle—human, spontaneous, unpretentious. It is packed with laughs that hit you below the belt."

On one of his travels—to Brunswick, Georgia, to visit an old friend, Wilbert Robinson, former manager of the Brooklyn Dodgers—McGeehan suffered a massive heart attack. After a week in the hospital, he seemed better and was permitted to leave for a nearby cottage at Sea Island Beach. Within days, his condition worsened and he was forced to reenter the hospital. Medical staff members were amazed at his energy; they disclosed that, despite the gravity of his condition, he demanded that a typewriter be brought to him so he could continue his writing. On 29 November 1933, just over a month after his first attack and a week after his fifty-fourth birthday, he was stricken again, and minutes later he died.

Over the years, McGeehan's high principles and unflinching honesty led him to attack some boxing promoters and others who exploited professional athletics for their own gain; his columns brought him a number of enemies. Yet the columns also set a new and enduring standard of excellence in the realm of thoughtful, authoritative sports commentary, and they remain his legacy to journalism.

Reference:

Lisle Bell, "*Trouble in the Balkans*," *Books* (6 September 1931): 11.

O. O. McIntyre

(18 February 1884-14 February 1938)

Jean Lange Folkerts
University of Texas at Austin

MAJOR POSITION HELD: Syndicated columnist (1922-1938).

BOOKS: *White Light Nights* (New York: Cosmopolitan Book Corporation, 1924);
Twenty-five Selected Stories of O. O. McIntyre (New York: Cosmopolitan Magazine, 1929);
Another "Odd" Book: 25 Selected Stories of O. O. McIntyre (New York: International Magazine Company, 1932);
The Big Town (New York: Dodd, Mead, 1935).

In the 1920s, Americans were enamored of New York. It was the city which most represented the struggles of the modern age, the dilemma of new values versus old, innovation in the arts and in politics, and the aspirations and the excitement of the "Roaring Twenties." Radicals and artists populated Greenwich Village, speakeasies abounded, and the nouveau riche frequented posh nightclubs. It was into this atmosphere that Oscar Odd McIntyre, newspaper writer and aspiring columnist, in 1922 brought his small-town view of the world and his desire to describe the city to the folks at home.

In 1929, McIntyre wrote in the preface to the collection of his articles from *Cosmopolitan* that he had never changed his original idea. "I write from a country town angle of a city's glamour and the metropolis has never lost its thrill for me. Things the ordinary New Yorker accepts casually are my dish—the telescope man on the curb, the Bowery lodging houses and drifters, . . . speakeasies on side streets, fake jewelry auction sales, cafeterias, chop houses, antique shops, $5 hair bobbing parlors—in short all the things we didn't have in our town." McIntyre's significance was in his ability to interpret the sights and sounds of New York to readers nationwide.

A plaque now marks the house in Plattsburg, Missouri, where McIntyre was born on 18 February 1884 to Henry Bell McIntyre, proprietor of the town's main hotel, and Frances Young McIntyre, who was from an old and respected Missouri family. McIntyre had two older sisters, Katie and Georgia; Georgia died at the age of eleven. McIntyre's

O. O. McIntyre (Culver Pictures)

mother died in 1887, when he was three years old. Faced with the task of raising two children by himself, Henry McIntyre took Oscar and Katie to live with their grandmother in Gallipolis, Ohio, when McIntyre was five. After he became famous, McIntyre never returned to either of his boyhood towns, despite his fond descriptions of them in his columns. (He did, however, buy a house—"Gatewood"—in absentia in Gallipolis, and he was buried in the cemetery there.)

McIntyre hated school and often skipped classes to play in a cave nearby; his grades were poor, and he later lamented his lack of formal education. His father usually came to Gallipolis in the summer and sometimes took the children to Plattsburg for a visit. But he was a quiet and stern man, and young McIntyre always viewed him with a certain amount of formality and dread. However,

McIntyre's sister, Kate, his closest boyhood companion
(Mr. and Mrs. Alf Resener)

he later wrote an article for *Cosmopolitan* describing his father as "one of the truly great Americans." McIntyre described his father as having a "strange combination of surliness and sweet temper," and praised him for being a good citizen. Henry McIntyre, who had hated newspeople "ever since some circulation men from the *St. Louis Post-Dispatch* had jumped their hotel bill, and got clear of the town," always pretended not to be proud of his son. But when he died, an iron box filled with clippings of his son's work was found in his house.

At school in Gallipolis, McIntyre started a newspaper, which contained both real and fictional items. "Since my earliest recollection I wanted to be a newspaper reporter and I cannot tell you why," McIntyre later said. "My father was a country hotel keeper and all of my people, mostly, were farmers. Every one of my cousins owns a farm."

McIntyre briefly realized his desire to be a newspaperman while he was still in Gallipolis. Jimmy Johnson, the *Journal*'s reporter, whom McIntyre admired greatly, became ill and McIntyre was hired temporarily to fill his spot. When Johnson died shortly thereafter, McIntyre replaced him at $5 a week. But the elder McIntyre was not impressed and sent him to business school in Cincinnati. Henry McIntyre was friendly with a Missouri congressman, who had promised to give his son a job in Washington if he could develop the necessary skills. Although McIntyre spent two years in the school in Cincinnati, he despised it as much as he had despised grammar school; he did not do well in his courses, except for typing. His father then brought him back to Plattsburg, determined to make a hotel keeper of his son. But McIntyre was unhappy and spent most of his time writing to newspapers looking for a job.

The accounts of McIntyre's next newspaper job vary. His biographer, Charles B. Driscoll, says that in the spring of 1904 the *East Liverpool* (Ohio) *Morning Tribune* offered him a job at $12 a week, and he accepted. The position was attractive for more than one reason: it was newspaper work, but it also brought the young McIntyre back to Ohio and 600 miles closer to a girl he had admired in Gallipolis, Maybelle Hope Small. But McIntyre found that he was lonely in Liverpool. Not wanting to quit his job without having one to replace it, he finally got a friend in Plattsburg to write to him, requesting that he come home because a relative was seriously ill; thus he was able to escape the town for a while, without losing his position. Once in Plattsburg, he spent his time looking for other jobs. The Liverpool publisher tried to get him to return, offering him a raise of $6 a week, but McIntyre remained in Plattsburg, sleeping until noon, loafing around the hotel, and drinking beer at a corner bar in the evening. Finally, his father "fired" McIntyre, paying him $20 in wages and telling him to leave. McIntyre sent telegrams to newspapers and received an offer from the *Dayton Herald* for $12 a week. He left immediately to take the position.

McIntyre omitted the *East Liverpool Herald* from his resume, claiming that the first newspaper job he had was the one with the *Dayton Herald*. After business college, he said, he returned to Plattsburg to be a clerk in his father's hotel but found "I had no talent for such work and after two weeks he took me around the side of the hotel, gave me $20 and suggested that travel broadened the mind." He said he sent nine telegrams to newspapers, and the only reply came from the *Dayton Herald*, which hired him as a police court reporter.

McIntyre's newspaper career was beginning during a period of dramatic change in the journalistic world. Newspapers were changing from the "wooden" writing developed by the Associated Press to a feature style characterized by the Scripps-McRae newspapers, such as the *Cincinnati Post*. While in Cincinnati, McIntyre had read the *Post*, and he adapted this style to his writing for the *Herald*. Within three weeks after taking the job, McIntyre was made city editor and put in charge of four reporters. He encouraged them to read the *Post* and taught them to look for the feature angle. He began to be regarded as a humorist, the newspaper became more lighthearted, and circulation grew.

The adaptation of *Cincinnati Post* style was to be more advantageous to McIntyre than he had imagined. In 1907, Ray Long, managing editor of the *Post*, visited Dayton and hired McIntyre for $25 a week. Long and McIntyre became friends for life.

Cincinnati was a corrupt city, and Lincoln Steffens, the muckraker, was uncovering that corruption in his famous series, "The Shame of the Cities." Long cooperated with Steffens and brought in Will Irwin, the exposer of patent medicines, and cartoonist Homer Davenport to help in the cleanup campaign. McIntyre was made assistant to the telegraph editor and then was promoted to telegraph editor. With this last promotion, McIntyre felt comfortable enough to ask Maybelle Small to marry him. But he was still uneasy, afraid his father would be proved right and he would be a failure, and he did not even ask for a day off in order to get married. The marriage took place on 18 February 1908, and the next day the editor told McIntyre he would have given him the day off—provided, of course, that it was not a busy day.

McIntyre was soon promoted to assistant managing editor; but by this time Ray Long had moved to the *Cleveland Press*, and the new managing editor was a man of difficult temperament. McIntyre did not respond well to Victor Morgan's dictatorial ways, and he was ready for a move. Long made the move first, going to New York to edit *Hampton's* magazine, and he hired McIntyre as his assistant. In 1911, when McIntyre went to New York City, he had progressed to the then magnificent sum of $65 a week. But the joy and the magazine were short-lived: when *Hampton's* folded, McIntyre was out of a job.

After searching the city for work, McIntyre finally found a job as copy editor on the *Evening Mail* at $35 a week. He admitted to his wife that he had been on the verge of writing to the *Cincinnati Post*, hoping to get his old job back, just at the point when the offer from the *Evening Mail* came. McIn-

O. O. McIntyre's wife, Maybelle Hope Small McIntyre, who assisted him with his column and acted as his business manager (Mr. and Mrs. Alf Resener)

tyre was promoted to assistant city editor and on 14 April 1912, when the *Titanic* went down and the survivors arrived in New York on the *Carpathia*, McIntyre was in charge of the reporters at the dock. Using techniques learned at the *Post*, McIntyre turned out a story so well done that it attracted attention throughout the city. But the newspaper was unwilling to recognize his strengths and instead focused on McIntyre's lifetime weakness: poor spelling. Poor spelling meant poor editing, and McIntyre was fired again.

While out of a job, McIntyre often talked to his wife about the possibility of writing a New York letter to the people back home. He needed a way to make money while writing the letter, and he managed to get some publicity jobs. Then the newspapers, informed that they would be printing columns containing generous dollops of publicity for commercial concerns, were given his column free of charge. McIntyre systematically sent copies of the column to several new newspapers each week, broadening the number of papers which carried his work. He also began to write personality sketches. He was making about $50 a week from the publicity accounts, when in 1915 he landed a publicity job for the Majestic Hotel, which in addition to paying him, allowed him to live in the hotel rent free. He was instructed to entertain as much as he liked, as long as he promoted the hotel. McIntyre created many stunts to publicize the Majestic. On Washington's Birthday, he sent out a story about a child who "had taken her toy hatchet and chopped down an expensive palm tree in the lobby." When skipping rope was in fashion, he hired "a dozen pretty girls, dressed them in attractive costumes, and had them photographed skipping on the Majestic's roof garden."

As McIntyre became better established, he asked the newspapers if they would pay him. He did not set a price, but he began to get small returns on the column. After an argument with the owner of the Majestic about whether his dog could continue to live in the hotel, McIntyre moved to the Ritz Carlton; by this time he had saved $50,000. He approached a few syndicates, but the publicity material in the column earned him a negative response until, in 1922, the McNaught syndicate signed him for $400 a week, plus profit sharing. During the same year, Long, who had become editor of *Cosmopolitan*, asked McIntyre to contribute a monthly column for the magazine. McIntyre left the country for the first time, traveling in Europe, and proving that his readers liked McIntyre, and not just New York. His columns from Paris and London were received as well as the letter from New York. For the next ten years he went to Europe once a year, and he also wrote from places such as Florida and Texas.

McIntyre wrote his newspaper column seven days a week. At the time of his death the column was syndicated in 375 dailies and 129 Sunday papers and brought him an income of $200,000 a year. McIntyre had not titled the "letter," but several newspapers started calling the column "New York Day by Day," and others picked up the name. Newspapers previously had used other heads, including "Once Overs," "Manhattan Minutes," "Breezy Brieflets," and "Sidewalks of New York."

McIntyre's "Recipe for Success," according to Driscoll, included a "faint nostalgia" for the small town. It was his "love of the old home town and loyalty toward its people and its simplicity" that earned McIntyre his reputation. Driscoll also said McIntyre's "faculties for knowing, feeling and expressing" contributed to his popularity. McIntyre's columns often drew on his experiences in Missouri and Ohio. In a *Cosmopolitan* column, he wrote about New Year's Day in Gallipolis: "I want to live over again a New Year's Day on which young men and women do not awaken with aching heads and burning thirsts. I want to hear the venerable pastor of our church pronounce his New Year blessing. I want to hear Aunt Nell Bovie play the pipe organ again with those sweet, sad, rising, swelling and tremulous notes."

McIntyre was especially well known for his columns about dogs; some claim the most mail he ever received was from the column "Billy in Dog Heaven." Writing about "My Dog" in *Another "Odd" Book* (1932), he said:

> For many years I have had a sneaking suspicion that a number of friends have regarded what they consider a foolish sentimentality of mine with a tinge of disgust. They think I am a nut about dogs.
>
> This is neither an explanation nor an *apologia*. I was born with an overwhelming love for all dumb animals—especially dogs. It is as natural as breathing and to see them suffer actually makes me ill.

McIntyre knew New York as well as he knew the small towns, Driscoll said. "O. O. knew his small and big towns, the two kinds of gossips, the two sets of values, and he strongly felt the contrast. . . . so precisely did he ring the bell that the customers in all kinds of towns and rural places, as well as in the big city, clipped out the column and pasted it on the mirror." But in a sketch of McIntyre in the *Saturday Evening Post*, J. Bryan III said New Yorkers objected to McIntyre's description of the city because "as every New Yorker eventually comes to realize, the place that McIntyre reports bears no closer relation to reality than, say, the Suwanee River of song bears to the Suwanee River of Florida." In McIntyre's New York, Bryan said, "Harlem adjoins Chinatown, and Greenwich Village is across the street from Hell's Kitchen. Here Lizzie Borden is arrested by squad car, and Diamond Jim Brady dines at the Stork Club." But Bryan conceded that on "a dozen Railroad Avenues, Main Streets and R.F.D. No. 3's," McIntyre's word was "gospel."

McIntyre's material came from his memory, his observations, his reading, and his mail. An average week resulted in about 3,000 letters from friends, celebrities, and people McIntyre never met. He answered letters from his friends and from some celebrities, and his secretary answered the

McIntyre receiving an early-morning visit from Irvin S. Cobb, Will Rogers, and publisher Amon Carter (caricature by H. T. Webster)

rest. All letters from celebrities were sent to Gallipolis, where they were placed in the public library.

Driscoll, who edited the syndicated column, said most of the mail was inspired by columns which talked about preserves, jellies, apples, or other hometown products and events; McIntyre always got packages of these items when they were mentioned. The publisher of the *Ft. Worth Star-Telegram* even sent watermelons. "Four months after the recollection of blackberry jelly had made his mouth water for a line or two, jars of it were still being sent him; the twelve-hundredth jar came from Tahiti," Bryan noted.

McIntyre's problems with spelling and punctuation seemed to extend to a problem with accuracy as well. Complaints were many about his inaccurate comments, and Walter Winchell once wrote in his own column:

> Whenever I make mistakes in this pillar, I will refer my critics to this item clipped from O. O. McIntyre:
> "Harlem's reigning sheik is Cab Calloway, a saddle-colored Negro out of a small

town in Missouri. He has been leading an orchestra in cabaret and vaudeville. His dicty (flashy) clothes in zebra patterns set the style pace for ebony swells along Lenox Avenue."

Cab is not saddle-colored. He was not born in a small town in Missouri. He does not wear dicty clothes in zebra patterns. He does not set the style pace for Harlem swells. He is not a sheik, but spends most of his time at home with his wife. Other than that, O. O. McIntyre is correct.

McIntyre was also accused of plagiarism: in 1935, when *Big Town* was published, Christopher Morley said some of it had been lifted from his *Saturday Review of Literature* column, "The Bowling Green." Morley claimed McIntyre had stolen from him for fifteen years. "I don't want to seem selfish if he needs to divot the Green now and then for his newspaper syndicate. . . . But when he gets into the bookshops, then I feel a certain sense of trade honor is involved." Morley said he worked hard on his own stuff, "and if people are going to read it, I'd prefer them to get it in the *Saturday Review . . .* under my own name than in the Hearst papers under his." Morley included about thirty parallels. For example, Morley's "floats an instant in the mind like a smoke ring, then spreads and thins and sifts apart" was compared to McIntyre's "floating for an instant in the public eye like a smoke ring and sifting apart." The manager of McIntyre's syndicate replied: "Why should the most successful columnist in the business take the copy of the most unsuccessful? . . . Mr. Morley, whose Bowling Green column is perhaps the least read in the history of journalism, is capitalizing on Mr. McIntyre's popularity." Bryan claimed that McIntyre, genuinely bewildered by the debate, said, "If it did happen, it happened unintentionally." Bryan said McIntyre "had no consciousness of guilt" but considered every phrase or paragraph once written to be in the public domain.

Some competing writers, and even some of McIntyre's friends, claimed he was as odd as his middle name implied. (McIntyre had been named after an uncle, who pronounced the name "Ud." McIntyre preferred to be called by this name rather than "Oscar.") Indeed, he was reclusive, afraid of microphones and large crowds, and wary of movie and advertising offers. Driscoll said McIntyre's fright when called upon to speak was "pathetic," and he remembered one incident where McIntyre had simply stood up, bowed, and sat down. "That was at an Old Home Week celebration in Cincinnati," he added. McIntyre admitted that he had only a few intimate friends and that he never went to public events unless he was sure they would interest him. "I will not make speeches, talk over the radio or otherwise parade myself. I do not believe people are particularly interested in a writer. It is his work that counts."

Bryan described McIntyre as a "genuinely shy man" who sat next to Joan Crawford after she had specifically requested his presence at lunch but "never addressed a remark to her, and answered her only in monosyllables." He became increasingly reclusive over the years and toward the end of his life did not go out much socially. Every evening he and Mrs. McIntyre would go for a ride in their chauffeur-driven automobile. Bryan said the trips never lasted less than three hours, and McIntyre did not talk much during the ride but whistled, watched the streets, and made notes. "But it is a fruitful night that yields three items."

McIntyre was considered odd in many ways. He was known to have sixty dressing gowns hanging in his closet, thirty pairs of pajamas to wear during the day when he wrote, and another thirty to sleep in. He owned 200 canes, an equal number of ties, 100 pairs of socks, and wore formal attire— including a silk top hat—when he went out in the evening. Driscoll claimed the accumulation of fine clothing represented an ever-present fear of a recurring loss of job.

McIntyre's oddities included a fear of doctors. He did not go to a physician during the last twenty years of his life, nor did he take medicine. Driscoll said he had developed an interest in Christian Science even before his marriage but that he also was something of a hypochondriac. As a young man he had ordered a variety of medicines by mail and was constantly worried about his health. He had a number of nose and throat operations which doctors later told him were unnecessary. This left him with not only a fear of physicians but a feeling of futility about them as well. Despite a series of illnesses, McIntyre did not change his mind about physicians, and he died of a heart attack at the age of fifty-three.

The success of McIntyre's column reveals a preoccupation in America with the conflicts between growing urbanization and rural values; people read "New York Day by Day" to see what the man from the small town had to say about the big city. In addition, the willingness of newspapers to accept the material which blurred publicity and news represented an age of developing ethical standards in journalism. Such practice soon would be discarded by reporters and columnists who were adopting new standards of professionalism.

Biographies:

Charles B. Driscoll, *The Life of O. O. McIntyre* (New York: Greystone Press, 1938);

J. Bryan III, "Gallipolis Boy Makes Good," in *Post Biographies of Famous Journalists*, edited by John E. Drewry (Athens: University of Georgia Press, 1942).

William L. McLean

(4 May 1852-30 July 1931)

Jacqueline Steck
Temple University

MAJOR POSITION HELD: Owner and publisher, *Philadelphia Evening Bulletin* (1895-1931).

William L. McLean bought the *Evening Bulletin* in 1895, when it was thirteenth in a field of thirteen newspapers circulating in the city. By his death in 1931, the *Bulletin* led the field and was considered one of the nation's most prestigious newspapers. Although the paper died, greatly lamented, in 1982, much of its distinguished history was due to the leadership and publishing acumen of McLean and his descendants.

William Lippard McLean was born 4 May 1852 in Mount Pleasant, Pennsylvania, a small town thirty-two miles southeast of Pittsburgh. As a young man of twenty, he secured a position in the circulation department of the *Pittsburgh Leader*. His job required him to travel about outlying areas of the city, and it was here he learned a fact of newspaper life that was to prove essential in his later management of the *Evening Bulletin*: the primacy of local news. Later he held other positions at the *Leader*, so that by the time he headed for Philadelphia, he had a good grasp of all the operations involved in producing a sound newspaper.

It was another Pittsburgh native who introduced McLean to Philadelphia journalism. Calvin Wells, a Pittsburgh iron manufacturer, had purchased the *Philadelphia Press*, a newspaper of 6,317 circulation. He hired McLean, then twenty-six, as secretary and treasurer of The Press Co., Limited. In a short time, the young man became business manager of the paper, which was edging up on its competitors. But by this time, McLean was determined to strike out on his own. In 1895, he left the *Press* and purchased the *Evening Bulletin*, the oldest afternoon newspaper in Philadelphia (it had been founded in 1847), with a circulation of only 6,000 copies daily.

When he took over the *Bulletin*, McLean promised that the newspaper would support the Republican party and sound currency. He followed these two promises; the paper was not a crusader nor an investigator. McLean maintained a conservative approach to news and editorials while yellow journalism was sweeping the nation. He introduced features offering advice on subjects as diverse as etiquette and the best automobile routes through the city. In McLean's first year with the paper, the circulation jumped to 33,625.

Shortly before the Spanish-American War, McLean became convinced that the United States would become involved, so he installed Hoe Quadruple rotary perfecting presses so that he could provide more readers with speedy war news. The investment paid off: the *Bulletin*'s circulation in 1897 was 59,281; in 1898, it was 113,973. "The 129 miles of the city's limits," said an item that appeared in the paper at this time, "are covered by Bulletin wagons drawn by fast horses, by messengers on foot and in trolley cars, and by sturdy-legged young men astride bicycles." However, as America approached the twentieth century, McLean decided that he needed more than his "sturdy-legged young men" to deliver the news quickly. In 1899 he imported two Daimler electric wagons from France and became the first American publisher to use automobiles to distribute papers. This enabled him to get the latest news to the city outskirts only thirty minutes after the *Bulletin* came off the press.

Speed in news delivery was only one of the hallmarks of the *Bulletin*, which continued to climb in circulation and in the affection of its readers. McLean saw Philadelphia as a vast amalgamation of independent and clannish neighborhoods, each wanting to see its local stories in the big-city paper. McLean obliged, offering intense and thorough coverage of the little villages that made up the metropolis.

By 1905, just ten years after McLean purchased it, the *Bulletin* boasted the largest circulation in Philadelphia: over 200,000 daily. The achievement was the result of clear analysis, unremitting work, and a keen insight into the nature of the community the paper served.

A story, probably apocryphal, was often told among *Bulletin* people that illustrated the attitude of Philadelphians toward the paper. Two men, the story goes, were sitting on a front porch one day as fire engines roared past on their way to a local conflagration.

"Let's go follow them and see where the fire is," said the first.

"Why bother?," rejoined the second. "Let's just wait and we can find out all about it in this afternoon's *Bulletin!*"

This kind of confidence was reflected in the circulation figures, which grew as Philadelphia grew. So popular did the paper become that the *Bulletin* used as its slogan, "In Philadelphia, nearly everybody reads the Bulletin." As circulation figures soared, some staffers suggested the word *nearly* should be deleted. McLean demurred: it might not be accurate. Other newspapers offered various circulation gimmicks: prizes, games, premiums; McLean offered solid coverage of the news. He saw the paper as a visitor in the family home, and his writers and editors were kept constantly aware of their guest status: the paper must never offend. This meant that an artist might be asked to draw more clothes on a comic-strip character or a writer might be asked to delete a rude word such as *lousy*. With McLean, his readers' feelings and sensibilities were paramount.

To serve his readers, he improved the paper's content with excellent editorial material and attractive features. While he continually urged top-notch local coverage, he never slighted national and international news. Elected a director of the Associated Press in 1896, he continued as an official in the organization until 1924, playing an active part in its reorganization from an Illinois to a New York corporation. During his tenure, AP achieved a membership of more than 1,200 newspapers. He was a director of the American Newspaper Publishers Association from 1889 to 1905. However, he would not accept a directorship in another business lest such involvement restrict the paper's freedom in printing the news or commenting on it.

In addition to his newspaper activities, McLean played a leading part in the cultural life of Philadelphia. He donated funds for a giant statue of Benjamin Franklin in the Franklin Memorial Institute; he presented the Tudor Room to the Pennsylvania Art Museum (now called the Philadelphia Art Museum) as a memorial to his wife; he gave a gymnasium to the Germantown YMCA as a memorial to his son Warden, who had been killed during military training in 1917. He was a member of the Union League, the Franklin Institute, the Fairmount Park Art Association, the Chamber of Commerce, and many other organizations in the city.

McLean was married in 1889 to Sarah Burd Warden, who died in 1921. When McLean died in 1931, he was survived by his son Robert, vice-president of the Bulletin Company, who succeeded him as a member of the board of directors of the Associated Press; William, Jr., treasurer of the *Bulletin*; and his daughter, Sarah (Mrs. John S. Williams). The trade journals of the newspaper business and other newspapers were lavish in their praise of McLean. Some commented on the fact that his had been one of the few newspapers not to print the false story on the signing of the Armistice on 7 November 1918. Other newspapers had printed it, and hundreds of thousands of people had poured into the streets cheering; schools had been dismissed, factories closed, and mothers had wept for joy. But the *Bulletin* had refused to credit the rumor, which the AP reported lacked confirmation. The *Bulletin*'s headline had read "Armistice Not Signed; False Rumor Stirs Nation." A stern editorial had castigated "Harum-Scarum News."

Other tributes recounted his publication of a book called *One Day*, in which all the contents of the

The 4 June 1928 edition of the Philadelphia Evening Bulletin *printed in book form to demonstrate the amount of material the paper's readers received each day for two cents. The book measures 5¼ by 7¾ inches and is 307 pages long.*

Bulletin of 4 June 1928, except the advertising, was published. That paper contained 102 columns of news, editorials, illustrations, and features, somewhat below the daily average for the month. In book form it made a volume of 307 pages, seven and three-quarters inches high, five and one-quarter inches wide, and one inch thick—a stunning demonstration of the material a daily newspaper published every twenty-four hours and sold for two cents a copy.

Of all the encomiums printed to honor the publisher, perhaps this paragraph from the *Philadelphia Record* of 30 July 1931 best summed up his contribution to journalism: "Conservative by inclination and habit, of thoughtful and judicial rather than crusading temperament, Mr. McLean pursued undeviatingly his ideal of a newspaper that should be a force for civic sanity and righteousness and progress, but at the same time should mold public opinion by quiet persuasion rather than by news emphasis or argumentative vigor." That was an appropriate eulogy for the man who gave Philadelphia the newspaper that "nearly everybody" read and most people loved.

Robert McLean was publisher of the *Bulletin* until 1964, when he was succeeded by Robert E. L. Taylor, his wife's nephew. That year both the *Bulletin* and the *Philadelphia Inquirer* suffered severe daily circulation drops, but by 1970 the *Bulletin* was selling 174,000 more papers a day than the *Inquirer*. Taylor retired in 1975 and was succeeded by William L. McLean III. Four years later McLean sold it to the Charter Company.

The *Bulletin* went out of business, to the sorrow of most Philadelphians, in January 1982. Like numerous other afternoon papers, it succumbed to the pressures of delivery during peak traffic hours and accelerating competition from the early evening TV news and newly aggressive suburban dailies. The most immediate reason for its demise was its loss in the advertising competition to the *Inquirer*, owned by Philadelphia Newspapers Inc., part of the Knight-Ridder organization. In a last-ditch attempt to stay in business, the paper, which had for decades been called the *Evening Bulletin*, became an all-day paper. The device failed, and the paper which in the years immediately following World War II had enjoyed the largest daily circulation among evening newspapers in America closed its doors.

Reference:

David G. Wittels, "The Paper That Was Tailored to a City (William L. McLean and the *Philadelphia Bulletin*)," in *More Post Biographies*, edited by John E. Drewry (Athens: University of Georgia Press, 1947), pp. 178-191

Frank A. Munsey

(21 August 1854-22 December 1925)

Ted Curtis Smythe
California State University, Fullerton

NEWSPAPERS OWNED: *New York Daily Continent* (1891); *New York Daily News* (1901-1904); *Washington Times* (1901-1917); *Boston Journal* (1902-1913); *Baltimore Evening News* (1908-1915, 1918-1922); *Philadelphia Evening Times* (1908-1914); *New York Press*, merged into *New York Sun* in 1916 (1912-1924); *New York Sun*, merged with the *New York Herald* in 1918, renamed *New York Herald* in 1920 (1916-1924); *New York Evening Sun*, renamed *New York Sun* in 1920 (1916-1925); *New York Telegram* (1918-1925); *New York Herald–European Edition* (1918-1924); *Baltimore Star*, merged with *Baltimore News* in 1921 (1921-1922); *Baltimore American* (1921-1923); *New York Globe*, merged with *New York Sun* in 1923 (1923-1925); *New York Evening Mail*, merged with *New York Telegram* in 1923 (1923-1925).

BOOKS: *Afloat in a Great City: A Story of Strange Incidents* (New York: Cassell, 1887);
The Boy Broker; or, Among the Kings of Wall Street (New York: Munsey, 1888);
A Tragedy of Errors (New York: Munsey, 1889);
Under Fire; or, Fred Worthington's Campaign (New

Frank A. Munsey (© Burr McIntosh)

York: Munsey, 1890); republished as *Under Fire: A Tale of New England Village Life* (New York: Munsey, 1897);
Derringforth (New York: Munsey, 1894).

PERIODICAL PUBLICATIONS: "Getting on in Journalism," *Munsey's*, 19 (May 1898): 214-224;
"Advertising in Some of Its Phases," *Munsey's*, 20 (December 1898): 476-486;
"Something More about Advertising," *Munsey's*, 20 (January 1899): 656-660;
"The Making and Marketing of Munsey's Magazine," *Munsey's*, 22 (December 1899): 323-343.

Frank A. Munsey was a vocal proponent of the application of business methods and concepts to the newspaper business from the turn of the century

into the 1920s. A man who made great sums of money in the magazine field, especially with *Munsey's*, he poured his efforts into creating a better journalism than he perceived existed in his day. That he failed in his efforts speaks more of the man than of his prescient insights into the problems of journalism. In his role as publisher of the *New York Herald* and other newspapers, he helped to elect a president and played an important role in politics.

Frank Andrew Munsey was born in Mercer, Maine, on 21 August 1854 to Andrew Chauncey and Mary Jane Munsey. His father was a farmer and, according to the Munsey genealogist, was a hard worker who held rigid opinions and possessed an intense nature. These characteristics seem to have been passed on to his son.

Munsey's first job was as a clerk in a grocery store in Lisbon Falls. This store was the site of the local post office and telegraph station. There young Munsey mastered the telegraph, thus acquiring a skill that enabled him to escape the drudgery of clerking in a general store. While still only sixteen, he left Lisbon Falls and became a telegraph operator at the Falmouth Hotel in Portland. From there he was sent to several other towns and cities in New England. While managing the Augusta, Maine, telegraph office, Munsey lived in the Augusta House, where he met many local politicians and businessmen. James G. Blaine noted his qualities of service and loyalty, and during political campaigns Blaine had especially sensitive telegrams sent only through Munsey. The young man never forgot Blaine's recognition and kindness.

Augusta was the home of the E. C. Allen Publishing House, which produced *Literary Companion* and other periodicals, all of which earned a large sum for the publisher. Allen lived in Augusta House, and Munsey often heard him talking about his business. Once Allen reportedly complained: "I have to build up anew every year or it will crumble away. What I ought to have done was to go to New York or Chicago and use the money that came in from subscriptions to found a great daily newspaper."

While Munsey was eagerly listening to Allen and acquiring information about the publishing business from Allen's subordinates, he also sought counsel on how to improve his writing and speaking. The superintendent of schools told him that he would never get rid of the colloquialisms he had acquired from farm and village, but Munsey did. He paid close attention to his speech and writing from that time on, carefully thinking of the correct word to use before speaking. This practice continued for years until he became confident in his ability with the language.

Finally Munsey decided to take the plunge and go to New York City to start a magazine. Undeterred by the many people—including Blaine—who warned against such a move, Munsey got promises of $2,500 from a stockbroker and $1,000 from a young man who had gone to New York from Augusta and added to the sum $500 that he had been saving toward such a day. He knew what he wanted to produce: a young person's magazine to be called *Golden Argosy*. He had a list of writers whom he had already contacted. The long serial selected to appear in the first issue was entitled "Do and Dare; or, A Brave Boy's Fight for Fortune," by Horatio Alger, Jr.

Munsey arrived in New York City on 23 September 1882. He was unknown, had little money ($40 was left from his original $500 savings after he had purchased manuscripts), little credit, and no magazine publishing experience. The manuscripts served as collateral for the printers and paper manufacturers he was importuning for credit. In need of the $3,500 that had been promised, Munsey wrote to the stockbroker, but received no reply. Repeated letters failed to get any response, and Munsey released his other funding source, the young man with the $1,000, from his obligation. Munsey then walked the streets seeking financial support. Publisher E. G. Rideout provided Munsey with a small office, and on 2 December 1882 the first weekly issue of the *Golden Argosy* was sent out, with Rideout as publisher. After five months Rideout went bankrupt, and Munsey took over the publication. Munsey was able to persuade others to come on board, even though the magazine was losing money and bills were piling up.

Malcolm Douglas, who later became well known as a playwright and theater owner, became editor. British children's magazines were the source of many of the *Golden Argosy* stories. One day Douglas reported to Munsey that he could find nothing appropriate for the *Golden Argosy*; Munsey promised to write a story that night, and the next day he delivered "Harry's Scheme; or, Camping among the Maples," about young men in the Maine woods. With no experience in writing, Munsey began a career as writer in addition to his other duties. At night he wrote; during the day he managed the office, sought manuscripts, held off paper and printing creditors, solicited advertising, and kept the books. It was an exhausting pace that he

would maintain for years. After four years of publishing, his $40 in cash had become $5,000 in debts; but Munsey, although harried, was happy, because he knew that credit was the lifeblood of his business.

At that point Munsey started writing a long serial story entitled "Afloat in a Great City." Because he had great faith in the story, he placed $10,000 worth of advertising (on credit) in New York newspapers and printed an additional 100,000 copies of the *Golden Argosy*, distributing them throughout the city and Brooklyn. The promotion worked: readers, captured by the story, sent in subscriptions, and for the first time income exceeded expenses by $100 a week. Then Munsey further expanded his enterprise by sending solicitors across the country; his credit boomed—as did his debts, which soon exceeded $95,000. Onward he pushed, seeking credit from new sources while paying off the oldest debtors. While he juggled finances during the day, at night he wrote another serial, "The Boy Broker," which added 20,000 to his circulation. In May 1887 Munsey was earning $1,500 a week profit on a circulation of $150,000. He was exultant: in five years of relentless pressure and exhausting work he had created a profitable publication.

It was, in the words of his biographer, George Britt, "fool's gold." The day of the juvenile weekly was dead. Such magazines received little advertising because children had little money to spend; in addition, children grew out of their publications, and one constantly had to find new readers to replace them. Munsey experimented with changes in price and size and concluded, when circulation continued to decline, that the juvenile weekly could never again be the great success it once had been. In 1888 he converted the magazine into an adult publication called *Argosy*.

In 1889 Munsey started *Munsey's Weekly* along the lines of the then popular comic weekly *Life*; it failed. In October 1891, after carefully reviewing his publication and his finances, Munsey dropped the word *Weekly* from the title and started issuing the magazine monthly.

Also in 1891 Munsey bought his first newspaper, the *New York Star*. He renamed it the *Daily Continent* and turned it into a tabloid, with pictures and feature stories. After losing $40,000 in four months, he sold the paper and went back to his magazines. The *Continent* became the *Morning Advertiser*.

While *Munsey's* sought a market, the country's economy turned sour. The panic of 1893 crushed the hopes of many businessmen, and Munsey's

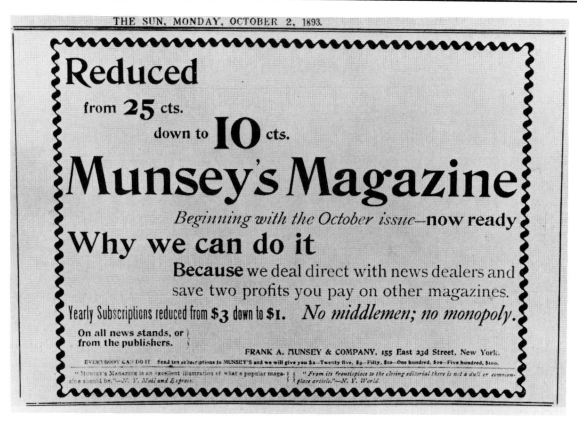

Advertisement for Munsey's Magazine, *announcing the 1893 price cut that made the magazine successful*

creditors called in their loans. One loan cost him eighteen percent interest to pay off. It was six years from the heady days of 1887, and he was desperate. Only a Munsey, it seems, could take the gamble that would win the day.

There were 80,000,000 people in the United States, but circulation of the general magazines was only 250,000. Munsey concluded that there was a large, untapped market that was not being reached because of high costs. Most magazines sold for twenty-five or thirty-five cents a copy; a few were cutting their prices to fifteen cents (*McClure's*) and twelve and a half cents (*Cosmopolitan*). Munsey decided to cut his price, and his October 1893 issue was sold for ten cents a copy or one dollar a year. This was a tremendous break with existing practice. It is true that the *Ladies' Home Journal* already sold for ten cents and claimed the largest circulation in the world, but it was a specialized-audience magazine; no general circulation publisher had sought to follow its lead.

Having made his decision, Munsey soon confronted the realities of magazine distribution. The American News Company, which together with its affiliates monopolized distribution of magazines in

the United States, refused to carry *Munsey's* for less than five and a half cents on each copy; this meant Munsey would receive only four and a half cents per copy. He had offered three and a half cents but retreated from that figure when the company gave its counteroffer. Munsey now said he would pay American News Company no more than three cents. He conferred with Charles A. Dana of the *New York Sun*, who suggested that Munsey start his own distribution system; Munsey formed the Red Star News Company. Still frustrated by the difficulty of getting newsstands to carry his magazine, he went to Dana again. This time Dana gave Munsey half-page ads in the *Sun* on credit. This strategy worked: the American News Company offered to carry *Munsey's* for four and a half cents. Munsey refused.

His paper supplier almost stopped the new enterprise before it had really gotten started when he spoke with Munsey about the large debt created by sales of the October and November editions. But Munsey persuaded him that the magazine would succeed—after all the October issue had sold 40,000 copies and the November issue 60,000.

Munsey knew that the future of the

magazine-publishing industry would involve large circulation with small profit on each piece sold. Dana had preached the same financial doctrine for years with the *Sun*; what set Munsey's concept apart was that his magazines would vigorously seek advertising. He later recalled: "I knew what the purchase of large quantities of paper meant in the way of lower prices. I knew what a printing plant of my own meant in the reduction of cost. I knew what perfect equipment throughout meant in the way of saving. I knew too that the great circulation toward which we were pushing with such tremendous strides meant that the advertisers of the country could not afford to remain out of *Munsey's Magazine*, and that from the advertising pages a big revenue must inevitably come." It did: advertising followed circulation. The circulation rose to 200,000 in four months; in one year circulation reached 275,000, and six months later it hit 500,000. One year after *Munsey's* began selling at ten cents there were only sixteen pages of advertising; nine months later there were eighty pages. Revenues from advertising soared. For the six months ending in March 1896 Munsey earned $163,273 from advertising alone. In 1905, for the first time, Munsey earned over one million dollars from his various publications, of which *Munsey's* was the flagship. And he continued to earn over a million dollars a year for the next several years.

Munsey's offered popular fiction and somewhat pedestrian articles by leaders in business and society, and every issue was profusely illustrated. Munsey made a fetish of illustrations. He coupled the halftone engraving, which had been possible in the magazine field for several years, with art and photography. The high-priced illustrated publications had for years avoided the halftone illustration, instead relying upon steel line engravings, usually of art or sketches by artists. Munsey understood that the halftone had reduced engraving costs so greatly that numerous illustrations could be used without breaking the editorial budget.

Munsey eschewed vulgar and critical articles. He saw America as a land of opportunity for all; if people would work hard and persevere, as he had, they too could make their way to success in this happy land. He admired big business, and the content of his magazine reflected this admiration. The vulgar was not a part of his personality, and he would not lower himself to appeal to people's passions through his magazine. Although some of the art he reproduced showed rather scantily clad women, it was tastefully done.

Munsey's demonstrated the success of the ten-cent magazine, and its enormous profits enabled Munsey to enter nonjournalistic fields where his business concepts and practices were highly successful. He began a grocery store in 1897 in a building he owned in New London, Connecticut, and from its success he built a chain of cash-and-carry grocery stores that offered customers quality goods at low prices. Large refrigeration units allowed the stores to carry perishable goods, which other grocery stores did not carry. Within a decade his Mohican chain of over fifty stores in New England was capitalized at $3,000,000, which specialists in the field considered far less than its true value.

Munsey got into the banking business partly through the same accidental process, when he erected a building with a ground floor section designed for a bank. No bank was interested in the site, so Munsey started his own, the Munsey Trust Company of Baltimore, in 1912. Other banks followed, including one in Washington, D.C., which enabled Munsey to be on hand when a crisis faced the new administration of President Woodrow Wilson in 1913. A major bank, with five branches and 55,000 depositors, was facing a run on its resources. Munsey responded to pleas for help from the administration that were ignored by other bankers and merged with the troubled bank, saving the institution and its depositors from ruin. Eventually the Munsey Trust Company made money from the action, but not before Munsey had expended over $1,250,000.

Munsey became a newspaper publisher again in November 1901 when he bought the *New York Daily News* and the *Washington Times*. When he bought the evening *Daily News* Munsey told a *Herald* reporter that he wanted to apply to the journalistic field what he had learned about chain operations from the grocery business. But Munsey lacked the skill, the time, and the desire to duplicate the *Daily News*'s earlier success, which had come from reaching the lower classes on the East Side. Instead Munsey made it Republican and a morning paper. After much experimenting, and some learning about journalistic practices, Munsey transferred the newspaper to his managing editor in June 1904; the paper died two years later. It was a relatively unmourned death since the *Daily News* had not been a power in politics or journalism, despite an early connection with Tammany Hall. Munsey reportedly invested $750,000 in the paper before its demise; it is not known how much he earned from it during the three years of his ownership.

In 1902, Munsey purchased the *Boston Journal* with its morning, evening, and Sunday editions.

The *Journal* was an old newspaper which was hidebound in nearly every respect. It was not doing well when Munsey bought it for $600,000, well over its proper valuation. After purchasing the paper he began to experiment with it: he changed publication schedules, typography, and the magazine section; he got rid of the Sunday edition by making it independent, then reinstated it. He changed the price of the paper several times. For about five months in 1911 he even cut all illustrations from the paper—a radical departure from the journalism of the day and the practice of Munsey, who had used halftone illustrations so successfully in his magazine. Munsey sold the paper in 1913.

In 1908 Munsey added the *Baltimore Evening News* and the *Philadelphia Evening Times* to his *Washington Times* and *Boston Journal*. The *Baltimore Evening News* remained a paying newspaper, partly because Munsey tended to keep his hands off of its daily administration; instead he hired Stuart Olivier as general manager and permitted him full control so long as the paper earned money. The *Washington Times* manager was Edgar D. Shaw, who also had great latitude in running his paper. The *New York Press*, purchased in 1912 to serve the Progressive party in New York, became the base for building Munsey's New York newspaper dynasty.

These papers remained as part of Munsey's chain until 1913, when the *Journal* was sold. In 1914, Munsey was offered $900,000 for the *Philadelphia Times*, to be paid over three years; but he wanted $1,200,000, so he sent the best men to New York and killed the paper. In 1915 he sold the *Baltimore Evening News* to Olivier. Two years later he sold the *Washington Times* to Arthur Brisbane. Despite Munsey's expenditures in erecting a fine building in Washington, D.C., the *Times* had made a small profit in 1909 and had been near to profit-making for several years. Olivier later turned the *Baltimore Evening News* back to Munsey when wartime operating costs sapped its profits. Munsey's dream of a national chain of newspapers was over. Now he would concentrate on New York City.

The decline of his chain idea was a loss in one sense: Munsey had articulated a far-reaching concept of chain journalism which would be supported by top newsmen and editors, men paid outstanding salaries because they were the best in their fields. He had spoken on this subject in 1902, claiming that "I shall be able to make good by the power of organization and by applying the methods that are now employed by our great business combinations, popularly known as the trusts. In my judgment it will not be many years—five or ten, perhaps—

before the publishing business of this country will be done by a few concerns, three or four at most." He was wrong, although he understood what William Randolph Hearst and E. W. Scripps, among others, were doing by establishing chains across the country. Munsey's journalism was not sensationalistic or personally political, as was Hearst's, nor did he seek to reach the working class in America's small cities, as did Scripps. He simply wanted to produce money-making, news-generating, Republican-supporting newspapers by using modern business practices. Important as those practices were in the new journalism of the day, content and style also played an important role in reaching the masses for advertisers.

The *New York Press* had been purchased in 1912 as a vehicle for promoting the candidacy of Theodore Roosevelt. In 1916 Munsey looked around New York City and began to seriously appraise the newspaper market. What he found caused him to buy, consolidate, and sell newspapers and to fundamentally shape the city's journalistic landscape. By 1924 he had purchased nine newspapers, seven of them in New York alone.

The papers that started him on this binge were the *New York Sun* and the *Evening Sun*, which he purchased in 1916 for over $3,000,000. He combined the *Press* with the *Sun* in order to provide the *Sun* with an Associated Press franchise. This was one of the effects of the Associated Press's protectionism, which allowed the established publishers in a city to block the sale of the AP service to newly created newspapers. Although both the United Press and the International News Service, respectively created by Scripps and Hearst, were available, neither was as complete as the Associated Press. It is difficult to know how important the Associated Press franchise was in killing the *Press*, because Munsey also merged and killed newspapers for circulation and advertising considerations.

After James Gordon Bennett, Jr., died in 1918, Munsey purchased the morning *Herald*, the evening *Telegram*, and the Paris edition of the *Herald* for $3,000,000 from the Bennett estate. He almost immediately consolidated the *Sun* and the *Herald* into one morning edition; he kept the *Evening Sun* and the *Telegram* operating separately. This arrangement could not exist forever, so in October 1920, just ten months after the consolidation, Munsey renamed the morning paper the *Herald*; the evening edition became just the *Sun*, while the *Telegram* continued as a barely profitable evening paper with good want ad income.

Munsey saw that there were far too many

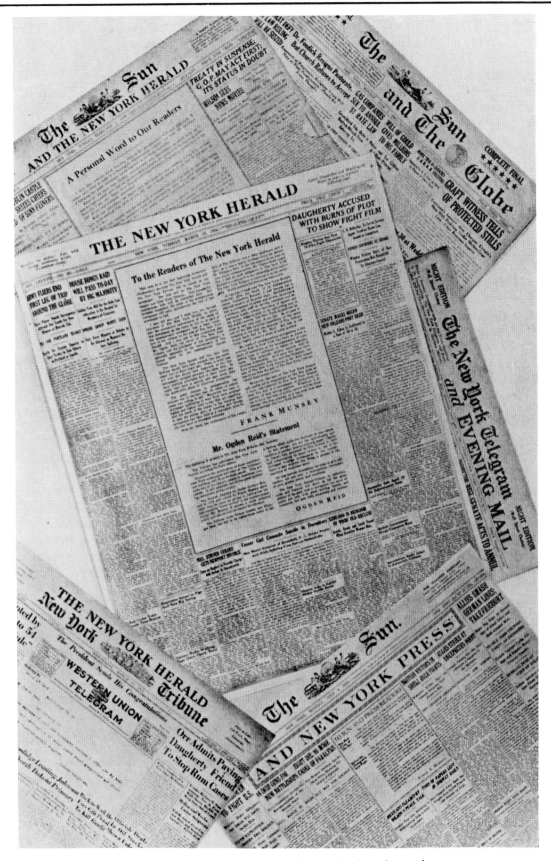

First issues of some of the papers Munsey bought and merged

evening newspapers in New York City. In 1923 he purchased the *New York Globe*, which was formerly the *Commercial Advertiser* and a successful afternoon paper, and consolidated it with the *Sun*. In doing so he created a massively successful newspaper that returned profits of about $1,500,000 annually. He also bought the *Evening Mail* and consolidated it with the *Telegram*. The result here, too, was a successful newspaper.

He then turned his attention to the morning field. The *New York Tribune*, which had a long and important history, although it was somewhat weakened by the changing market in New York, seemed available. He attempted to buy the *Tribune* to merge it with the *Herald*, but he failed. Instead Mrs. Ogden Reid asked to buy the *Herald* from Munsey. Munsey recognized that there was no economic need for the competing morning papers; in addition, despite his having spent enormous sums promoting the *Herald*, it still was losing money. In 1924 he sold the *Herald* for $5,000,000. Mrs. Reid then consolidated the paper into the *Tribune* under her son Ogden, its publisher. Thus the *New York Herald* finally passed from the scene, except for the appearance of its title in the nameplate of what had been its greatest competitor through the years.

While Munsey was busy consolidating the newspaper field in New York, he also remembered his *Baltimore Evening News*, which had been returned to him when the buyer had failed with it. In an effort to bolster the *Evening News*, he purchased both the *Baltimore American* and the *Baltimore Star* in 1921, combining the *Star* with the *News*. Within two years Munsey had sold both newspapers to Hearst, the *Evening News* in 1922 and the *American* in 1923.

When Munsey died in December 1925 he owned only two newspapers; both were evening papers in New York, the *Sun* and the *Telegram*. Both were quite successful at the time. He also owned four magazines—*Munsey's, Argosy, Flynn's Weekly Detective Fiction*, and *All Story Weekly*.

Munsey, who had never married, left no direct heirs. His estate was valued at $19,747,687 in 1929, although it was greatly reduced by the time it was liquidated. Munsey's one living sister and her son and daughter were remembered in his will, as were

some of his most important and faithful employees. Some of the estate was given to various public service institutions. What was left was given to the Metropolitan Museum of Art; the bequest was estimated at over $1,000,000 in 1929, although the depression reduced that figure by forty-one percent.

The young man who had arrived in New York City in 1882 with $40 in cash to start a young person's magazine died at the age of seventy-one, wealthy, but generally a failure in newspaper journalism. He had owned eighteen newspapers at one time or another, but had truly succeeded with only the two that remained at his death. He had used his newspapers to fight for editorial crusades he felt were important and for political figures such as Theodore Roosevelt and Warren G. Harding. He had undertaken unpopular stands on political and economic issues that cost him dearly in subscribers and advertising, but he had never flinched. He had also created the Sunday afternoon edition, which nearly always was successful with his papers and was copied in some metropolitan centers. He is credited with having established the "agate line" as the standard unit of measurement in newspaper advertising.

Still, Frank A. Munsey is remembered largely for his successful magazine career and for his killing of major New York newspapers. The fact that most of those newspapers would have failed if they had not been merged was lost on most journalistic observers. To them, Munsey was never a real newspaperman.

Biography:
George Britt, *Forty Years—Forty Millions. The Career of Frank A. Munsey* (New York: Farrar & Rinehart, 1935).

References:
D. O. S. Lowell, *The Munsey-Hopkins Genealogy* (Boston: Privately printed, 1920);
Frank Luther Mott, *A History of American Magazines, 1885-1905*, volume 5 (Cambridge, Mass.: Harvard University Press, 1957).

Lucius W. Nieman

(13 December 1857-1 October 1935)

Gail L. Barwis

MAJOR POSITION HELD: Editor and president, *Milwaukee Journal* (1882-1935).

Newspaperman: this one word was all Lucius W. Nieman wanted said of his noted career as founder and editor of one of the country's leading daily newspapers, the *Milwaukee Journal*. A man who prized brevity, accuracy, and fairness, Nieman helped to elevate the standards of journalism not only during his lifetime but also through the present day. Under the terms of an endowment made to Harvard University by his widow, the distinguished Nieman Fellowships annually provide working newspapermen with the opportunity to increase their journalistic competence through a year's study in a field of their choice.

Nieman's successor as editor and president of the *Milwaukee Journal*, Harry J. Grant, described his predecessor in a speech to the Nieman Fellows at Harvard in April 1941: "Lucius William Nieman abhorred pretense and avoided 'guff'—his term for the modern 'bunk.' There was no land of make-believe in his world. He called for a straightforward, factual story." And, added Grant, "his story should be written in such terms."

Nieman was born 13 December 1857 in the small Wisconsin settlement of Bear Creek in Sauk County. His father, Conrad, died when he was two, and his mother, Sara Elizabeth, took Nieman and his older sister, Vidette, to live with her parents, William and Susan Cuppernall Delamatter. Nieman's mother died after a few years, and his grandmother became the guiding force in his life.

As a child Nieman demonstrated a keen interest in the newspaper business, and with his grandmother's help he got his first job at age twelve as a printer's devil at the *Waukesha Freeman*, an influential weekly run by her friend Theron Haight, a former teacher.

Nieman lived with the Haights and not only learned to set type and carry out the sundry duties of a printer's devil but also developed his reading and reasoning skills. Billy Sixty, whom Nieman later groomed from a golf caddy to be one of his closest confidants on the *Journal*, recounted a story dating from Nieman's apprentice days that demonstrated

Lucius Nieman (State Historical Society of Wisconsin)

the young journalist's resourcefulness:

It appears that a rival paper was about to print a story said to be sensational. The *Freeman* did not know its nature, but the owners speculated a good deal about it.

In those days the two papers exchanged society notes and it was one of Nieman's jobs to take *Freeman* proofs to the offices of the other paper. On one of his trips, he noticed a galley of type lying on one of the tables. Inspection led him to believe that it was the sensational story, all nicely inked. At the last moment before leaving, he leaned casually over the table and took a legible impression of the type on his white shirt front. Dashing back to the *Freeman* office, he panted, "If you want to read that story, just read my shirt."

By the time he was fifteen Nieman was ready to move to the big city, Milwaukee, where he got a job in the composing room of the *Milwaukee Sentinel*, the largest English-language daily in the city. Nieman wanted to write, however, and asked to become a reporter. Advised by the editor to get more education, he enrolled at Carroll College in Waukesha and took up residence again with his grandmother, who had moved to that city. While at Carroll, Nieman wrote dispatches for the *Sentinel* as the paper's Waukesha correspondent. After a year and a half, he returned to Milwaukee as a full-time reporter for the *Sentinel*.

When he was seventeen he was sent to Madison to cover the 1875 state legislative session. Denounced on the floor of the senate because of his tendency to pry into questionable dealings between legislators and men of power in the state, Nieman returned to Milwaukee when the session was over and was rewarded with the city editor's job. Within a year he was named managing editor of the *Sentinel*, a job he kept until 1880.

Nieman's natural genius for straight thinking and for ferreting out the news was recognized by more senior members of his profession. Grant, in reflecting on Nieman's early career, said, "At 21 . . . he had become a 'newspaperman' and did his best to collect, edit and print the news fully and truthfully. There were no side issues, no secret concessions or compromises of any sort, and this was the cornerstone of his success, because newspapers at that time were largely political organs or tools in the hands of wealthy men with outside interests to which their newspapers were subservient."

Nieman grew frustrated with restraints being placed on him as editor at the *Sentinel*, and he accepted the challenge to revive the dying *St. Paul Dispatch* in Minnesota. Within a year Nieman had turned the paper's editorial and financial situation around and was offered a one-third interest in the paper. But, homesick for Milwaukee, he declined and returned to the *Sentinel*. Shortly thereafter the *Sentinel* was bought by a Republican, Horace Rublee, who wanted it to be a political mouthpiece rather than a hard-hitting nonpartisan newspaper. Nieman soon left to find a paper more suited to his Democratic temperament.

He found what he was looking for in the floundering *Daily Journal*, a paper begun by two Democrats, Peter V. Deuster and Michael Kraus, as an English version of the German daily *Seebote*. The

Daily Journal's first edition was 16 November 1882. Three weeks later—two days before his twenty-fifth birthday—the enterprising Nieman had bought Deuster's half-interest for a modest price and had set himself up as the co-owner, editor, reporter, and sometime typesetter of the *Daily Journal*.

In his first editorial on 11 December, Nieman told the reading public: "The Journal will be independent and aggressive, but always with a due regard to the sanctities of private life. It will oppose every political 'machine' and cabal, venal politicians of every stripe, every form of oppression, and at the same time give all the news for two cents. It will be the people's paper, and will recognize that its field is Milwaukee and the state at large." For half a century Nieman attempted to put into practice the philosophy he set forth in his first editorial. Harry Grant said of Nieman, "A wholesome respect for facts helped form his editorial opinion and gave him courage as an editor to meet issues in a way that made his decisions seem simple and inevitable, and in no way courageous. He was conducting a newspaper and its duty was to print the news; the news was a presentation of available facts, and that was all there was to it."

Nieman was never averse to taking a stand, even when it was unpopular, yet he was willing to present readers with two sides of an issue. When the *Journal* for a brief time was the official Democratic paper of Wisconsin, he insisted upon publishing all political news and developments, whether favorable to his party or not. Under Nieman's direction, the *Journal* took a strong stand against judges having political affiliations, for electing U.S. senators and even the president by direct popular vote, and for municipal home rule.

The *Journal* distinguished itself in its early years for both concise and thorough reporting. At the turn of the century telegraph news was usually given undeserved prominence simply because it was more expensive to obtain. Nieman stopped the practice of padding these wire stories and gave them only the play appropriate to the subject.

Nieman cared about words. Often he would request that a particularly sensitive story be sent to him in proof so that he would be sure the accompanying headline did not give the wrong impression. When he would settle down to getting a thing "right," he would labor over the proper phrasing. "Somehow, the word dropped out of the hat in time to make the press, but often not until a half dozen co-workers had come near nervous prostration," recalled one employee. In the early days Nieman would stand in the pressroom until he had read the paper through. If anything was wrong, the press would be stopped and the type in error removed. Nieman would then dash upstairs to the composing room, reset the type himself, and carry it back down in a composing stick.

Nieman was innovative not only in the careful, judicious use of words but also in the manner in which he reported the news. In his early legislative correspondence he got away from the routine and superficial means of reporting in vogue at the time. He analyzed bills, outlined their essential provisions, and wrote careful and objective summaries on their progress.

Nieman's sense of news was apparent in his sensitivity to people: he knew what made them tick. Politicians were often surprised to find their plans revealed in the *Journal* when they had tried to keep them secret, but Nieman explained, "When you've been around where those fellows talk with each other as much as I have, you know how their minds work."

Nieman's resourcefulness helped him not only to capture the news of the day but also to target it to the right audience. From early in his career Nieman was mindful of the importance of women as readers. This was reflected both in the paper's content and in the hiring of female reporters in days when a woman in the newsroom was cause for raised eyebrows beneath green eyeshades. Nieman figured, and accurately so, that an evening paper was left at home for the women to read after the men of the household had finished with it, whereas a morning paper was often taken on the trolley to work and never seen by the distaff side. By 1890 the *Journal* had hired Milwaukee's first woman editorial writer, Mary Stewart, and its first full-time woman reporter, Ida Mae Jackson. Also serving on the staff at the turn of the century were Zona Gale and Edna Ferber, both of whom later gained prominence as novelists. These women covered hard news as well as women's features and occasionally even earned a by-line, a rare occurrence for any reporter in those days.

Another early innovation of the *Journal* was the Green Sheet, instituted around 1890 as a sports summary wraparound for the final street edition. Discontinued during World War I for lack of newsprint, it was revived in the early 1920s as a two-page daily feature section printed on green paper. Its gossipy content was aimed to fight the sensationalism of the *Journal*'s Hearst-owned competitor, the *Wisconsin News*. In the late 1920s, however, under the editorship of Larry Lawrence, the Green Sheet became a family rather than a sensational feature page and was made a part of home-delivered editions as well as street sales. In 1934 it was expanded to four pages. Today the Green Sheet remains one of the hallmarks of the paper.

Whether it be women on the editorial staff or a green-colored feature page, Nieman was willing to gamble on a new idea and stick with it until it became a success. He was also willing to work to bring about success. Nieman once said, "Only a journalist has office hours. A newspaperman never rests." He worked long hours and expected no less from those under him. Perry Olds said of him, "He could give you more work than you could possibly do. And you did it. He would order a story for nine in the morning that you were sure you couldn't manage in less than a week—and the story was on his desk at nine. The usual reward," he added, "was one sharp glance and one smile—and you were good for another twenty-four hours without sleep. You got the feeling you were living the news and you reveled in it."

Before starting the day Nieman would stop by the composing room and ask the foreman, "How's the space?", referring to the day's allotment of news space. Later, when the dispatch department took over the duty of determining space, Nieman continued his practice of asking the composer. One day a printer, upon being queried by Nieman in his usual fashion, replied that the editor should check with so-and-so in the dispatch room. "Is he a printer?" asked Nieman. "No," was the answer. "Well, how can a man know anything about space if he's not a printer?" retorted Nieman.

In 1892 a large fire broke out in the city and threatened the building which housed the *Journal*'s bitterest rival, the *Sentinel*. Nieman went over to the *Sentinel* and upon going in met Albert Huegin, the general manager. He and Nieman were not on speaking terms—for business, not personal reasons—but Nieman put out his hand and said, "Hello, Al. It looks like the fire's coming this way. I just wanted to let you know that if it does, you can come over and use our presses and equipment to get out the morning paper." The *Sentinel* building was saved, but the offer stood as a credit to Nieman.

One cause for which the *Journal* fought hard and won—but later regretted having done so—was the defeat of a bill known as the Bennett Law, proposed in 1899, that would have required all public and private schools in the state to teach reading, writing, arithmetic, and American history in English, not German. The bill failed, but during World War I the *Journal* recognized the danger of division in America against which the author of the Bennett Law had sought to safeguard the schools. Nieman in an editorial publicly acknowledged that the paper had been mistaken in its fight and urged against teaching German to any child below high-school age for fear such teaching would foster disloyalty.

On 29 November 1900 Nieman married Agnes Elizabeth Gunther Wahl, a leader of Milwaukee's social and intellectual life. She was the daughter of Christian Wahl, who had been one of Milwaukee's most public-spirited citizens and the father of the city's public park system. Mrs. Nieman is said to have been Nieman's closest friend as well as his devoted wife. The couple had no children, but their niece, Faye McBeath, was their substitute daughter and served on the *Journal* staff for many years.

Prior to and during World War I, the *Journal* engaged F. Perry Olds, a recent graduate of Harvard College, to translate German articles and editorials printed by the one German daily and ten German weeklies in the city. Perry translated more than 5,000,000 words from German sources; the paper printed 750,000 of them and made the translations available to other newspapers. These translations provided readers with a clear sense of the propaganda being used to gain support for Germany in the United States. As a result, in 1919 the *Journal* was awarded the Pulitzer Prize for the "most disinterested and meritorious service rendered by any American newspaper during the year." The award resulted from the *Journal*'s "strong and courageous campaign for Americanism in a constituency where foreign elements made such a policy hazardous from a business point of view." Editorially the *Journal* wrote that the honor of the prize belonged to the state, not the paper: "Wisconsin, which has been so misrepresented and so maligned and so misunderstood, is awarded the Pulitzer medal for its patriotism in the Great War."

A man who in his teen years had impressed the editor of the *Sentinel* by his unusually neat attire as a composing-room worker, Nieman maintained a gentlemanly demeanor throughout his career. He was an enthusiastic bicyclist and horseman in his early days and later became a devotee of golf, bridge, and whist. The man who worked most closely with him, Harry Grant, described Nieman as "a little diffident with strangers, but a very choice friend to those who got to know him."

A few years after World War I ended, Nieman turned most of the daily operation of the paper over to Grant. A stroke had left him nearly paralyzed and dumb. According to Billy Sixty, Nieman had for many years kept a confidential file in his office. Into it went scraps of personal information about people in public life, evidence of graft or faithlessness. The material was sealed in linen envelopes with captions written in shorthand by his secretary. When Nieman gave up active management of the paper, the material was turned over to one man, who was told to destroy whatever could not be put in the open files. Ninety-five percent of the material was destroyed. That person often remarked that anyone with blackmail proclivities could have realized a "cool million" out of the slips that were burned.

By 1924, when the *Journal* moved into its present quarters on Fourth and State streets, Neiman had recovered enough to participate briefly in the cornerstone-laying ceremony. He was then sixty-seven. According to *Journal* historian Robert Wells, "The cane he had once swung so jauntily was now a necessity. His hairline had retreated to mid-scalp. He was a bit stooped, but he was still a sprightly dresser with his pearl gray spats and his pince-nez glasses suspended on a ribbon."

Eight years later, Nieman was on hand for the paper's fiftieth anniversary celebration. The event was jubilant, even though the Depression had taken its toll on the city and on the paper. Between 1929 and 1933 the value of Milwaukee-made products declined from $700 million to $272 million, and the number of wage earners from 94,000 to 55,000. *Journal* employees were given no raises in 1931, workers began to be laid off in 1932, and salaries were cut in 1933 for those fortunate enough to still have jobs. The legalization of "3.2 percent" beer in 1933, however, put Milwaukee back on its feet. With the reopening of the city's breweries, 8,500 jobs were created, and the beer capital of the world began to pull itself out of the Depression.

Nieman lived to see his *Journal* awarded the second of five Pulitzers in its first 100 years for a cartoon by Ross Lewis in 1934. The remaining three awards, in 1953, 1966, and 1977, were given for the type of public service, investigative work that was and is the *Journal*'s trademark.

At the time of his death on 1 October 1935, Nieman's estate was valued at about $10,000,000, a little less than half representing his *Journal* stock. Aside from specific bequests to two employees, three-quarters of the estate was left to his wife and one-quarter to his niece. The *Journal* stock was to be sold within five years with half the profits going to his wife and half to Miss McBeath. But four months after his death, Nieman's wife died on 5 February 1936. She had willed the bulk of her estate to Harvard University to "promote and elevate the standards of journalism." Harvard president James B. Conant accepted. The will was contested by two half uncles and a half aunt of Mrs. Nieman's, but they lost the case, and the Nieman Foundation began to provide fellowships to working journalists in 1938. Nine fellowships were awarded the first year and about twelve each succeeding year.

Harvard created the endowment by selling Nieman's stock to Harry Grant, who had long wished to establish an employee-ownership plan at the paper. Grant used his stock, along with that of Nieman's heirs and a third principal stockholder, to create the stock pool which was offered to employees and which continues today to provide financial stability to one of the most successful employee-owned newspapers in the world.

In tribute to Nieman after his death, the paper's primary competitor, the *Sentinel*, printed a signed editorial by its publisher, Paul Bock: "Mr. Nieman's ability, his courage, and his energy in building up one of the leading newspapers of the land were recognized throughout the newspaper world. His newspaper will live after him and be his monument."

Bock's prediction has been realized. The newspapering ideals fostered by Lucius W. Nieman are perpetuated today not only through the Nieman Fellowships but also through the daily publication of the award-winning newspaper he founded.

References:

Will C. Conrad, Kathleen F. Wilson, and Dale Wilson, *The Milwaukee Journal: The First Eighty Years* (Madison: University of Wisconsin Press, 1964);

Harry J. Grant, "Lucius W. Nieman, Newspaperman" (Cambridge, Mass.: Nieman Foundation, Harvard University, 1941);

Robert W. Wells, *The Milwaukee Journal: An Informal Chronicle of Its First 100 Years* (Milwaukee: Journal Company, 1981).

Adolph S. Ochs

Susan G. Barnes
University of Tennessee

BIRTH: Cincinnati, Ohio, 12 March 1858, to Julius and Bertha Ochs.

MARRIAGE: 28 February 1883 to Effie Miriam Wise; child: Iphigene.

MAJOR POSITIONS HELD: Owner and publisher, *Chattanooga Times* (1878-1935); owner and publisher, *The Tradesman* (1879-1899); general manager and chairman of the executive committee, Southern Associated Press (1891-1894); owner and publisher, *New York Times* (1896-1935); owner and publisher, *Philadelphia Times*, merged with *Philadelphia Public Ledger* in 1902 (1901-1913); director and executive committee member, Associated Press (1908-1935).

AWARDS AND HONORS: M.A., Yale University, 1922; LL.D., Columbia University, 1924; Litt.D., University of Chattanooga, 1925; Litt.D., New York University, 1926; Litt.D., Lincoln Memorial University, 1928; LL.D., Dartmouth College, 1932;

Chevalier of the Order of the Legion of Honor, France, 1919, Officer, 1924; National Institute of Social Science gold medal, 1929; American Philosophical Society member, 1931; Tennessee Newspaper Hall of Fame, 1969.

DEATH: Chattanooga, Tennessee, 8 April 1935.

BOOK: *Address by Adolph S. Ochs before the Pulitzer School of Journalism, Columbia University* (New York: Privately printed, 1925).

PERIODICAL PUBLICATION: "Standards of Journalism," *Journal of the National Institute of Social Sciences*, 12 (1927): 7-10.

When Adolph Simon Ochs began his journalism career in 1869, he earned $1.50 a week delivering newspapers in Knoxville, Tennessee. At his death sixty-six years later, he had built the *New York Times* to a half-million daily circulation and made it one of the most respected newspapers in the world.

Adolph Ochs (Culver Pictures)

Ochs was a man of little formal education, ending his sporadic schooling permanently at the age of fifteen. He was heaped with honorary university degrees late in his life after creating a publishing empire that today produces books, magazines, trade journals, and scholarly reference works as well as newspapers. The *New York Times* building, housing the editorial offices of many of these publications, occupies a good portion of the most valuable real estate in midtown Manhattan.

That empire, and the remarkable journalism career on which it was built, began when Adolph Ochs, and later his brothers George and Milton, began delivering the *Knoxville Chronicle* in the east Tennessee city of 3,000 where their father had been very briefly successful in the dry goods business. Julius and Bertha Ochs, German Jews who came to America during Europe's mid-nineteenth-century political unrest, reared six children in Knoxville, but not without severe financial trials in the aftermath of the Civil War. Julius Ochs—soldier, bookkeeper, merchant, public servant, and unpaid rabbi—was a wanderer of considerable intellect but little business acumen. It was the task of his eldest

son, Adolph, to give the Ochs family the financial independence and position of respect that it still enjoys.

The success of this former Knoxville newspaper carrier reads like a prototype "rags-to-riches" story. Adolph Ochs at age twenty was owner and publisher of his own newspaper in Chattanooga, Tennessee. At age thirty-eight Ochs purchased a controlling interest in the *New York Times* based on the success he enjoyed in reviving the *Chattanooga Times* in 1878. Once a respected journal during the Civil War, the *New York Times* in 1896 was all but finished after a period of bad management and uncertain editorial policy. Young Ochs had watched his father flounder from occupation to occupation and had vowed, therefore, to concentrate his own efforts in the field he knew best, the "newspaper game." Backed only by his reputation as a small-town Tennessee publisher, Ochs proceeded to make the *Times* once again the *news* paper for New Yorkers and the world. In an age of screaming headlines and yellow journalism, the *Times* became under the Ochs banner a newspaper for "intelligent, thoughtful people." A quarter-century after Ochs acquired it, the *Times*, in its owner's estimation, was not just a newspaper but an institution, one that had successfully separated news from opinion.

It was difficult for Adolph Ochs himself to comprehend his own accomplishments. In a letter to his uncle Oscar Levy in 1881, shortly after the *Chattanooga Times* had begun to show a profit, Ochs wrote, "Does it not puzzle you, when you stop to think of it, how I ever came to be a newspaper man. It is even to me." That his entire family would be so deeply involved in journalism was no less a surprise to Julius Ochs, who had always tried but failed miserably to provide the best for his family. Biographers of Julius Ochs labeled him a failure; "a greater misfit can hardly be imagined," wrote Gerald White Johnson of the aimless intellectual who was Adolph Ochs's father. However, the success of Julius Ochs would ultimately be measured in the successes of his children. In 1887, the year before his death, Julius Ochs wrote in his memoirs "My subsequent history is submerged in the achievements of my children." In rearing those children Julius and Bertha Ochs instilled in them a strong sense of right and wrong, a respect for their Jewish faith and for morality, a penchant for decisive, independent action, and an unshakable family loyalty—all qualities that surfaced in Adolph Ochs's operation of the *New York Times*.

In truth, it would appear that the only endeavor at which Julius Ochs was ever successful was the upbringing of his children. Julius immigrated to Louisville, Kentucky, in 1845 from his home in Fürth, Bavaria. Fluent in French, Italian, Spanish, and Hebrew, as well as German and English, Ochs became a French teacher at a girls' school in Mt. Sterling, Kentucky.

Ochs enlisted in the United States Army during the Mexican War but never got into the fighting. As the war ended he found himself in Natchez, Mississippi. He opened a relatively successful dry goods business, met his future wife, and developed a loathing for slavery that separated Julius and Bertha Ochs politically the rest of their lives. As a fifteen-year-old student at Heidelberg Seminary in Germany, Bertha Levy had been forced to leave her homeland to live with an uncle in Natchez after she took part in a demonstration at the graves of some slain revolutionaries. She became steeped in Southern thought and tradition and later caused her husband considerable discomfort in aiding the Confederacy during the Civil War.

The couple were married in Nashville, Tennessee, where Ochs had opened another dry goods business. Bertha's friends were inclined to think she had "driven her ducks to the wrong market" in

Ochs in his cadet's uniform during his brief period as a student at East Tennessee University in Knoxville

marrying Julius and noted that she was giving embroidery lessons soon after the marriage to make ends meet.

The couple moved to Cincinnati, where four of their surviving six children were born (their first son, Louis, died in infancy)—Adolph in 1858, Nannie in 1860, George in 1861, and Milton in 1864. Ochs was in Nashville to open a branch of a wholesale jewelry house when the Civil War broke out. He rushed north to join the Union army, serving as a member of the Cincinnati home guard charged with keeping open the bridge over the Ohio River to Kentucky.

It was over the very bridge her husband guarded that Bertha was caught smuggling quinine to rebel troops camped near her family's home in Covington, Kentucky, just across the river. She had concealed the illegal drugs in the diapers of her son George, and later Adolph Ochs would delight in reducing George to tears by saying that it was actually he, Adolph, who was the war's youngest smuggler.

At the end of the war, Julius and Bertha Ochs found it desirable to settle in an area where neither would feel adverse effects of their wartime sentiments. Such a place was Knoxville, a city that had been "equally divided" in sympathy between North and South. In late 1864 Ochs opened a dry goods store on Gay Street, selling "Clothing, Boots, Shoes, Hats, Caps, Hosiery, Notions, Stationery, and Cigars." A year later he opened two more stores. The value of goods in one store alone was $30,000, a sum "considerable in those days," Ochs pointed out in his memoirs.

The Ochs family had its first permanent home, a veritable mansion, on Cumberland Avenue, where they were hosts to lavish parties and evenings of the music Julius loved, as well as an eighty-one-acre farm four miles from the city. Besides assuming numerous civic offices, Julius became the first rabbi for the fledgling Jewish congregation, Beth El, which met in the back of a vinegar store, the members seated on pickle barrels to hear sermons in German and English. The Ochs children attended Professor Bradford's Hampden-Sydney Academy; Julius, like his father before him, insisted that his children be well educated. George took music lessons, and Bertha taught the girls "fancy work."

The idyllic existence was not to continue. In 1867 a postwar financial panic swept the nation, the soldiers and their fat pay envelopes all went home, and the Ochs dry goods company was saddled with a warehouse full of merchandise bought at inflated wartime prices that it could not sell. Ochs declared personal bankruptcy on 30 October 1868. The mansion on Cumberland and the farm in the country gone, the family moved to an unpainted, rented house just east of downtown on Water Street. For the next eleven years, Julius Ochs had no really steady income.

"I retained nothing save my good name," wrote Julius, "a clear conscience, and the respect of my friends and neighbors." He also retained the fierce loyalty of his family, and his sons were quick to step in to help the family finances. Out of dire financial necessity, and not from some burning inner desire to fulfill an inherent talent, Adolph Ochs, at age eleven, entered the "newspaper game." He became a carrier for the new *Knoxville Chronicle*, with a route that took him over four square miles of East Knoxville in the early morning darkness. The paper, founded by Capt. William Rule and H. C. Tarwater, was at first published only once a week, but soon it became a daily, raising Adolph's income from 25 cents to $1.50 a week from his fifty customers. His brother George also had a route, and the boys would arise at 3:00 A.M. to go to the *Chronicle* office on Gay Street to hand-fold their papers as they came off the press. The work was a hardship, since the boys had to be at the Bell House Public School by 7:00 A.M., but it was a necessary evil for the debt-plagued Ochses.

"My work was not a matter of choice," Adolph Ochs wrote in 1933 to his Chattanooga carrier boys, "but it was a welcome little contribution to my family's needs." From that early experience on the *Chronicle*, "I thus learned to work, be helpful, and to do my work conscientiously. . . . I regard it as a fortunate episode in my life that I began so early to work and be helpful to my family." In fact, the Ochs boys' lot in life was not much different from that of others in the postwar South, when entire families had to pitch in to survive economic hardships. However, few proved to be as successful in the Horatio Alger mold as Adolph Ochs.

The hardships that the family had known shaped the character of the eldest Ochs son. He had watched his brilliant but ineffectual father drift along with little purpose and had resolved to accomplish much more with his own life. Though he possessed some of his father's idealism, Adolph was endowed with a healthy dose of *chutzpah* from his mother. The woman who had defied German authority in Europe so long ago favored Adolph over her other children, recognizing, perhaps, the special qualities that would make him such a success. Adolph became, even as a young boy, "a little father figure . . . even to his own father."

Julius, however, did not watch his young sons go off to help support the family without some feeling of regret. He would arise with them in the early morning and walk with them in the dark to the *Chronicle* office, "a kind of humble apology, his way of letting them know that he shared the discomforts that resulted from his misfortunes." In return, the boys handed over their pay envelopes each week, unopened, from which they received a "small weekly allowance as spending money." Julius also expected them to remain in school. During the times that their work schedules prevented formal schooling, Julius tutored them at home.

Adolph continued his paper route for two years and did his work "conscientiously, and in wet weather I saw that the paper was put in a dry place," he recalled in 1933. "So excellent was my service on my route, I received a nice little Christmas present from everyone on my route." However, the financial burden on the family was worsening, and Julius took his eldest son to live with Bertha's brother Oscar in Providence, Rhode Island. Adolph worked in his uncle's drugstore, but lost the job for selling a customer borax instead of sal soda. (In 1881, as a successful publisher in Chattanooga, Ochs assured his uncle that he was much more dependable, "not the same boy I was in Providence.") He worked for a while as a cash boy in a grocery store and attended Warner's Business School. In only a few months, he was back in Knoxville, working as an office boy for Capt. Rule's *Chronicle*.

Adolph Ochs in 1872 still only earned $1.50 a week to sweep floors, clean lamps, empty cuspidors, and take crude practical jokes from the older staff members, but he no longer had to walk the early morning streets of Knoxville carrying papers. He also began to learn the printing trade, watching H. C. Collins run the presses and hand-set type until well after midnight, when Collins and young Ochs would walk home together past the First Presbyterian Church graveyard, an area Ochs was afraid to pass by alone. Ochs performed his tasks so well that he was soon promoted to delivery boy at $3 a week, which he handed over to his father in its entirety until he became a real newspaperman—a printer's devil—at fifteen.

The full-time job meant that Ochs had to quit school for good, having finished only a few intermittent months in the preparatory grades at East Tennessee University, forerunner of the University of Tennessee. Ochs was, remembered Collins, a quick learner, finishing the four-year printing apprenticeship in half the normal time. Ochs learned lessons from Collins that followed him throughout his life; the chief one was that no matter what the content, if a paper was poorly printed, it would not be read. At the *Chattanooga Times* and later at the *New York Times*, Ochs refined printing processes to an art and showed a marked lack of tolerance for typographical errors. Able to hand-set type faster and more accurately than anyone else at the *Chronicle*, Ochs later maintained an affinity for the "back shop" of his newspapers. Late in his life, negotiating a contract with the unionized printers of the *New York Times*, he said, "I still feel I am on the wrong side of this table. I belong with the boys from the composing room."

After three years as Collins's helper, Ochs felt that he had learned all he could of his trade, and the financial pinch at home was worse than ever. He decided to seek his fortune in California and gathered recommendations from Capt. Rule and other Knoxville businessmen. Rule called him a "young man worthy of confidence and esteem . . . quick to comprehend and faithful to execute whatever may be entrusted to him," with "intellect capable of reaching the highest point of mental achievement." S. C. Ramage, editor of a rival Knoxville paper, said he was "a young man of unusual promise to society and his fellow man." His fellow *Chronicle* printers, inscribing a book of Thomas Hood's poems as a going-away gift, predicted that Adolph Ochs would eventually be counted "among the nation's honored sons."

Those high words of praise got the young newspaperman only as far as Louisville, where he boarded with cousins and landed a job as typesetter on Henry Watterson's *Courier-Journal*. He was soon promoted to assistant composing room foreman and eventually to reporter. Ochs's first—and only—major assignment was to cover the burial of Andrew Johnson at Greeneville, Tennessee, in July 1875. Adolph Ochs, premier typesetter, proved to be a rather dull writer, convincing him that his talents lay in the business and mechanical operations of journalism. Judging from his later handwritten correspondence, it does not appear that Ochs's lack of formal education was a handicap to his writing. Some of his biographers have claimed that his ungrammatical prose kept Ochs from pursuing a writing career and embarrassed him throughout his life, but his letters to his family and business associates are grammatical, though rather stilted and formal.

Whatever the reason (most likely homesickness), Ochs gave up a reporting career with the *Courier-Journal* and returned to Knoxville in less than a year without ever seeing the Pacific. While in Louisville, he had sent almost all of his money home to his mother after she wrote him that she was "ashamed to send the children to school" because they had "no decent shoes and no stockings, and their clothes are almost past mending." It was clear to the seventeen-year-old Ochs that it was up to him to keep the family from disintegrating.

However, he chose not to return to the *Chronicle*, where his brothers were still newsboys and he would be only a printer's devil again. At almost eighteen he thought he should be "more than an office boy grown up" and joined the staff of John Fleming's new *Knoxville Tribune* as assistant to the composing room foreman. There his typesetting talents and "grim application to business" attracted the attention of the *Tribune*'s business manager, Franc M. Paul, who promoted Ochs to be his assistant. The connection led Ochs to his first venture as a publisher in Chattanooga. He often talked with Paul about his ambition to have his own newspaper, citing as his ideal Horace Greeley, who had risen from poverty to the ownership of the powerful *New York Tribune*. Ochs did not envy "the young man or young woman born with a golden spoon in the mouth" but held in awe those successful entrepreneurs who had risen from humble beginnings. An Ochs-owned newspaper, though, seemed impossible given the family's financial circumstances.

Paul, a former editor of the *Chattanooga Rebel*, had gained a reputation for rehabilitating failing newspapers and putting new ventures on sound financial footing. That reputation helped him convince Ochs in 1876 to join him in Chattanooga as "business solicitor"—advertising manager—for the *Daily Dispatch*, a sheet that had been barely surviving in the rough frontier town 100 miles south of Knoxville. Ochs had no money at all to sink into the venture, and Paul and editor J. E. MacGowan had only a few hundred dollars in capital. Since Ochs's uncle, Samuel Bissinger, had moved to Chattanooga and could provide him a place to live, the young man decided to join Paul and MacGowan in the venture.

It was fortunate that Ochs had guaranteed room and board in his new home, because the *Dispatch* folded after only a few months. It was so poorly printed as to be almost unreadable; and a large proportion of Chattanooga's population was illiterate anyway, dooming the newspaper almost from the start. Paul went back to Knoxville to work for the *Tribune*, but MacGowan and Ochs were too poor to return with him. However, Ochs had so impressed the paper's creditors with his business sense that he was appointed receiver for the bankrupt venture and eventually liquidated every cent of debt incurred by the *Dispatch*.

The *Dispatch*'s job-printing operation remained intact after the newspaper's failure, and Ochs set about putting the old Gordon handpress to use. While settling the *Dispatch*'s debts he had noted that the rough-and-tumble river town—it had an aura not unlike that of the Wild West—had no city directory. Ochs and David Harris, another printer left jobless by the *Dispatch*'s failure, went to every store, bank, mansion, and shack to record its location and the residents' occupations for their *Chattanooga City Directory*. The directory served two purposes: it revealed new avenues for expansion in the city that old-line Chattanoogans had overlooked, and it introduced an enterprising young printer to some of the most influential businessmen and financiers in the city. Ochs and Harris did all the work on the directory themselves, setting type, reading proofs, running the handpress, and distributing the book. The venture gave Ochs enough profit to keep him from starving for six months, and he managed to send $2 a week home to his family in Knoxville.

The year 1878 was not an auspicious one for newspapers in Chattanooga. The *Dispatch* was gone, and the remaining paper, the *Chattanooga Times*, had dwindled to a circulation of 250. Its owner, S. A. Cunningham, was looking for a buyer. Ochs, age nineteen, desperately wanted to be that buyer. He convinced MacGowan and four other printers left out of work by the *Dispatch*'s failure that they should try to take over the ailing paper, though the six men had only $3 among them. Cunningham was asking $800 for sole ownership of the *Times*, and Ochs went into action, using the contacts he had made in preparing the *Chattanooga City Directory* to secure financing. With his talent for convincing other people, usually men much older and more experienced than himself, of his ability to succeed at whatever he tried, Ochs persuaded Cunningham to sell him a half interest in the paper for $250. He secured an option to buy the other half in two years at a price to be fixed according to the paper's worth at that time. Ochs borrowed the purchase price and working capital of $300 from the First National Bank of Chattanooga with a note cosigned by local businessman Eb James. After paying his staff of eight (not including himself) a short week's salary, Ochs was left with $37.50, $25.00 of which was used to subscribe to the Western Associated Press. On 2 July 1878, Julius Ochs traveled from Knoxville for the signing of ownership papers for the *Times*—not for any ceremonial reasons but because his son, at twenty, was still not old enough to conduct legal transactions.

The *Chattanooga Times* under new publisher and part-owner Adolph Ochs was a shoestring operation. There was one reporter; an office staff of one; five men in the composing room; a foreman who was proofreader and pressman; part-time editor MacGowan; and Ochs, who was editorial supervisor, business manager, and advertising salesman. The payroll was $100 per week, with no compensation going to the owner-publisher except for bare essentials. All profits were plowed back into the *Times*, and at the end of the year the paper had taken in $12,000 with expenses of only $10,000. Circulation and advertising had improved dramatically, as had the appearance and content of the paper. Ochs had expanded national and international coverage in the *Times* with the addition of the wire service and was constantly upgrading his equipment to improve readability. Unlike other small-town papers of the late 1870s, the *Times* did not depend on any one political party or business interest for its survival, raising its editorial voice instead for the benefit of all "business, commercial and productive, of Chattanooga, and of the mineral and agricultural districts" of the area. The *Times* adopted conservative Democratic party allegiance (the only Republicans in Chattanooga at the time were freed slaves who could not read) but reserved the right of independent policy.

The *Chattanooga Times* under Ochs became the leading voice for promoting growth and progress of the city. He advocated a nonpartisan city government, which became a reality. He pushed for the building of a sewer system, the founding of the University of Chattanooga, improvement of schools and theaters, and later the establishment of the Chickamauga and Lookout Mountain National Parks. He sang the praises of the area in the columns of the *Times* and attracted new business, becoming recognized as a leader in the postwar South's Reconstruction. The people of Chattanooga, who, Ochs was convinced, wanted such a progressive, impartial voice in a newspaper, supported the *Times* and made it a financial success, though not without some sleepless nights being spent by the publisher.

Pouring all of the profits back into the paper, Ochs was usually perilously short of cash. He was able in 1880 to buy the other half of the paper outright from Cunningham for about $5,000. Ochs had brought his entire family to Chattanooga in 1879, after all their household goods had been auctioned to pay their debts, and his two brothers and father were employed by the *Times*. Adolph Ochs, at age twenty-two, had become one of Chattanooga's leading citizens. In January 1882 he was successful enough to pay $5,000 for a large red-brick house at Cedar and Fifth Streets, in which he installed the five other Ochs offspring and both parents. George was able to graduate from the University of Tennessee in Knoxville, and Milton could attend Chickering Institute in Cincinnati. Nannie, from her brother's largess, attended Virginia Intermont College in Bristol; Ada and Mattie, the younger girls, went to a private seminary in Chattanooga.

The family was always grateful to Ochs for rescuing them from the poverty they had known in Knoxville. "Adolph, even when we were little children, was the pride of the household," wrote George in his memoirs, "a pattern of filial and fraternal devotion, and in his early years gave promise of the high destiny which lay before him." He "never wavered as the guiding spirit of our household. His energy, his ability, his industry, his unselfish helpfulness to each member of the family, were an inspiration." Adolph Ochs remained devoted to his family throughout his newspaper career both in Chattanooga and in New York, so much so that the *New York Times* has been called a "towering totem to nepotism."

Adolph Ochs's imposing home, under the able direction of Bertha, became a social center for prominent Chattanoogans whom Ochs had impressed with his success and for visiting dignitaries, eventually including President Grover Cleveland. Ochs traveled widely on the free railroad pass accorded members of the press. It was on a trip to Cincinnati that he met Effie Miriam Wise, the daughter of Rabbi Isaac M. Wise, the leader of the Reform Jewish movement in the United States in which the Ochs family was active. The two were married in February 1883. The new Mrs. Ochs was content to let her mother-in-law continue to manage the household and busied herself with writing book reviews for her husband's newspaper. Their only surviving child (two died in infancy), Iphigene, was born in 1892.

It seemed that, with the birth of his daughter, the life of Adolph Ochs was complete. He had been instrumental in the reconstruction of his adopted city and was one of its most prominent citizens. His high praise for Chattanooga through the pages of the *Times*—the paper was called "the Builder of Chattanooga"—had attracted outside investments and new business to the city, setting off a land speculation boom that reached a pinnacle in 1886.

Ochs himself had been drawn into the speculative fever and had bought large tracts of land around the city while also signing notes for others to do so. Consequently his cash reserves were stretched thin when it was discovered that the iron ore deposits on much of the land were too sulfurous to produce high quality steel. Land prices dropped, and the enterprising young businessman found himself in nearly the same fix in which his father had been twenty years before.

However, Adolph Ochs still had a going business—the newspaper—bringing in handsome profits. Extricating himself from his land deals, he resolved never again to enter into any business venture in which he was not an expert. To still any community gossip about his precarious financial position, he built a new plant for the *Times*, complete with the newest equipment and a gold dome, with $150,000 in borrowed money. It was the most impressive building in Chattanooga, but its proud owner was diligently looking for another ailing newspaper to rejuvenate as he had the *Times*, hoping to improve his cash flow. In arranging the loans for his new *Times* office and in looking for his second newspaper, Ochs traveled frequently to New York. There he made the acquaintances that would eventually lead him to the purchase of the *New York Times*.

By 1895 Ochs had all but abandoned the idea of buying another Southern newspaper. The panic of 1893 had left his finances even more precarious, forcing him to mortgage the new *Times* building, which he had vowed never to do. He confided to his wife that he felt he was only "a country newspaperman burdened with debt." His negotiations to buy the ailing *New York Mercury* had failed, largely because he had hotly opposed the free coinage of silver in his *Chattanooga Times* editorial pages, and the *Mercury* partners wanted the New York paper to maintain opposition to the gold standard. Unwilling to compromise his principles, Ochs had broken off negotiations when Harry Alloway, Wall Street reporter for the *New York Times*, tipped him off that the paper that had built its reputation for accurate reporting during the Civil War might be for sale.

Some six years before, Ochs had casually remarked to Alloway that the *New York Times* "offered the greatest opportunity in American journalism." Founded by George Jones and Henry Raymond in 1851, the *Times* had begun to fade after Jones's death in 1891. A group of staff members, headed by editor Charles R. Miller, had bought the paper from Jones's heirs for $1,000,000, but almost immediately their working capital was depleted by the panic of 1893. The yellow penny press of the city was throwing a new sensation at New Yorkers every day, and the respectable—and more expensive—*Times* found it impossible to compete.

When Ochs, just turned thirty-eight, received Alloway's message about the possible sale of the paper, the "country newspaperman" was ecstatic. It never occurred to him that he might not have the reputation or knowledge to revitalize the most venerable newspaper in America; it also was no problem to him that he was already heavily in debt. He rushed to New York to convince Miller that Adolph Ochs could save the *New York Times*.

In a letter to Effie upon his arrival, he wrote, "I doubt if there are many men in these United States who are as subject to the caprices of circumstances as I am. Here I am in New York less than twenty-four hours ready to negotiate for the leading and most influential newspaper in America. . . . Now for the supreme gall of a country newspaperman burdened with debt. Alloway thinks I am the man—the ideal man—for *The Times*."

Miller, upon meeting the young Southern publisher, thought so, too. Miller and the other owners were particularly concerned that the paper, "an institution of great and honorable tradition," should be bought by someone capable of carrying on that tradition. They did not want to see the *Times* sink to the level of the yellow press, but with a circulation of only 9,000, it was losing $1,000 a day; its total debt stood at $300,000. After a long interview with Ochs, who once again displayed his ability to impress older and wiser men, Miller was convinced that Ochs was the man to save the *Times*.

The offer made to Ochs to run the paper for a group of investors and to keep it strictly independent and of high quality—a yearly salary of $50,000—was attractive. But Ochs was determined to come into sole possession of the *Times*. There were stockholders and creditors to satisfy, however, and a receiver was appointed for the paper until Ochs could make his legal and financial arrangements. The many important personages who had been entertained at the red-brick house in Chattanooga were called upon to repay the kindness shown them there, and they all responded with words of high praise for Ochs. President Grover Cleveland wrote in his own hand: "In your management of The Chattanooga Times you have demonstrated such a faithful adherence to Democratic principles and have so bravely supported the ideas and policies which tend to the safety of our country as well as our party that I should be glad to see you in a larger sphere of usefulness." Other recommen-

dations came from H. S. Chamberlain of the First National Bank of Chattanooga, Melville E. Stone of the Associated Press, W. B. Somerville of Western Union, Gen. Joseph Wheeler of the Alabama congressional delegation, Clark Howell of the *Atlanta Constitution*, Bishop Isaac Joyce of the Chattanooga Methodist Episcopal Church, railroad and mining executives, and many others. Their praises convinced the *Times* owners that Ochs's plan to issue 10,000 shares of stock in the company, with enough shares placed in escrow to revert to his ownership at the end of three consecutive profitable years to make him majority stockholder, was a good one. He took over operation of the *Times* on 18 August 1896.

He mortgaged everything he had to raise the $75,000 to make the plan workable. The other shares of stock were bought by industrialists who saw them as a good, if speculative, investment. The only investor who really stood to lose if the venture failed was Ochs himself, and he stood to lose everything. His family back in Tennessee, with the possible exception of his wife, thought him quite daft for undertaking such a burden. Julius Ochs, bad businessman though he was, was not there to advise his son, having died of chronic bronchitis in 1888. Bertha, a woman endowed with a "brilliant intellect" and a "logical, clear mind" of her own, seriously considered having her son committed. Ochs placed his brother George in charge of his Chattanooga operations, making Milton managing editor of the *Chattanooga Times*, and turned all his efforts toward making the New York paper a success.

At first it seemed almost impossible; New York was not Chattanooga, and the newspaper competition was considerably stiffer. The *Herald* boasted the best foreign news coverage in the world, an expensive luxury the *Times* could not hope to duplicate. The *World* and the *Journal* were "wildly sensational" and cost only a penny, while the *Times* was priced at three cents. Ochs was not intimidated. He retained Miller as editor, and in the *Times*'s first issue under Ochs's ownership, the paper's new proprietor promised to "conduct a high standard newspaper, clean, dignified and trustworthy" for "thoughtful, pure-minded people." Competitors at first laughed at the "All the News That's Fit to Print" motto, introduced 25 October 1896, as they had at Jones's and Raymond's "It Does Not Soil the Breakfast Cloth" phrase earlier. When they found that Ochs adhered to the tenets of high principle and common decency in all his dealings and not just in his newspaper, the amusement died.

Ochs refused to run comics in his paper; instead, he instigated a Sunday pictorial magazine, which became the pioneer in rotogravure sections for Sunday papers. As perhaps a nod to his wife's interest in literature, he made the Saturday book-review section a regular feature, later shifting it to the Sunday edition and eventually making it a separate major publication. Letters to the editor occupied a prominent place, and readers soon began to recognize publication of their comments as a special honor and privilege. The *Times* adopted the preciseness and formality of its publisher, who called everyone from the editor to the office boy "Mister." The *Times* still maintains that editorial style for second references to everyone except criminals and sports figures.

The reading public soon expressed its approval of the *Times* concept. Circulation doubled in the first year of Ochs's ownership, and losses were cut to $200 a day. But the paper was, nevertheless, still losing money. It was therefore difficult for Ochs to turn down an offer from New York's Tammany Hall to carry its $150,000 yearly advertising. Even though the Tammany machine assured Ochs that it would not interfere in editorial policies, Ochs was convinced that the mere presence of such ads would plant doubt in his readers' minds as to the *Times*'s independence. He worked at dispelling rumors that he had been brought to New York by any special interest group to buy the *Times* as a mouthpiece. Ochs always kept his advertising and editorial policies strictly separated, a policy commonplace for respectable newspapers today but one that was highly irregular in the 1890s.

While the *Times* was making its dignified gains in circulation, to 25,000 in 1898, disaster struck. The Spanish-American War, probably caused at least in part by sensational reporting on events in Cuba in the *World* and *Journal*, began. Rival papers poured money into special correspondents, photographs, and showmanship that the *Times* could not hope to match. *Times* advertising linage dropped, and the operating deficit rose to $78,000, higher than the previous year. At this point Ochs made possibly the boldest move of his career, cutting the price of his paper to a penny when his advisers advocated raising the cost to a nickel. He believed that there was a large audience for his kind of paper and that the people who bought the yellow sheets did so because they were cheap. In the years before demographic, statistical market analyses, Ochs relied on his instinct that there was a public waiting to be served by a respectable paper, and he was right. The *New York Times* circulation jumped to 76,000 the next year, and by the third year of operation, the

paper showed a profit of $50,000. It was, Ochs said, a "vindication of the reader."

Ochs became the majority stockholder of the *New York Times* on 1 July 1900. At the silver anniversary of his ownership, in 1921, the paper boasted a gross income of $100,000,000 for those twenty-five years. Most of that money, like the income of the *Chattanooga Times*, was put directly back into the operation of the newspaper; in 1933, on his seventy-fifth birthday, Ochs could boast that not one dollar of new capital had ever been put into the paper. One of Ochs's first moves had been to buy new equipment to make the paper more readable. The innovative rotogravure unit purchased in 1914 grew until it required its own production plant, built in 1925 on West Forty-fourth Street near the imposing *Times* building constructed by Ochs on Forty-third. The area now known as Times Square had been "decidedly second-rate" when Ochs had moved in 1905 into what was to become a New York landmark. Ochs, the *Knoxville Tribune*'s most accurate and swiftest hand typesetter, kept his *New York Times* equipped with the most modern machines for composition and printing. The paper employed a staff of 3,000 in 1933 and printed a million copies of the Sunday *Times*, much of the work being done in the paper's new Brooklyn plant opened that year.

The accomplishments of Adolph Ochs's *New York Times* were not just physical and mechanical. Ochs may not have been a skillful writer or accomplished journalist himself, but he had an innate sense for talent in others. In addition to retaining Charles Miller as his editor in chief, in 1904 Ochs hired the dapper Carr V. Van Anda as managing editor of the *Times*. Van Anda, wrote Ochs in 1921, had a "genius for news-gathering and marvelous appreciation of news value and fidelity to fairness and thoroughness." Ochs also singled out for praise business manager Louis Wiley, who helped Ochs keep the paper afloat from the beginning of his ownership. William C. Reick, Arthur R. Greaves, and Henry Loewenthal were valued reporters in the early news department. Ochs and the *Times* put up $500,000 for the publication of the first *Dictionary of American Biography*. After being given a "second class" (nonvoting) membership in the new Associated Press upon his purchase of the *Times*—AP director Joseph Pulitzer had claimed the *Times* would fail soon anyway and did not rate full membership—Ochs later became a member of the wire service executive committee. He expanded its service to include wireless transmissions from Europe, having underwritten the work of the inventor Marconi. Ochs and the *Times* also financed

Front page of the New York Times *for 3 April 1917, with the full text of President Wilson's request to Congress for a declaration of war* exploration of the North and South Poles by Admirals Byrd and Peary. Charles A. Lindbergh owed much of the success of his first transatlantic flight in 1927 to financial help and publicity from the *New York Times*. Through his columns in the *Times*, Will Rogers became a household name.

Perhaps the greatest challenge to the *Times* under Ochs came with the reporting of World War I. Taking the opportunity to firmly cement its position as a newspaper of record, the *Times* distinguished itself by being the only American paper to publish the entire texts of government White Papers and official documents; it won a 1918 Pulitzer Prize for publishing the complete text of the Treaty of Versailles. The paper also deployed a larger corps of foreign correspondents to cover more war news than any of its competitors. As early as 1907, Ochs had teamed with the *London Times* to form the first transatlantic news service using Marconi's wireless telegraph, and the link served his paper well during the war. The *Times* often published more special dispatches from the combat zone than all other American papers combined. Ochs had recognized the historical implications of the *New York Times* in 1913, before the war began, when the paper began cross-referencing and indexing every item that appeared in its pages. (In 1927, the *Times* began printing a special limited daily edition on pure rag stock and permanently binding those copies.)

Before the United States entered the war, the *Times* had taken the editorial position that the Germans were in the wrong. However, the paper reported both Allied and German sides of the conflict so thoroughly that both groups of supporters in America claimed the paper was biased for the other. Ochs's brother George, acutely conscious of his German heritage during the war, legally changed his surname to Ochs-Oakes and that of his two sons to Oakes, much to the despair of the rest of the family. It was true that the Ochs family, along with many other German Americans at the time, suffered the wrath of many of their fellow Americans who questioned their loyalty. That criticism reached a zenith when, near the end of the war and with the Germans clearly losing, *Times* editor Miller wrote an editorial endorsing the Austrians' proposal for "non-binding" peace talks. The paper was flooded with angry protests accusing the *Times* of "running up the white flag." The *New York Herald* began an advertising campaign telling the public to "Read an American paper."

The incident was crushing to Ochs, who took great pride in the way his German Jewish family had assimilated itself into the mainstream of American life. A trustee of the Reform congregation of Temple Emanu-El in New York, Ochs was close to many prominent clergymen, particularly of the Methodist Church in Tennessee. Even though his stand cost him some popularity among other Jews, he had refused to advocate Zionism, saying that once in America, everyone became an American. Therefore, public reaction to the Miller editorial caused Ochs to sink deeper into a mental depression that had begun in 1916 and was to follow him through the remaining years of his life.

Ochs's periods of depression seemed to observers to indicate that the same man who could build great newspapers from ashes and continue to make bold investments of huge sums of borrowed money had difficulty living comfortably with prosperity. When his melancholia first began, Ochs had built circulation of the New York paper to almost 328,000. The Chattanooga paper continued to do well, and he had sold his *Philadelphia Public Ledger*, purchased in 1902, to Cyrus Curtis for a handsome profit. His daughter had graduated from Barnard College, much to the delight of her father, who set a great store by the higher education he never had. It appeared that the "country newspaperman" could only be happy when molding a new publication.

His depression did not completely debilitate him during the rest of his life, though it was worse in 1925 and 1929 than during other years. He began to leave important decisions concerning the *Times* to his son-in-law, Arthur Hays Sulzberger, while he traveled around the country accepting awards and honorary university degrees. His lack of education had always been an embarrassment to him. In addressing the 1925 graduating class of the Columbia School of Journalism, he asked the graduates almost wistfully, "I wonder if you appreciate the good fortune that is yours in that you have the advantage of a college education? A college education will not make a newspaper man, or any other kind of professional man, of you, but it will make a better qualified man of you, whatever your occupation."

So strong was his faith in education that he shook off his illness in 1926 to chair a committee to raise $4,000,000 for Hebrew Union College, founded in Cincinnati by his father-in-law. He devoted the latter part of his life to other causes, particularly the "Hundred Neediest Cases" charity of the *New York Times*. He had begun appeals for donations to the city's six most prominent charities through his news columns in 1911; in twenty years the fund netted $3,000,000 plus uncounted assistance in donated clothing and adopted children.

Ochs and his wife, Effie, returning from a trip on the liner
Majestic *(Bettmann Archive)*

His contribution of $400,000 for the building of the Julius and Bertha Ochs Memorial Temple in Chattanooga reaffirmed his devotion to the religious faith of his parents.

Writing in 1931 for Will Durant's book *On the Meaning of Life*, Ochs emphasized his affinity for benevolence: "Suffice it for me to say that I inherited good health and sound moral principles; I found pleasure in work that came to my hand and in doing it conscientiously; I found joy and satisfaction in being helpful to my parents and others, and in thus making my life worth while found happiness and consolation." In 1933 he was well enough to celebrate his golden wedding anniversary and his seventy-fifth birthday. Tributes from friends and world leaders poured in.

Ochs's refusal to adopt extreme positions pervaded the editorial policy of the *Times*. The paper's editorial page reflected the philosophy of the publisher that there was usually something to be said on both sides of any question. A self-proclaimed conservative Democrat, Ochs was cautious in supporting political figures, lending overt approval only to Grover Cleveland's candidacy through the Chat-

tanooga paper and to Woodrow Wilson during the war and during Wilson's fight for the League of Nations. By the time Franklin Roosevelt took office, the Democrats had become too liberal for Ochs, and the *Times* became the archenemy of the New Deal.

For all his success in New York, Adolph Ochs was, at heart, a Southerner. Even during the Depression, when the Chattanooga paper began to be a drain on the resources of the New York paper, he refused to cut his ties with his first triumph. He labored over his will, making sure that the Chattanooga paper would remain in his family as long as the *New York Times* did, and he tried to ensure that there would always be Ochses in command on West Forty-third Street. He was an active member of New York's Tennessee Society, telling visiting Tennessee Governor Henry Horton in 1928, "Distance has not diminished our love for Tennessee. On the contrary, it has grown more fervent as memory recalls happy days spent in its delightful environment. There is no more favored spot on earth than . . . the State of Tennessee."

"He never cut his roots [in the Reconstruction South]," wrote Harrison Salisbury of Ochs. It was there that Ochs went in 1935 to die. It was spring in Chattanooga, the dogwoods were blooming, and Ochs had just turned seventy-seven. He determined to make a trip back to the red-brick house at Cedar and Fifth Streets, away from the bodyguards he had hired for his grandchildren in New York in the wake of the Lindbergh kidnapping, away from Times Square, away from Hillandale, his country home in White Plains. He had just emerged, almost miraculously, from his deepest depression, brought on by the country's worsening economic condition and the rise of Hitler in Europe. He had been hospitalized, unable to make even an abbreviated round of his beloved *Times* offices, only a few weeks before he announced that he was going to Chattanooga.

He arrived in Chattanooga on 7 April and went to visit his sister Ada, wife of Harry C. Adler and mother of *New York Times* general manager Julius Ochs Adler. The next morning he went to the offices of the *Chattanooga Times*, greeting old friends and employees. At noon, his nurse, his brother Milton, and editor R. E. Walker accompanied him to lunch at a restaurant a few blocks from the *Times* building. As the waiter passed out menus, Milton turned and said, "What do you think you'll have, Adolph?" Ochs did not answer; in two hours he was dead of a cerebral hemorrhage.

Adolph Ochs was buried on 12 April in Temple Israel Cemetery, Mount Hope, New York, not far from his country home. On that day, work ceased at both the *Chattanooga Times* and *New York Times*. Flags in New York City and Tennessee flew at half-staff. The Associated Press wire fell silent all over the world for two minutes. President Roosevelt and other world leaders sent condolences to Mrs. Ochs. Perhaps the most fitting epitaph for the "country newspaperman" came in 1950, however, with the publication of the first volume of the papers of Thomas Jefferson, which the *New York Times* had underwritten. "Dedicated to Adolph S. Ochs," it read, "who by the example of a responsible press enlarged and fortified the Jeffersonian concept of a free press."

Biographies:

G. W. Johnson, *An Honorable Titan: A Biographical Study of Adolph S. Ochs* (Westport, Conn.: Greenwood Press, 1970);

LXXV: Biography of Adolph S. Ochs at 75th Birthday (Cincinnati: Hebrew Union University, American Jewish Archives, 1933).

References:

Meyer Berger, *The Story of the New York Times,*

1851-1951 (New York: Simon & Schuster, 1951);

Brownlow's Knoxville Whig and Rebel Ventilator, 23 November 1864;

Chattanooga Times, 12 March 1918;

E. H. Davis, *History of the New York Times, 1851-1921* (New York: The New York Times, 1921);

Goodspeed's History of Hamilton, Knox and Shelby Counties of Tennessee (Nashville, Tenn.: Charles and Randy Elder Booksellers, 1974)

Julius Ochs, *A Memoir of Julius Ochs: An Autobiography* (New York: Privately printed, 196?);

H. E. Salisbury, *Without Fear or Favor: The New York Times and Its Times* (New York: Times Books, 1980);

W. M. Schuyler, ed., *The Life and Letters of George Washington Ochs-Oakes* (New York: Schuyler, 1933);

Gay Talese, *The Kingdom and the Power* (New York: World, 1969).

Papers:

Adolph Ochs's papers are held at the Hebrew Union University, American Jewish Archives, Cincinnati, Ohio; the University of Tennessee Library, Special Collections, Knoxville, Tennessee; and Yale University, New Haven, Connecticut.

Fremont Older
(30 August 1856-3 March 1935)

Billy E. Deal
University of South Carolina

MAJOR POSITIONS HELD: City editor, *San Francisco Morning Call* (1894); managing editor, *San Francisco Bulletin* (1895-1918); editor, *San Francisco Evening Call* (1918-1929); editor in chief, *San Francisco Evening Call-Bulletin* (1929-1935); president, Hearst Publications Fiction Board (1932-1935).

BOOKS: *My Own Story* (San Francisco: Call Publishing, 1919; revised and enlarged edition, New York: Macmillan, 1926);

Growing Up (San Francisco: San Francisco Call-Bulletin, 1931);

The Life of George Hearst, California Pioneer, by Older and Cora Baggerly Older (San Francisco: Privately printed, 1933).

It has been said of Fremont Older that he influenced more journalists during his lifetime than any other man. His efforts in social, governmental, and penal reform are as legendary as his editorial exploits. For forty years, second only to William Randolph Hearst, he was one of the most powerful newspapermen on the West Coast. In the age of personal journalism, he was perhaps the perfect example. He was a muckraker, a crusader, a cigar-chewing, bombastic, tenacious teacher who had a reverential respect for truth and decency. But above all, Fremont Older was an editor: a newspaperman's editor. "He was not only a brilliant editor," wrote his protégé, Bruce Bliven, "he was the kindliest of men." His patient nurturing of

Fremont Older

best do the story got the story.

Older had only three years of formal schooling. He was self-educated with a passion for Charles Dickens, Mark Twain, Horace Greeley, and Montaigne. Colorful, unpredictable, and impatient, he developed a speech to match his frenzied life-style. If he could not think of a word to fit a situation, he simply invented one. He is credited with coining such expressions as *higher-ups*, *gangster*, and *mutt*, and popularizing the use of *Extra!* to promote an unscheduled edition of his paper.

Known as the Great Reformer, Older was venerated and vilified for his tireless efforts to clean up city government in turn-of-the-century San Francisco, for his campaign to abolish capital punishment, for passionate pleas for gun control, and for his personal dedication to prison reform. He was ahead of his time in his beliefs and was constantly perplexed by the failure of the San Francisco populace to embrace his fervor for reform.

But through it all he made the *San Francisco Bulletin* the most powerful newspaper in the West for two decades (1895-1918), then turned his talents to Hearst's *Evening Call* and duplicated his feat. Older's fame outside journalistic circles was mostly confined to the West Coast, although he was repeatedly linked with Arthur Brisbane, editor of Hearst's *New York Evening Journal*, as one of the "two greatest editors in the country."

Fremont Older was born on 30 August 1856 in Freedom Township, Wisconsin, where his parents, Emory and Celia Marie Augur Older, were living on his maternal grandfather's farm. He was named for John Charles Frémont, the Pathfinder. His father died shortly after returning from the Civil War, leaving his young family to fend for itself in the Wisconsin wilds. After a time, Older was sent to live with his grandparents, who had moved to Omro, Wisconsin; while he worked on farms in the area, his mother enjoyed a brief success as an itinerant bookseller. She sent copies of the books to Older, and one of them—*The Life of Horace Greeley*—inspired in him the dream of becoming an editor. Older and his brother Herbert enrolled at Ripon College in 1868, a few months after Fremont's twelfth birthday. A year later, when his mother could not support him any longer, Fremont dropped out of school and took a job as a printer's devil at the *Courant* in Berlin, Wisconsin.

But the young Older was a restless wanderer who was still unsure of his niche in life. He moved frequently, lugging a trunk in which he kept all of his belongings, often walking forty miles a day to reach a destination. He worked as a cabin boy on a

promising talent and his uncanny ability to "see a story" made him the father figure of West Coast newspapers, and he assembled a group of writers and artists on the *San Francisco Bulletin* whose aggregate accomplishments are perhaps unmatched in American journalism. Among those whose talents Older could solicit were Sinclair Lewis, Robert Ripley, Rube Goldberg, William O. McGeehan, Eustace Cullinan, Edgar T. Gleeson, Lowell Otus Reese, Robert L. Duffus, Maxwell Anderson, Carl Hoffman, Rose Wilder Lane, Bessie Beatty, Ernest J. Hopkins, Lemuel F. Parton, Ralph E. Renaud, Bruce Bliven, John P. Coghlan, and Kathleen Norris.

Curiously, Older was not noted as a writer and, indeed, did little writing until late in his career, and then only at the behest of Hearst. But as an editor he possessed the enthusiasm and stamina to ferret out a story and the intuition to pick the best writer to report it. His drama critic might be sent to cover a three-alarm fire while the women's editor was shadowing a suspected criminal: whoever could river steamer, a roustabout on the Mississippi, and a printer's devil at several newspapers in Wisconsin, Illinois, and Minnesota; for a month, the fifteen-year-old typesetter ran the *Oconto* (Wisconsin) *Free Press* by himself while the editor served a jail term for libeling a political opponent. Finally he headed for California, where his mother had moved after her remarriage in 1869, arriving in San Francisco in 1873. He promptly went to work setting type for the *Morning Call*, where his latest hero, Mark Twain, had toiled before him. Still gripped by wanderlust, Older set out for Virginia City, Nevada, and the *Territorial Enterprise*, another Twain stopping point. He returned to San Francisco in 1874 and joined the madcap crew of the *Daily Mail*, where he began a lifelong friendship with Arthur McEwen, who would join him later as a mainstay at the *Bulletin*. But the *Daily Mail* was short-lived, and Older was on the move again. After spending some months homesteading 160 acres in Mendocino County, he went to Redwood City, where he worked as a reporter for the *Weekly Journal* and then as editor and business manager of the *Times-Gazette*. During this period he married a woman named Emma Finger, but the marriage soon ended in separation and divorce. Older realized the importance of his early experience and would later tell young reporters who came to him for advice: "Try getting a start first on a small-town newspaper. Don't attempt to break in first on a large daily. You get a closer and more intimate touch with life in a small town."

It was this "touch of life" that brought Older his big break. In 1884 he was offered a job with the *Alta California* in San Francisco and eagerly took it. He applied his special feel to a police story, which was read by John Pratt, a dapper Englishman who had known Dickens. Pratt, the editor of the *Morning Call*, liked Older's style. He offered him a job, and Older quickly was back with the paper he had first served as a printer on his arrival in San Francisco.

It was during his tenure with Pratt that Older acquired his favorite story, one which he would use to intimidate many a young reporter later in life. Pratt was frustrated by the lack of enthusiasm of a young cub reporter. Older suggested that Pratt send him out with the newly formed Salvation Army. Upon his return, the cub produced two pitiful columns. Pratt groaned, "You were with them for three weeks. Didn't you observe anything? At night, where did they hang the bass drum?" The cub did not know, and was promptly fired. Forever afterward, when Fremont thought one of his reporters had not put enough detail into a story, he would roar: "Where did they hang the bass drum?"

Older's wife, Cora Baggerly Older

Soon Older was acknowledged one of the top reporters in San Francisco, and his personal life began to blossom. He soon married again: Cora Baggerly was the perfect mate for Older, and they worked side by side for many years. Cora was an astute journalist in her own right, ultimately producing the official biographies of George Hearst and his son, William Randolph Hearst. They were married on 22 August 1893 and were nearly inseparable until Older's death in 1935. Older's marriage brought him a bit closer to polite society, but he still had the country boy look, according to his biographer, Evelyn Wells: "long-legged, lanky, with heavy black hair beginning to desert his high forehead, a dominant nose, mouth firmly contoured under the sweeping Western mustache, and deep-set, dark eyes which smoldered and were tender, benign, or without mercy, flashing the signal-lights of his multitudinous moods."

After a brief stint with the *Post*, Older returned to the *Call* as city editor, only to stand by helplessly as the paper was sold. But a former owner of the *Call*, R. A. Crothers, quickly bought the *Bul-*

letin on behalf of his sister and offered Older the job of managing editor at $45 a week. This was the beginning of one of the most significant partnerships in American journalism. Unfortunately, Crothers, a refined, quiet man who preferred poetry to reform, could never appreciate Older's radical sensationalism, often remarking that there was nothing in his paper that he could read.

Older was thirty-nine years old when he finally settled down to run the down-and-out *Bulletin*, which had a circulation of only 9,000. Although his life had not been professionally productive from a career standpoint, it had prepared him well for his ensuing battles with San Francisco police, mobs, political bosses, and grafters.

Older wasted no time in sprucing up the tired old *Bulletin*. He later wrote:

> The office of the *Bulletin* was on Clay street, between Sansome and Montgomery, in a building that was almost on the verge of tumbling down. It had been there for more than thirty years. We had only one old press, and that was wholly inadequate for handling a circulation of any size. Our type was set by hand.
>
> It was almost impossible to make improvements because we had no money. We were running so close on revenue that Crothers was constantly worried for fear we should encounter losses that would destroy our hopes of success.
>
> I worked desperately hard in the beginning. I had a staff of only five men besides myself, and I acted as managing editor, city editor, book reviewer, dramatic critic and exchange editor, thus doing the work of several men. I lived, breathed, ate, slept and dreamed nothing but the paper. My absorbing thought was the task of making it go.
>
> I was utterly ruthless in my ambition. My one desire was to stimulate the circulation, to develop stories that would catch the attention of readers. The character of the stories did not matter. They might make people suffer, might wound or utterly ruin someone. That made no difference to me; it was not even in my mind. I cared only for results, for success to the paper and to myself.
>
> It was not long before the paper began to respond to the strong pressure I put upon it. We had only two competitors in the evening field, the *Post* and the *Report*, and I had the satisfaction of seeing our circulation slowly creep upward, until we had passed the *Post*

and were becoming a serious rival of the *Report*.

In the best style of the sensational period of yellow journalism, Older quickly transformed the *Bulletin* into a readable sheet. His headlines asked provocative questions, his editorials inspired thought, and circulation went up.

Older soon moved the *Bulletin* into a better location downtown and was experimenting with artwork on a chalk plate when a story broke in the spring of 1895 that would send the *Bulletin* on its way to justifying its slogan: "Largest circulation of any afternoon paper west of Chicago!" It was called the "Murder of the Century," and it was one of the most hideous crimes sedate San Francisco had ever witnessed. Two young women had been murdered by a prominent, successful young man, Theodore Durant. The Durant case became just the circulation builder Older needed. The crime had many angles, and Older played them all, using the "Extra!" for the first time to keep his readers informed up to the minute on all developments. At the trial, Older cautioned his reporters to break for the door before it could be sealed when the verdict came in. The reporter, Henry Brooke, did as ordered and barely escaped before the judge ordered the doors closed. While other reporters were trapped inside the courtroom, the *Bulletin* was being hawked on every street corner with an "Extra!" carrying the news of Durant's conviction. That boosted the *Bulletin*'s circulation past the 20,000 mark and permanently into the lead.

One year after Older had taken over the *Bulletin*, it was producing a Saturday edition of twenty-four pages of bright and sparkling news, articles, poetry, editorials, and the paper's first novel, complete in one edition, "The Purple Emperor." In March 1896 Older began his first continued serial, publishing a chapter every Saturday of *Weir of Hermiston*, the last work of Robert Louis Stevenson.

Older, sensing that his readers wanted more than traditional news, quickly developed a complete sports page and a woman's section and devoted more space to art and drama. At a time when the leading papers on the East Coast were filled with irresponsible reports on the war in Cuba, the *Bulletin* was content to concentrate on local scandal.

Even during the peak of his career with the *Bulletin*, Older's name never appeared on the masthead of the paper, and he never wrote signed articles. Yet he was the *Bulletin*'s best source of ideas, sitting behind a cluttered, battered desk in a tiny office, waving the ubiquitous cigar, and shouting instructions to his reporters. He would think of ideas for editorials and pass them on to writers such as Robert Duffus and Eustace Cullinan to produce. His liberal use of type sizes and faces (often creating a new font just to get the right "feel" for a special story), his sensational layouts, his development of the serial, and his early use of artwork made the *Bulletin* one of the most readable newspapers in America. His headlines reflected the yellow journalism period, and like Pulitzer and Hearst, he saw the attraction in lurid stories of sex, murder, and violence.

Older was partial to the editorial page, where he ran this squib: "Editorials are the special excellence of the *Bulletin*. Its timely utterances, vigorous, comprehensive and pointed, ever sounding the note of warning and jealously guarding the interest of the people, make the *Bulletin* the terror of evil doers and the shield of the citizens." The editorials were fierce and protective, straight-spoken and kindly, interesting in matters vital or small. If not the words, they were the voice of Fremont Older.

It was at this point that Older began to look to greater heights. Spurred by Hearst's efforts, Older wanted to take on the Southern Pacific Railroad, the dominant force in California society. The railroad held a vicelike grip on the state, appointing politicians, running businesses, and paying off newspapers on a regular basis. Graft and corruption were rampant. Older thought the first step in cleaning up the government was to have an influence in politics, and he handpicked popular, honest, successful, and rich James Phelan to run for mayor. With the *Bulletin*'s support, Phelan won the race and was reelected twice, proving to be one of the finest mayors in San Francisco history.

Older continued to experiment with the layout of his pages, using six-inch type and screaming headlines. To appeal to women, he introduced a Sunday magazine in 1896. The male audience still had the best sports section in town, which was supervised by Hiland Baggerly, Older's brother-in-law.

Older insisted on the "cleanest" sheet—freest from typographical errors—on the coast, and he got it. One of his specialties was the "dingbat" head, made of one large and two small lines, a certain circulation getter. His favorite was a "stepped" or double head in type running the full width of the page. He began using single-column subheads under the scarehead, as many as five to a story. Every front page attracted new readers, and each

was carefully planned. Older was a master of the sensational layout and was a driving force behind the use of art. Good photographic reproduction was still uncommon in newspapers at the turn of the century, and Older preferred good drawings to poor photography. At one time he had twenty-five artists working for the *Bulletin*. Older showed his disdain for sexual bias when he named Virginia Brastow city editor of the *Bulletin*, a bold move in those days. Older's treatment of his reporters was also unique. He allowed them to edit their own copy, lay out their own sheets, and even write their own heads. Older trusted their judgment, and they returned it with conscientious and excellent work.

Older moved into his first great crusade when Phelan refused to run for a fourth term and Eugene E. Schmitz was elected mayor in 1901. Schmitz was totally corrupt and was controlled by Abraham Ruef, a diminutive lawyer with a handlebar mustache—the "boss" of the San Francisco underworld. In a running battle that would last for nearly eight years and see several attempts on Older's life, the *Bulletin* led the fight to rid San Francisco of graft and corruption. European newspapers sent correspondents to cover the proceedings, and *McClure's* magazine called Older "one of the greatest living editors." Then a strange thing began to happen that would puzzle Older the rest of his life. The people began to ridicule and criticize Older and the *Bulletin*. They had had enough bad news, enough continual stirring up of political muck. It was a public apathy Older would never be able to understand, although he would finally come to accept it.

At one point Older was kidnapped and hustled out of town on a train bound for Los Angeles. The plan, revealed later, was for Older to be killed in the mountains north of Los Angeles. But a young attorney recognized Older, realized something was happening, and called the *Morning Call* with the story. "Older Kidnapped" the headline screamed, and when the train stopped in Santa Barbara, police surrounded it and rescued Older. Perhaps Older's greatest disappointment on the occasion was that his paper had been scooped by a competitor!

After years of fighting Ruef, Schmitz, and Southern Pacific boss Patrick Calhoun, Older was able to elicit only the conviction of Ruef. At this point he turned his entire life around, confounding his closest friends, many of whom would never again feel as if they knew him. After working so hard to convict Ruef, he realized that Ruef was only a victim of the system. It was not just one man who was responsible for all the corruption, but many;

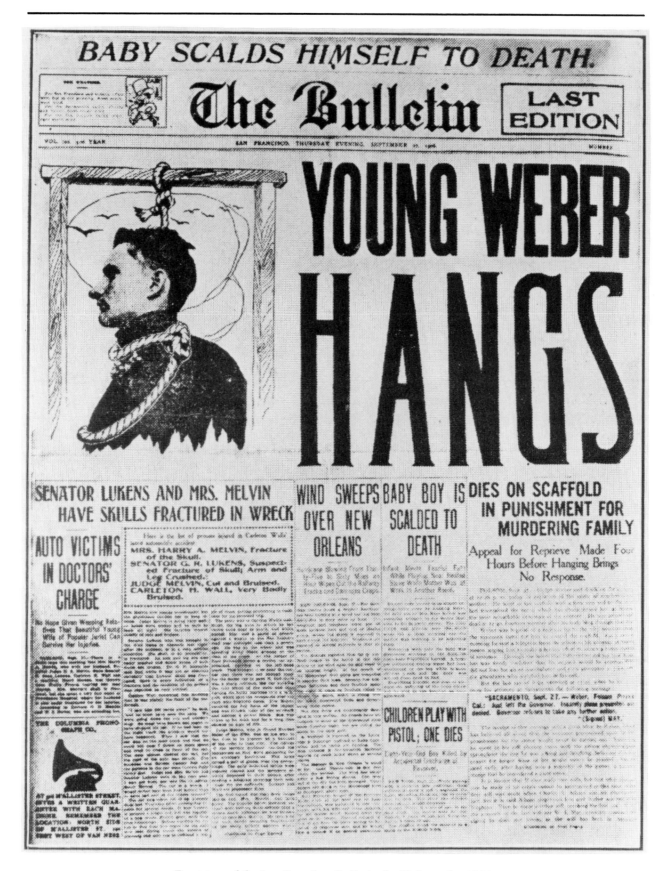

Front page of the San Francisco Bulletin *for 27 September 1906*

and if all were not sentenced, then none should be. So Older embarked on a campaign to free Abraham Ruef with the same vigor he had applied to his conviction. Noting how he had fought to strip Ruef of his freedom and had won, Older wrote:

> I thought over my own life, and the many unworthy things I had done to others, the injustice, the wrongs I had been guilty of, the human hearts I had wantonly hurt, the sorrows I had caused, the half truths I had told, and the mitigating truths I had withheld, the lies I had allowed to go undenied.
>
> And then I saw myself also stripped, that is stripped of all pretense, sham, self righteousness, holding the key to another man's cell. I dropped the key. I never want to hold it again. Let it be taken up and held by those who feel they are justified in holding it. I want no more jail keys. For the rest of my life I want to get a little nearer to the forgiving spirit that Christ expressed. . . .
>
> Think it over. Think of your own life. Think of the lives of those around you, and see if you cannot discern that we are all guilty. And then think whether or not you believe that society will be benefitted by denying Ruef a parole. . . .

It was about this time that Older began his almost fanatical interest in prison reform and abolishment of capital punishment. He kept a steady stream of paroled felons coming to Woodhills, his ranch outside of San Francisco. Here Older and Cora would counsel the criminals and give them work, food, and a place to live until they moved on. Neighbors began to call it "Convict Canyon," but Older was oblivious to the taunts because he could see the results. Jack Black, a convicted safecracker serving a thirty-year sentence, was paroled at Older's request. He turned into an accomplished speaker and writer about his decision to "go straight" and became one of Older's most trusted friends and even his bodyguard. Another convict, Donald Lowrie, was rescued by Older and convinced to write a serial, "My Life in Prison." It was tremendously successful, and Lowrie became a celebrity, but finally slipped back into his old habits. There were many others, some who benefited from Older's help and some who did not, but the editor never quit trying.

Cora and Fremont Older at Woodhills, their ranch in Santa Clara County, California

His most famous crusade was also his most disappointing, and the one which led to his leaving the *Bulletin*. As America moved toward World War I in 1916, a Preparedness Parade was held in San Francisco. A bomb was exploded during the parade, killing ten people and mangling fifty more. Emotions were running high as the city came to grips with prowar and antiwar sentiments, and a known rabble-rouser named Tom Mooney was quickly made a suspect in the bombing. A rapid series of events led to his arrest along with four cohorts. It soon became clear to Older, after viewing a total mockery of a trial, that Mooney and the others had been framed. Mooney was convicted and sentenced to die, and Older and the *Bulletin* began campaigning feverishly for Mooney's freedom as they had for Ruef's. It was perhaps the most unpopular campaign of Older's career, but he was steadfast in his belief in Mooney's innocence.

Finally totally incriminating evidence against the district attorney and the star witness forced President Wilson to request a review of the Mooney case. Tom Mooney was an international figure—Older's crusade had brought pleas for leniency from as far away as Russia—but still his sentence was only commuted to life. He was still serving his sentence when Fremont Older died, but Older never relented in his quest to free Mooney.

Eventually Crothers ordered Older to abandon the case. At this point, William Randolph Hearst called with this message: "Come to the *Call*. Bring the Mooney case with you." Although Older did not like Hearst, he admired him as a newspaperman and had been offered jobs by Hearst many times before. On 16 July 1918, Older left the *Bulletin* and joined the *Call* as editor. He had returned to the first paper he had worked for in San Francisco. Older said later that he always had felt some inner compulsion to return to the *Call*.

He soon proved that he still had his old touch. When Older had joined the *Bulletin* in 1895, the circulation was 9,000; when he left it was 100,000 and had been as high as 111,000. In 1918, the *Call* was at 99,000; after one year under Older, it had moved 12,000 ahead of the sinking *Bulletin*.

Far from the unforgiving, accusing muckraker he had been in the beginning, Older was mellower and said he did not blame anybody for anything. His life revolved around Woodhills, where he spent weekends and evenings with Cora, commuting by train the round trip of 100 miles to San Francisco five days a week. He had developed a passion for automobiles and always had the latest one available, though the rest of their life was sim-

ple. They lived in quiet luxury but ate modestly (both were vegetarians), and Older's chief pleasures came from reading passages from Dickens nightly and taking a morning dip in his pool. He worked more patiently with young writers and would rejoice when he found a promising one. His fascination with books became more intense, but he still preferred to reread Dickens. He once called a reporter at one o'clock in the morning to meet him at a restaurant. The reporter came immediately (they always did), whereupon Older began to read passages from Montaigne, whom he had just discovered.

He became a father confessor for men and women from all walks of life. Some of his most devoted followers were those whom he had hounded in his early years—prostitutes, petty criminals, crooked politicians. Anyone who knew him felt he could be trusted; Abraham Ruef even asked him to manage his money while he was in prison. Even friends on rival newspapers would discuss their plans with him before carrying out some circulation-building stunt, knowing that Older would not betray their trust. At this point, when someone asked him to describe himself, he said, "Six feet, two inches in height; weight twotwenty; erect but old looking; mustache; bald; dark grey-green suit; green tie; light green, soft hat."

Older developed serial writing into one of the fine arts of journalism, simultaneously chiding his writers for clichés and predictable phrases. He preferred spontaneous writing to too-careful grammatical construction. "Never believe a man who punctuates a love letter properly," he said. He urged journalism professors to look for students with "word sense" and observed that "nearly everyone thinks he can write but very few can."

After showing early promise as a writer then doing virtually no writing for nearly twenty-four years, Older began his literary career at age sixty-three by dictating his autobiography, *My Own Story* (1919). Urged by Hearst to write a regular column for the *Call*, he reluctantly agreed, and it turned out to be the most enjoyable facet of his professional life in his last years. He found that he actually enjoyed writing and covered a variety of subjects and opinions.

In 1929 the *Call* and *Bulletin* were merged, and, at seventy-two, Older became the editor in chief. The first paper he had worked on as a reporter in San Francisco was the *Call*. He had first been a managing editor on the *Bulletin*. Now they were one. Reflecting on this, Older said, "When we held a conference in my office over the bones of the old *Bulletin*, I felt as if I were sitting alongside my own ghost." For several years, Older was also fiction editor for the Hearst chain. He began to spend more time questioning the meaning of life with his close friend Clarence Darrow and enjoying the small pleasures of Woodhills. On 3 March 1935, he accompanied his wife to a flower show in Sacramento. While driving home, he collapsed and died at the wheel. With him passed an era of journalism that bore his mark.

Perhaps Older's greatest contribution to American journalism was his dedication to reform and the proper use of the press to attain it. His insistence on sound journalistic principles, combined with a sincere and humane interest in political and social reform, established him as a believable and objective editor. His cultivation of an excellent group of writers attests to his credibility among his staff—as well as his eye for talent. Like Pulitzer, Older was an unwavering advocate of style (accuracy and excellence in writing). Like Hearst, he was dynamic and highly visible. But unlike either, Older

was a kind, compassionate man who could communicate at all levels of society. His personal joys and pursuits were simple, belying his relentless professional crusades. Above all, Older established sound criteria to be used by his successors in fighting for reform without sacrificing journalistic principles. A cut above the muckrakers in professional class, he was no less powerful as a journalist.

Biography:
Evelyn Wells, *Fremont Older* (New York: Appleton-Century, 1936).

References:
Bruce Bliven, "My Most Unforgettable Character," *Reader's Digest*, 85 (August 1964): 129-133;
Robert L. Duffus, *The Tower of Jewels* (New York: Norton, 1960);
Kenneth Stewart and John Tebbel, *Makers of Modern Journalism* (New York: Prentice-Hall, 1952).

Charles Edward Russell
(25 September 1860-23 April 1941)

Warren T. Francke
University of Nebraska at Omaha

MAJOR POSITIONS HELD: Managing editor, *Davenport Gazette* (1881-1883); night editor, *Minneapolis Tribune* (1883); managing editor, *Minneapolis Journal* (1884); managing editor, *Detroit Tribune* (1886); Chicago correspondent, *New York World* (1887-1889); reporter, assistant city editor, *New York Herald* (1889-1894); Sunday supplement editor, city editor, *New York World* (1894-1897); managing editor, *New York Journal and American* (1897-1900); publisher, *Chicago American* (1900-1902).

BOOKS: *Such Stuff as Dreams* (Indianapolis: Bowen-Merrill, 1901);
The Twin Immortalities and Other Poems (Chicago: Hammersmark, 1904);
The Greatest Trust in the World (New York: Ridgway-Thayer, 1905);
The Uprising of the Many (New York: Doubleday, Page, 1907);

Thomas Chatterton, the Marvelous Boy: The Story of a Strange Life, 1752-1770 (New York: Moffat, Yard, 1908; London: Richards, 1909);
Lawless Wealth: The Origin of Some Great American Fortunes (New York: B. W. Dodge, 1908);
Songs of Democracy (New York: Moffat, Yard, 1909);
Why I Am a Socialist (New York: Hodder, Stoughton, Doran, 1910);
Business: The Heart of the Nation (New York: John Lane, 1911);
The Passing Show of Capitalism (Girard, Kans.: The Appeal to Reason, 1912);
Stories of the Great Railroads (Chicago: Kerr, 1912);
Doing Us Good and Plenty (Chicago: Kerr, 1914);
The Story of Wendell Phillips: Soldier of the Common Good (Chicago: Kerr, 1914);
These Shifting Scenes (New York: Hodder, Stoughton, Doran, 1914);
Unchained Russia (New York: Appleton, 1918);
After the Whirlwind: A Book of Reconstruction and Prof-

Charles E. Russell (Underwood & Underwood)

itable Thanksgiving (New York: Doran, 1919);

Bolshevism and the United States (Indianapolis: Bobbs-Merrill, 1919);

The Story of the Non-Partisan League: A Chapter in American Evolution (New York & London: Harper, 1920);

The Outlook for the Philippines (New York: Century, 1922);

Railroad Melons, Rates and Wages: A Handbook Of Railroad Information (Chicago: Kerr, 1922);

The Hero of the Filipinos: The Story of José Rizal, Poet, Patriot, and Martyr, by Russell and E. B. Rodriguez (New York & London: Century, 1923);

Julia Marlowe: Her Life and Art (New York & London: Appleton, 1926);

The American Orchestra and Theodore Thomas (Garden City: Doubleday, Page, 1927);

A Rafting on the Mississip' (New York & London: Century, 1928);

From Sandy Hook to 62° (New York & London: Century, 1929);

An Hour of American Poetry (Philadelphia & London: Lippincott, 1929);

Charlemagne (Boston & New York: Houghton Mifflin, 1930; London: Butterworth, 1931);

Haym Salomon and the Revolution (New York: Cosmopolitan, 1930);

Blaine of Maine: His Life and Times (New York: Cosmopolitan, 1931);

Bare Hands and Stone Walls (New York: Scribners, 1933);

A Pioneer Editor in Early Iowa: A Sketch of the Life of Edward Russell by His Son (Washington, D.C.: Ransdell, 1941).

PERIODICAL PUBLICATIONS: "William Randolph Hearst," *Harper's Weekly,* 48 (21 May 1904): 790-792;

"The Greatest Trust in the World," *Everybody's,* 12-13 (February-September 1905);

"Soldiers of the Common Good," *Everybody's,* 13-16 (April 1906-June 1907);

"Wall Street Greed and Railroad Ruin," *Ridgway's* (29 December 1906): 172-200;

"The Growth of Caste in America," *Cosmopolitan,* 42 (March 1907): 524-534;

"The American Language," *Saturday Evening Post* (15 June 1907): 6-7;

"Swinburne and Music," *North American Review* (November 1907): 427-441;

"A Burglar in the Making," *Everybody's,* 18 (June 1908): 753-760;

"Tenements of Trinity Church," *Everybody's,* 19 (July 1908): 47-57;

"Chaos and Bomb Throwing in Chicago," *Hampton's,* 24 (March 1910): 307-320;

"Revolution," *Pearson's* (February 1913): 129-139;

"The Keeping of the Kept Press," *Pearson's* (January 1914): 33-43;

"The Magazine Soft Pedal," *Pearson's* (February 1914): 179-189;

"The Associated Press and Calumet," *Pearson's* (April 1914): 437-448;

"The Farmer's Battle," *Pearson's* (May 1915): 516-527;

"New Socialist Alignment," *Harper's,* 136 (March 1918): 563-570;

"Radical Press in America," *Bookman,* 49 (July 1919): 513-518;

"British Propaganda in America," *American Irish Review* (March 1924): 1, 7;

"The American Grand Orchestra," *Century,* 116 (June 1928): 167-175;

"Old Reporter Looks at the Mad-House World," *Scribner's,* 94 (October 1933): 225-230.

When Charles Edward Russell sat as city editor for Joseph Pulitzer's *New York World* in the middle of the 1890s, a lustrous staff of reporters knew him as "Iron-faced Charlie." But he crowned himself the "city room caliph" when recalling it as "the best job I ever had." Russell went even further in one of his several autobiographies: "After a newspaper experience of more than 25 years that had at one end the post of deputy assistant mailing clerk and at the other the post of publisher, I can place my hand upon my heart and declare that the best job on earth is that of the city editor of a New York daily." He brushed off as trivial his other titles—publisher, managing editor, editorial writer—and declared the city editor "the real captain of the ship, the only person in the establishment that has any real power, and the only producer of results."

Russell's claim is disputable, even in regard to his own career, but it hints at both the aspirations and the frustrations of a reform-minded journalist who worked more fully at the center of the experiences called New Journalism, yellow journalism, and muckraking than perhaps any other journalist. From his father's *Davenport Gazette* to newspapers owned by Bennett, Pulitzer, and Hearst, he carried the abolitionist fervor of his ancestors into new battles for social justice. Yet at the apparent height of his power, as publisher of the *Chicago American*, critics labeled him an apologist for the owner, William Randolph Hearst; and in 1902, after only two years in the position, he resigned on the brink of a nervous breakdown. Although he returned for another year with Hearst in New York, his subsequent newspaper career, with minor exceptions, consisted of contributions to the *New York Call* and other Socialist publications. He became, from 1905 to 1916, one of the most prolific and persistent magazine muckrakers and an active Socialist party member and candidate. By his own testimony, the motivation for his muckraking and the basis for his socialism could be found in his experiences as a newspaper man. What separated Russell from so many progressive reformers who emerged from the Midwest, practiced newspaper journalism, and evolved into magazine muckrakers was that he stepped over the line from literature to activism and from liberal to radical politics.

Reporters under Russell nicknamed him "Iron-faced Charlie" in apparent response to his grim demeanor and gruff efficiency. George Creel, chairman of the World War I Committee on Public Information, referred to Russell's rough exterior and martinet quality as an editor, but wrote to President Wilson when recommending him for an appointment that "Russell is one of the best newspapermen in the country, and a writer of rare ability." The pioneer publicist "Poison" Ivy Lee, who worked under Russell on the *New York Journal*, praised his training and noted, "Though you were very strict and sometimes forbidding, . . . I always felt that you were square." When Russell became a Socialist candidate for governor of New York, another former colleague, J. C. Hammond, predicted that a hundred or so New York newsmen, "battle-scarred reporters, men who have risen in the ranks and once worked under the direction of 'Uncle Charlie,'" would put political principles aside to pay tribute to Russell with their votes. The consensus seemed to be that Russell was not only a great reporter and writer but also an outstanding news executive—talents that seldom mixed in one man. Another contemporary, I. F. Marcossen, summarized Russell's outstanding gift as his "swift and accurate appraisal of men."

Russell's heritage was one common to journalistic reformers of the New Journalism-yellow journalism-muckraking eras. His paternal grandfather, William Russell, gave up a position as a distillery clerk in England to become a temperance lecturer, known both for his oratory and his written appeals. His maternal grandfather, the Reverend William Rutledge, joined in the fight against alcohol. Both became active abolitionists, providing links in the underground railway, when they settled on the eastern edge of Iowa. William Russell and his son Edward, Charles's father, arrived in LeClaire, near Davenport on the Mississippi River, in 1848; Edward married Lydia Rutledge, the clergyman's daughter, in 1852.

Edward Russell wrote antislavery articles for the weekly *LeClaire Express* and for the *National Era* magazine, where Harriet Beecher Stowe's *Uncle Tom's Cabin* had first been published. He became editor of the LeClaire weekly in 1858. When the *Express* failed a year later, he moved to Davenport for a job in the county recorder's office and began writing for the daily *Davenport Gazette*, which he bought in 1862, two years after Charles Edward Russell was born. An early backer of Abraham Lincoln, Edward Russell was active in Republican politics, winning an appointment as postmaster. He was also dedicated to crusading journalism, and Charles had vivid memories of a lynch mob threatening "the editorial nigger-stealer" and the railroads cutting off the *Gazette*'s coal supply.

Later in life, Russell believed that his father's patience and persistence in drawn-out struggles against slavery and the railroads influenced his own approach to social problems. His father's opponents ranged from antiabolitionists who shot at him on the way home from the office to railroad owners who would eventually force him out of the newspaper business. But Edward retained the *Gazette* long enough for Russell to advance from a twelve-year-old who arose at 3:30 A.M. to wrap papers in the mailing room to a twenty-one-year-old managing editor who ran the paper while his postmaster father wrote editorials.

Russell wore other titles on the Davenport daily, from city editor with no staff of reporters to telegraph editor, but he contributed his first writing as a teenaged typesetter. When his father's editorial on a fire alarm swindle spilled to the composing-room floor, it required rewriting. As he recalled in the last of his more than thirty books, *A Pioneer Editor in Early Iowa: A Sketch of the Life of Edward Russell* (1941), Russell sprinkled the short piece with terms such as "thieves" and "scoundrels," and soon he faced two threats of libel suits and a red-faced German armed with a club.

While his father provided a model of moral courage, Russell's dreams of journalistic success were spun from the tales of a tramp printer named Scotty, who not only taught the boy tricks of copy editing and headline writing but also name-dropped Greeley, Dana, and Bennett into yarns of New York as the mecca of journalism. Scotty insisted that the only headlines worth writing were written in New York and said of New York news stories: "It isn't newspaper writing, it's literature." He also convinced a wide-eyed Charles that "the true glory of newspaper work lay in the unraveling of murder mysteries." So the father instilled a lofty idealism and the tramp printer a romantic vision in the boy.

The experience on the *Gazette* was interrupted by schooling at St. Johnsbury Academy in Vermont, which Russell later praised for its offerings in Latin, science, rhetoric, and political economy, but criticized for its chapel requirement. Doubtful that salvation was available only through the Congregational church, he absorbed the agnostic tracts of Robert Ingersoll. Russell also came to admire Wendell Phillips, the abolitionist who would later serve as the subject for one of his biographies, and Wendell Phillips Stafford, an orator whose proclamation that "Man's gifts are lent to serve the common good" became the student's motto. He read Henry George, and he observed the power of the Fairbanks Scale family in St. Johnsbury. They justified their rule, it seemed to a doubtful Russell, by "the great Trickle and Filter Theory of social existence,"

which assumed that some of their wealth would eventually trickle down to those below.

When Russell returned to Davenport in 1881 to manage the paper, he helped Henry J. Philpott, editor of the *Des Moines Leader*, found the Iowa State Free Trade League, and he lectured and wrote on behalf of free trade. In the same year he read an article in the *Atlantic Monthly* which he later recognized as pivotal in his development. It was "The Story of a Great Monopoly," the first of H. D. Lloyd's works on Standard Oil and John D. Rockefeller, and it convinced Russell that opposition to corporate power was the next great work after the defeat of slavery. This cause took on added personal significance a year later when the *Gazette* fell into financial difficulties and was purchased by the Rock Island Railroad, a leading opponent of Edward Russell's plan for a Hennepin Canal from the Great Lakes to the Mississippi River.

From 1883 to 1886, Russell moved rapidly from one Midwestern newspaper to another. After writing editorials for the free trade, antimonopoly *St. Paul Pioneer Press*, he became a reporter and then night editor on the *Minneapolis Tribune*. In 1884 he was hired as managing editor of the *Minneapolis Journal*, for which he covered two national political conventions. Also in 1884 he married Abby Osborn Rust of St. Johnsbury. Minnesota colleagues jokingly awarded him the title, which he treasured, of "Pork and Poetry" editor. It reflected both his wide-ranging early assignments, from livestock to the arts, and his lifelong interests. According to one biographer, these contrasting interests pointed up a lifelong dilemma: whether to focus on the exposure of political and economic problems or to emphasize his other devotion to art, music, and literature. In this early stage, the former seemed to dominate, as Russell moved on for a brief stay as managing editor of the *Detroit Tribune* in 1886 and then to New York, "the city of my dreams."

In *These Shifting Scenes* (1914) Russell confessed that he had never imagined that the former managing editor of three Midwestern dailies would have trouble finding a job. But he struggled jobless through a hot summer, free-lancing poems, paragraphs, and puns, and sending editorials back to Detroit before landing a reporting job on the *Commercial Advertiser*, which paid thirty-two cents a column space rates, but no time allowance. A reporter could lose money when an unproductive assignment required fares on the elevated railroad. But he admired the editor, George Cary Eggleston, and on covering the Jefferson Market police court, he claimed, "I know of no spectacle more instructive than that bare and filthy court of a morning." He saw its clientele as the product of the injustices of the tenements, and he insisted in another autobiography, *Bare Hands and Stone Walls* (1933), that "the only education I ever had that amounted to anything was when I was a police reporter on the East Side of New York." He learned not from Fifth Avenue but from the slums of Mulberry Bend.

A demand from the *Commercial Advertiser* that he discover the names of strike leaders for other than news purposes led him to apply again with Joseph Pulitzer's *New York World*. "Are you suggestive? . . . I am looking for suggestive men," Pulitzer said, and when Russell assured him he was, Pulitzer told him to see Col. John A. Cockerill, the managing editor. After a few months, Russell was named Chicago correspondent and sent to cover the events that culminated in the Haymarket bombing and the hanging of strike leaders in 1887. He later recalled the pressures and paranoia that plagued reporters during those chaotic months in Chicago and characterized the inflammatory newspaper coverage as the "literature of lunacy." However, Russell's own later heroic treatment of Albert Parsons, the labor editor he credited with rescuing reporters from a mob, contrasts with his description in the 12 November 1887 *World*. Published a day after the hangings, his account calls Parsons "a hoarse-voiced, hatchet-faced and restless printer," "one of the most blatant of the haranguers," and, like several of the other leaders, "cool" and "bloodthirsty."

He considered his coverage of the 1888 Republican nominating convention in Chicago another major learning experience—"The delegates could have stayed home" as reporters focused on the smoke-filled rooms. But he wanted to return to Mecca, so in 1889 Russell joined the *New York Herald*, under the absentee ownership of James Gordon Bennett, Jr. His tenure there was highlighted by sensational disaster coverage and by investigating the sort of "murder mysteries" romanticized by the old tramp printer. The *Herald* paid $8 a column and double for exclusive news. After Russell and three other reporters traveled a tortuous route to cover the Johnstown flood and had gone sixty-five hours without sleep, he outwitted the others by monopolizing the only Western Union wire and sending back a story that made him the focus of another newspaper's account of his triumph—a success that led some to label him one of New York's top reporters. His unraveling of the mystery of a missing mother and children won Russell space for almost two columns "at $16 per." In 1892 he was named assistant city editor; working

under William Reick, Russell was reponsible for the Brooklyn edition.

Russell next moved back to the *World* as city editor from 1894 to 1897, a period in which he also assisted Arthur Brisbane with the Sunday supplement. Not only was the city editor's post on a competitive New York daily generally "the best job on earth," but Russell felt particularly blessed with "the greatest staff that ever worked upon a newspaper." David Graham Phillips, another muckraker-to-be, led his list, and he singled out a Phillips Thanksgiving piece on a home for incurables as a prime example of that old tramp printer's claim that the best New York journalism was true art. "Life as it is and portrayed with vividness and conviction to the reader—what better literature?" Russell asked in *These Shifting Scenes*. His staff included many others who became successful editors and authors, including local colorists Rudolph Block (who wrote as Bruno Lessing) and Jacob Dreyfus.

The "great talent" of Russell and Brisbane was credited by Don Carlos Seitz, a later Pulitzer editor and biographer, for surging circulation which surpassed 600,000 on several dates in 1896. Though working amid the extremes of competition and yellow journalism, Russell referred detachedly to the excesses of the day as the "Bedlam period of New York journalism." He cited the fads that followed one after the other, such as "freaking"—beginning each story with a single-word exclamation ("Blood!" or "Crash!") or ending stories about Irishmen with the line "A Great Day for Ireland!," even when the item involved the death of a philanthropist named Mulrooney, who had swallowed a chicken bone. But Russell blamed all this on an anonymous night editor and seemed pleased that the latter incident "laid freaking low for seven years."

Russell chose to leave Pulitzer, who had grown more erratic and demanding, in 1897 for a managing editor's post with William Randolph Hearst's *New York Journal*. A biographer speculated that money and by-lines, two scarce rewards for even top Pulitzer men at the time Hearst began his raids, won Russell over. Brisbane warned him against risking a promising future by going to Hearst, but then he himself joined Russell on the *Journal* six weeks later.

In 1900 Hearst appointed Russell publisher of his recently established *Chicago American*. Russell later described the job of publisher as being "no more than a high-priced lackey," and a history of the *American* accuses Russell of merely performing a public relations job for Hearst in Chicago.

Russell's wife, Abby, died in 1901, leaving him

one son, John Edward. Russell took medical leave from his publisher's post in 1902. This "nervous breakdown," caused by the cumulative pressures of employment under Pulitzer and Hearst, was followed by a year-long vacation, then another year for Hearst in New York.

One incident reveals Russell as a naive pawn of yellow journalism. A reporter fired for filing a false interview told Russell he had been ordered to do so as part of the paper's policy of pleasing Hearst. Russell allegedly refused to even discuss the matter. A *New York Post* writer portrayed Russell during 1904, his last year with Hearst, as conspicuous by his quietness in the buzzing hive of the *New York Journal* newsroom. The staff held Russell in "affectionate awe," thanks to his utter sincerity and a physical image dominated by a huge head, a dark face, and melancholy eyes which gave the impression of "a deep and rather pessimistic reflection." In 1904 Russell wrote an article for *Harper's Weekly* which Ferdinand Lundberg labels "a puff for Hearst." In the article, Russell painted a heroic Hearst whose primary motives were "to fight for the weak, to represent the unrepresented, to better conditions, to protect the unprotected," and so on; in short, his Hearst is motivated by a "generous idealism." Two years later and two years removed from full-time employment by Hearst, Russell wrote to a friend that his old boss had grown more reactionary by the month, and "no doubt his chief impulse all the time was his own ambition."

Russell had planned to concentrate on the cultural side of his dual interests by studying Swinburne's poetry and writing about its relationship to music, when he happened to sit in on regulatory hearings in Chicago; the hearings had grown out of the *American*'s exposures, under his leadership, of city water thefts by the meat packing houses. He reluctantly put poetry and music aside and promised Erman Ridgway an article for *Everybody's* magazine. The result was "The Greatest Trust in the World," which ran monthly from February through September 1905. Thus began a period of investigative exposure which would eventually make Russell one of the most prolific and certainly the most persistent of muckrakers. When other muckraking periodicals ceased publishing or converted to less controversial content, *Hampton's* carried his articles. When *Hampton's* was undone by a railroad conspiracy, he turned to the last of the muckraking magazines, *Pearson's*, and continued until early 1917. His exposure of the beef trust preceded Upton Sinclair's novel *The Jungle* (1906), and was defended by Sinclair when critics attacked

the series while Russell traveled in Europe to write his "Soldiers of the Common Good" articles for *Everybody's* in 1906 and 1907.

The reporting techniques and writing style that Russell brought to magazine muckraking had been developed during his newspaper days from Davenport, Iowa, to Park Row in New York. His literary background contributed generally, of course, but several writers provide identifiable influences. By his own account, H. D. Lloyd's ideas awakened him, and Lloyd's epigrammatic style made an impact as well. The "tour-guide reporting" often associated with Charles Dickens and adopted by many reporters in the 1870s appears clearly in Russell's article on "Tenements of Trinity Church" in the July 1908 *Everybody's*, where he wrote: "We will imagine that we guide a party of inquiring and well-fed tourists to whom the tenement house is merely a name. . . . Come, then, into the filthy little back yards at the rear of No. 20 Clarkson Street, and, looking over the rotting fences, you may discover a peculiarity of many of the houses in this region."

His newspaper experiences became the subject for "The Keeping of the Kept Press" in the January 1914 *Pearson's* and "The Associated Press and Calumet," which followed in April. Billed as an insider's "truth about how newspapers are made," "The Keeping of the Kept Press" argued that independent reporting was declining under the growing influence of the great "Controlling Interests." Citing examples from his experiences with Pulitzer and Hearst, Russell charged both reactionary and progressive papers with "perverting and poisoning" public opinion. He described advertiser pressures on editors, "don't print" lists in newspaper offices, and attacks by the "Interests" on those who defied their influence. The Associated Press article, quoted liberally in Sinclair's *The Brass Check* (1920), outlines the same controls over the AP and compares AP coverage of strikes with "the Facts" and affidavits. In a letter to Sinclair, Russell claimed the AP "made a loud squeal" and "blacklisted me for some years afterward."

If he was blacklisted, the article might share the blame with the fact that he formally announced his allegiance to socialism in 1908, despite warnings from colleagues that it would weaken his influence as a journalist. In 1909 he married Theresa Hirschl of Chicago; that same year, he met with William English Walling and others to plan the conference that initiated the National Association for the Advancement of Colored People. Russell served as a board member, fundraiser, publicist, contributor to

The Crisis, and convention chairman; these and other N.A.A.C.P. activities may have prompted the awarding of an honorary degree by Howard University in 1923.

The Socialist party nominated him for governor of New York in 1910 and 1912, for mayor of New York City in 1913, and for United States senator from New York in 1914. Running for governor in 1910, he said that experiences as a *New York Herald* reporter in 1892 had caused his conversion; he cited "untold misery" among tenement dwellers when coal prices rose sharply, and recalled gazing in horror at the mutilation of a pretty girl in a sweatshop. He received between four and five percent of the vote in his campaigns. Between 1908 and 1916, he contributed to five Socialist publications, particularly the daily *New York Call* and the *Coming Nation*. Russell tried unsuccessfully to make the *Call* entertaining and newsworthy, so readers would not need to "buy another journal to know what's going on." He lost his chance for the Socialist presidential nomination in 1916 when he supported the Allied cause in World War I.

Drummed out of the Socialist party, he accepted European assignments for the Newspaper Enterprise Association in 1916, helped George Creel with the wartime news bureaus, and still found time to aid the Non-Partisan League in starting its 65,000-circulation newspaper, the *Non-Partisan Leader*, in Fargo, North Dakota. In 1917 he became a national director of the American Federation of Labor and joined a new political movement, the Social Democratic League of America. Although expelled by the Socialists, Russell was named to the Root Commission to Russia as a representative of United States Socialists and workers. In *Unchained Russia* (1918), he forecast, "To the last syllable of recorded time, mankind is likely to have cause to lament that in the years 1917 and 1918 the people of the United States did not understand the people of Russia and the people of Russia did not understand the people of the United States."

Other books followed, including the Pulitzer Prize-winning *The American Orchestra and Theodore Thomas* (1927). In the last twenty years before his death in 1941, the aesthete apparently dominated the political activist in Russell's makeup, at least as reflected in his writing. However, he supported Irish and Filipino independence, fought capital punishment, and spoke out for German Jews in the late 1930s. As early as 1901 he had published a volume of poetry, *Such Stuff as Dreams*; and he maintained a close friendship with the actress Julia Marlowe, which led to a biography in 1926. He

continued being fascinated with the relationship between music and poetry which began with his early study of Swinburne. Yet, when summing up his full and varied life, Russell wrote, "I like to muckrake. It isn't as calm and peaceful a pursuit as analyzing the amphibrach foot, but it seems to have more relation to living men and to be of immeasurably more use." The usefulness of his muckraking could be measured; new regulation of the beef trust and the end of Trinity Church's role as slumlord were among the more dramatic results.

Biography:

Donald Henry Bragaw, "Soldier for the Common Good: The Life and Career of Charles Edward Russell," Ph.D. dissertation, Syracuse University, 1970.

References:

Oliver Carlson, *Brisbane: A Candid Biography* (New York: Stackpole, 1937);

David Mark Chalmers, *The Social and Political Ideas of the Muckrakers* (New York: Citadel Press, 1964);

Louis Filler, *Crusaders for American Liberalism* (New York: Harcourt, Brace, 1939);

Homer A. King, *Pulitzer's Prize Editor: A Biography of John A. Cockerill* (Durham, N.C.: Duke University Press, 1965);

Ferdinand Lundberg, *Imperial Hearst* (New York: Equinox, 1936);

I. F. Marcossen, *David Graham Phillips and His Times* (New York: Dodd, Mead, 1932);

C. C. Regier, *The Era of the Muckrakers* (Chapel Hill: University of North Carolina Press, 1932);

Don C. Seitz, *Joseph Pulitzer: His Life and Letters* (New York: Simon & Schuster, 1924);

Upton Sinclair, *The Brass Check* (Pasadena, Cal.: Sinclair, 1920);

Harvey Swados, *Years of Conscience* (Cleveland: World, 1962);

W. A. Swanberg, *Citizen Hearst* (New York: Scribners, 1961);

Swanberg, *Pulitzer* (New York: Scribners, 1967);

Arthur and Lila Weinberg, *The Muckrakers* (New York: Simon & Schuster, 1961);

Frank Marshall White, "Charles Edward Russell," *Human Life* (December 1908): 11-12.

Papers:

Charles Edward Russell's papers are in the Library of Congress.

E. W. Scripps

Eric M. Odendahl
San Diego State University
and
Philip B. Dematteis

BIRTH: Rushville, Illinois, 18 June 1854, to James Mogg and Julia Osborn Scripps.

MARRIAGE: 7 October 1885 to Nackie Benson Holtsinger; children: James George Osborn, John Paul Holtsinger, Dorothy Blair, Edward Willis McLean, Robert Paine, Nackey Elizabeth.

MAJOR POSITION HELD: City editor, *Detroit Evening News* (1875-1878).

NEWSPAPERS OWNED: *Cleveland Penny Press* (1878-1889, 1892-1926), *St. Louis Chronicle* (1880-1908), *Cincinnati Post* (1883-1926), *Detroit Evening News* (1888-1890); *Kentucky Post* (Covington) (1890-1914), *San Diego Sun* (1893-1926), *Los Angeles Record* (1895-1920), *Kansas City World* (1897-1908), *Seattle Star* (1899-1920), *Akron Press* (1899-1925), *Chicago Press* (1900), *Des Moines News* (1902-1924), *Spokane Press* (1902-1920), *Tacoma Times* (1903-1920), *Toledo News-Bee* (1903-1926), *San Francisco News* (1903-1926), *Sacramento Star* (1904-1925), *Columbus Citizen* (1904-1926), *Fresno Tribune* (1905-1912), *Portland News* (1906-1920), *Evansville Press* (1906-1926), *Terre Haute Post* (1906-1926), *Denver Express* (1906-1926), *Pueblo Sun* (1906-1910), *Memphis Press* (1906-1926), *Nashville News* (1906-1907), *Dallas Dispatch* (1906-1920), *Oklahoma City News* (1906-1926), *Oakland Mail* (1909-1910), *Houston Post* (1911-1926), *Chicago Day Book* (1911-1917), *Philadelphia News-Post* (1912-1914), *El Paso Post* (1921-1926), *Knoxville News* (1921-1926), *Washington Daily News* (1921-1926), *Fort Worth Press* (1921-1926), *Norfolk Post* (1921-1926), *Birmingham Post* (1921-1926), *New Mexico State Tribune* (1922-1926), *Baltimore Post* (1922-1926), *Indianapolis Times* (1922-1926), *Youngstown Telegram* (1922-1926), *Pittsburgh Press* (1923-1926), *Akron Times* (1925-1926).

OTHER ENTERPRISES OWNED: Newspaper Enterprise Association (1902), United Press Associations (1907), Newspaper Supply Company (1909),

E. W. Scripps at Miramar, his ranch near San Diego

Science Service (1921), United Features Syndicate (1923), United News Pictures (1924).

DEATH: Aboard his yacht, the *Ohio*, off Monrovia, Liberia, 12 March 1926.

BOOKS: *Damned Old Crank: A Self-Portrait of E. W. Scripps*, edited by Charles R. McCabe (New York: Harper, 1951);
I Protest: Selected Disquisitions of E. W. Scripps, edited

by Oliver Knight (Madison: University of Wisconsin Press, 1966).

E. W. Scripps, the Illinois farm boy who grew up to build the first major newspaper chain in the United States and to found what later became United Press International, was a paradox. He based his success on his support for the working class, yet he paid his own employees low wages and amassed a fortune of $50,000,000. He professed faith in the "common people," but he was anything but common: he was an extreme individualist who wore rough work clothes even on formal occasions and had as his motto, "Whatever is, is wrong." He was a large and burly man who instilled fear in others with his gaze; but he was sickly all of his life, and those who met him were impressed by the limpness of his handshake. He was a hypochondriac who wore a skullcap indoors to ward off colds and moved to the desert for his health; but he claimed that he smoked forty cigars and drank a gallon of whiskey a day, in spite of doctors' warnings. He was a womanizer who engaged in numerous affairs in his younger days; but he was a puritan who was filled with disgust at his own weakness, and married a minister's daughter to whom he was devoted for the rest of his life. He was a crusader for democracy and liberal political causes, yet he was a self-proclaimed autocrat who insisted on ruling his business enterprises and his family with an iron hand. Such a contradictory personality is difficult to summarize; perhaps Scripps did it best himself when he proudly accepted the label of "damned old crank." Historian Oliver Knight, who edited the "disquisitions" Scripps dictated after his semiretirement, assessed Scripps as

> a vigorous thinker who was in a position to leave an impress upon the thought patterns of his time; a humanist of some stature; a philosopher who generalized from experience and empathy; a social critic of penetrating view; an idealist who reared his head into the clouds but let not the fog obscure the reality; an experimenter, even with his nearest and dearest, to see what would happen to human beings under certain conditions; a shrewd analyst of his time and of the drift in time; and a minor prophet.
>
> He also was a contrary old bastard.

At one time or another during his life, Scripps owned a controlling interest in fifty-two newspapers. None of these were first-rank papers, and a few were failures; but most were solid, profitable enterprises which managed to compete successfully in their markets. The majority of the Scripps papers were established in smaller but growing industrial cities in the Midwest; Scripps tended to stay away from the East. He also started several papers in the Far West, but these were his least successful ones, probably because of the lower level of industrialization in that region at the time. His papers championed the right of workers to organize, attacked political corruption, crusaded for public ownership of utilities, and supported liberal politicians such as Theodore Roosevelt and Woodrow Wilson. The Scripps papers were tightly edited, with a wide variety of items and features to hold reader interest; Scripps eschewed circulation-building gimmicks such as contests. In addition to his newspaper chain, Scripps established a wire service, the United Press, as a nonexclusive rival to the Associated Press, and three feature syndicates, the Newspaper Enterprise Association, the Science Service, and the United Features Syndicate. Outside of journalism, he was instrumental in the creation of the Scripps Institution of Oceanography in La Jolla, California.

Scripps was born 18 June 1854 on a farm near Rushville in Schuyler County, Illinois, the last of thirteen children of his father's three marriages. James Mogg Scripps had come to America in 1844 after failing as a bookbinder in London. On his way to Illinois he married Julia Osborn, a schoolteacher, in Cleveland. The farm on which they settled had been purchased by his father, William Armiger Scripps, who had remained in England. The city-bred James Mogg Scripps avoided working the farm as long as he could, taking up and failing in several other trades. Finally Julia, who had grown up in the country, took charge and turned the farm into a fairly profitable enterprise.

There is some mystery about the proper spelling of E. W. Scripps's middle name. He is usually referred to—even in some family documents—as Edward Wyllis Scripps; he generally signed his own name as Edward W. or simply E. W. Scripps. But on the one known occasion when he used his full name—in signing a will in 1906—he spelled his middle name "Willis."

Scripps's childhood was not particularly happy. His mother did not spare the rod on her son, perhaps because he was unwanted; she was forty and James Mogg was fifty-two when Scripps was born—as he later put it—"of an accident, the last expiring flame of passion burned to ashes in the aged bodies of my parents." He was sickly, rebellious, and unpopular; other children called him "Turkey Egg" because of his unruly mop of bright red hair. He

Scripps's boyhood home on the family farm near Rushville, Illinois (courtesy Edwin A. Dyson, Rushville Times*)*

turned to his sister, Ellen Browning Scripps, for most of his mothering. She was eighteen years older than he, homely, strong-willed but of a gentle disposition. He later declared that she "had more to do with the shaping and development of my character than all other influences that have borne me." Their special relationship continued for the rest of Scripps's life.

Scripps learned to read when he was four or five years old, and thereafter a great deal of his solitary childhood was spent in the company of books from his father's extensive library. In spite of this, he did not do well in school, where he rebelled against the teachers and refused to study his lessons; he never learned the multiplication table past seven.

His formal education ended when he was fifteen, because his father fell ill with a lingering and finally fatal disease. Since the other four boys had left home, Scripps had to take over the running of the farm. It was then that he began his Tom Sawyer-like practice of getting others to do the work while he had the ideas. He hired other Rushville boys to do the field work, which he turned into a contest; while they competed to see who could complete the hoeing first, he sat in a corner of the field with his head buried in a book. Scripps's refusal to do anything himself that he could get someone else

to do as well or better lasted throughout his career.

By the time he was eighteen, the idea of a journalistic career had taken hold in Scripps's mind, even though his real dream was to become a man of letters. Newspapering seemed more realistic than literature, however, since Scripps's half brother, James E. Scripps, was then part-owner and editor of the *Detroit Advertiser and Tribune,* and Ellen B. and several of his other relatives worked there. Journalism was a family tradition: Scripps's grandfather, William Armiger Scripps, had been editor of *True Briton* and publisher of the London *Daily Sun;* some of Scripps's cousins had started newspapers in Schuyler County; and another cousin, John Locke Scripps, had been one of the founders of the *Chicago Tribune.*

James E., however, was nineteen years older than Scripps, and the two had little in common; the older half brother did not want the younger one to come to work for him. Their dying father arranged for Scripps to take a teaching job at the Newberry School near Rushville. Before he could begin his duties, however, an opportunity arose for Scripps to go to Detroit to become a clerk in a drugstore being started by a cousin from England. When Scripps arrived in Detroit in November 1872, the drugstore was not yet ready to open; another half brother, Will, who was foreman of the job printing shop at the *Advertiser and Tribune*, persuaded James E. to let Scripps join the paper temporarily as an office boy. A few weeks later, a management shakeup left James E. and Will in control of the *Advertiser and Tribune*'s job printing business, the only profitable part of the paper. Scripps went to work for them, learning to set type and run a press.

On Easter Sunday 1873, the *Advertiser and Tribune* building burned to the ground. James E. used his half of the $20,000 insurance money to establish the *Detroit Evening News*, an experimental four-page, condensed newspaper that sold for two cents a copy instead of the nickel charged by other Detroit papers. Ellen was made exchange editor of the *News*, and Scripps was assigned a delivery route. Selling cheap newspapers led Scripps to discover that "a newspaper that had the patronage of the working class had a better business opportunity than a newspaper that had to depend upon the upper class alone for its patronage. There were at least ninety-five possible readers for a one-cent paper to every five possible readers for a five-cent paper." The *News* was also helped by the depression of 1873, which suddenly made the nickel papers too expensive even for many in the upper classes. Scripps expanded his routes and hired other boys to start new ones until he had 2,000 subscribers in the city; then he went to work building an equivalent circulation in the countryside. In the process, he later claimed, he pioneered out-of-town home delivery, a practice that became standard with daily papers.

With a steady income assured from his circulation business, Scripps decided in 1874 to move into the editorial side of the paper. He spent a year running errands and rewriting stories to improve his grammar and spelling, and finally persuaded James E. to make him city editor. He instructed his staff of three to seven reporters to "raise as much hell as possible," and he began running exposés in the paper. To escape personal liability in the resulting libel suits, James E. incorporated the paper in 1877 as the Detroit Evening News Association and distributed shares in the company to the members of the family. Scripps received one share in return for the $600 from his country circulation which he had turned over to James E. He later parlayed that one share of stock into a publishing empire.

By this time, the former country boy had become a loudly dressed, cigar-smoking, hard-drinking rake, whose sexual escapades were followed by strong guilt reactions. His habits reached a point of excess while he was serving as legislative correspondent in Lansing during the winter of 1877-1878. Seeking a rest, he traveled to Europe with his half brother George H. Scripps in the spring. It was while there, he said later, that he formed his determination to rise above the common herd and become a master of men.

During their absence, James E. had decided to start what he called a "cordon" of cheap newspapers in the Midwest, beginning in Cleveland. When they returned from Europe in the fall, George H. helped Scripps talk James E. into letting Scripps be the editor of the Cleveland paper, which was to be called the *Penny Press*. Scripps put up his one share of *News* stock as collateral for a twenty percent interest in the new paper. He quickly moved to take complete control of the *Penny Press* by placing the composing room under his authority rather than that of the business manager; this allowed him to determine the amount of space that would be devoted to news as opposed to advertising. Scripps made this arrangement the rule on every paper he owned: the editor was to be in charge of the composing room, and hence of the paper. The first issue of the *Cleveland Penny Press* was published on 2 November 1878. The politically independent, four-page paper was aimed at the working class, with a wide variety of short, concise stories—many of them involving crime, suicides, and paternity suits. A mainstay of the paper was a column of miscellany by Ellen, sent each day from Detroit. Scripps and his cousin, John Sweeney, the business manager, had to borrow an extra $2,500 from James E. and George H. to get the paper started; but by the end of 1879 the debt had been repaid and the *Penny Press* was making money.

Scripps was plagued with chronic bronchitis, and his condition was not improved by his heavy drinking and smoking. He also continued his pattern of sexual escapades followed by guilt and self-loathing, and took up rowing to try to sublimate his sexual energy. He began delegating more and more responsibility at the newspaper and spending less time in the office; it was characteristic of Scripps to be enthusiastic about starting projects and then to lose interest once they were under way.

Needing a new challenge, as well as a change of scene for his health, Scripps convinced James E. to back him in a paper in St. Louis. He left Cleveland in May 1880; the *St. Louis Chronicle* began publication on 31 July. At about the same time, James E. added the *Buffalo Telegraph* and the *Cincinnati Penny Paper* (which he renamed the *Penny Press*) to the family's joint holdings. The *Chronicle* was a failure for various reasons: St. Louis was too large and conservative for a Scripps-type paper that was better suited to a smaller, booming industrial city; Scripps tried to start the paper on too large a scale; and, perhaps most important, it was in competition with Joseph Pulitzer's *Post-Dispatch*. The *Chronicle* limped along until Scripps finally sold it in 1908. The paper's failure, combined with Scripps's tendency to blame everyone but himself for the debacle, further strained the relationship between him and James E.

Scripps returned to Cleveland in the spring of 1881 to train Robert F. Paine to be the new editor of the *Penny Press*. Almost immediately he was hit with a criminal libel suit claiming that a story in the paper implied that a rival publisher had had venereal disease; Scripps feared that he would go to prison, but after twenty-nine hours of deliberation, the jury found him not guilty. Meanwhile, his health continued to deteriorate. Given the erroneous diagnosis that his weight loss and coughing up blood were caused by tuberculosis, Scripps traveled with Ellen to Algeria for his health in November 1881. The hemorrhaging stopped and Scripps's weight went from 120 to 180 pounds (he was six feet tall). He and Ellen then traveled in Europe, the Mediterranean, and the Holy Land. While on the tour, Scripps immersed himself in the arts and began to dream again of a literary career; but James E., in a series of letters, persuaded him to return to the family business. He and Ellen came back from Europe in June 1883.

During their absence, the Scrippses' *Cincinnati Penny Press* had been renamed the *Penny Post*. Scripps decided that this was the paper he wanted for his own, acquired fifty-five percent of the stock, and dropped the word *Penny* from the title. He moved the paper to more reputable offices and continued his formula of numerous, concise news items and features combined with attacks on political corruption. He was fortunate to have as his advertising manager the young Milton A. McRae, who had been transferred from the *Detroit Evening News* a few months before Scripps took over the *Post*. Scripps said later, "I am willing to concede that I might have failed with the *Post* had I not had such a lieutenant as McRae in the business office." Historian Oliver Knight points out that Scripps and McRae "were almost complete opposites in nature and temperament. Where Scripps detested trade, McRae was a businessman. Where Scripps wanted to be in the background, McRae loved being out front. Where Scripps did not care for association with famous or rich personages, McRae was in his element with them." McRae was to be Scripps's

Milton A. McRae, Scripps's right-hand man for twenty-two years

right-hand man for twenty-two years.

Two incidents within two months of Scripps's arrival in Cincinnati almost succeeded in ending his enterprise before it had really begun. The first was the arrival in August of a woman who had been his mistress in Cleveland and St. Louis; she threatened to expose their past relationship if he did not take her back. Instead, Scripps had her arrested for disorderly conduct and called in reporters from rival papers: "I told the plain-clothes detective and the three reporters that for some time, up to a period of three or four years before, the woman who was present and I had been intimate. I said that the period of intimacy had closed by mutual consent and she now had remained determined to take up the old relations and make a disagreeable scene. The story was a short enough one. It was sufficiently sordid and vulgar to cause me considerable pain in relating it." The story appeared in the *Enquirer*, the *Commercial Gazette*, and the *Times-Star* the next day, and Scripps feared that he was ruined in Cincinnati; but he found to his disgust that he was neither condemned for his past indiscretion nor applauded for his bravery in standing up to blackmail. The woman left town, and Scripps—temporarily—swore off women.

The second incident, occurring almost immediately afterward, was a criminal libel suit against *Post* editor R. B. Ross and a reporter for a story accusing the city health officer of corruption. The health officer was represented in court by Thomas C. Campbell, the head of the Democratic political machine in Cincinnati. Inside the courthouse, a gang of Campbell thugs attacked McRae and Ross and then turned on Scripps. Although he was no fighter, Scripps had learned several years before how to contort his face into a particularly menacing expression; he also reached into his pocket as if going for a gun. The thugs fled. Scripps gave full editorial support to his employees, and the case ended in a hung jury.

Scripps and McRae were able to pay off a $10,000 debt and begin showing a profit by February 1884, when the paper's circulation reached 20,000. With the *Post* well on its way, Scripps spent most of 1884 in St. Louis, trying again to make a go of the *Chronicle*. He also resumed his woman-chasing, this time with upper-class society belles whom he had previously considered to be "nice girls" and untouchable; his disgust at his own weakness was combined with further disillusionment about human nature. His heavy drinking continued, and he developed neurotic symptoms of anxiety and hypochondria.

For a rest, Scripps spent the first four months of 1885 touring the South and meeting Democratic leaders. He returned to Cincinnati in May, determined to rid himself of his personal weaknesses. He left the *Post* under McRae's direction and rented rooms in a country house sixteen miles north of the city, where he intended to lead a monastic existence of reading and exercise. Instead, he met eighteen-year-old Nackie Holtsinger, the daughter of a West Chester minister, at a church social. They were married on 7 October 1885; Scripps's philandering apparently ended forever at that time. Scripps did not inform his relatives of the marriage until afterward, but in December, he took Ellen, James E. and his wife, and one of James E.'s daughters on a vacation in Mexico with him and his bride. In the spring, Scripps and Nackie moved into a country house in West Chester. Scripps figured his net worth then at $250,000, and he had an income of $20,000 a year. He was particularly proud of the fact that the *Post* had by that time surpassed James E.'s *Detroit Evening News* in circulation.

Scripps around the time of his marriage in 1885

Scripps adopted the life-style of a country squire at West Chester. From a sense of noblesse oblige he made the grounds of his home into a public park for the benefit of his neighbors. He dressed in rough work clothes, with his pants (he refused to call them "trousers") stuffed into high boots; he refused to change into more formal attire for his periodic trips into Cincinnati, which caused McRae considerable embarrassment when they dined in restaurants. Indoors, Scripps constantly wore a skullcap in the belief that this would prevent the chronic colds to which he was subject. He insisted on being in total command over everyone in his domain: his wife, his servants, and his children. His first child, James George, was born on 19 July 1886; Nackie was almost immediately pregnant again, but the child died at birth. John Paul was born in 1888 and Dorothy Blair (Dolla) was born in 1890. Jim, even as a baby, had a refractory disposition that infuriated Scripps; determined to bend the

Nackie Holtsinger Scripps, shortly after her marriage to E. W. Scripps

child to his will, he dealt so harshly with the boy that Nackie called him a brute. When Jim grew up, he told Scripps that for years he had "cherished the hope of some day growing large enough to give me a licking." While he never carried out that ambition, Jim was to seize part of his father's publishing empire.

Scripps began to move toward building that empire in 1887. James E. was in failing health and was forced to give up control of the family papers in Detroit, Cleveland, Cincinnati, and St. Louis (the Buffalo paper had been sold). He, Scripps, George H., and Sweeney signed what they called the Quadripartite Agreement, pledging that they would not sell any of their stock to outsiders and that if any of them died, half of his stock would be purchased by the remaining signers. As soon as James E. left for a two-year trip to Europe, thinking that peace had been achieved, Scripps began his drive for more power. Through a series of maneuvers, Scripps, then thirty-four, was able to make himself dominant in all four newspaper companies by September 1888. The following month, he adopted the name Scripps League for the chain.

Scripps moved quickly to revamp the operations of all four papers. Starting with the *Cincinnati*

Post, he dropped the muckraking, crusading policy and made them boomers of the cities in which they were located, making friends instead of enemies of the community leaders. For economy, he centralized both the buying of materials and the writing of editorials and plowed most of the profits back into the expansion of the papers. He established the New York Advertising Bureau to obtain national advertising for the papers and the New York News Bureau to obtain news from New York, Chicago, Washington, and Europe, in addition to the home cities of the League papers. Total readership, Scripps estimated, had reached 300,000 by 1889.

Scripps's fortunes changed, however, when James E. returned from Europe in August 1889. Outraged by Scripps's risky expansion of his beloved *Detroit Evening News*, James E. began a year-long battle that resulted in Scripps being dropped from the management of the Detroit and Cleveland papers. In 1890 Scripps pulled the Cincinnati and St. Louis papers out of the family organization; Ellen went with him, while George H. remained loyal to James E.

Calling his new organization the Scripps-McRae League and leaving McRae in charge, Scripps threw all his energies for the next two years into building a home, Miramar, on 400 acres in the desert north of San Diego, California. The location appealed to him because of its isolation and because the climate was similar to that of Algeria, the only place he had ever felt really healthy. As he began building Miramar in February 1891, Scripps felt that he did not have much to worry about financially with "a tolerably free income of $30,000 to $50,000 annually"—just one year's income amounting to what most people in those days considered to be enough to retire on comfortably for the rest of their lives. What started out to be a cheap winter house grew into an eight-year project, and Scripps expanded his landholdings to 2,100 acres. The forty-seven-room ranch house, with three turrets, a patio, and fountains in the center, was patterned after the dream house of Maximilian and Carlota, the emperor and empress of Mexico during the period of French rule. Scripps built dams to collect water, planted 700 acres of eucalyptus trees, and experimented with various types of citrus trees and cactus plants. He spent the winters at Miramar and the summers at West Chester until 1900, when he moved into Miramar on a year-round basis. The Scrippses had three more children during the 1890s: Edward Willis McLean was born in 1891, Robert Paine in 1895, and Nackey Elizabeth in 1898; Edward died at Miramar in 1899.

Aerial view of Miramar

In 1892, Scripps was ready to get back into journalism on an active basis. That year George H. broke with James E. and came over to Scripps's side, giving Scripps control once again of the *Cleveland Press*. In 1893, he bought the *San Diego Sun*. In 1895 Scripps and George H. combined their stock and made an agreement with McRae under which Scripps had control of the papers as editor in chief, McRae ran the business side as general manager, and the three pooled their salaries and dividends. The two Scripps half brothers each took two-fifths, and McRae got one-fifth. The Scripps-McRae League added the *Kansas City World* in 1897; it failed due to competition from William Rockhill Nelson's powerful *Star*. The *Akron Press* was added in 1899. In 1900 Scripps experimented with an adless paper, the *Chicago Press*, but William Randolph Hearst's *American* drove the *Press* out of business within the year. George H. died in 1900 and left all his stock to Scripps; James E. contested the will in a protracted legal battle.

Scripps founded the Newspaper Enterprise Association in 1902 as an adjunct to the *Cleveland Press*. The NEA supplied news, features, and editorials to the Scripps papers. Scripps's dream was to use the NEA to transform the papers in his chain into a single national newspaper, but his independent editors merely treated it as a source of syndicated material. Also in 1902, the Scripps-McRae League added the *Des Moines News*; the *Toledo News-Bee* was acquired in 1903. In a settlement of their legal dispute in 1903, James E. received George H.'s thirty-two percent stock in the *Detroit Evening News* while Scripps agreed to take that amount in other papers.

Scripps became interested in science in 1903 as a result of a visit to a University of California temporary research station near San Diego. With his usual enthusiasm for a new project, he took on the task of establishing permanent facilities: he contributed money himself, persuaded Ellen to contribute, and got the city of San Diego to donate 170 acres of idle land it owned in the suburb of La Jolla. The facility was named the Scripps Institution for Biological Research in 1912; in 1925, the university changed the name to the present Scripps Institution of Oceanography.

Meanwhile, the Scripps-McRae League continued to expand. The *Columbus Citizen* was acquired in 1904. Six papers were started in 1906: in

Indiana, the *Evansville Press* and the *Terre Haute Post*; in Colorado, the *Denver Express* and the *Pueblo Sun*; in Tennessee, the *Memphis Press* and the *Nashville News*; and the *Dallas Dispatch* and the *Oklahoma City News*. At the same time, apart from the League, Scripps was adding nine West Coast papers to the *San Diego Sun*: the *Los Angeles Record*, the *Seattle Star*, the *Spokane Press*, the *Tacoma Times*, the *San Francisco News*, the *Sacramento Star*, the *Fresno Tribune*, the *Portland News*, and the *Oakland Mail*.

The founding of all these newspapers provided great opportunity for success for young men in Scripps's organization. The method was simple: a young editor and business manager would be advanced about $25,000 in a city of 50,000 to 100,000 population selected by Scripps. Scripps did not want to invest too much in any enterprise because "it has long been my conviction that, everything else being equal, the more money spent in the establishment of a new newspaper and its conduct, the less its prospects for success." The men's salaries would be $25 a week until the money advanced was used up. Scripps took the loss if the paper failed; if it was profitable, the editor and business manager received a large block of stock—while Scripps retained fifty-one percent so he could keep full control. Scripps explained his reasoning: "We employ only very young men, men who have not elsewhere, under other employment, earned a right to prestige—young men who have practically been working for us at apprentice wages while they are doing their best work; and further we do not load ourselves up with older men who are employed simply on account of their prestige long after the period of their greatest usefulness." These papers, mainly afternoon ones, were published for the common man. Scripps wrote to his editors that "I have constituted myself the advocate of that large majority of people who are not so rich in worldly goods and native intelligence as to make them equal, man for man, in the struggle with the wealthier and more intellectual class." Scripps returned to his original formula of crusades and exposés of corruption. In 1905, he reduced McRae's power by "kicking him upstairs" to become chairman of the board; McRae retired in 1907.

It was also in 1907 that Scripps founded the United Press. The roots of UP went back to 1897, when Scripps had gotten into a dispute with the Associated Press. AP offered to supply some of his newspapers with the wire service, but not all of them. This was because AP operated under a membership program which, Scripps felt, made it impossible for a new paper to be started in any city where there were AP members. So he began a Midwestern agency, the Scripps-McRae Association, in 1897 and an Eastern service, the Publishers' Press Association, in 1904. He also operated the Scripps News Association for his papers on the West Coast. A merger and reorganization of these three agencies brought about the establishment of the United Press Associations in 1907.

"Among other motives in founding the UP was the altruistic one. I do not believe in monopolies," Scripps wrote. "I believe that monopolists suffer more than their victims in the long run. I did not believe it would be good for journalism in this country if there should be one big news trust such as the founders of the Associated Press fully expected to set up." Another motive, perhaps, was the fact that James E. Scripps had been one of the founders of the modern AP in 1900.

The manager of United Press was twenty-four-year-old Roy W. Howard, who had worked for the *Indianapolis News* and the *Indianapolis Star* before moving over to Pulitzer's *Post-Dispatch*. Extremely ambitious, and feeling that he had been unfairly

Roy W. Howard, president of United Press and Scripps's partner in the Scripps-Howard League

passed over for a telegraph editor's job, Howard quit the *Post-Dispatch* and joined the Scripps *Cincinnati Post*. He moved to New York as special correspondent for the *Post*, and his aggressiveness elevated him to news manager of Publisher's Press in 1906. When UP was founded the following year, Howard kept the job as news manager. He was just the kind of man Scripps wanted as a top executive in his organization. "His manner was forceful, and the reverse from modest," Scripps recalled later. "Gall was written all over his face. It was in every tone and every word he voiced. There was ambition, self-respect, and forcefulness coming out of every pore in his body."

Scripps went into partial retirement in early 1908, turning the business side of his papers over to his son Jim. Scripps still controlled the news policies until 1911, when he handed those over to his son John, who was married to McRae's daughter.

The early dream of a literary life returned to Scripps as his "retirement" began. It was then that he started to write his "disquisitions," partly because "I have still secretly hugged the hope that I was really a philosopher and an original genius who could possibly, and even probably, produce at least some matter which would be of great value to the public, if ever submitted to." While dictating his disquisitions at Miramar, Scripps corresponded with people he regarded as intellectuals, such as Clarence Darrow, Lincoln Steffens, William Allen White, Max Eastman, and William Jennings Bryan. Many such persons came to visit him at the ranch. Scripps produced about 500 disquisitions between 1908 and his death in 1926. Some were loosely edited by Charles R. McCabe into a book, *Damned Old Crank: A Self-Portrait of E. W. Scripps* (1951). The most complete and objective work on Scripps is a 1966 book edited by Oliver Knight, *I Protest*, which centers around selections from Scripps's disquisitions.

The Scripps-McRae League continued to add newspapers to its holdings. The *Houston Post* was started in 1911. The same year, Scripps tried again to establish an adless paper in Chicago: the *Day Book*, edited by Negley Cochran, with Carl Sandburg as a reporter. The *Day Book* had moderate success but was driven out of business in 1917 by the rising cost of newsprint during World War I. Scripps started the *Philadelphia News-Post* in 1912 and considered turning it into an adless paper, but killed it in 1914. Scripps had stated the importance of separating advertisers from any control over the editorial content of his newspapers in a 1910 letter: "A newspaper fairly and honestly conducted in the

ONE CENT—LAST EDITION—ONE CENT

TROOPS PUSH ON THROUGH MEXICO
THOUSAND STRIKE AT PULLMAN CO.

THE DAY BOOK

An Adless Newspaper, Daily Except Sunday

VOL. 5, NO. 144   Chicago, Thursday, March 16, 1916   398

SAM INSULL'S DREAM OF UNIFICATION

One Vast Public Utility Trust to Which Commonwealth Edison Will Supply the Juice—Unified Politics Controlled by the Same Influence.

BY N. D. COCHRAN

Now that Vic Lawson has given us a line on the steps about to be taken toward the organization of one big public utility trust in Chicago, I can predict with reasonable assurance other events that we may look for as part of the game.

You see these things are all worked out in advance. Even last year steps were taken to stage a Billy Sunday revival early next year. That means the good people will be stirred up by a strenuous crusade against Vice and Crime. The newspapers will be full of it, and you will see long rows of automobiles near the tabernacle, while the eminently respectable rich help boost the game along and get their morals laundered.

In the meantime we'll have a busy morals squad, crusades against cabarets and dancing and a generally active interest by the rich in the private morals of the poor.

There will be political organization, too. Big Biz needs a politic.

Front page of Scripps's second experimental adless newspaper in Chicago

interest of the great masses of the public must at all times antagonize the selfish interests of that very class which furnishes the larger part of a newpaper's income, and occasionally so antagonize this class as to cause it not only to cease patronage, to a greater or lesser extent, but to make actually offensive warfare against the newspaper." A newspaper with no advertising at all would eliminate this possibility; but Scripps was never able to make this goal a reality.

John Scripps died in 1914; in 1916, Scripps's daughter Nackey eloped with one of Scripps's former secretaries, for whom Scripps had an intense dislike. Scripps decided to leave Miramar to escape the situation, and in 1917 he moved to Washington, D.C., to supervise his newspapers' coverage of World War I. The war produced a change in Scripps's political thinking: from a radical whose cry had been "God damn the rich and God help the poor," he became a conservative admirer of big business for its contributions to the war effort. His support for Woodrow Wilson's war policies brought him into conflict with his son Jim.

Overwork, renewed hard drinking, and stress from his family problems probably combined to produce a stroke that partially paralyzed Scripps in November 1917. He went to Florida to recuperate and took up residence on the *Kemah*, a ninety-six-foot gasoline-powered yacht. Later, he stayed briefly in a rented house near Annapolis.

It was son Jim who showed his father's trait of wanting to be in control. When Scripps moved his other son, Robert P., into the organization as editor in chief, Jim forced a split. Like his father, he was able to resolve family disputes by the simple expedient of controlling stock. Pooling his stock with that of others, Jim in 1920 was able to remove five West Coast papers—the *Portland News*, the *Tacoma Times*, the *Spokane Press*, the *Seattle Star*, and the *Los Angeles Record*—as well as the *Dallas Dispatch* from the chain. Jim died in 1921; his father did not get the papers back because Jim's widow formed the Scripps-Canfield League, which later became known simply as the Scripps League. B. H. Canfield had been Jim's chief editorial lieutenant.

Work on the disquisitions sparked Scripps's interest in science, and he formed the Science Service, a specialized news agency, in 1921. The Scripps Foundation for Population Research was also founded that year.

With the agreement of McRae, the old partnership was dissolved and Scripps formed a new one. His one surviving son, Robert P., became a partner with Roy Howard. The ambitious Howard had moved from president of United Press to chairman of what became in 1922 the Scripps-Howard newspaper chain.

Robert P. had a larger yacht, the *Ohio*, built for his father in 1922. Powered by two diesel engines, the yacht was about 180 feet long with a large library and living room; it could cruise nonstop for 10,000 miles. Scripps virtually lived on the *Ohio* for the last few years of his life. By this time he was estranged from his wife, who, he felt, had sided with Jim and Nackey against him in their family disputes.

Even though the West Coast papers had been split away, the larger chain continued to grow. By 1925 United Features Syndicate and United News Pictures (its name was changed to Acme Newspictures in 1926) had been added along with twelve more newspapers—the *Akron Times*, the *New Mexico State Tribune*, the *Baltimore Post*, the *Pittsburgh Press*, the *El Paso Post*, the *Indianapolis Times*, the *Youngstown Telegram*, the *Knoxville News*, the *Washington Daily News*, the *Fort Worth Press*, the *Nor-*

folk Post, and the *Birmingham Post*. In September of that year Scripps tried to put himself in perspective with other newspaper giants of the time:

> At this date William Randolph Hearst is recognized as the greatest of American newspapermen. I own more newspapers than Hearst, but Hearst owns bigger newspapers than mine. I really do not know what Hearst is worth in the way of money, and to be perfectly frank, I do not know what I am worth. I only feel pretty sure that Hearst controls newspaper property valued at two or three times the value I put on my newspaper holdings.
>
> But Hearst's star actually arose after I had retired from business, or thought I had retired, some thirty-five years ago.
>
> All the old great journalists of New York [Greeley, Bennett, and Dana] have disappeared, followed by Pulitzer.
>
> The greatest figures in New York journalism today are, I suppose, William Randolph Hearst of the *Journal* and *American*, Adolph Ochs of the New York *Times*, and Frank Munsey who, besides several newspapers, owns, I believe, a string of grocery stores. I think that the Jew, Ochs, has more ready money than any other newspaperman in the United States. I think his net profits are perhaps larger than mine and Hearst [*sic*] put together.
>
> I consider myself a glittering example of what may happen to a man if he succeeds in living long enough. Victor Lawson was another equally good example.
>
> Neither Lawson nor myself were ever very articulative. Victor Lawson died the other day about the age of seventy-four. I am now seventy-one years old. It is only because Lawson and I lasted so long that the tide of fortune carried us so far.

Scripps was to last only another six months after he wrote that assessment. He died of apoplexy while entertaining friends aboard the *Ohio* off Monrovia, Liberia, on 12 March 1926. In accordance with his wishes, he was buried at sea. Nackie Holtsinger Scripps died in 1930. The controlling interest in Scripps's enterprises went to Robert P. Scripps, and on his death in 1938, it was divided among his six children. Roy Howard remained powerful in the organization. Scripps-Howard continued to found and buy newspapers; most of these were, as in E. W. Scripps's day, located in second- and third-class cities. An exception was the *New York*

The Ohio, *the yacht on which Scripps lived the last years of his life and on which he died*

Telegram, purchased in 1927 and merged with the Pulitzers' failing *World* in 1931 under Howard's direction.

A number of papers were killed or sold during the Depression, leaving the total at nineteen in 1940. The *New York Sun* was combined with the *World-Telegram* in 1950. The United Press gained in stature under the leadership of presidents Karl Bickel and Hugh Baillie; it was merged with Hearst's International News Service in 1958 to form the present United Press International. The United Features Syndicate offered leading columnists such as Raymond Clapper and Marquis Childs. Howard died in 1964, and his brainchild, the *New York World-Telegram and Sun*, went under three years later. In the West, the family of Jim Scripps developed small dailies in Utah, Montana, Oregon, and Idaho, while John Paul Scripps—the son of Scripps's son John—built a chain of small newspapers in California.

In a tribute to Scripps, muckraker Lincoln Steffens wrote: "He is a great man and individual. There are no others like him: energy, vision, courage, wisdom. He thinks his own thoughts absolutely. He sees straight. He sees the line he is on and his thinking sticks to that. I regard Scripps as one of the two or three great men of my day. He is on to himself and the world, plays the game and despises it. He is sincere and not cynical . . . he avoided other rich men, so as to escape from being one; he knew the danger his riches carried for himself, for his papers, and for his seeing. Rough, almost ruthless force, but restrained by clear, even shrewd insight; an executive capable of fierce action, restrained by the observation that a doer must not do many things himself but must use his will to make others do them. And he did that all right. Read some of the letters to his editors, the young fellows he was driving so hard and letting alone."

Roy Howard put the matter more succinctly: "There is no journalistic slide rule to measure him by. He was unique."

Biographies:

Gilson Gardner, *Lusty Scripps: The Life of E. W. Scripps* (New York: Vanguard Press, 1932);

Negley D. Cochran, *E. W. Scripps* (New York: Harcourt, Brace, 1933).

References:

Max Eastman, "My Friend E. W.," *Freeman* (11 January 1954);

"Life and Death of Edward W. Scripps, Pioneer Genius of Free Press," *Editor and Publisher* (20 March 1926);

Milton A. McRae, *Forty Years in Newspaperdom: The Autobiography of a Newspaper Man* (New York: Brentano, 1924);

William E. Ritter, "The Relation of E. W. Scripps to Science," *Science* (25 March 1927);

Ritter, "Science Service and E. W. Scripps' Philosophy of Life," *General Science* (25 December 1926);

Lincoln Steffens, *The Autobiography of Lincoln Steffens* (New York: Harcourt, Brace, 1931).

Papers:

E. W. Scripps's papers are at his home, Miramar, near San Diego, California, and at the Edward W. Scripps Trust, Cincinnati, Ohio.

Frank L. Stanton

(22 February 1857-7 January 1927)

Bruce M. Swain
University of Georgia

MAJOR POSITION HELD: Columnist, *Atlanta Constitution* (1890-1927).

BOOKS: *Songs of a Day and Songs of the Soil* (New York: Alden, 1892);

Songs of the Soil (New York: Appleton, 1894);

Comes One with a Song (Indianapolis: Bowen-Merrill, 1898);

Songs from Dixie Land (Indianapolis: Bowen-Merrill, 1900);

Up from Georgia (New York: Appleton, 1902);

Little Folks down South (New York: Appleton, 1904);

Just from Georgia, compiled by Marcelle Stanton Megahee (Atlanta: Byrd, 1927).

PERIODICAL PUBLICATIONS: "At Andersonville," *New England Magazine* (June 1891): 434;

"Look Aloft," *Outlook* (28 September 1895): 519;

"Thankful Soul," *Outlook* (28 March 1896): 600;

"June Dreams," *Spectator* (25 April 1896): 581;

"So Many," *Outlook* (29 May 1897): 253;

"With the Colored Regiment Band," *Century* (June 1899): 328.

Frank L. Stanton, author of some of the most popular poems and songs of his era, for thirty-six years delivered his rhymed optimism each day on the editorial page of the *Atlanta Constitution*. Although the *Constitution* championed the emerging New South, Stanton's writing—with its frequent use of Negro and poor white or "cracker"· dialects—presented the old order with nostalgic fondness. As an article in the *Nation* said shortly after his death, Stanton represented "the sentiments of his own race both in the South where he sang and elsewhere among that large population which likes to be reminded at a distance of the plantation and the pickaninny, with remarkable fidelity." His "Just from Georgia" column led to his being designated the first poet laureate of Georgia in 1925. But, despite that distinction and the national popularity of "Mighty Lak a Rose" and others of his poems, Stanton sometimes claimed not to be a poet. "Still," he told an interviewer, "if a feller goes fishing every day of his life, he is bound to get a nibble now and then." First and foremost, Stanton was a journalist, beginning his apprenticeship as a copyboy on the *Savannah Morning News* at age twelve and working in a newsroom until he died at sixty-nine.

Frank Lebby Stanton was born in Charleston, South Carolina, on 22 February 1857 to parents with strong connections to both journalism and the Old South. His father, Valentine Stanton, was a printer. The father of his mother, Catherine Parry Stanton, had been a wealthy cotton planter on Kiawah Island, South Carolina. For at least some of his early childhood his family lived on a farm, where his duties included herding cattle. The enviable simplicity of country living was a theme he would later return to time and time again in his writing.

Stanton credited his mother with the easy swing of his verse, the attribute that destined many of his poems to become popular songs. "I was brought up on Charles Wesley and Isaac Watts," he said in reference to her habit of reading to him from the Methodist hymnal. He was less receptive to other elements of his mother's Methodism. He was no teetotaler, and near the end of his life he told his biographer, Wightman F. Melton: "When I was a small boy over there in South Carolina and my mother used to sing me the old hymns of the Wesleys and Isaac Watts, it was all clear enough to me that a man who dies shall live again, but during a long life of rubbing elbows with the world, doubts have crept in." However, one of the posthumous tributes he received was from a Methodist bishop, Warren A. Candler: "He will be remembered most for religious poems inspired by the sublime simplicities of the genuine Christian life, however slow he may have been to claim such a life for himself."

In 1862 the family moved to Savannah, Georgia, where Stanton attended public school until his schooling was interrupted by the Civil War, in which his father served as a Confederate soldier. Stanton completed his education privately, without a tutor. Much of that early self-education was apparently devoted to reading the works of Shakespeare and other classics. Stanton possessed a remarkable memory: according to several commentators, he was capable later in life of quoting from memory entire Shakespearean dramas, as well as his own earlier work and other material. One contemporary article related an incident in which that capacity was tested by a man who read aloud a poem Stanton had never heard before. While he read, Stanton read some prose that was also new to him. When both men finished Stanton immediately recited both the prose and the poetry verbatim. Another admirer reported having heard him recite Byron's entire *Childe Harold* without a mistake.

His first poem, "To Lizzy," was written when he was eleven. The next year he went to work at the *Savannah Morning News* as a copyboy, then moved into the back shop to work as a printer's devil. If a study of American literature seems to indicate that a newspaper office is a splendid school for writers, the *Morning News* of that era would seem to have been a particularly promising environment for an aspiring literary journalist. The editor was William Tappan Thompson, author of *Major Jones's Courtship* (1843), a book of Southern humor; among

the reporters was Joel Chandler Harris. The youngster in the printing shop who submitted verses to the paper caught Harris's eye. Harris, who was at the time himself experimenting with poetry, encouraged Stanton in those early attempts. Harris left the Savannah paper for the *Atlanta Constitution* soon thereafter, but the paths of the two men were to cross years later.

Although several histories report that he remained at the Savannah paper, where he reached the position of reporter and feature writer, until 1887, Stanton told interviewer Walter Chambers of *American Magazine* in 1925 that there was a period of nearly ten years during which he drifted from town to town as a traveling printer. "I would work at the type cases all day," he told Chambers, "and at night go out walking close to the soil." (That habit, Chambers noted, was one he continued after he had obtained a job on the *Atlanta Constitution* and risen to national prominence: "Every clear day, when he leaves the *Constitution* office he goes for a ride out into the country, where the car is stopped in some by-road and he strolls around in the green fields of spring, or on the carpet of leaves in autumn.") At age thirty he was still deciding between regular employment and the footloose life of an itinerant printer. He might well have followed the second course but for some brotherly advice and an advertisement by a country editor looking for an assistant. His brother lectured him that he could soon be on the editorial staff of the *Constitution* if he would quit "running around the country with no objective." Although Stanton remembered "laughing till I fell off the log," the advice proved prophetic. The ad was from the owner of the *Smithville News*, who promised Stanton that he would be allowed to write a column if he joined the southeast Georgia paper.

It was a fortuitous move for him. In 1887 he became owner and editor of the *News* and on 15 January of that year he married Leona Jossey, who inspired many of his poems. They had three children. Under his leadership the *News* became one of the most noted weeklies in the state. According to Charles W. Hubner in *The Library of Southern Literature*, the paper became known for its "racy editorials, its witty comment on current events, its sparkling humor, and its graphic dialect verse and stories." Stanton was having the time of his life. With the full consent of local subscribers, he was writing stories that placed them in comical, highly fictional situations. The entertaining copy soon came to the attention of his old friend Harris, who by then was a mainstay of the editorial page of the *Constitution*. "Mr. Smith, of Smithville" became a standard favorite reprint for Harris's *Constitution* readers. Stanton's handiwork also came to the attention of John Temple Graves of the *Rome Daily Tribune*, who lured him to northwest Georgia in 1888 as night editor.

His sojourn at Rome was to be as brief as his stint in Smithville, however: Harris was instrumental in arranging an offer for Stanton to come to the *Constitution*, which Stanton accepted in 1889. He was assigned reportorial work and feature stories for a short while, but joined Harris on the editorial-page staff within a year. His job there was to write a column and to handle the exchange papers the *Constitution* received from Georgia weeklies.

From Harris he received his only direction concerning the column: "Whirl in and write the same sort of stuff you reeled off down yonder, in the piney places where you met the mockingbirds. We all, up here, are just plain home-folks, kind of like children that crawled in under the tent of the big circus, and when we look back to where you and lots of us came from, we are apt to feel that we're a long ways from home. Make your column home-like." The managing editor, Clark Howell, concurred in that approach.

For many years Stanton and Harris shared an office at the newspaper and were neighbors as well. From the author of the Uncle Remus tales Stanton learned a valuable lesson: develop sources among the older blacks if attempting to describe their lives. Many of his dialect poems were based, Stanton said later, on the sayings of one elderly black friend of his, whom he identified only as "Brother Dickey"—and in his writings as "Brer William." It was also Harris who suggested the name for his column, "Just from Georgia." The column featured Stanton's poems, prose, anecdotes, brief essays, humorous sayings, and items borrowed from other newspapers. But it was the short poems with which he introduced his column each day that became his trademark.

Newsroom observers recalled that it was a simple matter to determine whether Stanton, writing with a soft lead copy pencil on copy paper, was laboring over a poem or a song: if it were the latter, he would be tapping his foot as he wrote.

He kept his promise to Harris and Howell to keep his writing "homey," and the column immediately caught on with the public. So popular was his writing with readers of the *Constitution* that he was continually the recipient of gifts. Among the presents arriving at his already dramatically cluttered desk were live possums, raccoons, sea turtles, and even wildcats. "Please accept this Georgia salamander which I am sending you by express," one fan wrote. "This salamander is the only one ever captured in Georgia. I suppose you'll know what to do with it, as I don't."

Stanton's humor was not the sort to produce guffaws; it was the tickling humor of the country-store philosopher beside the pot-bellied stove. Sometimes he borrowed philosophical statements from the rural weeklies he monitored for the *Constitution*. On other days he included "Briefs from Billville," fictional news items from a small and utterly pleasant Georgia village that existed only in his imagination. "Our literary society has suspended for the plowing season," his Billville column of 24 February 1925 reported. "Now there will be some real work done." When his friend and fellow *Constitution* writer Don Marquis tried to interview him about the imaginary town, Stanton was not receptive. "I see myself letting you go there!" he told Marquis. "First thing I know someone will be sneaking a railroad through Billville if I start letting outsiders in." Tourists, he told Marquis, would frighten away the villagers.

His reluctance to allow change to arise in the imaginary Billville may well have reflected Stanton's attitude toward the changes that were sweeping the South during his tenure at the *Constitution*. Henry W. Grady, the legendary editor, had died shortly after Stanton arrived at the paper, but in his twelve years at the *Constitution* he had made the paper outspoken in its support of the New South: industrialization, diversification of crops, and an end to the Negro illiteracy, servitude, and poverty that had been an institution for more than a century. Like Henry Watterson at the *Louisville Courier-Journal*, Grady informed his fellow white Southerners in no uncertain terms that, ready or not, they were faced with a new social order—one that required black and white to live together in peace if their region were to survive economically. Harris and Howell continued the course set by Grady; but Stanton's writing hardly reflected his newspaper's editorial position, despite his close friendship with Harris. Instead, his message seemed to glorify the old order. He did not actually oppose change, but he reminded readers incessantly of the past. His poem "Old Times in Georgy" begins:

> Old times in Georgy—them's the times for me!
> No times now like them times, an' never-more will be!

Long before the railroads, an' steamers
                                 blowin' free,
How I like to dream o' them—dear old times
                                        to me!

Nor, apparently, was he persuaded that an agriculture-based society was economically unsound—as he argued in "Down on the Old Plantation":

In spite of politics an' sich
        A-worryin' of the nation,
We're doin' well in Georgy lan'
        Down on the ol' plantation.
We're fixin' now fer cotton white
        To fleece the fiel's from left to right,
An' take ol' Georgy out o'sight
        Down on the ol' plantation!

Stanton was not reluctant to write in his facsimile of Negro dialect, and even included the word "nigger" in his poems—as in the first stanza of "The Colored Dancing Match":

'Twuz in de dancin' season w'en de fros' wuz
                                        layin' roun'
En de rabbit wuz a-gwine lak a gray ghos'
                                cross de groun'—
W'en de lazies'er niggers wuz a-comin' ter de
                                        scratch—
Dat we took de whole plantation wid de
                        cullud Dancin' Match.

As infuriatingly convincing evidence of racism as such lines might appear to present-day blacks, they evidently were not perceived as such at the time. In fact, in an introduction to *Just From Georgia* (1927), a posthumous collection of Stanton's poetry, *Constitution* editorial writer James A. Holloman suggested that Stanton used "the language of the upland Negro . . . to concentrate about him the sympathy of those who had been taught to despise him."

Stanton could certainly never be said to be sympathetic to the lynch mob tactics by which blacks were being suppressed at the time by some whites resisting racial equality. While still at the *Smithville News* he had written a powerful attack on the brutality of the mob. "I took a walk along about dusk one day," he told Chambers thirty-seven years later, "and came across a place where a Negro had been lynched a few hours before. The poor man's wife and her little girl were sittin' on a log cryin'. My heart went out to them, and that's how I happened to write a poem called 'Lynched,' and also another one called 'They've Hung Bill Jones.' " One of his

shortest works, "Lynched" is not in dialect:

The tramp of horse adown a sullen glen,
Dark forms of stern, unmerciful masked
                                        men;
A clash of arms, a cloven prison door,
And a man's cry for mercy! . . . Then high
                                        o'er
The barren fields, dim outlined in the storm,
The swaying of a lifeless human form.
And close beside, in horror and affright,
A widowed woman wailing to the night!

"*They've Hung Bill Jones*" begins:

They've hung Bill Jones to the sycamore tree,
        An' his wife an' his mother is a-weepin';
An' his children's come from the house to see,
        An' the col' wind a-wailin' an' a-creepin'!

"Lynched" and "They've Hung Bill Jones" were part of a real drama, in that Stanton and others claimed that the poems saved the life of a condemned prisoner. A western governor told reporters that after refusing to commute a death sentence, he had picked up a collection of Stanton poems—ten years old at the time—and had come across the two antilynching poems. Stirred, he had reversed his decision. Stanton told Chambers that once the story had been carried by wire services to newspapers across the country, "fifteen or twenty men" came to his office claiming to be the one whose life had been spared. One woman, he reported, claimed to have walked from a western state to thank him for the life of her husband.

If Stanton did not shy away from that violent aspect of race relations in the South of his day, it was surely one of the few instances in which he did not attempt to put a happy face on reality. One of his most popular poems, "Keep A-Goin'," perhaps best captures his approach to life. It begins:

Ef you strike a thorn or rose,
        Keep a-goin'!
Ef it hails or ef it snows,
        Keep a-goin'!
'Tain't no use to sit an' whine
When the fish ain't on your line;
Bait your hook an' keep a-tryin'—
        Keep a-goin'!

Such unremitting optimism was no accident in the work of Stanton, who partially attributed to it the success of his column. He said the column caught on because of its "homey" quality and because "I didn't put my troubles into it. I sang about the sunshine often when the rain was round my eyes, though the sad note just will creep in at times." The sad note crept into one of his best-known bits of writing, "Jest A-Wearyin' fer You," which was prompted by his loneliness when his wife was out of town:

> Jest a-wearyin' fer you—
> All the time a-feelin' blue;
> Wishin' fer you, wonderin' when
> You'll be comin' home again;
> Restless—don't know what to do—
>   Jest a-wearyin' fer you.

Shortly after he had moved to Atlanta to join the *Constitution* staff the sickness of his son Frank led to the writing of his most popular song, "Sweetes' Li'l Feller," which is often referred to as "Mighty Lak a Rose." Looking down into the child's feverish face his grandmother remarked, "Isn't he the sweetest little fellow? He's just like a rose!" Stanton later recalled, "I went into my room, picked up a piece of copy paper, and the poem wrote itself." He chose to write it, as he usually did, in dialect, but its international appeal was not diminished thereby. Stanton told one interviewer that he had received more than ten thousand letters and personal calls expressing appreciation of the poem, some from England and India. That song began:

> Sweetes' li'l feller—
> Everybody knows;
> Dunno what ter call 'im,
> But he mighty lak' a rose!

"Keep A-Goin' " and "Sweetes' Li'l Feller" would probably have brought him a good income for life, had Stanton been worldly-wise. That was not the case; he rarely, if ever, copyrighted his work. Each of his two most famous poems brought him only $150. The first time he learned "Mighty Lak a Rose" had been set to music was when he heard a friend singing it to himself. Stanton learned that an eminent American composer, Ethelbert Nevin, who had just died, had published the song. Stanton wrote to his widow, who dispatched to Atlanta "a nice young fellow" who offered him $150. "I happened to be a little short of cash," Stanton remembered, "so I took the $150." "Jest A-wearyin' for You" was set to music by composer Carrie Jacobs Bond.

Stanton, who had been too shy to ask the *Constitution* cashier for his paycheck for his first three weeks on the job, did once venture to New York City at the invitation of a publisher who had sent him fifty dollars. "I decided to make some money," he told Chambers. " 'I'll go to New York,' I said to myself, 'and make enough money to buy me a farm down South, where I can live forever.' " But he found the pace in New York hectic and became heartsick at the children he saw living in tenements. He was back on the train to Atlanta within a month.

His lack of interest in financial reward for his work extended to his avoidance of public accolades. At one time he was described as the most widely known man in Georgia, though he seldom ventured beyond his men's club or his *Constitution* office, where he received a constant stream of well-wishers and persons seeking help. One attempt to fete him at a *Constitution* dinner fell through when he heard the orchestra strike up "Mighty Lak a Rose" and fled. When Gov. Clifford Walker named him poet laureate on 22 February, his birthday, in 1925, he pleaded ill health and did not attend the public ceremony.

Within fifteen years of his arrival at the *Constitution*, six books of Stanton's poetry were in print. The first to appear was *Songs of a Day* (1892), portions of which were republished in *Songs of the Soil* (1894). In his introduction to *Songs of a Day*, Harris drew attention to the daily pressures under which Stanton operated: "It should be said, not by way of apology, but by way of explanation, that the poems in this little volume are the flowers that have sprung up in the wilderness of daily newspaper work, blooming unexpectedly, even to the author, between paragraphs or side by side with the results of the most arduous routine work."

Carl Holliday, in his *History of Southern Literature* (1906), dealt bluntly with the pitfalls of grinding out any writing under daily deadline pressure: "It cannot be claimed that Mr. Stanton's poetry is perfect in artistic form. He has his mannerisms; errs sometimes in grammar; uses words, figures, phrases that have become shop-worn by too frequent repetition; and manifests other occasional flaws and defects, usually due to hasty work and over-crowded production." At least, he suggested, Stanton brought poetry into the lives of common people and thus helped prepare them for higher forms of verse. The *Nation*, however, did not accept the argument that critics should remember that Stanton's poetry was produced amid "the heat and hurry of newspaper work." In its review of *Songs of the Soil* the magazine remarked: "We see no reason why any wide-awake country editor should not produce five, six, or even seven of these poems in a morning without seriously interfering with business."

Hardly a review of Stanton's work failed to touch on his optimistic outlook. In his introduction to *Songs of the Soil* Harris made much of it, contrasting it with the conditions that led others to despair for the future: "It is a bold voice, too, for it persists in singing night and day, neither seeking nor avoiding an audience. If the world listens, well and good: if not, pleasant dreams for the sake of the old times! But the world listens. The newspapers pick up the songs and send them far and wide, till the voice of the singer is carried over the continent and into the isles of the sea. People say, 'Who is this man that goes on singing day after day as if there had never been a singer in the world before him?' They find that he has the root of the matter in him, and so they listen gladly." A year later Hubner condensed the governing motif of Stanton's work for *A Library of Southern Literature*, again emphasizing the rosy hue:

> In his theory of life the darkest hour is always just before daybreak. Joy follows sorrow and glorifies its shadows. Life is, indeed, worth living, provided we live it in the sunshine of love, in an atmosphere of cheer and good will, in intercourse with kind hearts, in applauding as well as in doing generous deeds; we must have faith in the ultimate happiness of everybody, and have absolute confidence in the overruling Providence, as ideally expressed by Browning:
>> "God's in his heaven,
>> "All's right with the world."

In a 1922 tribute to Stanton in the *Christian Index*, the Reverend John F. Purser lauded him for the daily doses of optimism he provided the public. Purser quoted labor organizer Eugene Debs as saying that it was Stanton's poetry that kept his heart and hopes aglow while he was in prison. "There is," Purser suggested, "more sound theology and Christian charity in 'Just from Georgia' than is often heard in some of our modern pulpits."

Stanton's rosy view was also amply evident in the bits of prose philosophy with which he interspersed the poetry in his column. Although these were often attributed to the "Old Deacon" or to "Brer William," they were clearly his own:

> Sometimes, after you've searched the hills for Happiness you discover her in the humble

valley, training a vine to blossom at a cabin door.

> Satan wuz a' angel in heaven, but lak de res' of us, he couldn't stan' prosperity.

> The chap who can whistle trouble out of town is a world-benefactor to count on.

> Old Trouble don't have a chance when Joy is the bandmaster and strikes up a lively tune.

> Growling at the weather never yet brought wet or dry. Since the Lord made it the wisest plan is to let him manage it.

> Folks dat say dis ole worl' is no fr'en' ter grace, wouldn't know grace ef dey met her in a Sunday hat, on de road ter preachin'.

Little has been written about Stanton since the tributes that followed his death. Some of his poems survived for years as popular songs, but his kind of newspaper column did not. *Outlook* noted in its obituary that "it might almost be said that the newspaper column as he knew it died with him." Like Edgar Guest of the *Detroit Free Press* and Eugene Field of the *Chicago Daily News*, Stanton enjoyed a fame that rested more on visibility than on poetic ability. Part of the dated quality of Stanton's writing can be traced to the sentimental optimism with which he may have outlived his era. As one columnist put it when he died, he continued singing "Sweet Little Woman of Mine" right into the days of the "Red Hot Momma."

Still, when he died at home after a brief illness in 1927, the *Constitution* obituary could make justifiable claims for the universal appeal of some of his work. His "This World," according to the *Constitution*, despite its being a single stanza of four lines, "is quoted wherever men foregather and regardless of which language they speak." It also adorns the tombstone of Frank Stanton in West View Cemetery in Atlanta:

> This world that we're a-livin' in
>   Is mighty hard to beat;
> You git a thorn with every rose,
>   But ain't the roses sweet!

References:
Edwin A. Alderman and Joel Chandler Harris, eds., *The Library of Southern Literature*, volume 11

(Atlanta: Martin & Hoyt, 1904), pp. 5061-5082;

Walter Chambers, "He Sings of Simple Things," *American Magazine*, 19 (February 1925): 118-126;

Mel R. Colquitt, "Frank L. Stanton," *Magazine of Poetry* (October 1892): 369-372;

"Columnist of the South," *Outlook* (19 January 1927): 74;

Current Literature, volume 34 (New York: Current Literature Publishing Co., 1903), p. 49;

"Georgia's Poet Laureate Sings a Joyous Note," *Christian Science Monitor*, 21 November 1925, p. B3;

Bertha Sheppard Hart, *Introduction to Georgia Writers* (Macon, Ga.: J. W. Burke, 1929), pp. 96, 115, 129-131;

Carl Holliday, *History of Southern Literature* (New York: Neale, 1906), pp. 370-371;

Lucian L. Knight, *Reminiscences of Famous Georgians*, volume 1 (Atlanta: Franklin-Turner, 1907), pp. 541-545;

Wightman F. Melton, ed., *Frank Lebby Stanton* (Atlanta: Georgia Division of Information and Publications, 1938);

Montrose J. Moses, *The Literature of the South* (New York: Crowell 1910), p. 472;

"Poems—New Editions and Criticism," *Review of Reviews* (December 1904): 759;

"Poet of Georgia," *Nation*, 124 (19 January 1927): 55-56;

The Reverend John F. Purser, "An Appreciation," *Christian Index*, 106 (16 February 1922): 3;

Review of *Songs of the Soil, Nation*, 59 (20 December 1894): 467-468;

Review of *Up from Georgia, Nation*, 75 (11 December 1902): 466;

"South Loses Sweet Singer as Frank L. Stanton Dies," *Atlanta Constitution*, 8 January 1927, pp. 1, 10.

Papers:

Frank L. Stanton's papers are in the Beinecke Rare Book and Manuscript Library, Yale University; Butler Library, Columbia University; Henry E. Huntington Library, San Marino, California; Margaret I. King Library, University of Kentucky; Lilly Library, Indiana University; Margaret Mitchell Memorial Library, Atlanta Historical Society; Newberry Library, Chicago; William R. Perkins Library, Duke University; the University of California-San Diego Library; and the Robert W. Woodruff Library, Emory University.

Melville Stone

Michael Kirkhorn
University of Kentucky

BIRTH: Hudson, Illinois, 22 August 1848, to Elijah and Sophia Louisa Creighton Stone.

MARRIAGE: 25 November 1869 to Martha Jameson McFarland; children: Herbert Stuart, Melville Edwin, Elizabeth Creighton.

MAJOR POSITIONS HELD: Founder and owner, *Chicago Daily News* (1875-1888); founder and owner, *Chicago Morning News* (1881-1888); general manager, Associated Press (1893-1921).

AWARDS AND HONORS: M.A., Yale University; LL.D., Knox College, Ohio Wesleyan University, Middlebury College, Columbia University.

DEATH: New York, 15 February 1929.

BOOK: *Fifty Years a Journalist* (Garden City & Toronto: Doubleday, Page, 1921; London: Heinemann, 1922).

Only forty-five years old when he was appointed general manager of the Associated Press, Melville Elijah Stone already had been a reporter, the owner of a foundry and machine shop, the owner of two Chicago newspapers, a convalescing world traveler, and a bank president. If he had done nothing else, he would be remembered as the founder of the *Chicago Daily News*, one of the city's great newspapers, but it was through his long association with the AP—"founded by six wrangling

Melville Stone (Associated Press)

away entirely all effort at thinking," Stone told the students. "I know many news editors who calmly catalogue events, saying this is news and that is not; and having done this, they go their way, assuming that they are master-workmen in the craft. They will say, for instance, that a hanging is always news, a railway accident is always news; in short, that any disaster by flood, or fire, or in the domestic circle is always news. Now, as a matter of fact, these things are episodes; they are the May-flies in the world of news. . . . They are in no sense contributions to the real history of the world." Stone quoted approvingly, from the previous century, the words of the statesman Fisher Ames, who found incomprehensible journalists' preoccupation with "taverns, and boxing matches, and elections, gouging and drinking, and love and murder, and running in debt, and running away, and suicides." Ames implored journalists to "banish as many murders, and horrid accidents, and monstrous births, and prodigies from their gazettes as their readers will permit them, and by degrees to coax them back to contemplate life and manners; to consider common events with some common sense; and to study Nature where she can be known, rather than in those of her ways where she really is, or is represented to be, inexplicable."

In 1914, the issuer and quoter of these admonitions was a man who for twenty-one years had been manager of the most relentless recorder of episodes in the history of the planet—the Associated Press. In his contradictoriness, Stone was typical of those who govern American news-gathering organizations. He knew that the products of thought and inquiry were more important than scuttlebutt, but, of necessity, he was a creature of deadlines and journalistic close calls. The remarkable thing is that his nature encompassed the contradictions and encompassed them happily.

Stone's was a hard-won happiness, legendarily American. His father, the Reverend Elijah Stone, was a Methodist circuit rider on the northern Illinois prairies. The $300 he earned each year would not support a family; Elijah Stone supplemented the family income by selling "Stone's Chinese Liniment for Man and Beast" and by making daguerreotype portraits. The Stone home was a stop on the Underground Railroad, the linked refuges through which escaped slaves passed in their flight from Southern bondage to liberty in the North.

When Stone was ten, Horace Greeley was a guest at his father's table and in his church; but Greeley cannot be given credit for inspiring Stone to enter journalism. More than a dozen members of

New York publishers" about three months before Stone was born—that he recorded his most enduring accomplishments. Stone wrote only one book, *Time* magazine's obituary writer observed. "But his monument, the Associated Press, is a great unbound volume, an unceasing history attuned alike to hamlet and metropolis."

Energetic and resourceful as a news executive, Stone also was a thoughtful observer of the workings of American journalism. In all the utterings of editors, publishers, managers, and owners, there may be no more elevating and optimistic view of the purposes of journalism than one expressed in a speech Stone delivered at Columbia University's Pulitzer School of Journalism on 12 January 1914. He argued that a newspaper which sought to make "fast friends" of its readers should avoid assembling the daily news from the "episodes of the hour." Instead, its reporters should relay news of recent accomplishments in science, ethics, politics, and economics. "It is easy to edit a newspaper if you put

Stone's parents, the Reverend Elijah Stone and Sophia Creighton Stone

his family, including his mother, Sophia Creighton Stone, had worked at journalism at one time or another.

In 1860 Elijah Stone was assigned to the pastorship of the old Des Plaines Street Methodist Church in Chicago, and Melville entered Chicago High School (later West Division High School) at Monroe Street near Halsted. In 1864 Stone was invited by a *Chicago Tribune* editor, the father of one of his classmates, to join the staff as a reporter during summer vacation. Stone considered becoming a lawyer, but the bloody and momentous Civil War news eclipsed tamer aspirations. From his earliest boyhood he had been an eager reader of the news; the uproars of his youth turned that excitement into ambition.

When Charles A. Dana came to town to buy the *Chicago Republican*, he hired away a number of *Tribune* staff members, including the seventeen-year-old Stone. For two years the *Republican* wavered; then it died. As a young reporter, Stone helped to cover the Democratic National Convention in New York in 1868, and there he had his first

taste of national political journalism. But before he was twenty years old he changed occupations.

Elijah Stone and his brother, Nathaniel F. Stone, an inventor who manufactured sawmill appliances, opened a business in Chicago. Melville Stone worked in the business, and in the process became editor and publisher of the *Sawyer and Mechanic*, a newspaper for readers interested in saw and flour milling. The paper soon folded, and Stone's father bought him an interest in the Lake Shore Iron Works, near Chicago's Lake Michigan beaches. Stone was soon able to buy out his partners and become the sole owner. Three months after his twenty-first birthday the successful young businessman—"Maker and Factor of Hardware"—married Martha J. McFarland. He was doing very well as a manufacturer of folding iron theater chairs when the great Chicago fire destroyed the theaters he was supplying and almost everything he owned.

Chicago banker Jonathan Young Scammon had purchased the remains of Dana's *Republican* and had decided to revive the paper, which would be called the *Inter-Ocean*. Scammon was the president of the Chicago Astronomical Society, of which Stone's brother Ormond was a member. Acting on Ormond's recommendation, Scammon appointed Stone managing editor of the new newspaper. But the exertions of Stone's youth had weakened him. At twenty-four he needed a leave of absence, granted by the *Inter-Ocean*, which he used to travel through the Southern states for five months. When he returned he resigned from the *Inter-Ocean* and became managing editor of the *Chicago Evening Mail*, which, upon its consolidation with the *Chicago Evening Post*, sent Stone to the national capital as Washington correspondent. In Washington, he also began corresponding for the *New York Herald*.

While he was reporting from Washington, Stone decided that Chicago needed a one-cent evening newspaper. Returning to Chicago, he resigned from the *Post and Mail*, found two partners, and, ignoring the discouraging jibes of his former colleagues and employers, published on Christmas Day 1875 the first issue of the *Chicago Daily News*—the first penny newspaper in the West—with the announcement that the paper would begin regular publication on New Year's Day.

He was resourceful. When he found that Chicago had a penny shortage, he had several barrels of copper coins shipped from the Philadelphia mint and persuaded merchants to sell goods for prices which required change in pennies—fifty-nine, sixty-nine, and ninety-nine cents.

The *Daily News* began regular publication the first day of 1876 and continued for a little more than a century to provide Chicago with independent, inquisitive, and intelligent reporting and commentary. The editorial department, Stone said, had "three offices to perform: First, to print news; second, to endeavour to guide public opinion aright; and, third, to furnish entertainment. . . . I believed it to be even a business mistake to invert this order and to make the entertainment of the reader of first importance." The important news was placed on the first page, and an effort was made to "present a true perspective of the world's real developing history."

Stone set unimpeachably high standards for his newspaper. He said that his editors must not pander "to the vitiated taste of the unthinking"; they must publish no "so-called sensational and exaggerated or scandalous material for the purpose of making sales." The *Daily News* was engaged, he said, "in something else than a mere business enterprise in which we would seek to provide anything and everything that the public might crave. There-

fore, a rule provided that in his relation to the public every man's activities were a proper subject for attention, while in his domestic relations he was entitled to privacy which no newspaper was privileged to invade." The paper would acknowledge and apologize for its errors and would seek integrity in decency: "Also a rule that nothing should be printed which a worthy young gentlewoman could not read aloud in the presence of a mixed company."

Soon the "fine lot of men," the "soldiers" who had devoted their efforts to the early progress of the *Daily News*, were joined by Victor F. Lawson, who had been a fellow student at Chicago High School and who worked at the Norwegian-American newspaper, the *Skandinaven*, in whose building the *Daily News* was produced. Lawson became business manager, beginning a harmonious relationship which permitted Stone to devote his time to the editorial department of the paper.

The *Daily News* soon attracted the attention, scornful and envious, of its competitors. The *Chicago Post and Mail*, owned by the McMullen brothers, eagerly copied stories from the *Daily News*. "No sooner would a dispatch appear in our early edition than it would be seized upon by that paper," Stone recalled. John J. Flinn, Stone's editorial assistant, concocted a dispatch about misery and violence in Servia, which was published in the noon edition of the *Daily News*. The story contained a proclamation supposedly uttered by the mayor of the "provincial town of Sovik," which ended with these words: "Er us siht la Etsll iws nel lum cmeht." At 3 P.M. the *Post and Mail* published the dispatch word for word. Only after the *Post and Mail* had sent the paper out to its readers did a friend of the McMullens' notice that backward the supposed foreign words read "The McMullens will steal this sure." The *Post and Mail* was "literally laughed to death." Less than two years later Stone bought what remained of the paper, and its Associated Press franchise, for $15,000.

As the *Daily News* developed, Stone and his editors devised their own form of sensationalism—but "not by parading the noisome details of commonplace crime, nor the silly so-called 'human-interest stories' of cats born with two heads, or like babble having no real value and only presented for the purpose of pandering to the prurient taste of groundlings." The "larger and better" sensationalizing he preferred was intended to "give an individual character to a paper, wake an echo, and conduce to betterment of the readers." This he called "detective journalism," and it brought Stone himself into action as a journalistic sleuth. "How we pursued public plunderers, and uncovered their misdeeds, and sent them to prison, constitutes a chapter in the history of Chicago of which no one connected with the paper has reason to be ashamed," Stone wrote.

One of these miscreants was the president of a Chicago savings bank which suddenly closed its doors upon 25,000 depositors, leaving liabilities of millions of dollars. The *Daily News* had been campaigning for state legislation which would provide for inspection and control of savings institutions. When Stone learned that the bank president had "decamped," he had the banker's movements traced to Canada. With a photograph of the banker and a facsimile of his signature, Stone went to Hamilton, Ontario, where he interviewed a railroad baggage clerk; the clerk passed Stone on to another clerk in Toronto. There Stone was informed that the banker and his family had traveled to Quebec and then had boarded a ship bound for Liverpool.

Stone telegraphed the information he had gathered to the Chicago police. Chief of Police M. C. Hickey cabled Scotland Yard to arrest the "absconding bank president," but the absconder and his wife and child left the ship in Ireland. Stone traveled to Europe, enlisting the help of police in London, Paris, and Berlin. Unable to find the elusive banker, Stone was about to give up when he received a cable saying that an associate of the banker had sailed for England. Confronting the associate, Stone obtained a promise that he would notify the editor when the banker was found. As a result, a *Daily News* reporter obtained a full confession from the banker at Cannstadt, Germany. The indictment against the banker was dismissed, but the Illinois legislature passed a law providing for inspection of savings banks. The *Daily News* engaged in this sort of detective journalism for years.

In 1881, having decided that it was "not enough" to own a leading afternoon newspaper, Lawson and Stone started the *Chicago Morning News*, a two-cent daily. The standards he had set for the *Daily News* were diligently observed in the new paper.

For the new paper, Stone performed an industrious and creative job of staff-building. Among the experts he hired to write, upon request, on special topics were Dr. Frank W. Reilly, head of the Illinois Board of Health, to write on sanitary and medical topics; Gilbert A. Pierce, later governor and United States senator from North Dakota, on national politics; William Morton Payne, later editor of the *Dial*, on literature; Professor James Laurence

Laughlin, of the University of Chicago, on finance; and Professor Richard T. Ely, of the University of Wisconsin, on sociology. Literary artists such as George Ade and Slason Thompson joined the staff, as well as caricaturist John T. McCutcheon and humorist Finley Peter Dunne.

Among Stone's special favorites was an old friend, Eugene Field, who was invited to join the *Daily News* after Stone accidentally discovered him working at the *Denver Tribune*. Field, a "newspaperman, not from choice, but because in that field he could earn his daily bread," and one "conscious of great capabilities" in literature, joined the staff as the writer of the column "Sharps and Flats." For $50 a week the prolific Field wrote a daily column 2,000 words in length—a column, Stone said, which "laughed and wept, sparkled and crackled

Inscription in a book presented to Stone by Eugene Field, who wrote the "Sharps and Flats" column for the Chicago Morning News

with jollity" and "swept the tenderest chords of the human soul." Field was a prankster, but occasionally Stone was able to beat him at his own game. Learning that Stone made it a practice to give a Thanksgiving turkey to every married staff member, the columnist asked to be given a suit of clothes instead. Stone complied by asking an old friend, the warden of the Illinois Penitentiary at Joliet, to send him a suit of prison stripes. With elaborate ceremony, the suit was presented to Field on Thanksgiving Day; it "surprised and delighted him beyond measure," Stone recalled.

In 1888, Victor Lawson offered to buy Stone's interest in the *Daily News*. Stone, whose health never was robust and who, in earlier years, had been prone to melancholy, agreed to sell for a price of $350,000, receiving an additional $100,000 for promising Lawson that he would not engage in journalism in Chicago for ten years. In his parting editorial, published on 16 May 1888, Stone claimed that his "arduous labour" as founder of the *Daily News* had impaired his health. With regret, "because circumstances thus force me to abandon the one ambition of my life and to sunder a thousand ties which seem well-nigh unbreakable," he said goodbye to his paper's readers. In his autobiography he revealed another motive. Informed that he had received a LL.D. degree in absentia from Middlebury College, Stone felt suddenly overtaken by doubts about the sufficiency of his formal education. "I felt as might one who had stolen the sacred relics from the altar of a Roman Catholic church," he wrote. "I had no education justifying such distinction." So when Lawson offered him a chance to enrich his education by escaping daily journalism, he said he "jumped at the chance. I felt like a prisoner to whom freedom was suddenly possible." Lawson wrote prophetically in the same issue of the *Daily News* which published Stone's farewell that Stone was "too young a man to long face a purposeless future," predicting that "new interests in proper time will engage his efficient abilities. . . ."

In a home on the Savoy shore of Lake Geneva, Switzerland, Melville and Martha Stone and their sons, Herbert Stuart and Melville Edwin, enjoyed their holiday. The boys entered a preparatory school at Lancy, and the family made tours to the North Cape, to the cataracts of the Nile, and as far east as Nizhni Novgorod in Russia. Stone took his family back to Chicago in 1890. He wanted to get back to work, and he wanted his sons to have American educations.

Stone was still at loose ends when some friends who were reorganizing the Globe National Bank

suggested that he apply his versatile administrative competence to the bank's problems by becoming its president. He insisted on an apprenticeship as vice-president, then assumed the presidency. His ability, integrity, and reputation attracted other opportunities for public service, and again he complied selflessly. As treasurer for an organization responsible for the building of the great drainage canal which was to carry Chicago's sewage away from the city's drinking water source in Lake Michigan, Stone marketed the bonds and directed a financial operation which required years of careful management. For this he expected and received no compensation. During this period he served as president of the Bankers' Club, of the Citizens' Association, of the Civil Service Reform League, of the Fellowship Club of Chicago, and as vice-president or member of other organizations.

Stone's old friend and associate Victor Lawson was a principal figure in the Western Associated Press; the Western AP was coexisting in uneasy alliance with the service's New York organization, which had been accused of distributing biased reports. Associated Press officers were also concerned about the inroads of an active rival, the United Press, which had begun to gather and distribute news in 1882. United Press's proficiency excited charges from members of the Western Associated Press, who accused eastern members of the Associated Press's Joint Executive Committee of being in connivance with United Press, to the Associated Press's detriment. Lawson was given the chairmanship of a committee which was to investigate the charges. The report his committee delivered in 1891 was stunning: it showed that national distribution of news was in the hands of a trust which operated according to a secret agreement between the United Press and members of the Joint Executive Committee of the New York and Western associations of the Associated Press. Stock had been given to committee members who participated in this scheme. Lawson's electrifying 10,000-word report was the first wedge in the bitter struggle to free the news from the control of the secret monopoly. Under Lawson's leadership, the Western association began to employ string correspondents to cover cities where the West was not represented. The Western Associated Press would become a national association.

The United Press, whose true power Lawson's investigation had revealed, still wished to do business with the Western AP, continuing the heretofore secret alliance. Playing upon the anxiety of the United Press officials, who wanted a new agreement before the secret Associated Press-United Press compact expired, Lawson persuaded them to sign a contract for a news exchange between the two organizations. The United Press would provide news from foreign nations, the Eastern seaboard and the Gulf states; a new organization, the Associated Press of Illinois, would provide news from the rest of the country. Overlooked by the United Press representatives was an innocently phrased clause which permitted the expansion beyond its eastern boundaries of the Associated Press of Illinois.

The Associated Press of Illinois would depart radically from the old pattern for a press association. It would be a nonprofit cooperative, collecting and distributing news for its member newspapers. Each paper would have a voice in the association's affairs. The news was to be presented truthfully and impartially. The charter, which was applied for on 10 November 1892, specified the organization's objectives: "to buy, gather and accumulate information and news; to vend, supply, distribute and publish the same; to purchase, erect, lease, operate and sell telegraph and telephone lines and other means of transmitting news; to publish periodicals; to make and deal in periodicals and other goods, wares and merchandise." Of this new and ambitious organization Melville E. Stone was named the first general manager.

Stone was no stranger to the workings of the Associated Press. In 1883 he had been elected a member of the board of directors and of the executive committee of the Western Associated Press. He had been a close observer of the embittering conflict between the Associated Press and the United Press. He confirmed the confidence which had been demonstrated by his appointment by leaving immediately for London, where he signed an agreement placing at the disposal of the Associated Press for ten years reports from Reuter's Telegram Company, the British news organization; Agence Havas of Paris, another news-gathering company; and their German equivalent, Continental-Telegraphen-Compagnie of Berlin.

In a speech at Franklin Institute in 1916, Stone recalled the intentions of the new Associated Press—"in form at least, an ideal news-gathering association." He said: "We believed that, with a self-governing people, it was all-important that they should be well informed: informed truthfully and honestly respecting the affairs of the day. There should be no chance that they should be misled, if it were possible to achieve such an end. There was a public duty, of a very high character, involved in the matter. Not alone, if you please, that the market

reports for the investor, or the merchant, or the farmer should be accurate, but—deeper and more important—in our political life, where the very business of government was at stake and vital, the truth, impartially, without bias or alien purpose, should be furnished for the guidance of the electorate. Obviously this was not to be secured from an agency operated by a few men, owning no responsibility to any one." In 1916, Stone was speaking of an organization which had grown from 65 charter members in 1893 to 900, and represented "every angle of every fad or ism outside the walls of Bedlam." He was speaking also of an organization which in twenty-three years had never paid a dollar of damages in a libel action. This immaculate record, evidence of the integrity of the organization, he ascribed to the vigilance of the Associated Press's member newspapers and of "the argus-eyed millions who read the despatches of The Associated Press. The very magnitude of its work tends to make truthfulness and impartiality imperative." Under the system of operation devised in 1892 and 1893, he said, the news "is automatically truthful and fair."

But a four-year struggle, coinciding with an economic panic and depression which crushed thousands of banks, businesses, factories, and railroads and left millions jobless and desperate, lay ahead before AP would be secure in its new identity and new approach to news gathering and distribution. Almost immediately after the new Associated Press was formed in 1893, Lawson, chairman of the executive committee, had to call a meeting to tell members that the news service was running a deficit and needed as much as $100,000 to challenge the United Press in the East and to stabilize its operations. As Lawson sat down, James E. Scripps, publisher of the *Detroit Evening News*, rose and launched a vehement attack on the United Press—"a syndicate of mercenary sharks who will . . . plunder the press of the country." Stone told the members that progress already had been made in the improvising of an Associated Press news-gathering operation in the East to replace the New York organization, which had been absorbed by the United Press. Before the meeting was over members had pledged $320,000; subsequent subscriptions increased that amount to $550,000. It must have been good news for Stone, who had accepted the general managership at a salary of $10,000 a year, and had to keep his bank presidency because not even that small amount was forthcoming immediately from the faltering AP.

A week later Stone and Lawson left for the

East Coast to enroll 100 newspapers then receiving United Press reports. They first hit the New York papers, where key men on three papers had once been associated with the Western Associated Press: John A. Cockerill, manager of the *Advertiser*; Horace White, director of the *Post*; and Joseph Pulitzer, owner of the *World*. Cockerill and Pulitzer joined, and when Lawson and Stone walked into White's office, the editor announced, "I am with you. I do not believe in an association which is controlled by three or four men." White helped to bring the *Brooklyn Eagle* and the *New York Staats-Zeitung* into AP. Other metropolitan and upstate papers followed. When they had finished in New York, Stone and Lawson moved on to Philadelphia and enrolled most of the papers there. On 28 March 1897, the United Press filed a petition of bankruptcy. A few weeks later the United Press discontinued its news operations.

Stone rejected at least one tempting offer in order to remain leader of the Associated Press's struggle. In 1897 Pulitzer offered Stone editorship of the *New York World*. The energetic Pulitzer, whose editors were never free of his intrusions, even offered to sail on his yacht to the China Sea and leave Stone undisturbed. Stone refused, replying that he could not desert his "public trust." (Assuming that Pulitzer had resented his refusal, Stone was surprised in 1911 to find that Pulitzer had directed in his will that Stone be a member of the advisory board of the Columbia University School of Journalism, founded with Pulitzer's donations.)

The AP, still in debt, had to contend with the penalties of success. Its critics called it a monopoly; it was accused in various states of acting in restraint of trade, and statutes were enacted to require AP to act as a public service corporation and serve all comers. In 1897 the *Chicago Inter-Ocean*, which once had employed Stone as managing editor, was bought by Chicago utility magnate Charles T. Yerkes, whose attempts to obtain extensions for his street railway franchises had been criticized by Lawson's *Daily News*. Yerkes appointed to the editorship George Wheeler Hinman, formerly a member of the staff of one of the most bitter enemies of Lawson and Stone from the days of the UP-AP dispute, William M. Laffan's *New York Sun*. The *Inter-Ocean* launched abusive attacks on Lawson, but the legal struggle did not begin until Stone noticed that the *Inter-Ocean* was using reporting syndicated by the Laffan News Bureau. The Laffan bureau had been designated an antagonist of the Associated Press and all subscribers were forbidden to use the Laffan service. As soon as the Associated Press penalized

the *Inter-Ocean* by suspending its service to the paper, Hinman applied to state courts for an injunction, arguing that the Associated Press was a public utility, obligated to provide service to any newspaper which sought it. By designating certain services antagonistic, Hinman said, the Associated Press was restraining trade. The Associated Press replied that it was a nonprofit cooperative which had a right to limit and govern its membership.

The initial rulings favored the Associated Press, but in 1900 the Supreme Court of Illinois reversed lower court decisions, ruling against the AP on every point. Citing the right, claimed in the Associated Press's charter, to erect, lease, or sell telegraph or telephone lines—a right never exercised—the Court ruled that the Associated Press was a public utility and therefore was not permitted to discriminate among subscribers. The decision was the undoing of the Associated Press as an Illinois corporation. On 22 May 1900, a certificate for the incorporation of the Associated Press was filed in New York. It bore the names of the six newspapers which had formed the Associated Press in 1848—the *Boston Journal*, the *New York Times*, the *Brooklyn Eagle*, the *Philadelphia Bulletin*, the *Washington Star*, and the *Dallas News*. The new organization, like the old, would be a nonprofit cooperative whose members would not buy news from the association but would act as part owners, each with an equal voice in the affairs of the service. On 12 September 1900, the Associated Press of Illinois dissolved itself. On 19 September the board of directors of the Associated Press—the New York corporation—confirmed the appointment of Melville E. Stone as general manager.

The next decade proved that the Associated Press's formula for news gathering and distribution would work to the advantage of the cooperative's members. This was a time which required daring and adventurous coverage (the destructive eruption of Mount Pelée on Martinique in 1902; the Russo-Japanese War in 1904-1905; the San Francisco earthquake in 1906; the Wright Brothers' flights) as well as reporting which provided a consistent record of the events of the world. Associated Press reporters, relaying information obtained sometimes at great risk, and relaying it impartially and fully, proved their value to member newspapers.

By 1910 Stone had other problems. In that year the Associated Press ran a small deficit ($2,742,492 in expenses, $2,728,888 in revenues), but it was the fifth deficit in seven years. Stone preferred not to worry about money; he had devoted his energy to the steady improvement of the Associated Press report. "Business details never captured his imagination and he was happier in the midst of a great news emergency than while struggling with the intricacies of a balanced budget," Oliver Gramling observed. The Associated Press's subscription fee was based on the population in each member's circulation area; if that system was retained, there would be no chance of revising it until 1910 population figures were released by the census bureau. In addition, small newspapers in outlying towns were complaining that their reports were arriving in garbled form, or not arriving at all.

A solution arrived from an entirely unexpected source. Stone was asked to interview a young man from Indiana named Kent Cooper. At first reluctant to entertain the notion that an outsider could help the Associated Press, Stone was immediately impressed by Cooper's knowledge of news transmission and by his suggestion that newspapers in isolated communities be given, over the telephone, abbreviated daily news reports by Associated Press employees in nearby bureaus. This strategy would silence the complaints and save the Associated Press money, Cooper said. The thirty-year-old Cooper had worked for the *Indianapolis Press*, had established the Indianapolis bureau of the Scripps-McRae Press Association, and then had started his own news service, the United Press News Association. He had sold that service to Scripps-McRae, which in 1907 had merged with two other agencies to form the United Press Associations (which should not be confused with the Associated Press's defunct rival). As Indianapolis bureau manager for the United Press Associations Cooper had experimented with a telephone talking circuit which would serve several small papers at the same time, and had convinced local telephone companies to adjust their rates in ways which would enable them to compete with the telegraph as a means of news distribution. This was the idea he presented to Stone.

In December 1910, Stone gave Cooper his first assignment. He was sent to Chicago to devise a talking circuit which would serve the remote *Houghton* (Michigan) *Gazette* and the *Marquette* (Michigan) *Journal*, two papers which had been receiving incomplete or garbled information by telegraph. News delivered over Cooper's circuit, which linked both papers simultaneously with Chicago, was received and printed efficiently and accurately. Within four months Cooper, given additional responsibility by Stone, had arranged for thirty-six additional newspapers to receive their news over telephone talking circuits.

Relieved by Cooper of that problem, Stone faced others. Ever since its victory over the United Press, the Associated Press had been the object of criticism of those who charged that it was a monopoly. Stone had been a persuasive defender of the cooperative's practices and purposes, but in 1911 his own heretofore immaculate reputation was attacked. The accusations against Stone, alarming in themselves, came from an impressive source— Frank B. Kellogg, later secretary of state, in 1911 a government attorney engaged in a prosecution of the Standard Oil Company under the Sherman antitrust law. During the litigation he wrote a statement which said that Stone "is controlled absolutely by the Standard Oil people" and accused Stone of deliberately distorting coverage of the trial. At the request of member newspapers, the board of directors appointed a five-member committee of inquiry, with Oswald Garrison Villard of the *New York Post* as its chairman, to investigate the allegations together with any other complaints about the integrity of the Associated Press report. Villard recalled later that "there were many charges going around in progressive circles as to its [Associated Press's] integrity and freedom from corporate influence," and the committee found "that the social relations of the general manager with . . . individuals prominent in powerful financial circles, and likewise the acceptance of decorations from foreign governments . . . had not unnaturally aroused unjust suspicion of the independence and impartiality of his administration of the news service." But the committee, following a long and thorough investigation, concluded that Stone had not been influenced by these social contacts and that he had remained devoted to the ideals of the Associated Press and to the strengthening of its service. When members of the committee presented to Kellogg the letter in which he had accused. Stone of misdoings, Kellogg— unable to persuasively defend the allegation and faced with a $100,000 libel suit by Stone—withdrew his charges and apologized.

Skillfully and gracefully, Stone countered other charges that the AP introduced bias or tainted the news. These charges were easily handled, for in each case Stone had only to demonstrate the unbiased and thorough nature of Associated Press reporting. The persistent demand that the AP regard itself as a common carrier, obliged to distribute news to all comers, required more adroitness. The Associated Press in no way resembled a railroad, which enjoyed some of the privileges as well as the responsibilities assigned by law to a common carrier, Stone said in one of his arguments against a charge that the Associated Press monopolized the news. The news service did not, for example, enjoy the right of eminent domain, as the railroads did. The Associated Press, Stone said, "is simply a voluntary union of a number of gentlemen for the employment of a certain staff of news reporters to serve them jointly. For its work it derives no advantage from the Government, from any state or municipality, from any corporation, or from any person. Its service is a purely personal one, and never, except under the long-since abolished slave laws, has any Government sought to compel personal service, save in cases of voluntarily assumed contracts, or of adjudgments for crime. The output of The Associated Press is not the news; it is its own story of the news." Anyone, Stone said, could have written a news article about the sinking of the battleship *Maine*. When Associated Press reporters wrote their version, Stone said, "Who shall say that they, or those who employed them, were not entitled to its exclusive use? And is this not equally true, whether the employer be one man, or ten men, or nine hundred men acting in co-operation?"

Subsequent years brought personal unhappiness, but Stone remained undisillusioned. Melville Edwin Stone died young, and Stone's other son, Herbert Stuart, was killed in the sinking by a German submarine of the liner *Lusitania*. In a letter to a friend, Stone said that he had told his son on the morning of the *Lusitania*'s sailing that German notices of possible attacks on ships carrying supplies or munitions ought to be regarded as threats. But, he had told Herbert, "while they might be provoked into such a threat with a view to deterring people from sailing, I was sure from my acquaintance with the Germans, that they were at least civilized and that no one born of a decent mother would participate in the destruction of the *Lusitania* in the way threatened. It was not that one doubted their warning, but that everybody doubted that a civilized nation, however much they threatened, would carry into execution so horrible an undertaking." After the sinking, the Associated Press's coverage of German affairs remained studiously dispassionate and impartial.

The entry of the United States into World War I brought censorship and also the threat of the unraveling of standards and practices governing international news gathering. Stone advised President Wilson to hire journalists to work on censorship boards—newspaperman George Creel was eventually given control over wartime censorship—and turned his attention to another sticky problem. By 1917 the pirating by other agencies of its reporting was so extensive that the Associated Press began legal action against a major offender, William Randolph Hearst's International News Service. On 26 April 1917, member newspapers were instructed to further protect the Associated Press's ownership of its reports against unauthorized publication: all Associated Press matter would have to be credited to the news service and all member newspapers would have to print, every day, notice of their affiliation with the service; no others could use Associated Press matter.

An active sixty-nine years of age, Stone went to Europe to observe AP coverage and to shift correspondents around to conform to the changes which would occur as Americans began fighting the Germans. A sergeant of marines escorted him through the muddy trenches. His frontline touring completed, he ordered stronger coverage in Italy and Russia and assigned reporters to General Pershing's headquarters in Europe.

Back in New York, Stone found that a war so cataclysmic in its scope and frequently so chaotic in the rapid advancing and retreating of large forces made extreme demands on his judgment. During the Germans' Somme offensive, an Associated Press correspondent cabled that Paris was being bombarded by an enormous cannon. Maps showed that the nearest German line was twenty-six miles from Paris, a distance greater than any known gun could fire a projectile. The dispatch was held up to allow the Associated Press to consult with experts. The War Department scornfully dismissed the report. Stone, however, trusted the correspondent, and, noting that he had taken time to verify his report, ordered that the dispatch be distributed. Forty-eight hours later, military authorities confirmed the report.

Stone's seventieth birthday was celebrated at the 1918 annual meeting of the Associated Press, and before long he was packing his bags again, to resume direction of the Associated Press report from Europe. He arrived just after United States soldiers and marines had stopped a German advance along the Marne in battles at Château-Thierry and Belleau Wood. He was in Paris during the Second Battle of the Marne, but he could hear the thunder of artillery fire. He returned to New York a few days before armistice negotiations were announced. At that moment the system he managed sped news to 1,033 newspapers over a 53,000-mile leased wire network.

Stone was at lunch with Associated Press

Stone shortly before his retirement as general manager of the Associated Press

president Frank Brett Noyes on 7 November 1918 when rumors of the signing of an armistice on that day began to spread through New York and other American cities. Without confirmation from its correspondents, the Associated Press transmitted no information other than to report, at Stone's direction, that the rumor had not been confirmed in Washington. Angry demonstrators shook their fists outside the windows of the Associated Press's offices at 51 Chambers Street, accusing the news service of siding with the Germans by refusing to announce a peace settlement. Finally, the State Department announced that no armistice had been signed that day; the end of the war came four days later. Once again the judgment of Associated Press correspondents and editors was vindicated.

As the war ended the Associated Press brought a lawsuit which provided a different sort of vindication. The Associated Press's contention that its reports should be regarded as private property, owned only by the organization and its membership, had been the subject of continuous dispute. Late in the war, the Associated Press learned that

the *Cleveland News* was selling Associated Press war reports to the International News Service, which resold the news to agencies and papers which were not members of the Associated Press. Affidavits attesting to the unauthorized sale of Associated Press reports were turned over to the federal district court in New York. The district court ruled for the Associated Press; the International News Service took the case to the United States Supreme Court, where the justices ruled that a commercial agency had no right to appropriate Associated Press dispatches after they had been printed by members of the cooperative. Elated, the board of directors followed up on the decision by once again instructing all members to credit dispatches by carrying the line *By The Associated Press* or by putting the logotype *AP* on the dateline of each story. The logotype was popular with newspapers, and in time the Associated Press came to be commonly known as AP.

In 1920, Stone, who had ended his wartime service by going to Paris to organize coverage of the peace conference, relinquished his duties as general manager to take an extended leave. When he went before the board of directors in 1921 to announce his retirement, he was still a commanding figure. He had avoided the office during the year of his leave, he told the directors, to learn whether his staff was able to carry on without him. He was satisfied with their competence and ready to retire. Stone was appointed counselor to the AP and Frederick Roy Martin replaced him as general manager; Cooper was named assistant general manager.

Stone retained his position as counselor—the title suggested a "fountainhead of wisdom," one AP board member said—until his death in New York City on 15 February 1929. A couple of members of the Villard committee which investigated Kellogg's charges did not like Stone personally, but they found his performance impeccable. Karl August Bickel, president of the United Press, said of Stone: "His unrelenting insistence upon impartiality, accuracy and absolute honesty in news created standards that have become universal in American journalism, and for that all Americans stand tremendously in his debt." Frank B. Noyes, president of the Associated Press, said:

> Melville E. Stone came into the fight for a news service that would be unsubservient to private interests, with a full sympathy for its object and an absolute belief that such a service was vital to an honorable American press.
>
> He was extraordinarily equipped for the part he was to play, both in the war with the opposition and in the constructive work of establishing, maintaining, and constantly developing a great world-wide news service. He was a tactician of the highest order, fertile of resource, ready to meet any emergency, perceiving unerringly the weak spot in the enemy line and deadly in his blows on that line, though in this war the blow took the form of persuasion of the enemy and the victory that of a new recruit to the cause of an unfettered press. . . .
>
> It is one thing, however, to win a fight for a principle and altogether another thing to put that principle into working practice. And this is where Stone's genius came into full play. His range of knowledge; his acquaintance with men of all stations of life and of all countries; his understanding of conditions throughout the world and his ability to call into instant service this knowledge, this acquaintance, and this understanding are simply marvelous. Under his direction the news arms of The Associated Press have year by year reached out until now the whole globe

contributes to its daily story of world happenings.

Noyes said that he and others in the AP's governing councils had had differences of opinion with Stone, but the arguments were never mean or petty. These were arguments, he said, about which course was the best, about "what was the right thing to do." "I suppose," Noyes said, "that every man who amounts to anything has enemies, and he [Stone] has a select assortment; but it seems to me that more people throughout the world regard Stone as a friend than any one else that I know of. It seems to be almost a law of nature that with him an acquaintance should be a friend."

It is hard, in this light, to avoid seeing Stone as a sort of hero of American journalism. A new, or revived, organization of any kind needs protection and nurturance. Stone's job, when he assumed the general managership of the Associated Press in 1893, and when he assumed the position again in New York in 1900, was to lead an organization which had adversaries to overcome, a reputation to maintain, and established services to be carried on without regard for distractions from other quarters. He provided that leadership without compromising his principles or the principles of the organization. He and Lawson overcame a news monopoly and so successfully struggled against claims that the Associated Press itself was a superseding monopoly that, finally, the United States Supreme Court was won over to their view that news—or at least the version of the news supplied to subscribers by a selected staff of reporters and editors—could be considered private property.

The loyalty of Stone's colleagues and staff was a repayment for the confidence he showed in their judgment and skill. "Much may be said," he observed, "and fairly, in criticism of our journalism, of a lack of perspective on the part of our journalists, of the pushing to the front of inconsequential things, of exaggeration and inaccuracy, but I think it fair to say, after all, that with rare exceptions American newspaper men generally are striving for a common end—for an honest, truthful, and dignified history of the day's doings—which shall be helpful and uplifting."

This loyalty could be an amusing annoyance. When Stone went to the Republican National Convention at Chicago in 1908, he was greeted by a procession of "old printers, dilapidated ex-reporters and editors, and other sorts of peripatetics, all in more or less derelict condition." That sort of thing happened to Stone constantly, but one observer was so impressed by this "plague" of respectful reminding that he wrote a poem about it:

> But there's a noble band of men who live on,
>   year on year;
> You meet them everywhere you go—they
>   seem to live on beer.
> You meet them in Chicago, at sea and
>   on land,
> In Timbuctoo and Hong Kong, at The
>   Hague and on the Strand.
> They never die, they never work, they turn
>   up night and day.
> You speak to them with cuss-words, but they
>   will not go away,
> They seldom wash, they never shave; they
>   have one shirt—or none;
> The tie by which they cling to life—they
>   "used to work for Stone."

In his lifetime, Stone enjoyed more eloquent tributes in more dignified settings, but this hacked-out bit of doggerel also is a tribute to a man who never was able to dismiss any other human being from his life.

References:

John Palmer Gavit, compiler, *M. E. S.: His Book* (New York & London: Harper, 1918);

Oliver Gramling, *AP: The Story of News* (New York & Toronto: Farrar & Rinehart, 1940);

"M. E. S." In Memoriam (New York: Associated Press, 1929);

Oswald Garrison Villard, *Fighting Years: Memoirs of a Liberal Editor* (New York: Harcourt, Brace, 1939).

Herbert Bayard Swope
(5 January 1882-20 June 1958)

Rosemarian V. Staudacher
Marquette University

MAJOR POSITIONS HELD: Reporter, *New York Herald* (1901-1903, 1904-1907); reporter, city editor, executive editor, *New York World* (1909-1928).

BOOKS: *Inside the German Empire* (New York: Century, 1917);
Journalism: An Instrument of Civilization (Geneva, N.Y.: Hobart College, 1924); republished in *An Introduction to Journalism,* edited by Lawrence Murphy (New York: Nelson, 1930).

OTHER: Louis Weitzenkorn, *Five Star Final*, preface by Swope (New York: French, 1931);
Dale Kramer, *Heywood Broun: A Biographical Portrait*, foreword by Swope (New York: A. A. Wynn, 1949);
Louis L. Snyder, ed., *A Treasury of Great Reporting*, preface by Swope (New York: Simon & Schuster, 1949);
"Aim of the New York World," in *Newsmen Speak*, edited by Edmond D. Coblentz (Berkeley: University of California Press, 1954), pp. 54-58.

Herbert Bayard Swope was called the greatest reporter of his time by Lord Northcliffe of the London *Daily Mail*. The accolade is all the more impressive when one considers that Swope's illustrious colleagues included Walter Lippmann, Damon Runyon, Heywood Broun, Alexander Woollcott, Franklin P. Adams, William Henry Chamberlin, Arthur Brisbane, and Richard Harding Davis. That Swope had a special impact upon journalism in his time is undeniable. He rose rapidly from obscurity to become a journalistic legend.

Herbert Bayard (pronounced "*by*-ard") Swope was born 5 January 1882 in St. Louis, Missouri, which was at that time the fourth largest city in the United States. His parents were Isaac and Ida Cohn Swope, both immigrants from Germany. He was the youngest of four children. As a child, Swope was something of a loner. His brother, Gerard, was nine years older, and his interests were widely different

Herbert Bayard Swope in 1937

was appalled and wrote Swope a letter outlining his many objections. Swope, not yet seventeen and in the throes of teenage growing pains, was acquiring a doubtful reputation as a ladies' man, gambler, and tippler. Gerard thought a stint in the Missouri National Guard or a healthful lumber camp, rather than a city room, might be just what his brother needed; Swope was not convinced.

Shortly after the death of their father in 1899, their mother went back to Germany, where Swope's sisters had moved after their marriages, and remained there most of the rest of her life. When the estate was settled, Swope, who had thoughts of attending Harvard, took his share and went to Germany, where he visited his family and went to some lectures at the University of Berlin. With that, his college aspirations ended.

Meanwhile Gerard, who had moved to Chicago, got Swope a job in the electrical shop where he was working. Swope hated every minute of the job and soon gave it up to return to St. Louis, where he had heard of an opening at the fairgrounds racetrack. Henry Ittleson, a family friend, felt Swope's time should be better spent and got the young man a job on the *St. Louis Post-Dispatch*. This first job in the newspaper field did not last very long: Swope was fired for spending more time at the racetrack than in the city room. The next step in his career was a job in Chicago on the daily *Inter Ocean*. That, too, was brief, for a recruiter from the *New York Herald* spotted Swope and offered him a job; Swope was just nineteen.

As a *Herald* reporter, Swope was unorthodox, flamboyant, bold, extravagant, and, in general, a thorn in the flesh of his editor. He was in love with New York, at that time a rowdy, uncultured metropolis teeming with life. He hung around a gaudy district known as the "Tenderloin," where bars, music, gambling, girls, sin, and crime abounded. Since the *Herald* almost never went to press before three or four o'clock in the morning, Swope, a young and energetic bachelor, slipped easily into the habit of never going to bed before sunrise. Once, coming in four hours late for work, he was challenged by city editor Leo Redding, to whom he replied blithely: "But Leo, whenever I come in, I'm still worth any two other men you've got on your staff." It was about this time that he struck up an acquaintance with John Barrymore, who was not yet an actor but had aspirations to become a painter. The two became roommates in a flat located over a Times Square restaurant. Barrymore was working as a cartoonist for the *Morning Telegraph*, but switched to the *Evening Journal*, where he illustrated

from Swope's. Yet, as Swope was growing up, it was Gerard who was to have a large influence in shaping his brother's character. From the beginning, Swope was an individualist. Graduated from Stoddard School at age twelve, he entered Central High School and was promptly expelled for poor behavior. He was later readmitted and finished high school with more attention to sports than to study, much to his brother's chagrin. Gerard, who was then studying electrical engineering at M.I.T., required a weekly report from Swope on his behavior.

Gangly and freckled, Swope had startling red hair, very white skin, and large blue eyes. He loved a good argument and more than once was banned from the lunch table by his mother when a discussion escalated into an argument and then into a shouting match. When he was eight, he discovered the excitement of horse racing at the St. Louis fairgrounds; this interest would stay with him all his life.

In 1897, Swope won a $50 prize in a department store essay contest, the first time he was paid for writing. In the fall of 1898, he told his brother that he wanted to become a newspaperman. Gerard

Arthur Brisbane's editorials. Sometimes Barrymore tagged along on Swope's assignments.

Swope was inclined to go his own way in a most distracting fashion, and, after a few disconcerting episodes, he was dismissed from the *Herald*. In 1903, he embarked upon a brief theatrical career as an advance man for a touring theater company, but when a reporter's job on the *New York Morning Telegraph* became available, he took it. It gave him access to horse racing, which pleased him, but he was not happy at the *Telegraph*. In 1904, *Herald* editor Redding agreed to rehire him.

His career had been highly undistinguished so far, but at this point, Swope decided to create for himself a singular image. He went in for bright yellow chamois gloves, spats, and a cane by day and white tie and tails to cover the theater and opera at night. He frequented the popular restaurants and gambling establishments, making contacts and friends everywhere. On one occasion, he was assigned to cover Prince Louis of Battenberg (later known as Mountbatten), a rear admiral in the British navy. Swope dutifully trailed his subject from fancy dinner parties to a slumming tour of Chinatown to a famous pub on Pell Street, where two singing waiters serenaded the royal guest. One of them, Izzy Baline, later changed his name to Irving Berlin; he and Swope became close friends.

Swope worked only sporadically at reporting, but when he did work, he could be outstanding. He once stated his criteria for a good reporter: "accuracy, judgment of news, sense of public duty, understanding of professional ethics and ability to write." His colleagues credited him with all of these qualities but generally agreed that he could do outstanding work only when he was "cornered." City editors concocted some ingenious schemes for cornering him. In the end, he was dropped from the *Herald* staff for the second time in 1907. Swope was not upset, having decided that the *Herald* was not much of a paper. It stymied his individualism, an unspeakable offense to the young man who had set out to be unique. For some time he drifted, running up bills and exhausting his credit, and continued to hang about with racetrack devotees, baseball promoters, and gamblers (including the notorious Arnold Rothstein).

In 1908, he met eighteen-year-old Margaret Honeyman Powell, variously known thereafter as Maggie, Pearl, and Pug. She was beautiful, talented, and totally enchanted by the dapper, man-of-the-world, unconventional Swope. Their courtship was stormy but ended in a marriage in 1912 that endured for forty-six years.

Swope and his bride, Margaret Powell Swope, on their honeymoon in 1912

Swope was unemployed through most of 1908 and 1909, although he did try a public relations career in partnership with Willis Carle Pratt, a former reporter on the *New York World* and the *Herald*. This enterprise was short-lived because clients were not forthcoming.

Finally, on 15 November 1909, city editor Sherman W. Morse of the *New York World* hired Swope. Swope considered Joseph Pulitzer, owner and publisher of the *World*, one of the four greatest journalists of the time—along with William Randolph Hearst, Adolph Ochs, and Lord Northcliffe—and subscribed completely to the *World*'s philosophy. It seemed that Swope had at last found his proper place in the world of journalism. The *World* had a circulation of more than 350,000 and cost one cent everywhere except on trains, where it cost two cents. Swope worked six days a week for $7 a day plus current space rates. Since he tended to write long stories, he liked space rates. For the first time in his life, Swope worked hard. He became interested in politics.

His diligence paid off and by 1912, at the age

of thirty, Swope, known as HBS, was one of the *New York World*'s most acclaimed reporters. He was assigned top stories, worked hard at them, and did a competent job. He was at Halifax, Nova Scotia, when survivors of the *Titanic*, which sank after striking an iceberg, were brought ashore.

Swope's most important story at that time, one which he later said was the most significant of his career, concerned the murder of Herman Rosenthal, a gambler who had revealed a scandal involving police protection of big-time gamblers. The *World* was the first newspaper to carry Rosenthal's affidavit. Before Rosenthal could appear before District Attorney Charles Seymour Whitman, he was shot and killed by four hired gunmen. The *World* ran a brief story at once and the next day used Rosenthal's own account of his relationship with Lt. Charles A. Becker, who was involved in the protection racket. Throughout the entire series of events, Swope, who knew all the persons involved, was probing, prompting, and urging action. He had the inside track on the story and even assisted in the investigation which followed. The corrupt police officer was found guilty of first-degree murder, but the conviction was later set aside. The four assailants were apprehended, tried, and convicted in separate proceedings; Swope covered their executions. Lieutenant Becker was tried on a second-degree murder charge in May 1914; he was found guilty and was executed in Sing Sing the next year. The case created a stir in New York. District Attorney Whitman was later elected governor, and it was thought that his successful prosecution of the Rosenthal case had great influence upon his election. Some credited Swope, because of his extensive involvement, with being the newspaperman who had made Whitman governor. Swope got a raise to $125 a week and began to be pointed out as a celebrity. He also gained considerable respect from the police department, which he neglected to return in kind; he once posted a notice in the *World*'s city room cautioning staff members "not to take oftentimes irresponsible utterances of the police as final or authoritative."

In 1914, Swope was sent to Germany. When the German submarine U-9 sank three British battleships, it was Swope who got a first-person account by telephone from Otto von Weddigen, the submarine commander. In December, Swope returned to the United States and was made city editor of the *World* at the suggestion of Morse, who was retiring. As city editor, Swope, in characteristic fashion, leaped wildly into every news story. James Barrett, a reporter, remarked: "He attacked the news with such zest that the staff was galvanized — also partly paralyzed and partly amused." Restless and eager to see for himself the progress of the First World War, Swope again went to Germany in 1916. The *World* bestowed upon him the title of special staff observer, and he produced a series of stories which won the first Pulitzer Prize for reporting in 1917. The series was published in book form as *Inside the German Empire* (1917).

Although he was thirty-five years old when the United States entered the war, Swope tried without success to get a commission as an officer in the army. Meanwhile, he was sent to Washington by the *World* on an undercover assignment to investigate the true state of affairs in the conduct of the war. Much impressed with the work of Bernard Baruch, head of the War Industries Board, Swope set out to interview him. His efforts produced nothing until Swope arranged a number of introductory letters from prestigious sources. In 1918 Swope joined the staff of the War Industries Board, and from then on his friendship with Baruch grew. It was said that Baruch had a talent for attracting to himself competent, colorful, and loyal men, and Swope was no exception.

On 4 December 1918, President Woodrow Wilson sailed for Paris to attend the peace conference. Although the *World* had veteran reporters in Europe, Swope made arrangements to cover the event himself. Once in Paris he enthusiastically supported Wilson's policies, to the chagrin of some of his colleagues on the *World* staff. Swope and his colleagues protested what they termed a "gag" rule in dissemination of news at the conference to Wilson, who then sided with the journalists against England and France and arranged to have a limited number of reporters attend the plenary sessions of the conference.

On 7 May, when the Allies presented the peace treaty to Count Ulrich von Brockdorff-Rantzau, Germany's representative, Swope did not have a press pass. He was not daunted. He arrived boldly in an American army vehicle flying a general officer's flag. He had borrowed it from his friend, Brig. Gen. Harry H. Bandholtz, General Pershing's provost marshal. Swope was sure nobody would stop a car that was clearly that of the chief of military police of the Allied Expeditionary Forces. At the portals of the Petit Trianon, Swope stepped out majestically, resplendent in the striped pants, cutaway coat, and tall hat of a top diplomat. He was followed by three only slightly less splendid correspondents carrying attaché cases. The entire retinue passed through to the front section reserved for the diplomatic corps, from which privileged spot Swope had a first-rate view of the proceedings.

Meanwhile, in the United States, Margaret had had a nervous breakdown, seemingly aggravated by his long absence. When Swope returned to the *World* office, Ralph Pulitzer, who had taken over the paper after his father's death in 1911, suggested the creation of a new position for him: Swope became executive editor, a post he was to fill for eight years. He attacked the new position with his usual frenzied vigor, and the *World* began to achieve a reputation for excitement, cockiness, competence, and innovation; Swope called it "sparkle." He told Heywood Broun: "What I try to do in my paper is to give the public part of what it wants and part of what it ought to have whether it wants it or not."

Swope was masterful on the telephone and often achieved through it what he could not accomplish in a personal meeting. His phone calls were a highly animated show, and his employees often stood ten deep to manage a word with him if and when he abandoned the phone.

High on Swope's list of editorial interests were crusades of all kinds. Among his more memorable ones was that against the Ku Klux Klan, which in the 1920s had achieved a certain status as a social and political force; the *World* received a Pulitzer Prize for its series exposing the Klan. He was also interested in the problems of blacks and commissioned Lester A. Walton, a black journalist and later a minister to Liberia, to do a series about Southern blacks migrating north.

On the lighter side, Swope hired magician Harry Houdini to supervise a Sunday feature section on the occult called "Red Magic." Walter Lippmann had met Houdini at Harvard and cultivated his friendship because both were interested in exposing charlatan mediums. Swope enjoyed claiming the "greats" of the day as *World* staff members and arranged to have H. G. Wells cover the Washington International Conference on Disarmament, which the *World* sponsored in 1922. He once obtained exclusive rights to a Kipling poem and even tried to persuade George Bernard Shaw to cover a championship prizefight.

When Swope became executive editor, the page opposite the editorial page had no special distinction; it was a conglomeration of society news, obituaries, reviews, ads, and notices. Swope coined the name Op Ed page and recruited writers to upgrade the page's content; soon he had engaged the services of Heywood Broun, Alexander Woollcott, Lawrence Stallings, Franklin P. Adams, Deems Taylor, Harry Hansen, and numerous others. The

result was the creation of a vital, exciting, and refreshing collection of good writing. Swope considered reporters to be the *World*'s most valuable employees; he gave them leeway in all matters and forgave transgressions that might have gotten other employees fired. His biggest problems were not with editorial workers but with the business department: the paper's management was abysmally frugal and did not reinvest profits in the business.

Swope took time out from his editorial activities in 1924 to accept an honorary degree from Hobart College.

In 1925, the *World* was financially sound and profitable; but that year marked a fatal mistake by its council, who raised the price from two to three cents. Swope and Arthur Krock, assistant to Ralph Pulitzer, opposed the increase. Within a year, the *World*'s circulation dropped by 60,000. In 1926 Colgate University awarded honorary degrees to both Herbert and Gerard Swope at the same ceremony; Gerard had become president of General Electric. Meanwhile, the *World* was losing another 20,000 in circulation. On 2 January 1927 the council reversed

Swope's children, Jane and Herbert, Jr., in 1927

*Swope with New York governor Alfred E. Smith in 1927. Swope
was a strong political supporter of Smith's.*

only half of the departed readers.

Along with his journalistic activities, Swope
was becoming more heavily involved in politics. He
had persuaded the Democrats to hold their 1924
national convention in New York City—the first
national convention of either major party to be held
there since 1868. Swope knew all the Democratic
leaders, but the man who most intrigued and inspired him was Alfred E. Smith, whom Swope considered something of a genius. Smith in turn saw in
Swope a man with no ulterior political or personal
motives who was informed, intelligent, and quick to
respond with opinions. Swope's tireless work for
Smith was at least partially responsible for Smith's
nomination for the presidency in 1928. On election
night, Swope was glued to the telephone in the
World office so that he could get firsthand election
returns. Smith's defeat was a heavy blow to him.

Several weeks before, Swope had decided to
leave the *World* staff and had issued a statement to
that effect on 16 October. The statement was a
shock to the world of journalists and hundreds of
other persons whose lives had been touched by
Swope. Walter Lippmann wrote Swope a letter supporting his decision to retire on the grounds that
Swope had outgrown the job. *New York Times* publisher Adolph Ochs, British publisher Lord Beaver-

its policy and reduced the price back to two
cents—a move which Swope also thought was a
mistake at that time. The price cut brought back

Swope at his desk in 1928, shortly before he left the New York World

Mock front page of the New York World *for 23 December 1928, prepared by Swope's staffers*

brook, and others expressed the hope that he would not retire from the field of journalism entirely. Paradoxically, at the same time Swope announced his departure, the *World* reached an all-time high circulation of 592,000.

It was Swope's hope that if the Pulitzers decided to sell the *World*, he would be given first opportunity to purchase it. He was counting on Baruch to back him. Ralph and Herbert Pulitzer evidently fostered the hope, at least verbally. In 1931, the *World* was sold, but not to Swope. Despite the best efforts of Swope and his backers, and of *World* employees, the *World* was sold to the Scripps-Howard chain. The publication resulting from the sale was the *World-Telegram*.

Some journalists of the day, including Woollcott, believed that Swope's departure from the *World* staff spelled its doom. The claim angered Swope, who often pointed out that he had resigned from the paper several years before its sale. Yet the belief persisted that after Swope's departure, the *World* lost much of its unique verve, that quality which Swope called "sparkle."

With the election of Franklin Delano Roose-

velt in 1932, Swope knew that Al Smith's political star had surely set and that his own chance for political prominence was gone. In the Democratic convention in Chicago that preceded Roosevelt's election, Swope was a veritable whirlwind. His allegiance still followed Al Smith even when it became apparent that Smith could not beat Roosevelt. Swope was everywhere, barging in unceremoniously on every caucus and meeting. When the inevitable happened, he was smart enough to repair his political fences. After the inauguration, he began to send informative notes to Roosevelt and those close to him. From time to time, he yielded to presidential invitations to visit the White House and made sure all his friends knew of it.

Roosevelt also appointed Swope to a diplomatic mission, but it turned out badly through no fault of Swope's. When representatives of sixty-six countries met in London in June 1933 for an economic conference, Assistant Secretary of State Raymond Moley suggested that Swope be appointed to accompany the American delegation as a public relations man, but the job was given to someone else. The conference was beset by problems because of disagreements among the nations, and Roosevelt sent Moley to England as his personal troubleshooter. Moley asked that Swope be sent with him, and this time Roosevelt agreed. Swope took his seventeen-year-old son, Herbert, along as his assistant. In England, the London *Daily News Chronicle* called Moley and Swope "Roosevelt's two mystery men" and said even the American delegates to the conference were confused about the status of the pair. There were hints that Swope was not a messenger for Roosevelt but a spy for J. P. Morgan. The conference soon broke up in confusion and disagreement.

Once out of journalism, Swope devoted considerable time and several hundred thousand dollars to the development of "Keewaydin," his Long Island estate with its quarter-mile beachfront and lavish stables for thoroughbred racehorses. He chose royal blue and scarlet for his racing colors. In 1934, when racing became legal in New York State, Swope became chairman of the state racing commission, a position he carried off with his usual color and dash. It added nothing to his financial situation but considerable to his jaunty reputation. Through his enthusiasm and innovative zest, racing became a respectable and popular sport. He remained on the commission until 1945.

The name "Keewaydin" was supposedly that given to the northwest wind by some long-extinct Indian tribe. The main structure on the estate was a three-story house with some twenty-seven rooms and eleven bathrooms. The huge library had two fireplaces. Twelve to fifteen staff members were employed to take care of the estate. Swope spent lavishly on improvements and called upon experts to achieve his carefully laid-out plans. He installed a year-round tennis court and a saltwater swimming pool which had its own telephone. Swope acquired a reputation for promoting, or at least tolerating, nude bathing, which from time to time created a stir in the neighborhood. Keewaydin was always filled with an assortment of guests who attended lavish dinner parties which began very late and ended at sunup.

Swope's favorite pastime was croquet, which he stoutly defended as a game which combined the "thrills of tennis, the problems of golf, and the finesse of bridge." He played the game viciously and plotted his shots carefully. It has been said that he once kept Al Smith waiting twenty minutes on the telephone while executing his turn at croquet. The croquet grounds were expertly kept, and the equipment used was the finest. Some of it was imported from England. The mallets were handmade

Keewaydin, Swope's estate at Sands Point, Long Island

Swope and his friend, financier and presidential adviser Bernard Baruch, at a prizefight in 1939

of ash or snakewood, and Swope kept his in an unheated room because he felt high temperatures might affect their balance.

It might have been expected that, having quit the *World*, Swope would take to writing on his own, but this was not the case. Book publishers and magazine editors hounded him. Even President Roosevelt dangled a journalistic plum before him in 1939 when he suggested, tongue-in-cheek, that Swope cover the visit of the king and queen of England to America. Swope declined; he thought the visit ill-timed and said so. Despite suggestions, urgings and coaxings, Swope wrote little for publication after leaving journalism. He did, however, write a tremendous number of personal letters, which he signed with a flourish in bright red ink. Cheerful notes went to family, friends, acquaintances, and even strangers. He was conscientious about congratulating newcomers to the writing field and encouraged young journalists. Patients in hospitals were deluged with cheery messages. After receiving one such siege of encouragement during a lengthy hospital stay, Ring Lardner wired Swope: "CAN YOU SUGGEST ANY WAY TO END THIS CORRESPONDENCE AMICABLY STOP MY PERSONAL PHYSICIAN SAYS EXCITEMENT

OF HEARING FROM YOU DAILY IS BAD FOR ME. . . ."

A decidedly eccentric personality, Swope saved every clipping or other memento about himself. Some he preserved lavishly in ornate frames. Old racing ticket stubs, theater bills, dog licenses, rubber bands, letters, invitations, and hundreds of other worthless items filled several bulging scrapbooks and nearly a hundred filing cabinets. It was said that he never threw anything away. Yet, despite his penchant for saving, he never preserved a complete file of the *World*.

Once detached from the *World,* Swope never found another newspaper opportunity suitable to him, although he explored many possibilities and once looked into backing for purchase of the *Washington Post*. He served for a while on a stockholder's committee of the Brooklyn-Manhattan Transit Company, was on the board of directors of the Columbia Broadcasting System, and ran a one-man public relations operation. Meanwhile, his friendship with Bernard Baruch continued to grow.

Swope was nearly sixty when the Japanese bombed Pearl Harbor. Immediately he telegraphed his offers of help to President Roosevelt and other officials in Washington. In a reorganization of the army's bureau of public relations, Swope was installed as a civilian deputy to Gen. Alexander G. Surles, its head. In July 1942, he was appointed part-time civilian consultant to Secretary of War Henry L. Stimson. After VE Day in 1945, civilian assistants in the army were cut and Swope's job as consultant was eliminated. In 1947, he was given the Medal of Merit, awarded to 404 civilians who had distinguished themselves in public service. Gen. Dwight Eisenhower, army chief of staff, presided at the award ceremony.

In the years that followed, Swope became interested in a great number of civic and charitable organizations, including Beekman Street Hospital, the Child Welfare Society, the Humane Society, the Citizen's Welfare Committee, and Freedom House, where he kept company with such luminaries as Henry Luce, Robert Patterson, and Norman Cousins.

Swope was seventy in 1952. His brother, Gerard, was nearly eighty and his close friend Bernard Baruch was eighty-two. The impact of his seventieth birthday had a strange effect upon Swope: the birthday messages he received plunged him into deep gloom. To make matters worse, three of his best friends died early that year. Swope's insomnia, which he had suffered for some time, worsened, and he became preoccupied with thoughts of death. Between bouts of depression, he

Swope at Hialeah Race Course in 1940. Jockey Eddie Arcaro is riding one of Swope's horses.

struggled to exhibit his old exuberance, even taking part in the journalistic excitement that swept the *New York Times* when President Eisenhower suffered a heart attack. Turner Catledge, *Times* managing editor, was spending the weekend at Keewaydin when the Eisenhower story broke. At once, all of Swope's telephones, which were numerous, became hotlines to the *Times* city room as staffers called Catledge for instructions. Swope, who loved the excitement, gave Catledge copious advice. For one brief moment, he was back in the journalistic whirl.

In the spring of 1958 he was hospitalized for what was announced as a hernia operation but was actually exploratory surgery. The notes Swope constantly wrote to himself began to contain memos about his symptoms. One month after he was dismissed from the hospital, he had to return, ostensibly because of a bout with diverticulitis. A large, cancerous tumor was removed from his stomach. Swope seemed to have little desire to recover; it was not long before he contracted pneumonia. He died on 20 June. His funeral was held at his Sands Point estate; two other services were held, one at Freedom House and the other at the Columbia University School of Journalism. At the latter, a *World* room was rededicated in Swope's name.

Among his contemporaries, Swope was admired and esteemed for his imagination, ingenuity, and aggressiveness. He had a way of seizing upon circumstances to turn them to his advantage. His boldness, brashness, and colorfulness barely outdid his ego.

Columnist Westbrook Pegler once described him as "All gall, divided into three parts—Herbert, Bayard and Swope." In a farewell communication upon the occasion of his resignation from the *World*, Ralph Pulitzer had referred to Swope's "brilliant intellect . . . amazing energy . . . and fine courage." At the same time, Walter Winchell wrote: "As I see it you began as the greatest reporter New York has known in a generation. But you were more than a reporter. You were also an editor of the most original sort." Adolph Ochs, who could not believe that Swope would not return to the newspaper field, wrote: "Your energy, enterprise and enthusiasm, combined with your uncanny news sense, have ever been inspiriting contributions in making New York newspapers alert and interesting. . . ."

An attempt to assess the evidence of Swope's genius reveals one rather surprising fact: almost nothing of what Swope wrote as a reporter found its way into permanence in books. Except in the yellowing files of the defunct *World*, little remains to attest to his alleged genius as "the greatest reporter New York has known in a generation." Biographer E. J. Kahn states that Swope "avoided writing for publication . . . in part because it was too much work and in part because he was not, as he may have been painfully aware, a consistently skillful writer. . . . But he liked to foster the belief in others that he was always on the point of engaging in some literary pursuit, and toward the end of his life he himself came to have a swollen concept of his own output." It would appear, then, that some of the accolades accorded Swope were exaggerated.

All the same, Swope had considerable impact upon the journalistic world. He was a "mover," one of those inventive, imaginative, exciting persons who was two jumps ahead of everyone else when things were happening. When nothing was happening, he made things happen. As an editor, he had intuition, insight, and imagination. He knew how to organize, direct, and inspire those on his staff who wrote well. The "sparkle" which he claimed for the *World* in its heyday was a happy intangible born of that unique talent with which he goaded others into productive excellence.

Biographies:
E. J. Kahn, *The World of Swope* (New York: Simon & Schuster, 1965);

Alfred Allan Lewis, *Man of the World; Herbert Bayard Swope: A Charmed Life of Pulitzer Prizes, Poker and Politics* (Indianapolis: Bobbs-Merrill, 1978).

References:
James W. Barrett, *Joseph Pulitzer and His World* (New York: Vanguard Press, 1941);
Bernard M. Baruch, *My Own Story* (New York: Holt, 1957);
Baruch, *The Public Years* (New York: Holt, Rinehart & Winston, 1960);
"Death of a Reporter," *Time* (30 June 1958): 40;
Donald Kirk, "Herbert Bayard Swope," M.A. thesis, Princeton University, 1959;
David Loth, *Swope of G. E.* (New York: Simon & Schuster, 1968);
G. Manning, "Swope Urges a Strict Censorship of Press in Time of War," *Editor and Publisher* (30 May 1931): 59;
"Swope of the World," *Newsweek* (30 June 1958): 49;
Stanley Walker, "Symphony in Brass," *Saturday Evening Post* (4 June 1938): 10-11;
Emily Smith Warner, *The Happy Warrior: A Biography of My Father* (New York: Doubleday, 1956).

Bert Leston Taylor

(13 November 1866-19 March 1921)

Norman H. Sims
University of Massachusetts, Amherst

MAJOR POSITIONS HELD: Reporter and columnist, *Chicago Journal* (1899-1901); columnist, *Chicago Tribune* (1901-1903, 1909-1921), *New York Telegraph* (1903-1904).

BOOKS: *Under Three Flags*, by Taylor and A. T. Thoits (Chicago: Rand McNally, 1896);
Line-O'-Type Lyrics (Evanston: W. S. Lord, 1902);
The Well in the Wood (Indianapolis: Bobbs-Merrill, 1904);
The Log of the Water Wagon; or, The Cruise of the Good Ship "Lithia," by Taylor and W. C. Gibson (Boston: H. M. Caldwell, c. 1905);

Monsieur d'En Brochette, by Taylor, Arthur Hamilton Folwell, and John Kendrick Bangs (New York: Keppler & Schwarzmann, 1905);
Extra Dry; Being Further Adventures of the Water Wagon, by Taylor and Gibson (New York: G. W. Dillingham, 1906);
The Charlatans (Indianapolis: Bobbs-Merrill, 1906);
A Line-O'-Verse or Two (Chicago: Reilly & Britton, 1911);
The Pipesmoke Carry (Chicago: Reilly & Britton, 1912);
Motley Measures (Chicago: Laurentian Publishers, 1913);

Bert Leston Taylor (©Chicago Tribune)

A Penny Whistle; Together with The Babette Ballads
(New York: Knopf, 1921);

The So-Called Human Race (New York: Knopf, 1922);

A Line o' Gowf or Two (New York: Knopf, 1923);

The East Window, and The Car Window (New York: Knopf, 1924);

Captain Kidd, Coin Collector, by Taylor and Walter Henry Lewis (N.p., n.d.);

The Explorers, by Taylor and Lewis (N.p., n.d.).

PERIODICAL PUBLICATIONS: "When It Is Hot," *Literary Digest,* 47 (26 July 1913): 145;

"Chicago Owns Up," *Literary Digest,* 47 (13 December 1913): 1198;

"F. P. A.," *American Magazine,* 77 (April 1914): 66-68;

"Anchor to Windward," *Canadian Magazine,* 43 (September 1914): 491-500;

"Dinosaur," *Literary Digest,* 54 (5 May 1917): 1338;

"B. L. T. by Himself," *Everybody's* (October 1920): 52-53;

"Behind the Door" and "In Statu Quo," *Current Opinion,* 72 (1922): 399.

Bert Leston Taylor began writing a humorous column for the *Chicago Journal* in 1899. The column soon moved to the *Tribune,* where it attracted a large and devoted audience. Among newspaper people, especially in Chicago, his initials — B. L. T. — and his column — "A Line o' Type or Two" — are still readily recognized. Taylor is remembered for his literary standards and for creating a column format that permitted reader participation.

Taylor's father, Albert Otis Taylor, had been a sailor on whaling ships and a captain in the navy during the Civil War, retiring in 1869. Captain Taylor worked from then until his death in 1918 at the *New York Herald,* much of the time in the advertising department. Captain Taylor met his wife, Katherine White Taylor, in Dublin, Ireland. Their eldest son, Bert Leston Taylor, was born 13 November 1866 while the family was visiting relatives in Goshen, Massachusetts.

In his columns, Taylor recalled childhood visits with his Aunt Jennie and Uncle Tim Lyman in their "rambling old farmhouse" where he was born. Near the end of his life he returned on a sentimental journey. "The farm house was gone," he wrote in *The East Window, and The Car Window* (1924); "on its site is a modern dwelling, inhabited by a professor, who preaches some doctrine or other in Northampton. All of Goshen hill has been combed and brushed and is now a mere resort for summer folk. I lingered long enough to turn the automobile around in the narrow road, and then we coasted down the long grade to Williamsburg, where my father was born, and his father before him."

Taylor grew up in New York City, attending the public schools and the College of the City of New York in 1881-1882. After college, Taylor worked at several New England newspapers, including the *Montpelier* (Vermont) *Argus and Patriot,* the *Manchester* (New Hampshire) *Union,* and the *Boston Traveler.* At smaller papers he apparently worked as a printer as well as a reporter. For a while before 1896, he reported for the *New York Herald,* where his father was employed. Taylor said the cornerstone of his education in journalism was laid by a stern city editor of the *Herald.* Awed by his first assignment — covering the opening of the excursion season on the Hudson River — Taylor asked the editor if a half-column of copy would be enough. "He placed a hand kindly on my shoulder," Taylor recalled, "and said: 'My boy, I have only eight columns for the entire city of New York.' It was better than a long lecture on the art of condensation."

On 16 November 1895 Taylor married Emma

Bonner of Providence, Rhode Island. They had two daughters, Alva Theits Taylor and Barbara Leston Taylor.

Taylor's migration westward produced a character type that can be seen as well in other newspaper humorists of his day. The *Springfield (Massachusetts) Republican* noted that Taylor came from the same Yankee stock as humorists Artemus Ward, Bill Nye, and Josh Billings and that he "took a large part of his fun from rural life and the rural press." Taylor "remained essentially true to the 'small town.'" In a foreword to a collection of "A Line o' Type or Two" columns, James R. Angell said Taylor had "a strong flavour of New England Yankee tempered by long sojourn in the Middle West and by a youth spent in New York—shrewd, alert, full of amusing tales and still more amusing turns of phrase."

Chicago Journal managing editor W. H. Turner and reporter Finley Peter Dunne had pioneered a daily feature on the front page called "A Little About Everything." It contained a few news items and jokes. Turner and Dunne fished for better contributions, using cash prizes for bait. Taylor won three consecutive weekly prizes. In 1899, Turner hired Taylor and gave him control of the column. His early contributions included imaginary reports of Theodore Roosevelt on a lion hunt in the West. During the following months the column was frequently filled with features and illustrations.

James Keeley, managing editor of the *Chicago Tribune*, noticed Taylor's work and sent for him. "What are they giving you on the *Journal*?," Keeley asked. "Well, they've raised me to thirty dollars but I'm worth more." "You're worth sixty dollars to me," Keeley said. Thus B. L. T. came to the *Tribune*, where his first "A Line o' Type or Two" column appeared on 21 January 1901. He wrote of the fabulous Sarah Bernhardt, teasing her for wearing a "gorgeous Paris gown" on a visit to the Chicago stockyards. Taylor rode Chicago's elevated commuter trains to work that winter and suffered the stale tobacco smoke, garlic odors, and alcoholic breaths in the sealed smoking cars. One of his paragraphs for the "Line" let readers overhear a conversation between two microbes riding the "el": *"We must escape or we are lost! Only the human race can live in such an atmosphere!"* Taylor was not sure about that: he usually referred to the species as "the so-called human race."

In 1903, Taylor returned to New York, where he wrote a column called "The Way of the World" for the *New York Telegraph* and in 1904 joined the

humor magazine *Puck* as an assistant editor. His popularity in Chicago remained strong, and Keeley supposedly lured B. L. T. back with a telegram that read: "You're worth ten thousand a year to me now. Come back." After his return in 1909, Taylor remained with the *Tribune* as commander in chief of "A Line o' Type or Two" until his death in 1921.

The man who took over Taylor's column at the *Journal*, Franklin P. Adams—a lifelong friend and later a columnist in New York—wrote poems much like Taylor's. One or two of them were about B. L. T., including this one about his career:

> In Goshen, Massachusetts, he,
> Some eight-and-forty years ago,
> The subject of this cameo,
> First saw the l. of d.
> I mean—why Truth attempt to smother?—
> Bert Leston Taylor, and none other.
>
> Soon after that ("that" means his birth)
> He took to writing things for print,
> Replete with merriment and mirth—
> A daily column stint.
> Duluth, New York, and points connecting,
> Were places of his young selecting.
>
> "How is your job?" a man inquired
> Of Taylor, in Duluth. "Oh, grand!
> A pipe!" said Bert . . . "Aha! you're fired.
> I am the boss. You're canned."
> So Taylor left that land hibernal
> And made for the Chicago "Journal."
>
> Where, penning trifles light as air—
> And healthful as the air and pure—
> The public said: "The guy is there.
> His stuff is Lit'rature."
> So now he runs "A Line-o'-Type or
> Two" in Chicago's Grytest Pyper.

Chicago and Bert Leston Taylor are sometimes mistakenly given credit for inventing the newspaper column. Henry B. Fuller, the novelist, wrote in a foreword to a collection of Taylor's columns that Taylor "was the first of our day's 'colyumists'—first in point of time, and first in point of merit." "Colyum" was a pressroom pronunciation that came to signify a collection of clippings and quips put together by a humorist such as Taylor or Don Marquis of the *New York Evening Sun*. The general newspaper column, meaning a space reserved for the comments of a certain writer, had been started earlier. The Southwestern frontier created the tradition of the tall tale, and with it the storyteller who used local dialect and played on the humor of rural life. Artemus Ward (Charles Farrar Browne), Josh Billings (Henry Wheeler Shaw), and M. Quad (Charles B. Lewis) represented that tradition. Another example was Opie Read, who published a humorous newspaper, the *Arkansaw Traveller*, in the 1880s. The front page usually carried a "column" by Read, while the inside material was clipped from other newspapers and humorous publications around the nation.

Eugene Field influenced the modern column more than any other Chicago writer. In the 1890s, the *Chicago Record* carried his "Sharps and Flats," a collection of brief paragraphs on subjects ranging from the theater to sports, written entirely by Field. The column was closely read because Field was notorious for his elaborate jokes; he was also famous for his poems and satires. After Field's death in 1895, Finley Peter Dunne and George Ade became well known for their storytelling columns. Dunne's semifictional character Mr. Dooley permitted him to criticize society while filtering out some of his personal cynicism. Ade's "Stories of the Streets and of the Town" originally appeared alongside Field's column. Ade drew his stories from the neighborhoods, rooming houses, and workplaces of a booming Chicago, creating in the process fictional characters such as Pink Marsh and Min Sargent. Taylor's "A Line o' Type or Two" drew upon all of these earlier models, incorporating poetry, short paragraphs on diverse subjects, and longer pieces of prose.

Like Field, Taylor was a humorous poet. He might begin the "Line" with a few stanzas like these, written during World War I:

Arms and the Colyum

I sing of arms and heroes, not because
I'm thrilled by what these heroes do
                              or die for:
The Colyum's readers think they make
                              its laws,
And I make out to give them what they
                              cry for.

And since they cry for stuff about the war,
Since war at this safe distance not to
                              them's hell,
I have to write of things that I abhor,
And far, strange battlegrounds like Ypres
                              and Przemysl.

War is an almost perfect rime for bore;
And, 'spite my readers (who have cursed
                              and blessed me),

Some day I'll throw the war junk on the floor,
And write of things that really interest me:

Of books in running brooks, and wilding
                              wings,
Of music, stardust, children, casements
                              giving
On seas unvext by wars, and other things
That help to make our brief life worth
                              the living.

I sing of arms and heroes, just because
All else is shadowed by that topic fearful;
But I've a mind to chuck it [Loud applause],
And tune my dollar harp to themes
                              more cheerful.

After the opening poem would come many items gathered by B. L. T.'s contributors around the country. The difference between the "column" by Field or Ade and the "colyum" by Taylor was the reader's contribution. Field and Ade filled all their allotted space themselves; the "colyumists" encouraged their readers to do some of the work.

"Running a column is as simple a matter as driving a golf-ball," Taylor explained; "you 'let the club-head do the work.' The club-head, you surmise, is the contributor, and observe how unwearyingly he performs. The question is, what sets him going?" Answering his own question, B. L. T. said, "He contributes because he yearns to express himself, and he needs a vehicle for his thinklets. But he is, generally, particular about his company; he likes to feel that he is a member of a family of choice intelligence." The contributors were travelers, bankers, professors, housewives—anyone who recognized the funny newspaper headline, the blooper, or the awkwardly worded business sign. Taylor received 80 to 100 letters a day; anyone who could write a few verses of comic poetry might "make the Line." Many of the items were similar to the fillers used today by the *New Yorker* magazine. They were signed with initials, and Taylor said he knew some contributors were prominent writers. Others remained anonymous forever.

Gleaned by R. J. S. from a Topeka church calendar: "Preaching at 8 p.m., subject 'A Voice from Hell.' Miss Holman will sing."

We have recorded the opinion that the Lum Tum Lumber Co. of Walla Walla, Wash., would make a good college yell; but the Wishkah Boom Co. of Wishkah, Wash., would do even better.

As to why hotelkeepers charge farmers less than they charge traveling men, one of our readers discovered the reason in 1899: The gadder takes a bunch of toothpicks after each meal and pouches them; the farmer takes only one, and when he is finished with it he puts it back.

I SHOT AN ARROW INTO THE AIR, IT WENT RIGHT THROUGH MISS BURROUGHS' HAIR

(From the Dallas Bulletin.)

We quote Miss Burroughs: "I don't think B. L. T. is so good any more—it takes an intelligent person to comprehend his meaning half the time."

If space remained, Taylor might write a literary satire or a parody running to considerable length.

"A Line o' Type or Two" had several traditional departments. Items culled from the rural press appeared in "The Enraptured Reporter" department. Gems from private correspondence were found in "The Second Post." Unusual bits of nomenclature and odd names fell into the "Academy of Immortals." Taylor's passion for correct language usage led to the formation of the "Cannery": worn-out words and phrases were "canned" and placed on a shelf in a jar. One of his own was preserved in the first jar. While working in New York, Taylor once referred to the Hudson River as the "Rhine of America." Next to it on the shelf were jars with "trusty blade," "in the last analysis," "trumpet call," "last but not least," "a shot rang out," and "absolutely." " 'Absolutely' is absolutely the most overworked word," he said. "Our language, to B. L. T., was an honest, living growth," wrote Henry B. Fuller; "deadwood, whether in thought or in the expression of thought, never got by, but was marked for the burning. The 'Cannery,' with its numbered shelves and jars, was a deterrent indeed." Readers and critics admired Taylor's use of the language. Charles Evans, Jr., a fellow reporter, recalled: "A man once said to me: 'I consider the daily reading of B. L. T.'s column equal to a liberal education in English.' The thought immediately came to me that whatever it was necessary for B. L. T. to do he did well; and as his chief business in life was the writing of English he did that with an accuracy, a beauty and grace of expression at which the rest of us could only marvel."

Taylor was enthusiastic about words, golf, his political independence, the North Woods, music, and typography. As a golfer, his friends described him as better at theory than practice. "Mr. Taylor's whole attitude towards the game and everything else in life impressed upon me the intrinsic value of sound methods," said Charles Evans, Jr.

Taylor did not hew to the political line of the *Chicago Tribune*. Joseph Medill Patterson, who managed the *Tribune* during part of B. L. T.'s tenure, said, "I don't think it was stipulated that he should have absolute independence of expression, but whether it was stipulated or not, he did have it. . . . He had the swing of the space, and he filled it as he wanted."

Many poems were devoted to his favorite pastime, backpacking through the Canadian forests. "His eyes were ever turning towards the north, to the cool silences of the woods, for there was in his nature a something shy, aloof, that found itself most at home out in the open, under the great pines," his friend Karleton Hackett said. The unmoving stillness of the North Woods seemed present in the tone of his work, like a quiet spot in the midst of a great city. His love of the woods was not without humor. "For years he was fascinated with the name Saskatchewan," according to Hackett. "He used to speak it aloud that others might sense its charm."

If the forest comforted him, so too did music. He was a regular concertgoer. As many columnists have since learned, the freedom of conducting a daily column is a great burden. "He lived under an intense nervous strain, his whole heart bound up in the 'Line' which was never absent from his thoughts day or night; and as he gave of himself without stint so he constantly had recourse to the restorative powers of music as necessary to his well-being," recalled Hackett.

Choosing the proper word for the "Line" was not enough. It had to be presented correctly, as well. "As a newspaper man he was peculiarly expert because he was a printer as well as a writer," Patterson pointed out. The "Line" was always a beautifully printed piece of work because B. L. T. directed its typographical layout himself. "His early life was spent on several small-town newspapers," Patterson explained, "where he learned to set type, and thus he learned the typographical effect of certain printing, and was aware of its value. He knew when to put something in italics, and he knew when to use the smaller or larger type. There is a real art about it, and he knew how to bring out the more pungent paragraphs, surrounding them with two sets of different type to give the different meanings."

Newspaper poets like Field, Adams, and Taylor have disappeared. Many of Taylor's best quips have lost their humor now because their references in the news are no longer understood. But one achievement has endured: B. L. T. brought his readers into intimate contact with his column. Few have achieved that since. Readers sought the glory of seeing their initials in the "Line"; today, some people get the same thrill if their letter to the editor is printed in the *New York Times*. "As the 'Column' grew in reputation, 'making the Line' became almost a national sport," Fuller said.

Taylor grew up in a world where the dominant "mass medium" was the newspaper, but where personal communication relied on the letter. Putting the two together was part of his genius. "In spirit B. L. T. was a letter-writer," wrote Henry Kitchell Webster in a memorial. "He wrote a letter just a column long every day. It came as personally from him, put us as much in possession of him, as if he had sent it to each of us in a sealed envelope." Little wonder, then, as Charles Evans, Jr., put it, that "thousands had found his column a sort of daily bread, and mind and heart were hungry when he laid aside his pen."

Many of Taylor's newspaper poems found their way into collections, especially the soothing and reflective series known as "the East Window." Explaining that "there is nothing between our East Window and the rim of the world," Taylor said he liked to sit by the window and contemplate the stillness of the universe. One such poem, "Canopus," was reprinted in *Poetry* magazine at his death:

When quacks with pills political would
            dope us,
When politics absorbs the livelong day,
I like to think about the star Canopus,
So far, so far away.

Greatest of visioned suns, they say who
             list 'em;
To weigh it science always must despair.
Its shell would hold our whole dinged
           solar system,
Nor ever know 'twas there.

When temporary chairmen utter speeches,
And frenzied henchmen howl their
           battle hymns,
My thoughts float out across the
          cosmic reaches
To where Canopus swims.

When men are calling names and
          making faces,
And all the world's ajangle and ajar,

I meditate on interstellar spaces
And smoke a mild seegar.

For after one has had about a week of
The arguments of friends as well as foes,
A star that has no parallax to speak of
Conduces to repose.

Taylor died at the age of fifty-four, on 19 March 1921, at his home in Chicago; he was survived by his wife and daughters. He had been ill with a bronchial condition for two weeks but continued to conduct his column until pneumonia developed. Taylor maintained a sense of humor through his last days. His final columns noted his illness. One quoted a typographical error in a Wisconsin newspaper advertisement: "Three-year-old cold for sale." B. L. T. added his quip: "We have one we will dispose of at a sacrifice and will throw in a prescription pint."

The "Line o' Type or Two" column containing B. L. T.'s last contributions was bordered in black the day after his death. Several previous B. L. T. columns were reprinted in the following weeks. The column was later conducted by a series of "Linemasters," including foreign correspondent Richard Henry Little, until 1936; reporter and drama critic Charles W. Collins, until 1951; and John T. McCutcheon, Jr., son of the famous *Tribune* cartoonist, until "A Line o' Type or Two" made its last appearance on 7 June 1969.

References:

Franklin P. Adams, "Bert Leston Taylor," *American Magazine*, 77 (April 1914): 68;

Adams, Foreword to *A Penny Whistle; Together with The Babette Ballads* (New York: Knopf, 1921);

James R. Angell, Foreword to *The East Window, and The Car Window* (New York: Knopf, 1924);

"Bert L. Taylor, 'Colyumist' of *The Chicago Tribune*," *Everybody's* (April 1916): 478-479;

Elmer Ellis, *Mr. Dooley's America* (New York: Knopf, 1941);

Charles Evans, Jr., Introduction to *A Line o' Gowf or Two* (New York: Knopf, 1923);

Henry B. Fuller, Foreword to *The So-Called Human Race* (New York: Knopf, 1922);

Ring Lardner, Foreword to *Motley Measures* (New York: Knopf, 1927);

William Trowbridge Larned, "The Mantle of Eugene Field," *Bookman*, 41 (March-August 1915): 44-57;

"The Lost 'Colyumist,'" *Literary Digest* (9 April 1921): 27;

John J. McPhaul, *Deadlines & Monkeyshines* (Englewood Cliffs, N.J.: Prentice-Hall, 1962);

Meeting in Memory of Bert Leston Taylor: Records of a Public Meeting Held in the Blackstone Theatre, *Chicago, 27 March 1921* (Chicago: Walter M. Hill, 1922);

Harriet Monroe, "The Death of 'B. L. T.,'" *Poetry,* 18 (May 1921): 97-98.

Charles H. Taylor
(14 July 1846-22 June 1921)

Dorothy H. Powell
Arkansas State University

MAJOR POSITIONS HELD: Manager, editor, publisher, *Boston Globe* (1873-1921).

Charles H. Taylor, whose newspaper innovations in the last quarter of the nineteenth century helped to change the character of American journalism, was editor and publisher of the *Boston Globe* for more than forty years. His introduction in New England of unbiased reporting, emphasis on local events and working-class issues, and courting of women and children as readers upset journalistic tradition in the 1870s and created patterns which became standard for twentieth-century newspapers.

The eldest of seven children, Charles Henry Taylor was born 14 July 1846 in Charlestown, a Boston suburb, where both his father, John Ingalls Taylor, and his grandfather, John Taylor, were employed in the Navy Yard; his mother was Abigail Russell Hapgood Taylor. He had completed Winthrop Grammar School and was near the end of his first year at Charlestown High School when the Civil War began. Too young at fifteen to join the army, he left school and went to work. His first job was with a printing firm where the *Christian Register* and the *Massachusetts Ploughman* were set into type. He experimented with two or three other jobs before becoming a printer's devil at the *Boston Traveller*.

Soon after his sixteenth birthday, Taylor attempted to volunteer for the army but was rejected because of nearsightedness. Determined, he went to another recruiting station, managed to pass the eye test, and enlisted on 13 August 1862 as a private in the Thirty-eighth Massachusetts Volunteer Regiment. After being wounded in the second battle at Port Hudson, Louisiana, in May 1863, he recuper-ated for fifteen weeks in a New Orleans hospital and was released on 20 September 1863.

Returning to the *Traveller* composing room, Taylor resumed his printer's apprenticeship and soon began to spend part of his lunch period as a volunteer reporter, covering the Charlestown police court. This effort led to occasional assignments as a substitute reporter on other stories. Meanwhile, at night he studied shorthand, a skill that he said enlarged his vocabulary, improved his pronunciation, and made him a good speller. By the time he was nineteen, he had become a regular member of the *Traveller's* reporting staff. On 7 February 1867 he married his childhood sweetheart, Georgiana Olivia Davis. Soon afterward, he became a correspondent for Horace Greeley's *New York Tribune*. He gained the *Tribune's* attention with a report of an Anti-Slavery Society meeting at which William Lloyd Garrison announced that the purpose of the society—and his lifework—had ended with the Emancipation Proclamation. Although the *Traveller* used only a few paragraphs of the story, the *Tribune* used his verbatim account of Garrison's speech. Taylor's position with the *Tribune* required him to cover major New England events, leading him into a wide acquaintance with public figures of Boston and Massachusetts. At twenty-three, he was recognized as the top newsman in Boston.

Seeking to broaden his experience, Taylor in 1869 became private secretary to Gov. William Claflin, who had been chairman of the Republican National Committee and manager of Ulysses S. Grant's campaign for the presidency. The connection with Claflin brought Taylor into contact with national figures as well as with state leaders. As a member of the governor's staff, he was given the title of colonel. At this time, he began to develop his

Chas. H. Taylor.

public speaking ability, often taking the rostrum at meetings of the Somerville post of the Grand Army of the Republic and at the Middlesex Club, which he helped to organize.

In 1871, Taylor was elected to the Massachusetts legislature as the Republican representative from Somerville, a position he apparently sought in order to expand his understanding of political methods and his acquaintance with state policymakers. With the added insights offered by the position, he continued as a correspondent for the *Tribune* and also began writing for the *Boston Sunday Times* and the *Cincinnati Times*.

In the summer of 1871, he began publication of *American Homes*, a ten-cent monthly magazine designed for family reading. The magazine had fiction, poetry, travel stories, departments for boys and girls, fashions, recipes, health notes, and a section called "Sabbath Thoughts." Taylor said that

during those days, he learned one of his most important lessons about public taste: "You can't reach the people in the press, in politics, in the church or anywhere else except with the human touch." In a little over a year, he had pushed the magazine to a circulation of 40,000; but the disastrous Boston fire of November 1872 destroyed the magazine's new quarters and its press, wiping out Taylor's investment and ending the publication. Friends came to his assistance, helping him to get elected clerk of the House, a post that paid $2,500 a year, three times his salary as a representative. In June 1873, he was offered the managership of the *Boston Globe* but declined; however, when the position was offered again two months later, after the legislature's term had closed, he accepted.

The *Globe* had been started on 4 March 1872 by Maturin Ballou, a literary man with real estate interests; Eben D. Jordan, a dry goods merchant; and others. In an already overcrowded Boston newspaper market, it was conceived as a morning counterpart to the evening *Transcript*, a circumspect literary newspaper. Initiated with a capitalization of $150,000, the *Globe* was in financial trouble before the end of a year. Circulation of the eight-page newspaper had not grown as expected—it probably never exceeded 8,000—and the depression of 1873 exacerbated its financial problems. When the backers approached Taylor, the initial investment was almost gone and the newspaper's revenues were $60,000 behind operating expenses.

Taylor, who at twenty-seven had little business experience, plunged into a five-year battle to turn the enterprise around financially. As the depression deepened, he cut the price from four cents to three. He struggled to increase advertising revenue, going himself to call on clients in New York and throughout New England and hiring the newspaper's first advertising salesman. After the *Globe*'s paper supplier cut off credit, Taylor faced a daily crisis to gather enough cash to buy newsprint for the press-run. While Taylor borrowed heavily and sold stock to whomever he could to maintain operations, the *Globe* was abandoned by all the original investors except Jordan. The newspaper had lost about $300,000 when in 1877 Taylor, borrowing $100,000 from friends, put into effect a reorganization plan that would extricate it from its financial problems and lead eventually to all the stock being held by him and Jordan.

As a result of the reorganization, Taylor was in full control, and he immediately began to change the *Globe* to attract readers being overlooked by Boston's established press. More than a half-million people then lived in the city and its environs. Thousands of them were Irish immigrants, recently arrived and cognizant that politics was the way to a place on the city payroll. They and those who had been there long enough to gain the benefits of Massachusetts's compulsary education laws were reading weekly story papers and dime novels because little in the daily press aroused their interest. To this working-class population, Taylor directed his new *Globe*. In October 1877 he started an eight-page Sunday edition designed especially for family reading. The following March he added an afternoon edition—called an "extra"—to bring fresh news to those whose reading time came later in the day. It was not a separate newspaper, in the style of the times, but was an extension of the morning edition: the features remained the same through both editions; only the news columns changed. In Taylor's view, the daily *Globe* was never two newspapers.

At the same time, he discarded the *Globe*'s Republican allegiance and announced that henceforth it would be a "live progressive Democratic newspaper," advocating measures "to advance the interests of the masses in the social and financial condition" and "to promote their moral and intellectual welfare." This change in direction was both pragmatic and consistent with Taylor's personal views. The *Boston Post*, the only other Democratic newspaper in the city, was ailing, and a replacement was timely. Also, Gen. Benjamin F. Butler was leading an exodus from the Republican party, and a mass of disaffected party members was accompanying him. Taylor, who had tilted with the Republican old guard since his days in the state house, could enthusiastically engage with the insurgents in an effort to unseat the Republican machine. The Boston Democratic Committee welcomed the announcement by asserting that it was "the duty of every Democrat in Massachusetts to aid personally in increasing the *Globe*'s circulation and influence." Sensing that the day of the party organ was past, however, he accompanied the shift in the *Globe*'s political viewpoint with an effort to make reporting bipartisan. He believed, he said, that the news columns should be entirely independent and give impartially the news of all parties, and he told reporters: "There are two sides to every story; get both of them."

While crime news and reports of trials continued to be its mainstay, the *Globe* began to cover social concerns being ignored by other Boston newspapers and their Brahmin readers. Taylor's reporters wrote about wage complaints of factory

girls in New Hampshire, labor unrest among longshoremen, the Catholics' desire to have priests admitted to local hospitals to administer last rites for the dying, and the interest of the Boston Irish in the condition of Ireland under British domination. He also developed a strong network of correspondents throughout New England to counter the disadvantage of being excluded from the Associated Press. Taylor eschewed the common practice of emphasizing telegraphed news and made the most of local stories. Told that the *Boston Herald* was sending a man to Europe, he is said to have blithely replied with the suggestion that the *Globe* "put another man in South Boston."

Taylor's news formula was simple: what was interesting to *Globe* readers was important; what was not interesting was not important. His aim, he said, was "to make the *Globe* a cheerful, attractive and useful newspaper that would enter the home as a kindly, helpful friend of the family." He also said he wanted "to help men, women and children to get some of the sunshine of life, to be, perhaps, a little better and happier because of the *Globe*."

Women, Taylor said, were a newspaper's most important readers, and he brought the basic ingredients of his magazine to the *Globe* to attract them. He urged the expansion of a column of social notes that had been begun soon after he took over the newspaper and the development of a "housekeeper's column." He touted the advantages of advertisements, which he said women read as news. "One of my principles," he explained later, "was to get the women to reading the *Globe*. When I could get the paper into the houses and the women reading it, I knew it would stay there. Men who hated the *Globe* on account of its politics would have to buy it if the women wanted it, and I chuckled to see those fellows carrying the *Globe* home at night."

For the whole family, Taylor began in 1879 to serialize fiction, something no other American newspaper had done. He cautioned the staff, however, never to start a story during the week and end it on a Sunday. "It isn't fair," he said, "to get people to reading something in a two-cent paper and make them buy a ten-cent paper in order to get the rest of it." Sporting events were played up, and soon reports of boys' baseball games began to appear. Breaking up the columns of type were illustrated news stories, which the *Globe* had first tried in 1875.

Taylor's efforts were showing results by 1880, when the newspaper produced a profit for the first time and circulation had climbed to about 30,000. That year, he assumed the title of editor as well as publisher, although he apparently delegated much

Taylor in 1881

of the responsibility in the newsroom; he had resolved, he said, never to get tired again. During the next two or three years, he fostered a strong news department and encouraged the hiring of young Harvard graduates, who brought bright, perceptive writing to the *Globe*'s pages. He also developed a business staff built around friends and acquaintances from Charlestown, his old hometown, and Somerville, where he had lived since 1869.

In the news columns, Taylor considered the coverage he arranged of the death and funeral of President Garfield in 1881 to be among his most significant accomplishments. The *Globe* was the only Boston newspaper to put out a midnight extra the night Garfield died, and Taylor spent the next two days preparing a souvenir edition to commemorate the funeral. He commissioned poems by John Boyle O'Reilly, Walt Whitman, Oliver Wendell Holmes, and others and prepared a full obituary. Four extra pages were added to accommodate the memorial. "It waked up all New England to see a Democratic paper come out with a magnificent tribute to a Republican President," Taylor said. "In appealing to the masses as I had done with the *Globe*, I had to offend some people as everyone has to do; but all had to take off their hats to the *Globe*'s Garfield number. I had calculated in the beginning that it

would take me ten years to get into a position where I could make the kind of newspaper that I wanted to make. But that day, at least, I made the *Globe* what I wanted it to be, and it carried the paper a long way down the road." Forty thousand extra copies of the newspaper were sold, and Taylor estimated that 10,000 of the new readers stayed on as regular customers.

The next year, Taylor approved the *Globe*'s first two-column headline when General Butler was elected governor. The *Globe* had something to celebrate, for it had been the only newspaper to support him. Butler was a controversial figure whose nomination and unsuccessful campaign for governor in 1879 had split the Massachusetts Democratic party. Taylor worked hard, personally and editorially, to mend the rift, amid unproven allegations that the general owned stock in the *Globe*. As governor, Butler advocated measures which the *Globe* supported—woman's suffrage, the secret ballot, elimination of the poll tax as a qualification for voting, the ten-hour workday, and protection of women and children in industry—but they proved unpopular, and he was defeated for reelection in 1883. When Butler's political caprices led him into a devisive effort to gain the Democratic nomination for the presidency in 1884, Taylor broke with him; the *Globe* came out for Grover Cleveland.

During the 1883 Massachusetts election and the 1884 presidential election, Taylor developed and refined a method of projecting outcomes which led to the *Globe*'s being considered the standard of accuracy on early returns. Rejecting partisan feeling, Taylor relied on statistical comparisons of previous voting patterns and current totals, precinct by precinct, to predict the winner. The system came to be adopted generally by journalists throughout the country.

At this time, Taylor's innovations attracted the attention of Joseph Pulitzer, ever alert to meet editors who could teach him something. Pulitzer came to Boston, and the two went to lunch. Recalling the incident, Taylor said: "Then I went up to his room and we stayed together every minute from that Friday until Monday morning, talking all the while about building up newspapers. From that time on for years, we kept in very close touch, often working out each other's ideas in our papers at the same time." Taylor's business acumen was held in high regard by Pulitzer, who offered him $100,000 a year to divide his time between the *Globe* and the *New York World* after Pulitzer's election to Congress in 1885. Taylor declined the proposition, prefer-

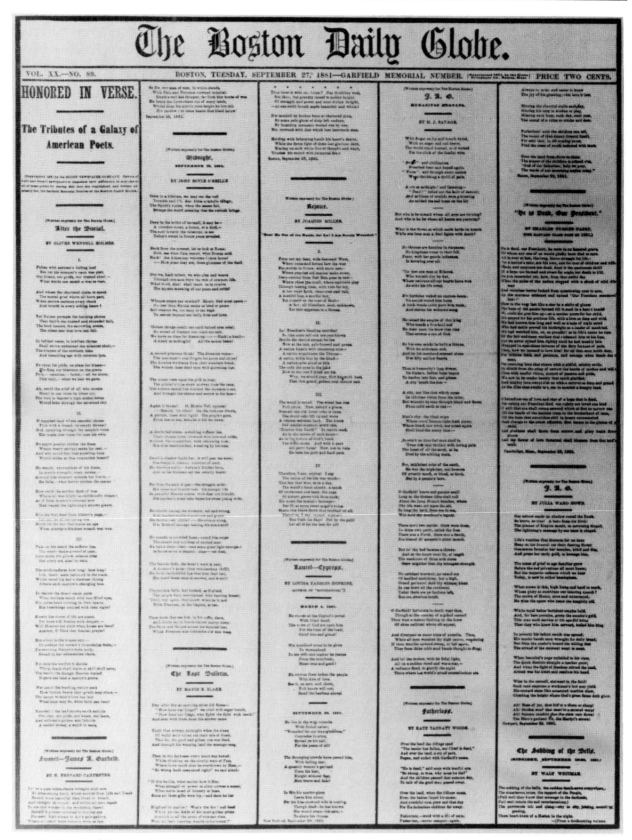

Front page of the Boston Globe *for 27 September 1881, with tributes to the assassinated President James A. Garfield commissioned by Taylor*

ring to devote himself to New England.

Throughout the 1880s, Taylor busied himself with promotion of his newspaper, adopting as a practice—at least temporarily—almost anything that would result in the *Globe*'s being talked about favorably and frequently. He advertised the newspaper and its features in other newspapers, being perhaps the first publisher to do so. He encouraged sporting events by offering *Globe* prizes to the winners. He celebrated the opening of a new *Globe* building by printing a coupon good for a five-cent ride on the city's horsecars. He boasted about circulation as it climbed toward 100,000 and ran monthly statements to show the increases. He invited well-known figures to write signed articles on topics of public interest for the *Globe*'s editorial page and experimented with signed contributions by staff members on that page. He broke with the journalistic tradition of anonymity when in 1886 he began to place staff by-lines on stories of major importance. The introduction of the reporters to readers apparently was a part of Taylor's design to make the *Globe* a "kindly friend of the family."

The *Globe*'s move into a new building in 1887 was the occasion for a celebration of Taylor's success. About 300 well-wishers—newspaper editors and publishers from across the country, city dignitaries, and state officials—gathered to congratulate him. Ten years after assuming command of the *Globe*, Taylor was in charge of a newspaper with an average daily circulation of 129,000. In reporting the affair, the *Globe* claimed that it was one of only a half-dozen newspapers in the United States then doing an annual business in excess of $1,000,000 a year and running as many as 20,000 want ads per month.

At forty-one, Taylor was beginning to adopt the bearing of a man of distinction. He had grown a full beard, replacing the moustache he had worn in earlier years. Slight of build—he was only five feet, seven inches tall—he dressed fashionably and wore black-rimmed nose glasses.

Meanwhile, the *Globe*'s editorial page continued to wander in search of focus. In one sense, Taylor had neglected it since the beginning, for he considered the news columns to be the most important part of the newspaper. To Taylor the editorial page was merely "a necessary evil," said James Morgan, who guided the page for almost fifty years. Polemics as regular fare had been dismissed from the *Globe* soon after Taylor took control, appearing only sporadically while a general climate of moderation began to dominate. Taylor, Morgan said, "simply could not mount the editorial tripod and

become oracular; and for several years he merely sat on the fence editorially." At last, in 1891 the mellow tone that Taylor wanted was crystallized in the friendly "Uncle Dudley" essays which began to appear in the Sunday newspaper. Not strictly editorials, the presentations offered a point of view to readers without foisting dogmatism upon them. Whether the "Uncle Dudley" approach was the brainchild of Taylor or Morgan is not clear, but it satisfied Taylor.

The editor's lack of stance likely was as much a result of his kindliness and ebullience as of equivocalness. He described his disposition as one which "has always led me to dwell on the virtues of men and institutions rather than upon their faults and limitations. My impulse has always been to build up rather than to join in tearing down." Taylor was a pragmatic man as well: what was good for Boston, for the working class, for downtown, was good for the *Globe*, and he could be expected to support it.

He was also influenced by loyalty to fellow members of the G.A.R. and to a coterie of friends who had supported him since his early days at the *Globe*. In 1887 he was able to dismiss allusions to corruption while he defended the West End Street Railway's efforts to consolidate horsecar lines and replace them with electric cars. Downtown Boston would benefit from the modernization, but also significant was the presence among the scheme's promoters of a fellow G.A.R. member, Congressman William T. Lovering, and two early *Globe* stockholders, Col. Jonas French and Henry H. Whitney. All were successful in business, an achievement Taylor admired, and were prominent in Democratic party affairs.

Taylor's interest in party politics waned in the 1890s. The turning points were the nomination of William Jennings Bryan as candidate for president in 1896 and the death soon afterward of young Massachusetts politician William Eustis Russell, to whom the editor was devoted. Rankled by the Democrats' nomination of Bryan and adoption of the free silver platform, which was vigorously opposed by Boston businessmen, Taylor considered deserting the party to support Republican William McKinley. He compromised, however, by merely refusing to endorse either presidential candidate and balancing news coverage between the two.

Russell—energetic, magnetic, and intelligent—had had Taylor's support through two unsuccessful campaigns and three terms as governor of Massachusetts. In 1890, the *Globe* called him a "candidate without a flaw." Russell reciprocated by naming Taylor an honorary member of his staff with the titular rank of general. Having continued to use the title of colonel since his days as a member of Governor Claflin's staff, Taylor enjoyed the promotion and used the new label both formally and informally the rest of his life. Taylor was almost paternal in his relationship with Russell and reacted emotionally to his death. The former governor's death and funeral provided the main stories in the *Globe* for days in the late summer of 1896, and Taylor himself wrote a eulogistic editorial attesting that "none knew him but to love him."

By the turn of the century, Taylor's period of newspaper innovation in Boston was ending. E. L. Grozier at the *Post* and William Randolph Hearst at the *American* were given laissez-faire to battle for the sensation-seeking mass audience, while the *Globe* settled down comfortably as the moderate, middle-class newspaper of New England.

For some time, Taylor had been lessening his responsibilities in the daily operations of the newspaper. Now he regularly spent Thursday afternoons at Keith's vaudeville theater. He continued to work at strengthening the Algonquin Club, an exclusive organization of businessmen, and its elegant quarters. He played golf often. He gratified a long interest in baseball by buying the Boston Red Sox. Seldom a traveler before—he had not been west of Chicago until 1896—he began to make annual trips to California. He became a frequent public speaker, with the growth of the newspaper industry in the United States a favorite topic. He was active also in the affairs of the Associated Press, serving as a vice-president in 1905-1906, and again in 1912-1914, and as a director from 1907 to 1912.

He was impatient with friends who did not share his pleasure in leisure time and varied activity. On a visit to Pulitzer at the New York editor's Bar Harbor estate in 1911, he was taken aback to be asked, "Taylor, do you know how many want ads we had in the *World* this morning?" Taylor conceded he did not. When recounting the episode, he added that he did not know how many want ads the *Globe* had published that day either.

In 1916 he rebuffed a suggestion that he seek the nomination for United States senator, as in 1910 he had rejected a proposal by the *Boston Post* that he be nominated as candidate for governor. He explained: "There is but one office that I really care for, and that is my present office in the *Boston Globe*."

Much of Taylor's genius as a newspaper maker lay in his ability to engender enthusiastic cooperation from employees in completing projects he conceived. On his last day in the *Globe* office, he began to outline an editorial for the staff to complete. After suffering a physical collapse, he sent the next morning for a writer to discuss with him the final details of this "Uncle Dudley" piece, which appealed for courage and leadership in the economic recession the nation was then experiencing. It was published a week before Taylor's death in June 1921. His wife had died in 1919 after a long illness; they were survived by three sons and two daughters.

There was contrariety in Taylor's view of journalism. He said that a newspaper "should take the roof off the world and let the people see in," but he concentrated the *Globe*'s attention on its own dooryard. Two years after Taylor's death, Boston was described as a "journalistic poor farm" by Oswald Garrison Villard of the *New York Evening Post*:

> It was General Charles H. Taylor of the *Boston Globe* who led the profession downward. It was also he who first understood how best to exploit the new-type residents of Boston. He built up his great journalistic success by several simple policies. He printed sensational headlines and "played up" crime. But what is a far more important explanation of his success, he issued orders that, if possible, every reader of the *Globe* must find his name in the paper at least once a year. Main Street must have its day in the journalistic court. Even today it prints long lists of "among those present" and gives pages and pages to clubs, societies and society news, to meetings of fraternal orders—anything which makes possible the printing of names, names, and names. In a city as self-centered as any parish, the *Globe* is as parochial as it knows how to be. . . . Bits of European news squeeze in as best they can; one must have the American habit of superficiality to be content with its American political news. To this must be added General Taylor's second recipe for sure success: Never say anything unfavourable of anybody in your daily if it can in any way be avoided; never give offence. It was his desire, too, that no "story" should appear in the *Globe* whose writer could not shake hands the next day with the man about whom he had written.
>
> That rule has long governed the *Globe*. General Taylor adopted it not merely because it was good business, but because he was himself a simple, sweet-natured person, utterly undiscriminating, utterly conventional, utterly ignorant that there were such things as deep economic currents and terrible economic injustices. A kindly employer,

whose gentle spirit of goodwill permeated his whole printing plant and made him very popular in the Associated Press and wherever newspaper publishers or writers met, General Taylor none the less became distinctly cynical in public and professional affairs and more and more materialistic. He was typical of many an idealist who, under the spell of this extraordinary cold-blooded and materialistic period in our history, has more and more yielded to the influence thereof.

A more kindly view was presented by Florence Finch Kelly, who worked for the *Globe* from 1881 until 1884, when she began a thirty-year career with the *New York Times*. She classed Taylor as a "genius" among journalists and said: "He was one of the greatest journalists of his period because he so definitely broke with the traditions of the past. He was determined to transmute into his paper his belief in democracy and his faith in human nature. All this showed a new viewpoint in newspapers. He introduced into American journalism a new note of tolerance, of free plain speech and of the objective point of view. He was one of the first newspaper publishers to have an inkling of and to attempt to

translate into actuality the 20th century conception of the newspaper as an instrument of social service. He did not see that conception in the fullness to which it later came. But he caught its outlines and glimpses of its possibilities. He made the *Globe* a prophecy of the newspapers of today."

Biography:

James Morgan, *Charles H. Taylor: Builder of the Boston Globe* (Boston: Privately printed, 1923).

References:

Robert Healy, *The Taylors & the Boston Globe* (Boston: Globe Newspaper Company, 1981), pp. 1-27;

Florence Finch Kelly, *Flowing Stream* (New York: Simon & Schuster, 1924), pp. 161-212, 471-516;

Louis M. Lyons, *Newspaper Story* (Cambridge, Mass.: Harvard University Press, 1971), pp. 1-219;

Don C. Seitz, *Joseph Pulitzer* (Garden City, N.Y.: Garden City Publishing Co., 1927), pp. 140, 152, 163, 408, 451;

Oswald Garrison Villard, "Boston, A Poor-Farm of Journalism," in his *Some Newspapers and Newspaper-Men* (New York: Knopf, 1923), pp. 95-111.

Carr Van Anda

(2 December 1864-28 January 1945)

Terry Hynes

California State University, Fullerton

MAJOR POSITIONS HELD: Reporter and night editor, *New York Sun* (1888-1904); managing editor, *New York Times* (1904-1932).

PERIODICAL PUBLICATION: "The Unsolved Riddle of the Solar System," *Science*, 74 (21 August 1931): 187-195.

Carr Van Anda, a master in the gathering and presentation of news, was the chief architect who carried out Adolph Ochs's avowed purpose to gather and publish "All the News That's Fit to Print." In the twenty-one years that he served actively as the managing editor of the *New York Times*, Van Anda applied his keen intelligence and quiet, energetic industriousness to the task of publishing a

daily newspaper of the highest quality, with the most complete and current information about major events.

Born 2 December 1864 in Georgetown, Ohio, Carr Vattel Van Anda was the only child of Frederick C. Van Anda, a lawyer, and Mariah E. Davis Van Anda. Raised in Wapakoneta, the seat of Auglaize County in the western part of Ohio, about 100 miles north of Cincinnati, Van Anda demonstrated as a boy an almost insatiable curiosity about math and science as well as a tinkerer's delight in working with mechanical equipment. Before he was ten, Van Anda compiled a publication by pasting together clippings from various periodicals and selling the product to relatives for ten cents a copy. Soon Van Anda moved beyond his small clipping paper to

publish the *Boy's Gazette* on a press he made himself, consisting of a pair of hinged boards and a wooden frame that held worn type salvaged from one of the local newspapers. After purchasing a more sophisticated and reliable toy printing press for $5 from another boy, the young Van Anda continued his newspaper publication with fewer mechanical difficulties and expanded his enterprise to job printing for local businesses. He used the profits for experiments in physics and chemistry and operated the printing plant, sometimes irregularly, until he went to college at sixteen.

In 1880, Van Anda entered Ohio University with the hope of becoming a mathematician or a professor of physics or Greek in an Eastern university. While attending college he was a correspondent for newspapers in Cleveland and Cincinnati. He left school after his sophomore year and went home to work for a year as foreman on one of the three Wapakoneta weeklies, the *Auglaize Republican*, a job which provided him with invaluable training in

the mechanical aspects of newspaper work.

After resigning from the *Republican*, Van Anda was employed as a typesetter on the *Cleveland Herald* in 1883. To make extra money he covered assignments as a reporter, and after the editors noticed the quality of his reporting, he was made telegraph editor of the paper. In this capacity Van Anda demonstrated what were to become characteristic professional traits—persistent hard work and almost uncanny insight into news events—when he scooped the other local papers with the news of Gen. Ulysses S. Grant's death on 23 July 1885. Van Anda and others at the paper had maintained an increasingly tense vigil over the wires for weeks, awaiting news about Grant, who for months had been suffering from cancer of the throat and was reportedly close to death at his home near Saratoga, New York. Finally even the *Herald*'s editor gave up the watch, but Van Anda persisted one more night. News of Grant's death began flashing over the wire at 5:00 A.M.; the *Herald* beat its competition to the street with the news by nearly two hours.

The *Herald* was sold to the *Cleveland Plain Dealer* in 1885. On 16 December Van Anda married Harriet L. Tupper. He remained with the *Plain Dealer-Herald* for approximately a year after the merger, then left to join the staff of Cleveland's other newspaper, the *Evening Argus*. When the *Argus* folded in 1886, Van Anda went east in search of big-city journalistic adventures in Baltimore, where his editor on the *Argus* had been night editor of the *Baltimore Sun*. When he interviewed for a position on the *Sun* in 1886, he was given the job of night editor. His wife died in December 1887, leaving him with a daughter, Blanche.

The lure of New York journalism brought Van Anda to that city, where he obtained a job as a combination reporter-copy editor on Charles A. Dana's *New York Sun* in March 1888. He remained with the *Sun* for sixteen years, serving as night editor after 1 January 1893. During this time he took complete charge of the paper whenever managing editor Chester S. Lord was away on vacation. Years later, when he was managing editor of the *Times*, Van Anda commented on the importance of the night editor's post on a morning newspaper: "The man most to be envied is the night editor. The night editor's work, always of world wide scope, is never dull. He is the appraiser of events. He is the keeper of a St. Peter's Ledger of the news of the day. To him the excellence of a newspaper is due. He can make it or mar it. The night editor passes finally on every item. He is the retriever of errors and must

Van Anda as night editor on the New York Sun

from the sensational distortions of "yellow" journals like those of Hearst and Pulitzer.

At the *Times* Van Anda was given a virtual free hand in exercising his finely honed news judgment and in displaying major news effectively; Ochs insisted that space be allocated to Van Anda's news first and to advertising afterward. Van Anda was further aided by Ochs's policy of pouring profits back into the paper in order to build the most competent international news-gathering organization possible. Meyer Berger, one of the *Times*'s historians, has noted that without Ochs's willingness to spend whatever it cost for such things as exclusive rights to stories about exploration, scientific advancements, and developments in aviation and transportation, Van Anda's capabilities would have been crippled and the leadership potential of the *Times* would never have been realized.

Two months after joining the *Times*, Van Anda had a chance to test his ability to bring a major international breaking story quickly to his readers' attention. On 14 April he achieved a clear beat concerning the naval victory scored by the Japanese over the Russian fleet off Port Arthur during the Russo-Japanese War. The *Times* received the information exclusively because of its 1901 agreement to exchange news with the *Times* of London. Lionel James, the London *Times*'s reporter at the scene, used his DeForest wireless equipment to dispatch the story of the Japanese victory from 150 miles at sea. The London *Times*, in accordance with its exchange agreement, cabled the news to the *New York Times* at once. When Van Anda received the cable in his office early on the morning of the fourteenth, he quickly wrote the headline and, as was his custom in such circumstances, stood over the printers as they set the story in type. Then he rode about the city on one of the horse-drawn delivery wagons to insure that newsstands displayed the paper prominently. Other New York newspapers were compelled to rewrite the *Times*'s version.

Although his title was managing editor, Van Anda, during all his years at the *Times*, maintained a night editor's schedule. He usually arrived at the office about one o'clock and spent the afternoon planning the next day's paper, conferring with staff members and receiving visitors. At six in the evening he ordinarily went home for dinner and, sometimes, a nap. By ten o'clock he was back at his desk, reading proofs, correcting mistakes, seeking clarification or more information for incomplete stories. He remained on the job until the last edition went to bed, rarely leaving before five in the morning and usually being the last person to go home.

always be on the lookout for shortcomings and neglected opportunities. He should be keen, alert, and well-informed. He must be sympathetic, imaginative, human. As he sits quietly reading proof slips, it is he who is framing the reflection of itself the world will see at the breakfast table. When you have achieved this post you have reached the highest place in your profession. It is true there are a few figures ahead of you, the managing editor and editor-in-chief, but these are only offices to absorb the profit of other people's work."

On 11 April 1898, Van Anda married Louise Shipman Drane of Frankfort, Kentucky. Their son, Paul, born in 1899, became a New York lawyer and a director of the New York Times Company.

Van Anda—referred to by staffers as "V.A." or "Boss"—became managing editor of the *New York Times* on 14 February 1904. He joined the staff at 41 Park Row, eleven months before the paper moved to the Times Tower at Times Square. By the time Van Anda arrived, Adolph Ochs had owned the *Times* more than seven years, having purchased it in August 1896. Ochs's goal was to produce a newspaper both enterprising and credible, yet free

Working twelve hours a day, seven days a week, Van Anda rarely took a vacation or even a day off in his twenty-one years as active managing editor.

The staff's attitude toward Van Anda is not easy to determine. Some found him cold, humorless, distant, and impersonal; his disapproving look was referred to as the "death ray." But staffers also respected his professionalism, efficiency, and sometimes uncanny insight into important news stories; and they appreciated his fairness, impartiality, and loyalty when they were in trouble. Some accounts claim that while Ochs recognized Van Anda's genius, he was sometimes resentful of Van Anda's power and his reputation among journalists.

Although it was not their primary intention to "scoop" the competition in the style of sensational newspapers, Van Anda and Ochs loved speed in news gathering and often made extraordinary efforts to beat other papers in reporting events Van Anda considered newsworthy. In some areas— for example, aviation—the *Times* promoted news events regarding mechanical or scientific developments which Van Anda believed significant or undeveloped. In 1910, Van Anda even outmaneuvered the *New York World* staff in reporting the first airplane flight from Albany to New York. The *World* had offered a $10,000 prize to the first person who could achieve the flight, but when pilot Glenn Curtiss had a week-long series of false starts out of Albany, the *World* openly began negotiating with another flyer to try to defeat him. In contrast, the *Times* hired a special train and filled it with reporters. When Curtiss finally and unexpectedly left the ground and stayed up, the *Times* train followed him to New York, noting and picturing every incident along the way. Under Van Anda's direction the story and pictures of the flight occupied six pages of the next day's *Times*, thus eclipsing the *World*, which had sponsored the flight.

Van Anda's energy, enthusiasm, and organizing ability when faced with a significant news event became almost legendary in the newspaper field. The *Times*'s coverage of the sinking of the *Titanic* in 1912 is a particularly vivid example. The White Star Line's newest and largest luxury ship was due in New York harbor Tuesday, 16 April, after its maiden voyage from Southampton, England. Early Monday morning, the *Times* received a brief Associated Press bulletin, cabled from Newfoundland, saying that the "unsinkable" steamship had struck an iceberg and needed help immediately. Van Anda instantly recognized the significance of the message. The paper's first edition had already been put to bed, but Van Anda reacted to the cable with an electricity that sparked a somewhat somnolent staff into speedy action. The front-page lead story for the mail edition was replaced with a new, briefer lead on the *Titanic* and topped with a headline saying that the ship was sinking in the Atlantic. By 3:30 A.M., after the staff completed further investigation and rechecked all available information, the headline on the last city edition reported the liner had sunk. This edition also contained background information on the passenger list and a picture of the ship reprinted from the Sunday edition.

Other papers hedged their accounts with reminders about the unsinkability of the *Titanic*. But the *Times* was guided by Van Anda's reasoning that the ship's silence after brief signals for help meant she was gone, and the paper blazed the conclusion in its stark headline. Even the White Star Line did not officially confirm the sinking until Monday night. Later that week, through Van Anda's efforts, a *Times* reporter accompanied Guglielmo Marconi on board the rescue ship *Carpathia* to talk with the surviving wireless man of the *Titanic* and the chief wireless operator of the *Carpathia*; thus the *Times* secured exclusive interviews regarding the last messages from the sinking ship. The Friday edition in which the interviews appeared devoted fifteen of its twenty-four pages to the *Titanic* disaster. Although credit for the *Times*'s superior coverage of the story over several days deserves to be shared by various staffers, including day city editor Arthur Greaves, it seems fair to say that Van Anda's driving force was the major catalyst in this event, as in many others.

Accounts by some of those who worked for him suggest that Van Anda saw reporting as a kind of intellectual game. He deduced possible alternatives based on the available evidence and risked his and the paper's reputations on the logic of his deductions. A major story like the *Titanic* illustrates this, but less world-shaking stories apparently elicited from Van Anda the same application of his sharp wits to intense dissection and analysis of the data. Edward Klauber, a night city editor of the *Times* under Van Anda and subsequently a vice-president of the Columbia Broadcasting System, once remarked of the Boss, "As a piece of mental gymnastics, he loved to trace down a piece of news. . . ."

Not all of Van Anda's ventures resulted in victory. In 1912, he secured exclusive rights to publish the stories of Roald Amundsen and Robert Falcon Scott about their respective attempts to reach the South Pole. When other papers pilfered the accounts, the *Times* sued for violation of copyright. Due to a technical error by the librarian of Congress

The New York Times.

VOL. LXI...NO. 19,586.   NEW YORK, TUESDAY, APRIL 16, 1912.—TWENTY-FOUR PAGES.   ONE CENT

TITANIC SINKS FOUR HOURS AFTER HITTING ICEBERG; 866 RESCUED BY CARPATHIA, PROBABLY 1250 PERISH; ISMAY SAFE, MRS. ASTOR MAYBE, NOTED NAMES MISSING

Col. Astor and Bride, Isidor Straus and Wife, and Maj. Butt Aboard.

"RULE OF SEA" FOLLOWED

Women and Children Put Over in Lifeboats and Are Supposed to be Safe on Carpathia.

PICKED UP AFTER 8 HOURS

Vincent Astor Calls at White Star Office for News of His Father and Leaves Weeping.

FRANKLIN HOPEFUL ALL DAY

Manager of the Line Insisted Titanic Was Unsinkable Even After She Had Gone Down.

HEAD OF THE LINE ABOARD

J. Bruce Ismay Making First Trip on Gigantic Ship That Was to Surpass All Others.

Biggest Liner Plunges to the Bottom at 2:20 A. M.

RESCUERS THERE TOO LATE

Except to Pick Up the Few Hundred Who Took to the Lifeboats.

WOMEN AND CHILDREN FIRST

Cunarder Carpathia Rushing to New York with the Survivors.

SEA SEARCH FOR OTHERS

The Californian Stands By on Chance of Picking Up Other Boats or Rafts.

OLYMPIC SENDS THE NEWS

Only Ship to Flash Wireless Messages to Shore After the Disaster.

The Lost Titanic Being Towed Out of Belfast Harbor.

CAPT. E. J. SMITH,
Commander of the Titanic.

PARTIAL LIST OF THE SAVED.

Includes Bruce Ismay, Mrs. Widener, Mrs. H. B. Harris, and an Incomplete name, suggesting Mrs. Astor's.

in framing the copyright application, the *Times* lost the case in the lower court and all the way to the United States Supreme Court. Van Anda, however, did not seem upset by the *Times's* legal defeat. Noting two other papers' accounts of the case, he asked his staffers: "Did you notice that they took the best part of a column to point out that, although the court let them off on a technicality, it was *The Times'* property and they really did steal it? If only they do that often enough!" Van Anda also took solace from the fact that at the end of the litigation, the *Times's* circulation had increased while those of the offending papers had declined.

In 1913, the *Times* moved from Times Square to more spacious quarters at 229 West Forty-third Street. At that time, its presses had a twenty-four-page limit; no one—except Van Anda—imagined that a larger paper would ever be necessary. But with the beginning of World War I, the *Times* found itself turning away up to $15,000 worth of advertising a day due to the lack of space. At Van Anda's urging, the printers began doubling up on the presses, increasing the paper to forty-eight and sometimes sixty-four pages. Circulation and revenues increased dramatically.

Reporting the events and issues of World War I was another major challenge for Van Anda and the *Times*. From the opening of the war in Europe in 1914, Van Anda realized the importance of official documents on events leading to the declaration of war. He published in full the first of these, the British "White Paper," consisting of 159 items of diplomatic correspondence between the British Foreign Office and the Central Powers. The correspondence, and the *Times's* guide to the diplomats involved, covered six pages of a Sunday edition in late August 1914. The *Times's* scoop in this case was twofold: not only was it the only newspaper to have the verbatim account, but it published the document before an official copy reached Washington. One day later, 24 August, the *Times* published the counterpart German official paper after two translators had worked on it for nearly a day. This document had been brought home by Frederic Wile, the *Times's* correspondent in Germany. Again, the *Times* was first; no other copy of this text had been received in the United States. Van Anda gave the same treatment, that is, complete verbatim quotation, to all the official papers of all the other countries engaged in the war. Throughout the war, unofficial documents, like the speeches of British Prime Minister Lloyd George, also were published in full in the *Times* under Van Anda's direction. This

was the beginning of the concept of the *Times* as a "newspaper of record."

The *Times* published detailed accounts of battles and, wherever possible, carried versions of both sides. This evenhanded approach to news led to criticism of the newspaper from supporters of both the Allies and the Central Powers. In addition, the Sunday rotogravure sections—produced on presses purchased in April 1914 at Van Anda's instigation—carried pages of war photographs. Van Anda's thirst for war news was further aided by the news exchange agreement worked out between the *Times* and the London *Chronicle*. Thus, in addition to publishing reports from *Times* war correspondents, Van Anda could provide supplementary information from the paper's British sources, especially *Chronicle* correspondent Sir Philip Gibbs. During the first year of the war, the *Times*, the *New York World*, and the *New York Tribune* consolidated their cable services to assure each other of adequate information because of the pressure on the limited communications facilities.

Again and again during the war, the competence and efficiency of Van Anda and his staff resulted in exceptional or exclusive coverage of major events. When the *Lusitania* was sunk by a German submarine off the Irish Coast on 7 May 1915, Van Anda put out a predawn extra, giving the entire front page to the story. In contrast to the emotionally charged reporting of this incident by some newspapers, the *Times's* account leaned on the facts as it had received them, leaving inferences and opinion to the editorial pages and the readers themselves. In December 1916, as a result of some inventive, cryptic cabling between Van Anda and Wythe Williams, the *Times's* chief correspondent in Paris, the *Times* published an exclusive on Joffre's retirement as chief of the French army and his succession by Nivelle instead of Pétain; it was nearly a week before French officials confirmed the story. In April 1917, Van Anda and Williams used the same cable code to communicate the news of Nivelle's succession by Pétain—another exclusive report for the *Times*.

Van Anda's enthusiasm and organizing ability were important elements in the beats achieved by the *Times*. Carbon copies of all war dispatches were delivered to Van Anda's desk; thus he often knew what was happening even before his own desk men could tell him. When an important dispatch arrived close to deadline, Van Anda would have the copy rushed to the composing room and would go there himself and set the headline directly into type with-

Front page of the New York Times *for 22 March 1918. Van Anda was the first newspaperman to realize that the final German offensive of World War I had begun.*

out the delay of having to write it out on paper first.

For its extraordinary efforts in the publication of war reports and documents, the *New York Times* in 1918 was rewarded with the first Pulitzer gold medal for "disinterested and meritorious service" by a newspaper.

When the German offensive began in late March 1918, Van Anda was one of the rare newspapermen to recognize it as the final win-or-lose struggle rather than as just another battle. When the first reports came in from the firing line, Van Anda, knowing that Ochs would support the added expense, cabled instructions to London and Paris that all future messages from the front and other important messages should be cabled at full commercial rates and, when warranted, at "double urgent" rates of seventy-five cents a word, thus giving these dispatches precedence over ordinary press reports and resulting in the *Times*'s generally being one day ahead of other newspapers in publishing major war news.

After the armistice, Van Anda gave the same detailed consideration and support to reporting postwar events that he had given to reports during the war. When an advance copy of the Versailles Treaty was brought to Washington in June 1919 and was being set in type for the *Congressional Record*, Van Anda opened twenty-four telephone and telegraph lines in New York to receive the document for complete publication in the next day's edition. The text of the treaty, published in no other newspaper, ran sixty-two columns, one-sixth of the forty-eight-page issue. In 1921, the *Times* was the only New York newspaper to publish the full text of the German reparations proposals, and it was the first to report that the French had officially rejected them.

Without war news to dominate the pages of the *Times*, Van Anda renewed the paper's coverage of developments in aviation and science. He assigned a special reporter to cover the nonstop transoceanic flight of John Alcock and Arthur Brown from Newfoundland in June 1919. When the British dirigible R-34 made its first westward nonstop crossing of the Atlantic in July 1919, Van Anda obtained stories from two of its passengers as part of his effort to give complete coverage to the event.

Van Anda's own knowledge of mathematics and physics probably led to his advantage over other newspapermen in seeing the importance of Einstein's theories. When various groups began testing Einstein's notions in 1919, Van Anda supervised the *Times*'s handling of the events. In the early 1920s, Van Anda saved Einstein from an embarrassing mistake by spotting an error in one of the equations Einstein had transcribed on a blackboard while lecturing mathematicians at Princeton. When Van Anda's calculations did not match the copy of the lecture he was editing for publication in the *Times*, his inquiry to Princeton finally brought word, after several levels of checking, that, indeed, Einstein had miscopied his notes onto the blackboard. Van Anda corrected the equation for the *Times*. On another occasion, Van Anda corrected a mathematician who gave a figure for the "diameter" of the universe in light years when he actually had meant to refer to its radius.

In late 1922, when the first brief messages about the discovery of the tomb of Tutankhamen came over the wires, Van Anda's imagination was sparked again, and he arranged for full and exclusive New York coverage of the opening of the tomb through a contractual arrangement with Lord Northcliffe's London *Times*. When the London *Times*'s correspondent in Egypt wrote his account after seeing the tomb for the first time, Van Anda gave it front-page coverage. Van Anda also proved enough of an Egyptologist to decipher some of the hieroglyphics on photographs showing the interior of the tomb and even corrected some experts regarding other translations and King Tut's genealogy.

Van Anda's news values were reflected in the attention he gave to major hard-news stories, such as the death of President Harding in 1923, which, through Van Anda's foresight, the *Times* covered in more complete detail and more rapidly than any other American newspaper. But Van Anda's sense of news extended also to sports events such as the Dempsey-Carpentier fight and to murder cases.

When publisher Adolph Ochs reviewed his twenty-five years of control of the *Times* on the paper's editorial page on 18 August 1921, he paid tribute to Van Anda's contribution to the newspaper's success "To Carr V. Van Anda . . . to whose exceptional newspaper experience, genius for newsgathering and marvelous appreciation of news value and fidelity to fairness and thoroughness, knowing no friend or foe when presiding over the news pages of *The Times*, the greatest measure of credit is due for the high reputation it has attained for the fullness, trustworthiness and impartiality of its news service. His vigilance and faithfulness to the very highest and best traditions of newspaper making make him a tower of strength to the organization."

After twenty-one years as managing editor of

the *New York Times*, Van Anda took a leave of absence in February 1925 because of ill health; he had developed double pneumonia while covering the King Tut story and never wholly recovered. His duties were assumed by assistant managing editor Frederick T. Birchall. He never actively returned to his position, but he retained the title of managing editor until his formal retirement in the spring of 1932, when Birchall was sent to Berlin as a *Times* correspondent; Edwin L. James, director of the *Times*'s foreign service, was brought back from Paris to become managing editor.

In the last years of his life, Van Anda continued to pursue his interests in math, physics, and astronomy. Although he disliked publicity to such an extent that he seldom allowed his name to appear in print, granted an interview, or consented to having any stories written about him while he was at the *Times*, in retirement he published some articles, including a scholarly paper, "The Unsolved Riddle of the Solar System," in *Science* magazine in 1931; in this article he refuted theories of the origin of the solar system proposed by Sir James Jeans and Dr. Harold Jeffreys of Cambridge University. Occasionally he provided the *Times* with a tip for a science news story. He lived most of the time on a farm in the Catskills until 1938, when he bought a 153-acre estate, the Mount, on Laurel Lake in Massachusetts.

Van Anda's second wife died of bronchial pneumonia in the couple's Park Avenue apartment on 17 February 1942. On the evening of 28 January 1945, Van Anda had a quiet dinner in his apartment with his brother-in-law, Paul Drane, director of the library of the *New York Sun*, and Drane's sister,

Judith Hewitt. After his guests had left, Van Anda received word that his daughter, Blanche, had been found dead in bed in the one-room apartment at the Hotel Fairfax where she had lived alone since 1941. Later the same night, Carr Van Anda, eighty, died of a heart attack, probably as a result of the shock of hearing of his daughter's death. When his estate was settled it was valued at more than $800,000, including $500,000 in *New York Times* stock.

In an editorial, the *Times* eulogized Van Anda as a "a legend in his lifetime" and noted further: "In any field he cared to enter he would have shone. It was the good fortune of journalism and of this newspaper that he chose journalism. . . . Unlike most intellectuals, he was a born organizer, able also to handle the unexpected. . . . His signature is written large across *The Times* today."

Biography:

Barnett Fine, *A Giant of the Press* (New York: Editor & Publisher, 1933); republished with changes and additions as *A Giant of the Press: Carr Van Anda* (Oakland, Cal.: Acme, 1968).

References:

Meyer Berger, *The Story of The New York Times, 1851-1951* (New York: Simon & Schuster, 1951);

Elmer Davis, *History of the New York Times, 1851-1921* (New York: The New York Times, 1921);

Obituary, *New York Times*, 29 January 1945, pp. 113;

Gay Talese, *The Kingdom and the Power* (New York: World Publishing Co., 1969).

Oswald Garrison Villard

(13 March 1872-1 October 1949)

Michael Kirkhorn
University of Kentucky

MAJOR POSITIONS HELD: Editor, *New York Evening Post* (1897-1918), *Nation* (1918-1932).

BOOKS: *John Brown, 1800-1859: A Biography Fifty Years After* (Boston & New York: Houghton Mifflin, 1910; London: Constable, 1910);
Germany Embattled: An American Interpretation (New York: Scribners, 1915; London: Low, 1915);
Some Newspapers and Newspaper-Men (New York: Knopf, 1923);
Prophets True and False (New York & London: Knopf, 1928);
Russia from A Car Window (New York: The *Nation*, 1929);
The Press Today (New York: The *Nation*, 1930);
Henry Villard: A True Fairy Tale (New York: Holt, 1931);
The German Phoenix: The Story of the Republic (New York: Smith & Haas, 1933);
Our Military Chaos: The Truth about Defense (New York & London: Knopf, 1939);
Fighting Years: Memoirs of a Liberal Editor (New York: Harcourt, Brace, 1939);
Inside Germany; with an Epilogue, England at War (London: Constable, 1939); also published as *Within Germany* (New York: Appleton-Century, 1940);
The Disappearing Daily: Chapters in American Newspaper Evolution (New York: Knopf, 1944);
Free Trade, Free World (New York: R. Schalkenbach Foundation, 1947).

Oswald Garrison Villard (Kaiden Studios)

OTHER: Henry Villard, *Lincoln on the Eve of '61: A Journalist's Story*, edited by Villard and Harold G. Villard (New York: Knopf, 1941).

A lifelong reformer, one of the five founders of the NAACP, editor over a period of thirty-five years of two liberal publications, the *New York Evening Post* and the *Nation*, Oswald Garrison Villard was also a sailor and a sailing journalist—the founder in 1907 of *Yachting* magazine and owner from 1918 to 1935 of the *Nautical Gazette*. Born in Wiesbaden, Germany, in 1872, he died in 1949 after spending his life defending and advancing his liberal beliefs, some of them inherited from his abolitionist grandfather, William Lloyd Garrison. His father, Henry Villard, was a newspaper publisher and one of the builders of the Northern Pacific Railroad. His fortune allowed Oswald Garrison Villard to pursue his interests with relative security, but the breadth of his zeal would have been impressive under any circumstances. He worked to improve the status of black Americans; he campaigned for the emancipation of women; he fought to keep the United States out of the First and Second World Wars; he stood up for conscientious objectors and for the victims of the suppression of

312

dissidents during World War I. He was against tariffs, trusts, Wall Street, and corrupt politics. He was a supporter of prison reform, birth control, and the independence of Ireland, and he wrote on behalf of Eugene Debs and Sacco and Vanzetti.

A youthful Civil War correspondent, Henry Villard had met Helen Frances (Fanny) Garrison at Dr. Dio Lewis's gymnasium where she, wearing a bloomer costume, was participating in the first girls' gymnastic class ever held in Boston. They married on 3 January 1866 and moved to Washington, where Henry Villard was capital correspondent for the *Chicago Tribune*. The Villards moved to Germany for Henry's health; Oswald Garrison Villard was born there on 13 March 1872. He would later have two brothers and a sister. After an interval in Boston the family moved to New York in 1876, when Henry Villard began the railroad career which would lead him over a period of thirteen years to the presidency of the Oregon Railway and Navigation Company and then of the Northern Pacific Railroad.

Oswald Garrison Villard's admiration for his parents was complete. His father he described as a deeply loving man, generous in his gifts to charities and philanthropies, indifferent to the size of a fortune built through the construction of ships and

railroads and the founding of electric light companies. His mother's strict principles were disarmingly concealed beneath her simplicity, her easy trusting nature, and her vivacity. Villard accompanied his parents across the continent in 1883 for the successive celebrations which acclaimed the completion of the Northern Pacific's transcontinental line, which was to lower the cost of living and cheapen bread in England and other European nations; but in his autobiography, *Fighting Years* (1939), he noted that this "spontaneous and wholehearted celebration" was held at the expense of 15,000 Chinese laborers, many lying in unmarked graves, and "warring Indians driven to despair by the greed of the white men and by the endless perfidy and betrayals of the government in Washington...."

Villard entered Harvard in 1889, graduated in 1893, and returned as a graduate student from 1894 to 1896, working as an assistant in the history department.

Villard began his newspaper career after leaving Harvard in 1896. In his autobiography Villard recalled how painful it was to relinquish "such a wonderfully stimulating atmosphere" for the hurly-burly of metropolitan journalism. His "spirit of adventure" carried him to the staff of the

Underwood & Underwood

Oswald Garrison Villard's parents, Henry and Fanny Garrison Villard

Philadelphia Press, where he learned a valuable lesson—"exactly what a newspaper office ought not to be; therefore when I came into authority on *The Evening Post* I always endeavored to make it the exact antithesis of the *Press*."

His apprenticeship was a rough one, particularly for the privileged son of a wealthy family. He worked twelve hours a day, six days a week, for a salary of $10. The *Press* was produced in a "shockingly broken-down structure, a perfect firetrap," with plaster fallen from the newsroom walls littering the floor and noisy staffers working at collapsed office furniture. "It was a bedlam," Villard recalled, "with men singing, whistling, talking, and yelling for copy boys." Apologizing to the *Press*'s loyal employees, Villard called the paper "a journalistic harlot. . . . It was absolutely subservient to its advertisers; it was a partisan Republican organ; it had a tremendously long list of sacred cows and a corresponding black list."

Villard joined his father's *New York Evening Post* on 24 May 1897, and immediately he was offered the opportunity to rescue the paper from its competitors. He found the paper's editor, the excitable Horace White, alarmed by the defection of editorial staff members to the competing *Commercial Advertiser*. White proposed that the *Evening Post* defend itself by installing as city editor the twenty-four-year-old newcomer Villard. Wisely, Villard refused to shoulder the burden alone. He asked instead for editorship of the Saturday feature section, from which vantage point he could analyze the paper's problems. Among the talented journalists perfectly satisfied to remain with the *Evening Post* Villard found Edwin L. Godkin, an inspirer of young newsmen, in Villard's estimation very nearly the living embodiment of the paper's spirit. Godkin was, Villard said, "the greatest editorial writer the American press has ever produced. No other leader writer in this country could match him in irony and sarcasm, in power of phraseology, in clarity and logic, in his masterly style, in his ability to dissect a proposition and to destroy it merely by restating it. Few other journalists have had such a prophetic vision."

Here, a fugitive from the shrillness and shabbiness of Philadelphia journalism, spending his days with journalists who were efficient, thoughtful, and idealistic, Villard found happiness. As a member of the editorial board Villard enjoyed "the generous kindliness of the older men, the sincere and earnest and enlightening discussions in the editorial council, the comradeship and the pride in our joint production. . . ." He admitted that the

paper appealed to members of the upper classes, but he ardently defended its popular purposes: "It served the whole people far more faithfully, for all its limitations, than many a paper which professed its devotion to the plain people and to the workers as such." His father had combined the *Evening Post* with the liberal weekly *Nation* when he bought the publications in 1881, and young Villard unreservedly admired some of the *Nation*'s editors, including Wendell Phillips Garrison, Villard's uncle and cofounder with Godkin of the *Nation*, and Hammond Lamont, "the pure and magnificent spirit" who edited the *Nation* from 1906 to 1909, when he died of bungled surgery. Under the influence of such men the *Evening Post* opposed the expansion of American power and influence in Cuba and the Philippines, arguing that imperial cruelty and devastation would coarsen and brutalize the American spirit. Both publications expressed distaste for the bumptious Theodore Roosevelt, who retorted by claiming that reading either publication steadily would produce a "fearful mental degeneracy."

At the *Evening Post*'s centennial in 1901 Villard recalled the paper's procession of eminent editors—William Leggett, William Cullen Bryant, Parke Godwin, John Bigelow, Carl Schurz, Godkin, and White. No daily ever had more distinguished editors, Villard said. Leggett, he reminded his listeners, had committed the paper to the abolition of slavery as early as 1835. A few years later, once again illustrating the paper's outspokenness, as well as revealing his own relish for pungent journalistic prose, Villard quoted Rollo Ogden's *Evening Post* editorial deriding William Randolph Hearst's stillborn candidacy for the presidency in 1904. "An agitator we can endure; an honest radical we can respect; a fanatic we can tolerate; but a low voluptuary trying to sting his jaded senses to a fresh thrill by turning from private to public corruption is a new horror in American politics. To set the heel of contempt upon it must be the impulse of all honest men."

In April 1902 Villard took an educational excursion into the South which had two direct results. One was his marriage on 18 February 1903 to Julia B. Sandford of Covington, Kentucky; the couple had a daughter, Dorothea Marshall, and two sons, Oswald Garrison, Jr., and Henry Hilgard. The other result was that, also in 1903, Villard became president of the board of directors of the Manassas Industrial School. This "small, struggling imitation of Hampton" Institute absorbed some of his energies for twenty-two years. It led him, he said, to a greater understanding of the problems of Ameri-

Four great editors of the New York Evening Post *during Villard's time with the paper: (top left) E. L. Godkin, (top right) Horace White, (bottom left) Wendell Phillips Garrison, (bottom right) Hammond Lamont*

can Negroes, prompted him a decade later to propose that President Wilson appoint a national race commission, and amplified an idealistic impulse into the conviction which placed Villard among the founders of the National Association for the Advancement of Colored People in 1909. The NAACP, "with its platform of the abolition of all caste distinctions based simply on race and color," should, Villard said, "be aggressive . . . be the watchdog of Negro liberties . . . allow no wrong to take place without its protesting and bringing all the pressure to bear that it possibly could."

The greatest "beat" of Villard's *Evening Post* career occurred in 1910, resulting in publication of an article implicating in a graft scandal Jotham P. Allds, Republican majority leader and president of the state legislature. The *Evening Post*'s crusade led, Villard thought, to the first graft conviction of a New York legislator—"something of an achieve-

ment in view of the many who had been, and were, notoriously corrupt." A reader's letter corrected Villard: Sen. Jasper Ward had been impeached and convicted in 1826—also because of revelations published by the *Evening Post*.

Villard supported women's suffrage and was one of eighty-four men to march in the first joint suffrage parade in New York City in 1911. The parade started out beneath the windows of the University Club, through which Villard observed "the faces of scoffing friends, who were doubtless much outraged at this latest proof of the insanity of that crank Villard." The marchers, he recalled, were "booed, hissed, and ridiculed without a moment's cessation."

Villard had heard Woodrow Wilson lecture in 1895 and, engaging him in debate over some differences the two had about abolitionists, had found him witty and interesting. He had placed the *Eve-*

ning Post behind Wilson's candidacy for the governorship of New Jersey. The paper supported Wilson's candidacy for the presidency in 1912, and Villard claimed some credit for Wilson's political education. When he told Wilson of the 5,000 homeless black children wandering the streets of Atlanta and of the seventeen-year-old Negro girl who was to be executed for murder, even though "she has had no chance to be anything else than what she is," Wilson declared that he would speak out against lynching and promised to appoint "colored men on their merits" to federal jobs.

Subsequent presidential decisions changed Villard's mind about Wilson. In 1913, after at first seeming receptive to the idea, Wilson refused to talk with Villard about the editor's proposal for a national race commission. Then Villard learned that Secretary of the Treasury William G. McAdoo had begun segregating white and black treasury clerks, that the president was replacing black officials with white, and that instead of appointing black Americans as ministers to Haiti and Santo Domingo, as had been customary, the administration was sending white men to occupy those posts. Wilson wrote to Villard, defending racial segregation as a means of protecting black federal workers from "friction and criticism." Predictably, the disappointed and indignant Villard took the president's statements out on the stump at mass meetings in several eastern cities. They were never close friends again.

Villard retained an amateur's enthusiasm for journalism. The opportunity to wield political influence from his editor's chair never interested him, he said, but from the beginning he had been "fettered" by "the thrill of getting the news, of being in touch with and recording the daily kaleidoscope of public life at home and abroad as well as the opportunity to champion reforms." In 1915, finding his paper shorthanded in Washington, the forty-three-year-old Villard leaped happily into the breach by appointing himself Washington correspondent. His ten months in Washington were, he said, "indubitably the most interesting experience of my newspaper career" and "as exciting as it could possibly be."

Pursuing "beats" and "scoops," Villard mixed with the mighty and sought the insider's tidbits of information. Taken together, those interviews, official notes, communiqués, and dispatches revealed to Villard's appreciative eye the pattern of political contest which intensified in Washington as the United States came closer to involvement in World War I. He remained a dismayed critic of Wilson and particularly of Wilson's unwillingness to chastise the British for preventing cargo ships leaving the United States from traveling without restriction to neutral ports. When he interviewed Robert Lansing, then counselor of the State Department, on 16 May, Villard obtained a statement, based on a diplomatic note Lansing had just written, charging that Great Britain's conduct was "unbearable." When Villard's story appeared, Secretary of State William Jennings Bryan and Lansing both denied the existence of the note. It was not the first time, Villard said, that a journalist "had been made use of to fly a trial balloon and if necessary to take the consequences." He was pleased anyway: the article provoked an apologetic response from the British Foreign Office, and the contentious Villard had the satisfaction of defending his ethical standards against Bryan, who angrily told him in private that he misunderstood "the ethics governing the obtaining of news in this city." The Lansing note was sent in "weak and emasculated" form five months later.

Villard, founder of the League to Limit Armaments, blamed Wilson for irresolutely allowing the United States to be drawn into the European conflict. Wilson, Villard said, had "neither the foresight nor the courage nor the understanding" to enforce neutrality and allowed the United States to become "tied up with the British war machine."

War—"the great tragedy"—came, and with it the ugliness and recriminations that Villard had feared. Wilson, he said, became a wartime "dictator," assuming "greater power by far than had ever been Abraham Lincoln's." Villard's response was cynical:

> This, we were assured, was proper, for the country was now actually fighting for its life as well as for the democratic doctrine in the world, for everlasting peace, and nobody and nothing must stand in the way of the holiest and noblest crusade since the quest of the grail.
>
> From the moment we embarked upon that crusade it was marked by a bitterness, a vindictiveness, a rage against all who opposed it, which in themselves should have given pause to those who really believed that out of such passions, out of wholesale murder, would come an all-cleansing spiritual victory.

The former Washington correspondent (he had left David Lawrence in his Washington position) feared—groundlessly, as it turned out—that the government might censor the *Evening Post* or the *Nation*. The lines were drawn, testing the loyalty of the dissenter's friends: "I soon discovered that half of mine were afraid that I would land in prison and that the other half was afraid that I would not." Villard, born in Germany and a lifelong student of its politics, was forced to respond to outrageous rumors and even had to rescue the family dachshund, Fritz, who was in danger of being stoned by children who had heard Villard referred to as "the Kaiser."

The public temperament was agitated and ignitable; very little further provocation was needed to turn scorn and suspicion into open hostility. The derision to which Villard was subjected was unfair. His *Germany Embattled: An American Interpretation* (1915) is anything but a pro-German tract; it is, instead, a dispassionate analysis of German character, *Kultur*, and politics, and it reminds Americans of their ancestral ties with Germany. At the end of the war, he argued, American opinion must be mobilized to safeguard the best interests of Germany, "for the claims of her people upon us cannot be denied, however we may reprobate her participation in the struggle or the policies of her General Staff." Germans are "bone of our bone and sinew of our sinew," Villard said. "They have enriched our national life; what we owe to them for the development of art and music is incalculable. . . ." Prussian militarism, however, "is a disease to be eradicated; the whole aggressive attitude of the ruling Germans who to-day embody the nation is the inevitable result of their militarism and autocracy. . . ." Villard feared that autocracy was spreading: "our President by himself, and our Congress, can involve the nation in war, ruin the hopes and aspirations of a generation, and plunge it into misery and grief without the consent of those so injured." But American institutions, imperfect as they are, have shown a generosity of spirit which has included Germans among those millions who immigrated to the United States, and the evidence they offer of the quest for "universal and permanent peace" should not, Villard insisted, be forgotten.

With war came the suppression of workers and the "strangling of the most precious thing in the world, the conscience of the individual"—military conscription. "Nothing could have been more ironic," Villard observed, "than the drafting of our Negroes to save the world for democracy when all over the South they were denied every vestige of democracy. . . ."

The war years also saw the end of the Villard family's association with the *Evening Post*. The deficit-ridden paper was sold, with Villard's approval, by the staff to Thomas A. Lamont. Villard bought the *Nation* and attended to its revival.

If Villard had attracted controversy as editor of the *Evening Post*, his invigoration of *The Nation* invited it. During the thirty-seven years of its connection with the newspaper, the *Nation* had become "more and more purely a literary journal." Villard wanted it to be a political journal again. He restored news features; printed more foreign correspondence; started a fortnightly international relations section which printed diplomatic papers, summaries from the foreign press, and book reviews; and added new staff members, including William MacDonald, Albert Jay Nock, Ludwig Lewisohn, Ernest H. Gruening, Suzanne La Follette, Norman Thomas, Raymond Gram Swing, and the four Van Dorens—Carl, Irita, Mark, and Dorothy. In 1918 the *Nation* was especially concerned to prevent the United States and the Allies from involving themselves in active opposition to the Russian revolution, but it was another matter that got the publication into trouble with the government. On 13 September the *Nation* was informed that it could not distribute its issue of 14 September. When he could get no satisfaction in New York, Villard went to Washington, where he learned from the Post Office Department's solicitor that a *Nation* article criticizing labor leader Samuel Gompers had offended postal officials who appreciated Gompers's efforts to control union unrest during the war. This, said Villard, gave "the most perfect proof of the lengths to which censorship, intended by Congress only to prevent the publication of vital military news or seditious articles, had already been stretched." Villard went to the White House and complained to a presidential assistant. The next day Wilson overruled the Post Office Department. As is always the case, Villard observed, the act of censorship increased circulation greatly.

The *Nation*'s staff decided that it would be necessary to cover the Paris peace conference, and Villard was selected to represent his publication. After a perilous passage during which his liner, the *Balmoral Castle*, was nearly swamped in heavy Atlantic seas, he arrived in London, where he found his name on a list of proscribed journalists and needed help in entering the country. For all his disagreements with Wilson, he was impressed by the almost godlike enthrallment which Wilson exerted over audiences in the Allied nations. Never had Villard seen a meeting "so moving and reverential" as that at which Wilson spoke in the Manchester Free Trade Hall on 30 December. "When that great crowd rose to its feet as Mr. Wilson appeared, there was an atmosphere around me—yes, all through the hall—that defied description. Reverence, profound gratitude, the feeling that there stood the savior of the world, the creator of a new and better universe—all of these feelings were expressed on every countenance. . . . It would have taken very little more for that audience to have gone down on its knees to Wilson."

Villard's political experience and his pacifism prevented him from sharing the enthusiasm felt by many correspondents attending the peace conference. He was disdainful about the spectacle—"uniforms without number, unending gilt and braid, and so many decorations for successful killing. . . ." When he looked into the conference room he saw none of the mothers and wives "who had given of their beloved . . . not one of the private soldiers who had borne the brunt of the fighting . . . no single representatives of the masses who had paid the price of the stupidities, the follies, the blunders, and the crimes of the statesmen and the generals there assembled. . . . Great territories involving the lives of millions of black men were to be turned over to new masters, yet there was hardly a dark skin visible. Worst of all, for the first time in modern history, a great peace was to be written without a single representative of the defeated peoples in the council chamber." He was tempted to agree with an English friend who suggested that all the political leaders present at the conference, except Wilson, should be guillotined because their scoffing cynicism would prevent any lasting peace from being established. "After it became clear that the plenary sessions were farces, and that the whole thing was going to be decided by the Big Four," reporters began to leave the conference, many of them "aching" to reach Germany—where, Villard observed, "the war blockade was being enforced and old men and women and children were daily dying . . . for lack of adequate food"—or Russia.

Villard reported on the meetings of the Socialist Second International at Bern and then, packing as much food and as many other useful items as he could into his soldier's trunk, he crossed the border into Germany—a journey forbidden to all reporters by the Allies. In Munich he found riots and bloodshed and hotel food so meager it was almost unrecognizable. Villard was in Munich when Bavarian president Kurt Eisner was assassinated. The assassination was followed by a call for a general strike; by the seizure of hostages from among the professional military and upper social classes, who had been Eisner's enemies; and by more rioting, curfew, and censorship. This violence, Villard said, was "the natural result of four years of

wholesale plundering and killing known as war." When, twenty years later as another world war began, he considered the evidence of brutality and atrocity he had witnessed in 1919, he reflected sadly that "the new Germany is not only without contrition for such acts but is being taught by its latest false gods that ruthlessness and purgings and mass murders are the highest aspiration a race of Aryans can possibly have."

When he returned to Paris Villard was invited to report on conditions in Germany to Secretary of State Lansing, Gen. Tasker Bliss, and Prime Minister Lloyd George. He had thought that his unauthorized journey would cause him more trouble, but even William C. Bullitt and Lincoln Steffens, who had just returned from Russia, envied him. "Instead of being shunned or looked at askance I was sought after, much invited, and entertained," he said. "Apparently it sometimes pays to defy Presidential ukases."

In Paris Villard found that there were now fourteen world wars being waged at the same time—one over each of Wilson's fourteen points. One at a time, Villard said, Wilson had given up the fine proclamations which comprised his peace plan. Cynicism and fatigue prevailed. Of Wilson's antagonism to the Russian Bolsheviks, Villard said, "Nothing more completely revealed Mr. Wilson's inadequacy for his Paris tasks, his mental tergiversations, his habitual refusal to face raw facts, than the treatment of Russia."

Villard returned home, and during the dark days of suppression in 1919 and 1920, when the government used all its devices to entrap and punish "reds," Villard used the *Nation* as a weapon against suppression. "Much has occurred under Adolf Hitler in Germany which could be paralleled by official misconduct in this country during this period," Villard said later.

Villard had published his first book when he was thirty-eight years old and only began to write books regularly in the mid-1920s. Several of his books consisted of political observations; in others he continued to explore one of the great mysteries of the twentieth century, Germany. He also was well known for his press criticism. His books on the press were published in 1926, 1930, and 1944.

In one of his essays he discussed his old newspaper, the *Evening Post*, and its avatar, Edwin L. Godkin. He repeated his conviction that the *Evening Post* had never been given credit for caring about common people, although it did. "Above all the editors of the *Evening Post* had too few social contacts beyond their own circles. They had little or no real understanding of the sufferings of the poor, of that labouring class who are without any margin between a bare existence and starvation. Perhaps they lacked heart somewhat, perhaps social imagination." Still, the paper was the unacknowledged defender of ordinary citizens' rights—"infinitely more so than many another which mulcted the people of their pennies by posing—for profit only—as the protagonist of the multitude." For all his polemical brilliance and masterful command of the great issues of his time, Godkin had the same faults as the newspaper he served: "To be absolutely independent and detached as an editor, to spare not even one's friends when they merit castigation, is to serve the State well but usually not to raise up multitudes to call one blessed. Yet one can but wonder if at some time in Mr. Godkin's life there had been hard places, if he could have lived in the Middle West and come to see for himself the pure, sound gold that lies underneath the commonness of exterior, the commonplacedness of much of the thinking of our rural and small-town multitudes, there might have come that fuller understanding and appreciation of American democracy which even this noble defender of it lacked."

Formerly a member of the board of directors and the executive committee of the Associated Press, Villard was unsparing in his criticism when he analyzed the workings of the wire service in his book *The Disappearing Daily* (1944). He liked the fact that the AP was a cooperative, nonprofit enterprise, but as a cooperative it was "at the mercy of the mass psychology of its members. . . . It usually takes no account of grim social situations until they result in violence or some sensational happening. . . . It is not concerned with the terrible plight of the sharecropper, or the migratory workers, or with the Negro situation, or with the special problems of labor and capital."

By 1935 Villard had severed his active connection with the *Nation* and disposed of his nautical magazines. He was very proud of his accomplishment as a "free journalist," and the conclusion of his autobiography leaves no doubt that, given a second chance, he would have chosen the same career. "Under freedom," Villard said, "the education of the unchained editor never stops. . . . That is one of the chief attractions and one of the great rewards of the profession—the joy of intense intellectual absorption in stimulating and exciting tasks which put the editor behind the scenes of politics and in touch with the men who work the governmental machinery." He admitted that "inherited means" had increased his freedom to travel, learn, and speak

freely through his own journal: "The ability to roam the world in order to see for myself the kinship of all peoples; the power to aid in some slight degree the suffering, the oppressed, the victims of prejudice, of injustice and cruelty everywhere; above all, the freedom to say one's soul is one's soul: these are the sole justifications of wealth which I have been able to discover."

Wealth, however, did not protect him from the great discouragements of his time. It had not been easy, he said, "to retain one's courage when bitterness, hatred, and medieval cruelty have entered into men's hearts and brute force . . . rules the world. Much of the great promise of my youth has been dispelled. All that hope and belief that we, in a country of unlimited riches and inexhaustible lands, were destined to be a tranquil, happy, uniquely prosperous people safe from all quarrels and embroilments of the Old World, have vanished. Our social problems have become those of the old countries—by our own folly and shortsightedness." Yet the ideals which the *Nation* had supported were those of humanity and would never perish. These were the ideals of justice, equality, freedom, security, and peace. And Villard still believed, on the eve of World War II, that those who take up the sword shall perish by it.

This conviction led to Villard's final parting with the *Nation* in 1940. From 1933 until June 1940, "in sickness or in health, whether I was here or in Europe," Villard had contributed a regular weekly column, "Issues and Men," to the *Nation*. In 1940 he wrote his last column. The editors, he said, had abandoned the *Nation*'s "steadfast opposition to all preparations for war, to universal military service, to a great navy, and to *all* war, for this in my judgment has been the chief glory of its great and honorable past."

Toward the end of his career Villard believed there were many accomplishments to celebrate. There had been "the marvelous alteration in the relations of men and women," a freeing of women from Victorian prudery, and therefore

the emancipation of society from unbearably degrading chains of falsity, sanctimonious hypocrisy, stupid prudery, and deliberate disregard of truth and the realities of life. . . .

In the generations to come, I believe, nothing will seem more incredible to historians of our time than that women should have been for centuries chained by law to human brutes whose very aspect was loathsome to them, whom they could not divorce, who would not divorce them, who made their lives a daily hell, indescribable in the refinements of its cruelty; nothing will seem more tragic perhaps than that those martyred women could not leave their husbands to fend for themselves because there were almost no decent economic opportunities for them to earn a livelihood.

Of the promise of democratic politics he was less hopeful. Forty-four years of journalism left him with little respect for most high officeholders. "Nothing in my life has been more disheartening than the discovery of how high officeholding eats into the characters and souls of human beings. . . ." Deceiving themselves by claiming that they are indispensable to their nations, freed from ordinary morality, believing that they are infallible, powerful politicians "change all their viewpoints by processes of self-delusion and rationalization until they convince themselves that they are as consistent as they are righteous, as true to themselves and to their beliefs as they are just."

Villard suffered a heart attack in 1944; he died in 1948.

Perseverance was perhaps Villard's great virtue. If his tenacious conviction in the pursuit of liberty and peace ever flagged, those intervals were not evident in the publications he edited. He had fast friends who respected his idealism and his accomplishments, and the sort of enemies he wanted.

He was a member of a generation which thought after World War I that it had seen the worst violence mankind could do to itself; yet he lived through another war even more hideous, destructive, and disillusioning in its consequences. Certainly the voice of a persevering idealist was valuable for others sensitive to the horrors of the early twentieth century, even though that voice could be self-righteous and unduly vitriolic. His political writing probably will not stand the test of time; his writing about the press is important for the standards it upholds and for the glimpses it provides of publications and journalists of his time. But it is his insistence on the goodness of mankind uncorrupted by the schemings of its chosen or unchosen leaders that remains inspiring. Of his career he observed on the last page of his autobiography that for all his failures, it could be said of him "that he did know how to fight and cared enough about the struggle to put into it all that he had to give during his fighting years—as his life's contribution to the country which he has sought to serve and the democracy for which he will never cease to strive."

Biographies:

Dolena Joy Humes, *Oswald Garrison Villard: Liberal of the 1920s* (Syracuse, N.Y.: Syracuse University Press, 1960);

Michael Wreszin, *Oswald Garrison Villard: Pacifist at War* (Bloomington: Indiana University Press, 1965).

Henry Watterson
(16 February 1840-22 December 1921)

Robert K. Thorp
Louisville Times

MAJOR POSITION HELD: Editor, *Louisville Courier-Journal* (1868-1919).

BOOKS: *A History of the Spanish-American War*, attributed to Watterson but ghostwritten by Young E. Allison (New York: Werner, 1898; London: Werner, 1899);

The Compromises of Life (New York: Fox & Duffield, 1906);

History of the Manhattan Club (New York: De Vinne Press, 1915);

"Marse Henry," 2 volumes (New York: Doran, 1919);

The Editorials of Henry Watterson, edited by Arthur Krock (New York: Doran, 1923).

OTHER: *Oddities in Southern Life and Character*, edited by Watterson (Boston & New York: Houghton Mifflin, 1883).

PERIODICAL PUBLICATIONS: "Abraham Lincoln," *Cosmopolitan*, 46 (March 1909): 363-375; "Mark Twain—An Intimate Memory," *American*

Henry Watterson (Culver Pictures)

Magazine, 70 (July 1910): 372-375;
"The Humor and Tragedy of the Greeley Campaign," *Century*, 85 (November 1912): 27-43.

"I was born in a party camp and grew to manhood on a political battlefield," Henry Watterson wrote in his reminiscences. He spent most of his life on the political battlefields, too, combining his zest for politics with his equally strong penchant for wanting to share his information and instruct an audience. With the *Louisville Courier-Journal* as his base for more than fifty years, he was one of the most famous political editors of his time. Not only were his editorials widely quoted and reprinted, but he gained wider recognition from his magazine articles, his lecture tours, his frequent forays into the bright society of New York and Washington and the capitals of Europe, and his diligent efforts in the highest councils of the Democratic party.

Watterson was born in Washington, D.C., early in the first Congressional term of his father, Harvey Watterson. Harvey held the Tennessee seat in the House formerly occupied by James Polk, who had been elected governor of Tennessee. The Watterson family was prominent in Tennessee Democratic circles; Harvey's father, William, had served with Andrew Jackson during the War of 1812, was a neighbor of Jackson's, and had worked in Jackson's campaigns. Harvey Watterson was not only Polk's successor; he was his anointed successor. Still, he thought 1840 "a bad year for Democrats. I am afraid my boy will grow up to be a Whig." There seemed little likelihood of that. The Wattersons saw a great deal of other Democrats, and some of young Henry's earliest recollections were of prominent Democrats — Jackson, Polk, Lewis Cass, and Franklin Pierce.

Watterson's life and career were so lengthy, and his activities so widespread and various, that he was acquainted with every man to occupy the White House from John Quincy Adams to Franklin D. Roosevelt, with the exception of the Whig William Henry Harrison, who, in that "bad year" of 1840, managed to capture Tennessee's electoral votes.

The Wattersons' sojourn in Washington was interrupted when Harvey, through his father's intervention, was sent on a special mission to Buenos Aires. This broke up the spirited antics of Harvey and his House colleague Franklin Pierce. Tabitha Black Watterson took their son back to McMinnville, Tennessee, in 1843 while Harvey went to Argentina to report on trade and the war between Argentina and Uruguay. For Henry, it was the beginning of instruction; his mother taught him to read and gave him piano lessons. He also had a serious case of scarlet fever, which weakened his eyes greatly and left them forever impaired. A later accident nearly blinded him in one eye, so that he always had vision problems. But from his mother he gained quickness of mind, and later he learned to scan pages quickly, saving his sight.

Harvey Watterson returned from Argentina after a year and was reelected to Congress, and the family moved back to Washington. Henry Watterson's education was largely informal: he had a music teacher in Washington, but his mother was his tutor until he was twelve, and he read widely on his own, in addition to absorbing the lore of politics by listening to adults talking about politics and politicians. He had the run of the Capitol and played at being a page, and he had books a kindly representative from Massachusetts helped him get from the Library of Congress. Watterson was present when that friend, John Quincy Adams, collapsed on the floor of the House, mortally stricken, in 1848.

In 1849, Harvey Watterson purchased the *Nashville Union*, once a Jackson organ and always Democratic. Watterson hung around the office, getting his first lessons in printing and journalism.

The *Union* was a moderate paper, not a supporter of Southern extremists, and Watterson was ever like his father in this respect. In 1851, Harvey was asked to return to Washington as assistant editor of the *Washington Union* and was in place for the 1852 campaign of his former drinking companion, Franklin Pierce. Henry Watterson's formal education consisted of four years, from ages twelve through sixteen, at the Academy of the Protestant Episcopal Church in Philadelphia, where he was editor of the *Ciceronian*, the school newspaper; he held the office for all four of his years at school, the rule calling for one-year tenure having been suspended for him. For Harvey Watterson and the *Union* times were not so auspicious, and Pierce's administration was less than he had hoped. The split came on the Kansas-Nebraska bill in 1854, and Harvey resigned. Pierce tried to placate him with the governorship of Oregon, but the Wattersons returned to Tennessee, where Harvey began to practice law.

When Watterson left school two years later, he joined the family in Tennessee and found almost instant success in journalism. His father gave him a printing press that summer of 1856, and Watterson began the *New Era*, a one-sheet broadside that, in its first issue, called on the Democrats to elect Buchanan, rout Frémont and the Black Republicans, and save the country. The *Nashville American*, more of a fire-eating paper, picked up the editorial, and it eventually was reprinted in the *Washington Union* and other papers in the East. After that heady beginning, Watterson managed to stick it out in McMinnville for two years, reporting the mundane events of the community. In 1858 he felt ready for New York. *Harper's Weekly* had accepted his poetry, and he wanted to get on with the literary career he felt was his. Charles A. Dana, Horace Greeley's assistant on the *Tribune*, hired Watterson at space rates, enough to keep him going. He got an assist, too, from Henry Raymond of the *Times*, who had heard Watterson play the piano and hired him as substitute music critic. Despite his partial success, his new friends, and the cultural ambience, Watterson was not at home in New York. He returned to more comfortable terrain late in 1858, made himself at home again in Washington's familiar Willard's Hotel, and was hired by the *Daily States* "on the strength of being my father's son and a very self-confident young gentleman." On that paper he received some journalistic training and further instruction in writing from a remarkable woman named Jane Casneau, who wrote the editorials. He spent his spare time in the Library of Congress and still was able to write occasional letters from Washington to the *Philadelphia Press*. He got additional income when, as he recalled in his memoirs, "without anybody's interposition I was appointed to a clerkship, a real 'sinecure,' in the Interior Department by Jacob Thompson, the secretary, my father's old colleague in Congress." All in all, he found life in Washington delightful. His parents were back in the capital and provided a social base, although they apparently needed his financial help. He had some interesting journalistic experiences, among them a trip to Harper's Ferry and an interview there with John Brown.

He also met Abraham Lincoln, forming a lifelong liking and respect for the man that was broken only by a few ill-chosen, and much regretted, epithets written during the Civil War. As a reporter for the *States*, Watterson was among the first to speak with the president-elect in the Capitol; later, he was hired to help the old Associated Press in its coverage of the inaugural ceremonies and stood by Lincoln's side "whilst he delivered his inaugural address."

But 1861 was a hard year for Watterson, for his heritage made him a rebel, even though "I had been an undoubting Union boy. Neither then nor afterward could I be fairly classified as a Secessionist." After the *States* went out of business early in the year, he resigned from the Department of the Interior and returned to Tennessee, even though "I retained my belief that secession was treason, that disunion was the height of folly and that the South was bound to go down in the unequal strife." Watterson was hardly a warrior; he was barely five feet tall and weighed less than 100 pounds. Still, he signed on in Nashville as an officer on the staff of Gen. Leonidas Polk. He fell ill on the first mission, a foray into Kentucky, and returned to Nashville and editorship of the *Nashville Banner* until the city fell in February 1862. Fleeing, he attached himself to Gen. Nathan Forrest, performing "mainly guerrilla service," he recalled. "But Fate, if not Nature, had decided that I was a better writer than fighter," and he went to Chattanooga to become editor of the *Rebel*. Biographer Joseph Frazier Wall points out that it was on the *Rebel* that Watterson began to develop the journalistic style that he used during the rest of his professional career, a style which would always have about it a tinge of extravagance. He lashed out at the North and called Lincoln "a man without mind or manners . . . a rude, vulgar, obscure, backwoods pettifogger . . . knock-kneed, shamble gaited, bow-legged . . . pigeon-toed, swobsided . . . a shapeless skeleton in a very tough, dirty, unwholesome skin . . . born and bred a rail-splitter . . . a rail-splitter still." This was a position which he would later recant. There was no distortion of war news in the pages of the *Rebel*. By the summer of 1863 Watterson was telling his readers that things were not going well for the South. Under his editorship, coverage in the *Rebel* was not limited to the city or county. It soon became the newspaper most widely read by the Confederate troops and eventually reached 8,000 circulation. However, because of its uncertain future, subscriptions were sold only by the month at one dollar.

After the fall of Chattanooga in the late summer of 1863, Watterson became chief of scouts on Gen. Albert S. Johnston's staff, keeping an eye on the Union army moving from Chattanooga to Atlanta. In Atlanta he was given a position as assistant editor of the *Atlanta Southern Confederacy*. When Atlanta fell to Union forces, he joined the military again and fled east. Soon, however, he decided that he no longer cared to be a part of the military forces. He then wrote to a friend on the *Montgomery Mail* and was offered the position of editor and the opportunity to become part owner. He readily accepted and retreated to Montgomery to live for a few months until he accepted an abortive mission to "slip through the Union lines" in an effort to get to Liverpool, England, and seek financial aid for the Confederacy. By the time he arrived in the North he realized the cause of the South was hopeless and headed for Cincinnati, where relatives and friends provided shelter throughout the remaining few months of the war.

In the early spring of 1865 he accepted the position as assistant amusements editor of the *Cincinnati Evening Times* and within a month was given the editorship and a salary of $75 a week, when the regular editor drowned in a boating accident. He also began his long friendship with Murat Halstead, editor of the *Cincinnati Commercial*. The war was difficult for one as frail and so torn by conflicting loyalties as Henry Watterson, but he made the best of it and, in typical fashion, even profited. He established himself as a bona fide soldier of the Confederate army, credentials that would serve him well in his political and journalistic battles; he gained valuable newspaper experience, especially in Chattanooga, where he had developed his style and made his own policies. In Chattanooga, too, he had met and courted the beautiful Rebecca Ewing, who was to become his wife. He had also met Walter N. Haldeman, owner of the *Courier* in Louisville, Kentucky, who had taken his newspaper south when federal troops arrived in his city. During the

Watterson shortly after the end of the Civil War

war, then, Watterson had added much to his practical education and had, in effect, secured his future.

Being a Southern Democrat on a Republican newspaper was less than desirable. Watterson marked time in Cincinnati, eager to get back to Tennessee, to Rebecca, to his family. The opportunity came when two friends asked him to join them in reviving the *Republican Banner* in Nashville. He quickly accepted, and in September 1865 his first editorials appeared in that publication. During the following three years, Watterson used the editorial pages of the *Banner* to begin his campaign of national reconciliation by calling for national harmony and an end to sectional differences. In what he called "The New Departure," he argued for diversified farming and invited investors of Northern wealth to develop Southern resources—a goal which Henry Grady of the *Atlanta Constitution* was later to popularize as "The New South." So successful was the *Republican Banner* that Watterson was able to save enough money to marry Rebecca on 20 December 1865 and to honeymoon in New Orleans.

He was also saving for a trip to Europe, long a dream, and he had money for that by the summer of 1866. They went first to London, where Watterson immediately fell among congenial people. A letter of introduction from a British lady in Montgomery led to dinner with Thomas Huxley and John Stuart Mill. Then they spent some days in Paris, the first of many visits there. Watterson enjoyed Europe; he liked to travel, to meet the great and the interesting, and to sample the good life.

He was looking for more of the good life when he made the decision to leave Nashville in the spring of 1868. He had risen to the top there, he thought, and it was time to find a sphere more in keeping with his talents and ambition. Louisville beckoned: Haldeman would like to have him on the *Courier*; there was also an offer from the *Journal*, once nationally famous as a Whig paper under the editorship of its founder, George D. Prentice. Prentice was old and ailing and willing to relinquish his place to a younger man, and Isham Henderson, the majority owner, liked Watterson. Watterson later said that he knew from the outset that the Louisville papers must merge, that the city could not support both of them as well as the *Democrat*. Watterson chose the moribund *Journal* and, when Haldeman declined to merge, began to attack the *Courier*. After he raised daily circulation from 1,800 to 10,000 and circulation of the weekly edition from 1,500 to 50,000, he suggested to Haldeman that they stop trying to ruin each other. Haldeman agreed, and the *Courier-Journal* first appeared on 8 November 1868. The *Democrat* was out of the race; its owner had died.

It has been said that Watterson was a thundering, fearless editorial writer because he wrote with the power of ownership. Actually, he wrote with the power granted by his agreement with Haldeman, for he never held more than one-third interest in the *Courier-Journal*. At times his interest was less, for he sold stock to Haldeman to support his flamboyant life-style and growing family. Watterson and Haldeman were a good team: they were in accord on the issues, and they knew what they wanted. The merger gave Haldeman a staunch Democratic editor; it gave Watterson an exceptional publisher who cared nothing for the limelight but did know how to make the money Watterson would spend so lavishly.

Watterson thought the editorial page was the heart and soul of a newspaper; without it a paper had no identity and became only a commodity to be mass produced and sold. Consequently, at times the *Courier-Journal* would have as many as ten editorial

writers—more than the number of reporters usually found in the newsroom.

With his business future in safe hands, Watterson could turn his attention to what he considered his vital missions: preserving the federal union and reforming and revitalizing the Democratic party in Kentucky.

Since Louisville was considered the "Gateway to the South" and was scarcely touched by the war, Watterson saw the city as the perfect place to continue his campaign for reconciliation between North and South. He constantly expressed his belief in the Union and industrialization of the South; fearing a strong centralized government, he argued for states' rights and a weak federal system, and a low tariff "for revenue only," a plan he advocated throughout his career.

Watterson thought the role of Kentucky would be central in setting the direction of the South during the Reconstruction years. He realized that if he and the *Courier-Journal* were to be a part of the postwar political movement in the state, he would have to bring his newspaper back into the mainstream of the Democratic party, from which it had drifted under Prentice. He found Kentucky Democrats "a riffraff of opportunists" and "selfish and short-sighted time servers." So he "sought to ride down the mass of ignorance which was at least for the time being mainly what I had to look to for a constituency."

Prentice and others tried to dissuade him from his course, but he was willing to risk his career and even his safety. The latter was in question when he tackled the issue of Negro testimony, which was barred by state law in trials of white persons. Watterson took up the cudgel in April 1869 and kept pounding at the legislature until the law was changed in 1872. He later remembered his fight as one on behalf of the Negro, but many of his editorials stress the advantages that changing the law would have for white people. However else it may be viewed, Watterson's fight was a "new departure" and he was a fiery liberal compared to the reactionary "Bourbon Democracy" he was attempting to reform and lead.

Part of his reforming was the attempt to persuade the meaner elements to be respectable and not harass the black populace. That would help with another goal: keeping the federal government out of the state, insofar as possible. Concerning the Negro, Watterson recalled, "I urged that he be taken out of the arena of agitation, and my way of taking him out was to concede him his legal and civil rights. The lately ratified Constitutional Amend-

A page of Watterson's handwriting, which was notorious for its illegibility. A tramp printer, assigned to set type for one of Watterson's Courier-Journal *editorials, supposedly walked off the job with the comment, "I have set all kinds of writing, but I never did learn how to set up music."*

ments, I contended, were the real Treaty of Peace between the North and South. The recognition of these Amendments in good faith by the white people of the South was indispensable to that perfect peace which was desired by the best people of both sections. The political emancipation of the blacks was essential to the moral emancipation of the whites. With the disappearance of the negro question as a cause of agitation, I argued, radicalism of the intense, prescriptive sort would die out; . . . the restoration of Constitutional Government would follow, being a matter of momentous concern to the body of the people both North and South." But as Watterson learned, Southern and Northern extremists both preferred to wave "the bloody shirt." Votes were what mattered.

In arguing for allowing Negro testimony Watterson wrote, "Equality before the law and political equality are two different sorts of equality in their conditions. The admission of the one is in reality a line of defense against the other." That editorial was published on 13 April 1869, after the Fourteenth Amendment had been ratified but about a year before the Fifteenth was adopted. (Kentucky rejected both.) In the same editorial, he declared, "By granting the purely legal privilege of testimony, Kentucky would have gained ground to resist the political encroachment of suffrage." Suffrage would be a bone of contention until the Fifteenth Amendment was adopted, for as he stated in an editorial on 12 December 1868, "Remove the bayonet from the South and enfranchise the negroes, and four-fifths of them will go just as they happen to be bought by money or by kindness." He rejected a proposal to grant suffrage in return for complete amnesty. His major bastion on the suffrage question was states' rights; but when the amendment was declared ratified on 30 March 1870, he accepted it, although not gracefully. To him it was an "outrage upon the States." Thereafter he counseled his fellow Democrats to stop making Negro suffrage a campaign issue; the amendment was a fact. He had been right, he said after an election in August of that year: the Negro vote had not been much of a factor.

It was at this point that Watterson revised his harangue and perhaps established himself as a champion of the black people. "Why should we quarrel with his ignorance?," he wrote. "Have we made any effort to instruct him? . . . Have we done anything to elevate him? . . . Is it not better to try and educate and instruct him, to make a better workman and a more useful citizen out of him?" He advocated working to improve the black people so that "they

will cease to be a disturbance and become an industrious and perhaps a prosperous class."

Watterson kept to this track in general, and the tone of the paper changed somewhat, being less inclined to name-calling. What he seemed to advise was largely benign neglect; let the Negro make his way as any free man should; let him establish his schools and get on about his business. Watterson did not favor the proposed amendment to the Civil Rights Bill that would ban racial discrimination in public accommodations, schools, colleges, and cemeteries; and he did not think Americans, even in the North, wanted "Cuffee and Dinah on a footing of perfect social equality."

While he was engaged in those battles on the Negro question and related issues, he also kept up his efforts to persuade Kentucky Democrats that he was indeed one of them and, moreover, to accept him as a leader. Likewise, there was the task of persuading the Northern wing of the party that the Southern wing was respectable; he wanted, in short, to reunite the party, to end the war.

Watterson saw the current change a little in 1872 in the liberal movement that culminated in Horace Greeley's nomination for the presidency at the Liberal Republican convention. The convention was dominated by newspapermen — Horace White of the *Chicago Tribune*, Murat Halstead of the *Cincinnati Commercial*, Samuel Bowles III of the *Springfield* (Massachusetts) *Republican*, and Whitelaw Reid of the *New York Tribune*. After great debate and political maneuvering the convention named Greeley, founder of the *New York Tribune*, as its candidate. Greeley was subsequently also nominated by the Democratic party. Even though Greeley's candidacy failed, some important links of reconciliation had been forged, and Watterson supported him editorially and with personal courtesies.

As far as Watterson was concerned, his political efforts bore their first bumper crop in 1876 when "a Democratic State Convention put its mark upon me as a Democrat by appointing me a Delegate at large to the National Democratic Convention of that year called to meet at St. Louis to put a Presidential ticket in the field." Watterson had fought for Samuel J. Tilden in the party's state convention and, consequently, the delegation went to the national convention committed to Tilden. Watterson realized that the Kentucky vote for a candidate would probably trigger the support of the other Southern states; therefore, it was essential to control the Kentucky delegation. The major problem was to fight off the challenge of Gen. Winfield

Scott Hancock. Watterson was elected chairman of the convention, made the keynote address, and was instrumental in overcoming the Hancock support. Tilden got the vote of the Kentucky delegation and, eventually, that of the other Southern states and received the presidential nomination.

The *New York Tribune* saw Kentucky's unity for Tilden as "a great triumph for Watterson, as it gives the best proof the party in his state has ever accorded him of his great influence and popularity." He went back to Kentucky to be hailed as "the state's foremost citizen," and several of the state's newspapers said he should have been nominated for the vice-presidency. The *Courier-Journal* said he was coming home as "a prophet in his own land." During the campaign, Watterson spent a month in New York writing dispatches, talking to reporters, and contacting wealthy businessmen for their support. He also spoke on behalf of Tilden throughout Kentucky and in the neighboring states of Indiana and Ohio. He was constantly bombarding the fraud

Cartoon by Thomas Nast published during the Hayes-Tilden electoral controversy, showing a fiery Watterson being cooled off by Cincinnati Commercial *editor Murat Halstead*

and corruption of the two Grant administrations while continuing to urge an end to sectionalism. He went to bed election night assured that Tilden had won. He was astounded when he learned that the Tilden votes in South Carolina, Florida, and Louisiana had been challenged and, later, that Tilden's election was overturned by the National Election Commission in favor of Rutherford Hayes. Watterson could mark 1876 for another reason: when E. P. Parsons, a congressman from Kentucky, died in August 1876, Watterson made his only effort to hold public office. Even though Watterson insisted that journalists should not hold political positions, he accepted the nomination and was elected to serve the remaining six months of Parson's term in the Forty-fourth Congress.

Thus, in eight years, Watterson had overcome fierce personal and political opposition. He did it through his forceful personality and his equally forceful editorials, which were widely circulated. He did it by appealing to the "better" elements in Kentucky and the South to put aside their passions, to work for the Union and for the return of economic prosperity. He had advocated, too, a policy of moderation toward the black population and had excoriated the crueler, bumptious whites who had a tendency to terrorize the Negroes.

Watterson was actively involved in all the national Democratic campaigns through 1892 as an official delegate from Kentucky and a member of select convention committees. At various times he served the conventions as chairman of the Committee on Resolutions or the Platform Committee, where he was able to insert planks on tariff reduction and oppose the "free silver" interests. He was so widely known that some Kentucky Democratic clubs bore his name.

By 1880, Watterson had established himself, through his newspaper, as a spokesman for the South and was gaining a widespread national reputation. The *Courier-Journal* could boast of the largest circulation of any Democratic newspaper west of the Alleghenies with a combined daily and weekly circulation of 150,000. His lecture tours, which began in 1877, were a means by which he expressed his interest in national political affairs and, being highly profitable, helped support his rather lavish life-style. His first lecture, "The Comicalities and Whimsicalities of Southern Life," was both humorous and serious. He explained to his audiences that the differences between the Northerner and the Southerner were "purely exterior," and that, when stripped of regional manners, speech, and customs, all Americans were the same.

And, he concluded, even the exterior differences were being swept away. By the 1880s his editorial fame was such that it assured him of audiences when he was on a speaking tour; and even though he was not a good speaker, the fact that he was a former Confederate soldier asking for sectional harmony and extolling the American union was appealing to Northern audiences.

His most popular speech, which he used the rest of his life, was his "Lincoln Speech." First given in 1894 to the Lincoln Union in Chicago, it included selections from the Lincoln-Douglas Debates, the first inaugural address, the Widow Bixley letter, and the Hampton Road conference to show that the assassinated president was the greatest American who ever lived.

Although he may have persuaded Kentuckians to remove the Negro from the political arena, Watterson himself never quite let go. The Negro is a topic arising a number of times in his reminiscences, in which he tells his readers that he viewed slavery as objectionable ("I cannot recall the time when I was not passionately opposed to slavery"). He assigns responsibility for slavery to both North and South, saying that the Civil War (he usually calls it the "War of Sections") had been precipitated by "an untenable and indefensible system of slave labor, for which the two sections were equally responsible." "The North, which brought the Africans here in its ships, finding slave labor unprofitable, sold its slaves to the South at a good price, and turned pious. The South took the bait and went crazy." Lincoln, he claims, "believed the North equally guilty with the South for the original existence of slavery."

Watterson discussed the Negro in his lectures, too, perhaps knowing that Northern audiences would be interested in hearing about the black man in the South. "The South in Light and Shade," for example, started with a lengthy recital of the foibles, whimsicalities, jokes, and peculiar characteristics of Southerners. Then the tone and subject became serious, with Watterson talking about the good people, both North and South. Then it was back to humor until an ending that included a soliloquy on the Negro and his place, past and present, and, finally, closing remarks on how the "aim of the Southron is to out-Yankee the Yankees . . . by the successful emulation of Yankee thrift." That was "Marse Henry" Watterson, the embodiment of the Southern colonel, charming the Northerners, bringing harmony to the land. He was always a strong man for union.

He was also for sound money and a "tariff for revenue only." The latter led to long and bitter exchanges with Grover Cleveland; the former almost ruined the *Courier-Journal* and put the Watterson-Haldeman team back to where it had started in 1868. William Jennings Bryan, with his policy of free silver, was the precipitating agent; Haldeman and Watterson were gold men. But even Kentucky sent a "silver" delegation to the convention that nominated Bryan in 1896. Haldeman promptly announced that the *Courier-Journal* would not support him. That was near-treason: the *Courier-Journal* was the voice of the party in the South, and its weekly edition circulated throughout the region; it spoke the South's language and carried its message to the North.

Watterson, in Europe supervising the education of his children and contemplating early retirement, cabled Haldeman to stick with his decision. "No compromise with dishonor," he roared. The party faithful roared back; subscribers deserted in droves. The weekly's circulation of 100,000 dwindled; the daily faltered as subscribers turned to the Silver Democrats' new paper in Louisville, the *Dispatch*. Kentucky went Republican for the first time, and William McKinley went to the White House. For Watterson there was no early retirement. He hurried home, and the partners began a four-year fight to save their newspaper. Watterson was to recall the fight as costing "more of labor and patience to save it from destruction than it had cost to create it thirty years before."

The *Courier-Journal* was saved by Watterson's editorial and personal efforts and by Haldeman's business acumen, part of that being his foresight in establishing the afternoon *Louisville Times*. Watterson had objected vehemently, but Haldeman had persisted, and the paper had appeared on 1 May 1884. Watterson did not acknowledge the birth and would not allow mention of the *Times* in his newspaper for nearly fifteen years, but its profits kept the *Courier-Journal* afloat in the dark days after 1896. So Watterson and the *Courier-Journal* gradually made their way back to the Democratic fold, supporting Bryan's candidacy in 1900, Alton B. Parker's in 1904, and Bryan's again in 1908. In that last year, Watterson was head of the Committee of the Daily Press, whose aim was to get Bryan a better reception than he had received in his earlier campaigns. By that time, the circulation of the *Courier-Journal* had returned to its previous level, and it again claimed to be the largest newspaper in the South.

Watterson may have been chastened by the 1896 drubbing and ensuing battles, but he was not cowed. He continued to give advice to all comers, including President Theodore Roosevelt and his successors, and he was again acknowledged as a power in the party. He always felt free to criticize the administration: before Theodore Roosevelt was elected vice-president and assumed the presidency after the assassination of McKinley, Watterson said Roosevelt was "youthful, well-balanced, a gentleman cowpuncher, a man of letters, and a clear-headed politician." But after assuming office, Roosevelt became "something of a crank; over-educated and overbred for practical affairs, affecting the cowboy among men of letters and a man of letters among the cowboys; with more of audacity than common sense." Yet they remained good friends.

Watterson was invited to meet Woodrow Wilson when the Princeton president was being eyed as a possible gubernatorial candidate; Watterson thus became one of his early supporters. He reserved the right to blow hot and cold, of course, and by convention time in 1912 he was blowing cold on Wilson. Still, he was a good Democrat and visited Wilson in the White House, still criticizing him.

Watterson seemed not much interested in the Progressive Era that preceded World War I. Arthur Krock, Washington correspondent and later editorial manager of the *Courier-Journal* and *Times*, in his commentary on the editorials he collected, said: "One reason why this volume is empty of comment on many important events from 1910 to 1914 is because the editor left the writing to others." For Watterson, Krock says, the two greatest topics of sociology and legislation were female suffrage and the prohibition of alcoholic beverages, and he opposed both with vigor and sarcasm. Watterson's memoirs reflect that; in 1919 he was still writing of "silly Sallies" and "crazy Janes." Even so, he saw himself as the woman's champion: "I have been fighting the woman's battle for equality in the things that count, all my life." But when the suffrage battle was ended, there remained feminism. "It is feminism, rather than suffragism, which is dangerous." Then, in an echo of his soliloquies on the Negro, he added: "I am not opposed to Votes for Women. But I would discriminate and educate, and even at that rate I would limit the franchise to actual taxpayers, and, outside of these, confine it to charities, corrections and schools, keeping woman away from the dirt of politics." Prohibition he opposed on grounds of infringement with personal liberty, and probably unconstitutional infringement at that.

But the big menace in Watterson's late years came from the Kaisers (he preferred the plural and the upper case). The *Courier-Journal* was awarded the second Pulitzer Prize given for editorial writing, and Watterson's pieces were the heart and soul of the commentary on the war. Usually cited is his ringing "To Hell with the Hapsburg and the Hohenzollern" from the "Vae Victis" editorial written on the American declaration of war. That editorial did not originate the denunciation; Watterson first used it in an editorial on 3 September 1914, when the war was only a month old. He worked it into other editorials, too, even through the long months when he was counseling prudence and restraint. After the sinking of the British passenger ship *Lusitania* by German submarines in May 1915, with the loss of 128 American lives, he was strained between his natural desire for isolationism and the urge to defend the nation's honor through retaliation. His frustration was best expressed in his editorial published in the *Courier-Journal* two days after the *Lusitania* disaster:

Truly, the Nation of the black hand and the bloody heart has got in its work. . . . Nothing in the annals of piracy can in wanton and cruel ferocity equal the destruction of the Lusitania. . . . But comes the query, what are we going to do about it? . . . Please God, as all men shall behold, we are a Nation; please God, as Europe and all the world shall know, we are Americans. . . . The *Courier-Journal* will not go the length of saying that the President shall convene the Congress and advise it to declare against these barbarians a State of War. This may yet become necessary. . . . Yet we are not wholly without reprisal for the murder of our citizens and the destruction of their property. There are many German ships—at least two German men-of-war—in the aggregate worth many millions of dollars, within our reach to make our losses—repudiated by Germany, good—and their owners—robbed by Germany, whole again.

We must not act in haste of passion. This catastrophe is too real—the flashlight it throws upon the methods and purposes of Germany is too appalling—to leave us in any doubt what awaits us as the bloody and brutal work goes on. Civilization should abjure its neutrality.

After Wilson asked Congress to declare war in April 1917, Watterson became openly belligerent and demanded action. In his "Vae Victis" editorial, which was a major factor in his winning a 1917 Pulitzer Prize, he said:

> Surely the time has arrived—many of us think it was long since overdue—for calling the braves to the colors. Nations must e'en take stock on occasion and manhood come to a showdown . . . .
>
> Like a bolt out of the blue flashed the war signal from the very heart of Europe. Across the Atlantic its reverberations rolled to find us divided, neutral and unprepared. . . . There followed the assassin sea monsters and the airship campaign of murder.
>
> All the while we looked on with either simpering idiocy, or dazed apathy. Serbia? It was no affair of ours. Belgium? Why should we worry? Food stuffs soaring—war stuffs roaring—everybody making money. . . . Even the *Lusitania* did not awaken us to a sense of danger and arouse us from the stupefaction of ignorant and ignoble self-complacency.

Then he encouraged Wilson to send "the Black Horse Cavalry sweeping the Wilhelmstrasse like lava down the mountainside" in order to rid the world of "Autocracy, Absolutism and the divine right of Kings."

When the United States did officially join the war, Watterson was seventy-seven years old and burdened with squabbling among the heirs of Haldeman, who had died in 1901. He took on top managerial duties after a court fight and a subsequent board meeting at which he was elected president of the two corporations that owned the newspapers. He was critically ill in the early months of 1918.

As World War I intensified, Watterson became more outspoken about the way the Wilson administration was prosecuting the war. He thought the war effort should be pressed harder on all fronts. He was particularly anguished by efforts to control dissent within the United States when Congress passed the Espionage Act and gave the postmaster general the authority to ban materials from the mail which might be considered treasonable or seditious. When it was suggested to him that, as a Democrat, he should support the president, Watterson remembered his role in electing Wilson and acidly remarked, "Things have come to a hell of a pass / When a man can't whip his own jackass." His unending support of the Allies during the war earned him both domestic and foreign praise. The French government gave him the Croix de Legion

d'honneur as "a mark of gratitude for service and friendship for France in the greatest crisis of its history," and Belgium awarded him "the dignity of Officer in the Order of the Crown as a token of . . . appreciation of the devotion you have shown to the cause of Belgium."

Watterson was ready to relinquish his control of the newspapers if a suitable buyer could be found. That turned out to be the wealthy lawyer who had represented the Watterson forces in the management dispute, Robert Worth Bingham, a former judge and former mayor. Watterson gladly sold his stock, and his friends did likewise; Watterson gave himself the title of editor emeritus and agreed to continue writing on whatever topics suited his fancy.

Wilson's League of Nations proposal was his main topic, but he did not fancy it. He viewed it as "this latest of Wilsonian hobbies" and "a fad." Its effect "can only be to tie our hands, not to keep the dogs away." For nine months, Bingham let Watterson write against the League, even though the newspaper was running its own editorials favoring Wilson's efforts. Ultimately, the new owner decided the arrangement must end. The announcement was made on 2 April 1919; the arrangement had endured only since the previous August.

Watterson kept busy. He opposed a third term for President Wilson, supporting James Cox for the Democratic nomination. He wrote his memoirs for the *Saturday Evening Post*, getting at the same time a good contract for their publication in book form. He sent a few harangues and other articles to the *New York Herald* and elsewhere. He arranged his papers and wrote his will.

Henry Watterson died in Jacksonville, Florida, on 22 December 1921, after a brief period of not feeling well. The Wattersons were visiting friends in Jacksonville, as they often did on their annual trip to Florida. It is not surprising that he died away from home; the Wattersons traveled a great deal, often to Europe, where they consorted with royalty. They were also friends with the elite in America: Watterson was on speaking—and dealing—terms with important politicians and with other leading newspapermen; he knew actors and authors and concert performers. He was a man who lived well and shared his zest and his enthusiasms. It is unlikely that the name of any newspaper editor since his time has been known to so many people.

Throughout his career, Watterson's written influence exceeded that of the editorial pages of the *Courier-Journal*. He was frequently quoted in other newspapers around the country. He was also asked

Front page of the Louisville Courier-Journal *for 13 September 1918. Watterson had called for the United States to enter World War I in a Pulitzer Prize-winning editorial, but he was extremely critical of President Wilson's handling of the war afterward.*

for his opinions on national issues and wrote regularly for national publications such as *Century* magazine, *Harper's Monthly*, *Harper's Weekly*, *Collier's Weekly*, the *Saturday Evening Post*, *Cosmopolitan*, and *American Magazine*.

By the last decade of the nineteenth century, Watterson was considered a national leader in journalism and was frequently asked what function he thought American newspapers should perform. In public statements, he said the cardinal principles of journalism were "disinterestedness, cleanliness and capacity." Journalists, he insisted, should "be sure to tell the truth and be sure to not be animated by unworthy motives in telling the truth." Journalism, he added, "should be a complete history of yesterday, neatly and justly told . . . should be a chronicle of life and thought . . . a reflection of the temper and tone of the people, done with absolute fidelity." But in private conversations with his fellow editors, he was more direct, suggesting that being a good editor means knowing "where all hell is going to break loose next and having a man there to report it."

In a sense, the problems and concerns of twentieth-century America passed him by. Watterson's politics never changed from nineteenth-century concerns, and he failed to grasp the significance of the Progressive movement in the 1910s. Oswald Garrison Villard, editor of the *New York Evening Post*, acknowledged that "Col. Watterson typified the opinions of the Border States, if not of the entire South, in the minds of most Northern editors. It was his opinion which was sought and quoted as the representative one of his part of the country." But in noting the change in the problems and mood of the country in the twentieth century, Villard indicated that the public is "wearied of the long editorial fulminations. It is no longer interested in the same degree in political events and political machinations. Once of absorbing interest to the newspaper public, they no longer arouse the enthusiasms, the bitter antagonisms or the intense loyalties of the seventies, eighties, and nineties. The emphasis in national life is shifting to matters industrial and economic which Col. Watterson barely sensed and perhaps never plumbed." In summarizing a long career two years after Watterson's death, Villard said:

> But these and other eccentricities and his offences against taste, like his long list of unfulfilled prophecies, were readily forgiven by the audience which hung upon his words. For them he was a licensed editorial libertine; his lapses were laughed aside as just one of

'Marse Henry's' pleasant idiosyncrasies. What other editor could so have abused a President as popular as Roosevelt and escaped unscathed? The truth is that the South took a pride in him as in any other noted Southern institution and the Haldeman family, with him the owners of the *Courier-Journal*, were wise enough to agree to complete editorial autonomy as his share in the publication and were shrewd enough to realize that he was their greatest asset and a national one. . . .

Probably Henry Watterson will be best remembered in the years to come by what he did to bring North and South together when to be a liberal Republican and politically independent took courage and character; by his efforts for true reconstruction, by his realization that even after Emancipation it is true that this nation cannot exist half slave and half free. With real individualities all but gone from the American press, it is a melancholy reflection that there is no editor remaining South of Mason and Dixon's line—indeed, anywhere—whose written or spoken word can deeply influence so many people, or voice the aspirations of a group, or any editor who can be so freely a law unto himself.

Biographies:

Isaac F. Marcosson, *"Marse Henry"* (New York: Dodd, Mead, 1951);

Joseph Frazier Wall, *Henry Watterson: Reconstructed Rebel* (New York: Oxford University Press, 1956).

References:

W. E. Beard, "Henry Watterson," *Tennessee Historical Magazine* (July 1931): 70-75;

Lena Logan, "Henry Watterson, the Border Nationalist," Ph.D. dissertation, University of Indiana, 1942;

Louisville *Courier-Journal*, "Marse Henry Edition," 2 March 1919, special Watterson section;

Leonard Niel Plummer, "The Political Leadership of Henry Watterson," Ph.D. dissertation, University of Wisconsin, 1940;

Joseph M. Rogers, "Henry Watterson," *Book Lover's Magazine* (March 1905): 13-16;

Ballard Smith, "Henry Watterson," *Harper's Weekly* (20 August 1887): 600;

Robert K. Thorp, " 'Marse Henry' and the Negro: a New Perspective," *Journalism Quarterly*, 46 (Autumn 1969): 467-474.

Oswald Garrison Villard, "Henry Watterson and his

Courier-Journal," in his *Some Newspapers and Newspapermen* (New York: Knopf, 1923), pp. 258-272.

Papers:
Henry Watterson's papers are in the Library of Congress.

William Allen White

Stephen Vaughn
University of Wisconsin, Madison

See also the White entry in *DLB 9, American Novelists, 1910-1945*.

BIRTH: Emporia, Kansas, 10 February 1868, to Dr. Allen and Mary Ann Hatton White.

EDUCATION: Presbyterian College, Emporia, 1884-1886; University of Kansas, 1886-1890.

MARRIAGE: 27 April 1893 to Sallie Lindsay; children: William Lindsay, Mary.

MAJOR POSITIONS HELD: Editor, *El Dorado* (Kansas) *Republican* (1890-1891); reporter, *Kansas City Journal* (1891-1892), *Kansas City Star* (1892-1895); editor and proprietor, *Emporia Daily and Weekly Gazette* (1895-1944).

AWARDS AND HONORS: Master of Arts, Columbia University, 1910; Gold Medal for Citizenship, Theodore Roosevelt Memorial Association, 1934; Pulitzer Prizes, 1923, 1946.

DEATH: Emporia, Kansas, 29 January 1944.

Culver Pictures

SELECTED BOOKS: *Rhymes by Two Friends*, by White and Albert Bigelow Paine (Fort Scott, Kans.: Izor, 1893);
The Real Issue (Chicago: Way & Williams, 1896);
The Court of Boyville (New York: Doubleday & McClure, 1899; London: Ward, Locke, 1904);
Stratagems and Spoils: Stories of Love and Politics (New York: Scribners, 1901);
In Our Town (New York: McClure, Phillips, 1906);
Some Essentials of an Education, Being an Address Delivered at Oberlin College, Oberlin, Ohio, June 19, 1907 (Emporia: *Emporia Gazette*, 1907);
Emporia and New York (Emporia, Kans.: *Emporia Gazette*, 1908);
The Massachusetts Ballot: The Hope of Party Government

(Emporia, Kans.: *Emporia Gazette*, 1908);
A Certain Rich Man (New York: Macmillan, 1909);
The Old Order Changeth: A View of American Democracy (New York: Macmillan, 1910);
A Theory of Spiritual Progress: An Address Delivered Before the Phi Beta Kappa Society of Columbia University in the City of New York (Emporia, Kans.: The *Gazette* Press, 1910);

God's Puppets (New York: Macmillan, 1916);

The Martial Adventures of Henry and Me (New York: Macmillan, 1918);

In the Heart of a Fool (New York: Macmillan, 1918);

Woodrow Wilson: The Man, His Times, and His Task (Boston & New York: Houghton Mifflin, 1924; London: Benn, 1926);

Politics: The Citizen's Business (New York: Macmillan, 1924);

The Editor and His People: Editorials by William Allen White, edited by Helen Ogden Mahin (New York: Macmillan, 1924);

Calvin Coolidge: The Man Who Is President (New York: Macmillan, 1925);

Some Cycles of Cathay (Chapel Hill: University of North Carolina Press; London: Milford, 1925);

Conflicts in American Public Opinion, by White and Walter E. Myer (Chicago: American Library Association, 1925);

Boys—Then and Now (New York: Macmillan, 1926);

Masks in a Pageant (New York: Macmillan, 1928);

Pages from the Nation: Selections from the Contributions of the Editorial Staff for the Decade 1918-28; Illustrated with Cartoons and Other Drawings (New York: The Tenth Anniversary Committee of *Nation* Readers, 1928);

Fifty Years Before and After: An Address Given to the Sixty-Second Annual Commencement of the University of Kansas, June 11, 1934 (Lawrence: Department of Journalism Press, University of Kansas, 1934);

What It's All About: Being a Reporter's Story of the Early Campaign of 1936 (New York: Macmillan, 1936);

Some of the Problems of Christian Education (N.p., 1936?);

Forty Years on Main Street, compiled by Russell H. Fitzgibbon (New York & Toronto: Farrar & Rinehart, 1937);

A Puritan in Babylon: The Story of Calvin Coolidge (New York: Macmillan, 1938);

Speaking for the Consumer (Emporia, Kans.: *Emporia Gazette*, 1938);

Change Under Freedom (Emporia, Kans: *Emporia Gazette*, 1939);

The Changing West: An Economic Theory About Our Golden Age (New York: Macmillan, 1939);

We Are Coming, Father Abraham! Speech before the Abraham Lincoln Association of Springfield, Ill., Monday Evening, Feb. 12 (Springfield, Ill.: Abraham Lincoln Association, 1940);

Objectives of the Committee to Defend America by Aiding the Allies (New York: The Committee to Defend America, 1940);

The Autobiography of William Allen White (New York: Macmillan, 1946).

OTHER: Herbst S. Harley, *Rome and the World Today: A Study, in Comparison with Present Conditions, of the Reorganization of Civilization under the Roman Empire which Brought to a War-Worn World Two Hundred Years of Peace*, foreword by White (New York & London: Putnam's, 1934);

"An Old Friend Speaks," in Richard B. Fowler, *Alfred M. Landon, or Deeds Not Deficits* (Boston: Page, 1936); simultaneously published as *Deeds Not Deficits: The Story of Alfred M. Landon* (Kansas City, Mo.: Punton, 1936);

Defense for America: The Views of Quincy Wright, Charles Seymour, Barry Bingham, edited with introduction by White (New York: Macmillan, 1940).

Probably no other newspaper writer in the first half of the twentieth century mirrored the values of small-town life more clearly and enthusiastically than did William Allen White. White's life spanned a remarkable period. He was born in Emporia, Kansas, on 10 February 1868, the same year Ulysses S. Grant was first elected president. The United States, still recovering from the devastation of the Civil War, was predominantly an agrarian society. When White died in early 1944, in the midst of World War II, America had become a mighty urban, industrialized nation, second to none in military strength.

Unlike many writers and intellectuals who fled the village for the excitement—and often despair—of the city, White lived most of his life in small-town Kansas. He wanted it no other way. As the very foundations of rural America crumbled, White celebrated life in his beloved Emporia. Although the circulation of his paper, the *Gazette*, never reached 8,000, White's superb writing talent brought him international recognition and made him a formidable figure in both Kansas and national affairs. For many Americans, this lifelong Republican, who strayed only occasionally from his party, came to symbolize respectable, middle-class, reform-minded liberalism. White was by no means a deep or original thinker, nor did he run far in advance of the prevailing opinion of his time. Rather, he was one of what George Herbert Palmer once called those "sensitive, responsive souls, of less creative power," but on whom "current ideals record themselves with clearness."

White grew up in the frontier environment of late-nineteenth-century Kansas in the small town of El Dorado, some sixty miles southwest of Emporia. The rough-and-tumble Kansas of those years, with its shootings, lynchings, cowboys, and gambling saloons, was not for the weak or faint-hearted. At first glance the short, roly-poly Will White, with his chubby face as "pink and white, fat and sweet, as featureless and innocent as a baby's bottom," seemed out of place. You would see him "as he comes rolling down the street," one of his contemporary critics wrote, "and . . . wonder that he ever did anything but sit in the shade of a tree, and drink lemonade." His clothes looked "as if they had been planned and cut out by the town tinner. His hat [was] the most impossible structure in the world." There was always that "half suppressed twinkle in his eye" that suggested "an overgrown boy. Altogether, you would say that the man was made of putty, were it not for a certain firmness about the jaw indicating that there [was] steel beneath this flabby exterior, and plenty of it, too. . . ."

That steel, that inner toughness, undoubtedly owed much to his ancestry. His family traced its origins to the original migration to Massachusetts in the 1630s. New England Puritanism, with its ideas about individualism and social responsibility for evil, deeply influenced the White family and was passed to William from his father, Allen. New England Puritanism, Will White believed, was at the core of the reform spirit in Kansas.

White was the only child of Mary Ann Hatton and Dr. Allen White to survive infancy. His parents were quite different from one another, and each in their own way influenced their son. They met in 1866 and married the following year. Allen, whose first marriage had recently ended in divorce, was forty-nine at Will's birth. A shrewd businessman, he looked on the frontier as a land of opportunity which offered the chance to escape the rigidity of Eastern society. Easygoing, something of a romantic, he considered himself a loyal Democrat. When he moved from Ohio to Kansas in 1854, he supported women's rights and prohibition, although he opposed the antislavery crusade.

White's parents, Dr. Allen and Mary Hatton White

The Hattons came from Ireland and first settled in Quebec, where Mary Ann was born on 3 January 1830. They later moved to Oswego, New York, where Susan B. Anthony converted the young Mary Ann into a strong advocate of woman's suffrage and equality. After Mary Ann's parents died she lived for a time with Mr. and Mrs. Robert Wright, devout Congregationalists. When the Wrights moved to Illinois, they sent the young girl to Knox College at Galesburg, a school founded by New England ministers and a center of abolitionism. By the time Mary Ann Hatton left Illinois in 1865 she had strong opinions about racial equality, and shortly after accepting a teaching position at Council Grove, Kansas, she shocked local sentiment by permitting a black child to stay in her class. Unlike her husband, she never felt completely at home on the frontier, which for her was a cultural and educational desert. She did, however, take an active interest in politics. Quick-witted, volatile, a believer in hard work, she was an aggressive Republican. Her son remembered her as a "captain of a woman" who was "still afraid of hell-fire and still hoped for wings."

Will White was a mixture of these two people. Volatile, romantic, sharp-witted, a lover of a good battle, he was described once as "a good friend and a good hater. Give him a choice of running his fat legs off for a friend or heaving a brick at an enemy and he would hesitate. In the end he would do the errand for his friend, but he would hurry it along in order that he might also have time to heave the brick." Politically, he leaned to the Democrats until his father's death in October 1882. From then on his allegiance to the Democratic party waned as he realized that the only way to influence Kansas politics was through the Republican party.

Although White never formally graduated from college, his years as a student were important. They offered him an opportunity to move away from the domination of his mother and time in which to begin to develop a working philosophy. For nine months, in late 1884 and early 1885 and for the first half of 1886, he attended Presbyterian College of Emporia. There he read Walt Whitman, Charles Dickens, the King James version of the Bible, and Ralph Waldo Emerson, whose "Self-Reliance" led White to what he called in his *Autobiography* (1946) his "first rebirth on earth." What emerged was an "Emersonian-Nazarenean philosophy" which White carried with him for the remainder of his life. While at Emporia, he met the future historian Vernon Parrington and made friends with Vernon L. Kellogg, who eventually

convinced White to enroll at the University of Kansas in Lawrence. At Lawrence, White was a good but not outstanding student, and his inability to pass a solid geometry course meant that he failed to receive a degree. He did encounter several professors who influenced his writing style, including Arthur Canfield, literary instructor and poet; W. H. Carruth, who also wrote poetry and taught German; and A. R. Marsh, a teacher of rhetoric and English literature. White's thinking about social and economic matters may also have been influenced by James H. Canfield, Arthur's brother, who taught history, sociology, and economics. Canfield was a maverick who championed views more radical than most Kansans were willing to accept, but his ideas had little noticeable effect on White until after the turn of the century.

While at the University of Kansas, White worked at various journalistic jobs and in the summer was a reporter for the *El Dorado Republican*. When he left the university in January 1890, he went to work for the *Republican* under editor Bent Murdock. White ran the paper for Murdock, who was in the Kansas senate, for more than a year and a half and used his spare time to write poetry, essays, and short stories under the pen name of Elder Twiggs. He studied Murdock's fine editorial style and copied it so successfully that many of his editorials were thought to have been written by Murdock. At some point while working for the *Republican*, perhaps in 1891, White's career plans crystallized and he decided to be both a newspaperman and a writer of literature.

When White began his journalistic career, he had only a superficial knowledge of the social forces changing America. For the United States, the late nineteenth century—the last decade in particular—was a time of dramatic change. At the center of this momentous transformation was the Industrial Revolution. Kansas was in the midst of rural America's revolt against industrial capitalism, and populism and the People's party were strong in White's home state. The Populists were deeply disturbed by the decline of rural life and by what they perceived to be exploitation by the banks, railroads, and mortgage companies, and they offered solutions to these problems. In the Omaha Platform of 1892, they called for free and unlimited coinage of silver at a ratio of sixteen to one with gold; increased government regulation of the economy, including ownership and regulation of the railroads and the telephone and telegraph systems; a more flexible currency controlled not by the national banks but by the federal government; postal savings banks; a graduated income tax; the end of alien landhold-ings; and the recovery of land held in excess of need by large corporations. Many Populists also favored the direct election of senators, the secret ballot, ini-tiative and referendum, a single-term presidency, shorter working days for labor, and restrictions on immigration. Many Kansans found this program attractive in the early 1890s. The panic of 1893 affected the entire country but was especially severe in Kansas, where as many as three-fourths of the farms in the center of the state were mortgaged. The panic forced large numbers of people to leave the state and saddled many of those who remained with heavy debt. With high interest rates and low prices for their produce, it was not surprising that farmers complained.

Although White ultimately came to support many of the reforms advocated by the Populists, as a twenty-two-year-old editor he saw a darker side to populism, and he became one of its most vocal crit-ics. He believed the Populist program was the work of a lunatic fringe, and he attacked the call for governmental control of monopoly as un-Amer-ican. He suggested that Populist leaders were fail-ures who had turned to politics because they were unable to succeed elsewhere and argued that they were too inexperienced to be trusted with the reins of government. White's opposition to populism grew from a belief that the "best people" should lead. He "considered himself to be a Lincolnesque type Republican," according to biographer Walter Johnson, and saw the Republican party not as a party "of the selfish rich" but as the instrument of the middle class. Clearly White did not consider Mary Elizabeth Lease, who advised farmers "to raise less corn and more HELL," to be one of the "best people." He likened her to a Kansas tornado—a hard, unattractive, shrewish woman "as sexless as a cyclone." In a short story for the *Republican* entitled "The Regeneration of Colonel Hucks" in 1891, White told of a man who left the Republican party and joined the Populists, only to learn the error of his ways and return to the GOP. This satire em-phasized the evils of populism, preached the virtues of the Republican party, and was reprinted in both the *Kansas City Journal* and the *Kansas City Star*. The essay gave White for the first time something more than local prominence and identified him as one of the Republican party's most effective spokesmen in the state if not the whole Midwest.

On the strength of "The Regeneration of Col-onel Hucks," both the *Journal* and the *Star* sought White's services. He and his mother moved to Kan-sas City, where he worked first for the *Journal*,

which he considered to be more solidly Republican. But he grew disillusioned with the paper, feeling that it was too reluctant to criticize the GOP and special-interest groups. He angrily quit the *Journal* in June 1892 after an editor sabotaged a scoop he had received in Wichita at the Populist state con-vention, where Jerry Simpson—the "Sockless Soc-rates of the Kansas Desert," White called him—had given the young writer an exclusive story.

White began working for the *Star* in Sep-tember 1892. Several people on this paper influ-enced his later career, but none was more impor-tant than the publisher, William Rockhill Nelson. White later modeled the *Emporia Gazette* after the *Star*. Nelson's paper was involved in numerous campaigns to improve local housing, playgrounds, and parks, and to expose political corruption, loan sharks, and deceptive medical practices. Nelson did not hesitate to publish news that might offend sub-scribers or advertisers. He tried to maintain a low profile, careful not to publicize himself too much in his own paper; above all, he believed an editor should not run for political office. Although White did run for office once, he generally followed Nel-son's example. When he witnessed an attempt on Nelson's life by Joe Davenport, an irate political boss, White learned that it required courage to run a paper devoted to public service.

On 27 April 1893, White married Sallie Lindsay, a Kansas City, Kansas, schoolteacher. The same year, *Rhymes by Two Friends*, written with Al-bert Bigelow Paine, was published.

White left Missouri and returned to Kansas in 1895; although he had many subsequent offers to leave—the *Chicago Tribune* once offered him $25,000 a year—he resided in small-town America for the remainder of his life.

If White's return from the city was unlike the route taken by many young writers who fled the small town permanently, he was not untouched by his urban experience. Lewis Gannett once observed that New York was "full of small-town boys trying their best to forget that they are small-town boys. . . . White made a career out of remembering it, but he remembered it with a city perspective."

White purchased the *Emporia Gazette* in 1895 after borrowing $3,000. He was only twenty-seven when he took over the paper. Within five years the loan was repaid and the *Gazette* was making its own way. Meanwhile, he continued his literary career: His second book, *The Real Issue* (1896), consisted of reworked stories which had appeared earlier in the *Republican*, the *Star*, and the *Gazette*.

White became much more than merely a re-

White's wife, Sallie Lindsay White, in 1894

porter of the news in Emporia; he was an integral part of nearly all aspects of the town's life. He helped connect Emporia with the larger flow of Kansas politics: as a member of the Kansas Republican state committee, he provided information about local conditions and names of people who could be trusted with party matters. He provided a bridge to economic forces beyond Emporia, too: for a time he assisted the Atchison, Topeka and Sante Fe Railroad, making recommendations as to how it might enhance its standing among Emporians; he encouraged other railroads to build through his town; and he was always ready to promote Emporia as an attractive location for new business.

Although White remained a small-town Kansas editor and booster for the next forty-nine years, he soon gained national stature and began to speak to a wider audience. He was first propelled into national prominence by a slashing editorial attack on William Jennings Bryan and the Populist platform in 1896. In "What's the Matter with Kansas," he sarcastically blamed the Populists for the state's wretched plight during the 1890s:

> Oh, this is a state to be proud of! We are a people who can hold up our heads! What we need is not more money, but less capital, fewer white shirts and brains, fewer men with business judgment, and more of those fellows who boast that they are "just ordinary clod hoppers, but they know more in a minute about finance than John Sherman"; we need more men who are "posted," who can bellow about the crime of '73, who hate prosperity, and who think because a man believes in national honor, he is a tool of Wall Street. . . .
>
> Give the prosperous man the dickens! Legislate the thriftless man into ease, whack the stuffing out of the creditors. . . .
>
> Whoop it up for the ragged trousers; put the lazy, greasy frizzle who can't pay his debts on the altar, and bow down and worship him. Let the state ideal be high. What we need is not the respect of our fellow men, but the chance to get something for nothing. . . .

The editorial was reprinted throughout the country by such papers as the *Chicago Times-Herald* and *Evening Post* and the *New York Sun*, and it was circulated in pamphlet form by the industrialist Mark Hanna. Soon the *Saturday Evening Post* and *McClure's* were writing to the twenty-eight-year-old editor seeking articles.

White's savage attacks on the Populists gained him a national reputation, but he later came to support much of the Populist program and became a strong voice for reform. When he arrived in Emporia from Kansas City he had found Vernon L. Parrington, later to become one of America's most influential historians and author of *Main Currents in American Thought* (1927-1930), teaching at the local college. Parrington argued that the industrial revolution and the growth of the cities had so altered the national landscape that new ideas were required to preserve American ideals. Parrington, however, like James Canfield, did not have an immediate impact on White; the two disagreed most of the summer and fall of 1896. White believed then, as did many other Americans, that William McKinley stood as a bulwark of democracy against that "dangerous un-American demagogue" Bryan. But White later decided that he had been wrong and Parrington had been right.

The person most influential in changing White's mind, the one who "shattered the foundations" of his political thinking, was Theodore

White at his desk during his early years with the Emporia Gazette *(Culver Pictures)*

Roosevelt, the man who as president did more than anyone else to popularize and make respectable the idea of reform. White first met Roosevelt on a trip east in 1897. Roosevelt, then assistant secretary of the navy, explained to White that business plutocracy was at the root of most political corruption and that men like Mark Hanna, McKinley's powerful supporter, were in politics to protect their interests from unfavorable legislation. Roosevelt later sent White a copy of his book *American Ideals* (1897), and his arguments must have come as a revelation because White later recalled that he realized he had only been a "protagonist of the divine rule of plutocracy." Roosevelt's career profited enormously from his exploits as a Rough Rider during the Spanish-American War. The war helped boost Roosevelt into the New York governorship. White enthusiastically endorsed Roosevelt's campaign and urged as early as September 1898 that he be made president. When Roosevelt came to Kansas in June of the following year, White publicized the tour and

suggested Roosevelt's name as a likely prospect for the White House in 1904. This relationship with Roosevelt grew stronger, and it played an important part in the next few years of White's career.

By the turn of the century White's editorials reflected an increasing spirit of reform as he joined the call for the regulation of monopolies and trusts. His conversion to the progressive ranks was not unqualified, however. He rejected the Bryan Democrats' call for the direct election of senators which, White said, would "elevate men to the Senate who are as cheap as the men elected governors. Any cheap screw," he maintained, could be governor. He also revealed his admiration of Mark Hanna, whom he called "a walking, breathing, living body of the American spirit."

The Whites' first child, William Lindsay, was born on 17 June 1900. He grew up to become a noted journalist and author.

White's fourth book, *Stratagems and Spoils* (several boyhood stories which originally appeared in

McClure's magazine were published in 1899 as *The Court of Boyville*), was published by Scribners in the autumn of 1901. It had been written over the previous two years and no longer truly reflected White's views on reform. In this work, White continued to jab at the Populists and pound the corrupt politicians. Society would be improved, he wagered, not by passing legislation to regulate business and industry but by the election of good men to political office. Improving society was a slow process and depended on individuals, not laws. Actually, by this time White believed government regulation of industry, transportation, and finance was necessary.

The change in White's thinking apparently had been wrought by Roosevelt. White was to have substantial influence in national politics throughout his career, but he never developed a closer relationship with a major political leader than he did with Roosevelt. He regretted that the former New York governor had buried himself in the vice-presidency; but that concern was short-lived as the bullet fired from the gun of the anarchist Leon F. Czolgosz ended McKinley's administration. Roosevelt had always been headed for big things, White believed, and he was finally at the helm. When asked why such a bitter foe of Bryan and the Populists now championed their causes, White replied that such objectives were at last being promoted by men of substance rather than by "long-haired reformers." "The movement was no longer the cry of the oppressed, but the demand of the aspiring." The call for reform had ceased to be indignant and was constructive. Liberalism had come to represent "not so much the attack of the have-nots upon the haves as the vision of a just and righteous relation between men; a plan to readjust obvious inequities by governmental agencies." Like the president, White was only slightly ahead of the average citizen in his views on social reform, however. He was not in the vanguard with men like Eugene Debs and Robert M. La Follette, nor did he engage in writing the type of muckraking exposé made famous by Lincoln Steffens and Ida M. Tarbell.

White suffered a breakdown from overwork early in 1902 and did not fully recover for several months, but by October he was back booming his support for Roosevelt to run in 1904. Only Roosevelt could tame the trusts and save Americans from the plutocracy ravaging the country. "Roosevelt is the hero of the average man," he wrote for the *Saturday Evening Post*; he has emerged "as the great national leader, bigger than any party, the epitome of his times, the great American."

The Whites' second child, Mary, was born in June 1904. Seventeen years later, tragically, she would become the subject of White's most famous editorial.

By the 1904 presidential campaign, White, then in his mid-thirties, exercised considerable influence in national affairs. He had the ear of the president. He reached a national audience through his magazine articles and *Gazette* editorials, which frequently were reprinted throughout the United States. *Gazette* circulation was then only about 2,000, but White's political influence in Kansas was strengthened by the *Kansas City Star*. The *Star*'s weekly edition had nearly a quarter-million readers, and the combined circulation of its morning and afternoon editions was slightly greater. The pages of this paper were open for White to promote political candidates and generally build a more progressive Kansas, and White used them often until the First World War.

White had become an open and adamant spokesman for reform throughout Kansas by early 1905. He supported a state-owned oil refinery and welcomed Ida Tarbell when she came to the state to investigate the practices of Standard Oil Company. He sensed a moral awakening in the American people and argued in the *Atlantic Monthly* that the Golden Rule should be applied to all phases of life. In "The Partnership of Society" for *American* magazine, he said progressivism emphasized the "altruistic" as opposed to the "egoistic" side of the human spirit; every man must be "his brother's keeper." In three articles for *Collier's* in the fall of 1906, he made the case for a direct primary system which would nominate candidates and thus bypass the traditional convention, which had been dominated by special interests.

White's emerging liberalism and the growing reform spirit among many Republicans threatened to split the party in Kansas. During the state convention in the summer of 1906, White organized a petition drive to have the party platform favor the direct primary and legislation outlawing free rail passes. He also encouraged Robert M. La Follette to speak in the state on progressivism and then used the *Kansas City Star* to publicize the growing insurgency within the party's ranks. Concerned conservatives within the party, sensitive to criticism and worried about growing opposition to their views, tried without success to establish a competitor to the *Gazette*.

Despite his willingness to publicize La Follette, White considered him too radical as the 1908 presidential campaign approached. He favored instead William Howard Taft, the rotund figure later to become chief justice of the Supreme Court. In an article for *American* magazine in May 1908, "Taft, A Hewer of Wood," he portrayed Roosevelt's hand-picked successor as the very essence of the average American and one who would work to continue Roosevelt's programs. Although he had traveled a long way intellectually since his attack on William Jennings Bryan and the Populists in 1896, he did not seriously consider supporting the Great Commoner against Taft in the fall campaign. Bryan simply did not have adequate support in the Midwest, White believed.

White continued his friendship with Roosevelt during the Taft years. When Roosevelt came to Osawatomie, Kansas, on 31 August 1910 to deliver his famous New Nationalism address, White helped shape both the content and tone of that speech. Very possibly he was responsible for the specific reforms Roosevelt advocated, reforms remarkably similar to the Kansas Republican platform which White, W. R. Stubbs, and Joseph L. Bristow had pushed through the party council the day before. Roosevelt's talk was part of a dedication ceremony for the John Brown Memorial Park to commemorate the Battle of Osawatomie between Brown and his followers and proslavery forces. Brown was still a controversial figure, however, and White convinced Roosevelt to limit his remarks. He also labored to promote Roosevelt to such influential groups as the Kansas Editorial Association and the Traveling Men's Association.

White's support for President Taft was short-lived. He became disenchanted over the Payne-Aldrich tariff, which raised duties, and the Ballinger-Pinchot affair. Gifford Pinchot, the chief of the U.S. Forest Service and good friend of former president Roosevelt, claimed that Taft's secretary of the interior, Richard Ballinger, was hostile to reform and had been involved in land fraud. Taft fired Pinchot, thus alienating Republican insurgents. Even though a later congressional investigation supported the president and Ballinger, it did not repair the political damage. White soon let it be known that he favored either Sen. Albert Beveridge or La Follette in 1912; and in January 1911 he helped La Follette start the National Progressive Republican League, which sought support for the former Wisconsin governor. White doubted La Follette's ability to defeat Taft, however, and after La Follette's tragic breakdown in early February 1912, he turned to his old friend Roosevelt. As the presidential nominating convention approached, White worked hard to gain support for the ex-president among the Kansas delegation and was

White with Theodore Roosevelt during the 1912 presidential campaign

even elected a Republican national committeeman. When Roosevelt failed to win the nomination, White bolted the party with Roosevelt and resigned from the national committee, thus ending any chance he may have had to work from the inside to influence the party in a more liberal direction.

White was terribly disappointed when Roosevelt came in second to Woodrow Wilson in the three-man race of 1912, but he was not hostile to the new president and had applauded Wilson as early as 18 April 1911 in an editorial. Early in the new president's term he praised Wilson for his progressive policies. White never seriously thought of switching to the Democratic party, though, because it was difficult, if not impossible, to influence Kansas politics outside of the Republican party; besides, he wondered about a party that had taken forty-six ballots to nominate a man of Wilson's qualities. When Roosevelt refused to accept the Progressive party's nomination in 1916, thus ensuring the party's collapse, White returned to the Republican party, where he found his influence diminished. He supported Charles Evans Hughes, but without enthusiasm.

There were other dimensions to White's career in addition to politics and editing a newspaper. He had agreed to serve on the board of regents of the University of Kansas in March 1905—the only political appointment he accepted during the progressive years. For the next seven years he actively participated in the affairs of that institution. White's experience as a regent further convinced him of the crucial importance education and schools had for democracy and increased his respect for academic freedom. He remained, however, strongly opposed to college football, which he believed was becoming too professionalized.

White's literary career was flourishing. *In Our Town* (1906), his fifth book, offered a sympathetic, if not idealized, depiction of small-town life. It remains one of White's most readable novels, and it received enthusiastic reviews. An admiring Mark Twain urged White to "talk again—the country is listening." White's fiction reflected the evolution of his progressive views. *A Certain Rich Man* (1909) summarized many of the author's beliefs. The work's main character, John Barclay, builds a huge fortune by manipulating stocks and becomes a corrupting influence in politics. Ultimately, though, Barclay is converted to the progressive cause. He gives up his fortune and dies attempting to rescue a drowning woman. Although the work is flawed and Barclay's conversion is unbelievable, the novel was nevertheless immensely popular, eventually selling 300,000 copies, 25,000 in the first month alone. Roosevelt, then on safari in Africa, wrote a long, glowing letter congratulating the author. White also publicized his ideas about reform in *The Old Order Changeth* (1910), a collection of articles written earlier for the *American* magazine. There he called for the initiative, referendum, and recall, along with the secret ballot, direct primaries, and publication of campaign expenses.

The responsibilities of being an editor and a community leader were taken seriously by White. He put great effort into his editorials at a time when other newspapers were neglecting their opinion pages. He never hesitated to change his mind editorially, although there were some matters on which he felt strongly. He was an ardent supporter of prohibition. He intensely disliked the yellow journalism associated with William Randolph Hearst and would not publish comic strips which he associated with this kind of reporting. He did not allow his paper to become a forum for religious or racial hatred and did not join in the attacks on the Catholic church that were so common in the Midwest. He became increasingly vigilant for questionable advertising and by 1909 had stopped running ads for patent medicines. The *Gazette* became a training ground for men who left it to become editors themselves. Roy Bailey of the *Salina Journal*; Rolla Clymer of the *El Dorado Times*; Oscar Stauffer, who operated a chain of papers including the *Topeka State Journal*; and John Redmond of the *Burlington Republican* all worked for the *Gazette*.

White did not like war, and when World War I began in Europe in the summer of 1914 he feared for the United States and for reform. At first he tried to stay neutral, but he became increasingly appalled by German ruthlessness—the invasion of Belgium, the sinking of the *Lusitania*, unrestricted submarine warfare. He decided as early as 1915 that isolation was impractical, if not impossible, and eventually concluded that the United States must join the struggle to destroy German militarism. After Congress declared war in 1917, White supported the war effort. "Having entered this war," he wrote, "we should not get out of [it] until the German princes are so crushed and conquered that the emperor and the military autocrats of Germany will not hold back one single shred of their pretense that in war they have a right to coerce neutrals and to put the planet in a state of war."

Substantial numbers of American and European intellectuals saw the war—as unfortunate as it might have been—as offering a chance for moral regeneration. White was no exception. Writing to the son of a friend, he said: "You are going into the most beautiful experience a man may have, the chance to serve a great cause in a great way. . . ." He concluded that only the birth of Christ and the discovery of America equaled this period in importance. Military service offered not only a chance to serve a great cause, White believed, but it also would help break down regional ties in the United States. He saw measures instituted during the war which he hoped would continue after a peace treaty had been signed: government control of business, price fixing, federal operation of railroads, arbitration of labor disputes, and taxes on inheritances.

White used his talented pen to assist the war effort. The Committee on Public Information, the government's official propaganda agency, asked him to write articles for a European audience. In July 1917, he and his friend Henry J. Allen traveled at the request of the Red Cross to investigate that organization's work in Europe. He wrote frequently to his wife on this trip; the correspondence was published under the title *The Martial Adventures of Henry and Me* (1918). White publicized the work of the Red Cross when he returned from Europe in October 1917. His articles were distributed by the Wheeler syndicate to such papers as the *St. Louis Post-Dispatch*, the *Kansas City Star*, the *Cincinnati Enquirer*, and the *San Francisco Examiner*.

About this time, too, White finished what proved to be his last novel, *In the Heart of a Fool* (1918). The work had been eight years in preparation, and during the last year of the war its theme of progressivism was not as timely as it would have been when White began the project. The book did not enjoy the success of *A Certain Rich Man*. The novel's thesis, White wrote, was that "this is essentially a spiritual not a material world and that in this spiritual world only spiritual rewards and punishments come as a result of spiritual virtue or spiritual lapses and that material gains and losses are in no way connected with a man's spiritual attitude." The whole point of the Great War, he said, was "the struggle of the world away from the gross materialism of Germany to a certain higher spiritual standard of life contained in the word, Democracy." He feared, perhaps with justification, that the average reader would not "detect the trend of the book."

White wanted to be a part of the American peace delegation to Paris, but, unable to secure a place, he resigned himself to covering the peace conference for the Wheeler syndicate. He also acted as a liaison for the Red Cross. His son, Bill, who served as his secretary, accompanied him to Europe. White met many people on this trip, including Norman Angell, with whom he became friends. He was impressed by the young Douglas MacArthur, with whom he dined at the general's headquarters in Germany. The terrible food shortages caused by the war moved White, and he wrote about this problem. He also worried about the rebuilding of German military strength, since Germany's industrial plant had been untouched. He endorsed Wilson's League of Nations and during the spring of 1919 fought for American entry into that organization as the best means of beginning a "new heaven and a new earth." Wilson's intransigence, he thought, defeated the League.

American liberals had long been fascinated by events in Russia, and White was no exception. He was slower than most, however, to turn away from Russia once the nature of the revolution became apparent. During the summer of 1920, when anti-Russian sentiment was strong, he still maintained sympathy. "I believe," he said, "in the Russian revolution and that the Russian people through their revolution will be able to conquer themselves and to rise after their own manner, following their own star to a vastly higher civilization through revolution to democracy than they ever could have risen through autocracy." Americans should remember the czars' exploitation, White argued: "Lenin and Trotsky represented the inexorable reaction of Russia to the age-long oppression of the old regime." He urged citizens to take a more active interest in Russian-American affairs and to learn as much as possible about that country.

Before the Republican national convention of 1920, White had opposed the party's move toward Warren G. Harding and had supported Kansas Governor Henry J. Allen and Leonard Wood for the nomination, although secretly his real choice was Herbert Hoover. He attended the convention in Chicago both as a reporter and as a delegate. He had little success influencing the party's platform; his call for government aid to maternity centers, industrial arbitration, and tougher enforcement of Prohibition fell, for the most part, on deaf ears. Once Harding won the nomination, White supported the Ohioan in the campaign but did so reluctantly. He believed the new president to be, even "at the height of his statesmanship, a mere bass drum, beating the time of the hour, carrying no tune, making no music, promoting no deep harmony. . . ." George Creel observed that White was a first-rate reporter between elections, "but where a Republican candidate has been decided upon he heaves a weary sigh, puts reporting by and takes up the burden of propaganda." White clearly, though, was upset by the direction American politics had taken. "What a God damned world!," he wrote to Ray Stannerd Baker. "Starvation on the one hand, and indifference on the other, pessimism rampant, faith quiescent, murder met with indifference; the lowered standard of civilization faced with universal complaisance, and the whole story so sad that nobody can tell it."

In May 1921, Mary White died after striking her head on a limb while riding her horse; she would have been seventeen years old the following month. Perhaps the most beautiful piece ever to flow from White's pen came after this deep personal tragedy in a moving tribute to her written the day after her funeral. Widely reprinted, it greatly enhanced White's reputation. It read in part:

> Her funeral yesterday at the Congregational Church was as she would have wished it; no singing, no flowers except the big bunch of red roses from her brother Bill's Harvard

White's daughter, Mary, a few weeks before her death in 1921

Hughes; and her brother Bill. It would have made her smile to know that her friend, Charley O'Brien, the traffic cop, had been transferred from Sixth and Commercial to the corner near the church to direct her friends who came to bid her good-bye.

A rift in the clouds in a gray day threw a shaft of sunlight upon her coffin as her nervous, energetic little body sank to its last sleep. But the soul of her, the glowing, gorgeous, fervent soul of her, surely was flaming in eager joy upon some other dawn.

White was slow to recover from the tragedy. He never completed a work he had begun on his relationship with Teddy Roosevelt, probably because Mary had been in and out of his study so often when he had started the manuscript. White's writing in the 1920s turned away from novels and toward biography. He finished a study of Woodrow Wilson in 1924, a man he admitted he did not like but of whose "type" he was "rather fond." A few years later, *Masks in a Pageant* (1928) brought together sketches of political figures that he had written over the past three decades. Included in the work were Grover Cleveland, Mark Hanna, Bryan, Roosevelt, Alfred E. Smith, and Calvin Coolidge.

White did not lose his head in the Red scare of the postwar years and in fact was thought by some to be dangerously radical because of his support for labor, his opposition to the Ku Klux Klan, and his efforts to stay the executions of Sacco and Vanzetti. Radicalism, White felt, should be combated through employment and a minimum wage rather than by force. In July 1922, he supported the nationwide strike of railroad shop workers after the Railroad Labor Board had cut their wages. His friend, Gov. Henry J. Allen, ordered White's arrest for violating an antipicketing law. White had refused to remove a poster in the *Gazette* window which read "We Are For the Striking Railroad Men 100 Per Cent. We Are For A Living Wage and Fair Working Conditions." Roundly criticized in the Kansas press, White defended his action in an editorial entitled "To an Anxious Friend." We should not fear freedom of utterance, he said, because "if there is freedom, folly will die of its own poison, and the wisdom will survive. . . . Reason never has failed men. Only force and repression have made the wrecks in the world." This editorial was reprinted in the *New York World* and elsewhere, and in May 1923, White received the Pulitzer Prize for this piece.

White felt uncomfortable in the atmosphere of intolerance in the early 1920s, and he denounced

classmen—heavens, how proud that would have made her!—and the red roses from the Gazette force, in vases, at her head and feet. A short prayer: Paul's beautiful essay on "Love" from the Thirteenth Chapter of First Corinthians; some remarks about her democratic spirit by her friend, John H. J. Rice, pastor and police judge, which she would have deprecated if she could; a prayer sent down for her by her friend, Carl Nau; and, opening the service the slow, poignant movement from Beethoven's Moonlight Sonata, which she loved; and closing the service a cutting from the joyously melancholy first movement of Tschaikovsky's Pathetic Symphony, which she liked to hear, in certain moods, on the phonograph; then the Lord's Prayer by her friends in the High School.

That was all.

For her pallbearers only her friends were chosen: her Latin teacher, W. L. Holtz; her High School principal, Rice Brown; her doctor, Frank Foncannon; her friend, W. W. Finney; her pal at the Gazette office, Walter the policies of A. Mitchell Palmer, the attorney general, saying that "If a man desires to preach any doctrine . . . and advocates the realization of his vision by lawful orderly constitutional means—let him alone. . . . The deportation business is going to make martyrs of a lot of idiots whose cause is not worth it." "My idea of one hundred percent Americanism," he wrote, "is an American who has intelligent faith enough in his country and his ideals to allow any other American however stupid and however crooked and however malicious to say what he pleases, to think what he pleases and to do what he pleases and to print what he pleases in controversy of American ideals and then laugh at the fool rather than to put him in jail. . . ."

White's revulsion against the wave of provincial patriotism perhaps peaked in September 1924 when he announced that he would run for governor of Kansas on an independent ticket to oppose the Ku Klux Klan. The Klan was enjoying a revival of its popularity in the 1920s, although its strength largely disappeared by the end of the decade. The KKK had begun organizing in Emporia in 1921 and had been able to elect the mayor. From the first, White had opposed the Klan and printed members' names in the *Gazette* whenever possible. These were "moral idiots," cowardly, mediocre men, he maintained. In announcing his candidacy, White noted that "the Ku Klux Klan is found in nearly every county. It represents a small minority of the citizenship and it is organized for purposes of terror. Its terror is directed at homes, law-abiding citizens, Negroes, Jews and Catholics. These groups in Kansas comprise more than one-fourth of our population. They are entitled to their full constitutional rights; their rights to life, liberty and the pursuit of happiness." Party regulars, aware of White's independence, were worried. Only a few papers, such as Victor Murdock's *Eagle* and the *Kansas City Star*, backed White. When the votes were counted he had come in third behind the winner, Ben S. Paulen, with less than twenty-five percent of the tally. Whatever the effect of White's efforts, the Klan's strength in Kansas soon diminished.

White supported Coolidge over La Follette in 1924, partly, one suspects, because he was sensitive about abandoning the Republican party again and partly because he felt more comfortable with Coolidge. White was by no means as advanced a liberal as La Follette. The Emporia editor put together a hasty biography, *Calvin Coolidge: The Man Who Is President* (1925). He was impressed by the president's Puritan background, his belief in temperance, moderation, hard work, and frugality.

"He represents exactly the mood of the people," White wrote. Later, in 1938, White wrote a more substantial biography of Coolidge, *A Puritan in Babylon*. This well-written work is generally considered to have been White's best piece of nonfiction and is an interesting account of the postwar decade.

Herbert Hoover had little trouble in winning White's support in 1928. Even though he went to the national convention pledged to Kansas senator Charles Curtis, White wrote a feature article on Hoover for *Collier's*. Historian Paul W. Glad maintains that White believed Hoover symbolized "the ultimate triumph of the progressive cause" and that he had done more than any other man in Coolidge's cabinet to check "the Wall Street crowd." White came to accept the business culture of the 1920s to a greater degree than most progressives. Influenced by the Harvard economist Thomas Nixon Carver, he believed the prosperity of the decade would make social justice more likely. Few writers labored harder to fuse progressivism with the business mystique of that time. Hoover, therefore, was a logical choice in 1928, and White provided him effective support during the campaign, not only by publicizing the future president's good qualities but also by attacking his opponent, Al Smith. White disliked Smith, who in so many ways personified urban life, because the New York governor opposed Prohibition and was too friendly with Tammany Hall.

White remained loyal to Hoover throughout his administration and believed the president had been made a scapegoat for the Great Depression. But he had few illusions about Hoover's leadership ability. Hoover was a good administrator, but too timid; he lacked Teddy Roosevelt's capacity to inspire opinion and generate the hope needed to pull the country to recovery. Although he considered Hoover's 1932 campaign doomed from the beginning, he supported the president for reelection. To have bolted the party would have weakened his influence with Republicans in Kansas and thus hurt the chances of his choice for governor, Alf Landon.

In 1936, Franklin Roosevelt told the Emporia editor jokingly that he could count on White's support "three and a half years out of every four." White supported most of Roosevelt's New Deal, but he also believed that Roosevelt was moving too fast. White backed Landon in 1936, but without much fervor. White's contribution to a preconvention pamphlet, *Deeds Not Deficits: The Story of Alfred M. Landon*, offered only tepid support for his fellow Kansan. Similarly, articles written on Landon's behalf for the *New York Times Magazine* and *Saturday Evening Post*—and published in book form in Sep-

The Whites with their son, Bill, in 1939 (Wide World)

tember 1936 under the title *What It's All About: Being A Reporter's Story of the Early Campaign of 1936* — were restrained. White was troubled by Landon's drift toward Old Guard reactionaries such as John Hamilton, and he was convinced that the overwhelming defeat at the polls came because the Republican party had allowed itself to be tainted by plutocracy. White was considerably more sympathetic to Wendell Willkie, whom he supported in 1940. Next to Teddy Roosevelt, among politicians White perhaps liked Willkie best.

Although the *Gazette*'s circulation never climbed to much over 7,000, by the 1930s White's reputation was international. Millions had read reprints of his editorials, many of which had been republished in *The Editor and His People* (1924), edited by Helen O. Mahin, and *Forty Years on Main Street* (1937), edited by Russell H. Fitzgibbon. Even if people were not aware of White, their reading habits may very well have been influenced by him. Between 1926 and 1944 he served as a judge for the Book-of-the-Month Club.

White was on good terms with both Hoover and Franklin Roosevelt, and because of his national following the Emporia editor was asked by both chief executives to help with matters relating to foreign affairs. In February 1930, Hoover appointed him to a Commission for the Study and Review of Conditions in Haiti. White, later an enthusiastic supporter of Roosevelt's Good Neighbor Policy, supported the commission's recommendation to gradually withdraw American marines from that country. After Roosevelt extended diplomatic recognition to the Soviet Union—as White had been urging throughout the 1920s—in 1933, White and his wife traveled there. Although he was disappointed at the lack of basic freedoms, White wrote favorably about the Soviets' accomplishments in changing Russian society.

White watched with horror as events in the late 1930s pushed the United States toward war. He served as honorary vice-chairman of the American Committee for Non-Participation in Japanese Aggression (he had traveled to China) and was a member of the American Boycott against Aggressor Nations. He also accepted the chair of the Union for

Concerted Peace Efforts, which sought to keep America out of the war while at the same time defeating Nazi Germany.

White refused to accept the arguments of groups, such as the America First Committee, who argued that the United States had no stake in the events in Europe. He had long argued that isolation from world affairs was an unrealistic and dangerous course for the United States to follow. He edited *Defense for America* (1940), a compilation of articles by community leaders calling for aid to the Allies and warning that a victory for Hitler would endanger American security. In addition, he chaired the Committee to Defend America by Aiding the Allies, an organization that had evolved from the earlier Nonpartisan Committee for Peace through the Revision of the Neutrality Act. By the summer of 1940, the CDAAA, with its almost 600 local chapters, was in the vanguard of the attempt to discredit the isolationists and promote support for aid to England. White genuinely did not want war for the United States, yet he was convinced that a German victory over Great Britain would mean war for America. Caught in this dilemma, White's leadership of the CDAAA, according to historian William M. Tuttle, Jr., was "inept and irresolute." Criticism of his leadership mounted, first over how the CDAAA should respond to Hoover's plan to

supply food to the defeated countries of Europe and then over how to deal with isolationists. The committee's activist New York state chapter was particularly troublesome. Members there had moved to block the reelection of the isolationist Republican congressman Hamilton Fish. When White learned of this effort after reading a column written by Bruce Catton, he immediately disavowed any connection between his organization—which was supposed to be nonpartisan—and the stop-Fish movement. Furthermore, he wrote to Fish only two weeks before the fall elections and stated that he hoped a straight Republican ticket would be elected. The result was confusion over just how far White was willing for the United States to go toward intervention. That confusion was compounded on 20 December 1940, when White wrote to Roy Howard, head of the Scripps-Howard newspaper chain, that if the United States became engaged in the fighting it "would defeat the end for which our Committee is organized to defend America by aiding Great Britain and would bring on a thirty year war. . . ." Plagued by attacks on his leadership and hindered by poor health, White resigned.

White's health continued to decline in his last years. He turned increasing attention to his *Autobiography*, which would win a Pulitzer Prize two years after his death. He did manage one last fling

The Emporia Gazette *office as it looked a year after White's death*

with Kansas politics, taking great interest in the 1942 gubernatorial campaign and calling for new blood in the state's Republican party. But if his spirit were still willing his body was not. In early April 1943, while in New York to meet with Book-of-the-Month Club judges, he suffered an influenza attack that developed into double pneumonia. In October, while at the Mayo clinic, he learned that he was dying of cancer. Finally, perhaps mercifully, on 29 January 1944, only a few days short of his seventy-sixth birthday, a heart attack silenced Will White's pen forever.

Although William Allen White wrote for a small-town newspaper, he became one of America's most influential journalists and a model to subsequent generations of writers. The school of journalism at the University of Kansas, for example, bears his name. That he was a prolific author and a master stylist accounts in part for his fame, but more than sheer volume or style explains his influence. Many people found White attractive because he seemed to reflect a way of life that was rapidly disappearing under the pressures of industrialization and urbanization. Yet he came to favor government regulation to make the modern economic system more just; he preached the need for tolerance when tolerance seemed inappropriate or even dangerous; and he rejected isolation in a world that had been made smaller by technology. He championed a brand of liberalism which seemed both respectable and responsible to many in his generation.

Letters:

Selected Letters of William Allen White, 1899-1943, edited by Walter Johnson (New York: Holt, 1947);

Letters of William Allen White and a Young Man, edited by Gil Wilson (New York: Day, 1948).

Bibliographies:

Walter Johnson and Alberta Pantle, "A Bibliography of the Published Works of William Allen White," *Kansas Historical Quarterly*, 15 (February 1947): 22-41;

Gary Mason and others, *A Bibliography of William Allen White*, 2 volumes (Emporia, Kans.: Teachers College Press, 1969).

Biographies:

Frank C. Clough, *William Allen White of Emporia* (New York: McGraw-Hill, 1941);

Everett Rich, *William Allen White: The Man from Emporia* (New York: Farrar & Rinehart, 1941);

David Hinshaw, *A Man from Kansas: The Story of William Allen White* (New York: Putnam's, 1945);

Walter Johnson, *William Allen White's America* (New York: Holt, 1947);

John DeWitt McKee, *William Allen White: Maverick on Main Street* (Westport, Conn.: Greenwood Press, 1975).

References:

Randolph C. Downes, ed., "Some Correspondence Between Warren G. Harding and William Allen White during the Presidential Campaign of 1920," *Northwest Ohio Quarterly*, 37 (1965): 121-132;

Joe L. Dubbert, "William Allen White's American Adam," *Western American Literature*, 7 (Winter 1973): 271-278;

Paul W. Glad, "Progressives and the Business Culture of the 1920s," *Journal of American History*, 53 (June 1966): 75-89;

George L. Groman, "W. A. White's Political Fiction: A Study in Emerging Progressivism," *Midwest Quarterly*, 8 (October 1966): 79-93;

Walter Johnson, *The Battle against Isolation* (Chicago: University of Chicago Press, 1944);

Jean L. Kennedy, "William Allen White: A Study of the Interrelationship of Press, Power and Party Politics," Ph.D. dissertation, University of Kansas, 1981;

Joe W. Kraus, "The Publication of William Allen White's *The Real Issue*," *Kansas Historical Quarterly*, 43 (1977): 193-202;

Robert S. La Forte, "Theodore Roosevelt's Osawatomie Speech," *Kansas Historical Quarterly*, 32 (1966): 187-200;

Philip Mangelsdorf, "When William Allen White and Ed Howe Covered the Republicans," *Journalism Quarterly*, 44 (1967): 454-460;

Richard L. McBane, "The Crisis in the White Committee," *Midcontinent American Studies Journal*, 4 (1963): 28-38;

Richard W. Resh, "A Vision in Emporia: William Allen White's Search for Community," *Mid-Continent American Studies Journal*, 10 (1969): 19-35;

John E. Semonche, "The 'American Magazine' of 1906-15: Principle vs. Profit," *Journalism Quarterly*, 40 (1963): 36-44;

Charles William Sloan, Jr., "Kansas Battles the Invisible Empire: The Legal Ouster of the KKK from Kansas, 1922-1927," *Kansas Historical Quarterly*, 40 (1974): 393-409;

Jack Wayne Traylor, "William Allen White and His

Democracy, 1919-1944," Ph.D. dissertation, University of Oklahoma, 1978;

Traylor, "William Allen White's 1924 Gubernatorial Campaign," *Kansas Historical Quarterly*, 42 (1976): 180-191;

William M. Tuttle, Jr., "Aid-to-the-Allies Short-of-War Versus American Intervention, 1940: A Reappraisal of William Allen White's Leadership," *Journal of American History*, 56 (March 1970): 840-858;

Tuttle, ed., "William Allen White and Verne Marshall: Two Midwestern Editors Debate Aid to the Allies Versus Isolationism," *Kansas Historical Quarterly*, 32 (1966): 201-209;

Lynda F. Worley, "William Allen White: Kansas Extraordinary," *Social Science*, 41 (1966): 91-98.

Papers:
William Allen White's letters, manuscripts, and other material are in the William Allen White Memorial Library at Kansas State Teachers College, Emporia.

Checklist for Further Reading

Aaron, Daniel. *Writers on the Left: Episodes in American Literary Communism.* New York: Harcourt, Brace & World, 1961.

Abrams, Alan E., ed. *Journalist Biographies Master Index.* Detroit: Gale Research, 1978.

Arndt, Karl J. R. and May Olson. *German-American Press Research from the American Revolution to the Bicentennial,* volume 3 of *German Language Press of Americas.* Detroit: Gale Research, 1980.

Bartow, Edith Merwin. *News and These United States.* New York: Funk & Wagnalls, 1952.

Baumgartner, Apollinaris W. *Catholic Journalism: A Study of Its Development in the United States, 1789-1930.* New York: Columbia University Press, 1931.

Beasley, Maurine H. *The First Women Washington Correspondents.* Washington, D.C.: George Washington University, 1976.

Beasley and Richard B. Harlow. *Voices of Change: Southern Pulitzer Winners.* Lanham, Md.: University Press of America, 1979.

Beasley and Sheila Silver. *Women in Media: A Documentary Source Book.* Washington, D.C.: Women's Institute for Freedom of the Press, 1977.

Becker, Stephen. *Comic Art in America: A Social History of the Funnies, the Political Cartoons, Magazine Humor, Sporting Cartoons, and Animated Cartoons.* New York: Simon & Schuster, 1959.

Bennion, Sherilyn Cox. "Reform Agitation in the American Periodical Press, 1920-29." *Journalism Quarterly,* 48 (Winter 1971): 652-659, 713.

Bent, Silas. *Newspaper Crusaders: A Neglected Story.* New York & London: Whittlesey House, McGraw-Hill, 1939.

Berger, Arthur. *Li'l Abner: A Study in American Satire.* New York: Twayne, 1970.

Bergman, Peter M. and Mort N. Bergman. *Chronological History of the Negro in America.* New York: Harper & Row, 1969.

Bessie, Simon Michael. *Jazz Journalism: The Story of the Tabloid Newspapers.* New York: Dutton, 1938.

Bleyer, Willard Grosvenor. *Main Currents in the History of American Journalism.* Boston: Houghton Mifflin, 1927.

Bliss, Robert M. "Development of Fair Comment as a Defense to Libel." *Journalism Quarterly,* 44 (Winter 1967): 627-637.

Blum, Eleanor. *Basic Books in the Mass Media.* Urbana: University of Illinois Press, 1972.

Brucker, Herbert. *The Changing American Newspaper.* New York: Columbia University Press, 1937.

Bullock, Penelope L. *The Afro-American Periodical Press, 1838-1909.* Baton Rouge: Louisiana State University Press, 1981.

Carroll, Wallace. *Persuade or Perish.* Boston: Houghton Mifflin, 1948.

Cater, Douglass. *The Fourth Branch of Government.* Boston: Houghton Mifflin, 1959.

Chafee, Zechariah, Jr. *Free Speech in the United States.* Cambridge, Mass.: Harvard University Press, 1941.

Chafee. *Government and Mass Communications,* two volumes. Chicago: University of Chicago Press, 1947.

Churchill, Allen. *Park Row.* New York & Toronto: Rinehart, 1958.

Commander, Lydia K. "The Significance of Yellow Journalism." *Arena,* 34 (August 1905): 150.

Conlin, Joseph R., ed. *The American Radical Press 1880-1960,* two volumes. Westport, Conn.: Greenwood Press, 1974.

Couperie, Pierre and others. *A History of the Comic Strip.* New York: Crown, 1968.

Creel, George. *How We Advertised America.* New York: Harper, 1920.

Cross, Harold L. *The People's Right to Know: Legal Access to Public Records and Proceedings.* New York: Columbia University Press, 1953.

Crozier, Emmet. *American Reporters on the Western Front, 1914-1918.* New York: Oxford University Press, 1959.

Daniels, Jonathan. *They Will Be Heard: America's Crusading Newspaper Editors.* New York: McGraw-Hill, 1965.

Dennis, Everette E. and Melvin Dennis. "100 Years of Political Cartooning." *Journalism History,* 1 (Spring 1974): 6-10.

Desmond, Robert W. *The Press and World Affairs.* New York: Appleton-Century, 1937.

Desmond. *Windows on the World: World News Reporting Nineteen Hundred to Nineteen Twenty.* Iowa City: University of Iowa Press, 1980.

Detweiler, Frederick G. *The Negro Press in the United States.* Chicago: University of Chicago Press, 1922.

Drewry, John E. *More Post Biographies.* Athens: University of Georgia Press, 1947.

Drewry. *Saturday Evening Post. Post Biographies of Famous Journalists.* Athens: University of Georgia Press, 1942.

Ellis, L. Ethan. *Newsprint: Producers, Publishers, Political Pressures.* New Brunswick, N.J.: Rutgers University Press, 1960.

Emery, Edwin. *History of the American Newspaper Publishers Association.* Minneapolis: University of Minnesota Press, 1950.

Emery, ed. *The Story of America as Reported by Its Newspapers, 1690-1965.* New York: Simon & Schuster, 1965.

Emery and Michael Emery. *The Press and America,* fourth edition. Englewood Cliffs, N.J.: Prentice-Hall, 1978.

Emery, Edwin and Henry Ladd Smith. *The Press and America*. New York: Prentice-Hall, 1954.

Emery, Michael C., R. Smith Schuneman, and Edwin Emery, eds. *America's Front Page News, 1690-1970*. New York: Doubleday, 1970.

Ernst, Morris. *The First Freedom*. New York: Macmillan, 1946.

Farrar, Ronald T. and John D. Stevens, eds. *Mass Media and the National Experience*. New York: Harper & Row, 1971.

Filler, Louis. *Crusaders for American Liberalism*. New York: Harcourt, Brace, 1939.

Fisher, Charles. *The Columnists*. New York: Howell, Soskin, 1944.

Forcey, Charles. *The Crossroads of Liberalism: Croly, Weyl, Lippmann, and the Progressive Era, 1900-1925*. New York: Oxford University Press, 1961.

Ford, Edwin H. and Edwin Emery, eds. *Highlights in the History of the American Press: A Book of Readings*. Minneapolis: University of Minnesota Press, 1954.

Gillmor, Donald M. *Free Press and Fair Trial*. Washington: Public Affairs Press, 1966.

Gordon, George N. *The Communications Revolution: A History of Mass Media in the United States*. New York: Hastings House, 1977.

Gramling, Oliver. *AP: The Story of News*. New York: Farrar & Rinehart, 1940.

Greene, Laurence. *America Goes to Press: The News of Yesterday*. Indianapolis: Bobbs-Merrill, 1936.

Gregory, Winifred, ed. *American Newspapers, 1821-1936: A Union List of Files Available in the United States and Canada*. New York: Wilson, 1937.

Hagelweide, Gert. *German Newspapers in Libraries and Archives: A Survey*. Düsseldorf: Droste Verlag, 1974.

Harrison, John M. and Harry H. Stein, eds. *Muckraking–Past, Present, and Future*. University Park: Pennsylvania State University Press, 1973.

Hausman, Linda Weiner. "Criticism of the Press in U.S. Periodicals, 1900-1939: An Annotated Bibliography." *Journalism Monographs*, 4 (August 1967).

Hess, Stephen and Milton Kaplan. *The Ungentlemanly Art: A History of American Political Cartoons*. New York: Macmillan, 1975.

Hocking, William E. *Freedom of the Press: A Framework of Principle*. Chicago: University of Chicago Press, 1947.

Hohenberg, John. *Foreign Correspondence: The Great Reporters and Their Times*. New York: Columbia University Press, 1964.

Hohenberg. *The Pulitzer Prizes: A History of the Awards in Books, Drama, Music, and Journalism Based on the Private Files over Six Decades*. New York: Columbia University Press, 1974.

Horn, Maurice and Richard E. Marschall, eds. *The World Encyclopedia of Cartoons*, two volumes. Detroit: Gale Research, 1980.

Hudson, Robert V. "Will Irwin's Pioneering Criticism of the Press." *Journalism Quarterly,* 47 (Summer 1970): 263-271.

Hughes, David Y. "The War of the Worlds in the Yellow Press." *Journalism Quarterly,* 43 (Winter 1966): 639-646.

Hughes, Helen M. *News and the Human Interest Story.* Chicago: University of Chicago Press, 1940.

Irwin, Will. *The American Newspaper,* edited by Clifford F. Weigle and David G. Clark. Ames: Iowa State University Press, 1969.

Jakes, John. *Great Women Reporters.* New York: Putnam's, 1969.

Johnson, Walter C. and Arthur T. Robb. *The South and Its Newspapers, 1903-1953: The Story of the Southern Newspaper Publishers Association and Its Part in the South's Economic Rebirth.* Chattanooga, Tenn.: Southern Newspaper Publishers Association, 1954.

Jones, Robert W. *Journalism in the United States.* New York: Dutton, 1947.

Karolevitz, Robert F. *Newspapering in the Old West: A Pictorial History of Journalism and Printing on the Frontier.* Seattle: Superior, 1965.

Knightley, Phillip. *The First Casualty: From the Crimea to Vietnam: The War Correspondent as Hero, Propagandist, and Myth Maker.* New York: Harcourt Brace Jovanovich, 1976.

Kobre, Sidney. *Development of American Journalism.* Dubuque, Iowa: Brown, 1969.

Kobre. *The Yellow Press and Gilded Age Journalism.* Tallahassee: Florida State University Press, 1964.

Lasswell, Harold D. *Propaganda Technique in the World War.* New York: Knopf, 1927.

Lee, Alfred McClung. *The Daily Newspaper in America: The Evolution of a Social Instrument.* New York: Macmillan, 1937.

Lee, James Melvin. *History of American Journalism.* Boston & New York: Houghton Mifflin, 1917.

Liston, Robert A. *The Right to Know: Censorship in America.* New York: Watts, 1973.

Lofton, John. *The Press as Guardian of the First Amendment.* Columbia: University of South Carolina Press, 1980.

Lyle, Jack, ed. *The Black American and the Press.* Los Angeles: Ward Ritchie, 1968.

Lyon, Peter. *The Wild, Wild West.* New York: Funk & Wagnalls, 1969.

Marbut, F. B. *News from the Capital: The Story of Washington Reporting.* Carbondale: Southern Illinois University Press, 1971.

Marty, Martin E. and others. *The Religious Press in America.* New York: Holt, Rinehart & Winston, 1963.

Marzolf, Marion. *Up from the Footnote: A History of Women Journalists.* New York: Hastings House, 1977.

Mathews, Joseph J. *Reporting the Wars.* Minneapolis: University of Minnesota Press, 1957.

McMurtrie, Douglas C. *A History of Printing in the United States.* New York: R. R. Bowker, 1936.

Mock, James R. *Censorship 1917*. Princeton, N.J.: Princeton University Press, 1941; London: Oxford University Press, 1941.

Mock and Cedric Larson. *Words That Won the War: The Story of the Committee on Public Information 1917-1919*. Princeton, N.J.: Princeton University Press, 1939.

Moran, James. *Printing Presses: History and Development from the Fifteenth Century to Modern Times*. Berkeley: University of California Press, 1973.

Morris, Joe Alex. *Deadline Every Minute: The Story of the United Press*. Garden City: Doubleday, 1957.

Morris, Richard B. and Louis L. Snyder, eds. *A Treasury of Great Reporting*. New York: Simon & Schuster, 1962.

Mott, Frank Luther. *American Journalism: A History: 1690-1960,* third edition. New York: Macmillan, 1962.

Mott and Ralph D. Casey, eds. *Interpretations of Journalism: A Book of Readings*. New York: Crofts, 1937.

Murrell, William. *A History of American Graphic Humor, 1865-1938,* two volumes. New York: Macmillan, 1938.

Myers, John M. *Print in a Wild Land*. Garden City: Doubleday, 1967.

Nelson, Harold L., ed. *Freedom of the Press from Hamilton to the Warren Court*. Indianapolis: Bobbs-Merrill, 1967.

Nelson and Dwight L. Teeter, Jr. *Law of Mass Communications: Freedom and Control of Print and Broadcast Media,* fourth edition. Mineola, N.Y.: Foundation Press, 1981.

Nevins, Allan. "American Journalism and Its Historical Treatment." *Journalism Quarterly,* 36 (Fall 1959): 411-422.

Nevins. *American Press Opinion, Washington to Coolidge*. Boston: Heath, 1928.

Oak, Vishnu V. *The Negro Newspaper,* volume 1 of *The Negro Entrepreneur*. Yellow Springs, Ohio: Antioch Press, 1948.

O'Brien, Frank M. *The Story of The Sun: New York, 1833-1913*. New York: Doran, 1918.

Ogilvie, William Edward. *Pioneer Agricultural Journalists: Brief Biographical Sketches of Some of the Early Editors in the Field of Agricultural Journalism*. Chicago: Arthur G. Leonard, 1927.

Park, Robert E. *The Immigrant Press and Its Control*. New York & London: Harper, 1922.

Park. "The Natural History of the Newspaper," in *The City,* by Park, Ernest W. Burgess, and Roderick D. McKenzie. Chicago: University of Chicago Press, 1925, pp. 80-98.

Payne, George H. *History of Journalism in the United States*. New York: Appleton-Century-Crofts, 1920.

Pickett, Calder M. *Voices of the Past: Key Documents in the History of American Journalism*. Columbus, Ohio: Grid, 1977.

Pitts, Alice Fox. *Read All About It! Fifty Years of ASNE*. Easton, Pa.: American Society of Newspaper Editors, 1974.

Pollard, James E. *The Presidents and the Press*. New York: Macmillan, 1947.

Presbrey, Frank. *The History and Development of Advertising*. Garden City: Doubleday, Doran, 1929.

Price, Warren C. *The Literature of Journalism: An Annotated Bibliography*. Minneapolis: University of Minnesota Press, 1959.

Price and Calder M. Pickett. *An Annotated Journalism Bibliography 1958-1968*. Minneapolis: University of Minnesota Press, 1970.

Ray, Royal H. "Economic Forces as Factors in Daily Newspaper Concentration." *Journalism Quarterly,* 29 (Winter 1952): 31-42.

Reilly, Sr. Mary Lona. *History of the Catholic Press Association, 1911-1968*. Metuchen, N.J.: Scarecrow Press, 1971.

Rivers, William L. *The Opinionmakers*. Boston: Beacon Press, 1965.

Rosewater, Victor. *History of Cooperative News-Gathering in the United States*. New York & London: Appleton, 1930.

Ross, Ishbel. *Ladies of the Press: The Story of Women in Journalism by an Insider*. New York & London: Harper, 1936.

Rucker, Bryce W. *The First Freedom*. Carbondale: Southern Illinois University Press, 1968.

Rucker, ed. *Twentieth Century Reporting at Its Best*. Ames: Iowa State University Press, 1964.

Salmon, Lucy. *The Newspaper and Authority*. New York: Oxford University Press, 1923.

Seldes, George. *Lords of the Press*. New York: Messner, 1938.

Sim, John C. *The Grass Roots Press: America's Community Newspapers*. Ames: Iowa State University Press, 1969.

Sloan, David. *The Pulitzer Prize Editorials: America's Best Editorial Writing, 1917-1979*. Ames: Iowa State University Press, 1980.

Snyder, Louis L., ed. *Masterpieces of War Reporting: The Great Moments of World War Two*. New York: Simon & Schuster, 1962.

Stein, M. L. *Under Fire: The Story of American War Correspondents*. New York: Messner, 1968.

Stevens, John D. and Hazel Dicken-Garcia. *Communication History*. Beverly Hills: Sage, 1980.

Stewart, Kenneth and John Tebbel. *Makers of Modern Journalism*. New York: Prentice-Hall, 1952.

Taft, William H. *Newspapers as Tools for Historians*. Columbia, Mo.: Lucas, 1970.

Tebbel, John W. *The Compact History of the American Newspaper*. New York: Hawthorn, 1969.

Tebbel. *The Media in America: A Social and Political History*. New York: Crowell, 1975.

Villard, Oswald Garrison. *The Disappearing Daily*. New York: Knopf, 1944.

Villard. *The Press Today*. New York: The *Nation*, 1930.

Villard. *Some Newspapers and Newspaper-Men.* New York: Knopf, 1923.

Watson, Elmo Scott. *A History of Newspaper Syndicates in the United States, 1865-1935.* Chicago: Publishers' Auxiliary, 1936.

Waugh, Coulton. *The Comics.* New York: Macmillan, 1947.

Weeks, Lyman H. *A History of Paper-Manufacturing in the United States, 1690-1916.* New York: Lockwood Trade Journal Co., 1916.

Weinfeld, William. "The Growth of Daily Newspaper Chains in the United States: 1923, 1926-1935." *Journalism Quarterly,* 13 (December 1936): 357-380.

Weisberger, Bernard A. *Reporters for the Union.* Boston: Little, Brown, 1953.

White, David M., ed. *Pop Culture in America.* New York: Watts, 1970.

Wittke, Carl. *The German-Language Press in America.* Lexington: University of Kentucky Press, 1957.

Wolseley, Roland E. *The Black Press, U.S.A.* Ames: Iowa State University Press, 1971.

Wood, James Playsted. *The Story of Advertising.* New York: Roland Press, 1958.

Contributors

Susan G. Barnes ....University of Tennessee
Gail L. Barwis...Appleton, Wisconsin
James Boylan ....University of Massachusetts, Amherst
Stephen D. Bray...Kentfield, California
Lea Ann Brown...Southern Illinois University
Richard M. Brown...Chapel Hill, North Carolina
Robert Carey ....University of Arkansas
Billy E. Deal...University of South Carolina
Philip B. Dematteis ....Columbia, South Carolina
John DeMers ....New Orleans, Louisiana
Wallace B. Eberhard ....University of Georgia
Ronald T. Farrar..University of Kentucky
James S. Featherston ....Louisiana State University
Jean Lange Folkers ....University of Texas at Austin
Warren T. Francke ....University of Nebraska at Omaha
Robert V. Hudson..Michigan State University
Terry Hynes ....California State University, Fullerton
A. J. Kaul...Western Kentucky University
Michael Kirkhorn..University of Kentucky
Alfred Lawrence Lorenz...Loyola University
William I. McReynolds...University of Colorado–Boulder
Susan G. Motes ....University of Alabama
David Paul Nord..Indiana University
Eric M. Odendahl ....San Diego State University
Alice A. Parsons ....Columbia, South Carolina
Dorothy H. Powell ....Arkansas State University
Daniel W. Pfaff...Pennsylvania State University
Sam G. Riley.....................................Virginia Polytechnic Institute and State University
Norman H. Sims ....University of Massachusetts, Amherst
William David Sloan ....University of Alabama
Ted Curtis Smythe...................................California State University, Fullerton
Lucas G. Staudacher...Marquette University
Rosemarian V. Staudacher..Marquette University
Jacqueline Steck ....Temple University
James Glen Stovall..University of Alabama
Bruce M. Swain ....University of Georgia
William H. Taft...University of Missouri
Robert K. Thorp..Louisville Times
Stephen Vaughn ....University of Wisconsin, Madison
Faye B. Zuckerman..................................California State University, Northridge

Cumulative Index

Dictionary of Literary Biography, Volumes 1-25
Dictionary of Literary Biography Yearbook, 1980, 1981, 1982
Dictionary of Literary Biography Documentary Series, Volumes 1-4

Cumulative Index

DLB before number: *Dictionary of Literary Biography*, Volumes 1-25
Y before number: *Dictionary of Literary Biography Yearbook*, 1980, 1981, 1982
DS before number: *Dictionary of Literary Biography Documentary Series*, Volumes 1-4

E

F

H

I

J

M

S

Y

Z